HOMER

THE HOMERIC STORIES
ILIAD AND ODYSSEY

DONE INTO ENGLISH PROSE BY

ANDREW LANG, M.A.

S. H. BUTCHER, M.A.

WALTER LEAF, Litt.D.

AND

ERNEST MYERS, M.A.

ABRIDGED EDITION

The Chautauqua Press

CHAUTAUQUA, NEW YORK

1909

888
H7iEla

THE ILIAD OF HOMER

BY

ANDREW LANG, M.A.
LATE FELLOW OF MERTON COLLEGE, OXFORD

WALTER LEAF, Litt.D.
LATE FELLOW OF TRINITY COLLEGE, CAMBRIDGE

AND

ERNEST MYERS, M.A.
LATE FELLOW OF WADHAM COLLEGE, OXFORD

COPYRIGHT, 1905,
BY THE MACMILLAN COMPANY.

Set up and electrotyped. Published February, 1905.
Reprinted April, 1906; October, 1907; January, April,
1909.

THE SACRED SOIL OF ILIOS IS RENT
   WITH SHAFT AND PIT; FOILED WATERS WANDER SLOW
THROUGH PLAINS WHERE SIMOIS AND SCAMANDER WENT
   TO WAR WITH GODS AND HEROES LONG AGO.
NOT YET TO DARK CASSANDRA LYING LOW
   IN RICH MYCENAE DO THE FATES RELENT;
THE BONES OF AGAMEMNON ARE A SHOW,
   AND RUINED IS HIS ROYAL MONUMENT.
THE DUST AND AWFUL TREASURES OF THE DEAD
   HATH LEARNING SCATTERED WIDE; BUT VAINLY THEE,
HOMER, SHE METETH WITH HER LESBIAN LEAD,
   AND STRIVES TO REND THY SONGS, TOO BLIND IS SHE
TO KNOW THE CROWN ON THINE IMMORTAL HEAD
   OF INDIVISIBLE SUPREMACY.

                                            A. L.

ATHWART THE SUNRISE OF OUR WESTERN DAY
   THE FORM OF GREAT ACHILLES, HIGH AND CLEAR,
   STANDS FORTH IN ARMS, WIELDING THE PELIAN SPEAR.
THE SANGUINE TIDES OF THAT IMMORTAL FRAY,
SWEPT ON BY GODS, AROUND HIM SURGE AND SWAY,
   WHERETHROUGH THE HELMS OF MANY A WARRIOR PEER,
   STRONG MEN AND SWIFT, THEIR TOSSING PLUMES UPREAR.
BUT STRONGER, SWIFTER, GOODLIER HE THAN THEY,
MORE AWFUL, MORE DIVINE. YET MARK ANIGH;
   SOME FIERY PANG HATH RENT HIS SOUL WITHIN,
   SOME HOVERING SHADE HIS BROWS ENCOMPASSETH.
WHAT GIFTS HATH FATE FOR ALL HIS CHIVALRY?
   EVEN SUCH AS HEARTS HEROIC OFTENEST WIN;
   HONOUR, A FRIEND, ANGUISH, UNTIMELY DEATH.

                                            E. M.

CONTENTS

PART I

	PAGE
INTRODUCTION	ix
HOMER AS A UNIVERSAL POET	xii
THE ILIAD	1
PRONUNCIATION OF PROPER NAMES	325

PART II

THE ODYSSEY	1
PRONUNCIATION OF PROPER NAMES	295

ILLUSTRATIONS

THE ILIAD

HOMER		*Frontispiece*
THE DEPARTURE OF BRISEIS FROM THE TENT OF ACHILLES	*facing page*	11
THE COUNCIL OF THE GODS	,, ,,	43
THE MEETING OF HECTOR AND ANDROMACHE	,, ,,	77
THE DESCENT OF DISCORD	,, ,,	135
THETIS BRINGING THE ARMOUR TO ACHILLES	,, ,,	243
THE FUNERAL PILE OF PATROKLOS	,, ,,	291
HECTOR'S BODY DRAGGED AT THE CAR OF ACHILLES	,, ,,	305

THE ODYSSEY

PENELOPE SURPRISED BY THE SUITORS	,, ,,	16
ODYSSEUS FOLLOWING THE CAR OF NAUSICAA	,, ,,	75
ODYSSEUS WEEPS AT THE SONG OF DEMODOCUS	,, ,,	94
ODYSSEUS GIVING WINE TO THE CYCLOPS	,, ,,	104
ODYSSEUS TERRIFIED BY THE GHOSTS	,, ,,	127
SCYLLA	,, ,,	141
PENELOPE CARRYING THE BOW OF ODYSSEUS TO THE SUITORS	,, ,,	246
ODYSSEUS KILLING THE SUITORS	,, ,,	261

INTRODUCTION

THE translation of the *Iliad* by Mr. Lang, Mr. Leaf, and Mr. Myers, first published in 1882, and that of the *Odyssey*, by Professor Butcher and Mr. Lang, issued three years earlier, have been generally accepted as the best versions of these great masterpieces yet made in English prose. This high reputation is due partly to their scholarly accuracy and faithfulness to the original, but perhaps more particularly to the literary skill of the translators. Their prose is simple but dignified; it has a touch of the archaic that reminds us of the Bible and Shakespeare, and gives us the sense of reading an ancient classic; and it has a smoothness, and grace, and rhythm that almost produce the effect of verse. In re-issuing both of the Homeric stories in a single volume, the intention is to encourage and facilitate the reading of these noble classics of antiquity by old and young. At present the knowledge of the *Iliad* and the *Odyssey* is confined too closely to the few who are able to read them in the original tongue. But, like the Bible, both these poems are so simple — so primitive indeed — in thought and expression that they are capable of adequate translation into the modern languages without loss of any great part of their power and beauty. It is to be hoped, therefore, that the publication in this form of these admirable versions will help to make a close acquaintance with the two noblest poems of antiquity possible for multitudes of people who are probably ignorant of the ancient tongue in which they were written, but who are not one whit less susceptible to their charm.

In adapting the translation of the *Iliad* to the purposes of this volume, it has been necessary to reduce it in bulk by about one-fifth, an operation rendered easy by the primitive character of the original poem. What I have struck out consists of some of the repetitions so plentifully used in Homer, and other similar matter unessential to the narrative, particularly passages that the average reader would find especially difficult. In a few instances, for the sake of clearness, I have replaced the allusive name of a god or hero by the simple name. No other changes have been made in the text of the translation, except in several cases where it was necessary to insert a few words to make the connection clearer.

Such notes of the translators as would be useful to young readers have been preserved, and I have added, in brackets, a few others that seemed to be required for the special public to which this volume is adapted. Other explanation the *Iliad* scarcely needs. The plot and its characters reveal themselves fully as the tale progresses, and allusions that are not quite clear at first soon become intelligible.

Nor did it seem wise to cumber these pages with discussion about the authorship and origin of the Homeric poems, points as to which little is definitely known. It is sufficient to say that they date from about the eighth century before Christ, that they seem to be based on the legends of an even earlier age, and that they are associated by tradition with the name of Homer. Like the more ancient portions of the Hebrew scriptures, they are precious memorials of primitive ages, of the early stages of civilization. In them we often find the plain records of cruelty and greed, of superstition and ignorance, but we see also the upspringing of the essential virtues: reverence for the unseen powers, charity and mutual helpfulness, love of honour and truth and manliness. Achilles and Odysseus, the most ancient heroes in the world's literature, have become for mankind two of the most typical: the one the ideal of manly valour, the other the ideal of manly wisdom and shrewdness. And the immortal tales that were woven about their names have never lost their charm for later generations, for they too are typical : the one of the passionate rivalry of war, the other of the steadfast love of country and family that draw the wanderer home through many perils.

G. R. CARPENTER.

COLUMBIA UNIVERSITY.

HOMER AS A UNIVERSAL POET

From Homer and the Study of Greek

Homer is a poet for all ages, all races, and all moods. To the Greeks the epics were not only the best of romances, the richest of poetry; not only their oldest documents about their own history, — they were also their Bible, their treasury of religious traditions and moral teaching. With the Bible and Shakespeare, the Homeric poems are the best training for life. There is no good quality that they lack; manliness, courage, reverence for old age and for the hospitable hearth; justice, piety, pity, a brave attitude toward life and death, are all conspicuous in Homer. He has to write of battles; and he delights in the joy of battle, and in all the movement of war. Yet he delights not less, but more, in peace; in prosperous cities, hearths secure, in the tender beauty of children, in the love of wedded wives, in the frank nobility of maidens, in the beauty of earth and sky and sea, and seaward murmuring river, in sun and snow, frost and mist and rain, in the whispered talk of boy and girl beneath oak and pine tree.

Living in an age where every man was a warrior, where every city might know the worst of sack and fire, where the noblest ladies might be led away for slaves, to light the fire and make the bed of a foreign master, Homer inevitably regards life as a battle. To each man on earth comes "the wicked day of destiny," as Malory unconsciously translates it, and each man must face it as hardily as he may.

Homer encourages them by all the maxims of chivalry and honour. His heart is with the brave of either side — with Glaucus and Sarpedon of Lycia no less than with Achilles and Patroclus. "Ah, friend," cries Sarpedon, "if once escaped from this battle we were for ever to be ageless and immortal, neither would I myself fight now in the foremost ranks, nor would I urge thee into the wars that give renown; but now— for assuredly ten thousand fates of death on every side beset us, and these may no man shun, nor none avoid—forward now let us go, whether we are to give glory or to win it!" And forth they go, to give and take renown and death, all the shields and helms of Lycia shining behind them, through the dust of battle, the singing of the arrows, the hurtling of spears, the rain of stones from the Locrian slings. And shields are smitten, and chariot horses run wild with no man to drive them, and Sarpedon drags down a portion of the Achaean battlement, and Aias leaps into the trench with his deadly spear, and the whole battle shifts and shines beneath the sun. Yet he who sings of the war, and sees it with his sightless eyes, sees also the Trojan women working at the loom, cheating their anxious hearts with broidery of gold and scarlet, or raising the song to Athene, or heating the bath for Hector, who never again may pass within the gates of Troy. He sees the poor weaving woman, weighing the wool, that she may not defraud her employers, and yet may win bread for her children. He sees the children, the golden head of Astyanax, his shrinking from the splendour of the hero's helm. He sees the child Odysseus, going with his father through the orchard, and choosing out some apple trees "for his very own." It is in the mouth of the ruthless Achilles, the fatal, the swift-footed hero with the hands of death, that Homer places the tenderest of his similes. "Wherefore weepest thou, Patroclus, like a fond little maid, that runs by her mother's side, praying her mother to take her up, snatching at her gown, and hindering her as she walks, and tearfully looking at her till her mother takes her up?—like her, Patroclus, dost thou softly weep."

Such are the moods of Homer, so full of love, of life, and all things living, so rich in all human sympathies, so readily moved when the great hound Argus welcomes his master, whom none knew after twenty years, but the hound knew him, and died in that welcome. With all this love of the real, which makes him dwell so fondly on every detail of armour, of implement, of art; on the divers-coloured gold-work of the shield, on the making of tires for chariot-wheels, on the forging of iron, on the rose-tinted ivory of the Sidonians, on cooking and eating and sacrificing, on pet dogs, on wasps and their ways, on fishing, on the boar hunt, on scenes in baths where fair maidens lave water over the heroes, on undiscovered isles with good harbours and rich land, on ploughing, mowing, and sowing, on the furniture of houses, on golden vases wherein the white dust of the dead is laid, — with all this delight in the real, Homer is the most romantic of poets. He walks with the surest foot in the darkling realm of dread Persephone, beneath the poplars on the solemn last beach of Ocean. He has heard the Siren's music, and the song of Circe, chanting as she walks to and fro, casting the golden shuttle through the loom of gold. He enters the cave of the Man Eater; he knows the unsunned land of the Cimmerians: in the summer of the North he has looked, from the fiord of the Laestrygons, on the Midnight Sun. He has dwelt on the floating isle of Aeolus, with its walls of bronze unbroken, and has sailed on those Phaeacian barks that need no help of helm or oar, that fear no stress, either of wind or tide, that come and go and return obedient to a thought and silent as a dream. He has seen the four maidens of Circe, daughters of wells and woods, and of sacred streams. He is the second-sighted man, and beholds the shroud that wraps the living who are doomed, and the mystic dripping from the walls of blood yet unshed. He has walked in the garden closes of Phaeacia, and looked on the face of gods who fare thither, and watched the weaving of the dance. He has eaten the honey-sweet fruit of the lotus, and from the hand of Helen he brings us that Egyptian nepenthe which puts all sorrow out of mind. His real world is as real as that in

Henry V, his enchanted isles are charmed with the magic of the *Tempest*. His young wooers are as insolent as Claudio, as flushed with youth; his beggar-men are brethren of Edie Ochiltree; his Nausicaa is sister to Rosalind, with a different charm of stately purity in love. His enchantresses hold us yet with their sorceries; his Helen is very Beauty: she has all the sweetness of ideal womanhood, and her repentance is without remorse. His Achilles is youth itself, glorious, cruel, pitiful, splendid, and sad, ardent, and loving, and conscious of its doom. Homer, in truth, is to be matched only with Shakespeare, and of Shakespeare he has not the occasional wilfulness, freakishness, and modish obscurity. He is a poet all of gold, universal as humanity, simple as childhood, musical now as the flow of his own rivers, now as the heavy plunging wave of his own Ocean.

ANDREW LANG.

THE ILIAD

BOOK I

How Agamemnon and Achilles fell out at the siege of Troy; and Achilles withdrew himself from battle, and won from Zeus a pledge that his wrong should be avenged on Agamemnon and the Achaians.

SING, goddess, the wrath of Achilles Peleus' son, the ruinous wrath that brought on the Achaians woes innumerable, and hurled down into Hades many strong souls of heroes, and gave their bodies to be a prey to dogs and all winged fowls; and so the counsel of Zeus wrought out its accomplishment from the day when first strife parted Atreides[1] king of men and noble Achilles.

Who among the gods set the twain at strife and variance? Apollo, the son of Leto and of Zeus; for he in anger at the king sent a sore plague upon the host, so that the folk began to perish, because Atreides[1] had done dishonour to Chryses the priest. For the priest had come to the Achaians' fleet ships to win his daughter's freedom, and brought a ransom beyond telling; and bare in his hands the fillet[2] of Apollo the Far-darter upon a golden staff; and made his prayer unto all the Achaians, and most of all to the two sons of Atreus, orderers of the host: "Ye sons of Atreus and all ye well-greaved[3] Achaians, now

---

[1] [Son of Atreus; here, Agamemnon.]   [2] [Band.]
[3] [Greaves, armour for the shins.]

may the gods that dwell in the mansions of Olympus grant you to lay waste the city of Priam, and to fare happily homeward; only set ye my dear child free, and accept the ransom in reverence to the son of Zeus, far-darting Apollo."

Then all the other Achaians cried assent, to reverence the priest and accept his goodly ransom; yet the thing pleased not the heart of Agamemnon son of Atreus, but he roughly sent him away, and laid stern charge upon him, saying: "Let me not find thee, old man, amid the hollow ships, whether tarrying now or returning again hereafter, lest the staff and fillet of the god avail thee naught. And her will I not set free; nay, ere that shall old age come on her in our house, in Argos, far from her native land, where she shall ply the loom and serve my couch. But depart, provoke me not, that thou mayest the rather go in peace."

So said he, and the old man was afraid and obeyed his word, and fared silently along the shore of the loud-sounding sea. Then went that aged man apart and prayed aloud to king Apollo, whom Leto of the fair locks bare: "Hear me, god of the silver bow! If ever I built a temple gracious in thine eyes, or if ever I burnt to thee fat flesh of thighs of bulls or goats, fulfil thou this my desire; let the Danaans pay by thine arrows for my tears."

So spake he in prayer, and Phoebus Apollo heard him, and came down from the peaks of Olympus wroth at heart, bearing on his shoulders his bow and covered quiver. And the arrows clanged upon his shoulders in his wrath, as the god moved; and he descended like to night. Then he sate him aloof from the ships, and let an arrow fly; and there was heard a dread clanging of the silver bow. First did he assail the mules and fleet dogs, but afterward, aiming at the men his piercing dart, he smote; and the pyres of the dead burnt continually in multitude.

Now for nine days ranged the god's shafts through the host;

but on the tenth Achilles summoned the folk to assembly, for in his mind did goddess Hera of the white arms put the thought, because she had pity on the Danaans when she beheld them perishing. Now when they had gathered and were met in assembly, then Achilles fleet of foot stood up and spake among them: "Son of Atreus, now deem I that we shall return wandering home again if war at once and pestilence must indeed ravage the Achaians. But come, let us now inquire of some soothsayer or priest, yea, or an interpreter of dreams — seeing that a dream too is of Zeus — who shall say wherefore Phoebus Apollo is so wroth, whether he blame us by reason of vow or hecatomb;[1] if perchance he would accept the savour of lambs or unblemished goats, and so would take away the pestilence from us."

So spake he and sate him down; and there stood up before them Kalchas son of Thestor, most excellent far of augurs, who knew both things that were and that should be and that had been before, and guided the ships of the Achaians to Ilios by his soothsaying that Phoebus Apollo bestowed on him. He made harangue and spake amid them: "Achilles, dear to Zeus, thou biddest me tell the wrath of Apollo, the king that smiteth afar. Therefore will I speak; but do thou make covenant with me, and swear that verily with all thy heart thou wilt aid me both by word and deed. For of a truth I deem that I shall provoke one that ruleth all the Argives with might, and whom the Achaians obey. For a king is more of might when he is wroth with a meaner man; even though for the one day he swallow his anger, yet doth he still keep his displeasure thereafter in his breast till he accomplish it. Consider thou, then, if thou wilt hold me safe."

And Achilles fleet of foot made answer and spake to him: "Yea, be of good courage, speak whatever soothsaying thou

[1] [Sacrifice of a hundred victims.]

knowest; for by Apollo, dear to Zeus, him by whose worship thou, O Kalchas, declarest thy soothsaying to the Danaans, no man while I live and behold light on earth shall lay violent hands upon thee amid the hollow ships; no man of all the Danaans, not even if thou mean Agamemnon, that now avoweth him to be greatest far of the Achaians."

Then was the noble seer of good courage, and spake: "Neither by reason of a vow is he displeased, nor for any hecatomb, but for his priest's sake to whom Agamemnon did despite, and set not his daughter free and accepted not the ransom; therefore hath the Far-darter brought woes upon us, yea, and will bring. Nor will he ever remove the loathly pestilence from the Danaans till we have given the bright-eyed damsel to her father, unbought, unransomed, and carried a holy hecatomb to Chryse; then might we propitiate him to our prayer."

So said he and sate him down, and there stood up before them the hero son of Atreus, wide-ruling Agamemnon, sore displeased; and his dark heart within him was greatly filled with anger, and his eyes were like flashing fire. To Kalchas first spake he with look of ill: "Thou seer of evil, never yet hast thou told me the thing that is pleasant. Evil is ever the joy of thy heart to prophesy, but never yet didst thou tell any good matter nor bring it to pass. And now with soothsaying thou makest harangue among the Danaans, how that the Far-darter bringeth woes upon them because, forsooth, I would not take the goodly ransom of the damsel Chryseis, seeing I am the rather fain to keep her own self within mine house. Yea, I prefer her before Klytaimnestra my wedded wife; in no wise is she lacking beside her, neither in favour nor stature, nor wit nor skill. Yet for all this will I give her back, if that is better; rather would I see my folk whole than perishing. Only make ye me ready a prize of honour forthwith, lest I alone of all the Argives be disprized, which thing beseemeth not; for ye all behold how my prize is departing from me."

To him then made answer fleet-footed goodly Achilles:
"Most noble son of Atreus, of all men most covetous, how
shall the great-hearted Achaians give thee a meed of honour?
We know naught of any wealth of common store, but what
spoil soe'er we took from captured cities hath been apportioned,
and it beseemeth not to beg all this back from the folk. Nay,
yield thou the damsel to the god, and we Achaians will pay
thee back threefold and fourfold, if ever Zeus grant us to sack
some well-walled town of Troy-land."

To him lord Agamemnon made answer and said: "Not in
this wise, strong as thou art, O godlike Achilles, beguile thou
me by craft; thou shalt not outwit me nor persuade me. Dost
thou wish, that thou mayest keep thy meed[1] of honour, for me
to sit idle in bereavement, and biddest me give her back? Nay,
if the great-hearted Achaians will give me a meed suited to my
mind, that the recompense be equal — but if they give it not,
then I myself will go and take a meed of honour, thine be it
or Aias', or Odysseus' that I will take unto me; wroth shall
he be to whomsoever I come. But for this we will take counsel hereafter; now let us launch a black ship on the great sea,
and gather picked oarsmen, and set therein a hecatomb, and
embark Chryseis of the fair cheeks herself, and let one of our
counsellors be captain, Aias or Idomeneus or goodly Odysseus,
or thou, Peleides,[2] most redoubtable of men, to do sacrifice for
us and propitiate the Far-darter."

Then Achilles fleet of foot looked at him scowling and said:
"Ah me, thou clothed in shamelessness, thou of crafty mind,
how shall any Achaian hearken to thy bidding with all his
heart, be it to go a journey or to fight the foe amain? Not
by reason of the Trojan spearmen came I hither to fight, for
they have not wronged me; never did they harry mine oxen
nor my horses, nor ever waste my harvest in deep-soiled Phthia,

[1] [Reward.]   [2] [Son of Peleus.]

the nurse of men; seeing there lieth between us long space of shadowy mountains and sounding sea; but thee, thou shameless one, followed we hither to make thee glad, by earning recompense at the Trojans' hands for Menelaos and for thee, thou dog-face! All this thou reckonest not nor takest thought thereof; and now thou threatenest thyself to take my meed of honour, wherefor I travailed much, and the sons of the Achaians gave it me. Never win I meed like unto thine, when the Achaians sack any populous citadel of Trojan men; my hands bear the brunt of furious war, but when the apportioning cometh then is thy meed far ampler, and I betake me to the ships with some small thing when I have fought to weariness. Now will I depart to Phthia, seeing it is far better to return home on my beaked ships; nor am I minded here in dishonour to draw thee thy fill of riches and wealth."

Then Agamemnon king of men made answer to him: "Yea, flee, if thy soul be set thereon. It is not I that beseech thee to tarry for my sake; I have others by my side that shall do me honour, and above all Zeus, lord of counsel. Most hateful art thou to me of all kings, fosterlings of Zeus; thou ever lovest strife and wars and fightings. Though thou be very strong, yet that I ween is a gift to thee of God. Go home with thy ships and company and lord it among thy Myrmidons; I reck not aught of thee nor care I for thine indignation; and this shall be my threat to thee: seeing Phoebus Apollo bereaveth me of Chryseis, her with my ship and my company will I send back; and mine own self will I go to thy hut and take Briseis of the fair cheeks, even that thy meed of honour, that thou mayest well know how far greater I am than thou, and so shall another hereafter abhor to match his words with mine and rival me to my face."

So said he, and grief came upon Peleus' son, and his heart within his shaggy breast was divided in counsel, whether to draw his keen blade from his thigh and set the company aside and so slay Atreides, or to assuage his anger and curb his soul. While yet he doubted thereof in heart and soul, and was drawing his great sword from his sheath, Athene came to him from heaven, sent forth of the white-armed goddess Hera, whose heart loved both alike and had care for them. She stood behind Peleus' son and caught him by his golden hair, to him only visible, and of the rest no man beheld her. Then Achilles marvelled, and turned him about, and straightway knew Pallas Athene; and terribly shone her eyes. He spake to her winged words, and said: "Why now art thou come hither, thou daughter of aegis-bearing[1] Zeus? Is it to behold the insolence of Agamemnon, son of Atreus? Yea, I will tell thee what I deem shall even be brought to pass: by his own haughtinesses shall he soon lose his life."

Then the bright-eyed goddess Athene spake to him again: "I came from heaven to stay thine anger, if perchance thou wilt hearken to me, being sent forth of the white-armed goddess Hera, that loveth you twain alike and careth for you. Go to now, cease from strife, and let not thine hand draw the sword; yet with words indeed revile him, even as it shall come to pass. For thus will I say to thee, and so it shall be fulfilled; hereafter shall goodly gifts come to thee, yea in threefold measure, by reason of this despite; hold thou thine hand, and hearken to us."

And Achilles fleet of foot made answer and said to her: "Goddess, needs must a man observe the saying of you twain, even though he be very wroth at heart; for so is the better way. Whosoever obeyeth the gods, to him they gladly hearken."

He said, and stayed his heavy hand on the silver hilt, and thrust the great sword back into the sheath, and was not disobedient to the saying of Athene; and she forthwith was

[1] [Aegis, the storm mantle of Zeus.]

departed to Olympus, to the other gods in the palace of aegis-bearing Zeus.

Then Peleus' son spake again with bitter words to Atreus' son, and in no wise ceased from anger: "Thou heavy with wine, thou with face of dog and heart of deer, never didst thou take courage to arm for battle among thy folk or to lay ambush with the princes of the Achaians; that to thee were even as death. Far better booteth it, forsooth, to seize for thyself the meed of honour of every man through the wide host of the Achaians that speaketh contrary to thee. But I will speak my word to thee, and swear a mighty oath therewith: verily by this staff that shall no more put forth leaf or twig, seeing it hath for ever left its trunk among the hills, verily shall longing for Achilles come hereafter upon the sons of the Achaians one and all; and then wilt thou in no wise avail to save them, for all thy grief, when multitudes fall dying before manslaying Hector. Then shalt thou tear thy heart within thee for anger that thou didst in no wise honour the best of the Achaians."

So said Peleides and dashed to earth the staff studded with golden nails, and himself sat down; and over against him Atreides waxed furious. Then in their midst rose up Nestor, pleasant of speech, the clear-voiced orator of the Pylians, he from whose tongue flowed discourse sweeter than honey. Two generations of mortal men already had he seen perish, that had been of old time born and nurtured with him in goodly Pylos, and he was king among the third. He made harangue to them and said: "Alas, of a truth sore lamentation cometh upon the land of Achaia. Verily Priam would be glad and Priam's sons, and all the Trojans would have great joy of heart, were they to hear all this tale of strife between you twain that are chiefest of the Danaans in counsel and chiefest in battle. Nay, hearken to me; ye are younger both than I. Of old days held I converse with better men even than you, and never did they make light of me. Even so hearken ye also, for better is it to hearken. Neither do thou, though thou art very great, seize from him his damsel, but leave her as she was given at the first by the sons of the Achaians to be a meed of honour; nor do thou, son of Peleus, think to strive with a king, might against might; seeing that no common honour pertaineth to a sceptred king to whom Zeus apportioneth glory. Though thou be strong, and a goddess mother bare thee, yet his is the greater place, for he is king over more. And thou, Atreides, abate thy fury; nay, it is even I that beseech thee to let go thine anger with Achilles, who is made unto all the Achaians a mighty bulwark of evil war."

Then lord Agamemnon answered and said: "Yea verily, old man, all this thou sayest is according unto right. But this fellow would be above all others, he would be lord of all and king among all and captain to all; wherein I deem none will hearken to him. Though the immortal gods made him a spearman, do they therefore put revilings in his mouth for him to utter?"

Then goodly Achilles brake in on him and answered: "Yea, for I should be called coward and man of naught, if I yield to thee in every matter, howsoe'er thou bid. To others give now thine orders, not to me. This, moreover, will I say to thee, and do thou lay it to thy heart. Know that not by violence will I strive for the damsel's sake, neither with thee nor any other; ye gave and ye have taken away. But of all else that is mine beside my fleet black ship, thereof shalt thou not take anything or bear it away against my will. Yea, go to now, make trial, that all these may see; forthwith thy dark blood shall gush about my spear."

Now when the twain had thus finished the battle of violent words, they stood up and dissolved the assembly beside the Achaian ships. Peleides went his way to his huts and trim ships with Menoitios' son[1] and his company; and Atreides

[1] Patroklos.

launched a fleet ship on the sea, and picked twenty oarsmen therefor, and embarked the hecatomb for the god, and brought Chryseis of the fair cheeks and set her therein; and Odysseus of many devices went to be their captain.

So these embarked and sailed over the wet ways; and Atreides bade the folk purify themselves. So they purified themselves, and cast the defilements into the sea and did sacrifice to Apollo, even unblemished hecatombs of bulls and goats, along the shore of the unvintaged sea; and the sweet savour arose to heaven eddying amid the smoke.

Thus were they busied throughout the host; but Agamemnon ceased not from the strife wherewith he threatened Achilles at the first; he spake to Talthybios and Eurybates that were his heralds and nimble squires: "Go ye to the tent of Achilles Peleus' son, and take Briseis of the fair cheeks by the hand and lead her hither; and if he give her not, then will I myself go, and more with me, and seize her; and that will be yet more grievous for him."

So saying he sent them forth, and laid stern charge upon them. Unwillingly went they along the beach of the unvintaged sea, and came to the huts and ships of the Myrmidons. Him found they sitting beside his hut and black ship; nor when he saw them was Achilles glad. So they in dread and reverence of the king stood, and spake to him no word, nor questioned him. But he knew in his heart, and spake to them: "All hail, ye heralds, messengers of Zeus and men, come near; ye are not guilty in my sight, but Agamemnon that sent you for the sake of the damsel Briseis. Go now, heaven-sprung Patroklos, bring forth the damsel, and give them her to lead away. Moreover, let the twain themselves be my witnesses before the face of the blessed gods and mortal men, yea and of him, that king untoward, against the day when there cometh need of me hereafter to save them all from shameful wreck. Of a truth he raveth with baleful mind, and hath not

THE DEPARTURE OF BRISEIS FROM THE TENT OF ACHILLES

knowledge to look before and after, that so his Achaians might battle in safety beside their ships."

So said he, and Patroklos hearkened to his dear comrade, and led forth from the hut Briseis of the fair cheeks, and gave them her to lead away. So these twain took their way back along the Achaians' ships, and with them went the woman all unwilling. Then Achilles wept anon, and sat him down apart, aloof from his comrades on the beach of the grey sea, gazing across the boundless main; he stretched forth his arms and prayed instantly[1] to his dear mother: "Mother, seeing thou didst of a truth bear me to so brief span of life, honour at the least ought the Olympian to have granted me, even Zeus that thundereth on high; but now doth he not honour me, no, not one whit. Verily Atreus' son, wide-ruling Agamemnon, hath done me dishonour; for he hath taken away my meed of honour and keepeth her of his own violent deed."

So spake he weeping, and his lady mother heard him as she sate in the sea-depths beside her aged sire. With speed arose she from the grey sea, like a mist, and sate her before the face of her weeping son, and stroked him with her hand, and spake and called on his name: "My child, why weepest thou? What sorrow hath entered into thy heart? Speak it forth, hide it not in thy mind, that both may know it."

Then with heavy moan Achilles fleet of foot spake to her: "Thou knowest it; why should I tell this to thee that knowest all! If indeed thou canst, guard thine own son; betake thee to Olympus and beseech Zeus by any deed or word whereby thou ever didst make glad his heart. For oft have I heard thee proclaiming in my father's halls and telling that thou alone amid the immortals didst save the son of Kronos, lord of the storm-cloud, from shameful wreck, when all the other Olympians would have bound him, even Hera and Poseidon and

---

[1] [Earnestly.]

Pallas Athene. Then didst thou, O goddess, enter in and loose him from his bonds, having with speed summoned to high Olympus him of the hundred arms whom gods call Briareus, and the blessed gods feared him withal and bound not Zeus. This bring thou to his remembrance and sit by him and clasp his knees, if perchance he will give succour to the Trojans; and for the Achaians, hem them among their ships' sterns about the bay, given over to slaughter; that they may make trial of their king and that even wide-ruling Agamemnon may perceive his blindness, in that he honoured not at all the best of the Achaians."

Then Thetis weeping made answer to him: "Ah me, my child, why reared I thee, cursed in my motherhood? Would thou hadst been left tearless and griefless amid the ships, seeing thy lot is very brief and endureth no long while; but now art thou made short-lived alike and lamentable beyond all men in an evil hour I bare thee in our halls. But I will go myself to snow-clad Olympus to tell this thy saying to Zeus, whose joy is in the thunder, if perchance he may hearken to me. But tarry thou now amid thy fleet-faring ships, and continue wroth with the Achaians, and refrain utterly from battle: for Zeus went yesterday to Okeanos, unto the noble Ethiopians for a feast, and all the gods followed with him; but on the twelfth day will he return to Olympus, and then will I fare to Zeus' palace of the bronze threshold, and will kneel to him and think to win him."

So saying she went her way and left him there, vexed in spirit for the fair-girdled woman's sake, whom they had taken perforce despite his will: and meanwhile Odysseus came to Chryse with the holy hecatomb. When they were now entered within the deep haven, they furled their sails and laid them in the black ship, and lowered the mast by the forestays and brought it to the crutch with speed, and rowed her with oars to the anchorage. Then they cast out the mooring stones and made fast the hawsers, and so themselves went forth on to the sea-beach, and forth they brought the hecatomb for the Fardarter Apollo, and forth came Chryseis withal from the seafaring ship. Then Odysseus of many counsels brought her to the altar and gave her into her father's arms, and spake unto him: "Chryses, Agamemnon king of men sent me hither to bring thee thy daughter, and to offer to Phoebus a holy hecatomb on the Danaans' behalf, wherewith to propitiate the king that hath now brought sorrow and lamentation on the Argives."

So saying he gave her to his arms, and he gladly took his dear child; and anon they set in order for the god the holy hecatomb about his well-builded altar; next washed they their hands and took up the barley meal. Then Chryses lifted up his hands and prayed aloud for them: "Hearken to me, god of the silver bow! Even as erst thou heardest my prayer, and didst me honour, and mightily afflictedst the people of the Achaians, even so now fulfil me this my desire: remove thou from the Daanans forthwith the loathly pestilence."

So spake he in prayer, and Phoebus Apollo heard him. Now when they had prayed and sprinkled the barley meal, first they drew back the victims' heads and slaughtered them and flayed them, and cut slices from the thighs and wrapped them in fat, making a double fold, and laid raw collops thereon, and the old man burnt them on cleft wood and made libation over them of gleaming wine. Now when the thighs were burnt and they had tasted the vitals, then sliced they all the rest and pierced it through with spits, and roasted it carefully, and drew all off again. So when they had rest from the task and had made ready the banquet, they feasted, nor was their heart aught stinted of the fair banquet. But when they had put away from them the desire of meat and drink, the young men crowned the bowls with wine, and gave each man his portion after the drink-offering had been poured into the cups.

So all day long worshipped they the god with music, singing the beautiful paean, the sons of the Achaians making music to the Far-darter; and his heart was glad to hear. And when the sun went down and darkness came on them, they laid them to sleep beside the ship's hawsers; and when rosy-fingered Dawn appeared, the child of morning, then set they sail for the wide camp of the Achaians; and Apollo the Far-darter sent them a favouring gale. They set up their mast and spread the white sails forth, and the wind filled the sail's belly and the dark wave sang loud about the stem as the ship made way, and she sped across the wave, accomplishing her journey. So when they were now come to the wide camp of the Achaians, they drew up their black ship to land high upon the sands, and set in line the long props beneath her; and themselves were scattered amid their huts and ships.

But he sat by his swift-faring ships, still wroth, even the heaven-sprung son of Peleus, Achilles fleet of foot; he betook him neither to the assembly that is the hero's glory, neither to war, but consumed his heart in tarrying in his place, and yearned for the war-cry and for battle.

Now when the twelfth morn thereafter was come, then the gods that are for ever fared to Olympus all in company, led of Zeus. And Thetis forgat not her son's charge, but rose up from the sea-wave, and at early morn mounted up to great heaven and Olympus. There found she Kronos' son of the far-sounding voice sitting apart from all on the topmost peak of many-ridged Olympus. So she sat before his face and with her left hand clasped his knees, and with her right touched him beneath his chin, and spake in prayer to king Zeus son of Kronos: "Father Zeus, if ever I gave thee aid amid the immortal gods, whether by word or deed, fulfil thou this my desire; do honour to my son, that is doomed to earliest death of all men: now hath Agamemnon king of men done him dishonour, for he hath taken away his meed of

honour and keepeth her of his own violent deed. But honour
thou him, Zeus of Olympus, lord of counsel; grant thou victory to the Trojans the while, until the Achaians do my son
honour and exalt him with recompense."

So spake she; but Zeus the cloud-gatherer said no word to
her, and sat long time in silence. But even as Thetis had
clasped his knees, so held she by him clinging, and questioned
him yet a second time: "Promise me now this thing verily,
and bow thy head thereto; or else deny me, seeing there is
naught for thee to fear; that I may know full well how I
among all gods am least in honour."

Then Zeus the cloud-gatherer, sore troubled, spake to her:
"Verily it is a sorry matter, if thou wilt set me at variance
with Hera, whene'er she provoketh me with taunting words.
Even now she upbraideth me ever amid the immortal gods,
and saith that I aid the Trojans in battle. But do thou now
depart again, lest Hera mark aught; and I will take thought
for these things to fulfil them. Come now, I will bow my
head to thee, that thou mayest be of good courage; for that, of
my part, is the surest token amid the immortals; no word
of mine is revocable nor false nor unfulfilled when the bowing
of my head hath pledged it."

Kronion [1] spake, and bowed his dark brow, and the ambrosial locks waved from the king's immortal head; and he made
great Olympus quake.

Thus the twain took counsel and parted; she leapt therewith into the deep sea from glittering Olympus, and Zeus fared
to his own palace. All the gods in company arose from their
seats before their father's face; neither ventured any to await
his coming, but they stood up all before him. So he sate him
there upon his throne; but Hera saw, and was not ignorant
how that the daughter of the Ancient of the sea, Thetis the

---

[1] [Son of Kronos; Zeus.]

silver-footed, had devised counsel with him. Anon with taunting words spake she to Zeus the son of Kronos: "Now who among the gods, thou crafty of mind, hath devised counsel with thee? It is ever thy good pleasure to hold aloof from me and in secret meditation to give thy judgments, nor of thine own good will hast thou ever brought thyself to declare unto me the thing thou purposest."

Then the father of gods and men made answer to her: "Hera, think not thou to know all my sayings; hard they are for thee, even though thou art my wife. But whichsoever it is seemly for thee to hear, none sooner than thou shall know, be he god or man. Only when I will to take thought aloof from the gods, then do not thou ask of every matter nor make question."

Then Hera the ox-eyed queen made answer to him: "Most dread son of Kronos, what word is this thou hast spoken? Yea, surely of old I have not asked thee nor made question, but in very quietness thou devisest all thou wilt. But now is my heart sore afraid lest thou have been won over by silver-footed Thetis, daughter of the Ancient of the sea, for she at early morn sat by thee and clasped thy knees. To her I deem thou gavest a sure pledge that thou wilt do honour to Achilles, and lay many low beside the Achaians' ships."

To her made answer Zeus the cloud-gatherer: "Lady, good lack! ever art thou imagining, nor can I escape thee. Abide thou in silence and hearken to my bidding, lest all the gods that are in Olympus keep not off from thee my visitation, when I put forth my hands unapproachable against thee."

He said, and Hera the ox-eyed queen was afraid, and sat in silence, curbing her heart; but throughout Zeus' palace the gods of heaven were troubled. Then Hephaistos the famed craftsman began to make harangue among them, to do kindness to his dear mother, white-armed Hera: "Verily this will be a sorry matter, neither any more endurable, if ye twain thus fight for mortals' sakes, and bring wrangling among the gods; neither will there any more be joy of the goodly feast, seeing that evil triumpheth. So I give counsel to my mother, though herself is wise, to do kindness to our dear father Zeus, that our father upbraid us not again and cast the banquet in confusion. What if the Olympian, the lord of the lightning, will to dash us from our seats! for he is strongest far. Nay, approach thou him with gentle words, then will the Olympian forthwith be gracious unto us."

So speaking he rose up and set in his dear mother's hand the two-handled cup, and spake to her: "Be of good courage, mother mine, and endure, though thou art vexed, lest I behold thee, that art so dear, chastised before mine eyes, and then shall I not be able for all my sorrow to save thee; for the Olympian is a hard foe to face. Yea, once ere this, when I was fain to save thee, he caught me by my foot and hurled me from the heavenly threshold; all day I flew, and at the set of sun I fell in Lemnos, and little life was in me."

He spake, and the white-armed goddess Hera smiled, and smiling took the cup at her son's hand. Then he poured wine to all the other gods from right to left, ladling the sweet nectar from the bowl. And laughter unquenchable arose amid the blessed gods to see Hephaistos bustling through the palace.

So feasted they all day till the setting of the sun; nor was their soul aught stinted of the fair banquet, nor of the beauteous lyre that Apollo held, and the Muses singing alternately with sweet voice.

Now when the bright light of the sun was set, these went each to his own house to sleep, where each one had his palace made with cunning device by famed Hephaistos the lame god; and Zeus the Olympian, the lord of lightning, departed to his couch where he was wont of old to take his rest, whenever sweet sleep visited him. There went he up and slept, and beside him was Hera of the golden throne.

c

BOOK II

How Zeus beguiled Agamemnon by a dream; and of the assembly of the Achaians and their marching forth to battle.

Now all other gods and chariot-driving men slept all night long, only Zeus was not holden of sweet sleep; rather was he pondering in his heart how he should do honour to Achilles and destroy many beside the Achaians' ships. And this design seemed to his mind the best, to wit, to send a baneful dream upon Agamemnon son of Atreus. So he spake, and uttered to him winged words: "Come now, thou baneful Dream, go to the Achaians' fleet ships, enter into the hut of Agamemnon son of Atreus, and tell him every word plainly as I charge thee. Bid him call to arms the flowing-haired Achaians with all speed, for now he may take the wide-wayed city of the Trojans. For the immortals that dwell in the halls of Olympus are no longer divided in counsel, since Hera hath turned the minds of all by her beseeching, and over the Trojans sorrows hang."

So spake he, and the Dream went his way when he had heard the charge. With speed he came to the Achaians' fleet ships, and went to Agamemnon son of Atreus, and found him sleeping in his hut, and ambrosial slumber poured over him. So he stood over his head in seeming like unto the son of Neleus, even Nestor, whom most of all the elders Agamemnon honoured; in his likeness spake to him the heavenly Dream:

"Sleepest thou, son of wise Atreus tamer of horses? To sleep all night through beseemeth not one that is a counsellor, to whom peoples are entrusted and so many cares belong. Now hearken straightway to me, for I am a messenger to thee from Zeus, who though he be afar yet hath great care for thee and pity. He biddeth thee call to arms the flowing-haired

Achaians with all speed, for now thou mayest take the wide-wayed city of the Trojans. For the immortals that dwell in the halls of Olympus are no longer divided in counsel, since Hera hath turned the minds of all by her beseeching, and over the Trojans sorrows hang by the will of Zeus. But do thou keep this in thy heart, nor let forgetfulness come upon thee when honeyed sleep shall leave thee."

So spake the Dream, and departed and left him there, deeming in his mind things that were not to be fulfilled. For indeed he thought to take Priam's city that very day; fond[1] man, in that he knew not the plans that Zeus had in mind, who was willed to bring yet more grief and wailing on Trojans alike and Danaans throughout the course of stubborn fights. Then woke he from sleep, and the heavenly voice was in his ears. So he rose up sitting, and donned his soft tunic, fair and bright, and cast around him his great cloak, and beneath his glistering feet he bound his fair sandals, and over his shoulder cast his silver-studded sword, and grasped his sires' sceptre, imperishable for ever, wherewith he took his way amid the mail-clad Achaians' ships.

Now went the goddess Dawn to high Olympus, foretelling daylight to Zeus and all the immortals; and the king bade the clear-voiced heralds summon to the assembly the flowing-haired Achaians. So did those summon, and these gathered with speed.

But first the council of the great-hearted elders met beside the ship of king Nestor the Pylos-born. And he that had assembled them told them his dream and framed this cunning counsel: "Come, let us now call to arms as we may the sons of the Achaians. But first I will speak to make trial of them as is fitting, and will bid them flee with their benched ships; only do ye from this side and from that speak to hold them back."

[1] [Foolish.]

So spake he and sate him down; and there stood up among them Nestor, who was king of sandy Pylos. He made harangue to them and said: "My friends, captains and rulers of the Argives, had any other of the Achaians told us this dream we might deem it a false thing, and rather turn away therefrom; but now he hath seen it who of all Achaians avoweth himself far greatest. So come, let us call to arms as we may the sons of the Achaians."

So spake he, and led the way forth from the council, and all the other sceptred chiefs rose with him and obeyed the shepherd of the host; and the people hastened to them. Even as when the tribes of thronging bees issue from some hollow rock, ever in fresh procession, and fly clustering among the flowers of spring, and some on this hand and some on that fly thick; even so from ships and huts before the low beach marched forth their many tribes by companies to the place of assembly. And in their midst blazed forth Rumour, messenger of Zeus, urging them to go; and so they gathered. And the place of assemblage was in an uproar, and the earth echoed again as the hosts sate them down, and there was turmoil. Nine heralds restrained them with shouting, if perchance they might refrain from clamour, and hearken to their kings, the fosterlings of Zeus. And hardly at the last would the people sit, and keep them to their benches and cease from noise. Then stood up lord Agamemnon bearing his sceptre, that Hephaistos had wrought curiously. Thereon he leaned and spake his saying to the Argives:

"My friends, Danaan warriors, men of Ares' company, Zeus hath bound me with might in grievous blindness of soul; hard of heart is he, for that erewhile he promised me and pledged his nod that not till I had wasted well-walled Ilios should I return; but now see I that he planned a cruel wile and biddeth me return to Argos dishonoured, with the loss of many of my folk. Shame is this even for them that come after to hear; how so goodly and great a folk of the Achaians thus vainly warred a bootless war, and fought scantier enemies, and no end thereof is yet seen. Already have nine years of great Zeus passed away, and our ships' timbers have rotted and the tackling is loosed; while there our wives and little children sit in our halls awaiting us; yet is our task utterly unaccomplished wherefor we came hither. So come, even as I shall bid let us all obey. Let us flee with our ships to our dear native land; for now shall we never take wide-wayed Troy."

So spake he, and stirred the spirit in the breasts of all throughout the multitude, as many as had not heard the council. And the assembly swayed like high sea-waves of the Icarian Main that east wind and south wind raise, rushing upon them from the clouds of father Zeus; and even as when the west wind cometh to stir a deep cornfield with violent blast, and the ears bow down, so was all the assembly stirred, and they with shouting hasted toward the ships; and the dust from beneath their feet rose and stood on high. And they bade each man his neighbour to seize the ships and drag them into the bright salt sea, and cleared out the launching-ways, and the noise went up to heaven of their hurrying homewards; and they began to take the props from beneath the ships.

Then would the Argives have accomplished their return against the will of fate, but that Hera spake a word to Athene: "Out on it, daughter of aegis-bearing Zeus, unwearied maiden! Shall the Argives thus indeed flee homeward to their dear native land over the sea's broad back? But they would leave to Priam and the Trojans their boast, even Helen of Argos, for whose sake many an Achaian hath perished in Troy, far away from his dear native land. But go thou now amid the host of the mail-clad Achaians; with thy gentle words refrain thou every man, neither suffer them to draw their curved ships down to the salt sea."

So spake she, and the bright-eyed goddess Athene disregarded not; but went darting down from the peaks of Olympus, and came with speed to the fleet ships of the Achaians. There found she Odysseus standing, peer of Zeus in counsel, neither laid he any hand upon his decked black ship, because grief had entered into his heart and soul. And bright-eyed Athene stood by him and said: "Heaven-sprung son of Laertes, Odysseus of many devices, will ye indeed fling yourselves upon your benched ships to flee homeward to your dear native land? But ye would leave to Priam and the Trojans their boast, even Helen of Argos, for whose sake many an Achaian hath perished in Troy, far from his dear native land. But go thou now amid the host of the Achaians, and tarry not; and with thy gentle words refrain every man, neither suffer them to draw their curved ships down to the salt sea."

So said she, and he knew the voice of the goddess speaking to him, and set him to run, and cast away his mantle, the which his herald gathered up, even Eurybates of Ithaca, that waited on him. And himself he went to meet Agamemnon son of Atreus, and at his hand received the sceptre of his sires, imperishable for ever, wherewith he took his way amid the ships of the mail-clad Achaians.

Whenever he found one that was a captain and a man of mark, he stood by his side, and refrained him with gentle words: "Good sir, it is not seemly to affright thee like a coward, but do thou sit thyself and make all thy folk sit down. For thou knowest not yet clearly what is the purpose of Atreus' son; now is he but making trial, and soon he will afflict the sons of the Achaians."

But whatever man of the people he saw and found him shouting, him he drave with his sceptre and chode him with loud words: "Good sir, sit still and hearken to the words of others that are thy betters; but thou art no warrior, and a weakling, never reckoned whether in battle or in council. In no wise can we Achaians all be kings here. A multitude of masters is no good thing; let there be one master, one king, to whom the son of crooked-counselling Kronos hath granted it."

So masterfully ranged he the host; and they hasted back to the assembly from ships and huts, with noise as when a wave of the loud-sounding sea roareth on the long beach and the main resoundeth.

Now all the rest sat down and kept their place upon the benches, only Thersites still chattered on, the uncontrolled of speech, whose mind was full of words many and disorderly, wherewith to strive against the chiefs idly and in no good order, but even as he deemed that he should make the Argives laugh. And he was ill-favoured beyond all men that came to Ilios. Bandy-legged was he, and lame of one foot, and his two shoulders rounded, arched down upon his chest; and over them his head was warped, and a scanty stubble sprouted on it. Hateful was he to Achilles above all and to Odysseus, for them he was wont to revile. But now with shrill shout he poured forth his upbraidings upon goodly Agamemnon. With him the Achaians were sore vexed and had indignation in their souls. But he with loud shout spake and reviled Agamemnon: "Atreides, for what art thou now ill content and lacking? Surely thy huts are full of bronze and many women are in thy huts, the chosen spoils that we Achaians give thee first of all, whene'er we take a town. Can it be that thou yet wantest gold as well, such as some one of the horse-taming Trojans may bring from Ilios to ransom his son, whom I perchance or some other Achaian have led captive? It is not seemly for one that is their captain to bring the sons of the Achaians to ill. Soft fools, base things of shame, ye women of Achaia and men no more, let us depart home with our ships, and leave this fellow here in Troy-land to gorge him with meeds of honour, that he may see whether our aid avail him aught or no; even he that hath now done dishonour to Achilles, a far better man than he; for he hath taken away his meed of honour and keepeth it by his own violent deed. Of a very surety is there no wrath at all in Achilles' mind, but he is slack; else this despite, thou son of Atreus, were thy last."

So spake Thersites, reviling Agamemnon shepherd of the host. But goodly Odysseus came straight to his side, and looking sternly at him with hard words rebuked him: "Thersites, reckless in words, shrill orator though thou art, refrain thyself, nor aim to strive singly against kings. For I deem that no mortal is baser than thou of all that with the sons of Atreus came before Ilios. Therefore were it well that thou shouldest not have kings in thy mouth as thou talkest, and utter revilings against them and be on the watch for departure. We know not yet clearly how these things shall be, whether we sons of the Achaians shall return for good or for ill. Therefore now dost thou revile continually Agamemnon son of Atreus, shepherd of the host, because the Danaan warriors give him many gifts, and so thou talkest tauntingly. But I will tell thee plain, and that I say shall even be brought to pass: if I find thee again raving as now thou art, then may Odysseus' head no longer abide upon his shoulders, nor may I any more be called father of Telemachos, if I take thee not and strip from thee thy garments, thy mantle and tunic that cover thy nakedness, and for thyself send thee weeping to the fleet ships, and beat thee out of the assembly with shameful blows."

So spake he, and with his staff smote his back and shoulders: and he bowed down and a big tear fell from him, and a bloody weal stood up from his back beneath the golden sceptre. Then he sat down and was amazed, and in pain with helpless look wiped away the tear. But the rest, though they were sorry, laughed lightly at him, and thus would one speak, looking at another standing by: "Go to, of a truth Odysseus hath wrought good deeds without number ere now, standing foremost in wise counsels and setting battle in array, but now is this thing the best by far that he hath wrought among the Argives, to wit, that he hath stayed this prating railer from his harangues. Never again, forsooth, will his proud soul henceforth bid him revile the kings with slanderous words."

So said the common sort; but up rose Odysseus waster of cities, with the sceptre in his hand. And by his side bright-eyed Athene in the likeness of a herald bade the multitude keep silence, that the sons of the Achaians, both the nearest and the farthest, might hear his words together and give heed to his counsel. He made harangue to them and said: "Now surely are the Achaians for making thee, O king, most despised among all mortal men, nor will they fulfil the promise that they pledged thee when they still were marching hither from horse-pasturing Argos; that thou shouldest not return till thou hadst laid well-walled Ilios waste. For like young children or widow women do they wail each to the other of returning home. Yea, here is toil to make a man depart disheartened. For he that stayeth away but one single month far from his wife in his benched ship fretteth himself when winter storms and the furious sea imprison him; but for us, the ninth year of our stay here is upon us in its course. Therefore do I not marvel that the Achaians should fret beside their beaked ships; yet nevertheless is it shameful to wait long and to depart empty. Be of good heart, my friends, and wait a while, until we learn whether Kalchas be a true prophet or no. For he foretold that we should war here nine years, but in the tenth year we should take the wide-wayed city. So spake the seer; and now are all these things being fulfilled. So come, abide ye all, ye well-greaved Achaians, even where ye are, until we have taken the great city of Priam."

So spake he, and the Argives shouted aloud, and all round the ships echoed terribly to the voice of the Achaians as they praised the saying of godlike Odysseus. And then spake among them knightly Nestor of Gerenia: "Out on it; in very truth ye hold assembly like silly boys that have no care for deeds of war. If any man is overmuch desirous to depart homewards, let him lay his hand upon his decked black ship, that before all men he may encounter death and fate. But do thou, my king, take good counsel thyself, and hearken to another that shall give it; the word that I speak, whate'er it be, shall not be cast away. Separate thy warriors by tribes and by clans, Agamemnon, that clan may give aid to clan and tribe to tribe. If thou do thus and the Achaians hearken to thee, then wilt thou know who among thy captains and who of the common sort is a coward, and who too is brave; for they will fight each after their sort. So wilt thou know whether it is even by divine command that thou shalt not take the city, or by the baseness of thy warriors and their ill skill in battle."

And lord Agamemnon answered and said to him: "Verily hast thou again outdone the sons of the Achaians in speech, old man. Ah, father Zeus and Athene and Apollo, would that among the Achaians I had ten such councillors; then would the city of king Priam soon bow beneath our hands, captive and wasted. But aegis-bearing Zeus, the son of Kronos, hath brought sorrows upon me, in that he casteth my lot amid fruitless wranglings and strifes. For in truth I and Achilles fought about a damsel with violent words, and I was first to be angry; but if we can only be at one in council, then will there no more be any putting off the day of evil for the Trojans, no not for an instant. But now go ye to your meal that we may join battle. Let each man sharpen well his spear and bestow well his shield, and let him well give his fleet-footed steeds their meal, and look well to his chariot on every side and take thought for battle, that all day long we may contend in hateful war. For of respite shall there intervene no, not a whit, only that the coming of night shall part the fury of warriors. On each man's breast shall the baldric of his covering shield be wet with sweat, and his hand shall grow faint about the spear, and each man's horse shall sweat as he draweth the polished chariot. And whomsoever I perceive minded to tarry far from the fight beside the beaked ships, for him shall there be no hope hereafter to escape the dogs and birds of prey."

So spake he, and the Argives shouted aloud, like to a wave on a steep shore, when the south wind cometh and stirreth it; even on a jutting rock, that is never left at peace by the waves of all winds that rise from this side and from that. And they stood up and scattered in haste throughout the ships, and made fires in the huts and took their meal. And they did sacrifice each man to one of the everlasting gods, praying for escape from death and the tumult of battle. But Agamemnon king of men slew a fat bull of five years to most mighty Kronion, and called the elders, the princes of the Achaian host, Nestor first and king Idomeneus, and then the two Aiantes[1] and Tydeus' son, and sixthly Odysseus peer of Zeus in counsel. And Menelaos of the loud war-cry came to him unbidden, for he knew in his heart how his brother toiled. Then stood they around the bull and took the barley meal. And Agamemnon made his prayer in their midst and said: "Zeus, most glorious, most great, god of the storm-cloud, that dwellest in the heaven, vouchsafe that the sun set not upon us nor the darkness come near, till I have laid low upon the earth Priam's palace smirched with smoke, and burnt the doorways thereof with consuming fire, and rent on Hector's breast his doublet cleft with the blade; and about him may full many of his comrades prone in the dust bite the earth."

So spake he, but not as yet would Kronion grant him fulfilment; he accepted the sacrifice, but made toil to wax unceasingly.

So when they had rest from the task and had made ready the banquet, they feasted, nor was their heart aught stinted

---

[1] [Aias (Ajax), the son of Telamon, and Aias, son of Oileus.]

of the fair banquet. But when they had put away from them the desire of meat and drink, then did knightly Nestor of Gerenia open his saying to them: "Most noble son of Atreus, Agamemnon king of men, let us not any more hold long converse here, nor for long delay the work that god putteth in our hands; but come, let the heralds of the mail-clad Achaians make proclamation to the folk and gather them throughout the ships; and let us go thus in concert through the wide host of the Achaians, that the speedier we may arouse keen war."

So spake he and Agamemnon king of men disregarded not. Straightway he bade the clear-voiced heralds summon to battle the flowing-haired Achaians. So those summoned and these gathered with all speed. And the kings, the fosterlings of Zeus that were about Atreus' son, eagerly marshalled them, and bright-eyed Athene in the midst, bearing the holy aegis that knoweth neither age nor death, whereon wave an hundred tassels of pure gold, all deftly woven and each one an hundred oxen worth. Therewith she passed dazzling through the Achaian folk, urging them forth; and in every man's heart she roused strength to battle without ceasing and to fight. So was war made sweeter to them than to depart in their hollow ships to their dear native land. Even as ravaging fire kindleth a boundless forest on a mountain's peaks, and the blaze is seen from afar, even so as they marched went the dazzling gleam from the innumerable bronze through the sky even unto the heavens.

And as the many tribes of feathered birds, wild geese or cranes or long-necked swans, on the Asian mead by Kaystrios' stream, fly hither and thither joying in their plumage, and with loud cries settle ever onwards, and the mead resounds; even so poured forth the many tribes of warriors from ships and huts into the Skamandrian plain. And the earth echoed terribly beneath the tread of men and horses. So stood they in the flowery Skamandrian plain, unnumbered as are leaves and flowers in their season. Even as the many tribes of thick flies that hover about a herdsman's steading[1] in the spring season, when milk drencheth the pails, even in like number stood the flowing-haired Achaians upon the plain in face of the Trojans, eager to rend them asunder. And even as the goatherds easily divide the ranging flocks of goats when they mingle in the pasture, so did their captains marshal them on this side and on that, to enter into the fray, and in their midst lord Agamemnon, his head and eyes like unto Zeus whose joy is in the thunder, and his waist like unto Ares and his breast unto Poseidon. Even as a bull standeth out far foremost amid the herd, for he is pre-eminent amid the pasturing kine, even such did Zeus make Atreides on that day, pre-eminent among many and chief amid heroes.

But Achilles lay idle among his seafaring ships, in sore wrath against Agamemnon Atreus' son, shepherd of the host; and his folk along the sea-shore sported with quoits and with casting of javelins and archery; and the horses each beside his own chariot stood idle, champing clover and parsley of the marsh, and their lords' chariots lay well covered up within the huts, while the men yearned for their warrior chief, and wandered hither and thither through the camp and fought not.

Now fleet Iris the wind-footed went to the Trojans, a messenger from aegis-bearing Zeus, with a grievous message. These were holding assembly at Priam's gate, being gathered all together both young men and old. And fleet-footed Iris stood hard by and spake to them; and she made her voice like to the voice of Polites son of Priam, who was the sentinel of the Trojans and was wont to sit trusting in his fleetness upon the barrow[2] of Aisyetes of old, and on the top thereof wait the sallying of the Achaians forth from their ships. Even in his likeness did fleet-footed Iris speak to Priam: "Old man, words

[1] [Farmstead.]   [2] [Grave-mound.]

beyond number are still pleasant to thee as erst in the days of peace; but war without respite is upon us. Of a truth have I very oft ere now entered into battles of the warriors, yet have I never seen so goodly a host and so great; for in the very likeness of the leaves of the forest or the sands of the sea are they marching along the plain to fight against the city. But, Hector, thee do I charge beyond all to do even as I shall say. Seeing that the allies are very many throughout Priam's great city, and diverse men, being scattered abroad, have diverse tongues; therefore let each one give the word to those whose chieftain he is, and them let him lead forth and have the ordering of his countrymen."

So spake she, and Hector failed not to know the voice of the goddess, and straightway dismissed the assembly, and they rushed to arms. And the gates were thrown open wide, and the host issued forth, footmen and horsemen, and mighty din arose.

BOOK III

How Menelaos and Paris fought in single combat; and Aphrodite rescued Paris. And how Helen and Priam beheld the Achaian host from the walls of Troy.

Now when they were arrayed, each company with their captains, the Trojans marched with clamour and with shouting like unto birds, even as when there goeth up before heaven a clamour of cranes which flee from the coming of winter and sudden rain, and fly with clamour towards the streams of ocean, bearing slaughter and fate to the Pigmy men, and in early morn offer cruel battle. But on the other side marched the Achaians in silence breathing courage, eager at heart to give succour man to man.

Even as when the south wind sheddeth mist over the crests of a mountain, mist unwelcome to the shepherd, but to the robber better than night, and a man can see no further than he casteth a stone; even so thick arose the gathering dust-clouds at their tread as they went; and with all speed they advanced across the plain.

So when they were now come nigh in onset on each other, godlike Alexandros[1] played champion to the Trojans, wearing upon his shoulders panther-skin and curved bow and sword; and he brandished two bronze-headed spears and challenged all the chieftains of the Argives to fight him man to man in deadly combat. But when Menelaos dear to Ares marked him coming in the forefront of the multitude with long strides, then even as a lion is glad when he lighteth upon a great carcase, a horned stag, or a wild goat that he hath found, being anhungered; and so he devoureth it amain, even though the fleet hounds and lusty youths set upon him; even thus was Menelaos glad when his eyes beheld godlike Alexandros; for he thought to take vengeance upon the sinner. So straightway he leapt in his armour from his chariot to the ground.

But when godlike Alexandros marked him appear amid the champions, his heart was smitten, and he shrank back into the host of his comrades, avoiding death. And even as a man that hath seen a serpent in a mountain glade starteth backward and trembling seizeth his feet beneath him, and he retreateth back again, and paleness hath hold of his cheeks, even so did godlike Alexandros for fear of Atreus' son shrink back into the throng of lordly Trojans. But Hector beheld and upbraided him with scornful words: "Ill Paris, most fair in semblance, thou deceiver woman-mad, would thou hadst been unborn and died unwed. Yea, that were my desire, and it were far better than thus to be our shame and looked at askance of all men. I ween that the flowing-haired Achaians laugh, deeming that a prince is our champion only because a goodly favour is his;

[1] [Paris.]

but in his heart is there no strength nor any courage. Art thou indeed such an one that in thy seafaring ships thou didst sail over the deep with the company of thy trusted comrades, and in converse with strangers didst bring back a fair woman from a far country, one that was by marriage daughter to warriors that bear the spear, that she might be a sore mischief to thy father and city and all the realm, but to our foes a rejoicing, and to thyself a hanging of the head? And canst thou not indeed abide Menelaos dear to Ares? Thou mightest see what sort of warrior is he whose lovely wife thou hast. Thy lyre will not avail thee nor the gifts of Aphrodite, those thy locks and fair favour, when thou grovellest in the dust. But the Trojans are very cowards: else ere this hadst thou donned a robe of stone[1] for all the ill thou hast wrought."

And godlike Alexandros made answer to him again: "Cast not in my teeth the lovely gifts of golden Aphrodite; not to be flung aside are the gods' glorious gifts that of their own good will they give; for by his desire can no man win them. But now if thou wilt have me do battle and fight, make the other Trojans sit down and all the Achaians, and set ye me in the midst, and Menelaos dear to Ares, to fight for Helen and all her wealth. And whichsoever shall vanquish and gain the upper hand, let him take all the wealth aright, and the woman, and bear them home. And let the rest pledge friendship and sure oaths; so may ye dwell in deep-soiled Troy, and let them depart to Argos pasture-land of horses, and Achaia home of fair women."

So spake he, and Hector rejoiced greatly to hear his saying, and went into the midst and restrained the battalions of the Trojans, with his spear grasped by the middle; and they all sate them down. But the flowing-haired Achaians kept shooting at him, aiming with arrows and casting stones. But

---

[1] *I.e.* been stoned by the people.

Agamemnon king of men cried aloud: "Refrain, ye Argives; shoot not, ye sons of the Achaians; for Hector of the glancing helm hath set himself to say somewhat."

So spake he, and they refrained from battle and made silence speedily. And Hector spake between the two hosts: "Hear of me, Trojans and well-greaved Achaians, the saying of Alexandros, for whose sake strife hath come about. He biddeth the other Trojans and all the Achaians to lay down their goodly armour on the bounteous earth, and himself in the midst and Menelaos dear to Ares to fight alone for Helen and all her wealth. And whichsoever shall vanquish and gain the upper hand, let him take all the wealth aright, and the woman, and bear them home; but let all of us pledge friendship and sure oaths."

So spake he, and they all kept silence and were still. Then in their midst spake Menelaos of the loud war-cry: "Bring ye two lambs, one white ram and one black ewe, for earth and sun; and let us bring one for Zeus. And call hither great Priam, that he may pledge the oath himself, seeing he hath sons that are overweening and faithless, lest any by transgression do violence to the oath of Zeus; for young men's hearts are ever lifted up. But wheresoever an old man entereth in, he looketh both before and after, whereby the best issue shall come for either side."

So spake he, and Achaians and Trojans were glad, deeming that they should have rest from grievous war. So they refrained their chariots to the ranks, and themselves alighted and doffed their arms. And these they laid upon the earth each close to each, and there was but small space between. And Hector sent two heralds to the city with all speed, to bring the lambs, and to call Priam. And lord Agamemnon sent forth Talthybios to go to the hollow ships, and bade him bring a ram; and he was not disobedient to noble Agamemnon.

Now Iris went with a message to white-armed Helen in the

likeness of her husband's sister, Laodike fairest favoured of Priam's daughters. And in the hall she found Helen weaving a great purple web of double fold, and embroidering thereon many battles of horse-taming Trojans and mail-clad Achaians, that they had endured for her sake at the hands of Ares. So fleet-footed Iris stood by her side and said: "Come hither, dear sister, that thou mayest see the wondrous doings of horse-taming Trojans and mail-clad Achaians. They that erst waged tearful war upon each other in the plain, eager for deadly battle, even they sit now in silence, and the battle is stayed, and they lean upon their shields, and the tall spears are planted by their sides. But Alexandros and Menelaos dear to Ares will fight with their tall spears for thee; and thou wilt be declared the dear wife of him that conquereth."

So spake the goddess, and put into her heart sweet longing for her former husband and her city and parents.

Forthwith she veiled her face in shining linen, and hastened from her chamber, letting fall a round tear; not unattended, for there followed with her two handmaidens, Aithre daughter of Pittheus and ox-eyed Klymene. Then came she straightway to the place of the Skaian gates. And the elders of the people sat at the Skaian gates. These had now ceased from battle for old age, yet were they right good orators, like grasshoppers that in a forest sit upon a tree and utter their lily-like[1] voice; even so sat the elders of the Trojans upon the tower. Now when they saw Helen coming to the tower they softly spake winged words one to the other: "Small blame is it that Trojans and well-greaved Achaians should for such a woman long time suffer hardships; marvellously like is she to the immortal goddesses to look upon. Yet even so, though she be so goodly, let her go upon their ships and not stay to vex us and our children after us."

So said they, and Priam lifted up his voice and called to

[1] Supposed to mean "delicate" or "tender."

Helen: "Come hither, dear child, and sit before me, that thou mayest see thy former husband and thy kinsfolk and thy friends. I hold thee not to blame; nay, I hold the gods to blame who brought on me the dolorous war of the Achaians — so mayest thou now tell me who is this huge hero, this Achaian warrior so goodly and great. Of a truth there are others even taller by a head; yet did mine eyes never behold a man so beautiful nor so royal; for he is like unto one that is a king."

And Helen, fair among women, spake and answered him: "Reverend art thou to me and dread, dear father of my lord; would that sore death had been my pleasure when I followed thy son hither, and left my home and my kinsfolk and my daughter in her girlhood and the lovely company of mine age-fellows. But that was not so, wherefore I pine with weeping. Now will I tell thee that whereof thou askest me and inquirest. This is wide-ruling Agamemnon, one that is both a goodly king and mighty spearman. And he was husband's brother to me, ah, shameless me."

And next the old man saw Odysseus, and asked: "Come now, tell me of this man too, dear child, who is he, shorter by a head than Agamemnon son of Atreus, but broader of shoulder and of chest to behold? His armour lieth upon the bounteous earth, and himself like a bell-wether rangeth the ranks of warriors. Yea, I liken him to a thick-fleeced ram ordering a great flock of white ewes."

Then Helen sprung of Zeus made answer to him: "Now this is Laertes' son, crafty Odysseus, that was reared in the realm of Ithaka, rugged though it be, and is skilled in all the ways of wile and cunning device."

Then sage Antenor made answer to her: "Lady, verily the thing thou sayest is true indeed, for erst came goodly Odysseus hither also on an embassage for thee, in the company of Menelaos dear to Ares; and I gave them entertainment and welcomed them in my halls, and learnt the aspect of both and their wise devices. Now when they mingled with the Trojans in the assembly, while all stood up Menelaos overpassed them all by the measure of his broad shoulders; but when both sat down, Odysseus was the more stately. And when they began to weave the web of words and counsel in the face of all, then Menelaos harangued fluently, in few words, but very clearly, seeing he was not long of speech, neither random, though in years he was the younger. But whenever Odysseus full of wiles rose up, he stood and looked down, with eyes fixed upon the ground, and waved not his staff whether backwards or forwards, but held it stiff, like to a man of no understanding; one would deem him to be churlish, and naught but a fool. But when he uttered his great voice from his chest, and words like unto the snowflakes of winter, then could no mortal man contend with Odysseus; then marvelled we not thus to behold Odysseus' aspect."

And thirdly the old man saw Aias, and asked: "Who then is this other Achaian warrior, goodly and great, pre-eminent among the Argives by the measure of his head and broad shoulders?"

And long-robed Helen, fair among women, answered: "This is huge Aias, bulwark of the Achaians. And on the other side amid the Cretans standeth Idomeneus like a god, and about him are gathered the captains of the Cretans. Oft did Menelaos dear to Ares entertain him in our house whene'er he came from Crete. And now behold I all the other glancing-eyed Achaians, whom well I could discern and tell their names; but two captains of the host can I not see, even Kastor tamer of horses and Polydeukes the skilful boxer, mine own brethren, whom the same mother bare. Either they came not in the company from lovely Lakedaimon; or they came hither indeed in their seafaring ships, but now will not enter into the battle of the warriors, for fear of the many scornings and revilings that are mine."

So said she; but them the life-giving earth held fast there in Lakedaimon, in their dear native land.

Meanwhile were the heralds bearing through the city the holy oath-offerings, two lambs and strong-hearted wine, the fruit of the earth, in a goat-skin bottle. And the herald Idaios bare the shining bowl and golden cups; and came to the old man and summoned him and said: "Rise, thou son of Laomedon. The chieftains of the horse-taming Trojans and mail-clad Achaians call on thee to go down into the plain, that ye may pledge a trusty oath. But Alexandros and Menelaos dear to Ares will fight with their long spears for the lady's sake; and let lady and treasure go with him that shall conquer. And may we that are left pledge friendship and trusty oaths and dwell in deep-soiled Troy, and they shall depart to Argos pasture-land of horses and Achaia home of fair women."

So said he, and the old man shuddered and bade his companions yoke the horses; and they with speed obeyed. Then Priam mounted and drew back the reins, and by his side Antenor mounted the splendid chariot. So the two drave the fleet horses through the Skaian gates to the plain. And when they had come even to the Trojans and Achaians, they went down from the chariots upon the bounteous earth, and marched into the midst of Trojans and Achaians. Then forthwith rose up Agamemnon king of men, and up rose Odysseus the man of wiles; and the lordly heralds gathered together the holy oath-offerings of the gods, and mingled the wine in a bowl, and poured water over the princes' hands. And Atreides put forth his hand and drew his knife that hung ever beside his sword's great sheath, and cut the hair from off the lambs' heads; and then the heralds portioned it among the chief of the Trojans and Achaians. Then in their midst Atreus' son lifted up his hands and prayed aloud: "Father Zeus, that rulest from Ida, most glorious, most great, and thou Sun that seest all things and hearest all things, and ye Rivers and thou Earth, and ye that in the underworld punish men outworn, whosoever sweareth falsely; be ye witnesses, and watch over the faithful oath. If Alexandros slay Menelaos, then let him have Helen to himself and all her possessions; and we will depart on our seafaring ships. But if golden-haired Menelaos slay Alexandros, then let the Trojans give back Helen and all her possessions and pay the Argives the recompense that is seemly, such as shall live among men that shall be hereafter. But if so be that Priam and Priam's sons will not pay the recompense unto me when Alexandros falleth, then will I fight on thereafter for the price of sin, and abide here till I compass the end of war."

So said he, and cut the lambs' throats with the pitiless knife. Them he laid gasping upon the ground, failing of breath, for the knife had taken their strength from them; and next they drew the wine from the bowl into the cups, and poured it forth and prayed to the gods that live for ever. And thus would say many an one of Achaians and Trojans: "Zeus most glorious, most great, and all ye immortal gods, which folk soe'er be first to sin against the oaths, may their brains be so poured forth upon the earth even as this wine, theirs and their children's; and let their wives be made subject unto strangers."

So spake they, but the son of Kronos vouchsafed not yet fulfilment. And in their midst Priam of the seed of Dardanos uttered his saying: "Hearken to me, Trojans and well-greaved Achaians. I verily will return back to windy Ilios, seeing that I can in no wise bear to behold with mine eyes my dear son fighting with Menelaos dear to Ares. But Zeus knoweth, and all the immortal gods, for whether of the twain the doom of death is appointed."

So spake the godlike man, and laid the lambs in his chariot, and entered in himself, and drew back the reins; and by his side Antenor mounted the splendid chariot. So they departed back again to Ilios; and Hector son of Priam and goodly Odysseus first meted out a space, and then they took the lots, and shook them in a bronze-bound helmet, to know whether of the twain should first cast his spear of bronze. And the people prayed and lifted up their hands to the gods; and thus would say many an one of the Achaians and Trojans: "Father Zeus, that rulest from Ida, most glorious, most great; whichsoe'er it be that brought this trouble upon both peoples, vouchsafe that he may die and enter the house of Hades; that so for us peace may be assured and trusty oaths."

So said they; and great Hector of the glancing plume shook the helmet, looking behind him; and quickly leapt forth the lot of Paris. Then the people sat them down by ranks where each man's high-stepping horses and inwrought armour lay. And upon his shoulders goodly Alexandros donned his beauteous armour, even he that was lord to Helen of the lovely hair. First upon his legs set he his greaves, beautiful, fastened with silver ankle-clasps; next upon his breast he donned the corslet of his brother Lykaon, and fitted it upon himself. And over his shoulders cast he his silver-studded sword of bronze, and then a shield great and sturdy. And on his mighty head he set a wrought helmet of horse-hair crest, whereover the plume nodded terribly, and he took him a strong spear fitted to his grasp. And in like wise warlike Menelaos donned his armour.

So when they had armed themselves on either side in the throng, they strode between Trojans and Achaians, fierce of aspect, and wonder came on them that beheld, both on the Trojans tamers of horses and on the well-greaved Achaians. Then took they their stand near together in the measured space, brandishing their spears in wrath each against other. First Alexandros hurled his far-shadowing spear, and smote on Atreides' round shield; but the bronze brake not through, for its point was turned in the stout shield. Next Menelaos son of Atreus lifted up his hand to cast, and made prayer to father Zeus: "King Zeus, grant me revenge on him that was first to do me wrong, even on goodly Alexandros, and subdue thou him at my hands; so that many an one of men that shall be hereafter may shudder to wrong his host that hath shown him kindness.

So said he, and poised his far-shadowing spear, and hurled, and smote on the round shield of the son of Priam. Through the bright shield went the ponderous spear and through the inwrought breastplate it pressed on; and straight beside his flank the spear rent the tunic, but he swerved and escaped black death. Then Atreides drew his silver-studded sword, and lifted up his hand and smote the helmet-ridge; but the sword shattered upon it into three, yea four, and fell from his hand. Thereat Atreides looked up to the wide heaven and cried: "Father Zeus, surely none of the gods is crueller than thou. Verily I thought to have gotten vengeance on Alexandros for his wickedness, but now my sword breaketh in my hand, and my spear sped from my grasp in vain, and I have not smitten him."

So saying, he leapt upon him and caught him by his horsehair crest, and swinging him round dragged him towards the well-greaved Achaians; and he was strangled by the embroidered strap beneath his soft throat, drawn tight below his chin to hold his helm. Now would Menelaos have dragged him away and won glory unspeakable, but that Zeus' daughter Aphrodite was swift to mark, and tore asunder for him the strap of slaughtered ox's hide; so the helmet came away empty in his stalwart hand. Thereat Menelaos cast it with a swing toward the well-greaved Achaians, and his trusty comrades took it up; and himself sprang back again eager to slay him with spear of bronze. But Aphrodite snatched up Paris, very easily as a goddess may, and hid him in thick darkness, and set him down in his fragrant perfumed chamber; and herself went to summon Helen. Her she found on the high tower, and about her the Trojan women thronged. So with her hand she plucked her perfumed raiment and shook it and spake to her in the likeness of an aged dame, a woolcomber that was wont to work for her fair wool when she dwelt in Lakedaimon, whom too she greatly loved. Even in her likeness fair Aphrodite spake: "Come hither; Alexandros summoneth thee to go homeward. There is he in his chamber and inlaid bed, radiant in beauty and vesture; nor wouldst thou deem him to be come from fighting his foe, but rather to be faring to the dance, or from the dance to be just resting and set down."

So said she, and stirred Helen's soul within her breast; and when now she marked the fair neck and lovely breast and sparkling eyes of the goddess, she marvelled straightway and spake a word and called upon her name: "Strange queen, why art thou desirous now to beguile me? Verily thou wilt lead me further on to some one of the peopled cities of Phrygia or lovely Maionia, if there too thou hast perchance some other darling among mortal men, because even now Menelaos hath conquered goodly Alexandros, and will lead me, accursed me, to his home. Therefore thou comest hither with guileful intent. Go and sit thou by his side, and depart from the way of the gods; neither let thy feet ever bear thee back to Olympus, but still be vexed for his sake and guard him till he make thee his wife or perchance his slave. But thither will I not go; all the women of Troy will blame me hereafter; and I have griefs untold within my soul."

Then in wrath bright Aphrodite spake to her: "Provoke me not, rash woman, lest in mine anger I desert thee, and hate thee even as now I love thee beyond measure, and lest I devise grievous enmities between both, even betwixt Trojans and Achaians, and so thou perish in evil wise."

So said she, and Helen sprung of Zeus was afraid, and went wrapped in her bright radiant vesture, silently, and the Trojan women marked her not; and the goddess led the way.

Now when they were come to the beautiful house of Alexan

dros the handmaidens turned straightway to their tasks, and the fair lady went to the high-roofed chamber; and laughter-loving Aphrodite took for her a chair and' brought it, even she the goddess, and set it before the face of Paris. There Helen took her seat, the child of aegis-bearing Zeus, and with eyes turned askance spake and chode her lord: "Thou comest back from battle; would thou hadst perished there, vanquished of that great warrior that was my former husband. Verily it was once thy boast that thou wast a better man than Menelaos dear to Ares, in the might of thine arm and thy spear. But go, now, challenge Menelaos dear to Ares to fight thee again face to face. Nay, but I, even I, bid thee refrain, nor fight a fight with golden-haired Menelaos man to man, neither attack him recklessly, lest perchance thou fall to his spear anon."

And Paris made answer to her and said: "Chide not my soul, lady, with cruel taunts. For now indeed hath Menelaos vanquished me with Athene's aid, but another day may I do so unto him; for we too have gods with us."

But Atreides the while strode through the hosts like to a wild beast, if anywhere he might set eyes on godlike Alexandros. But none of the Trojans or their famed allies could discover Alexandros to Menelaos dear to Ares. Yet surely did they in no wise hide him for kindliness, could any have seen him; for he was hated of all even as black death. So Agamemnon king of men spake among them there: "Hearken to me, Trojans and Dardanians and allies. Now is victory declared for Menelaos dear to Ares; give ye back Helen of Argos and the possessions with her, and pay ye the recompense such as is seemly, that it may live even among men that shall be hereafter." So said Atreides, and all the Achaians gave assent.

THE COUNCIL OF THE GODS

BOOK IV

How Pandaros wounded Menelaos by treachery; and Agamemnon exhorted his chief captains to battle.

Now the gods sat by Zeus and held assembly on the golden floor, and in the midst the lady Hebe poured them their nectar: they with golden goblets pledged one another, and gazed upon the city of the Trojans. Than did Kronos' son essay to provoke Hera with vexing words, and spake maliciously: "Twain goddesses hath Menelaos for his helpers, even Hera and Athene. Yet these sit apart and take their pleasure in beholding; but beside that other ever standeth laughter-loving Aphrodite and wardeth off fate from him, and now hath she saved him as he thought to perish. But of a truth the victory is to Menelaos dear to Ares; so let us take thought how these things shall be; whether once more we shall arouse ill war and the dread battle din, or put friendship between the foes. Moreover if this were welcome to all and well pleasing, may the city of king Priam yet be an habitation, and Menelaos take back Helen of Argos."

So said he, but Athene and Hera murmured thereat, who were sitting by him and devising ills for the Trojans. Now Athene held her peace and said not anything, for wrath at father Zeus, and fierce anger gat hold upon her: but Hera's breast contained not her anger, and she spake: "Most dread son of Kronos, what word is this thou hast spoken? How hast thou the will to make my labour void and of none effect, and the sweat of my toil that I sweated, when my horses were wearied with my summoning of the host, to be the plague of Priam and his sons? Do as thou wilt; but we other gods do not all approve thee."

Then in sore anger Zeus the cloud-gatherer spake to her: "Good lack, how have Priam and Priam's sons done thee such great wrong that thou art furiously minded to sack the established citadel of Ilios? Perchance wert thou to enter within the gates and long walls and devour Priam raw, and Priam's sons and all the Trojans, then mightest thou assuage thine anger. Do as thou art minded, only let not this quarrel hereafter be to me and thee a sore strife between us both. And this moreover will I say to thee, and do thou lay it to thy heart; whene'er I too be of eager mind to lay waste a city where is the race of men that are dear to thee, hinder thou not my wrath, but let me be, even as I yield to thee of free will, yet with soul unwilling. For of all cities beneath sun and starry heaven that are the dwelling of mortal men, holy Ilios was most honoured of my heart, and Priam and the folk of Priam of the good ashen spear. For never did mine altar lack the seemly feast, even drink-offering and burnt-offering, the worship that is our due."

Then Hera the ox-eyed queen made answer to him: "Of a surety three cities are there that be dearest far to me, Argos and Sparta and wide-wayed Mykene; these lay thou waste whene'er they are found hateful to thy heart; not for them will I stand forth, nor do I grudge thee them. For even if I be jealous and would forbid thee to overthrow them, yet will my jealousy not avail, seeing that thou art stronger far than I. Still must my labour too not be made of none effect; for I also am a god, and my lineage is even as thine, and Kronos the crooked counsellor begat me to the place of honour in double wise, by birthright, and because I am named thy spouse, and thou art king among all the immortals. Let us indeed yield each to other herein, I to thee and thou to me, and the rest of the immortal gods will follow with us; and do thou with speed charge Athene to betake her to the fierce battle din of Trojans and Achaians, and to essay that the Trojans may first take upon them to do violence to the Achaians in their triumph, despite the oaths."

So said she, and the father of men and gods disregarded not, and roused Athene that already was set thereon; and from Olympus' heights she darted down. Even as the son of Kronos the crooked counsellor sendeth a star, a portent for mariners or a wide host of men, bright shining, and therefrom are scattered sparks in multitude; even in such guise sped Pallas Athene to earth, and leapt into their midst; and astonishment came on them that beheld, on horse-taming Trojans and well-greaved Achaians. Then the goddess entered the throng of Trojans in the likeness of a man, even Antenor's son Laodokos, a stalwart warrior, and sought for godlike Pandaros the son of Lykaon, if haply she might find him. Him found she, the noble and stalwart, standing, and about him the stalwart ranks of the shield-bearing host that followed him. So she came near and spake winged words: "Wilt thou now hearken to me, thou wise son of Lykaon? Then wouldst thou take heart to shoot a swift arrow at Menelaos, and wouldst win favour and glory before all the Trojans, and before king Alexandros most of all. Surely from him first of any wouldst thou receive glorious gifts, if perchance he see Menelaos, Atreus' warrior son, vanquished by thy dart and brought to the grievous pyre. Go to now, shoot at glorious Menelacs, and vow to Apollo, the son of light, the lord of archery, to sacrifice a goodly hecatomb of firstling lambs when thou art returned to thy home."

So spake Athene, and persuaded his fool's heart. Forthwith he unsheathed his polished bow of horn of a wild ibex. He laid it down when he had well strung it, by resting it upon the ground; and his staunch comrades held their shields before him, lest the warrior sons of the Achaians should first set on them, ere Menelaos, Atreus' warrior son, were smitten. Then opened he the lid of his quiver and took forth a feathered arrow, never yet shot, a source of grievous pangs; and anon he laid the bitter dart upon the string and vowed to Apollo, the son of light, the lord of archery, to sacrifice a goodly hecatomb of firstling lambs when he should have returned to his home.

Then he took the notch and string of ox's-sinew together, and drew, bringing to his breast the string, and to the bow the iron head. So when he had now bent the great bow into a round, the horn twanged, and the string sang aloud, and the keen arrow leapt eager to wing his way amid the throng.

But the blessed gods immortal forgat not thee, Menelaos; and before all the daughter of Zeus, the driver of the spoil, who stood before thee and warded off the piercing dart. She turned it just aside from the flesh, even as a mother driveth a fly from her child that lieth in sweet slumber; and with her own hand guided it where the golden buckles of the belt were clasped and the doubled breastplate met them. So the bitter arrow lighted upon the firm belt; through the inwrought belt it sped and through the curiously wrought breastplate it pressed on and through the taslet[1] he wore to shield his flesh, a barrier against darts; and this best shielded him, yet it passed on even through this. Then did the arrow graze the warrior's outermost flesh, and forthwith the dusky blood flowed from the wound.

As when some woman of Maionia or Karia staineth ivory with purple, to make a cheek-piece for horses, and it is laid up in the treasure chamber, and many a horseman prayeth for it to wear; but it is laid up to be a king's boast, alike an adornment for his horse and a glory for his charioteer; even in such wise, Menelaos, were thy shapely thighs stained with blood and thy legs and thy fair ankles beneath.

Thereat shuddered Agamemnon king of men when he saw the black blood flowing from the wound. And Menelaos dear to Ares likewise shuddered; but when he saw how thread[2] and barbs were without, his spirit was gathered in his breast again. Then lord Agamemnon moaned deep, and spake among them, holding Menelaos by the hand; and his comrades made moan

[1] An apron or belt set with metal, worn below the corslet.
[2] By which the iron head was attached to the shaft.

the while: "Dear brother, to thy death, meseemeth, pledged I these oaths, setting thee forth to fight the Trojans alone before the face of the Achaians; seeing that the Trojans have so smitten thee, and trodden under foot the trusty oaths. I shall have sore sorrow for thee, Menelaos, if thou die and fulfil the lot of life. Yea in utter shame should I return to thirsty Argos, seeing that the Achaians will forthwith bethink them of their native land, and so should we leave to Priam and the Trojans their boast, even Helen of Argos."

But golden-haired Menelaos encouraged him and said: "Be of good courage, neither dismay at all the host of the Achaians. The keen dart lighted not upon a deadly spot; my glistering belt in front stayed it, and the kirtle of mail beneath, and the taslet that the coppersmiths fashioned."

Then lord Agamemnon answered him and said: "Would it may be so, dear Menelaos. But the leech shall feel the wound, and lay thereon drugs that shall assuage thy dire pangs."

So saying he spake to godlike Talthybios, his herald: "Talthybios, with all speed call Machaon hither, the hero son of Asklepios the noble leech, to see Menelaos, Atreus' warrior son, whom one well skilled in archery, some Trojan or Lykian, hath wounded with a bow-shot, to his glory and our grief."

And when Machaon was come where was golden-haired Menelaos wounded, and all as many as were chieftains gathered around him in a circle, the godlike hero came and stood in their midst, and anon drew forth the arrow from the clasped belt; and as it was drawn forth the keen barbs were broken backwards. Then he loosed the glistering belt and the kirtle of mail beneath and taslet that the coppersmiths fashioned; and when he saw the wound where the bitter arrow had lighted, he sucked out the blood and cunningly spread thereon soothing drugs.

While these were tending Menelaos of the loud war-cry, the ranks of shield-bearing Trojans came on; so the Achaians donned their arms again, and bethought them of the fray. Now wouldest thou not see noble Agamemnon slumbering, nor cowering, nor unready to fight, but very eager for glorious battle. He left his horses and his chariot adorned with bronze; and his squire kept apart the snorting steeds; and he straitly charged him to have them at hand whenever weariness should come upon his limbs with marshalling so many; and thus on foot ranged he through the ranks of warriors. And whomsoever of all the fleet-horsed Danaans he found eager, he stood by them and by his words encouraged them: "Ye Argives, relax not in any wise your impetuous valour; for father Zeus will be no helper of liars, but as these were first to transgress against the oaths, so shall their own tender flesh be eaten of the vultures, and we shall bear away their dear wives and little children in our ships, when once we take the stronghold."

But whomsoever he found shrinking from hateful battle, these he chode sore with angry words: "Ye Argives, warriors of the bow, ye men of dishonour, have ye no shame? Why stand ye thus dazed like fawns that are weary with running over the long plain and so stand still, and no valour is found in their hearts at all? Even thus stand ye dazed, and fight not. Is it that ye wait for the Trojans to come near where your good ships' sterns are drawn up on the shore of the grey sea, to see if Kronion will stretch his arm over you indeed?"

As when on the echoing beach the sea-wave lifteth up itself in close array before the driving of the west wind; out on the deep doth it first raise its head, and then breaketh upon the land and belloweth aloud and goeth with arching crest about the promontories, and speweth the foaming brine afar; even so in close array moved the battalions of the Danaans without pause to battle. Each captain gave his men the word, and the rest went silently; thou wouldest not deem that all the great host following them had any voice within their breasts; in silence feared they their captains. On every man

glittered the inwrought armour wherewith they went clad.
But for the Trojans, like sheep beyond number that stand in
the courtyard of a man of great substance, to be milked of their
white milk, and bleat without ceasing to hear their lambs' cry,
even so arose the clamour of the Trojans through the wide
host. For they had not all like speech nor one language, but
their tongues were mingled, and they were brought from many
lands. These were urged on of Ares, and those of bright-eyed
Athene, and Terror and Rout, and Strife whose fury wearieth
not, sister and friend of murderous Ares. She now cast common discord in their midst, as she fared through the throng
and made the lamentation of men to wax.

Now when they were met together and come unto one spot,
then clashed they targe and spear and fury of bronze-clad
warrior; the bossed shields pressed each on each and mighty
din arose. Then were heard the voice of groaning and the
voice of triumph together of the slayers and the slain, and the
earth streamed with blood. As when two winter torrents flow
down the mountains to a watersmeet and join their furious
flood within the deep ravine from their great springs, and the
shepherd heareth the roaring far off among the hills: even so
from the joining of battle came there forth shouting and travail.
Antilochos first slew a Trojan warrior in full array, valiant
amid the champions, Echepolos son of Thalysios; him was he
first to smite upon the ridge of his crested helmet, and he drave
the spear into his brow and the point of bronze passed within
the bone; darkness clouded his eyes, and he crashed like a
tower amid the press of fight. As he fell lord Elephenor
caught him by the foot, Chalkodon's son, captain of the great-hearted Abantes, and dragged him from beneath the darts, eager
with all speed to despoil him of his armour. Yet but for a
little endured his essay; great-hearted Agenor saw him haling
away the corpse, and where his side was left uncovered of his
buckler as he bowed him down, there smote he him with

bronze-tipped spear-shaft and unstrung his limbs. So his life departed from him, and over his corpse the task of Trojans and Achaians grew hot; like wolves leapt they one at another, and man lashed at man.

Next Telamonian Aias smote Anthemion's son. Scanty was his span of life by reason of the spear of great-hearted Aias that laid him low. For as he went he first was smitten on his right breast beside the pap; straight through his shoulder passed the spear of bronze, and he fell to the ground in the dust like a poplar-tree, that hath grown up smooth in the lowland of a great marsh, and its branches grow upon the top thereof. In such fashion did heaven-sprung Aias slay Simoeisios son of Anthemion; then at him Antiphos of the glancing corslet, Priam's son, made a cast with his keen javelin across the throng. Him he missed, but smote Odysseus' valiant comrade Leukos in the groin as he drew the corpse his way, so that he fell upon it and the body dropped from his hands. Then Odysseus was very wroth at heart for the slaying of him, and strode through the forefront of the battle harnessed in flashing bronze, and went and stood hard by and glanced around him, and cast his bright javelin; and the Trojans shrank before the casting of the hero. He sped not the dart in vain, but smote Demokoon, Priam's bastard son that had come to him from tending his fleet mares in Abydos. Him Odysseus, being wroth for his comrade's sake, smote with his javelin on one temple; and through both temples passed the point of bronze, and darkness clouded his eyes, and he fell with a crash and his armour clanged upon him. Then the forefighters and glorious Hector yielded, and the Argives shouted aloud, and drew the bodies unto them, and pressed yet further onward. But Apollo looked down from Pergamos, and had indignation, and with a shout called to the Trojans: "Arise, ye Trojans, tamers of horses; yield not to the Argives in fight; not of stone nor iron is their flesh that it should resist the piercing bronze when they are smitten. Moreover Achilles, son of Thetis of the fair tresses, fighteth not, but amid the ships broodeth on his bitter anger."

So spake the dread god from the city; and the Achaians likewise were urged on of Athene, most glorious, as she passed through the throng wheresoever she beheld them slackening.

Next was Diores son of Amarynkeus caught in the snare of fate; for he was smitten by a jagged stone on the right leg hard by the ankle, and the caster thereof was captain of the men of Thrace, Peiroos son of Imbrasos that had come from Ainos. The pitiless stone crushed utterly the two sinews and the bones; back fell he in the dust, and stretched out both his hands to his dear comrades, gasping out his soul. Then he that smote him, even Peiroos, sprang at him and pierced him with a spear beside the navel; so all his bowels gushed forth upon the ground, and darkness clouded his eyes. But even as Peiroos departed from him Thoas of Aitolia smote with a spear his chest above the pap, and the point fixed in his lung. Then Thoas came close, and plucked out from his breast the ponderous spear, and drew his sharp sword, wherewith he smote his belly in the midst, and took his life. Yet he stripped not off his armour; for his comrades, the men of Thrace that wear the top-knot, stood around, their long spears in their hands, and albeit he was great and valiant and proud they drave him off from them and he gave ground reeling. So were the two captains stretched in the dust side by side, he of the Thracians and he of the mail-clad Epeians; and around them were many others likewise slain. Many Trojans that day and many Achaians were laid side by side upon their faces in the dust.

BOOK V

How Diomedes by his great valour made havoc of the Trojans, and wounded even Aphrodite and Ares by the help of Athene.

But now to Tydeus' son Diomedes Athene gave might and courage, for him to be pre-eminent amid all the Argives and win glorious renown. She kindled flame unwearied from his helmet and shield, like to the star of summer that above all others glittereth bright after he hath bathed in the ocean stream. In such wise kindled she flame from his head and shoulders and sent him into the midst, where men thronged the thickest.

Now there was amid the Trojans one Dares, rich and noble, priest of Hephaistos; and he had two sons, Phegeus and Idaios, well skilled in all the art of battle. These separated themselves and assailed him face to face, they setting on him from their car and he on foot upon the ground. And when they were now come near in onset on each other, first Phegeus hurled his far-shadowing spear; and over Tydeides' left shoulder the spear point passed, and smote not his body. Then next Tydeides made a spear-cast, and the javelin sped not from his hand in vain, but smote his breast between the nipples, and thrust him from the chariot. So Idaios sprang away, leaving his beautiful car, and dared not to bestride his slain brother; else had neither he himself escaped black fate: but Hephaistos guarded him and saved him in a veil of darkness, that he might not have his aged priest all broken with sorrow. And the son of great-hearted Tydeus drave away the horses and gave them to his men to take to the hollow ships. But when the great-hearted Trojans beheld the sons of Dares, how one was fled, and one was slain beside his chariot, the spirit of all was stirred. But bright-eyed Athene took impetuous Ares by the hand and spake to him and said: "Ares, Ares, blood-stained

bane of mortals, thou stormer of walls, can we not now leave
the Trojans and Achaians to fight, on whichsoever it be that
father Zeus bestoweth glory? But let us twain give place, and
escape the wrath of Zeus."

So saying she led impetuous Ares from the battle. Then
she made him sit down beside loud Skamandros, and the
Danaans pushed the Trojans back.

So they laboured in the violent mellay; but of Tydeides
man could not tell with whom he were joined, whether he consorted with Trojans or with Achaians. For he stormed across
the plain like a winter torrent at the full, that in swift course
scattereth the causeys;[1] neither can the long lines of causeys hold it in, nor the fences of fruitful orchards stay its
sudden coming when the rain of heaven driveth it; and before
it perish in multitudes the fair works of the sons of men.
Thus before Tydeides the serried battalions of the Trojans were
overthrown, and they abode him not for all they were so many.

But when Lykaon's glorious son marked him storming across
the plain, overthrowing battalions before him, anon he bent his
crooked bow against Tydeides, and smote him as he sped onwards, hitting hard by his right shoulder the plate of his corslet; the bitter arrow flew through and held straight upon its
way, and the corslet was dabbled with blood. Over him then
loudly shouted Lykaon's glorious son: "Bestir you, great-
hearted Trojans, urgers of horses; the best man of the Achaians
is wounded, and I deem that he shall not for long endure the
violent dart."

So spake he boasting; yet was the other not vanquished of
the swift dart, only he gave place and stood before his horses
and his chariot and spake to Sthenelos son of Kapaneus:
"Haste thee, dear son of Kapaneus; descend from thy chariot,
to draw me from my shoulder the bitter arrow."

---

[1] [Causeways.]

So said he, and Sthenelos leapt from his chariot to earth and stood beside him and drew the swift shaft right through, out of his shoulder; and the blood darted up through the pliant tunic. Then Diomedes of the loud war-cry prayed thereat: "Hear me, daughter of aegis-bearing Zeus, unwearied maiden! If ever in kindly mood thou stoodest by my father in the heat of battle, even so now be thou likewise kind to me, Athene. Grant me to slay this man, and bring within my spear-cast him that took advantage to shoot me, and boasteth over me, deeming that not for long shall I see the bright light of the sun."

So spake he in prayer, and Pallas Athene heard him, and made his limbs nimble, his feet and his hands withal, and came near and spake winged words: "Be of good courage now, Diomedes, to fight the Trojans; for in thy breast I have set thy father's courage undaunted, even as it was in knightly Tydeus, wielder of the buckler. Moreover I have taken from thine eyes the mist that erst was on them, that thou mayest well discern both god and man. Therefore if any god come hither to make trial of thee, fight not thou face to face with any of the immortal gods; save only if Aphrodite daughter of Zeus enter into the battle, her smite thou with the keen bronze."

So saying bright-eyed Athene went her way and Tydeides returned and entered the forefront of the battle; even though erst his soul was eager to do battle with the Trojans, yet now did threefold courage come upon him, as upon a lion whom some shepherd in the field guarding his fleecy sheep hath wounded, being sprung into the fold, yet hath not vanquished him; he hath roused his might, and then cannot beat him back, but lurketh amid the steading, and his forsaken flock is affrighted; so the sheep are cast in heaps, one upon the other, and the lion in his fury leapeth out of the high fold; even so in fury mingled mighty Diomedes with the Trojans.

BOOK V

Him Aineias beheld making havoc of the ranks of warriors, and went his way along the battle and amid the hurtling of spears, seeking godlike Pandaros, if haply he might find him. Lykaon's son he found, the noble and stalwart, and stood before his face, and spake a word unto him. "Pandaros, where now are thy bow and thy winged arrows, and the fame wherein no man of this land rivalleth thee, nor any in Lykia boasteth to be thy better? Go to now, lift thy hands in prayer to Zeus and shoot thy dart at this fellow, whoe'er he be that lordeth it here and hath already wrought the Trojans much mischief, seeing he hath unstrung the knees of many a brave man; if indeed it be not some god wroth with the Trojans, in anger by reason of sacrifices; the wrath of god is a sore thing to fall on men."

And Lykaon's glorious son made answer to him: "Aineias, counsellor of the mail-clad Trojans, in everything liken I him to the wise son of Tydeus; I discern him by his shield and crested helmet, and by the aspect of his horses; yet know I not surely if it be not a god. But if it be the man I deem, even the wise son of Tydeus, then not without help of a god is he thus furious, but some immortal standeth beside him with a cloud wrapped about his shoulders and turned aside from him my swift dart even as it lighted. For already have I shot my dart at him and smote his right shoulder right through the breastplate of his corslet, yea and I thought to hurl him headlong to Aidoneus, yet I vanquished him not; surely it is some wrathful god. Already have I aimed at two princes, Tydeus' and Atreus' sons, and both I smote and surely drew forth blood, yet only roused them the more. Therefore in an evil hour I took from the peg my curved bow on that day when I led my Trojans to lovely Ilios, to do noble Hector pleasure. But if I return and mine eyes behold my native land and wife and great palace lofty-roofed, then may an alien forthwith cut my head from me if I break not this bow with mine hands and cast it upon the blazing fire; worthless is its service to me as air."

Then Aineias captain of the Trojans answered him: "Nay, talk not thus; naught shall be mended before that we with horses and chariot have gone to face this man, and made trial of him in arms. Come then, mount upon my car that thou mayest see of what sort are the steeds of Tros, well skilled for following or for fleeing hither or thither very fleetly across the plain; they will e'en bring us to the city safe and sound, even though Zeus hereafter give victory to Diomedes son of Tydeus. Come therefore, take thou the lash and shining reins, and I will stand upon the car to fight; or else withstand thou him, and to the horses will I look."

To him made answer Lykaon's glorious son: "Aineias, take thou thyself the reins and thine own horses; better will they draw the curved car for their wonted charioteer, if perchance it hap that we must flee from Tydeus' son; lest they go wild for fear and will not take us from the fight, for lack of thy voice, and so the son of great-hearted Tydeus attack us and slay us both and drive away the whole-hooved horses. So drive thou thyself thy chariot and thy horses, and I will await his onset with my keen spear." So saying mounted they upon the well-dight chariot, and eagerly drave the fleet horses against Tydeides. And Sthenelos, the glorious son of Kapaneus, saw them, and anon spake to Tydeides winged words: "Diomedes son of Tydeus, dear to mine heart, I behold two stalwart warriors eager to fight against thee, endued with might beyond measure. The one is well skilled in the bow, even Pandaros, and he moreover boasteth him to be Lykaon's son; and Aineias boasteth himself to be born son of great-hearted Anchises, and his mother is Aphrodite. Come now, let us give place upon the chariot, neither rage thou thus, I pray thee, in the forefront of battle, lest perchance thou lose thy life."

Then stalwart Diomedes looked sternly at him and said:

"Speak to me no word of flight, for I ween that thou shalt not at all persuade me; not in my blood is it to fight a skulking fight or cower down; my force is steadfast still. I have no mind to mount the chariot, nay, even as I am will I go to face them; Pallas Athene biddeth me not be afraid. And as for these, their fleet horses shall not take both back from us again, even if one or other escape. And this moreover tell I thee, and lay thou it to heart: if Athene rich in counsel grant me this glory, to slay them both, then refrain thou here these my fleet horses, and bind the reins tight to the chariot rim; and be mindful to leap upon Aineias' horses, and drive them forth from the Trojans amid the well-greaved Achaians. For they are of that breed whereof farseeing Zeus gave to Tros recompense for Ganymede his child, because they were the best of all horses beneath the daylight and the sun."

In such wise talked they one to the other, and anon those other twain came near, driving their fleet horses. First to him spake Lykaon's glorious son: "O thou strong-souled and cunning, son of proud Tydeus, verily my swift dart vanquished thee not, the bitter arrow; so now will I make trial with my spear if I can hit thee."

He spake and poised and hurled his far-shadowing spear, and smote upon Tydeides' shield; right through it sped the point of bronze and reached the breastplate. So over him shouted loudly Lykaon's glorious son: "Thou art smitten on the belly right through, and I ween thou shalt not long hold up thine head; so thou givest me great renown."

But mighty Diomedes unaffrighted answered him: "Thou hast missed, and not hit; but ye twain I deem shall not cease till one or other shall have fallen and glutted with blood Ares the stubborn god of war."

So spake he and hurled; and Athene guided the dart upon his nose beside the eye, and it pierced through his white teeth. So the hard bronze cut through his tongue at the root and the point issued forth by the base of the chin. He fell from his chariot, and his splendid armour gleaming clanged upon him, and the fleet-footed horses swerved aside; so there his soul and strength were unstrung.

Then Aineias leapt down with shield and long spear, fearing lest perchance the Achaians might take from him the corpse; and strode over him like a lion confident in his strength, and held before him his spear and the circle of his shield, eager to slay whoe'er should come to face him, crying his terrible cry. Then Tydeides grasped in his hand a stone — a mighty deed — such as two men, as men now are, would not avail to lift; yet he with ease wielded it all alone. Therewith he smote Aineias on the hip where the thigh turneth in the hip-joint, and this men call the "cup-bone." So he crushed his cup-bone, and brake both sinews withal, and the jagged stone tore apart the skin. Then the hero stayed fallen upon his knees and with stout hand leant upon the earth; and the darkness of night veiled his eyes. And now might Aineias king of men have perished, but that Aphrodite daughter of Zeus was swift to mark. About her dear son wound she her white arms, and spread before his face a fold of her radiant vesture, to be a covering from the darts, lest any of the fleet-horsed Danaans might hurl the spear into his breast and take away his life.

So was she bearing her dear son away from battle; but the son of Kapaneus forgat not the behest that Diomedes of the loud war-cry had laid upon him; he refrained his own whole-hooved horses away from the tumult, binding the reins tight to the chariot-rim, and leapt on the sleek-coated horses of Aineias, and drave them from the Trojans to the well-greaved Achaians, and gave them to Deïpylos his dear comrade whom he esteemed above all that were his age-fellows, because he was like-minded with himself; and bade him drive them to the hollow ships. Then did the hero mount his own chariot and take the shining reins and forthwith drive his strong-hooved horses in quest of Tydeides, eagerly. Now Tydeides had made onslaught with pitiless weapon on Kypris,[1] knowing how she was a coward goddess and none of those that have mastery in battle of the warriors. Now when he had pursued her through the dense throng and come on her, then great-hearted Tydeus' son thrust with his keen spear, and leapt on her and wounded the skin of her weak hand; straight through the ambrosial raiment that the Graces themselves had woven her pierced the dart into the flesh, above the springing of the palm. Then flowed the goddess's immortal blood, such ichor as floweth in the blessed gods; for they eat no bread neither drink they gleaming wine, wherefore they are bloodless and are named immortals. And she with a great cry let fall her son: him Phoebus Apollo took into his arms and saved him in a dusky cloud, lest any of the fleet-horsed Danaans might hurl the spear into his breast and take away his life. But over her Diomedes of the loud war-cry shouted afar: "Refrain thee, thou daughter of Zeus, from war and fighting. Is it not enough that thou beguilest feeble women? But if in battle thou wilt mingle, verily I deem that thou shalt shudder at the name of battle, if thou hear it even afar off."

So spake he, and she departed in amaze and was sore troubled: and wind-footed Iris took her and led her from the throng tormented with her pain, and her fair skin was stained. There found she impetuous Ares sitting, on the battle's left; and his spear rested upon a cloud, and his fleet steeds. Then she fell on her knees and with instant prayer besought of her dear brother his golden-frontleted steeds: "Dear brother, save me and give me thy steeds, that I may win to Olympus, where is the habitation of the immortals. Sorely am I afflicted with a wound wherewith a mortal smote me, even Tydeides, who now would fight even with father Zeus."

[1] Aphrodite.

So spake she, and Ares gave her his golden-frontleted steeds: and she mounted on the chariot sore at heart. By her side mounted Iris, and in her hands grasped the reins and lashed the horses to start them; and they flew onward nothing loth. Thus soon they came to the habitation of the gods, even steep Olympus. There wind-footed fleet Iris loosed the horses from the chariot and stabled them, and set ambrosial forage before them; but fair Aphrodite fell upon Dione's knees that was her mother. She took her daughter in her arms and stroked her with her hand, and spake and called upon her name: "Who now of the sons of heaven, dear child, hath entreated thee thus wantonly, as though thou wert a wrong-doer in the face of all?"

Then laughter-loving Aphrodite made answer to her: "Tydeus' son wounded me, high-hearted Diomedes, because I was saving from the battle my dear son Aineias, who to me is dearest far of all men. For no more is the fierce battle-cry for Trojans and Achaians, but the Danaans now are fighting even the immortals."

Then the fair goddess Dione answered her: "Be of good heart, my child, and endure for all thy pain; for many of us that inhabit the mansions of Olympus have suffered through men, in bringing grievous woes one upon another."

So saying with both hands she wiped the ichor from the arm; her arm was comforted, and the grievous pangs assuaged. But Athene and Hera beheld, and with bitter words provoked Zeus the son of Kronos. Of them was the bright-eyed goddess Athene first to speak: "Father Zeus, wilt thou indeed be wroth with me whate'er I say? Verily I ween that Kypris was urging some woman of Achaia to join her unto the Trojans whom she so marvellously loveth; and stroking such an one of the fair-robed women of Achaia, she tore upon the golden brooch her delicate hand."

So spake she, and the father of gods and men smiled, and called unto him golden Aphrodite and said: "Not unto thee, my child, are given the works of war; but follow thou after the loving tasks of wedlock, and to all these things shall fleet Ares and Athene look."

Now while they thus spake in converse one with the other, Diomedes of the loud war-cry leapt upon Aineias, knowing full well that Apollo himself had spread his arms over him; yet reverenced he not even the great god, but still was eager to slay Aineias and strip from him his glorious armour. So thrice he leapt on him, fain to slay him, and thrice Apollo beat back his glittering shield. And when the fourth time he sprang at him like a god, then Apollo the Far-darter spake to him with terrible shout: "Think, Tydeides, and shrink, nor desire to match thy spirit with gods; seeing there is no comparison of the race of immortal gods and of men that walk upon the earth."

So said he, and Tydeides shrank a short space backwards, to avoid the wrath of Apollo the Far-darter. Then Apollo set Aineias away from the throng in holy Pergamos where his temple stood. There Leto and Archer Artemis healed him in the mighty sanctuary, and gave him glory; but Apollo of the silver bow made a wraith like unto Aineias' self, and in such armour as his; and over the wraith Trojans and goodly Achaians each hewed the others' bucklers on their breasts, their round shields and fluttering targes.

Then to impetuous Ares said Phoebus Apollo: "Ares, Ares, blood-stained bane of mortals, thou stormer of walls, wilt thou not follow after this man and withdraw him from the battle, this Tydeides, who now would fight even with father Zeus? First in close fight he wounded Kypris in her hand hard by the wrist, and then sprang he upon myself like unto a god."

So saying he sate himself upon the height of Pergamos, and baleful Ares entered among the Trojan ranks and aroused them in the likeness of fleet Akamas, captain of the Thracians. On the heaven-nurtured sons of Priam he called saying: "O ye sons of Priam, the heaven-nurtured king, how long will ye yet suffer your host to be slain of the Achaians? Shall it be even until they fight about our well-built gates? Low lieth the warrior whom we esteemed like unto goodly Hector, even Aineias son of Anchises great of heart. Go to now, let us save from the tumult our valiant comrade."

So saying he aroused the spirit and soul of every man. Thereat Sarpedon sorely chode noble Hector: "Hector, where now is the spirit gone that erst thou hadst? Thou saidst forsooth that without armies or allies thou wouldest hold the city, alone with thy sisters' husbands and thy brothers; but now can I not see any of these neither perceive them, but they are cowering like hounds about a lion; and we are fighting that are but allies among you."

So spake Sarpedon, and his word stung Hector to the heart. Forthwith he leapt from his chariot in his armour to the earth, and brandishing two keen spears went everywhere through the host, urging them to fight, and roused the dread battle-cry. So they were rallied and stood to face the Achaians: and the Argives withstood them in close array and fled not. Even as a wind carrieth the chaff about the sacred threshing-floors when men are winnowing, and the chaff-heaps grow white — so now grew the Achaians white with falling dust which in their midst the horses' hooves beat up into the brazen heaven, as fight was joined again, and the charioteers wheeled round. Thus bare they forward the fury of their hands: and impetuous Ares drew round them a veil of night to aid the Trojans in the battle, ranging everywhere. And Apollo himself sent forth Aineias from his rich sanctuary and put courage in the heart of him, shepherd of the hosts. So Aineias took his place amid his comrades, and they were glad to see him come among them alive and sound and full of valiant spirit. Yet they questioned him not at all, for all the toil forbade them that the god of the silver bow was stirring and Ares bane of men and Strife raging insatiably.

And on the other side the two Aiantes and Odysseus and Diomedes stirred the Danaans to fight; yet these of themselves feared neither the Trojans' violence nor assaults, but stood like mists that Kronos' son setteth in windless air on the mountain tops, at peace, while the might of the north wind sleepeth and of all the violent winds that blow with keen breath and scatter apart the shadowing clouds. Even so the Danaans withstood the Trojans steadfastly and fled not. And Atreides ranged through the throng exhorting instantly: "My friends, quit you like men and take heart of courage, and shun dishonour in one another's eyes amid the stress of battle. Of men that shun dishonour more are saved than slain, but for them that flee is neither glory found nor any safety."

So saying he darted swiftly with his javelin and smote a foremost warrior, even great-hearted Aineias' comrade Deïkoon son of Pergasos, whom the Trojans held in like honour with Priam's sons, because he was swift to do battle amid the foremost. Him lord Agamemnon smote with his dart upon the shield, and it stayed not the spear, but the point passed through, so that he drave it through the belt into his nethermost belly: and he fell with a crash and his armour clanged upon him.

Then did Aineias slay two champions of the Danaans, even the sons of Diokles, Krethon and Orsilochos. Like them, two lions on the mountain tops are nurtured by their dam in the deep forest thickets; and these harry the kine and goodly sheep and make havoc of the farmsteads of men, till in their turn they too are slain at men's hands with the keen bronze; in such wise were these twain vanquished at Aineias' hands and fell like tall pine-trees.

But Menelaos dear to Ares had pity of them in their fall, and strode through the forefront, harnessed in flashing bronze, brandishing his spear; and Ares stirred his courage, with intent that he might fall beneath Aineias' hand. But Antilochos, great-hearted Nestor's son, beheld him, and strode through the forefront; because he feared exceedingly for the shepherd of the host, lest aught befall him and disappoint them utterly of their labour. So those two were now holding forth their hands and sharp spears each against the other, eager to do battle; when Antilochos came and stood hard by the shepherd of the host. But Aineias faced them not, keen warrior though he was, when he beheld two men abiding side by side; so these haled away the corpses to the Achaians' host, and laid the hapless twain in their comrades' arms, and themselves turned back and fought on amid the foremost.

But Hector marked them across the ranks, and sprang on them with a shout, and the battalions of the Trojans followed him in their might : and Ares led them on and dread Enyo, she bringing ruthless turmoil of war, the while Ares wielded in his hands his monstrous spear, and ranged now before Hector's face, and now behind.

Then Diomedes of the loud war-cry shuddered to behold him; and even as a shiftless man crossing a great plain cometh on a swift-streaming river flowing on to the sea, and seeing it boil with foam springeth backwards, even so now Tydeides shrank back and spake to the host: "Friends, how marvel we that noble Hector is a spearman and bold man of war! Yet ever is there beside him some god that wardeth off destruction; even as now Ares is there by him in likeness of a mortal man. But with faces towards the Trojans still give ground backwards, neither be desirous to fight amain with gods."

Now the Argives before the face of Ares and mail-clad Hector neither turned them round about toward their black ships, nor charged forward in battle, but still fell backward, when they heard of Ares amid the Trojans. But when the white-armed goddess Hera marked them making havoc of the Argives in the press of battle, anon she spake winged words to Athene: "Out on it, thou daughter of aegis-bearing Zeus, unwearied maiden!

Was it for naught we pledged our word to Menelaos, that he should not depart till he had laid waste well-walled Ilios, — if thus we let baleful Ares rage? Go to now, let us twain also take thought of impetuous valour."

So said she, and the bright-eyed goddess Athene disregarded not. So Hera the goddess queen, daughter of Kronos, went her way to harness the gold-frontleted steeds. And Athene, daughter of aegis-bearing Zeus, cast down at her father's threshold her woven vesture many-coloured, that herself had wrought and her hands had fashioned, and put on her the tunic of Zeus the cloud-gatherer, and arrayed her in her armour for dolorous battle. About her shoulders cast she the tasselled aegis terrible, whereon is Panic as a crown all round about, and Strife is therein and Valour and horrible Onslaught withal, and therein is the dreadful monster's Gorgon head, dreadful and grim, portent of aegis-bearing Zeus. Upon her head set she the two-crested golden helm with fourfold plate, bedecked with men-at-arms of a hundred cities. Upon the flaming chariot set she her foot, and grasped her heavy spear, great and stout, wherewith she vanquisheth the ranks of men, even of heroes with whom she of the awful sire is wroth. Then Hera swiftly smote the horses with the lash; self-moving groaned upon their hinges the gates of heaven whereof the Hours are warders, to whom is committed great heaven and Olympus, whether to throw open the thick cloud or set it to. There through the gates guided they their horses patient of the lash. And they found the son of Kronos sitting apart from all the gods on the topmost peak of many-ridged Olympus. Then the white-armed goddess Hera stayed her horses and questioned the most high Zeus, the son of Kronos, and said: "Father Zeus, hast thou no indignation with Ares for these violent deeds? How great and goodly a company of Achaians hath he destroyed recklessly and in unruly wise, unto my sorrow. But here in peace Kypris and Apollo of the silver bow take their pleasure, having set on this mad one that knoweth not any law. Father Zeus, wilt thou at all be wroth with me if I smite Ares and chase him from the battle in sorry plight?"

And Zeus the cloud-gatherer answered and said to her: "Go to now, set upon him Athene driver of the spoil, who most is wont to bring sore pain upon him."

So spake he, and the white-armed goddess Hera disregarded not, and lashed her horses; they nothing loth flew on between earth and starry heaven. As far as a man seeth with his eyes into the haze of distance as he sitteth on a place of outlook and gazeth over the wine-dark sea, so far leap the loudly neighing horses of the gods. Now when they came to Troy and the two flowing rivers, even to where Simoeis and Skamandros join their streams, there the white-armed goddess Hera stayed her horses and loosed them from the car and poured thick mist round about them, and Simoeis made ambrosia spring up for them to graze. So the goddesses went their way with step like unto turtle-doves, being fain to bring succour to the men of Argos. And when they were now come where the most and most valiant stood, thronging about mighty Diomedes tamer of horses, in the semblance of ravening lions or wild boars whose strength is nowise feeble, then stood the white-armed goddess Hera and shouted in the likeness of great-hearted Stentor with voice of bronze, whose cry was loud as the cry of fifty other men: "Fie upon you, Argives, base things of shame, so brave in semblance! While yet noble Achilles entered continually into battle, then issued not the Trojans even from the Dardanian gate; for they had dread of his terrible spear. But now fight they far from the city at the hollow ships."

So saying she aroused the spirit and soul of every man. And to Tydeides' side sprang the bright-eyed goddess Athene. That lord she found beside his horses and chariot, cooling the wound that Pandaros with his dart had pierced, for his sweat vexed it by reason of the broad baldrick of his round shield; therewith was he vexed and his arm grew weary, so he was lifting up the baldrick and wiping away the dusky blood. Then the goddess laid her hand on his horses' yoke, and said: "Of a truth Tydeus begat a son little after his own likeness. Tydeus was short of stature, but a man of war."

And stalwart Diomedes made answer to her and said: "I know thee, goddess daughter of aegis-bearing Zeus: therefore with my whole heart will I tell thee my thought and hide it not. Neither hath disheartening terror taken hold upon me, nor any faintness, but I am still mindful of thy behest that thou didst lay upon me. Thou forbadest me to fight face to face with all the blessed gods, save only if Zeus' daughter Aphrodite should enter into battle, then to wound her with the keen bronze. Therefore do I now give ground myself and have bidden all the Argives likewise to gather here together; for I discern Ares lording it in the fray."

Then the bright-eyed goddess Athene answered him: "Diomedes son of Tydeus, thou joy of mine heart, fear thou, for that, neither Ares nor any other of the immortals; so great a helper am I to thee. Go to now, at Ares first guide thou thy whole-hooved horses, and smite him hand to hand, nor have any awe of impetuous Ares, raving here, a curse incarnate, the renegade that of late in converse with me and Hera pledged him to fight against the Trojans and give succour to the Argives, but now consorteth with the Trojans and hath forgotten these."

So speaking, with her hand she drew back Sthenelos and thrust him from the chariot to earth, and instantly leapt he down; so the goddess mounted the car by noble Diomedes' side right eagerly. The oaken axle creaked loud with its burden, bearing the dread goddess and the man of might. Then Athene grasped the whip and reins; forthwith against

Ares first guided she the whole-hooved horses. Now he was stripping huge Periphas, most valiant far of the Aitolians, Ochesios' glorious son. Him was blood-stained Ares stripping; and Athene donned the helm of Hades, that terrible Ares might not behold her. Now when Ares scourge of mortals beheld noble Diomedes, he left huge Periphas lying there, where at the first he had slain him and taken away his life, and made straight at Diomedes tamer of horses. Now when they were come nigh in onset on one another, first Ares thrust over the yoke and horse's reins with spear of bronze, eager to take away his life. But the bright-eyed goddess Athene with her hand seized the spear and thrust it up over the car, to spend itself in vain. Next Diomedes of the loud war-cry attacked with spear of bronze; and Athene drave it home against Ares' nethermost belly, where his taslets were girt about him. There smote he him and wounded him, rending through his fair skin, and plucked forth the spear again. Then brazen Ares bellowed loud as nine thousand warriors or ten thousand cry in battle as they join in strife and fray. Thereat trembling gat hold of Achaians and Trojans for fear, so mightily bellowed Ares insatiate of battle.

Even as gloomy mist appeareth from the clouds when after heat a stormy wind ariseth, even so to Tydeus' son Diomedes brazen Ares appeared amid clouds, faring to wide heaven. Swiftly came he to the gods' dwelling, steep Olympus, and sat beside Zeus son of Kronos with grief at heart, and shewed the immortal blood flowing from the wound, and piteously spake to him winged words: "Father Zeus, hast thou no indignation to behold these violent deeds? For ever cruelly suffer we gods by one another's devices, in shewing men grace. With thee are we all at variance, because thou didst beget that reckless maiden and baleful, whose thought is ever of iniquitous deeds. For all the other gods that are in Olympus hearken to thee, and we are subject every one; only her thou chastenest not, neither in deed nor word, but settest her on, because this pestilent one is thine own offspring. Now hath she urged on Tydeus' son, even overweening Diomedes, to rage furiously against the immortal gods. Kypris first he wounded in close fight, in the wrist of her hand, and then assailed he me, even me, with the might of a god. Howbeit my swift feet bare me away; else had I long endured anguish there amid the grisly heaps of dead, or else had lived strengthless from the smitings of the spear."

Then Zeus the cloud-gatherer looked sternly at him and said: "Nay, thou renegade, sit not by me and whine. Most hateful to me art thou of all gods that dwell in Olympus: thou ever lovest strife and wars and battles. Truly thy mother's spirit is intolerable, unyielding, even Hera's; her can I scarce rule with words. Therefore I deem that by her prompting thou art in this plight. Yet will I no longer endure to see thee in anguish; mine offspring art thou, and to me thy mother bare thee."

So spake he and bade Paieon heal him. And Paieon laid assuaging drugs upon the wound. Even as fig juice maketh haste to thicken white milk, that is liquid but curdleth speedily as a man stirreth, even so swiftly healed he impetuous Ares. And Hebe bathed him, and clothed him in gracious raiment, and he sate him down by Zeus son of Kronos, glorying in his might.

Then fared the twain back to the mansion of great Zeus, even Hera and Athene, having stayed Ares scourge of mortals from his man-slaying.

BOOK VI

How Diomedes and Glaukos, being about to fight, were known to each other, and parted in friendliness. And how Hector returning to the city bade farewell to Andromache his wife.

So was the dread fray of Trojans and Achaians left to itself, and the battle swayed oft this way and that across the plain, as they aimed against each other their bronze-shod javelins, between Simoeis and the streams of Xanthos.

Now had the Trojans been chased again by the Achaians, dear to Ares, up into Ilios, in their weakness overcome, but that Priam's son Helenos, far best of augurs, stood by Aineias' side and Hector's, and spake to them: "Aineias and Hector, seeing that on you lieth the task of war in chief of Trojans and Lykians, because for every issue ye are foremost both for fight and counsel, stand ye your ground, and range the host everywhither to rally them before the gates, ere yet they fall fleeing in their women's arms, and be made a rejoicing to the foe. Then when ye have aroused all our battalions we will abide here and fight the Danaans, though in sore weariness; for necessity presseth us hard: but thou, Hector, go into the city, and speak there to thy mother and mine; let her gather the aged wives to bright-eyed Athene's temple in the upper city, and with her key open the doors of the holy house; and let her lay the robe, that seemeth to her the most gracious and greatest in her hall and far dearest unto herself, upon the knees of beauteous-haired Athene; and vow to her to sacrifice in her temple twelve sleek kine, that have not felt the goad, if she will have mercy on the city and the Trojans' wives and little children. So may she perchance hold back Tydeus' son from holy Ilios, the furious spearman, the mighty deviser of rout, whom in good sooth I deem to have proved himself mightiest of the Achaians. Never in this wise feared we Achilles, prince of men, who they say is born of a goddess; nay, but he that we see is beyond measure furious; none can match him for might."

So spake he, and Hector disregarded not his brother's word, but leapt forthwith from his chariot in his armour to earth, and brandishing two sharp spears passed everywhere through the host, rousing them to battle, and stirred the dread war-cry. So they were rallied and stood to face the Achaians, and the Argives gave ground and ceased from slaughter, and deemed that some immortal had descended from starry heaven to bring the Trojans succour, in such wise rallied they. Then Hector called to the Trojans with far-reaching shout: "O high-souled Trojans and ye far-famed allies, quit you like men, my friends, and take thought of impetuous courage, while I depart to Ilios and bid the elders of the council and our wives pray to the gods and vow them hecatombs."

So saying Hector of the glancing helm departed, and the black hide beat on either side against his ankles and his neck, even the rim that ran uttermost about his bossed shield.

Now Glaukos son of Hippolochos and Tydeus' son met in the mid-space of the foes, eager to do battle. Thus when the twain were come nigh in onset on each other, to him first spake Diomedes of the loud war-cry: "Who art thou, noble sir, of mortal men? For never have I beheld thee in glorious battle ere this, yet now hast thou far outstripped all men in thy hardihood, seeing thou abidest my far-shadowing spear. Luckless are the fathers whose children face my might. But if thou art some immortal come down from heaven, then will not I fight with heavenly gods. But if thou art of men that eat the fruit of the field, come nigh, that anon thou mayest enter the toils of destruction."

Then Hippolochos' glorious son made answer to him: "Great-hearted Tydeides, why enquirest thou of my generation? Even as are the generations of leaves such are those likewise of men; the leaves that be the wind scattereth on the earth, and the forest buddeth and putteth forth more again, when the season of spring is at hand; so of the generations of men one putteth forth and another ceaseth. Yet if thou wilt, have thine answer, that thou mayest well know our lineage, whereof many men have knowledge. Hippolochos, son of Bellerophon, begat me, and of him do I declare me to be sprung; he sent me to Troy and bade me very instantly to be ever the best and to excel all other men, nor put to shame the lineage of my fathers that were of noblest blood in Ephyre and in wide Lykia. This is the lineage and blood whereof I avow myself to be."

So said he, and Diomedes of the loud war-cry was glad. He planted his spear in the bounteous earth and with soft words spake to the shepherd of the host: "Surely then thou art to me a guest-friend of old times through my father: for goodly Oineus of yore entertained noble Bellerophon in his halls and kept him twenty days. Moreover they gave each the other goodly gifts of friendship; Oineus gave a belt bright with purple, and Bellerophon a gold two-handled cup. Therefore now am I to thee a dear guest-friend in midmost Argos, and thou in Lykia, whene'er I fare to your land. So let us shun each other's spears, even amid the throng; Trojans are there in multitudes and famous allies for me to slay, whoe'er it be that God vouchsafeth me and my feet overtake; and for thee are there Achaians in multitude, to slay whome'er thou canst. But let us make exchange of arms between us, that these also may know how we avow ourselves to be guest-friends by lineage."

So spake the twain, and leaping from their cars clasped each the other by his hand, and pledged their faith. But now Zeus son of Kronos took from Glaukos his wits, in that he made exchange with Diomedes Tydeus' son of golden armour for bronze, the price of five score oxen for the price of nine.

Now when Hector came to the Skaian gates and to the oak-tree, there came running round about him the Trojans' wives and daughters, enquiring of sons and brethren and friends and husbands. But he bade them thereat all in turn pray to the gods; but sorrow hung over many.

But when he came to Priam's beautiful palace, adorned with polished colonnades — and in it were fifty chambers of polished stone, builded hard by one another, wherein Priam's sons slept beside their wedded wives; and for his daughters over against them on the other side within the courtyard were twelve roofed chambers of polished stone builded hard by one another, wherein slept Priam's sons-in-law beside their chaste wives — then came there to meet him his bountiful mother, leading with her Laodike, fairest of her daughters to look on; and she clasped her hand in his, and spake, and called upon his name: "My son, why hast thou left violent battle to come hither. Surely the sons of the Achaians — name of evil! — press thee hard in fight about thy city, and so thy spirit hath brought thee hither, to come and stretch forth thy hands to Zeus from the citadel. But tarry till I bring thee honey-sweet wine, that thou mayest pour libation to Zeus and all the immortals first, and then shalt thou thyself also be refreshed if thou wilt drink. When a man is awearied wine greatly maketh his strength to wax, even as thou art awearied in fighting for thy fellows."

Then great Hector of the glancing helm answered her: "Bring me no honey-hearted wine, my lady mother, lest thou cripple me of my courage and I be forgetful of my might. But go thou to the temple of Athene, driver of the spoil, with offerings, and gather the aged wives together; and the robe that seemeth to thee the most gracious and greatest in thy palace, and dearest unto thyself, that lay thou upon the knees of beauteous-haired Athene, and vow to her to sacrifice in her temple twelve sleek kine, that have not felt the goad, if she will have mercy on the city and the Trojans' wives and little children. So go thou to the temple of Athene, driver of the spoil; and I will go after Paris, to summon him, if perchance he will hearken to my voice. Would that the earth forthwith might swallow him up! The Olympian fostered him to be a sore bane to the Trojans and to great-hearted Priam, and to Priam's sons. If I but saw him going down to the gates of death, then might I deem that my heart had forgotten its sorrows."

So said he, and she went unto the hall, and called to her handmaidens, and they gathered the aged wives throughout the city. Then she herself went down to her fragrant chamber where were her embroidered robes, the work of Sidonian women, whom godlike Alexandros himself brought from Sidon, when he sailed over the wide sea, that journey wherein he brought home high-born Helen. Of these Hekabe took one to bear for an offering to Athene, the one that was fairest for adornment and greatest, and shone like a star, and lay nethermost of all. Then went she her way and the multitude of aged wives hasted after her.

And Hector was come to Alexandros' fair palace, that himself had builded with them that were most excellent carpenters then in deep-soiled Troy-land; these made him his chamber and hall and courtyard hard by to Priam and Hector, in the upper city. There entered in Hector dear to Zeus, and his hand bare his spear, eleven cubits long: before his face glittered the bronze spear-point, and a ring of gold ran round about it. And he found Paris in his chamber busied with his beauteous arms, his shield and breastplate, and handling his curved bow; and Helen of Argos sate among her serving-women and appointed brave handiwork for her handmaidens. Then when Hector saw him he rebuked him with scornful words: "Good sir, thou dost not well to cherish this rancour in thy heart. The folk are perishing about the city and high wall in battle, and for thy sake the battle-cry is kindled and war around this city; yea thyself wouldest thou fall out with another, didst thou see him shrinking from hateful war. Up then, lest the city soon be scorched with burning fire."

And godlike Alexandros answered him: "Hector, since in measure thou chidest me and not beyond measure, therefore will I tell thee; lay thou it to thine heart and hearken to me. Not by reason so much of the Trojans, for wrath and indignation, sate I me in my chamber, but fain would I yield me to my sorrow. Even now my wife hath persuaded me with soft words, and urged me into battle; and I moreover, even I, deem that it will be better so; for victory shifteth from man to man. Go to then; tarry awhile, let me put on my armour of war; or else fare thou forth, and I will follow; and I think to overtake thee."

So said he, but Hector of the glancing helm answered him not a word. But Helen spake to him with gentle words: "My brother, even mine that am a dog, mischievous and abominable, would that on the day when my mother bare me at the first, an evil storm-wind had caught me away to a mountain or a billow of the loud-sounding sea, where the billow might have swept me away before all these things came to pass. Howbeit, seeing the gods devised all these ills in this wise, would that then I had been mated with a better man, that felt dishonour and the multitude of men's reproachings. But as for him, neither hath he now sound heart, nor ever will have; thereof deem I moreover that he will reap the fruit. But now come, enter in and sit thee here upon this bench, my brother, since thy heart chiefly trouble hath encompassed, for the sake of me, that am a dog, and for Alexandros' sin; on whom Zeus bringeth evil doom, that even in days to come we may be a song in the ears of men that shall be hereafter."

Then great Hector of the glancing helm answered her: "Bid me not sit, Helen, of thy love; thou wilt not persuade me. Already my heart is set to succour the men of Troy, that have great desire for me that am not with them. But rouse thou this fellow, yea let himself make speed, to overtake me yet within the city. For I shall go into mine house to behold my housefolk and my dear wife, and infant boy; for I know not if I shall return home to them again, or if the gods will now overthrow me at the hands of the Achaians."

So spake Hector of the glancing helm and departed; and anon he came to his well-stablished house. But he found not white-armed Andromache in the halls; she with her boy and fair-robed handmaiden had taken her stand upon the tower, weeping and wailing. And when Hector found not his noble wife within, he came and stood upon the threshold and spake amid the serving women: "Come tell me now true, my serving women. Whither went white-armed Andromache forth from the hall? Hath she gone out to my sisters or unto my brothers' fair-robed wives, or to Athene's temple, where all the fair-tressed Trojan women propitiate the awful goddess?"

Then a busy housedame spake in answer to him: "Hector, seeing thou straitly chargest us tell thee true, neither hath she gone out to any of thy sisters or thy brothers' fair-robed wives, neither to Athene's temple, where all the fair-tressed Trojan women are propitiating the awful goddess; but she went to the great tower of Ilios, because she heard the Trojans were hard pressed, and great victory was for the Achaians. So hath she come in haste to the wall, like unto one frenzied; and the nurse with her beareth the child."

So spake the housedame, and Hector hastened from his house back by the same way down the well-builded streets. When he had passed through the great city and was come to the Skaian gates, whereby he was minded to issue upon the plain, then came his dear-won wife, running to meet him, even Andromache daughter of great-hearted Eëtion. So she met him now, and with her went the handmaid bearing in her bosom the tender boy, the little child, Hector's loved son, like unto a beautiful star. Him Hector called Skamandrios, but all the folk Asty-

THE MEETING OF HECTOR AND ANDROMACHE

anax; for only Hector guarded Ilios.[1] So now he smiled and gazed at his boy silently, and Andromache stood by his side weeping, and clasped her hand in his, and spake and called upon his name. "Dear my lord, this thy hardihood will undo thee, neither hast thou any pity for thine infant boy, nor for me forlorn that soon shall be thy widow; for soon will the Achaians all set upon thee and slay thee. But it were better for me to go down to the grave if I lose thee; for never more will any comfort be mine, when once thou, even thou, hast met thy fate, but only sorrow. Nay, Hector, thou art to me father and lady mother, yea and brother, even as thou art my goodly husband. Come now, have pity and abide here upon the tower, lest thou make thy child an orphan and thy wife a widow."

Then great Hector of the glancing helm answered her: "Surely I take thought for all these things, my wife; but I have very sore shame of the Trojans and Trojan dames with trailing robes, if like a coward I shrink away from battle. Moreover mine own soul forbiddeth me, seeing I have learnt ever to be valiant and fight in the forefront of the Trojans, winning my father's great glory and mine own. Yea of a surety I know this in heart and soul; the day shall come for holy Ilios to be laid low, and Priam and the folk of Priam of the good ashen spear. Yet doth the anguish of the Trojans hereafter not so much trouble me, neither Hekabe's own, neither king Priam's, neither my brethren's, the many and brave that shall fall in the dust before their foemen, as doth thine anguish in the day when some mail-clad Achaian shall lead thee weeping and rob thee of the light of freedom. So shalt thou abide in Argos and ply the loom at another woman's bidding, and bear water from fount Messeis or Hypereia, being grievously entreated, and sore constraint shall be laid upon thee. And then shall one say that beholdeth thee weep: 'This is the wife of Hector, that

---

[1] Astyanax = "City King."

was foremost in battle of the horse-taming Trojans when men fought about Ilios.' Thus shall one say hereafter, and fresh grief will be thine for lack of such an husband as thou hadst to ward off the day of thraldom. But me in death may the heaped-up earth be covering, ere I hear thy crying and thy carrying into captivity."

So spake glorious Hector, and stretched out his arm to his boy. But the child shrunk crying to the bosom of his fair-girdled nurse, dismayed at his dear father's aspect, and in dread at the bronze and horse-hair crest that he beheld nodding fiercely from the helmet's top. Then his dear father laughed aloud, and his lady mother; forthwith glorious Hector took the helmet from his head, and laid it, all gleaming, upon the earth; then kissed he his dear son and dandled him in his arms, and spake in prayer to Zeus and all the gods, "O Zeus and all ye gods, vouchsafe ye that this my son may likewise prove even as I, pre-eminent amid the Trojans, and as valiant in might, and be a great king of Ilios. Then may men say of him, 'Far greater is he than his father' as he returneth home from battle; and may he bring with him blood-stained spoils from the foeman he hath slain, and may his mother's heart be glad."

So spake he, and laid his son in his dear wife's arms; and she took him to her fragrant bosom, smiling tearfully. And her husband had pity to see her, and caressed her with his hand, and spake and called upon her name: "Dear one, I pray thee be not of oversorrowful heart; no man against my fate shall hurl me to Hades; only destiny, I ween, no man hath escaped, be he coward or be he valiant, when once he hath been born. But go thou to thine house and see to thine own tasks, the loom and distaff, and bid thine handmaidens ply their work; but for war shall men provide, and I in chief of all men that dwell in Ilios."

So spake glorious Hector, and took up his horse-hair crested helmet; and his dear wife departed to her home, oft looking back, and letting fall big tears. Anon she came to the well-stablished house of man-slaying Hector, and found therein her many handmaidens, and stirred lamentation in them all. So bewailed they Hector, while yet he lived, within his house: for they deemed that he would no more come back to them from battle, nor escape the fury of the hands of the Achaians.

Neither lingered Paris long in his lofty house, but clothed on him his brave armour, bedight with bronze, and hasted through the city, trusting to his nimble feet. Even as when a stalled horse, full-fed at the manger, breaketh his tether and speedeth at the gallop across the plain, being wont to bathe him in the fair-flowing stream, exultingly; and holdeth his head on high, and his mane floateth about his shoulders, and he trusteth in his glory, and nimbly his limbs bear him to the haunts and pasturages of mares; even so Priam's son Paris, glittering in his armour like the shining sun, strode down from high Pergamos laughingly, and his swift feet bare him. Forthwith he overtook his brother noble Hector, even as he was on the point to turn him away from the spot where he had dallied with his wife. To him first spake godlike Alexandros: "Sir, in good sooth I have delayed thee in thine haste by my tarrying, and came not rightly as thou badest me."

And Hector of the glancing helm answered him and said: "Good brother, no man that is rightminded could make light of thy doings in fight, seeing thou art strong: but thou art wilfully remiss and hast no care; and for this my heart is grieved within me, that I hear shameful words concerning thee in the Trojans' mouths, who for thy sake endure much toil. But let us be going; all this will we make good hereafter, if Zeus ever vouchsafe us to set before the heavenly gods that are for everlasting the cup of deliverance in our halls, when we have chased out of Troy-land the well-greaved Achaians."

BOOK VII

Of the single combat between Aias and Hector, and of the burying of the dead, and the building of a wall about the Achaian ships.

So spake glorious Hector and issued from the gates, and with him went his brother Alexandros; and both were eager of soul for fight and battle. Even as God giveth to longing seamen fair wind when they have grown weary of beating the main with polished oars, and their limbs are fordone with toil, even so appeared these to the longing Trojans.

Now when the goddess bright-eyed Athene marked them making havoc of the Argives in the press of battle, she darted down from the crests of Olympus to holy Ilios. But Apollo rose to meet her, for he beheld her from Pergamos, and would have victory for the Trojans. So the twain met each the other by the oak-tree. To her spake first king Apollo son of Zeus: "Why now art thou come thus eagerly from Olympus, thou daughter of great Zeus, and why hath thy high heart sent thee? Surely it is to give the Danaans unequal victory in battle! seeing thou hast no mercy on the Trojans, that perish. But if thou wouldest hearken to me — and it were far better so — let us now stay battle and warring for the day; hereafter shall they fight again, till they reach the goal of Ilios, since thus it seemeth good to your hearts, goddesses immortal, to lay waste this city."

And the goddess bright-eyed Athene made answer to him: "So be it, Far-darter; in this mind I likewise came from Olympus to the midst of Trojans and Achaians. But come, how thinkest thou to stay the battle of the warriors?"

And king Apollo, son of Zeus, made answer to her: "Let us arouse the stalwart spirit of horse-taming Hector, if so be he will challenge some one of the Danaans in single fight man to man to meet him in deadly combat. So shall the bronze-greaved Achaians be jealous and stir up one to fight singly with goodly Hector."

So spake he and the bright-eyed goddess Athene disregarded not. Now Helenos Priam's dear son understood in spirit their resolve that the gods in counsel had approved; and he went to Hector and stood beside him, and spake a word to him: "Hector son of Priam, peer of Zeus in counsel, wouldest thou now hearken at all to me? for I am thy brother. Make the other Trojans sit, and all the Achaians, and thyself challenge him that is best of the Achaians to meet thee man to man in deadly combat. It is not yet thy destiny to die and meet thy doom; for thus heard I the voice of the gods that are from everlasting."

So said he, and Hector rejoiced greatly to hear his saying, and went into the midst and refrained the battalions of the Trojans with his spear grasped by the middle; and they all sate them down: and Agamemnon made the well-greaved Achaians sit. And Athene withal and Apollo of the silver bow, in the likeness of vulture birds, sate them upon a tall oak holy to aegis-bearing father Zeus, rejoicing in their warriors; and the ranks of all of them sate close together, bristling with shields and plumes and spears. Even as there spreadeth across the main the ripple of the west wind newly risen, and the sea grows black beneath it, so sate the ranks of Achaians and Trojans upon the plain. And Hector spake between both hosts: "Hearken to me, Trojans and well-greaved Achaians, that I may speak what my mind within my breast biddeth me. Our oaths of truce Kronos' son, enthroned on high, accomplished not; but evil is his intent and ordinance for both our hosts, until either ye take fair-towered Troy or yourselves be vanquished beside your seafaring ships. But in the midst of you are the chiefest of all the Achaians; therefore now let the man whose heart biddeth him fight with me come hither from among you all to be your champion against goodly Hector. And this declare I, and be Zeus our witness thereto; if that man slay me with the long-edged sword, let him spoil me of my armour and bear it to the hollow ships, but give back my body to my home, that Trojans and Trojans' wives may give me my due of burning in my death. But if I slay him and Apollo vouchsafe me glory, I will spoil him of his armour and bear it to holy Ilios and hang it upon the temple of far-darting Apollo, but his corpse will I render back to the well-decked ships, that the flowing-haired Achaians may entomb him, and build him a barrow beside wide Hellespont. So shall one say even of men that be late born, as he saileth in his benched ship over the wine-dark sea: 'This is the barrow of a man that died in days of old, a champion whom glorious Hector slew.' So shall a man say hereafter, and this my glory shall never die."

So spake he and they all were silent and held their peace; to deny him they were ashamed, and feared to meet him. But at the last stood up Menelaos and spake amid them and chiding upbraided them, and groaned deep at heart: "Ah me, vain threateners, ye women of Achaia and no more men, surely all this shall be a shame, evil of evil, if no one of the Danaans now goeth to meet Hector. Nay, turn ye all to earth and water, sitting there each man disheartened, helplessly inglorious; against him will I myself array me; and from on high the threads of victory are guided of the immortal gods."

So spake he and donned his fair armour. And now, O Menelaos, had the end of life appeared for thee at Hector's hands, seeing he was stronger far, but that the princes of the Achaians started up and caught thee. And Atreus' son himself, wide-ruling Agamemnon, took him by his right hand and spake a word and called upon his name: "Thou doest madly, Menelaos fosterling of Zeus; yet is it no time for this thy madness. Draw back, though it be with pain, nor think for contention's sake to fight with one better than thou, with Hector

Priam's son, whom others beside thee abhor. Yea, this man even Achilles dreadeth to meet in battle, wherein is the warrior's glory; and Achilles is better far than thou. Go therefore now and sit amid the company of thy fellows; against him shall the Achaians put forth another champion. Fearless though he be and insatiate of turmoil, I ween that he shall be fain to rest his knees, if he escape from the fury of war and terrible fray."

So spake the hero and persuaded his brother's heart with just counsel; and he obeyed. So his squires thereat with gladness took his armour from his shoulders; and Nestor stood up and spake amid the Argives: "Fie upon it, verily sore lamentation cometh on the land of Achaia. Verily old Peleus driver of chariots would groan sore, that goodly counsellor of the Myrmidons and orator, who erst questioned me in his house, and rejoiced greatly, inquiring of the lineage and birth of all the Argives. If he heard now of those that all were cowering before Hector, then would he lift his hands to the immortals, instantly praying that his soul might depart from his limbs down to the house of Hades. Would to God I were thus young and my strength were sound; then would Hector of the glancing helm soon find his combat. But of those of you that be chieftains of the host of the Achaians, yet desireth no man of good heart to meet Hector face to face."

So the old man upbraided them, and there stood up nine in all. Far first arose Agamemnon king of men, and after him rose Tydeus' son stalwart Diomedes, and after them the Aiantes clothed with impetuous might, and after them Idomeneus and Idomeneus' brother-in-arms Meriones, peer of Enyalios slayer of men, and after them Eurypylos Euaimon's glorious son; and up rose Thoas Andraimon's son and goodly Odysseus. So all these were fain to fight with goodly Hector. And among them spake again knightly Nestor of Gerenia: "Now cast ye the lot from the first unto the last, for him that shall be chosen;

for he shall in truth profit the well-greaved Achaians, yea and he shall have profit of his own soul, if he escape from the fury of war and terrible fray."

So said he, and they marked each man his lot and cast them in the helmet of Agamemnon Atreus' son; and the hosts prayed and lifted up their hands to the gods. And thus would one say, looking up to wide heaven: "O father Zeus, vouchsafe that the lot fall upon Aias or Tydeus' son, or else on the king of Mykene rich in gold."

So spake they, and knightly Nestor of Gerenia shook the helmet, and there leapt forth the lot that themselves desired, even the lot of Aias. And Aias saw and knew the token upon the lot, and rejoiced in heart, and spake: "My friends, verily the lot is mine, yea and myself am glad at heart, because I deem that I shall vanquish goodly Hector. But come now, while I clothe me in my armour of battle, pray ye the while to Kronos' son king Zeus, in silence to yourselves, that the Trojans hear you not — nay rather, openly if ye will, for we have no fear of any man soever. For none by force shall chase me, he willing me unwilling, neither by skill; seeing I hope that not so skill-less, either, was I born in Salamis nor nurtured."

So said he, and they prayed to Kronos' son, king Zeus; and thus would one speak, looking up to wide heaven: "O father Zeus that rulest from Ida, most glorious, most great, vouchsafe to Aias victory and the winning of great glory. But if thou so lovest Hector indeed, and carest for him, grant unto either equal prowess and renown."

So said they, while Aias arrayed him in flashing bronze. And when he had now clothed upon his flesh all his armour, then marched he as huge Ares coming forth, when he goeth to battle amid heroes whom Kronos' son setteth to fight in fury of heart-consuming strife. So rose up huge Aias, bulwark of the Achaians, with a smile on his grim face: and went with long strides of his feet beneath him, shaking his far-shadowing spear. Then moreover the Argives rejoiced to look upon him, but sore trembling came upon the Trojans, on the limbs of every man, and Hector's own heart beat within his breast. But in no wise could he now flee nor shrink back into the throng of the host, seeing he had challenged him to battle. And Aias came near bearing his tower-like shield of bronze, with sevenfold ox-hide, and stood near to Hector, and spake to him threatening: "Hector, now verily shalt thou well know, man to man, what manner of princes the Danaans likewise have among them, even after Achilles, render of men, the lion-hearted. But he amid his beaked seafaring ships lieth in sore wrath with Agamemnon shepherd of the host; yet are we such as to face thee, yea and many of us. But make thou beginning of war and battle."

And great Hector of the glancing helm answered him: "Aias of the seed of Zeus, son of Telamon, chieftain of the host, tempt not thou me like some puny boy or woman that knoweth not deeds of battle. But I well know wars and slaughterings. To right know I, to left know I the wielding of my tough targe; therein I deem is stalwart soldiership. And I know how to charge into the mellay of fleet chariots, and how in close battle to join in furious Ares' dance. Howbeit, I have no mind to smite thee, being such an one as thou art, by spying thee unawares; but rather openly, if perchance I may hit thee."

He spake, and poised his far-shadowing spear, and hurled and smote Aias' dread shield of sevenfold hide upon the uttermost bronze, the eighth layer that was thereon. Through six folds went the stubborn bronze cleaving, but in the seventh hide it stayed. Then heaven-sprung Aias hurled next his far-shadowing spear, and smote upon the circle of the shield of Priam's son. Through the bright shield passed the violent spear, and through the curiously wrought corslet pressed it on; and straight forth beside the flank the spear rent his doublet;

but he swerved aside and escaped black death. Then both together with their hands plucked forth their long spears and fell to like ravening lions or wild boars whose might is nowise feeble. Then Priam's son smote the shield's midst with his dart, but the bronze brake not through, for the point turned back; but Aias leapt on him and pierced his buckler, and straight through went the spear and staggered him in his onset, and cleft its way unto his neck, so that the dark blood gushed up. Yet even then did not Hector of the glancing helm cease from fight, but yielded ground and with stout hand seized a stone lying upon the plain, black and rugged and great; therewith hurled he and smote Aias' dread shield of sevenfold ox-hide in the midst upon the boss, and the bronze resounded. Next Aias lifted a far greater stone, and swung and hurled it, putting might immeasurable therein. So smote he the buckler and burst it inwards with the rock like unto a millstone, and beat down his knees; and he was stretched upon his back, pressed into his shield; but Apollo straightway raised him up. And now had they been smiting hand to hand with swords, but that the heralds, messengers of gods and men, came, one from the Trojans, one from the mail-clad Achaians, even Talthybios and Idaios, both men discreet. Between the two held they their staves, and herald Idaios spake a word, being skilled in wise counsel: "Fight ye no more, dear sons, neither do battle; seeing Zeus the cloud-gatherer loveth you both, and both are men of war; that verily know we all. But night already is upon us: it is well withal to obey the hest[1] of night."

Then Telamonian Aias answered and said to him: "Idaios, bid ye Hector to speak those words; of his own self he challenged to combat all our best. Let him be first, and I will surely follow as he saith."

Then great Hector of the glancing helm said to him: "Aias,

[1] [Behest.]

seeing God gave thee stature and might and wisdom, and with
the spear thou art excellent above all the Achaians, let us now
cease from combat and battle for the day; but hereafter will
we fight until God judge between us, giving to one of us the
victory. But come, let us give each the other famous gifts,
that men may thus say, Achaians alike and Trojans: 'These,
having fought for sake of heart-consuming strife, parted again
reconciled in friendship.'"

So said he, and gave him his silver-studded sword, with
scabbard and well-cut baldrick; and Aias gave his belt bright
with purple. So they parted, and one went to the Achaian
host, and one betook him to the throng of Trojans. And these
rejoiced to behold him come to them alive and sound, escaped
from the fury of Aias and his hands unapproachable; and they
brought him to the city saved beyond their hope. And Aias on
their side the well-greaved Achaians brought to noble Agamemnon, exulting in his victory.

So when these were come unto the huts of Atreides, then did
Agamemnon king of men slay them an ox, a male of five years
old, for the most mighty son of Kronos. This they flayed and
made ready, and divided it all, and minced it cunningly, and
pierced it through with spits, and roasted it carefully, and drew
all off again. Then as soon as they had rest from the task and
had made ready the meal, they began the feast, nor was their
soul aught stinted of the equal banquet. And the hero son of
Atreus, wide-ruling Agamemnon, gave to Aias slices of the
chine's full length for his honour. And when they had put
from them the desire of meat and drink, then first the old man
began to weave the web of counsel, even Nestor whose rede[1] of
old time was proved most excellent. He made harangue among
them and said: "Son of Atreus and ye other princes of the
Achaians, seeing that many flowing-haired Achaians are dead,

[2] [Counsel.]

and keen Ares hath spilt their dusky blood about fair-flowing Skamandros, and their souls have gone down to the house of Hades; therefore it behoveth thee to make the battle of the Achaians cease with daybreak; and we will assemble to wheel hither the corpses with oxen and mules; so let us burn them; and let us heap one barrow about the pyre, rearing it from the plain for all alike; and thereto build with speed high towers, a bulwark for our ships and for ourselves. In the midst thereof let us make gates well compact, that through them may be a way for chariot-driving. And without let us dig a deep foss hard by, to be about it and to hinder horses and footmen, lest the battle of the lordly Trojans be heavy on us hereafter."

So spake he and all the chiefs gave assent. But meanwhile there was in the high town of Ilios an assembly of the Trojans, fierce, confused, beside Priam's gate. To them discreet Antenor began to make harangue: "Hearken to me, Trojans and Dardanians and allies, that I may tell you that my soul within my breast commandeth me. Lo, go to now, let us give Helen of Argos and the wealth with her for the sons of Atreus to take away. Now fight we in guilt against the oaths of faith; therefore is there no profit for us that I hope to see fulfilled, unless we do thus."

So spake he and sate him down; and there stood up among them noble Alexandros, lord of Helen beautiful-haired; he made him answer and spake winged words: "Antenor, these words from thee are no longer to my pleasure; yet thou hast it in thee to devise other sayings more excellent than this. But if indeed thou sayest this in earnest, then verily the gods themselves have destroyed thy wit. But I will speak forth amid the horse-taming Trojans, and declare outright; my wife will I not give back; but the wealth I brought from Argos to our home, all that I have a mind to give, and add more of mine own substance."

So spake he and sate him down, and there stood up among

them Priam of the seed of Dardanos, the peer of gods in counsel; he made harangue to them, and said: "Hearken to me, Trojans and Dardanians and allies, that I may tell you that my soul within my breast commandeth me. Now eat your supper throughout the city as of old, and take thought to keep watch, and be wakeful every man. And at dawn let Idaios fare to the hollow ships to tell to Atreus' sons Agamemnon and Menelaos the saying of Alexandros, for whose sake strife is come about: and likewise to ask them this wise word, whether they are minded to refrain from noisy war till we have burned our dead; afterwards will we fight again, till heaven part us and give one or other victory."

So spake he, and they hearkened diligently to him and obeyed: and at dawn Idaios fared to the hollow ships. He found the Danaans in assembly, the men of Ares' company, beside the stern of Agamemnon's ship; and so the loud-voiced herald stood in their midst and said unto them: "Atreides and ye other princes of the Achaians, Priam and all the noble Trojans bade me tell you — if perchance it might find favour and acceptance with you — the saying of Alexandros, for whose sake strife hath come about. The wealth that Alexandros brought in his hollow ships to Troy — would he had perished first!—all that he hath a mind to give, and to add more thereto of his substance. But the wedded wife of glorious Menelaos he saith he will not give; yet verily the Trojans bid him do it. Moreover they bade me ask this thing of you; whether ye are minded to refrain from noisy war until we have burned our dead; afterwards will we fight again, till heaven part us and give one or other victory."

So said he and they all kept silence and were still. But at the last spake Diomedes of the loud war-cry in their midst: "Let no man now accept Alexandros' substance, neither Helen's self; known is it, even to him that hath no wit at all, how that the issues of destruction hang already over the Trojans."

So spake he, and all the sons of the Achaians shouted, applauding the saying of horse-taming Diomedes. And then lord Agamemnon spake to Idaios: "Idaios, thyself thou hearest the saying of the Achaians, how they answer thee; and the like seemeth good to me. But as concerning the dead, I grudge you not to burn them; for dead corpses is there no stinting, when they once are dead, of the swift propitiation of fire. And for the oaths let Zeus be witness, the loud-thundering lord of Hera."

So saying he lifted up his sceptre in the sight of all the gods, and Idaios departed back to holy Ilios. Now Trojans and Dardanians sate in assembly, gathered all together to wait till Idaios should come; and he came and stood in their midst and declared his message. Then they made them ready very swiftly for either task, some to bring the dead, and some to seek for wood. And on their part the Argives hasted from their well-decked ships, some to bring the dead and some to seek for wood.

Now the sun was newly beating on the fields as he climbed heaven from the deep stream of gently-flowing Ocean, when both sides met together. Then was it a hard matter to know each man again; but they washed them with water clean of clotted gore, and with shedding of hot tears lifted them upon the wains. But great Priam bade them not wail aloud; so in silence heaped they the corpses on the pyre, stricken at heart; and when they had burned them with fire departed to holy Ilios. And in like manner on their side the well-greaved Achaians heaped the corpses on the pyre, stricken at heart, and when they had burned them with fire departed to the hollow ships.

And when day was not yet, but still twilight of night, then was the chosen folk of the Achaians gathered together around the pyre, and made one barrow about it, rearing it from the plain for all alike; and thereto built they a wall and lofty towers, a bulwark for their ships and for themselves. In the midst thereof made they gates well-compacted, that through them might be a way for chariot-driving. And without they dug a deep foss beside it, broad and great, and planted a palisade therein.

Thus toiled the flowing-haired Achaians: and the gods sate by Zeus, the lord of lightning, and marvelled at the great work of the mail-clad Achaians. And Poseidon shaker of earth spake first to them: "O father Zeus, is there any man throughout the boundless earth that will any more declare to the immortals his mind and counsel? Seest thou not how the flowing-haired Achaians have now again built them a wall before their ships, and drawn a foss around it, but gave not excellent hecatombs to the gods? Verily the fame thereof shall reach as far as the dawn spreadeth, and men will forget the wall that I and Phoebus Apollo built with travail for the hero Laomedon."

And Zeus the cloud-gatherer said to him, sore troubled: "Out on it, far-swaying Shaker of earth, for this thing thou sayest. Well might some other god fear this device, one that were far feebler than thou in the might of his hands: but thine shall be the fame as far as the dawn spreadeth. Go to now, hereafter when the flowing-haired Achaians be departed upon their ships to their dear native land, then burst thou this wall asunder and scatter it all into the sea, and cover the great sea-beach over with sand again, that the great wall of the Achaians be brought to naught."

BOOK VIII

How Zeus bethought him of his promise to avenge Achilles' wrong on Agamemnon: and therefore bade the gods refrain from war, and gave victory to the Trojans.

Now Dawn the saffron-robed was spreading over all the earth, and Zeus whose joy is in the thunder let call an assembly of the gods upon the topmost peak of many-ridged Olympus, and himself made harangue to them and all the gods gave ear: "Hearken to me, all gods and all ye goddesses, that I may tell you what my heart within my breast commandeth me. One thing let none essay, be it goddess or be it god, to wit, to thwart my saying; approve ye it all together, that with all speed I may accomplish these things. Whomsoever I shall perceive minded to go, apart from the gods, to succour Trojans or Danaans, chastened in no seemly wise shall he return to Olympus, or I will take and cast him into misty Tartaros, right far away, where is the deepest gulf beneath the earth; there are the gate of iron and threshold of bronze, as far beneath Hades as heaven is high above the earth: then shall he know how far I am mightiest of all gods. Go to now, ye gods, make trial that ye all may know. Fasten ye a rope of gold from heaven, and all ye gods lay hold thereof and all goddesses; yet could ye not drag from heaven to earth Zeus, counsellor supreme, not though ye toiled sore. But once I likewise were minded to draw with all my heart, then should I draw you up with very earth and sea withal. Thereafter would I bind the rope about a pinnacle of Olympus, and so should all those things be hung in air. By so much am I beyond gods and beyond men."

So saying he let harness to his chariot his bronze-shod horses, fleet of foot, with flowing manes of gold; and himself clad him with gold upon his flesh, and grasped the whip of gold, well-wrought, and mounted upon his car, and lashed the horses to start them; they nothing loth sped on between earth and starry heaven. So fared he to many-fountained Ida, mother of wild beasts, even unto Gargaros, where is his demesne and fragrant altar. There did the father of men and gods stay his horses, and unloose them from the car, and cast thick mist about them; and himself sate on the mountain-tops rejoicing in his glory, to behold the city of the Trojans and ships of the Achaians.

Now the flowing-haired Achaians took meat hastily among the huts and thereafter arrayed themselves. Likewise the Trojans on their side armed them throughout the town — a smaller host, yet for all that were they eager to fight in battle, of forceful need, for their children's sake and their wives'. And the gates were opened wide and the host issued forth, footmen and horsemen; and mighty din arose.

So when they were met together and come unto one spot, then clashed they targe and spear and fury of bronze-clad warrior; the bossed shields pressed each on each, and mighty din arose. Then were heard the voice of groaning and the voice of triumph together of the slayers and the slain, and the earth streamed with blood.

Now while it yet was morn and the divine day waxed, so long from either side lighted the darts amain and the people fell. But when the sun bestrode mid-heaven, then did the Father balance his golden scales, and put therein two fates of death that layeth men at their length, one for horse-taming Trojans one for mail-clad Achaians; and he took the scale-yard by the midst and lifted it, and the Achaians' day of destiny sank down. So lay the Achaians' fates on the bounteous earth, and the Trojans' fates were lifted up towards wide heaven. And the god thundered aloud from Ida, and sent his blazing flash amid the host of the Achaians; and they saw and were astonished, and pale fear 'gat hold upon all.

Then had Idomeneus no heart to stand, neither Agamemnon,

neither stood the twain Aiantes, men of Ares' company. Only Nestor of Gerenia stood his ground, he the Warden of the Achaians; neither he of purpose, but his horse was fordone, which noble Alexandros, beauteous-haired Helen's lord, had smitten with an arrow upon the top of the crest where the foremost hairs of horses grow upon the skull; and there is the most deadly spot. So the horse leapt up in anguish and the arrow sank into his brain, and he brought confusion on the steeds as he writhed upon the dart. While the old man leapt forth and with his sword began to hew the traces, came Hector's fleet horses through the tumult, bearing a bold charioteer, even Hector. And now had the old man lost his life, but that Diomedes of the loud war-cry was swift to mark. Terribly shouted he, summoning Odysseus: "Heaven-born son of Laertes, Odysseus of many wiles, whither fleest thou with thy back turned, like a coward in the throng? Beware lest as thou fleest one plant a spear between thy shoulders. Nay, stand thy ground, till we thrust back from the old man his furious foe."

So spake he, but much-enduring noble Odysseus heard him not, but hastened by to the hollow ships of the Achaians. Yet Tydeides, though but one, mingled amid the fighters in the forefront, and took his stand before the steeds of the old man, Neleus' son, and spake to him winged words, and said: "Old man, of a truth young warriors beset thee hard; and thy force is abated, and old age is sore upon thee, and thy squire is but a weakling, and thy steeds are slow. Come then, mount upon my car, that thou mayest see of what sort are the steeds of Tros, well skilled for following or fleeing hither or thither very fleetly across the plain, even those that erst I took from Aineias inspirer of fear. Thine let our squires tend, and these let us guide straight against the horse-taming Trojans, that even Hector may know whether my spear also rageth in my hands."

So said he, and knightly Nestor of Gerenia disregarded not.

Then the two squires tended Nestor's horses, even Sthenelos the valiant and kindly Eurymedon: and the other twain both mounted upon Diomedes' car. And Nestor took into his hands the shining reins, and lashed the horses; and soon they drew nigh Hector. Then Tydeus' son hurled at him as he charged straight upon them: him missed he, but his squire that drave his chariot, Eniopeus, high-hearted Thebaios' son, even him as he held the reins, he smote upon the breast beside the nipple. So he fell from out the car, and his fleet-footed horses swerved aside; and there his soul and spirit were unstrung. Then sore grief encompassed Hector's soul for sake of his charioteer. Yet left he him there lying, though he sorrowed for his comrade, and drave in quest of a bold charioteer; and his horses lacked not long a master, for anon he found Iphitos' son, bold Archeptolemos, and him he made mount behind his fleet horses, and gave the reins into his hands.

Then had destruction come and deeds beyond remedy been wrought, and so had they been penned in Ilios like lambs, had not the father of gods and men been swift to mark. So he thundered terribly and darted his white lightning and hurled it before Diomedes' steeds to earth; and there arose a terrible flame of sulphur burning, and the two horses were affrighted and cowered beneath the car. And the shining reins dropped from Nestor's hands, and he was afraid at heart and spake to Diomedes: "Come now Tydeides, turn back thy whole-hooved horses to flight: seest thou not that victory from Zeus attendeth not on thee? Now doth Kronos' son vouchsafe glory to this Hector, for the day; hereafter shall he grant it us likewise, if he will. A man may not at all ward off the will of Zeus, not though one be very valiant; he verily is mightier far."

Then Diomedes of the loud war-cry answered him: "Yea verily, old man, all this thou sayest is according unto right. But this is the sore grief that entereth my heart and soul;

Hector some day shall say as he maketh harangue amid the Trojans: 'Tydeides betook him to the ships in flight before my face.' So shall he boast — in that day let the wide earth yawn for me."

So spake he and turned the whole-hooved horses to flight, back through the tumult; and the Trojans and Hector with wondrous uproar poured upon them their dolorous darts. And over him shouted loudly great Hector of the glancing helm: "Tydeides, the fleet-horsed Danaans were wont to honour thee with the highest place, and meats, and cups brimful, but now will they disdain thee; thou art after all no better than a woman. Begone, poor puppet; not for my flinching shalt thou climb on our towers, neither carry our wives away upon thy ships; ere that will I deal thee thy fate."

So said he, and Tydeides was of divided mind, whether to wheel his horses and fight him face to face. Thrice doubted he in heart and soul, and thrice from Ida's mountains thundered Zeus the lord of counsel, and gave to the Trojans a sign, the turning of the course of battle. And Hector with loud shout called to the Trojans: "Trojans and Lykians and Dardanians that love close fight, be men, my friends, and bethink you of impetuous valour. I perceive that of good will Kronion vouchsafest me victory and great glory, and to the Danaans destruction. Fools, that devised these walls weak and of none account; they shall not withhold our fury, and lightly shall our steeds overleap the delved foss. But when I be once come amid the hollow ships, then be thought taken of consuming fire, that with fire I may burn the ships and slay the men."

So spake he and shouted to his steeds, and said: "Xanthos, and thou Podargos, and Aithon and goodly Lampos, now pay me back your tending, even the abundance that Andromache, great-hearted Eëtion's daughter, set before you of honey-hearted wheat, and mingled wine to drink at the heart's bidding.

Pursue ye now and haste, that we may seize Nestor's shield, the fame whereof now reacheth unto heaven, how that it is of gold throughout, armrods and all; and may seize moreover from horse-taming Diomedes' shoulders his richly dight breastplate that Hephaistos wrought cunningly. Could we but take these, then might I hope this very night to make the Achaians to embark on their fleet ships."

And now had he burned the trim ships with blazing fire, but that queen Hera put it in Agamemnon's heart himself to bestir him and swiftly arouse the Achaians. So he went his way along the huts and ships of the Achaians, holding a great cloak of purple in his stalwart hand, and stood by Odysseus' black ship of mighty burden, that was in the midst, so that a voice could be heard to either end. Then shouted he in a piercing voice, and called to the Danaans aloud: "Fie upon you, Argives, ye sorry things of shame, so brave in semblance! Whither are gone our boastings when we said that we were bravest, the boasts ye uttered vaingloriously when in Lemnos, as ye ate your fill of flesh of tall-horned oxen and drank goblets crowned with wine, and said that every man should stand in war to face fivescore yea tenscore Trojans? yet now can we not match one, even this Hector that anon will burn our ships with flame of fire. O Father Zeus, didst ever thou blind with such a blindness any mighty king, and rob him of great glory? Nay, Zeus, this hope fulfil thou me; suffer that we ourselves at least flee and escape, neither suffer that the Achaians be thus vanquished of the Trojans."

So spake he, and the Father had pity on him as he wept, and vouchsafed him that his folk should be saved and perish not. Forthwith sent he an eagle — surest sign among winged fowl — holding in his claws a fawn, the young of a fleet hind; beside the beautiful altar of Zeus he let fall the fawn, where the Achaians did sacrifice unto Zeus lord of all oracles. So when they saw that the bird was come from Zeus, they sprang the more upon the Trojans and bethought them of the joy of battle.

Now could no man of the Danaans, for all they were very many, boast that he before Tydeus' son had guided his fleet horses forth, and driven them across the trench and fought man to man; first by far was Tydeides to slay a warrior of the Trojans in full array, even Agelaos son of Phradmon. Now he had turned his steeds to flee; but as he wheeled the other plunged the spear into his back between his shoulders, and drave it through his breast. So fell he from his chariot, and his armour clanged upon him.

And after him came Atreus' sons, even Agamemnon and Menelaos, and after them the Aiantes clothed upon with impetuous valour, and after them Idomeneus and Idomeneus' brother in arms Meriones, peer of Enyalios slayer of men, and after them Eurypylos, Euaimon's glorious son. And ninth came Teukros, stretching his back-bent bow, and took his stand beneath the shield of Aias son of Telamon. And so Aias would stealthily withdraw the shield, and Teukros would spy his chance; and when he had shot and smitten one in the throng, then fell such an one and gave up the ghost, and Teukros would return, and as a child beneath his mother, so gat he him to Aias; who hid him with the shining shield.

And Agamemnon king of men rejoiced to behold him making havoc with his stalwart bow of the battalions of the Trojans, and he came and stood by his side and spake to him, saying: "Teukros, dear heart, thou son of Telamon, prince of the host, shoot on in this wise, if perchance thou mayest be found the salvation of the Danaans and glory of thy father Telamon.

And noble Teukros made answer and said to him: "Most noble son of Atreus, why urgest thou me that myself am eager? Verily with such strength as is in me forbear I not, but ever since we drave them towards Ilios I watch with my bow to slay the foemen. Eight long-barbed arrows have I now sped, and all are buried in the flesh of young men swift in battle; only this mad dog can I not smite."

He said, and shot another arrow from the string right against Hector; and his heart was fain to smite him. Yet missed he once again, for Apollo turned the dart away; but Archeptolemos, Hector's bold charioteer, he smote on the breast beside the nipple as he hasted into battle: so he fell from his car and his fleet-footed horses swerved aside; and there his soul and spirit were unstrung. Then sore grief encompassed Hector's soul for his charioteer's sake; yet left he him, though he sorrowed for his comrade, and bade Kebriones his own brother, being hard by, take the chariot reins; and he heard and disregarded not. And himself he leapt to earth from the resplendent car, with a terrible shout; and in his hand he caught a stone, and made right at Teukros, and his heart bade him smite him. Now Teukros had plucked forth from his quiver a keen arrow, and laid it on the string; but even as he drew it back, Hector of the glancing helm smote him with the jagged stone, as he aimed eagerly against him, even beside his shoulder, where the collarbone fenceth off neck and breast, and where is the most deadly spot; and he brake the bowstring, and his hand from the wrist grew numb, and he stayed fallen upon his knee, and his bow dropped from his hand. But Aias disregarded not his brother's fall, but ran and strode across him and hid him with his shield. Then two trusty comrades bent down to him, even Mekisteus son of Echios and goodly Alastor, and bare him, groaning sorely, to the hollow ships. And once again the Olympian aroused the spirit of the Trojans. So they drove the Achaians straight toward the deep foss, and amid the foremost went Hector exulting in his strength. And even as when a hound behind wild boar or lion, with swift feet pursuing snatcheth at him, at flank or buttock, and watcheth for him as he wheeleth, so Hector pressed hard on the flowing-haired Achaians, slaying ever the hindmost, and they fled on. But when they were passed in flight through palisade and foss, and many were fallen beneath the Trojans' hands, then halted they and tarried beside the ships, calling one upon another, and lifting up their hands to all the gods prayed each one instantly. But Hector wheeled round his beauteous-maned steeds this way and that, and his eyes were as the eyes of Gorgon or Ares bane of mortals.

Now at the sight of them the white-armed goddess Hera had compassion, and anon spake winged words to Athene: "Out on it, thou child of aegis-bearing Zeus, shall not we twain any more take thought for the Danaans that perish, if only for this last time? Now will they fill up the measure of evil destiny and perish by one man's onslaught; seeing that he is furious now beyond endurance, this Hector son of Priam, and verily hath wrought many a deed of ill."

And the bright-eyed goddess Athene made answer to her, "Yea in good sooth, may this fellow yield up strength and life, and perish at the Argives' hands in his native land; only mine own sire is furious, with no good intent, headstrong, ever sinful, the foiler of my purposes. But now make thou ready our whole-hooved horses, while I enter into the palace of aegis-bearing Zeus and gird me in my armour for battle, that I may see if Priam's son, Hector of the glancing helm, shall be glad at the appearing of us twain amid the highways of the battle. Surely shall many a Trojan likewise glut dogs and birds with fat and flesh, fallen dead at the ships of the Achaians."

So said she, and the white-armed goddess Hera disregarded not. But when father Zeus beheld from Ida, he was sore wroth, and sped Iris golden-winged to bear a message: "Go thy way, fleet Iris, turn them back, neither suffer them to face me; for in no happy wise shall we join in combat. For thus will I declare, and even so shall the fulfilment be; I will maim their fleet horses in the chariot, and them will I hurl out from the car, and will break in pieces the chariot; neither within the courses of ten years shall they heal them of the wounds the thunderbolt shall tear; that the bright-eyed one may know the end when she striveth against her father. But with Hera have I not so great indignation nor wrath: seeing it ever is her wont to thwart me, whate'er I have decreed."

So said he, and whirlwind-footed Iris arose to bear the message, and departed from the mountains of Ida unto high Olympus. And even at the entrance of the gates of Olympus many-folded she met them and stayed them, and told them the saying of Zeus.

And father Zeus drave from Ida his fair-wheeled chariot and horses unto Olympus, and came unto the session of the gods. For him also the noble Shaker of Earth unyoked the steeds, and set the car upon the stand, and spread a cloth thereover; and far-seeing Zeus himself sate upon his golden throne, and beneath his feet great Olympus quaked. Only Athene and Hera sate apart from Zeus, and spake no word to him neither questioned him. But he was ware thereof in his heart, and said, "Why are ye thus vexed, Athene and Hera? Surely ye are not wearied of making havoc in glorious battle of the Trojans, for whom ye cherish bitter hate! Howsoever, seeing that my might is so great and my hands invincible, all the gods that are in Olympus could not turn me: and for you twain, trembling erst gat hold upon your bright limbs ere that ye beheld war and war's fell deeds. For thus will I declare, and even so had the fulfilment been—never had ye, once smitten with the thunderbolt, fared on your chariots back unto Olympus where is the habitation of the immortals."

So spake he, and Athene and Hera murmured, that were sitting by him and devising ills for the Trojans. Now Athene held her peace, and said not anything, for wrath at father Zeus, and fierce anger gat hold upon her; but Hera's heart contained not her anger, and she spake: "Most dread son of Kronos, what word is this thou hast said? Well know we, even we, that thy might is no wise puny; yet still have we pity for the Danaan spearmen, that now shall perish and fill up the measure of grievous fate."

And Zeus the cloud-gatherer answered and said: "At morn shalt thou behold most mighty Kronion, if thou wilt have it so, O Hera, ox-eyed queen, making yet more havoc of the vast army of Argive spearmen; for headlong Hector shall not refrain from battle till that Peleus' son fleet of foot have arisen beside the ships, that day when these shall fight amid the sterns in most grievous stress, around Patroklos fallen. Such is the doom of heaven. And for thine anger reck I not, not even though thou go to the nethermost bounds of earth and sea, where sit Iapetos and Kronos and have no joy in the beams of Hyperion the Sun-god, neither in any breeze, but deep Tartaros is round about them. Though thou shouldest wander till thou come even thither, yet reck I not of thy vexation, seeing there is no thing more unabashed than thou."

So said he, but white-armed Hera spake him no word. And the sun's bright light dropped into Ocean, drawing black night across Earth the grain-giver. Against the Trojans' will daylight departed, but welcome, thrice prayed for, to the Achaians came down the murky night.

Now glorious Hector made an assembly of the Trojans, taking them apart from the ships, beside the eddying river, in an open space where was found a spot clear of dead. And they came down from their chariots to the ground to hear the word that Hector, dear unto Zeus, proclaimed. He in his hand held his spear eleven cubits long; before his face gleamed the spearhead of bronze, and a ring of gold ran round about it. Thereon he leaned and spake to the Trojans, saying: "Hearken to me, Trojans and Dardanians and allies. I thought but now to make havoc of the ships and all the Achaians and depart back again to windy Ilios; but dusk came too soon, and that in chief hath now saved the Argives and the ships beside the beach of the sea. So let us now yield to black night, and make our supper ready; unyoke ye from the chariots your fair-maned horses, and set fodder beside them. And from the city bring kine and goodly sheep with speed; and provide you with honey-hearted wine, and corn from your houses, and gather much wood withal, that all night long until early-springing dawn we may burn many fires, and the gleam may reach to heaven; lest perchance even by night the flowing-haired Achaians strive to take flight over the broad back of the sea. Verily must they not embark upon their ships unvexed, at ease: but see ye that many a one of them have a wound to nurse even at home, being stricken with arrow or keen-pointed spear as he leapeth upon his ship; that so many another man may dread to wage dolorous war on the horse-taming men of Troy. And let the heralds dear to Zeus proclaim throughout the city that young maidens and old men of hoary heads camp round the city on the battlements builded of the gods; and let the women folk burn a great fire each in her hall; and let there be a sure watch set, lest an ambush enter the city when the host is absent. Howbeit for the night will we guard our own selves, and at morn by daybreak, arrayed in our armour, let us awake keen battle at the hollow ships. I will know whether Tydeus' son stalwart Diomedes shall thrust me from the ships back to the wall, or I shall lay him low with my spear and bear away his gory spoils. To-morrow shall he prove his valour, whether he can abide the onslaught of my spear. Would that I were immortal and ageless all my days and honoured like as Athene is honoured and Apollo, so surely as this day bringeth the Argives ill."

So Hector made harangue, and the Trojans clamoured applause. And they loosed their sweating steeds from the yoke, and tethered them with thongs, each man beside his chariot; and from the city they brought kine and goodly sheep with speed, and provided them with honey-hearted wine and corn from their houses, and gathered much wood withal. And from the plain the winds bare into heaven the sweet savour. But these with high hopes sate them all night along the highways of the battle, and their watchfires burned in multitude. Even as when in heaven the stars about the bright moon shine clear to see, when the air is windless, and all the peaks appear and the tall headlands and glades, and from heaven breaketh open the infinite air, and all stars are seen, and the shepherd's heart is glad; even in like multitude between the ships and the streams of Xanthos appeared the watchfires that the Trojans kindled in front of Ilios. A thousand fires burned in the plain and by the side of each sate fifty in the gleam of blazing fire. And the horses champed white barley and spelt, and standing by their chariots waited for the throned Dawn.

BOOK IX

How Agamemnon sent an embassage to Achilles, beseeching him to be appeased; and how Achilles denied him.

THUS kept the Trojans watch; but the Achaians were holden of heaven-sent panic, handmaid of palsying fear, and all their best were stricken to the heart with grief intolerable. Like as two winds stir up the main, the home of fishes, even the north wind and the west wind that blow from Thrace, coming suddenly; and the dark billow straightway lifteth up its crest and casteth much tangle out along the sea; even so was the Achaians' spirit troubled in their breast.

But Atreides was stricken to the heart with sore grief, and went about bidding the clear-voiced heralds summon every man by name to the assembly, but not to shout aloud; and himself he toiled amid the foremost. So they sat sorrowful in assembly, and Agamemnon stood up weeping like unto a fountain of dark water that from a beetling cliff poureth down its black stream; even so with deep groaning he spake amid the Argives and said: "My friends, leaders and captains of the Argives, Zeus son of Kronos hath bound me with might in grievous blindness of soul; hard of heart is he, for that erewhile he promised and gave his pledge that not till I had laid waste well-walled Ilios should I depart, but now hath planned a cruel wile, and biddeth me return in dishonour to Argos with the loss of many of my folk. Such meseemeth is the good pleasure of most mighty Zeus, that hath laid low the heads of many cities, yea and shall lay low; for his is highest power. So come, even as I shall bid let us all obey; let us flee with our ships to our dear native land, for now shall we never take wide-wayed Troy."

So said he, and they all held their peace and kept silence. Long time were the sons of the Achaians voiceless for grief, but at the last Diomedes of the loud war-cry spake amid them and said: "Atreides, with thee first in thy folly will I contend, where it is just, O king, even in the assembly; be not thou wroth therefor. My valour didst thou blame in chief amid the Danaans, and saidst that I was no man of war but a coward; and all this know the Argives both young and old. But the son of crooked-counselling Kronos hath endowed thee but by halves; he granted thee to have the honour of the sceptre above all men, but valour he gave thee not, wherein is highest power. Sir, deemest thou that the sons of the Achaians are thus indeed cowards and weaklings as thou sayest? If thine own heart be set on departing, go thy way; the way is before thee, and thy ships stand beside the sea, even the great multitude that followed thee from Mykene. But all the other flowing-haired Achaians will tarry here until we lay waste Troy. Nay, let them too flee on their ships to their dear native land; yet will we twain, even I and Sthenelos, fight till we attain the goal of Ilios; for in God's name are we come."

So said he, and all the sons of the Achaians shouted aloud, applauding the saying of horse-taming Diomedes. Then knightly Nestor arose and said amid them: "Tydeides, in battle art thou passing mighty, and in council art thou best among thine equals in years; none of all the Achaians will make light of thy word nor gainsay it. Now let us yield to black night and make ready our meal; and let the sentinels bestow them severally along the deep-delved foss without the wall. This charge give I to the young men; and thou, Atreides, lead then the way, for thou art the most royal. Spread thou a feast for the councillors; that is thy place and seemly for thee. Thy huts are full of wine that the ships of the Achaians bring thee by day from Thrace across the wide sea; all entertainment is for thee, being king over many. In the gathering of many shalt thou listen to him that deviseth the most excellent counsel; sore need have all the Achaians of such as is good and prudent, because hard by the ships our foemen are burning their watch-fires in multitude; what man can rejoice thereat? This night shall either destroy or save the host."

So said he, and they gladly hearkened to him and obeyed. Forth sallied the sentinels in their harness. Seven were the captains of the sentinels, and with each went fivescore young men bearing their long spears in their hands; and they took post midway betwixt foss and wall, and kindled a fire and made ready each man his meal.

Then Atreides gathered the councillors of the Achaians, and led them to his hut, and spread before them an abundant feast. So they put forth their hands to the good cheer that lay before them. And when they had put away from them the desire of meat and drink, then the old man first began to weave his counsel, even Nestor, whose rede of old time was approved the best. He spake to them and said: "Most noble son of Atreus, Agamemnon king of men, in thy name will I end and with thy name begin, because thou art king over many hosts, and to thy hand Zeus hath entrusted sceptre and law, that thou mayest take counsel for thy folk. Thee therefore more than any it behoveth both to speak and hearken, and to accomplish what another than thou may say. No other man shall have a more excellent thought than this that I bear in mind from old time even until now, since the day when thou, O heaven-sprung king, didst go and take the damsel Briseis from angry Achilles' hut by no consent of ours. Nay, I right heartily dissuaded thee; but thou yieldedst to thy proud spirit, and dishonouredst a man of valour whom even the immortals honoured; for thou didst take and keepest from him his meed of valour. Still let us even now take thought how we may appease him and persuade him with gifts of friendship and kindly words."

And Agamemnon king of men answered and said to him: "Old sir, in no false wise hast thou accused my folly. Fool was I, I myself deny it not. Worth many hosts is he whom Zeus loveth in his heart, even as now he honoureth this man and destroyeth the host of the Achaians. But seeing I was a fool in that I yielded to my sorry passion, I will make amends and give a recompense beyond telling. In the midst of you all I will name the excellent gifts; seven tripods untouched of fire, and ten talents of gold and twenty gleaming caldrons, and twelve stalwart horses, winners in the race, that have taken prizes by their speed. No lackwealth were that man whose substance were as great as the prizes my whole-hooved steeds have borne me off. And seven women will I give, skilled in excellent handiwork, Lesbians whom I chose me from the spoils the day that he himself took stablished Lesbos, surpassing womankind in beauty. These will I give him, and with them shall be she whom erst I took from him, even the daughter of Briseus. All these things shall be set straightway before him; and if hereafter the gods grant us to lay waste the great city of Priam, then let him enter in when we Achaians be dividing the

spoil, and lade his ship full of gold and bronze, and himself
choose twenty Trojan women, the fairest that there be after
Helen of Argos. And if we win to the richest of lands, even
Achaian Argos, he shall be my son and I will hold him in like
honour with Orestes, my stripling boy that is nurtured in all
abundance. Three daughters are mine in my well-builded hall,
Chrysothemis and Laodike and Iphianassa; let him take of them
which he will, without gifts of wooing, to Peleus' house; and
I will add a great dower such as no man ever yet gave with his
daughter. And seven well-peopled cities will I give him, Kardamyle and Enope and grassy Hire and holy Pherai and Antheia
deep in meads, and fair Aipeia and Pedasos land of vines. And
all are nigh to the salt sea, on the uttermost border of sandy
Pylos; therein dwell men abounding in flocks and kine, men that
shall worship him like a god with gifts, and beneath his sway
fulfil his prosperous ordinances. All this will I accomplish so
he but cease from wrath. Let him yield; Hades I ween is not to
be softened neither overcome, and therefore is he hatefullest of
all gods to mortals. Yea, let him be ruled by me, inasmuch as
I am more royal and avow me to be the elder in years."

Then knightly Nestor of Gerenia answered and said: "Most
noble son of Atreus, Agamemnon king of men, now are these
gifts not lightly to be esteemed that thou offerest king Achilles.
Come therefore, let us speed forth picked men to go with all
haste to the hut of Peleus' son Achilles. Lo now, whomsoever
I appoint let them consent. First let Phoinix dear to Zeus lead
the way, and after him great Aias and noble Odysseus; and
for heralds let Odios and Eurybates be their companions. And
now bring water for our hands, and bid keep holy silence, that
we may pray unto Zeus the son of Kronos, if perchance he will
have mercy upon us."

So said he, and spake words that were well-pleasing unto
all. Forthwith the heralds poured water on their hands, and
the young men crowned the bowls with drink and gave each

man his portion after they had poured the libation in the cups. And when they had made libation and drunk as their heart desired, they issued forth from the hut of Agamemnon son of Atreus. And knightly Nestor of Gerenia gave them full charge, with many a glance to each, and chiefest to Odysseus, how they should essay to prevail on Peleus' noble son.

So the twain went along the shore of the loud-sounding sea, making instant prayer to the earth-embracer, the Shaker of the Earth, that they might with ease prevail on Aiakides' great heart. So they came to the huts and ships of the Myrmidons, and found their king taking his pleasure of a loud lyre, fair, of curious work, with a silver cross-bar upon it. Therein he was delighting his soul, and singing the glories of heroes. And over against him sate Patroklos alone in silence, watching till Aiakides should cease from singing. So the twain came forward, and noble Odysseus led the way, and they stood before his face; and Achilles sprang up amazed with the lyre in his hand, and left the seat where he was sitting, and in like manner Patroklos when he beheld the men arose. Then Achilles fleet of foot greeted them and said: "Welcome; verily ye are friends that are come — sore indeed is the need — even ye that are dearest of the Achaians to me even in my wrath."

So spake noble Achilles and led them forward, and made them sit on settles and carpets of purple; and anon he spake to Patroklos being near: "Bring forth a greater bowl, thou son of Menoitios; mingle stronger drink, and prepare each man a cup, for dearest of men are these that are under my roof."

Then put they forth their hands to the good cheer lying before them. And when they had put from them the desire of meat and drink, Aias nodded to Phoinix. But noble Odysseus marked it, and filled a cup with wine and pledged Achilles: "Hail, O Achilles! The fair feast lack we not either in the hut of Agamemnon son of Atreus neither now in thine; for feasting is there abundance to our heart's desire, but our thought is not for matters of the delicious feast; nay, we behold very sore destruction, thou fosterling of Zeus, and are afraid. Now is it in doubt whether we save the benched ships or behold them perish, if thou put not on thy might. Nigh unto ships and wall have the high-hearted Trojans and famed allies pitched their camp, and kindled many fires throughout their host, and ween that they shall no more be withheld but will fall on our black ships. And Zeus son of Kronos sheweth them signs upon the right by lightning, and Hector greatly exulteth in his might and rageth furiously, trusting in Zeus, and recketh not of god nor man, for mighty madness hath possessed him. He prayeth bright Dawn to shine forth with all speed, for he hath passed his word to smite off from the ships the ensigns' tops, and to fire the hulls with devouring flame, and hard thereby to make havoc of the Achaians confounded by the smoke. Therefore am I sore afraid in my heart lest the gods fulfil his boastings, and it be fated for us to perish here in Troy-land, far from Argos pasture-land of horses. Up then! if thou art minded even at the last to save the failing sons of the Achaians˙ from the war-din of the Trojans. Eschew thy grievous wrath; Agamemnon offereth thee worthy gifts, so thou wilt cease from anger. Lo now, hearken thou to me, and I will tell thee all the gifts that in his hut Agamemnon promised thee. But if Agamemnon be too hateful to thy heart, both he and his gifts, yet have thou pity on all the Achaians that faint throughout the host; these shall honour thee as a god, for verily thou wilt earn exceeding great glory at their hands. Yea now mightest thou slay Hector, for he would come very near thee in his deadly madness, because he deemeth that there is no man like unto him among the Danaans that the ships brought hither."

And Achilles fleet of foot answered and said unto him: "Heaven-sprung son of Laertes, Odysseus of many wiles, in

openness must I now declare unto you my saying, even as I am
minded and as the fulfilment thereof shall be, that ye may not
sit before me and coax this way and that. For hateful to me
even as the gates of hell is he that hideth one thing in his
heart and uttereth another: but I will speak what meseemeth
best. Not me, I ween, shall Agamemnon son of Atreus persuade, nor the other Danaans, seeing we were to have no thank
for battling with the foemen ever without respite. He that
abideth at home hath equal share with him that fighteth his
best, and in like honour are held both the coward and the
brave; death cometh alike to the untoiling and to him that
hath toiled long. Neither have I any profit for that I endured
tribulation of soul, ever staking my life in fight. Even as a
hen bringeth her unfledged chickens each morsel as she winneth
it, and with herself it goeth hard, even so I was wont to watch
out many a sleepless night and pass through many bloody days
of battle, warring with folk for their women's sake. Twelve cities
of men have I laid waste from ship-board, and from land eleven,
throughout deep-soiled Troy-land; out of all these took I many
goodly treasures and would bring and give them all to Agamemnon son of Atreus, and he staying behind amid the fleet ships
would take them and portion out some few but keep the most.
Now some he gave to be meeds of honour to the princes and
the kings, and theirs are left untouched; only from me of all
the Achaians took he my darling lady and keepeth her. But
why must the Argives make war on the Trojans? why hath
Atreides gathered his host and led them hither? is it not for
lovely-haired Helen's sake? Do then the sons of Atreus alone
of mortal men love their wives? surely whatsoever man is good
and sound of mind loveth his own and cherisheth her, even as
I too loved mine with all my heart, though but the captive of
my spear. But now that he hath taken my meed of honour
from mine arms and hath deceived me, let him not tempt me
that know him full well; he shall not prevail. Nay, Odysseus,

let him take counsel with thee and all the princes to ward from the ships the consuming fire. Verily without mine aid he hath wrought many things, and built a wall and dug a foss about it wide and deep, and set a palisade therein ; yet even so can he not stay murderous Hector's might. But so long as I was fighting amid the Achaians, Hector had no mind to array his battle far from the wall, but scarce came unto the Skaian gates and to the oak-tree ; there once he awaited me alone and scarce escaped my onset. But now, seeing I have no mind to fight with noble Hector, I will to-morrow do sacrifice to Zeus and all the gods, and store well my ships when I have launched them on the salt sea — then shalt thou see, if thou wilt and hast any care therefor, my ships sailing at break of day over Hellespont, the fishes' home, and my men right eager at the oar; and if the great Shaker of the Earth grant me good journey, on the third day should I reach deep-soiled Phthia. There are my great possessions that I left when I came hither to my hurt; and yet more gold and ruddy bronze shall I bring from hence, and fair-girdled women and grey iron, all at least that were mine by lot ; only my meed of honour hath he that gave it me taken back in his despitefulness, even lord Agamemnon son of Atreus. To him declare ye everything even as I charge you, openly, that all the Achaians likewise may have indignation, if haply he hopeth to beguile yet some other Danaan, for that he is ever clothed in shamelessness. Verily not in my face would he dare to look, though he have the front of a dog. Neither will I devise counsel with him nor any enterprise, for utterly he hath deceived me and done wickedly ; but never again shall he beguile me with fair speech — let this suffice him. Let him begone in peace ; Zeus the lord of counsel hath taken away his wits. Hateful to me are his gifts, and I hold him at a straw's worth. Not even if he gave me ten times, yea twenty, all that now is his, and all that may come to him otherwhence, even all the revenue of Orchomenos or Egyptian

Thebes where the treasure-houses are stored full; it — Thebes of the hundred gates, whence sally forth two hundred warriors through each with horses and chariots — nay, nor gifts in number as sand or dust; not even so shall Agamemnon persuade my soul till he have paid me back all the bitter despite. And the daughter of Agamemnon son of Atreus will I not wed, not were she rival of golden Aphrodite for fairness and for handiwork matched bright-eyed Athene — not even then will I wed her; let him choose him of the Achaians another that is his peer and is more royal than I. For if the gods indeed preserve me and I come unto my home, then will Peleus himself seek me a wife. Many Achaian maidens are there throughout Hellas and Phthia, daughters of princes that ward their cities; whomsoever of these I wish will I make my dear lady. Very often was my high soul moved to take me there a wedded wife, a help meet for me, and have joy of the possessions that the old man Peleus possesseth. For not of like worth with life hold I even all the wealth that men say was possessed of the well-peopled city of Ilios in days of peace gone by, before the sons of the Achaians came; neither all the treasure that the stone threshold of the archer Phoebus Apollo encompasseth in rocky Pytho. For kine and goodly flocks are to be had for the harrying, and tripods and chestnut horses for the purchasing; but to bring back man's life neither harrying nor earning availeth when once it hath passed the barrier of his lips. For thus my goddess mother telleth me, Thetis the silver-footed, that twain fates are bearing me to the issue of death. If I abide here and besiege the Trojans' city, then my returning home is taken from me, but my fame shall be imperishable; but if I go home to my dear native land, my high fame is taken from me, but my life shall endure long while, neither shall the issue of death soon reach me. Moreover I would counsel you all to set sail homeward, seeing ye shall never reach your goal of steep Ilios; of a surety far-seeing Zeus holdeth his hand over her and her folk are of good courage. So go your way and tell my answer to the princes of the Achaians, even as is the office of elders, that they may devise in their hearts some other better counsel, such as shall save them their ships and the host of the Achaians amid the hollow ships: since this counsel availeth them naught that they have now devised, by reason of my fierce wrath. But let Phoinix now abide with us and lay him to rest, that he may follow with me on my ships to our dear native land to-morrow, if he will; for I will not take him perforce."

So spake he, and they all held their peace and were still, and marvelled at his saying; for he denied them very vehemently. But at the last spake to them the old knight Phoinix, bursting into tears, because he was sore afraid for the ships of the Achaians: "If indeed thou ponderest departure in thy heart, glorious Achilles, and hast no mind at all to save the fleet ships from consuming fire, because that wrath hath entered into thy heart; how can I be left of thee, dear son, alone thereafter? To thee did the old knight Peleus send me the day he sent thee to Agamemnon forth from Phthia, a stripling yet unskilled in equal war and in debate wherein men wax pre-eminent. Therefore sent he me to teach thee all these things, to be both a speaker of words and a doer of deeds. Yea, I reared thee to this greatness, thou godlike Achilles, with my heart's love; for with none other wouldest thou go unto the feast, neither take meat in the hall, till that I had set thee upon my knees and stayed thee with the savoury morsel cut first for thee, and put the wine-cup to thy lips. Oft hast thou stained the doublet on my breast with sputtering of wine in thy sorry helplessness. Thus I suffered much with thee, and much I toiled, being mindful that the gods in nowise created any issue of my body; but I made thee my son, thou godlike Achilles, that thou mayest yet save me from grievous destruction. Therefore, Achilles, rule thy high spirit; neither beseemeth it thee to have a ruthless heart. Nay, even the very gods can bend, and theirs withal is loftier majesty and honour and might. Nay, come for the gifts; the Achaians shall honour thee even as a god. But if without gifts thou enter into battle the bane of men, thou wilt not be held in like honour, even though thou avert the fray."

And Achilles fleet of foot made answer and said to him: "Phoinix my father, thou old man fosterling of Zeus, such honour need I in no wise; for I deem that I have been honoured by the judgment of Zeus, which shall abide upon me amid my beaked ships as long as breath tarrieth in my body and my limbs are strong. Moreover I will say this thing to thee and lay thou it to thine heart; trouble not my soul by weeping and lamentation, to do the pleasure of warrior Atreides; neither beseemeth it thee to cherish him, lest thou be hated of me that cherish thee. It were good that thou with me shouldest vex him that vexeth me. Be thou king even as I, and share my sway by halves, but these shall bear my message. So tarry thou here and lay thee to rest in a soft bed, and with break of day will we consider whether to depart unto our own, or to abide."

He spake, and nodded his brow in silence unto Patroklos to spread for Phoinix a thick couch, that the others might bethink them to depart from the hut with speed. Then spake to them Aias, Telamon's godlike son, and said : " Heaven-sprung son of Laertes, Odysseus of many wiles, let us go hence; for methinks the purpose of our charge will not by this journey be accomplished; and we must tell the news, though it be no wise good, with all speed unto the Danaans, that now sit awaiting. But Achilles hath wrought his proud soul to fury within him — stubborn man, that recketh naught of his comrades' love, wherein we worshipped him beyond all men amid the ships — unmerciful! Yet doth a man accept recompense of his brother's murderer or for his dead son; and so the man-slayer for a great price abideth in his own land, and the kinsman's heart is appeased, and his proud soul, when he hath taken the recompense. But for thee, the gods have put within thy breast a spirit implacable and evil, by reason of one single damsel. And now we offer thee seven damsels, far best of all, and many other gifts besides; entertain thou then a kindly spirit, and have respect unto thine home; because we are guests of thy roof, sent of the multitude of Danaans, and we would fain be nearest to thee and dearest beyond all other Achaians, as many as there be."

And Achilles fleet of foot made answer and said to him: "Aias sprung of Zeus, thou son of Telamon, prince of the folk, thou seemest to speak all this almost after mine own mind; but my heart swelleth with wrath as oft as I bethink me of those things, how Atreides entreated me arrogantly among the Argives, as though I were some worthless sojourner. But go ye and declare my message; I will not take thought of bloody war until that wise Priam's son, noble Hector, come to the Myrmidons' huts and ships, slaying the Argives, and smirch the ships with fire. But about mine hut and black ship I ween that Hector, though he be very eager for battle, shall be refrained."

So said he, and they took each man a two-handled cup, and made libation and went back along the line of ships; and Odysseus led the way. And Patroklos bade his fellows and handmaidens spread with all speed a thick couch for Phoinix; and they obeyed and spread a couch as he ordained, fleeces and rugs and fine flock of linen. Then the old man laid him down and tarried for bright Dawn.

Now when those were come unto Atreides' huts, the sons of the Achaians stood up on this side and on that, and pledged them in cups of gold, and questioned them; and Agamemnon king of men asked them first: "Come now, tell me, Odysseus full of praise, thou great glory of the Achaians; will he save the ships from consuming fire, or said he nay, and hath wrath yet hold of his proud spirit?"

And steadfast goodly Odysseus answered him: "Most noble son of Atreus, Agamemnon king of men, he yonder hath no mind to quench his wrath, but is yet more filled of fury, and spurneth thee and thy gifts. He biddeth thee take counsel for thyself amid the Argives, how to save the ships and folk of the Achaians. And for himself he threateneth that at break of day he will launch upon the sea his trim well-benched ships. Moreover he said that he would counsel all to sail for home, because ye now shall never reach your goal of steep Ilios; surely far-seeing Zeus holdeth his hand over her and her folk are of good courage. Even so said he, and here are also these to tell the tale that were my companions, Aias and the two heralds, both men discreet. But the old man Phoinix laid him there to rest, even as Achilles bade him, that he may follow with him on his ships to his dear native land to-morrow, if he will; for he will not take him perforce."

So said he, and they all held their peace and were still, marvelling at his saying, for he harangued very vehemently. Long were the sons of the Achaians voiceless for grief, but at the last Diomedes of the loud war-cry spake amid them: "Most noble son of Atreus, Agamemnon king of men, would thou hadst never besought Peleus' glorious son with offer of gifts innumerable; proud is he at any time, but now hast thou yet far more encouraged him in his haughtiness. Howbeit we will let him bide, whether he go or tarry; hereafter he shall fight, whenever his heart within him biddeth and god arouseth him. Come now, even as I shall say let us all obey. Go ye now to rest, full to your hearts' desire of meat and wine, wherein courage is and strength; but when fair rosy-fingered Dawn appeareth, array thou with all speed before the ships thy folk and horsemen, and urge them on; and fight thyself amid the foremost."

So said he, and all the princes gave assent, applauding the saying of Diomedes tamer of horses. And then they made libation and went every man to his hut, and there laid them to rest and took the boon of sleep.

BOOK X

How Diomedes and Odysseus slew Dolon, a spy of the Trojans, and themselves spied on the Trojan camp, and took the horses of Rhesos, the Thracian king.

Now beside the ships the other leaders of the whole Achaian host were sleeping all night long, by soft Sleep overcome, but Agamemnon son of Atreus, shepherd of the host, sweet Sleep held not, so many things he debated in his mind. And even as when the lord of fair-tressed Hera lighteneth, fashioning either a mighty rain unspeakable, or hail, or snow, when the flakes sprinkle all the ploughed lands, or fashioning perchance the wide mouth of bitter war, even so oft in his breast groaned Agamemnon, from the very deep of his heart, and his spirits trembled within him. And whensoever he looked toward that Trojan plain, he marvelled at the many fires that blazed in front of Ilios, and at the sound of flutes and pipes, and the noise of men; but whensoever to the ships he glanced and the host of the Achaians, then rent he many a lock clean forth from his head, to Zeus that is above, and greatly groaned his noble heart.

And this in his soul seemed to him the best counsel, to go first of all to Nestor son of Neleus, if perchance he might contrive with him some right device that should be for the warding off of evil from all the Danaans.

Then he rose, and did on his doublet about his breast, and beneath his shining feet he bound on fair sandals, and thereafter clad him in the tawny skin of a lion fiery and great, a skin that reached to the feet, and he grasped his spear.

And even in like wise did trembling fear take hold on Menelaos, (for neither on his eyelids did Sleep settle down,) lest somewhat should befall the Argives, who verily for his sake over wide waters were come to Troy-land, with fierce war in their thoughts.

With a dappled pard's skin first he covered his broad shoulders, and he raised and set on his head a casque of bronze, and took a spear in his strong hand. Then went he on his way to rouse his brother, that mightily ruled over all the Argives, and as a god was honoured by the people. Him found he harnessing his goodly gear about his shoulders, by the stern of the ship, and glad to his brother was his coming. Then Menelaos of the loud war-cry first accosted him: "Wherefore thus, dear brother, art thou arming? Wilt thou speed forth any of thy comrades to spy on the Trojans? Nay, terribly I fear lest none should undertake for thee this deed, even to go and spy out the foeman alone through the ambrosial night; needs must he be a man right hardy of heart."

Then the lord Agamemnon answered him and spake: "Need of good counsel have I and thou, Menelaos fosterling of Zeus, of counsel that will help and save the Argives and the ships, since the heart of Zeus hath turned again. Surely on the sacrifices of Hector hath he set his heart rather than on ours. For never did I see, nor heard any tell, that one man devised so many terrible deeds in one day, as Hector, dear to Zeus, hath wrought on the sons of the Achaians, unaided; though no dear son of a goddess is he, nor of a god. He hath done deeds that methinks will be a sorrow to the Argives, lasting and long, such evils hath he devised against the Achaians. But go now, run swiftly by the ships, and summon Aias and Idomeneus, but I will betake me to noble Nestor, and bid him arise, if perchance he will be fain to go to the sacred company of the sentinels and lay on them his command. For to him above others would they listen, for his own son is chief among the sentinels, he and the brother in arms of Idomeneus, even Meriones, for to them above all we entrusted this charge."

Then Menelaos of the loud war-cry answered him: "How meanest thou this word wherewith thou dost command and exhort me? Am I to abide there with them, waiting till thou comest, or run back again to thee when I have well delivered to them thy commandment?"

Then the king of men, Agamemnon, answered him again: "There do thou abide lest we miss each other as we go, for many are the paths through the camp. But call aloud, wheresoever thou goest, and bid men awake, naming each man by his lineage, and his father's name, and giving all their dues of honour, nor be thou proud of heart. Nay rather let us ourselves be labouring, for even thus did Zeus from our very birth dispense to us the heaviness of toil."

So he spake, and sent his brother away, having clearly laid on him his commandment. Then went he himself after Nestor, the shepherd of the host, whom he found by his hut and black ship, in his soft bed: beside him lay his arms, a shield, and two spears, and a shining helmet. Beside him lay his glittering girdle wherewith the old man was wont to gird himself when he harnessed him for war, the bane of men, and led on the host, for he yielded not to grievous old age. Then he raised him on his elbow, lifting his head, and spake to the son of Atreus, inquiring of him with this word: "Who art thou that farest alone by the ships, through the camp in the dark night, when other mortals are sleeping? Seekest thou one of thy mules, or of thy comrades? speak, and come not silently upon me. What need hast thou?"

Then the king of men, Agamemnon, answered him: "O Nestor, son of Neleus, great glory of the Achaians, thou shalt know Agamemnon, son of Atreus, whom above all men Zeus

hath planted for ever among labours, while my breath abides
within my breast, and my knees move. I wander thus, for
that sweet sleep rests not on mine eyes, but war is my care,
and the troubles of the Achaians. Yea, greatly I fear for the
sake of the Danaans, nor is my heart firm, but I am tossed
to and fro, and my heart is leaping from my breast, and my
good knees tremble beneath me. But if thou wilt do aught,
since neither on thee cometh sleep, let us go thither to the
sentinels, that we may see them, lest they be fordone with
toil, and so are slumbering, and have quite forgotten to keep
watch. And hostile men camp hard by, nor know we at all
but that they are keen to do battle in the night."

Then knightly Nestor of Gerenia answered him: "Verily
will I follow after thee, but let us also rouse others again, both
the son of Tydeus, spearman renowned, and Odysseus, and
swift Aias, and the strong son of Phyleus. But well it would
be if one were to go and call those also, the godlike Aias, and
Idomeneus the prince; for their ships are furthest of all, and
nowise close at hand. But Menelaos will I blame, dear as he
is and worshipful, yea, even if thou be angry with me, nor
will I hide my thought, for that he slumbereth, and to thee
alone hath left the toil; now should he be toiling among all
the chiefs and beseeching them, for need no longer tolerable is
coming upon us."

And the king of men, Agamemnon, answered him again:
"Old man, another day I even bid thee blame him, for often
is he slack, and willeth not to labour, yielding neither to un-
readiness nor heedlessness of heart, but looking toward me,
and expecting mine instance. But now he awoke far before
me, and came to me, and him I sent forward to call those concerning whom thou inquirest. But let us be gone, and them
shall we find before the gates, among the sentinels, for there
I bade them gather."

Then knightly Nestor of Gerenia answered him: "So will

none of the Argives be wroth with him or disobey him, whensoever he doth urge any one, and give him his commands."

So spake he, and did on his doublet about his breast, and beneath his bright feet he bound goodly shoon, and all around him buckled a purple cloak, with double folds and wide, and thick down all over it.

And he took a strong spear, pointed with sharp bronze, and he went among the ships of the mail-clad Achaians. Then Odysseus first, the peer of Zeus in counsel, did knightly Gerenian Nestor arouse out of sleep, with his voice, and quickly the cry came all about his heart, and he came forth from the hut and spake to them saying: "Wherefore thus among the ships and through the camp do ye wander alone, in the ambrosial night; what so great need cometh upon you?"

Then knightly Nestor of Gerenia answered him: "Laertes' son, be not wroth, for great trouble besetteth the Achaians. Nay follow, that we may arouse others too, even all that it behoveth to take counsel, whether we should fly, or fight."

So spake he, and Odysseus of the many counsels came to the hut, and cast a shield about his shoulders, and went after them.

And they went to seek Diomedes, son of Tydeus, and him they found outside his hut, with his arms, and around him his comrades were sleeping with their shields beneath their heads, but their spears were driven into the ground erect on the spikes of the butts, and afar shone the bronze, like the lightning of father Zeus. Now that hero was asleep, and under him was strewn the hide of an ox of the field, but beneath his head was stretched a shining carpet. Beside him went and stood knightly Nestor of Gerenia and stirred him with a touch of his foot, and aroused him, chiding him to his face, saying: "Wake, son of Tydeus, why all night long dost thou sleep? Knowest thou not that the Trojans on the high place of the plain are camped near the ships, and but a little space holdeth them apart?"

So spake he, and Diomedes sprang swiftly up out of sleep, and spake to him winged words: "Hard art thou, old man, and from toil thou never ceasest. Now are there not other younger sons of the Achaians, who might rouse when there is need each of the kings, going all around the host? but thou, old man, art indomitable."

And him knightly Nestor of Gerenia answered again, "Nay verily, my son, all this that thou sayest is according unto right. Noble sons have I, and there be many of the host, of whom each man might go and call the others. But a right great need hath assailed the Achaians. For now to all of us it standeth on a razor's edge, either pitiful ruin for the Achaians, or life. But come now, if indeed thou dost pity me, rouse swift Aias, and the son of Phyleus, for thou art younger than I."

So spake he, and Diomedes cast round his shoulders the skin of a great fiery lion, that reached to his feet, and he grasped his spear, and started on his way, and roused the others from their place and led them on.

Now when they had come among the assembled sentinels, they found not the leaders of the sentinels asleep, but they all sat wide awake with their arms. And even as hounds keep difficult guard round the sheep in a fold, having heard a hardy wild beast that cometh through the wood among the hills, and much clamour riseth round him of hounds and men, and sleep perisheth from them, even so sweet sleep did perish from their eyes, as they watched through the wicked night, for ever were they turning toward the plains, when they heard the Trojans moving.

And that old man was glad when he saw them, and heartened them with his saying, and calling out to them he spake winged words: "Even so now, dear children, do ye keep watch, nor let sleep take any man, lest we become a cause of rejoicing to them that hate us."

So saying he sped through the moat, and they followed
with him, the kings of the Argives, who had been called to
the council. And with them went Meriones, and the glorious
son of Nestor, for they called them to share their counsel. So
they went clean out of the delved foss, and sat down in the
open, where the mid-space was clear of dead men fallen, where
fierce Hector had turned again from destroying the Argives,
when night covered all. There sat they down, and declared
their saying each to the other, and to them knightly Nestor
of Gerenia began discourse: "O friends, is there then no man
that would trust to his own daring spirit, to go among the
great-hearted Trojans, if perchance he might take some strag-
gler of the enemy, yea, or hear perchance some rumour among
the Trojans, and what things they devise among themselves,
whether they are fain to abide there by the ships, away from
the city, or will retreat again to the city, now that they have
conquered the Achaians? All this might such an one learn,
and back to us come scathless: great would be his fame under
heaven among all men, and a goodly gift will be given him.
For all the best men that bear sway by the ships, each and all
of them will give him a black ewe, with her lamb at her foot,
and ever will he be present at feasts and clan-drinkings."

So spake he, and thereon were they all silent, holding their
peace, but to them spake Diomedes of the loud war-cry:
"Nestor, my heart and manful spirit urge me to enter the
camp of the foemen hard by, even of the Trojans: and if some
other man will follow with me, more comfort and more courage
will there be. If two go together, one before another per-
ceiveth a matter, how there may be gain therein; but if one
alone perceive aught, even so his wit is shorter, and weak his
device."

So spake he, and many were they that wished to follow
Diomedes. The two Aiantes were willing, men of Ares' company, and Meriones was willing, and right willing the son of

Nestor, and the son of Atreus, Menelaos, spearman renowned, yea and the hardy Odysseus was willing to steal into the throng of Trojans, for always daring was his heart within him. But among them spake the king of men, Agamemnon: "Diomedes son of Tydeus, joy of mine heart, thy comrade verily shalt thou choose, whomsoever thou wilt, the best of them that be here, for many are eager. But do not thou, out of reverent heart, leave the better man behind, and give thyself the worse companion, yielding to regard for any, and looking to their lineage, even if one be more kingly born."

So spake he, but was in fear for the sake of fair-haired Menelaos. But to them again answered Diomedes of the loud war-cry: "If indeed ye bid me choose myself a comrade, how then could I be unmindful of godlike Odysseus, whose heart is passing eager, and his spirit so manful in all manner of toils; and Athene loveth him. But while he cometh with me, even out of burning fire might we both return, for he excelleth in understanding."

Then him again answered the steadfast noble Odysseus: "Son of Tydeus, praise me not overmuch, neither blame me aught, for thou speakest thus among the Argives that themselves know all. But let us be going, for truly the night is waning, and near is the dawn, and the stars have gone onward, and the night has advanced more than two watches, but the third watch is yet left."

So spake they, and harnessed them in their dread armour. To the son of Tydeus did Thrasymedes steadfast in war give a two-edged sword (for his own was left by his ship) and a shield, and about his head set a helm of bull's hide, without cone or crest, that is called a skull-cap, and keeps the heads of stalwart youths. And Meriones gave Odysseus a bow and a quiver, and a sword, and on his head set a helm made of leather, and with many a thong was it stiffly wrought within, while without the white teeth of a boar of flashing tusks were arrayed thick set on either side, well and cunningly, and in the midst was fixed a cap of felt.

So when these twain had harnessed them in their dread armour, they set forth to go, and left there all the best of the host. And to them did Pallas Athene send forth an omen on the right, a heron hard by the way, and they beheld it not with their eyes, through the dark night, but they heard its shrill cry. And Odysseus was glad in the omen of the bird, and prayed to Athene: "Listen to me, thou child of aegis-bearing Zeus, that ever in all toils dost stand by me, nor doth any motion of mine escape thee: but now again above all be thou friendly to me, Athene, and grant that we come back with renown to the ships, having wrought a great work, that shall be sorrow to the Trojans."

Next again prayed Diomedes of the loud war-cry: "Listen now likewise to me, thou child of Zeus, unwearied maiden, and follow with me as when with my father thou didst follow, even noble Tydeus, into Thebes, when he went forth as a messenger from the Achaians. Even so now stand thou by me willingly, and protect me. And to thee will I sacrifice a yearling heifer, broad of brow, unbroken, that never yet hath man led below the yoke. Her will I sacrifice to thee, and gild her horns with gold."

So spake they in their prayer, and Pallas Athene heard them. And when they had prayed to the daughter of mighty Zeus, they went forth on their way, like two lions, through the dark night, amid the slaughter, amid the slain men, through the arms and the black blood.

Nay, nor the stout-hearted Trojans did Hector suffer to sleep, but he called together all the best of them, all that were chiefs and leaders of the Trojans, them did he call together, and contrived a crafty counsel: "Who is there that would promise and perform for me this deed, for a great gift? yea his reward shall be sufficient. For I will give him a chariot, and two horses of arching neck, the best that be at the swift ships of the Achaians, to whosoever shall dare the deed, and for himself shall win glory. And the deed is this; to go near the swift-faring ships, and seek out whether the swift ships are guarded, as of old, or whether already, being subdued beneath our hands, the foes are devising of flight among themselves, and have no care to watch through the night, being fordone with dread weariness."

So spake he, but they were all silent and held their peace. Now there was among the Trojans one Dolon, the son of Eumedes the godlike herald, and he was rich in gold, and rich in bronze: and verily he was ill favoured to look upon, but swift of foot. So he spake then a word to the Trojans and to Hector: "Hector, my heart and manful spirit urge me to go near the swift-faring ships, and spy out all. But come, I pray thee, hold up the staff, and swear to me, that verily thou wilt give me the horses and the chariots bedight with bronze that bear the noble son of Peleus. But to thee I will prove no vain spy, nor disappoint thy hope. For I will go straight to the camp, until I may come to the ship of Agamemnon, where surely the chiefs are like to hold council, whether to fight or flee."

So spake he, and Hector took the staff in his hand, and sware to him: "Now let Zeus himself be witness, the loud-thundering lord of Hera, that no other man of the Trojans shall mount those horses, but thou, I declare, shalt rejoice in them for ever."

So spake he, and sware a bootless oath thereto, and aroused Dolon to go. And straightway he cast on his shoulders his crooked bow, and did on thereover the skin of a grey wolf, and on his head a helm of ferret-skin, and took a sharp javelin, and went on his way to the ships from the host. But he was not like to come back from the ships and bring word to Hector.

But when he had left the throng of men and horses, he went

forth eagerly on the way, and Odysseus of the seed of Zeus was ware of him as he approached, and said unto Diomedes : " Lo, here is some man, Diomedes, coming from the camp, I know not whether as a spy to our ships, or to strip certain of the dead men fallen. But let us suffer him to pass by us a little way on the plain, and thereafter may we rush on him and take him speedily, and if it chance that he outrun us by speed of foot, ever do thou hem him in towards the ships and away from the camp, rushing on him with thy spear, lest in any wise he escape towards the city."

So they spake, and turning out of the path they lay down among the bodies of the dead; and swiftly Dolon ran past them in his witlessness. But when he was as far off as is the length of the furrow made by mules, these twain ran after him, and he stood still when he heard the sound, supposing in his heart that they were friends come from among the Trojans to turn him back, at the countermand of Hector. But when they were about a spear-cast off, or even less, he knew them for foemen, and stirred his swift limbs to fly, and speedily they started in pursuit.

And as when two sharp-toothed hounds, well skilled in the chase, press ever hard on a doe or a hare through a wooded land, and it runs screaming before them, even so Tydeus' son and Odysseus the sacker of cities cut Dolon off from the host, and ever pursued hard after him. But when he was just about to come among the sentinels, in his flight towards the ships, then Athene poured strength into the son of Tydeus, that none of the mail-clad Achaians might boast himself the first to smite, and he come second. And strong Diomedes leaped upon him with the spear, and said : " Stand, or I shall overtake thee with the spear, and methinks that thou shalt not long avoid sheer destruction at my hand."

So spake he, and threw his spear, but of his own will he missed the man, and passing over his right shoulder the point of the polished spear stuck fast in the ground: and Dolon stood still, in great dread and trembling, and the teeth chattered in his mouth, and he was green with fear. Then the twain came up with him, panting, and gripped his hands, and weeping he spake: "Take me alive, and I will ransom myself, for within our house there is bronze, and gold, and smithied iron, wherefrom my father would do you grace with ransom untold, if he should learn that I am alive among the ships of the Achaians."

Then Odysseus of the many counsels answered him and said: "Take courage, let not death be in thy mind, but come speak and tell me truly all the tale, why thus from the host dost thou come all alone among the ships, through the black night, when other mortals are sleeping? Comest thou to strip certain of the dead men fallen, or did Hector send thee forth to spy out everything at the hollow ships, or did thine own spirit urge thee on?"

Then Dolon answered him, his limbs trembling beneath him: "With many a blind hope did Hector lead my wits astray, who vowed to give me the whole-hooved horses of the proud son of Peleus, and his car bedight with bronze: and he bade me fare through the swift black night, and draw nigh the foemen, and seek out whether the swift ships are guarded, as of old, or whether, already, being subdued beneath our hands, they are devising of flight among themselves, and have no care to watch through the night, being fordone with dread weariness."

And smiling thereat did Odysseus of the many counsels make him answer: "Verily now thy soul was set on great rewards, even the horses of the wise son of Aiakos, but hard are they for mortal men to master, and hard to drive, for any but Achilles only, whom a deathless mother bare. But come, tell me all this truly, all the tale: where when thou camest hither didst thou leave Hector, shepherd of the host, and where lie his warlike gear, and where his horses? And how are disposed the

K

watches, and the beds of the other Trojans? And what counsel take they among themselves; are they fain to abide there nigh the ships afar from the city, or will they return to the city again, seeing that they have subdued unto them the Achaians?"

Then Dolon son of Eumedes made him answer again: "Lo, now all these things will I recount to thee most truly. Hector with them that are counsellors holdeth council by the barrow of godlike Ilos, apart from the din, but as for the guards whereof thou askest, oh hero, no chosen watch nor guard keepeth the host. As for all the watch fires of the Trojans — on them is necessity, so that they watch and encourage each other to keep guard; but, for the allies called from many lands, they are sleeping and to the Trojans they leave it to keep watch, for no wise near dwell the children and wives of the allies."

Then Odysseus of the many counsels answered him and said: "How stands it now, do they sleep amidst the horse-taming Trojans, or apart? tell me clearly, that I may know."

Then answered him Dolon son of Eumedes: "Verily all this likewise will I recount to thee truly. Towards the sea lie the Karians, and Paionians of the bended bow, and the Leleges and Kaukones, and noble Pelasgoi. And towards Thymbre the Lykians have their place, and the haughty Mysians, and the Phrygians that fight from chariots, and Maionians lords of chariots. But wherefore do ye inquire of me throughly concerning all these things? for if ye desire to steal into the throng of Trojans, lo, there be those Thracians, new comers, at the furthest point apart from the rest, and among them their king Rhesos, son of Eïoneus. His be the fairest horses that ever I beheld, and the greatest, whiter than snow, and for speed like the winds. And his chariot is fashioned well with gold and silver, and golden is his armour that he brought with him, marvellous, a wonder to behold; such as it is in no wise fit for mortal men to bear, but for the deathless gods. But bring me now to the swift ships, or leave me here, when ye have bound me with a ruthless bond, that ye may go and make trial of me whether I have spoken to you truth, or lies."

Then strong Diomedes, looking grimly on him, said: "Put no thought of escape, Dolon, in thy heart, for all the good tidings thou hast brought, since once thou hast come into our hands. For if now we release thee or let thee go, on some later day wilt thou come to the swift ships of the Achaians, either to play the spy, or to fight in open war, but if subdued beneath my hands thou lose thy life, never again wilt thou prove a bane to the Argives."

He spake, and that other with strong hand was about to touch his chin, and implore his mercy, but Diomedes smote him on the midst of the neck, rushing on him with the sword, and cut through both the sinews, and the head of him still speaking was mingled with the dust. And they stripped him of the casque of ferret's skin from off his head, and of his wolf-skin, and his bended bow, and his long spear, and these to Athene the Giver of Spoil did noble Odysseus hold aloft in his hand, and he prayed and spake a word: "Rejoice, O goddess, in these, for to thee first of all the immortals in Olympus will we call for aid; nay, but yet again send us on against the horses and the sleeping places of the Thracian men."

So spake he aloud, and lifted from him the spoils on high, and set them on a tamarisk bush, and raised thereon a mark right plain to see, gathering together reeds, and luxuriant shoots of tamarisk, lest they should miss the place as they returned again through the swift dark night.

So the twain went forward through the arms, and the black blood, and quickly they came to the company of Thracian men. Now they were slumbering, fordone with toil, but their goodly weapons lay by them on the ground, all orderly, in three rows, and by each man his pair of steeds. And Rhesos slept in the midst, and beside him his swift horses were bound with thongs to the topmost rim of the chariot. Him Odysseus spied from afar, and showed him unto Diomedes : " Lo, Diomedes, this is the man, and these are the horses whereof Dolon that we slew did give us tidings. But come now, put forth thy great strength ; it doth not behove thee to stand idle with thy weapons : nay, loose the horses ; or do thou slay the men, and of the horses will I take heed."

So spake he, and into that other bright-eyed Athene breathed might, and he began slaying on this side and on that, and hideously went up their groaning, as they were smitten with the sword, and the earth was reddened with blood. And like as a lion cometh on flocks without a herdsman, on goats or sheep, and leaps upon them with evil will, so set the son of Tydeus on the men of Thrace, till he had slain twelve. But whomsoever the son of Tydeus drew near and smote with the sword, him did Odysseus of the many counsels seize by the foot from behind, and drag him out of the way, with this design in his heart, that the fair-maned horses might lightly issue forth, and not tremble in spirit, when they trod over the dead ; for they were not yet used to dead men. But when the son of Tydeus came upon the king, he was the thirteenth from whom he took sweet life away, as he was breathing hard, for an evil dream stood above his head that night through the device of Athene. Meanwhile the hardy Odysseus loosed the whole-hooved horses, and bound them together with thongs, and drave them out of the press, smiting them with his bow, since he had not taken thought to lift the shining whip with his hands from the chariot : then he whistled for a sign to noble Diomedes.

But Diomedes stood and pondered what most daring deed he might do, whether he should take the chariot, where lay the armour, and drag it out by the pole, or lift it upon high, and so bear it forth, or whether he should take the life away from yet more of the Thracians. And while he was pondering this in his heart, then Athene drew near, and stood, and spake to noble Diomedes: "Bethink thee of returning, O son of great-hearted Tydeus, to the hollow ships, lest perchance thou come thither in flight, and perchance another god rouse up the Trojans likewise."

So spake she, and he observed the voice of the utterance of the goddess, and swiftly he sprang upon the steeds, and Odysseus smote them with his bow, and they sped to the swift ships of the Achaians.

Nay, nor a vain watch kept Apollo of the silver bow, when he beheld Athene caring for the son of Tydeus; in wrath against her he stole among the crowded press of Trojans, and aroused a counsellor of the Thracians, Hippokoon, the noble kinsman of Rhesos. And he started out of sleep, when he beheld the place desolate where the swift horses had stood, and beheld the men gasping in the death struggle; then he groaned aloud, and called out by name to his comrade dear. And a clamour arose and din unspeakable of the Trojans hasting together, and they marvelled at the terrible deeds, even all that the heroes had wrought, and had gone thereafter to the hollow ships.

But when those others came to the place where they had slain the spy of Hector, there Odysseus, dear to Zeus, checked the swift horses, and Tydeus' son, leaping to the ground, set the bloody spoil in the hands of Odysseus, and again mounted, and lashed the horses, and they sped onward nothing loth. But Nestor first heard the sound, and said: "O friends, leaders and counsellors of the Argives, shall I be wrong or speak sooth? for my heart bids me speak. The sound of swift-footed horses strikes upon mine ears. Would to god that Odysseus and that strong Diomedes may even instantly be driving the whole-hooved horses from among the Trojans; but terribly I fear in mine heart lest the bravest of the Argives suffer aught through the Trojans' battle din."

Not yet was his whole word spoken, when they came themselves, and leaped down to earth, but gladly the others welcomed them with hand-clasping, and with honeyed words. And first did knightly Nestor of Gerenia make question : "Come, tell me now, renowned Odysseus, great glory of the Achaians, how ye twain took those horses? Was it by stealing into the press of Trojans? Or did some god meet you, and give you them? Wondrous like are they to rays of the sun. Ever with the Trojans do I mix in fight, nor methinks do I tarry by the ships, old warrior as I am. But never yet saw I such horses, nor deemed of such. Nay, methinks some god must have encountered you and given you these. For both of you doth Zeus the cloud-gatherer love, and the maiden of aegis-bearing Zeus, bright-eyed Athene."

And him answered Odysseus of the many counsels : "O Nestor, son of Neleus, great glory of the Achaians, lightly could a god, if so he would, give even better steeds than these, for the gods are far stronger than we. But as for these new-come horses, whereof, old man, thou askest me, they are Thracian, but their lord did brave Diomedes slay, and beside him all the twelve best men of his company. The thirteenth man was a spy we took near the ships, one that Hector and the other haughty Trojans sent forth to pry upon our camp."

So spake he, and drave the whole-hooved horses through the foss, laughing ; and the other Achaians went with him joyfully. But when they had come to the well-built hut of the son of Tydeus, they bound the horses with well-cut thongs, at the mangers where the swift horses of Diomedes stood eating honey-sweet barley.

And Odysseus placed the bloody spoils of Dolon in the stern of the ship, that they might make ready a sacred offering to Athene. But for themselves, they went into the sea, and washed off the thick sweat from shins, and neck, and thighs. But when the wave of the sea had washed the thick

THE DESCENT OF DISCORD

sweat from their skin, and their hearts revived again, they went into polished baths, and were cleansed.

And when they had washed, and anointed them with olive oil, they sat down at supper, and from the full mixing bowl they drew off the honey-sweet wine, and poured it forth to Athene.

BOOK XI

Despite the glorious deeds of Agamemnon, the Trojans press hard on the Achaians, and the beginning of evil comes on Patroklos.

Now Dawn arose from her couch beside proud Tithonos, to bring light to the immortals and to mortal men. But Zeus sent forth fierce Discord unto the fleet ships of the Achaians, and in her hands she held the signal of war. And she stood upon the huge black ship of Odysseus, that was in the midst, to make her voice heard on either side, both to the huts of Aias, son of Telamon, and to the huts of Achilles, for these twain, trusting in their valour and the might of their hands, had drawn up their trim ships at the two ends of the line. There stood the goddess and cried shrilly in a great voice and terrible, and mighty strength she set in the heart of each of the Achaians, to war and fight unceasingly. And straightway to them war grew sweeter than to depart in the hollow ships to their dear native land.

Then each man gave in charge his horses to his charioteer, to hold them in by the foss, well and orderly, and themselves as heavy men at arms were hasting about, being harnessed in their gear, and unquenchable the cry arose into the Dawn. And long before the charioteers were they arrayed at the foss, but after them a little way came up the drivers. And among them the son of Kronos aroused an evil din, and from above rained down dew danked with blood out of the upper air, for that he was about to send many strong men down to Hades.

But the Trojans on the other side, on the high ground of the plain, gathered them around great Hector, and noble Polydamus, and Aineias that as a god was honoured by the people of the Trojans, and the three sons of Antenor, Polybos, and noble Agenor, and young Akamas like unto the immortals. And Hector in the foremost rank bare the circle of his shield. And as from amid the clouds appeareth glittering a baneful star, and then again sinketh within the shadowy clouds, even so Hector would now appear among the foremost ranks, and again would be giving command in the rear, and all in bronze he shone, like the lightning of aegis-bearing father Zeus.

And even as when reapers over against each other drive their swaths through a rich man's field of wheat or barley, and thick fall the handfuls, even so the Trojans and Achaians leaped upon each other, destroying, and neither side took thought of ruinous flight; and equal heads had the battle, and they rushed on like wolves. And woful Discord was glad at the sight, for she alone of the gods was with them in the war; for the other gods were not beside them, but in peace they sat within their halls, where the goodly mansion of each was builded in the folds of Olympus. And they all were blaming the son of Kronos, lord of the storm-cloud, for that he willed to give glory to the Trojans. But of them took the father no heed, but aloof from the others he sat apart, glad in his glory, looking toward the city of the Trojans, and the ships of the Achaians, and the glitter of bronze, and the slayers and the slain.

So long as morning was, and the sacred day still waxed, so long did the shafts of both hosts strike, and the folk fell, but about the hour when a woodman maketh ready his meal, in the dells of a mountain, when he hath tired his hands with

felling tall trees, and weariness cometh on his soul, and desire
of sweet food taketh his heart, even then the Danaans by their
valour brake the battalions, and called on their comrades
through the lines. And in rushed Agamemnon first of all,
where thickest clashed the battalions, there he set on, and
with him all the well-greaved Achaians. Footmen kept slaying footmen as they were driven in flight, and horsemen slaying horsemen with the sword, and from beneath them rose up
the dust from the plain, stirred by the thundering hooves of
horses. And the lord Agamemnon, ever slaying, followed after,
calling on the Argives. And as when ruinous fire falleth on
dense woodland, and the whirling wind beareth it everywhere,
and the thickets fall utterly before it, being smitten by the
onset of the fire, even so beneath Agamemnon son of Atreus
fell the heads of the Trojans as they fled; and many strong-
necked horses rattled empty cars along the highways of the
battle, lacking their noble charioteers; but they on the earth
were lying, far more dear to the vultures than to their wives.

But Hector did Zeus draw forth from the darts and the dust,
from the man-slaying, and the blood, and the din, and the son
of Atreus followed on, crying eagerly to the Danaans. And
past the tomb of ancient Ilos, son of Dardanos, across the mid
plain, past the place of the wild fig-tree they sped, making for
the city, and ever the son of Atreus followed shouting, and his
invincible hands were defiled with gore. But when they were
come to the Skaian gates, and the oak-tree, there then they
halted, and awaited each other. But some were still in full
flight through the mid plain, like kine that a lion hath scattered, coming on them in the dead of night; all hath he
scattered, but to one sheer death appeareth instantly, and he
breaketh her neck first, seizing her with strong teeth, and thereafter swalloweth greedily the blood and all the guts; even so
lord Agamemnon son of Atreus followed hard on the Trojans,
ever slaying the hindmost man, and they were scattered in

flight, and on face or back many of them fell from their chariots beneath the hands of Agamemnon, for mightily he raged with the spear. But when he was nowabout coming below the city, and the steep wall, then did the father of men and gods sit him down on the crests of many-fountained Ida, from heaven descending, with the thunderbolt in his hands.

Then sent he forth Iris of the golden wings, to bear his word: "Up and go, swift Iris, and tell this word unto Hector: So long as he sees Agamemnon, shepherd of the host, raging among the foremost fighters, and ruining the ranks of men, so long let him hold back, but bid the rest of the host war with the foe in strong battle. But when, or smitten with the spear or wounded with arrow shot, Agamemnon leapeth into his chariot, then will I give Hector strength to slay till he come even to the well-timbered ships, and the sun go down, and sacred darkness draw on."

So swift-footed Iris spake to Hector the words of Zeus and departed, but Hector with his harness leaped from the chariot to the ground, and, shaking his sharp spears went through all the host, stirring up his men to fight, and he roused the dread din of battle. And they wheeled round, and stood and faced the Achaians, while the Argives on the other side strengthened their battalions. And battle was made ready, and they stood over against each other, and Agamemnon first rushed in, being eager to fight far in front of all.

Tell me now, ye Muses that inhabit mansions in Olympus, who was he that first encountered Agamemnon, whether of the Trojans themselves, or of their allies renowned? It was Iphidamas, son of Antenor, great and mighty, who was nurtured in Thrace rich of soil, the mother of sheep; he it was that then encountered Agamemnon son of Atreus. And when they were come near in onset against each other, Atreus' son missed, and his spear was turned aside, but Iphidamas smote him on the girdle, below the corslet, and himself pressed on, trusting to his heavy hand, but pierced not the gleaming girdle, for long ere that the point struck on the silver, and was bent like lead. Then wide-ruling Agamemnon caught the spear with his hand and drew it toward him furiously, like a lion, and snatched it out of the hand of Iphidamas, and smote his neck with the sword, and unstrung his limbs. So even there he fell, and slept a sleep of bronze most piteously. Then did Agamemnon son of Atreus strip him, and went bearing his goodly harness into the throng of the Achaians.

Now when Koön beheld him, Koön Antenor's eldest son, illustrious among men, strong sorrow came on him, covering his eyes, for his brother's fall: and he stood on one side with his spear, and unmarked of noble Agamemnon smote him on the mid-arm, beneath the elbow, and clean through went the point of the shining spear. Then Agamemnon king of men shuddered, yet not even so did he cease from battle and war, but rushed against Koön, grasping his wind-nurtured spear. Verily then Koön seized right lustily by the foot Iphidamas, his brother, and his father's son, and called to all the best of his men; but him, as he dragged the dead through the press, beneath his bossy shield Agamemnon wounded with a bronze-shod spear, and unstrung his limbs, and drew near and cut off his head over Iphidamas. There the sons of Antenor, at the hands of Agamemnon the king, filled up the measure of their fate, and went down within the house of Hades.

But Agamemnon ranged among the ranks of men, with spear, and sword, and great stones for throwing, while yet the blood welled warm from his wound. But when the wound waxed dry, and the blood ceased to flow, then keen pangs came on the might of the son of Atreus. Then leaped he into his chariot, and bade his charioteer drive to the hollow ships, for he was sore vexed at heart. And he called in a piercing voice, and shouted to the Danaans: "O friends, leaders and counsellors of the Argives, do ye now ward from the seafaring ships the harsh din of battle, for Zeus the counsellor suffers me not all day to war with the Trojans."

So spake he, and his charioteer lashed the fair-maned steeds toward the hollow ships, and they flew onward nothing loth, and their breasts were covered with foam, and their bellies were stained with dust, as they bore the wounded king away from the war.

But Hector, when he beheld Agamemnon departed, cried to the Trojans and Lykians with a loud shout: "Ye Trojans and Lykians, and Dardanians that war in close fight, be men, my friends, and be mindful of your impetuous valour. The best man of them hath departed and to me hath Zeus, the son of Kronos, given great renown. But straightway drive ye the whole-hooved horses against the mighty Danaans, that ye may be the masters and bear away the higher glory."

So spake he, and aroused the might and spirit of every man. Himself with high thoughts he fared among the foremost, and fell upon the fight, like a roaring blast, that leapeth down and stirreth the violet-coloured deep. There whom first, whom last did he slay, even Hector, son of Priam, when Zeus vouchsafed him renown?

Asaios first, and Autonoos, and Opites, and Dolops, son of Klytios, and Opheltios, and Agelaos, and Aisymnos, and Oros, and Hipponoos steadfast in the fight; these leaders of the Danaans he slew, and thereafter smote the multitude, even as when the West Wind driveth the clouds of the white South Wind, smiting with deep storm, and the wave swelleth huge, rolling onward, and the spray is scattered on high beneath the rush of the wandering wind; even so many heads of the host were smitten by Hector.

There had ruin begun, and deeds remedeless been wrought, and now would all the Achaians have fled and fallen among the ships, if Odysseus had not called to Diomedes, son of Tydeus: "Tydeus' son, what ails us that we forget our impetuous valour? Nay, come hither, friend, and take thy stand by me, for verily it will be shame if Hector of the glancing helm take the ships."

And to him strong Diomedes spake in answer: "Verily will I abide and endure, but short will be all our profit, for Zeus, the cloud-gatherer, clearly desireth to give victory to the Trojans rather than to us."

He spake, and drave Thymbraios from his chariot to the ground, smiting him with the spear in the left breast, and Odysseus smote Molion the godlike squire of that prince. These then they let be, when they had made them cease from war, and then the twain fared through the crowd with a din, as when two boars full of valour fall on the hunting hounds; so rushed they on again, and slew the Trojans, while gladly the Achaians took breath again in their flight from noble Hector.

But Hector quickly spied them among the ranks, and rushed upon them shouting, and with him followed the battalions of the Trojans. And beholding him, Diomedes of the loud war-cry shuddered, and straightway spake to Odysseus that was hard by: "Lo, on us this ruin, even mighty Hector, is rolling: let us stand, and await him, and ward off his onset."

So spake he, and swayed and sent forth his far-shadowing spear, and smote him nor missed, for he aimed at the head, on the summit of the crest, and bronze by bronze was turned, nor reached his fair flesh, for it was stopped by the threefold helm with its socket, that Phoebus Apollo to Hector gave. But Hector sprang back a wondrous way, and mingled with the throng, and he rested, fallen on his knee, and leaned on the ground with his stout hand, and dark night veiled his eyes.

But while Tydeus' son was following after his spear-cast, far through the foremost fighters, where he saw it sink into the earth, Hector gat breath again, and leaping back into his chariot drave out into the throng, and avoided black Fate. Then rushing on with his spear mighty Diomedes spake to him: "Dog, thou art now again escaped from death; yet came ill very nigh thee: but now hath Phoebus Apollo saved thee, to whom thou must surely pray when thou goest amid the clash of spears. Verily I will slay thee yet when I meet thee hereafter, if any god is helper of me too. Now will I make after the rest, whomsoever I may seize."

So spake he, and stripped the son of Paeon, spearman renowned. But Alexandros, the lord of fair-tressed Helen, aimed with his arrows at Tydeides, shepherd of the host; leaning as he aimed against a pillar on the barrow, by men fashioned, of Ilos, son of Dardanos, an elder of the people in time gone by. Now Diomedes was stripping the shining corslet of strong Agastrophos from about his breast, and the shield from his shoulders, and his strong helmet, when Paris drew the centre of his bow; nor vainly did the shaft fly from his hand, for he smote the flat of the right foot of Diomedes, and the arrow went clean through, and stood fixed in the earth; and right sweetly laughing Paris leaped up from his lair, and boasted, and said: "Thou art smitten, nor vainly hath the dart flown forth; would that I had smitten thee in the nether belly, and taken thy life away. So should the Trojans have breathed again from their trouble, they that shudder at thee, as bleating goats at a lion."

But him answered strong Diomedes, no wise dismayed: "Bowman, reviler, proud in thy bow of horn, thou gaper after girls, verily if thou madest trial in full harness, man to man, thy bow and showers of shafts would nothing avail thee, but now thou boastest vainly, for that thou hast grazed the sole of my foot. I care not, more than if a woman had struck me or a senseless boy, for feeble is the dart of a craven man and a worthless. In other wise from my hand, yea, if it do but touch, the sharp shaft flieth, and straightway layeth low its man, and torn are the cheeks of his wife, and fatherless his children, and he, reddening the earth with his blood, doth rot away, more birds than women round him."

So spake he, and Odysseus, spearman renowned, drew near, and stood in front of him, and Diomedes sat down behind him, and drew the sharp arrow from his foot, and a sore pang passed through his flesh. Then sprang he into his car, and bade his charioteer drive back to the hollow ships, for he was hurt at heart. Then Odysseus, spearman renowned, was left alone, nor did one of the Argives abide by him, for fear had fallen on them all. Then in heaviness he spoke to his own great-hearted spirit: "Ah me, what thing shall befall me! A great evil it is if I flee, in dread of the throng; yet worse is this, if I be taken all alone, for the other Danaans hath Kronion scattered in flight. But wherefore doth my heart thus converse with herself? for I know that they are cowards, who flee the fight, but whosoever is a hero in war, him it mainly behoves to stand stubbornly, whether he be smitten, or whether he smite another."

While he pondered thus in heart and spirit, the ranks came on of the Trojans under shield, and hemmed him in the midst, setting among them their own bane. And even as when hounds and young men in their bloom press round a boar, and he cometh forth from his deep lair, whetting his white tusk between crooked jaws, and round him they rush, and the sound of the gnashing of tusks ariseth, and straightway they await his assault, so dread as he is, even so then round Odysseus, dear to Zeus, rushed the Trojans. And first he wounded noble Deïopites, from above, in the shoulder, leaping on him with sharp spear, and next he slew Thoon and Ennomos, and next Chersidamas, being leapt down from his chariot, he smote with the spear on the navel beneath the bossy shield, and he fell in the dust and clutched the ground with the hollow of his hand. These left he, and wounded Charops, son of Hippasos, with the spear, the brother of high-born Sokos. And to help him came Sokos, a godlike man, and stood hard by him, and spake saying: "O renowned Odysseus, insatiable of craft and toil, to-day shalt thou either boast over two sons of Hippasos, as having slain two such men of might, and stripped their harness, or smitten by my spear shalt lose thy life."

So spake he, and smote him on the circle of his shield; through the shining shield passed the strong spear, and through the fair-dight corslet it was thrust, and tore clean off the flesh of the flanks, but Pallas Athene did not suffer it to mingle with the bowels of the hero, and Odysseus knew that the dart had in nowise lighted on a deadly spot, and drawing backward, he spake unto Sokos: "Ah, wretched one, verily sheer destruction is come upon thee. Surely thou hast made me to cease from warring among the Trojans, but here to thee I declare that slaying and black Fate will be upon thee this day, and beneath my spear overthrown shalt thou give glory to me, and thy soul to Hades of the noble steeds."

He spake, and the other turned, and started to flee, and in his back as he turned he fixed the spear, between the shoulders, and drave it through the breast. Then he fell with a crash, and noble Odysseus boasted over him: "Ah, Sokos, son of wise-hearted Hippasos the tamer of horses, the end of death hath come upon and caught thee, nor hast thou avoided. Ah, wretch, thy father and lady mother shall not close thine eyes in death, but birds that eat flesh raw shall tear thee, shrouding thee in the multitude of their wings. But to me, if I die, the noble Achaians will yet give due burial."

So spake he, and drew the mighty spear of wise-hearted Sokos forth from his flesh, and from his bossy shield, and his blood flowed forth when the spear was drawn away, and afflicted his spirit. And the great-hearted Trojans when they beheld the blood of Odysseus, with clamour through the throng came all together against him. But he gave ground, and shouted unto his comrades: thrice he shouted then, as loud as man's mouth might cry, and thrice did Menelaos dear to Zeus hear his call, and quickly he spake to Aias that was hard by him: "Aias, of the seed of Zeus, child of Telamon, lord of the hosts, the shout of Odysseus of the hardy heart rings round me, like as though the Trojans were oppressing him alone among them, and had cut him off in the strong battle. Nay, let us speed into the throng, for better it is to rescue him. I fear lest he suffer some evil, being alone among the Trojans, so brave as he is, and lest great sorrow for his loss come upon the Danaans."

So spake he, and led the way, and the other followed him, a godlike man. Then found they Odysseus dear to Zeus, and the Trojans beset him like tawny jackals from the hills round a wounded horned stag, that a man hath smitten with an arrow from the bow-string, and the stag hath fled from him by speed of foot, as long as the blood is warm and his limbs are strong, but when the swift arrow hath overcome him, then do the ravening jackals rend him in the hills, in a dark wood, and then god leadeth a murderous lion thither, and the jackals flee before him, but he rendeth them, so then, round wise-hearted Odysseus of the crafty counsels, did the Trojans gather, many and mighty, but that hero thrusting on with the spear held off the pitiless day. Then Aias drew near, bearing his shield like a tower, and stood thereby, and the Trojans fled from him, where each man might. Then warlike Menelaos led Odysseus out of the press, holding him by the hand, till the squire drave up the horses.

Then Aias leaped on the Trojans, and slew Doyrklos, bastard son of Priam, and thereafter wounded he Pandokos, and he wounded Lysandros, and Pyrasos, and Pylartes. And as when a brimming river cometh down upon the plain, in winter flood from the hills, swollen by the rain of Zeus, and many dry oaks and many pines it sucketh in, and much soil it casteth into the sea, even so renowned Aias charged them, pursuing through the plain, slaying horses and men. Nor wist Hector thereof at all, for he was fighting on the left of all the battle, by the banks of the river Skamandros, whereby chiefly fell the heads of men, and an unquenchable cry arose, around great Nestor and warlike Idomeneus. And Hector with them was warring, and terrible things did he, with the spear and in horsemanship, and he ravaged the battalions of the young men. Nor would the noble Achaians have yet given ground from the path, if Alexandros, the lord of fair-tressed Helen, had not stayed Machaon shepherd of the host in his valorous deeds, and smitten him on the right shoulder with a three-barbed arrow. Therefore were the Achaians, breathing valour, in great fear, lest men should seize Machaon in the turning of the fight.

Then Idomeneus spake to noble Nestor: "O Nestor, son of Neleus, great glory of the Achaians, arise, get thee up into thy chariot, and with thee let Machaon go, and swiftly drive to the ships the whole-hooved horses. For a leech is worth many other men, to cut out arrows, and spread soothing medicaments."

So spake he, nor did knightly Nestor of Gerenia disobey him, but straightway gat up into his chariot, and with him went Machaon, son of Asklepios the good leech, and he lashed the horses, and willingly flew they forward to the hollow ships, where they desired to be.

But Kebriones, the charioteer of Hector, beheld the Trojans driven in flight, and spake to him, and said: "Hector, here do we contend with the Danaans, at the limit of the wailful war, but, lo, the other Trojans are driven in flight confusedly, men and horses. And Aias son of Telamon is driving them; well I know him, for wide is the shield round his shoulders. Nay, let us too urge thither the horses and chariot, there where horsemen and footmen thickest in the forefront of evil strife are slaying each other, and the cry goes up unquenchable."

So spake he, and smote the fair-maned horses with the shrill-sounding whip, and they felt the lash, and fleetly bore the swift chariot among the Trojans and Achaians, treading on the dead, and the shields, and with blood was sprinkled all the axle-tree beneath, and the rims round the car with the drops from the hooves of the horses, and with drops from the tires about the wheels. And Hector was eager to enter the press of men, and to leap in and break through, and evil din of battle he brought among the Danaans, and brief space rested he from smiting with the spear. Nay, but he ranged among the ranks of other men, with spear, and sword, and with great stones, but he avoided the battle of Aias son of Telamon.

Now father Zeus, throned in the highest, roused dread in Aias, and he stood in amaze, and cast behind him his sevenfold shield of bull's hide, and gazed round in fear upon the throng, like a wild beast, turning this way and that, and slowly retreating step by step. And as when hounds and country folk drive a tawny lion from the mid-fold of the kine, and suffer him not to carry away the fattest of the herd; all night they watch, and he in great desire for the flesh maketh his onset, but takes nothing thereby, for thick the darts fly from strong hands against him, and the burning brands, and these he dreads for all his fury, and in the dawn he departeth with vexed heart; even so at that time departed Aias, vexed at heart, from among the Trojans, right unwillingly, for he feared sore for the ships of the Achaians. And as when a lazy ass going past a field hath the better of the boys with him, an ass that hath had many a cudgel broken about his sides, and he fareth into the deep crop, and wasteth it, while the boys smite him with cudgels, and feeble is the force of them, but yet with might and main they drive him forth, when he hath had his fill of fodder, even so did the high-hearted Trojans and allies, called from many lands, smite great Aias, son of Telamon, with darts on the centre of his shield, and ever followed after him. And Aias would now be mindful of his impetuous valour, and turn again, and hold at bay the battalions of the horse-taming Trojans, and once more he would turn him again to flee. Yet he hindered them all from making their way to the fleet ships, and himself stood and smote between the Trojans and the Achaians, and the spears from strong hands stuck some of them in his great shield, fain to win further, and many or ever they reached his white body stood fast halfway in the earth, right eager to sate themselves with his flesh.

So they fought like unto burning fire.

But the mares of Neleus all sweating bare Nestor out of the battle, and also carried they Machaon, shepherd of the host. Then the noble Achilles, swift of foot, beheld and was ware of him, for Achilles was standing by the stern of his great ship, watching the dire toil, and the woful rout of battle. And straightway he spake to his own comrade, Patroklos, calling to him from beside the ship, and he heard, and from the hut he came, like unto Ares; and this to him was the beginning of evil. Then the strong son of Menoitios spake first to Achilles: "Why dost thou call me, Achilles, what need hast thou of me?"

Then swift-footed Achilles answered him and spake: "Noble son of Menoitios, dear to my heart, now methinks that the Achaians will stand in prayer about my knees, for need no longer tolerable cometh upon them. But go now, Patroklos dear to Zeus, and ask Nestor who is this that he bringeth wounded from the war. Verily from behind he is most like Machaon, that child of Asklepios, but I beheld not the eyes of the man, for the horses sped past me, straining forward eagerly."

So spake he, and Patroklos obeyed his dear comrade, and started and ran past the ships, and the huts of the Achaians.

Now when they came to the hut of the son of Neleus, they lighted down on the bounteous earth, and the squire, Eurymedon, loosed the horses of that old man from the car, and they dried the sweat from their doublets, standing before the breeze, by the shore of the sea, and thereafter came they to the hut, and sat them down on chairs. And fair-tressed Hekamede mixed for them a mess, Hekamede that the old man won from Tenedos, when Achilles sacked it, and she was the daughter of great-hearted Arsinoos, and her the Achaians chose out for him, because always in counsel he excelled them all. First she drew before them a fair table, polished well, with feet of cyanus, and thereon a vessel of bronze, with onion, for relish to the drink, and pale honey, and the grain of sacred barley, and beside it a right goodly cup, that the old man brought from home, embossed with studs of gold, and four handles there were to it, and round each two golden doves were feeding, and to the cup were two feet below. Another man could scarce have lifted the cup from the table, when it was full, but Nestor the Old raised it easily. In this cup the woman, like unto the goddesses, mixed a mess for them, with Pramnian wine, and therein grated cheese of goats' milk, with a grater of bronze, and scattered white barley thereover, and bade them drink, whenas she had made ready the mess.

So when the twain had drunk, and driven away parching thirst, they took their pleasure in discourse, speaking each to the other. Now Patroklos stood at the doors, a godlike man, and when the old man beheld him, he arose from his shining chair, and took him by the hand, and led him in, and bade him be seated. But Patroklos, from over against him, was for refusing, and spake and said: "No time to sit have I, old man, fosterling of Zeus, nor wilt thou persuade me. Revered and dreaded is he that sent me forth to ask thee who this man is that thou bringest home wounded. Nay, but I know myself, for I see Machaon, shepherd of the host. And now will I go back again, a messenger, to speak a word to Achilles. And well dost thou know, old man, fosterling of Zeus, how terrible a man he is; lightly would he blame even one that is blameless."

Then knightly Nestor of Gerenia answered him again: "Wherefore is Achilles thus sorry for the sons of the Achaians, for as many as are wounded with darts? He knoweth not at all what grief hath arisen in the camp: for the best men lie in the ships, wounded by shaft or smitten by spear. Wounded with the shaft is strong Diomedes, son of Tydeus, and smitten is Odysseus, spearman renowned, and Agamemnon, and this other have I but newly carried out of battle, wounded with an arrow from the bowstring. But Achilles, for all his valiance, careth not for the Danaans, nor pities them at all. Doth he wait till the fleet ships hard by the shore shall burn in the consuming fire, and till we be slain one upon another? Nay, but even now speak thou thus and thus to wise-hearted Achilles, if perchance he will obey thee. Who knows but that, God helping, thou mightst stir his spirit with thy persuading? and good is the persuasion of a friend. But if in his heart he be shunning some oracle of God, and his lady mother hath told him somewhat from Zeus, natheless let him send forth thee, and let the rest of the host of the Myrmidons follow with thee, if perchance any light shall arise from thee to the Danaans; and let him give thee his fair harness, to bear into the war, if perchance the Trojans may take thee for him, and withhold them from the strife, and the warlike sons of the Achaians might take breath, being wearied; for brief is the breathing time in battle. And lightly might ye, being unwearied, drive men wearied in the war unto the city, away from the ships and the huts."

So spake he, and roused his heart within his breast, and he started and ran by the ships to Achilles of the seed of Aiakos.

BOOK XII

How the Trojans and allies broke within the wall of the Achaians.

STILL they fought confusedly, the Argives and Trojans. Nor were the foss of the Danaans and their wide wall above long to protect them, the wall they had builded for defence of the ships, and the foss they had drawn round about; for neither had they given goodly hecatombs to the gods, that it might guard with its bounds their swift ships and rich spoil.

Then war and the din of war sounded about the well-builded wall, and the beams of the towers rang beneath the strokes; while the Argives, subdued by the scourge of Zeus, were penned and driven in by the hollow ships, in dread of Hector, the mighty maker of flight, but he, as aforetime, fought like a whirlwind. And as when, among hounds and hunting men, a boar or lion wheeleth him about, raging in his strength, and these array themselves in fashion like a tower, and stand up against him, casting many javelins from their hands; but never is his stout heart confused nor afraid, and his courage is his bane, and often he wheeleth him about, and maketh trial of the ranks of men, and wheresoever he maketh onset there the ranks of men give way, even so Hector went and besought his comrades through the press, and spurred them on to cross the dyke. But his swift-footed horses dared not, but loud they neighed, standing by the sheer edge, for the wide foss affrighted them, neither easy to leap from hard by, nor to cross, for overhanging banks stood round about it all on either hand, and above it was furnished with sharp stakes that the sons of the Achaians had planted there, thick set and great, a bulwark against hostile men. Thereby not lightly might a horse enter, drawing a well-wheeled chariot; but the footmen were eager, if they might accomplish it. Then Polydamas drew near valiant Hector, and spake to him: "Hector and ye other leaders of the Trojans and allies, foolishly do we drive our fleet horses through the dyke; nay right hard it is to cross, for sharp stakes stand in it, and over against them the wall of the Achaians. Thereby none may go down and fight in chariots, for strait is the place wherein, methinks, we might come by a mischief. For if Zeus that thunders on high is utterly to destroy them in his evil will, and is minded to help the Trojans, verily then I too would desire that even instantly this might be, that the Achaians should perish here nameless far from Argos : but and if they turn again, and we flee back from among the ships, and rush into the delved ditch, then methinks that not even one from among us to bear the tidings will win back to the city before the force of the Achaians when they rally. But come as I declare, let us all obey. Let our squires hold the horses by the dyke, while we being harnessed in our gear as foot soldiers follow all together with Hector, and the Achaians will not withstand us, if indeed the bands of death be made fast upon them."

So spake Polydamas, and his wise word pleased Hector well, and straightway in his harness he leaped from his chariot to the ground. Nor were the other Trojans gathered upon the chariots, but they all leaped forth, when they beheld goodly Hector. There each gave it into the charge of his own charioteer, to keep the horses orderly there by the foss. And they divided, and arrayed themselves, and ordered in five companies they followed with the leaders.

Now they that went with Hector and noble Polydamas, these were most, and bravest, and most were eager to break the wall, and fight by the hollow ships ; and with them followed Kebriones for the third, for Hector had left another man with his chariot, a weaker warrior than Kebriones. The second company Paris led, and Alkathoos, and Agenor : and the third company Helenos led, and godlike Deiphobos, — two sons of Priam, — the third was the warrior Asios, Asios Hyrtakos' son, whom his tall sorrel steeds brought out of Arisbe, from the river Selleëis. And of the fourth company was the brave son of Anchises leader, even Aineias ; and with him were two sons of Antenor, Archelochos and Akamas, both well skilled in all warfare.

And Sarpedon led the glorious allies, and to be with him he chose Glaukos and warlike Asteropaios, for they seemed to him to be manifestly the bravest of all after himself, but he was excellent, yea, above all the host. And these when they had arrayed one another with well-fashioned shields of bulls' hide, went straight and eager against the Danaans, nor deemed that they could longer resist them, but that themselves should fall on the black ships.

Then the rest of the Trojans and the far-famed allies obeyed the counsel of blameless Polydamas, but Asios, son of Hyrtakos, leader of men, willed not to leave his horses there, and his squire the charioteer, but with them he drew near the swift ships, fond man! for never was he, avoiding evil Fates, to return, rejoicing in his horses and chariot, back from the ships to windy Ilios. Nay, ere that the Fate of ill name overshadowed him, by the spear of Idomeneus, the haughty son of Deukalion. For Asios went against the left flank of the ships, whereby the Achaians returned out of the plain with chariots and horses: there he drave through his horses and his car, nor found he the doors shut on the gates, and the long bar, but men were holding them open if perchance they might save any of their comrades fleeing out of the battle towards the ships. Straight thereby held he his horses with unswerving aim, and his men followed him, crying shrilly, for they deemed that the Achaians could no longer hold them off, but that themselves would fall on the black ships: fools, for in the gates they found two men of the bravest, the high-hearted sons of the warrior Lapithae, one the son of Peirithoos, strong Polypoites, and one Leonteus, peer of Ares the bane of men. These twain stood in front of the lofty gates, like high-crested oak trees in the hills, that for ever abide the wind and rain, firm fixed with roots great and long; even so these twain, trusting to the mightiness of their hands, abode the coming of great Asios, and fled not. But straight came the Trojans against the well-builded wall, holding their shields of dry bulls' hide on high, with mighty clamour, round the prince Asios, and Iamenos, and Orestes, and Adamas, son of Asios, and Thoon, and Oinomaos. But the other twain for a while, being within the wall, urged the well-greaved Achaians to fight for the ships; but when they saw the Trojans assailing the wall, while the Danaans cried and turned in flight, then forth rushed the twain, and fought in front of the gates like wild boars that in the mountains abide the assailing crew of men and dogs, and charging on either flank they crush the wood around them, cutting it at the root, and the clatter of their tusks waxes loud, till one smite them and take their life away: so clattered the bright bronze on the breasts of the twain, as they were smitten in close fight, for right hardily they fought, trusting to the host above them, and to their own strength.

For the men above were casting with stones from the well-builded towers in defence of themselves and of the huts, and of the swift-faring ships. And like snowflakes the stones fell earthward, flakes that a tempestuous wind, as it driveth the dark clouds, rains thickly down on the bounteous earth: so thick fell the missiles from the hands of Achaians and Trojans alike, and their helms rang harsh and their bossy shields, being smitten with mighty stones. Verily then Asios, son of Hyrtakos, groaned and smote both his thighs, and indignantly he spake: "Father Zeus, verily thou too dost greatly love a lie, for I deemed not that the Achaian heroes could withstand our might and our hands invincible. But they like wasps of nimble body, or bees that have made their dwellings in a rugged path, and leave not their hollow hold, but abide and keep the hunters at bay for the sake of their little ones, even so these men have no will to give ground from the gates, though they are but two, ere they slay or be slain."

So spake he, nor with his speech did he persuade the mind of Zeus, for his will was to give renown to Hector.

The young men who followed with Polydamas and Hector, they that were most in number and bravest, and most were eager to break the wall and set the ships on fire, these still stood doubtful by the foss, for as they were eager to pass over a bird had appeared to them, an eagle of lofty flight, skirting the host on the left hand. In its talons it bore a blood-red monstrous snake, alive, and struggling still; yea, not yet had it forgotten the joy of battle, but writhed backward and smote the bird that held it on the breast, beside the neck, and the bird cast it from him down to the earth, in sore pain, and dropped it in the midst of the throng; then with a cry sped away down the gusts of the wind. And the Trojans shuddered when they saw the gleaming snake lying in the midst of them; an omen of aegis-bearing Zeus.

Then verily Polydamas stood by brave Hector, and spake: "Hector, ever dost thou rebuke me in the assemblies, though I counsel wisely; since it by no means beseemeth one of the people to speak contrary to thee, in council or in war, but always to increase thy power; but now again will I say all that seemeth to me to be best. Let us not advance and fight with the Danaans for the ships. For even thus, methinks, the end will be, if indeed this bird hath come for the Trojans when they were eager to cross the dyke, this eagle of lofty flight, skirting the host on the left hand, bearing in his talons a blood-red monstrous snake, yet living; then straightway left he hold of him, before he reached his own nest, nor brought him home in the end to give to his nestlings. Even so shall we, though we burst with mighty force the gates and wall of the Achaians, and the Achaians give ground, even so we shall return in disarray from the ships by the way we came; for many of the Trojans shall we leave behind, whom the Achaians will slay with the sword, in defence of the ships. Even so would a soothsayer interpret that in his heart had clear knowledge of omens, and whom the people obeyed."

Then Hector of the glancing helm lowered on him and said: "Polydamas, that thou speakest is no longer pleasing to me; yea, thou knowest how to conceive another counsel better than this. But if thou verily speakest thus in earnest, then the gods themselves have utterly destroyed thy wits; thou that bidst us forget the counsels of loud-thundering Zeus, that himself promised me, and confirmed with a nod of his head! But thou bidst us be obedient to birds long of wing, whereto I give no heed, nor take any care thereof, whether they fare to the right, to the dawn and to the sun, or to the left, to mist and darkness. Nay, for us, let us trust to the counsel of mighty Zeus, who is king over all mortals and immortals. One omen is best, to fight for our own country. And wherefore dost thou fear war and battle? For if all the rest of us be slain by the ships of the Argives, yet needst thou not fear to perish, for thy heart is not warlike, nor enduring in battle. But if thou dost hold aloof from the fight, or winnest any other with thy words to turn him from war, straightway by my spear shalt thou be smitten, and lose thy life."

So spake he, and led on, and they followed with a wondrous din; and Zeus that joyeth in the thunder roused from the hills of Ida a blast of wind, which bare the dust straight against the ships; and he made weak the heart of the Achaians, but gave renown to the Trojans and to Hector. Trusting then in his omens, and their might, they strove to break the great wall of the Achaians. They dragged down the machicolations[1] of the towers, and overthrew the battlements, and heaved up the projecting buttresses, that the Achaians set first in the earth, to be the props of the towers. These they overthrew, and hoped to break the wall of the Achaians. Nor even now did the Danaans give ground from the path, but closed up the battlements with shields of bulls' hides, and cast from them at the foemen as they went below the walls.

Now the two Aiantes went everywhere on the towers, ever urging, and arousing the courage of the Achaians. One they

---

[1] [Projecting galleries.]

BOOK XII

would accost with honeyed words, another with hard words of them, would rebuke, whomsoever they saw utterly giving ground even of the fight: "O friends, whosoever is eminent, or whosoever of the of middle station among the Argives, ay, or lower yet, for in no wise are all men equal in war, now is there work for all, and this yourselves well know. Let none turn back to the ships, for that he hath heard one threatening aloud; nay, get ye forward, and cheer another on, if perchance Olympian Zeus, the lord of lightning, will grant us to drive back the assault, and push the foe to the city."

So these twain shouted in the front, and aroused the battle of the Achaians. But as flakes of snow fall thick on a winter day, when Zeus the Counsellor hath begun to snow, showing forth these arrows of his to men, and he hath lulled the winds, and he snoweth continually, till he hath covered the crests of the high hills, and the uttermost headlands, and the grassy plains, and rich tillage of men; and the snow is scattered over the havens and shores of the grey sea, and only the wave as it rolleth in keeps off the snow, but all other things are swathed over, when the shower of Zeus cometh heavily, so from both sides their stones flew thick, some towards the Trojans, and some from the Trojans against the Achaians, while both sides were smitten, and over all the wall the din arose.

Yet never would the Trojans, then, and renowned Hector have broken the gates of the wall, and the long bar, if Zeus the Counsellor had not roused his son Sarpedon against the Argives, like a lion against the kine of crooked horn. Straightway he held forth his fair round shield, of hammered bronze, that the bronze-smith had hammered out, and within had stitched many bulls' hides with rivets of gold, all round the circle, this held he forth, and shook two spears; and sped on his way, like a mountain-nurtured lion, that long lacketh meat, and his brave spirit urgeth him to make assail on the sheep, and come even against a well-builded homestead. Nay, even if he find herds

this. By
themselvereby, guarding the sheep with hounds and spears, yet
us for*ie no mind to be driven without an effort from the stead-
prom'but he either leapeth on a sheep, and seizeth it, or himself
is smitten in the foremost place with a dart from a strong
hand. So did his heart then urge on the godlike Sarpedon
to rush against the wall, and break through the battlements.
And instantly he spake to Glaukos, son of Hippolochos:
"Glaukos, wherefore have we twain the chiefest honour, —
seats of honour, and messes, and full cups in Lykia, and all
men look on us as gods? And wherefore hold we a great
demesne by the banks of Xanthos, a fair demesne of orchard-
land, and wheat-bearing tilth? Therefore now it behoveth us
to take our stand in the first rank of the Lykians, and encounter fiery battle, that certain of the well-corsleted Lykians may
say, 'Verily our kings that rule Lykia be no inglorious men,
they that eat fat sheep, and drink the choice wine honey-sweet:
nay, but they are also of excellent might, for they war in the
foremost ranks of the Lykians.' Ah, friend, if once escaped
from this battle we were for ever to be ageless and immortal,
neither would I fight myself in the foremost ranks, nor would
I send thee into the war that giveth men renown, but now —
for assuredly ten thousand fates of death do every way beset
us, and these no mortal may escape nor avoid — now let us go
forward, whether we shall give glory to other men, or others to
us."

So spake he, and Glaukos turned not apart, nor disobeyed
him, and they twain went straight forward, leading the great
host of the Lykians.

Then Menestheus son of Peteos shuddered when he beheld
them, for against his tower they went, bringing with them
ruin; and he looked along the tower of the Achaians if perchance he might see any of the leaders, that would ward off
destruction from his comrades, and he beheld the two Aiantes,
insatiate of war, standing there, and Teukros hard by, newly

come from his hut; but he could not cry to be heard of them,
so great was the din, and the noise went up unto heaven of
smitten shields and helms with horse-hair crests, and of the
gates, for they had all been shut, and the Trojans stood beside
them, and strove by force to break them, and enter in. Swiftly
then to Aias he sent the herald Thoötes: "Go, noble Thoötes,
and run, and call Aias: or rather the twain, for that will be
far the best of all, since quickly here will there be wrought utter
ruin. For hereby press the leaders of the Lykians, who of old
are fierce in strong battle. But if beside them too war and toil
arise, yet at least let the strong Telamonian Aias come alone
and let Teukros the skilled bowman follow with him."

So spake he, and the herald listened and disobeyed him not,
but started and ran by the wall of the mail-clad Achaians, and
came, and stood by the Aiantes.

Nor did the strong Telamonian Aias disobey, but instantly
spake winged words to the son of Oileus: "Aias, do ye twain
stand here, thyself and strong Lykomedes, and urge the
Danaans to war with all their might; but I go thither, to take
my part in battle, and quickly will I come again, when I have
well aided them."

So spake Telamonian Aias and departed, and Teukros went
with him, his brother by the same father, and with them Pan-
dion bare the bended bow of Teukros.

Now when they came to the tower of great-hearted Menestheus, passing within the wall, — and to men sore pressed they
came, — the foe were climbing upon the battlements, like a
dark whirlwind, even the strong leaders and counsellors of the
Lykians; and they hurled together into the war and the battle-
cry arose. Now first did Aias Telamon's son slay a man, Epi-
kles great of heart, the comrade of Sarpedon. With a jagged
stone he smote him, a great stone that lay uppermost within
the wall, by the battlements. Not lightly could a man hold it
in both hands, however strong in his youth, of such mortals as

now are, but Aias lifted it, and cast it from above, and shattered the helm of fourfold crest, and broke the bones of the head, and he fell like a diver from the lofty tower, and his life left his bones. And Teukros smote Glaukos, the strong son of Hippolochos, as he came on, with an arrow from the lofty wall; even where he saw his shoulder bare he smote him, and made him cease from delight in battle. Back from the wall he leapt secretly, lest any of the Achaians should see him smitten, and speak boastfully. But sorrow came on Sarpedon when Gla ' ›s departed, so soon as he was aware thereof, but he forgot · the joy of battle. He aimed at Alkmaon, son of Thestor, with the spear, and smote him, and drew out the spear. A..d Alkmaon following the spear fell prone, and his bronze arms rang round him. Then Sarpedon seized with strong hands the battlement, and dragged, and it all gave way together, while above the wall was stripped bare, and made a path for many.

Then Aias and Teukros did encounter him: Teukros smote him with an arrow, on the bright baldric of his covering shield, about the breast, but Zeus warded off the Fates from his son, that he should not be overcome beside the ships' sterns. Then Aias leaped on and smote his shield, nor did the spear pass clean through, yet shook he Sarpedon in his eagerness. He gave ground a little way from the battlement, yet retreated not wholly, since his heart hoped to win renown. Then he turned and cried to the godlike Lykians: "O Lykians, wherefore thus are ye slack in impetuous valour. Hard it is for me, stalwart as I am, alone to break through, and make a path to the ships, nay, follow hard after me, for the more men, the better work."

So spake he, and they, dreading the rebuke of their king, pressed on the harder around the counsellor and king. And the Argives on the other side made strong their battalions within the wall, and mighty toil began for them. For neither could the strong Lykians burst through the wall of the

Danaans, and make a way to the ships, nor could the warlike Danaans drive back the Lykians from the wall, when once they had drawn near thereto. But as two men contend about the marches of their land, with measuring rods in their hands, in a common field, when in narrow space they strive for equal shares, even so the battlements divided them, and over those they smote the round shields of ox hide about the breasts of either side, and the fluttering bucklers. And many were wounded in the flesh with the ruthless bronze, whensoever the back of any of the warriors was laid bare as he turned, ay, and many clean through the very shield. Yea, everywhere the towers and battlements swam with the blood of men shed on either side, by Trojans and Achaians. But even so they could not put the Argives to rout, but they held their ground, as an honest woman that laboureth with her hands holds the balance, and raises the weight and the wool together, balancing them, that she may win scant wages for her children; so evenly was strained their war and battle, till the moment when Zeus gave the greater renown to Hector, son of Priam, who was the first to leap within the wall of the Achaians. In a piercing voice he cried aloud to the Trojans: "Rise, ye horse-taming Trojans, break the wall of the Argives, and cast among the ships fierce blazing fire."

So spake he, spurring them on, and they all heard him with their ears, and in one mass rushed straight against the wall, and with sharp spears in their hands climbed upon the machicolations of the towers. And Hector seized and carried a stone that lay in front of the gates, thick in the hinder part, but sharp at point: a stone that not the two best men of the people, such as mortals now are, could lightly lift from the ground on to a wain, but easily he wielded it alone, for the son of crooked-counselling Kronos made it light for him. And as when a shepherd lightly beareth the fleece of a ram, taking it in one hand, and little doth it burden him, so Hector lifted the stone, and bare it straight against the doors that closely guarded the stubborn-set portals, double gates and tall, and two cross bars held them within, and one bolt fastened them. And he came, and stood hard by, and firmly planted himself, and smote them in the midst, setting his legs well apart, that his cast might lack no strength. And he brake both the hinges, and the stone fell within by reason of its weight, and the gates rang loud around, and the bars held not, and the doors burst this way and that beneath the rush of the stone. Then glorious Hector leaped in, with face like the sudden night, shining in wondrous mail that was clad about his body, and with two spears in his hands. No man that met him could have held him back when once he leaped within the gates: none but the gods, and his eyes shone with fire. Turning towards the throng he cried to the Trojans to overleap the wall, and they obeyed his summons, and speedily some overleaped the wall, and some poured into the fair-wrought gateways, and the Danaans fled in fear among the hollow ships, and a ceaseless clamour arose.

BOOK XIII

Poseidon stirreth up the Achaians to defend the ships. The valour of Idomeneus.

Now Zeus, after that he had brought the Trojans and Hector to the ships, left them to their toil and endless labour there. To Troy no more at all he turned his shining eyes, for he deemed in his heart that not one of the Immortals would draw near, to help either Trojans or Danaans.

But the mighty Earth-shaker held no blind watch, who sat and marvelled on the war and strife, high on the topmost crest of wooded Samothrace, for thence all Ida was plain to see; and plain to see were the city of Priam, and the ships of the Achaians. Thither did he go from the sea and sate him down, and he had pity on the Achaians, that they were subdued to the Trojans, and strong was his anger against Zeus.

Then forthwith he went down from the rugged hill, faring with swift steps, and the high hills trembled, and the woodland, beneath the immortal footsteps of Poseidon as he moved. Three strides he made, and with the fourth he reached his goal, even Aigae, and there was his famous palace in the deeps of the mere, his glistering golden mansions builded, imperishable for ever. Thither went he, and let harness to the car his bronze-hooved horses, swift of flight, clothed with their golden manes. He girt his own golden array about his body, and seized the well-wrought lash of gold, and mounted his chariot, and forth he drove across the waves. And the sea beasts frolicked beneath him, on all sides out of the deeps, for well they knew their lord, and with gladness the sea stood asunder, and swiftly they sped, and the axle of bronze was not wetted beneath, and the bounding steeds bare him on to the ships of the Achaians.

Now there is a spacious cave in the depths of the deep mere, between Tenedos and rugged Imbros; there did Poseidon, the Shaker of the earth, stay his horses, and loosed them out of the chariot, and cast before them ambrosial food to graze withal, and golden tethers he bound about their hooves, tethers neither to be broken nor loosed, that there the horses might continually await their lord's return. And he went to the host of the Achaians.

Now the Trojans like flame or storm-wind were following in close array, with fierce intent, after Hector, son of Priam. With shouts and cries they came, and thought to take the ships of the Achaians, and to slay thereby all the bravest of the host. But Poseidon, that girdleth the world, the Shaker of the earth, was urging on the Argives, and forth he came from the deep salt sea, in form and untiring voice like unto

Kalchas. First he spake to the two Aiantes, that themselves were eager for battle: "Ye Aiantes twain, ye shall save the people of the Achaians, if ye are mindful of your might, and reckless of chill fear. For verily I do not otherwhere dread the invincible hands of the Trojans, that have climbed the great wall in their multitude, nay, the well-greaved Achaians will hold them all at bay; but hereby verily do I greatly dread lest some evil befall us, even here where that furious one is leading like a flame of fire, Hector, who boasts him to be son of mighty Zeus. Nay, but here may some god put it into the hearts of you twain, to stand sturdily yourselves, and urge others to do the like; thereby might ye drive him from the fleet-faring ships, despite his eagerness, yea, even if the Olympian himself is rousing him to war."

Therewith the Shaker of the world, the girdler of the earth, struck the twain with his staff, and filled them with strong courage, and their limbs he made light, and their feet, and their hands withal. Then, even as a swift-winged hawk speeds forth to fly, poised high above a tall sheer rock, and swoops to chase some other bird across the plain, even so Poseidon sped from them, the Shaker of the world. And of the twain Oileus' son, the swift-footed Aias, was the first to know the god, and instantly he spake to Aias, son of Telamon: "Aias, since it is one of the gods who hold Olympus, that in the semblance of a seer commands us now to fight beside the ships — not Kalchas is he, the prophet and soothsayer, for easily I knew the tokens of his feet and knees as he turned away, and the gods are easy to discern — lo, then mine own heart within my breast is more eagerly set on war and battle, and my feet beneath and my hands above are lusting for the fight."

Then Aias, son of Telamon, answered him saying: "Even so, too, my hands invincible now rage about the spear-shaft, and wrath has risen within me, and both my feet are swift beneath me; yea, I am keen to meet, even in single fight, the ceaseless rage of Hector son of Priam."

So they spake to each other, rejoicing in the delight of battle, which the god put in their heart. Then the girdler of the earth stirred up the Achaians that were in the rear and were renewing their strength beside the swift ships. Their limbs were loosened by their grievous toil, yea, and their souls filled with sorrow at the sight of the Trojans, that had climbed over the great wall in their multitude. And they looked on them, and shed tears beneath their brows, thinking that never would they escape destruction. But the Shaker of the earth right easily came among them, and urged on the strong battalions of warriors. Teukros first he came and summoned, and Leïtos, and the hero Peneleos, and Thoas, and Deïpyros, and Meriones, and Antilochos, lords of the war-cry, all these he spurred on with winged words: "Shame on you, Argives, shame, ye striplings, in your battle had I trusted for the salvation of our ships. But if you are to withdraw from grievous war, now indeed the day doth shine that shall see us conquered by the Trojans. Lo, the mighty Hector of the loud war-cry is fighting at the ships, and the gates and the long bar he hath burst in sunder."

On this wise did the Earth-enfolder call to and spur on the Achaians. And straightway they made a stand around the two Aiantes, strong bands that Ares himself could not enter and make light of, nor Athene that marshals the host. Yea, they were the chosen best that abode the Trojans and goodly Hector, and spear on spear made close-set fence, and shield on serried shield, buckler pressed on buckler, and helm on helm, and man on man. The horse-hair crests on the bright helmet-ridges touched each other as they nodded, so close they stood each by other, and spears brandished in bold hands were interlaced; and their hearts were steadfast and lusted for battle.

Then the Trojans drave forward in close array, and Hector led them, pressing straight onwards, like a rolling rock from a cliff, that the winter-swollen water thrusteth from the crest of a hill, having broken the foundations of the stubborn rock with its wondrous flood; leaping aloft it flies, and the wood echoes under it, and unstayed it runs its course, till it reaches the level plain, and then it rolls no more for all its eagerness, — even so Hector for a while threatened lightly to win to the sea through the huts and the ships of the Achaians, slaying as he came, but when he encountered the serried battalions, he was stayed when he drew near against them. But they of the other part, the sons of the Achaians, thrust with their swords and double-pointed spears, and drave him forth from them, that he gave ground and reeled backward. Then he cried with a piercing voice, calling on the Trojans: "Trojans, and Lykians, and close-fighting Dardanians, hold your ground, for the Achaians will not long ward me off, nay, though they have arrayed themselves in fashion like a tower. Rather, methinks, they will flee back before the spear, if verily the chief of gods has set me on, the loud-thundering lord of Hera."

Therewith he spurred on the heart and spirit of each man; and Deïphobos, the son of Priam, strode among them with high thoughts, and held in front of him the circle of his shield, and lightly he stepped with his feet, advancing beneath the cover of his shield. Then Meriones aimed at him with a shining spear, and struck, and missed not, but smote the circle of the bulls'-hide shield, yet no whit did he pierce it; nay, well ere that might be, the long spear-shaft snapped in the socket. Now Deïphobos was holding off from him the bulls'-hide shield, and his heart feared the lance of wise Meriones, but that hero shrunk back among the throng of his comrades, greatly in wrath both for the loss of victory, and of his spear, that he had shivered. So he set forth to go to the huts and the ships of the Achaians, to bring a long spear, that he had left in his hut.

Meanwhile the others were fighting on, and there arose an

inextinguishable cry. First Teukros, son of Telamon, slew a man, the spearman Imbrios, the son of Mentor rich in horses. Then Teukros rushed forth, most eager to strip his armour, and Hector cast at him as he came with his shining spear. But Teukros, steadily regarding him, avoided by a little the spear of bronze; so Hector struck Amphimachos, son of Kteatos, son of Aktor, in the breast with the spear, as he was returning to the battle. With a crash he fell, and his armour rang upon him.

Then verily was Poseidon wroth at heart, when his son's son fell in the terrible fray.[1] So he set forth to go by the huts and the ships of the Achaians, to spur on the Danaans, and sorrows he was contriving for the Trojans. Then Idomeneus, spearman renowned, met him on his way from his comrade that had but newly returned to him out of the battle, wounded on the knee with the sharp bronze. Then the mighty Shaker of the earth addressed him, in the voice of Thoas, son of Andraimon, that ruled over the Aitolians in all Pleuron, and mountainous Kalydon, and was honoured like a god by the people: "Come, take thy weapons and away: herein we must play the man together, if any avail there may be, though we are no more than two. Ay, and very cowards get courage from company, but we twain know well how to battle even with the brave."

Therewith the god went back again into the strife of men, but Idomeneus, so soon as he came to his well-builded hut, did on his fair armour about his body, and grasped two spears, and set forth like the lightning that Kronion seizes in his hand and brandishes from radiant Olympus, showing forth a sign to mortal men, and far seen are the flames thereof. Even so shone the bronze about the breast of Idomeneus as he ran, and Meriones, his good squire, met him, while he was still near his hut, — he was going to bring his spear of bronze, — and mighty Idomeneus

---

[1] **Kteatos**, father of Amphimachos, was Poseidon's son.

spake to him: "Meriones son of Molos, fleet of foot, dearest of my company, wherefore hast thou come hither and left the war and strife? Art thou wounded at all, and vexed by a dart's point, or dost thou come with a message for me concerning aught? Verily I myself have no desire to sit in the huts, but to fight."

Then wise Meriones answered him again, saying: "I have come to fetch a spear, if perchance thou hast one left in the huts, for that which before I carried I have shivered in casting at the shield of proud Deïphobos."

Then Idomeneus, leader of the Cretans, answered him again: "Spears, if thou wilt, thou shalt find, one, ay, and twenty, standing in the hut, against the shining side walls, spears of the Trojans whereof I have spoiled their slain. Yea, it is not my mood to stand and fight with foemen from afar, wherefore I have spears, and bossy shields, and helms, and corslets of splendid sheen."

Thus he spake, and Meriones, the peer of swift Ares, quickly bare the spear of bronze from the hut, and went after Idomeneus, with high thoughts of battle. And even as Ares, the bane of men, goes forth into the war, and with him follows his dear son Panic, stark and fearless, that terrifies even the hardy warrior; and these twain leave Thrace, and harness them for fight with the Ephyri, or the great-hearted Phlegyans, yet hearken not to both peoples, but give honour to one only; like these gods did Meriones and Idomeneus, leaders of men, set forth into the fight, harnessed in gleaming bronze. And Meriones spake first to Idomeneus saying: "Child of Deukalion, whither art thou eager to enter into the throng: on the right of all the host, or in the centre, or on the left? Ay, and no other where, methinks, are the flowing-haired Achaians so like to fail in fight."

Then Idomeneus, the leader of the Cretans, answered him again: "In the centre of the ships there are others to bear the brunt, the two Aiantes, and Teukros, the best bowmen of the

Achaians, ay, and a good man in close fight; these will give Hector Priam's son toil enough, howsoever keen he be for battle; yea, though he be exceeding stalwart. But guide us twain, as thou sayest, to the left hand of the host, that speedily we may learn whether we are to win glory from others, or other men from us."

So he spake, and Meriones, the peer of swift Ares, led the way, till they came to the host, in that place whither he bade him go.

And when the Trojans saw Idomeneus, strong as flame, and his squire with him, and their glorious armour, they all shouted and made for him through the press. Then their mellay began, by the sterns of the ships. And as the gusts speed on, when shrill winds blow, on a day when dust lies thickest on the roads, and the winds raise together a great cloud of dust, even so their battle clashed together, and all were fain of heart to slay each other in the press with the keen bronze. And the battle, the bane of men, bristled with the long spears, the piercing spears they grasped, and the glitter of bronze from gleaming helmets dazzled the eyes, and the sheen of new-burnished corslets, and shining shields, as the men thronged all together. Right hardy of heart would he have been that joyed and sorrowed not at the sight of this labour of battle.

Thus the two mighty sons of Kronos, with contending will, were contriving sorrow and anguish for the heroes. Zeus desired victory for the Trojans and Hector, giving glory to swift-footed Achilles; yet he did not wish the Achaian host to perish utterly before Ilios, but only to give renown to Thetis and her strong-hearted son. But Poseidon went among the Argives and stirred them to war, stealing secretly forth from the grey salt sea: for he was sore vexed that they were overcome by the Trojans, and was greatly in wrath against Zeus. Verily both were of the same lineage and the same place of birth, but Zeus was the elder and the wiser. Therefore also Poseidon avoided to give open aid, but secretly ever he spurred them on, throughout the host, in the likeness of a man.

Even then Idomeneus, though his hair was flecked with grey, called on the Danaans, and leaping among the Trojans, roused their terror. For he slew Othryoneus of Kabesos and dragged him by the foot across the fierce mellay. But Asios came to his aid, on foot before his horses that the charioteer guided so that still their breath touched the shoulders of Asios. And the desire of his heart was to cast at Idomeneus, who was beforehand with him, and smote him with the spear in the throat, below the chin, and drove the point straight through. And he fell as an oak falls, or a poplar, or tall pine tree, that craftsmen have felled on the hills with new whetted axes, to be a ship's timber; even so he lay stretched out before the horses and the chariot, groaning, and clutching the bloody dust. And the charioteer was amazed, and kept not his wits, as of old, and dared not turn his horses and avoid out of the hands of foemen; and Antilochos the steadfast in war smote him, and pierced the middle of his body with a spear. Nothing availed the corslet of bronze he was wont to wear, but he planted the spear fast in the midst of his belly. Therewith he fell gasping from the well-wrought chariot, and Antilochos, the son of great-hearted Nestor, drave the horses out from the Trojans, among the well-greaved Achaians. Then Deïphobos, in sorrow for Asios, drew very nigh Idomeneus, and cast at him with his shining spear. But Idomeneus steadily watching him, avoided the spear of bronze, being hidden beneath the circle of his shield, and the spear of bronze flew over. And his shield rang sharply, as the spear grazed thereon. Yet it flew not vainly from the heavy hand of Deïphobos, but smote Hypsenor, son of Hippasos, the shepherd of the hosts, in the liver, beneath the midriff, and instantly unstrung his knees. And Deïphobos boasted over him terribly, crying aloud: "Ah, verily, not unavenged lies Asios, nay, methinks, that even on his road to Hades, strong Warden of the gate, he will rejoice at heart, since, lo, I have sent him escort for the way!"

So spake he, but grief came on the Argives by reason of his boast, and stirred above all the soul of the wise-hearted Antilochos, yet, despite his sorrow, he was not heedless of his dear comrade, but ran and stood over him, and covered him with his buckler. Then two trusty companions, Mekisteus, son of Echios, and goodly Alastor, stooped down and lifted him, and with heavy groaning bare him to the hollow ships.

And Idomeneus relaxed not his mighty force, but ever was striving, either to cover some one of the Trojans with black night, or himself to fall in warding off death from the Achaians, There the dear son of Aisyetes, fosterling of Zeus, even the hero Alkathoos, was slain. This Alkathoos did Poseidon subdue to Idomeneus, throwing a spell over his shining eyes, and snaring his glorious limbs; so that he might neither flee backwards, nor avoid the stroke, but stood steady as a pillar, or a tree with lofty crown of leaves, when the hero Idomeneus smote him in the midst of the breast with the spear, and rent the coat of bronze about him, that aforetime warded death from his body, but now rang harsh as it was rent by the spear. And he fell with a crash, and the lance fixed in his heart, that, still beating, shook the butt-end of the spear. And Idomeneus boasted terribly, and cried aloud: "Deïphobos, are we to deem it fair acquittal that we have slain three men for one, since thou boastest thus? Nay, sir, but stand thou up also thyself against me, that thou mayst know what manner of son of Zeus am I that have come hither!"

Thus he spake, but the thoughts of Deïphobos were divided, whether he should retreat, and call to his aid some one of the great-hearted Trojans, or should try the adventure alone. And on this wise to his mind it seemed the better, to go after Aineias, whom he found standing the last in the press, for

Aineias was ever wroth against goodly Priam, for that Priam gave him no honour, despite his valour among men. So Deïphobos stood by him, and spake winged words to him: "Aineias, thou counsellor of the Trojans, now verily there is great need that thou shouldst succour thy sister's husband, if any care for kin doth touch thee. Nay follow, let us succour Alkathoos, thy sister's husband, who of old did cherish thee in his hall, while thou wert but a little one, and now, lo, spear-famed Idomeneus hath stripped him of his arms!"

So he spake, and roused the spirit in the breast of Aineias, who went to seek Idomeneus, with high thoughts of war. But fear took not hold upon Idomeneus, as though he had been some tender boy, but he stood at bay, like a boar on the hills that trusteth to his strength, and abides the great assailing throng of men in a lonely place. Even so stood spear-famed Idomeneus at bay against Aineias, that came to the rescue, and gave ground no whit, but called on his comrades, glancing to Askalaphos, and Aphareus, and Deïpyros, and Meriones, and Antilochos, all masters of the war-cry; them he spurred up to battle, and spake winged words: "Hither, friends, and rescue me, all alone as I am, and terribly I dread the onslaught of swift-footed Aineias, that is assailing me; for he is right strong to destroy men in battle, and he hath the flower of youth, the greatest avail that may be."

So he spake, and they all, being of one spirit in their hearts, stood hard by each other, with buckler laid on shoulder. But Aineias, on the other side, cried to his comrades, glancing to Deïphobos, and Paris, and noble Agenor, that with him were leaders of the Trojans; and then the hosts followed them, as sheep follow their leader to the water from the pasture.

Then they rushed in close fight around Alkathoos with their long spears, and round their breasts the bronze rang terribly, as they aimed at each other in the press, while two men of war beyond the rest, Aineias and Idomeneus, the peers of Ares, were each striving to hew the flesh of the other with the pitiless bronze. Now Aineias first cast at Idomeneus, who steadily watching him avoided the spear of bronze, and the point of Aineias went quivering in the earth, since vainly it had flown from his stalwart hand. But Idomeneus smote Oinomaos in the midst of the belly, and brake the plate of his corslet, and the bronze let forth the bowels through the corslet, and he fell in the dust and clutched the earth in his palms. And Idomeneus drew forth the far-shadowing spear from the dead, but could not avail to strip the rest of the fair armour from his shoulders, for the darts pressed hard on him. Nay, and his feet no longer served him firmly in a charge, nor could he rush after his own spear, nor avoid the foe. Wherefore in close fight he still held off the pitiless day of destiny, but in retreat his feet no longer bore him swiftly from the battle. And as he was slowly departing, Deïphobos aimed at him with his shining spear, for verily he ever cherished a steadfast hatred against Idomeneus. But this time, too, he missed him, and smote Askalaphos, the son of Enyalios, with his dart, and the strong spear passed through his shoulder, and he fell in the dust, and clutched the earth in his outstretched hand.

Now the people rushed in close fight around Askalaphos, and Deïphobos tore from Askalaphos his shining helm, but Meriones, the peer of swift Ares, leaped forward and smote the arm of Deïphobos with his spear, and from his hand the vizored casque fell clanging to the ground. And Meriones sprang forth instantly, like a vulture, and drew the strong spear from the shoulder of Deïphobos, and fell back among the throng of his comrades. But the own brother of Deïphobos, Polites, stretched his hands round his waist, and led him forth from the evil din of war, even till he came to the swift horses, that waited for him behind the battle and the fight. These bore him heavily groaning to the city, worn with his hurt, and the blood ran down from his newly wounded arm.

So they fought like flaming fire, but Hector, beloved of Zeus, had not heard nor knew at all that, on the left of the ships, his host was being subdued by the Argives, and soon would the Achaians have won renown, so mighty was the Holder and Shaker of the earth that urged on the Argives; yea, and himself mightily defended them. But Hector kept where at first he had leaped within the walls and the gate, and broken the serried ranks of shield-bearing Danaans, even where were the ships of Aias and Protesilaos, drawn up on the beach of the hoary sea, while above the wall was builded lowest, and thereby chiefly the heroes and their horses were raging in battle.

Now never at all did Aias, the swift son of Oileus, depart from the side of Aias, son of Telamon, nay, not for an instant, but even as in fallow land two wine-dark oxen with equal heart strain at the shapen plough, and round the roots of their horns springeth up abundant sweat, and nought sunders them but the polished yoke, as they labour through the furrow, till the end of the furrow brings them up, so stood the two Aiantes close by each other. Now verily did many and noble hosts of his comrades follow with the son of Telamon, and bore his shield when labour and sweat came upon his limbs. But the Lokrians followed not with the high-hearted son of Oileus, for their hearts were not steadfast in close brunt of battle, seeing that they had no helmets of bronze, shadowy with horse-hair plumes, nor round shields, nor ashen spears, but trusting in bows and well-twisted slings of sheep's wool, they followed with him to Ilios. Therewith, in the war, they shot thick and fast, and brake the ranks of the Trojans. So the one party in front contended with the Trojans, and with Hector arrayed in bronze, while the others from behind kept shooting from their ambush, and the Trojans lost all memory of the joy of battle, for the arrows confounded them.

There then right ruefully from the ships and the huts would

the Trojans have withdrawn to windy Ilios, had not Polydamas come near valiant Hector and said: "Behold all about thee the circle of war is blazing, but the great-hearted Trojans, now that they have got down the wall, are some with their arms standing aloof and some are fighting; few men against a host, being scattered among the ships. Nay, withdraw thee, and call hither all the best of the warriors. Thereafter shall we take all counsel carefully, whether we should fall on the ships of many benches, if indeed god willeth to give us victory, or after counsel held, should return unharmed from the ships. For verily I fear lest the Achaians repay their debt of yesterday, since by the ships there tarrieth a man insatiate of war, and never, methinks, will he wholly stand aloof from battle."

So spake Polydamas, and his safe counsel pleased Hector well, who spake to him winged words and said: "Polydamas, do thou stay here all the best of the host, but I will go thither to face the war, and swiftly will return again, when I have straitly laid on them my commands."

So he spake, and set forth, in semblance like a snowy mountain, and shouting aloud he flew through the Trojans and allies. And they all sped to Polydamas, the kindly son of Panthoos, when they heard the voice of Hector. But he went seeking Deïphobos, and the strong prince Helenos, and Adamas son of Asios, and Asios son of Hyrtakos, among the warriors in the foremost line, if anywhere he might find them. But them he found not at all unharmed, nor free of bane, but, lo, some among the sterns of the ships of the Achaians lay lifeless, slain by the hands of the Argives, and some were within the wall wounded by thrust or cast. But one he readily found, on the left of the dolorous battle, goodly Alexandros, the lord of fair-tressed Helen, heartening his comrades and speeding them to war. And he drew near to him, and addressed him with words of shame: "Thou evil Paris, fairest of face, thou that lustest for women, thou seducer, where, prithee, are Deïphobos, and the strong prince Helenos, and Adamas son of Asios, and Asios son of Hyrtakos, and where is Othryoneus? Now hath all high Ilios perished utterly. Now, too, thou seest, is sheer destruction sure."

Then godlike Alexandros answered him again saying: "Hector, since thy mind is to blame one that is blameless, some other day might I rather withdraw me from the war, since my mother bare not even me wholly a coward. For from the time that thou didst gather the battle of thy comrades about the ships, from that hour do we abide here, and war with the Danaans ceaselessly; and our comrades concerning whom thou inquirest are slain. Only Deïphobos and the strong prince Helenos have both withdrawn, both of them being wounded in the hand with long spears, for Kronion kept death away from them. But now lead on, wheresoever thy heart and spirit bid thee, and we will follow with thee eagerly, nor methinks shall we lack for valour, as far as we have strength; but beyond his strength may no man fight, howsoever eager he be."

So spake the hero, and persuaded his brother's heart, and they went forth where the war and din were thickest, round Kebriones, and noble Polydamas, and Phalkes, and Orthaios, and godlike Polyphetes, and Palmys, and Askanios, and Morys, son of Hippotion, who had come in their turn, out of deep-soiled Askanie, on the morn before, and now Zeus urged them to fight. And these set forth like the blast of violent winds, that rushes earthward beneath the thunder of father Zeus, and with marvellous din doth mingle with the salt sea, and therein are many swelling waves of the loud roaring sea, arched over and white with foam, some vanward, others in the rear; even so the Trojans arrayed in van and rear and shining with bronze, followed after their leaders.

BOOK XIV

How Sleep and Hera beguiled Zeus to slumber on the heights of Ida, and Poseidon spurred on the Achaians to resist Hector, and how Hector was wounded.

YET the cry of battle escaped not Nestor, albeit at his wine, but he spake winged words to the son of Asklepios : "Bethink thee, noble Machaon, what had best be done; lo, louder waxes the cry of the strong warriors by the ships. Nay, now sit where thou art, and drink the bright wine, till Hekamede of the fair tresses shall heat warm water for the bath, and wash away the clotted blood, but I will speedily go forth and come to a place of outlook."

Therewith he took the well-wrought shield of his son, horse-taming Thrasymedes, which was lying in the hut, all glistering with bronze, for the son had the shield of his father. And he seized a strong spear, with a point of keen bronze, and stood outside the hut, and straightway beheld a deed of shame, the Achaians fleeing in rout, and the high-hearted Trojans driving them, and the wall of the Achaians was overthrown. And as when the great sea is troubled with a dumb wave, and dimly bodes the sudden paths of the shrill winds, but is still unmoved nor yet rolled forward or to either side, until some steady gale comes down from Zeus, even so the old man pondered, — his mind divided this way and that, — whether he should fare into the press of the Danaans of the swift steeds, or go after Agamemnon, son of Atreus, shepherd of the host. And thus as he pondered, it seemed to him the better counsel to go to the son of Atreus.

Now the kings, the fosterlings of Zeus, encountered Nestor, as they went up from the ships, even they that were wounded with the bronze, Tydeus' son, and Odysseus, and Agamemnon, son of Atreus. For far apart from the battle were their ships drawn up, on the shore of the grey sea, for these were the first they had drawn up to the plain, but had builded the wall in front of the hindmost. For in no wise might the beach, wide as it was, hold all the ships, and the host was straitened. Wherefore they drew up the ships row within row, and filled up the wide mouth of all the shore that the headlands held between them. Therefore the kings were going together, leaning on their spears, to look on the war and fray, and the heart of each was sore within his breast. And the old man met them, even Nestor, and caused the spirit to fail within the breasts of the Achaians.

And mighty Agamemnon spake and accosted him: "O Nestor, son of Neleus, great glory of the Achaians, wherefore dost thou come hither and hast deserted the war, the bane of men? Lo, I fear the accomplishment of the word that dread Hector spake, and the threat wherewith he threatened us, speaking in the assembly of the Trojans, namely, that never would he return to Ilios from the ships, till he had burned the ships with fire, and slain the men."

Then Nestor of Gerenia the knight answered him, saying: "Verily these things are now at hand, and being accomplished. For, lo, the wall is overthrown, wherein we trusted that it should be an unbroken bulwark of the ships and of our own bodies. But let us take counsel, how these things may best be done, if wit may do aught: but into the war I counsel not that we should go down, for in no wise may a wounded man do battle."

Then Agamemnon king of men answered him again: "Let us drag down the ships that are drawn up in the first line near to the sea, and speed them all forth to the salt sea divine, and moor them far out with stones, till the divine night comes, if even at night the Trojans will refrain from war, and then might we drag down all the ships. For there is no shame in fleeing from ruin, yea, even in the night. Better doth he fare who flees from trouble, than he that is overtaken."

Then, looking on him sternly, spake Odysseus of many counsels: "Atreus' son, what word hath passed the door of thy lips? Man of mischief, sure thou shouldst lead some other inglorious army, not be king among us, to whom Zeus hath given it, from youth even unto age, to wind the skein of grievous wars, till every man of us perish. Art thou indeed so eager to leave the wide-wayed city of the Trojans, the city for which we endure with sorrow so many evils? Be silent, lest some other of the Achaians hear this word, that no man should so much as suffer to pass through his mouth, none that understandeth in his heart how to speak fit counsel, none that is a sceptred king, and hath hosts obeying him so many as the Argives over whom thou reignest. For the Achaians will not make good the war, when the ships are drawn down to the salt sea, but will look round about to flee, and withdraw from battle. There will thy counsel work a mischief, O marshal of the host!"

Then the king of men, Agamemnon, answered him: "Odysseus, right sharply hast thou touched my heart with thy stern reproof: nay, I do not bid the sons of the Achaians to drag, against their will, the well-timbered ships to the salt sea. Now perchance there may be one who will utter a wiser counsel than this of mine, — a young man or an old, — welcome would it be to me."

Then Diomedes of the loud war-cry spake also among them: "The man is near, — not long shall we seek him, if ye be willing to be persuaded of me, and each of you be not resentful at all, because in years I am the youngest among you. Let us go down to the battle, wounded as we are, since we needs must; and then might we hold ourselves aloof from the battle, beyond the range of darts, lest any take wound upon wound; but the others will we spur on, even them that aforetime gave place to their passion, and stand apart, and fight not."

So he spake, and they all heard him readily, and obeyed him. And they set forth, led by Agamemnon the king of men.

Now the renowned Earth-shaker held no vain watch, but went with them in the guise of an ancient man, and he seized the right hand of Agamemnon, Atreus' son, and uttering winged words he spake to him, saying: "Atreides, now methinks the ruinous heart of Achilles rejoices in his breast, as he beholds the slaughter and flight of the Achaians, since he hath no wisdom, not a grain. Nay, even so may he perish likewise, and god mar him. But with thee the blessed gods are not utterly wroth, nay, even yet methinks the leaders and rulers of the Trojans will cover the wide plain with dust, and thyself shalt see them fleeing to the city from the ships and the huts."

So spake he, and shouted mightily, as he sped over the plain. And loud as nine thousand men, or ten thousand cry in battle, when they join the strife of war, so mighty was the cry that the strong Shaker of the earth sent forth from his breast, and great strength he put into the heart of each of the Achaians, to strive and war unceasingly.

Now Hera of the golden throne stood on the peak of Olympus, and saw with her eyes, and anon knew him that was her brother and her lord's going to and fro through the glorious fight, and she rejoiced in her heart. And she beheld Zeus sitting on the topmost crest of many-fountained Ida, and to her heart he was hateful. Then she took thought, the ox-eyed lady Hera, how she might beguile the mind of aegis-bearing Zeus. And this seemed to her in her heart to be the best counsel, namely to fare to Ida, when she had well adorned herself, if perchance a sweet sleep and a kindly she could pour on his eyelids and his crafty wits. And she set forth to her bower, that her dear son Hephaistos had fashioned, and therein had made fast strong doors on the pillars, with a secret bolt, that no other god might open. There did she enter in and closed the shining doors. With ambrosia first did she cleanse every stain from her winsome body, and anointed her with olive oil, ambrosial, soft, and of a sweet savour; if it were but shaken, in the bronze-floored mansion of Zeus, the savour thereof went right forth to earth and heaven. Therewith she anointed her fair body, and combed her hair, and with her hands plaited her shining tresses, fair and ambrosial, flowing from her immortal head. Then she clad her in her fragrant robe that Athene wrought delicately for her, and therein set many things beautifully made, and fastened it over her breast with clasps of gold. And she girdled it with a girdle arrayed with a hundred tassels, and she set earrings in her pierced ears, earrings of three drops, and glistering, therefrom shone grace abundantly. And with a veil over all the peerless goddess veiled herself, a fair new veil, bright as the sun, and beneath her shining feet she bound goodly sandals. But when she had adorned her body with all her array, she went forth from her bower, and called Aphrodite apart from the other gods, and spake to her, saying: "Wilt thou obey me, dear child, in that which I shall tell thee? or wilt thou refuse, with a grudge in thy heart, because I succour the Danaans, and thou the Trojans?"

Then Aphrodite the daughter of Zeus answered her: "Hera, goddess queen, daughter of mighty Kronos, say the thing that is in thy mind, my heart bids me fulfil it, if fulfil it I may, and if it may be accomplished."

Then with crafty purpose the lady Hera answered her: "Give me now Love and Desire wherewith thou dost overcome all the Immortals, and mortal men. For I am going to visit the limits of the bountiful Earth, and Okeanos, father of the gods, and mother Tethys, who reared me well and nourished me in their halls, having taken me from Rhea, when far-seeing Zeus imprisoned Kronos beneath the earth and the unvintaged sea. Them am I going to visit, and their endless strife will I loose, for already this long time they hold apart from each other, since wrath hath settled in their hearts. If with words I might persuade their hearts, and bring them back to love, ever should I be called dear to them and worshipful."

Then laughter-loving Aphrodite answered her again: "It may not be, nor seemly were it, to deny that thou askest, for thou sleepest in the arms of Zeus, the chief of gods."

Therewith from her breast she loosed the broidered girdle, fair-wrought, wherein are all her enchantments; therein are love, and desire, and loving converse, that steals the wits even of the wise. This girdle she laid in her hands, and spake, and said: "Lo now, take this girdle and lay it up in thy bosom, this fair-wrought girdle, wherein all things are fashioned; methinks thou wilt not return with that unaccomplished, which in thy heart thou desirest."

So spake she, and the ox-eyed lady Hera smiled, and smiling laid up the zone within her breast.

Then the daughter of Zeus, Aphrodite, went to her house, and Hera, rushing down, left the peak of Olympus, and sped over the snowy hills of the Thracian horsemen, even over the topmost crests, nor grazed the ground with her feet, and from Athos she fared across the foaming sea, and came to Lemnos, the city of godlike Thoas. There she met Sleep, the brother of Death, and clasped her hand in his, and spake and called him by name: "Sleep, lord of all gods and of all men, if ever thou didst hear my word, obey me again even now, and I will be grateful to thee always. Lull me, I pray thee, the shining eyes of Zeus beneath his brows. And gifts I will give to thee, even a fair throne, imperishable for ever, a golden throne, that Hephaistos the Lame, mine own child, shall fashion skilfully, and will set beneath it a footstool for the feet, for thee to set thy shining feet upon, when thou art at a festival. Nay come, and I will give thee one of the younger of the Graces, to wed and to be called thy wife."

So she spake, and Sleep was glad, and answered and said: "Come now, swear to me by the inviolable water of Styx, and with one of thy hands grasp the bounteous earth, and with the other the shining sea, that all may be witnesses to us, even all the gods below that are with Kronos, that verily thou wilt give me one of the younger of the Graces, even Pasithea, that myself do long for all my days."

So spake he, nor did she disobey, the white-armed goddess Hera; she sware as he bade her, and called all the gods by name, even those below Tartaros that are called Titans. But when she had sworn and ended that oath, the twain left the citadel of Lemnos, and of Imbros, clothed on in mist, and swiftly they accomplished the way. To many-fountained Ida they came, the mother of wild beasts, to Lekton, where first they left the sea, and they twain fared above the dry land, and the topmost forest waved beneath their feet. There Sleep halted, ere the eyes of Zeus beheld him, and alighted on a tall pine tree, the loftiest pine that then in all Ida rose through the nether to the upper air. But Hera swiftly drew nigh to topmost Gargaros, the highest crest of Ida, and Zeus the cloud-gatherer beheld her. And as he saw her, so love came over his deep heart, and he stood before her, and spoke, and said: "Hera, with what desire comest thou thus hither from Olympus, and thy horses and chariot are not here, whereon thou mightst ascend?"

Then with crafty purpose lady Hera answered him: "I am going to visit the limits of the bountiful Earth, and Okeanos, father of the gods, and mother Tethys, who reared me well and cherished me in their halls. Them am I going to visit, and their endless strife will I loose, for already this long time they hold apart from each other, since wrath hath settled in their hearts. But my horses are standing at the foot of many-fountained Ida, my horses that shall bear me over wet and dry. And now it is because of thee that I am thus come hither, down from Olympus, lest perchance thou mightest be wroth with me hereafter, if silently I were gone to the mansion of deep-flowing Okeanos."

Then Zeus, the gatherer of the clouds, answered her and

said: "Hera, thither mayst thou go on a later day. For never once as thus did the love of goddess or woman so mightily overflow and conquer the heart within my breast."

Thus slept the Father in quiet on the crest of Gargaros, by Sleep and love overcome. But sweet Sleep started and ran to the ships of the Achaians, to tell his tidings to the god that holdeth and shaketh the earth. And he stood near him, and spake winged words: "Eagerly now, Poseidon, do thou aid the Danaans, and give them glory for a little space, while yet Zeus sleepeth, for over him have I shed soft slumber, and Hera hath beguiled him."

So he spake, and passed to the renowned tribes of men, and still the more did he set on Poseidon to aid the Danaans, who straightway sprang far afront of the foremost, and called to them: "Argives, are we again to yield the victory to Hector, son of Priam, that he may take our ships and win renown? Nay, even so he saith and declareth that he will do, for that Achilles by the hollow ships abides angered at heart. But for him there will be no such extreme regret, if we spur us on to aid each the other. Nay come, as I command, let us all obey. Let us harness us in the best shields that are in the host, and the greatest, and cover our heads with shining helms, and take the longest spears in our hands, and so go forth. Yea, and I will lead the way, and methinks that Hector, son of Priam, will not long await us, for all his eagerness. And whatsoever man is steadfast in battle, and hath a small buckler on his shoulder, let him give it to a worse man, and harness him in a larger shield."

So spake he, and they heard him eagerly and obeyed him. And them the kings themselves arrayed, wounded as they were, Tydeus' son, and Odysseus, and Agamemnon, son of Atreus. They went through all the host, and made exchange of weapons of war. The good arms did the good warrior harness him in, the worse he gave to the worse. But when they had done on the shining bronze about their bodies, they started on the march, and Poseidon led them, the Shaker of the earth, with a dread sword of fine edge in his strong hand, like unto lightning; wherewith it is not permitted that any should mingle in woful war, but fear holds men afar therefrom. But the Trojans on the other side was renowned Hector arraying. Then did they now strain the fiercest strife of war, even dark-haired Poseidon and glorious Hector, one succouring the Trojans, the other with the Argives. And the sea washed up to the huts and ships of the Argives, and they gathered together with a mighty cry. Not so loudly bellows the wave of the sea against the land, stirred up from the deep by the harsh breath of the north wind, nor so loud is the roar of burning fire in the glades of a mountain, when it springs to burn up the forest, nor calls the wind so loudly in the high leafy tresses of the trees, when it rages and roars its loudest, as then was the cry of the Trojans and Achaians, shouting dreadfully as they rushed upon each other.

First glorious Hector cast with his spear at Aias, who was facing him full, and did not miss, striking him where two belts were stretched across his breast, the belt of his shield, and of his silver-studded sword; these guarded his tender flesh. And Hector was enraged because his swift spear had flown vainly from his hand, and he retreated into the throng of his fellows, avoiding Fate.

Then as he was departing the great Telamonian Aias smote him with a huge stone; for many stones, the props of swift ships, were rolled among the feet of the fighters; one of these he lifted, and smote Hector on the breast, over the shield-rim, near the neck, and made him spin like a top with the blow, that he reeled round and round. And even as when an oak falls uprooted beneath the stroke of father Zeus, and a dread savour of brimstone arises therefrom, and whoso stands near and beholds it has no more courage, for dread is the bolt of great Zeus, even so fell mighty Hector straightway in the dust. And the spear fell from his hand, but his shield and helm were made fast to him, and round him rang his arms adorned with bronze.

Then with a loud cry they ran up, the sons of the Achaians, hoping to drag him away, and they cast showers of darts. But not one availed to wound or smite the shepherd of the host; before that might be the bravest gathered about him, Polydamas, and Aineias, and goodly Agenor, and Sarpedon, leader of the Lykians, and noble Glaukos, and of the rest not one was heedless of him, but they held their round shields in front of him, and his comrades lifted him in their arms, and bare him out of the battle, till he reached his swift horses that were standing waiting for him, with the charioteer and the fair-dight chariot at the rear of the combat and the war. These toward the city bore him heavily moaning. Now when they came to the ford of the fair-flowing river, of eddying Xanthos, that immortal Zeus begat, there they lifted him from the chariot to the ground, and poured water over him, and he gat back his breath, and looked up with his eyes, and sitting on his heels kneeling, he vomited black blood. Then again he sank back on the ground, and black night covered his eyes, the stroke still conquering his spirit.

BOOK XV

Zeus awakening, biddeth Apollo revive Hector, and restore the fortunes of the Trojans. Fire is thrown on the ship of Protesilaos.

Now when they had sped in flight across the palisade and trench, and many were overcome at the hands of the Danaans, the rest were stayed, and abode beside the chariots in confusion, and pale with terror, and Zeus awoke, on the peaks of Ida, beside Hera of the golden throne. Then he leaped up, and stood, and beheld the Trojans and Achaians, those in flight, and these driving them on from the rear, even the Argives, and among them the prince Poseidon. And Hector he saw lying on the plain, and around him sat his comrades, and he was gasping with difficult breath, and his mind wandering, and was vomiting blood, for it was not the weakest of the Achaians that had smitten him. Beholding him, the father of men and gods had pity on him, and terribly he spoke to Hera, with fierce look: "O thou ill to deal with, Hera, verily it is thy crafty wile that has made noble Hector cease from the fight, and has terrified the host. Nay, but yet I know not whether thou mayst not be the first to reap the fruits of thy cruel treason, and I beat thee with stripes. Dost thou not remember, when thou wert hung from on high, and from thy feet I suspended two anvils, and round thy hands fastened a golden bond that might not be broken? And thou didst hang in the clear air and the clouds, and the gods were wroth in high Olympus, but they could not come round and unloose thee."

So spake he, and the ox-eyed lady Hera shuddered, and spake unto him winged words, saying: "Let earth now be witness hereto, and wide heaven above, and that falling water of Styx, the greatest oath and the most terrible to the blessed gods, and thine own sacred head, and our own bridal bed, whereby never would I forswear myself, that not by my will does earth-shaking Poseidon trouble the Trojans and Hector, and succour them of the other part. Nay, it is his own soul that urgeth and commandeth him, and he had pity on the Achaians, when he beheld them hard pressed beside the ships. I would even counsel him also to go even where thou, lord of the storm-cloud, mayst lead him."

So spake she, and the father of gods and men smiled, and answering her he spake winged words: "If thou, of a truth, O ox-eyed lady Hera, wouldst hereafter abide of one mind with me among the immortal gods, thereon would Poseidon, howsoever much his wish be contrariwise, quickly turn his mind otherwhere, after thy heart and mine. But if indeed thou speakest the truth and soothly, go thou now among the tribes of the gods, and call Iris to come hither, and Apollo, the renowned archer, that Iris may go among the host of mail-clad Achaians and tell Poseidon the prince to cease from the war, and get him unto his own house. But let Phoebus Apollo spur Hector on to the war, and breathe strength into him again, and make him forget his anguish, that now wears down his heart, and drive the Achaians back again, when he hath stirred in them craven fear. Let them flee and fall among the many-benched ships of Achilles son of Peleus, and he shall rouse his own comrade, Patroklos; and him shall renowned Hector slay with the spear, in front of Ilios, after that he has slain many other youths, and among them my son, noble Sarpedon. In wrath therefor shall goodly Achilles slay Hector. From that hour verily will I cause a new pursuit from the ships, that shall endure continually, even until the Achaians take steep Ilios, through the counsels of Athene. But before that hour neither do I cease in my wrath, nor will I suffer any other of the Immortals to help the Danaans there, before I accomplish that desire of the son of Peleus, as I promised him at the first, and confirmed the same with a nod of my head, on that day when the goddess Thetis clasped my knees, imploring me to honour Achilles, the sacker of cities."

So spake he, nor did the white-armed goddess Hera disobey him, and she sped down from the hills of Ida to high Olympus, and went among the gathering of the immortal gods. And she called Apollo without the hall, and Iris, that is the messenger of the immortal gods, and she spake winged words, and addressed them, saying: "Zeus bids you go to Ida as swiftly as may be, and when ye have gone, and looked on the face of Zeus, do ye whatsoever he shall order and command."

And these twain came before the face of Zeus the cloud

gatherer, and stood there, and he was nowise displeased at heart when he beheld them, for that speedily they had obeyed the words of his dear wife. And to Iris first he spake ·winged words: "Go, get thee, swift Iris, to the prince Poseidon, and tell him all these things, nor be a false messenger. Command him to cease from war and battle, and to go among the tribes of the gods, or into the bright sea. But if he will not obey my words, but will hold me in no regard, then let him consider in his heart and mind, lest he dare not for all his strength to abide me when I come against him, since I deem me to be far mightier than he, and elder born."

So spake he, nor did the wind-footed fleet Iris disobey him, but went down the hills of Ida to sacred Ilios. And as when snow or chill hail fleets from the clouds beneath the stress of the North Wind born in the clear air, so fleetly she fled in her eagerness, swift Iris, and drew near the renowned Earth-shaker and spake to him the message of Zeus. And he left the host of the Achaians, and passed to the sea, and sank, and sorely they missed him, the heroes of the Achaians.

Then Zeus, the gatherer of the clouds, spake to Apollo, saying: "Go now, dear Phoebus, to Hector of the helm of bronze. Let glorious Hector be thy care, and rouse in him great wrath even till the Achaians come in their flight to the ships, and the Hellespont. And from that moment will I devise word and deed wherewithal the Achaians may take breath again from their toil."

So spake he, nor was Apollo deaf to the word of the Father, but he went down the hills of Ida like a fleet falcon, the bane of doves, that is the swiftest of flying things. And he found the son of wise-hearted Priam, noble Hector, sitting up, no longer lying, for he· had but late got back his life, and knew the comrades around him, and his gasping and his sweat had ceased, from the moment when the will of aegis-bearing Zeus began to revive him. Then far-darting Apollo stood near him, and spake to him: "Hector, son of Priam, why dost thou sit fainting apart from the others? Is it perchance that some trouble cometh upon thee?"

Then, with faint breath answered him Hector of the glancing helm: "Nay, but who art thou, best of the gods, who enquirest of me face to face? Dost thou not know that by the hindmost row of the ships of the Achaians, Aias of the loud war-cry smote me on the breast with a stone, as I was slaying his comrades, and made me cease from mine impetuous might? And verily I deemed that this very day I should pass to the dead, and the house of Hades, when I had gasped my life away."

Then prince Apollo the Far-darter answered him again: "Take courage now, so great an ally hath the son of Kronos sent thee out of Ida, to stand by thee and defend thee, even Phoebus Apollo of the golden sword, me who of old defend thee, thyself and the steep citadel. But come now, bid thy many charioteers drive their swift steeds against the hollow ships, and I will go before and make smooth all the way for the chariots, and will put to flight the Achaian heroes."

So he spake, and breathed great might into the shepherd of the host, and even as when a stalled horse, full fed at the manger, breaks his tether and speedeth at the gallop over the plain exultingly, being wont to bathe in the fair-flowing stream, and holds his head on high, and the mane floweth about his shoulders, and he trusteth in his glory, and nimbly his knees bear him to the haunts and pasture of the mares, even so Hector lightly moved his feet and knees, urging on his horsemen, when he heard the voice of the god. But as when hounds and country folk pursue a horned stag, or a wild goat, that steep rock and shady wood save from them, nor is it their lot to find him, but at their clamour a bearded lion hath shown himself on the way, and lightly turned them all despite their eagerness, even so the Danaans for a while followed on always in their companies, smiting with swords and double-pointed spears, but when they saw Hector going up and down the ranks of men, then were they afraid, and the hearts of all fell to their feet.

Then to them spake Thoas, son of Andraimon, far the best of the Aitolians, skilled in throwing the dart, and good in close fight, and in council did few of the Achaians surpass him, when the young men were striving in debate; he made harangue and spake among them: " Alas, and verily a great marvel is this I behold with mine eyes, how he hath again arisen, and hath avoided the Fates, even Hector. Surely each of us hoped in his heart, that he had died beneath the hand of Aias, son of Telamon. But some one of the gods again hath delivered and saved Hector, who verily hath loosened the knees of many of the Danaans, as methinks will befall even now, for not without the will of loud-thundering Zeus doth he rise in the front ranks, thus eager for battle. But come, as I declare let us all obey. Let us bid the throng turn back to the ships, but let us as many as avow us to be the best in the host, take our stand, if perchance first we may meet him, and hold him off with outstretched spears, and he, methinks, for all his eagerness, will fear at heart to enter into the press of the Danaans."

So spake he, and they heard him eagerly, and obeyed him. They that were with Aias and the prince Idomeneus, and Teukros, and Neriones, and Meges the peer of Ares, called to all the best of the warriors and sustained the fight with Hector and the Trojans, but behind them the multitude returned to the ships of the Achaians.

Now the Trojans drave forward in close ranks, and with long strides Hector led them, while in front of him went Phoebus Apollo, his shoulders wrapped in cloud, and still he held the fell aegis, dread, circled with a shaggy fringe, and gleaming, that Hephaistos the smith gave to Zeus, to bear for the terror of men; with this in his hands did he lead the host.

Now the Argives abode them in close ranks, and shrill the cry arose on both sides, and the arrows leaped from the bowstrings, and many spears from stalwart hands, whereof some stood fast in the flesh of young men swift in fight, but many halfway, ere ever they reached the white flesh, stuck in the ground, longing to glut themselves with flesh. Now so long as Phoebus Apollo held the aegis unmoved in his hands, so long the darts smote either side amain, and the folk fell. But when he looked face to face on the Danaans of the swift steeds, and shook the aegis, and himself shouted mightily, he quelled their heart in their breast, and they forgot their impetuous valour. And as when two wild beasts drive in confusion a herd of kine, or a great flock of sheep, in the dark hour of black night, coming swiftly on them when the herdsman is not by, even so were the Achaians terror-stricken and strengthless, for Apollo sent a panic among them, but still gave renown to the Trojans and Hector.

And Hector smote his horses on the shoulder with the lash, and called aloud on the Trojans along the ranks. And they all cried out, and level with his held the steeds that drew their chariots, with a marvellous din, and in front of them Phoebus Apollo lightly dashed down with his feet the banks of the deep ditch, and cast them into the midst thereof, making a bridgeway long and wide as is a spear-cast, when a man throws to make trial of his strength. Thereby the Trojans poured forward in their battalions, while in their van Apollo held the splendid aegis. And most easily did he cast down the wall of the Achaians, as when a boy scatters the sand beside the sea, first making sand buildings for sport in his childishness, and then again, in his sport, confounding them with his feet and hands; even so didst thou, archer Apollo, confound the long toil and labour of the Argives, and among them rouse a panic fear.

So they were halting, and abiding by the ships, calling each to other; and lifting their hands to all the gods did each man pray vehemently, and chiefly prayed Nestor, the Warder of the Achaians, stretching his hand towards the starry heaven: "O father Zeus, if ever any one of us in wheat-bearing Argos did burn to thee fat thighs of bull or sheep, and prayed that he might return, and thou didst promise and assent thereto, of these things be thou mindful, and avert, Olympian, the pitiless day, nor suffer the Trojans thus to overcome the Achaians."

So spake he in his prayer, and Zeus, the Lord of counsel, thundered loudly, hearing the prayers of the ancient son of Neleus.

But the Trojans when they heard the thunder of aegis-bearing Zeus, rushed yet the more eagerly upon the Argives, and were mindful of the joy of battle. And as when a great wave of the wide sea sweeps over the bulwarks of a ship, the might of the wind constraining it, which chiefly swells the waves, even so did the Trojans with a great cry bound over the wall, and drave their horses on, and at the hindmost row of the ships were fighting hand to hand with double-pointed spears, the Trojans from the chariots, but the Achaians climbing up aloft, from the black ships with long pikes that they had lying in the ships for battle at sea, jointed pikes shod at the head with bronze.

Now the Trojans, like ravening lions, rushed upon the ships, fulfilling the behests of Zeus, that ever was rousing their great wrath, but softened the temper of the Argives, and took away their glory, while he spurred on the others. For the heart of Zeus was set on giving glory to Hector, the son of Priam, that withal he might cast fierce-blazing fire, unwearied, upon the beaked ships, and so fulfil all the presumptuous prayer of Thetis; wherefore wise-counselling Zeus awaited, till his eyes should see the glare of a burning ship. For even from that hour was he to ordain the backward chase of the Trojans from the ships, and to give glory to the Danaans. With this design was he rousing Hector, Priam's son, that himself was right eager, against the hollow ships. For short of life was he to be, yea, and already Pallas Athene was urging against him the day of destiny, at the hand of the son of Peleus. And fain he was to break the ranks of men, trying them wheresoever he saw the thickest press, and the goodliest harness. Yet not even so might he break them for all his eagerness. Nay, they stood firm, and embattled like a steep rock and a great, hard by the hoary sea, a rock that abides the swift paths of the shrill winds, and the swelling waves that roar against it. Even so the Danaans steadfastly abode the Trojans and fled not away. But Hector shining with fire on all sides leaped on the throng, and fell upon them, as when beneath the storm-clouds a fleet wave reared of the winds falls on a swift ship, and she is all hidden with foam, and the dread blast of the wind roars against the sail, and the sailors fear, and tremble in their hearts, for by but a little way are they borne forth from death, even so the spirit was torn in the breasts of the Achaians.

So again keen battle was set by the ships. Thou wouldst deem that unwearied and unworn they met each other in war, so eagerly they fought. And in their striving they were minded thus; the Achaians verily deemed that never would they flee from the danger, but perish there, but the heart of each Trojan hoped in his breast, that they should fire the ships, and slay the heroes of the Achaians. With these imaginations they stood to each other, and Hector seized the stern of a seafaring ship, a fair ship, swift on the brine, that had borne Protesilaos to Troia, but brought him not back again to his own country. Now round his ship the Achaians and Trojans warred on each other hand to hand, nor far apart did they endure the flights of arrows, nor of darts, but standing hard each by other, with one heart, with sharp axes and hatchets they fought, and with great swords, and double-pointed spears. And many fair brands, dark-scabbarded and hilted, fell to the ground, some from the hands, some from off the shoulders of warring men, and the black earth ran with blood. But Hector, after that once he had seized the ship's stern, left not his hold, keeping the ensign in his hands, and he called to the Trojans: "Bring fire, and all with one voice do ye raise the war-cry; now hath Zeus given us the dearest day of all, — to take the ships that came hither against the will of the gods, and brought many woes upon us, by the cowardice of the elders, who withheld me when I was eager to fight at the sterns of the ships, and kept back the host. But if even then far-seeing Zeus did harm our wits, now he himself doth urge and command us onwards."

So spake he, and they set yet the fiercer on the Argives. And Aias no longer abode their onset, for he was driven back by the darts, but he withdrew a little, — thinking that now he should die, — on to the oarsman's bench of seven feet long, and he left the decks of the trim ship. There then he stood on the watch, and with his spear he ever drave the Trojans from the ships, whosoever brought unwearied fire, and ever he shouted terribly, calling to the Danaans: "O friends, Danaan heroes, men of Ares' company, play the man, my friends, and be mindful of impetuous valour. Do we deem that there be allies at our backs, or some wall stronger than this to ward off death from men? Verily there is not hard by any city arrayed with towers, whereby we might defend ourselves, having a host that could turn the balance of battle. Nay, but we are set down in the plain of the mailèd men of Troy, with our backs against the sea, and far off from our own land. Therefore is safety in battle, and not in slackening from the fight."

So spake he, and rushed on ravening for battle, with his keen spear. And whosoever of the Trojans was coming against the ship with blazing fire, to pleasure Hector at his urging, him would Aias wound, awaiting him with his long spear, and twelve men in front of the ships at close quarters did he wound.

BOOK XVI

How Patroklos fought in the armour of Achilles, and drove the Trojans from the ships, but was slain at last by Hector.

So they were warring round the well-timbered ship, but Patroklos drew near Achilles, shepherd of the host, and he shed warm tears, even as a fountain of dark water that down a steep cliff pours its cloudy stream. And noble swift-footed Achilles when he beheld him was grieved for his sake, and accosted him, and spake winged words, saying: "Wherefore weepest thou, Patroklos, like a fond little maid, that runs by her mother's side, and bids her mother take her up, snatching at her gown, and hinders her in her going, and tearfully looks at her, till the mother takes her up? like her, Patroklos, dost thou let fall soft tears. Hast thou aught to tell to the Myrmidons, or to me myself, or is it some tidings out of Phthia that thou alone hast heard? Or dost thou lament for the sake of the Argives, — how they perish by the hollow ships through their own transgression? Speak out, and hide it not within thy spirit, that we may both know all."

But with a heavy groan didst thou speak unto him, O knight Patroklos: "O Achilles, son of Peleus, far the bravest of the Achaians, be not wroth, seeing that so great calamity has beset the Achaians. For verily all of them that aforetime were the best are lying among the ships, smitten and wounded. Smitten is the son of Tydeus, strong Diomedes, and wounded is Odysseus, spearman renowned, and Agamemnon; and smitten is Eurypylos on the thigh with an arrow. And about them the leeches skilled in medicines are busy, healing their wounds, but thou art hard to reconcile, Achilles. Never then may such wrath take hold of me as that thou nursest; thou brave to the hurting of others.

What other men later born shall have profit of thee, if thou dost not ward off base ruin from the Argives? Pitiless that thou art, the knight Peleus was not then thy father, nor Thetis thy mother, but the grey sea bare thee, and the sheer cliffs, so untoward is thy spirit. But if in thy heart thou art shunning some oracle, and thy lady mother hath told thee somewhat from Zeus, yet me do thou send forth quickly, and make the rest of the host of the Myrmidons follow me, if yet any light may arise from me to the Danaans. And give me thy harness to buckle about my shoulders, if perchance the Trojans may take me for thee, and so abstain from battle, and the warlike sons of the Achaians may take breath, wearied as they be, for brief is the breathing in war. And lightly might we that are fresh drive men wearied with the battle back to the citadel, away from the ships and the huts."

So he spake and besought him, in his unwittingness, for truly it was to be his own evil death and fate that he prayed for. Then to him in great heaviness spake swift-footed Achilles : "Ah me, Patroklos of the seed of Zeus, what word hast thou spoken? Neither take I heed of any oracle that I wot of, nor yet has my lady mother told me somewhat from Zeus, but this dread sorrow comes upon my heart and spirit, from the hour that a man wishes to rob me who am his equal, and to take away my prize, for that he excels me in power. A dread sorrow to me is this, after all the toils that my heart hath endured. The maiden that the sons of the Achaians chose out for me as my prize, and that I won with my spear when I sacked a well-walled city, her has mighty Agamemnon the son of Atreus taken back out of my hands, as though I were but some sojourner dishonourable. But we will let bygones be bygones. No man may be angry of heart for ever, yet verily I said that I would not cease from my wrath, until that time when to mine own ships should come the war-cry and the battle. But do thou on thy shoulders my famous harness, and lead the war-loving Myrmidons to the fight, to ward off destruction from the ships, lest they even burn the ships with blazing fire, and take away our desired return. But when thou hast driven them from the ships, return, and even if the loud-thundering lord of Hera grant thee to win glory, yet long not thou apart from me to fight with the war-loving Trojans; thereby wilt thou minish mine honour. Neither do thou, exulting in war and strife, and slaying the Trojans, lead on toward Ilios, lest one of the eternal gods from Olympus come against thee; right dearly doth Apollo the Far-darter love them. Nay, return back when thou hast brought safety to the ships, and suffer the rest to fight along the plain. For would, O father Zeus, and Athene, and Apollo, would that not one of all the Trojans might escape death, nor one of the Argives, but that we twain might avoid destruction, that alone we might undo the sacred coronal of Troy."

So spake they each to other, but Aias no longer abode the onset, for he was overpowered by darts; the counsel of Zeus was subduing him, and the shafts of the proud Trojans; and his bright helmet, being smitten, kept ringing terribly about his temples: for always it was smitten upon the fair-wrought cheek-pieces. Moreover his left shoulder was wearied, as steadfastly he held up his glittering shield, nor yet could they make him give ground, as they pressed on with their darts around him. And ever he was worn out with difficult breath, and much sweat kept running from all his limbs, nor had he a moment to draw breath, so on all sides was evil heaped on evil.

Tell me now, ye Muses that have mansions in Olympus, how first fire fell on the ships of the Achaians. Hector drew near, and the ashen spear of Aias he smote with his great sword, hard by the socket, behind the point, and shore it clean away, and the son of Telamon brandished in his hand no more than a pointless spear, and far from him the head of bronze fell ringing on the ground.

And Aias knew in his noble heart, and shuddered at the
deeds of the gods, even how Zeus that thundereth on high did
utterly cut off from him avail in war, and desired victory for
the Trojans. Then Aias gave back out of the darts. But the
Trojans cast on the swift ship unwearying fire, and instantly the
inextinguishable flame streamed over her: so the fire begirt
the stern, whereon Achilles smote his thighs, and spake to
Patroklos: "Arise, Patroklos of the seed of Zeus, commander
of the horsemen, for truly I see by the ships the rush of the
consuming fire. Up then, lest they take the ships, and there
be no more retreat; do on thy harness speedily, and I will
summon the host."

So spake he, while Patroklos was harnessing him in shining
bronze. His goodly greaves, fitted with silver clasps, he first
girt round his legs, and next did on around his breast the well-
dight starry corslet of the swift-footed son of Aiakos. And
round his shoulders he cast a sword of bronze, with studs of
silver, and next took the great and mighty shield, and on his
proud head set a well-wrought helm with a horse-hair crest, and
terribly nodded the crest from above. Then seized he two
strong lances that fitted his grasp, only he took not the spear
of the noble son of Aiakos, heavy, and huge, and stalwart, that
none other of the Achaians could wield. And Patroklos bade
Automedon to yoke the horses speedily, even Automedon
whom most he honoured after Achilles, the breaker of the ranks
of men, and whom he held trustiest in battle to abide his call.
And for him Automedon led beneath the yoke the swift horses,
Xanthos and Balios, that fly as swift as the winds, the horses
that the harpy Podarge bare to the West Wind, as she grazed
on the meadow by the stream of Okeanos. And in the side-
traces he put the goodly Pedasos, that Achilles carried away,
when he took the city of Eetion; and being but a mortal steed,
he followed with the immortal horses.

Meanwhile Achilles went and harnessed all the Myrmidons

in the huts with armour, and they gathered like ravening wolves with strength in their hearts unspeakable. And among them all stood warlike Achilles urging on the horses and the targeteers. And he aroused the heart and valour of each of them, and the ranks were yet the closer serried when they heard the prince. And as when a man builds the wall of a high house with close-set stones, to avoid the might of the winds, even so close were arrayed the helmets and bossy shields, and shield pressed on shield, helm on helm, and man on man, and the horse-hair crests on the bright helmet-ridges touched each other when they nodded, so close they stood by each other.

And straightway they poured forth like wasps that have their dwelling by the wayside, and that boys are ever wont to vex, always tormenting them in their nests beside the way in childish sport, and a common evil they make for many. With heart and spirit like theirs the Myrmidons poured out now from the ships, and a cry arose unquenchable, and Patroklos called on his comrades, shouting aloud: "Myrmidons, ye comrades of Achilles son of Peleus, be men, my friends, and be mindful of your impetuous valour, that so we may win honour for the son of Peleus, that is far the bravest of the Argives by the ships, and whose close-fighting squires are the best. And let wide-ruling Agamemnon the son of Atreus learn his own blindness of heart, in that he nothing honoured the best of the Achaians."

So spake he, and aroused each man's heart and courage, and all in a mass they fell on the Trojans, and the ships around echoed wondrously to the cry of the Achaians. But when the Trojans beheld the strong son of Menoitios, himself and his squire, shining in their armour, the heart was stirred in all of them, and the companies wavered, for they deemed that by the ships the swift-footed son of Peleus had cast away his wrath, and chosen reconcilement: then each man glanced round, to see where he might flee sheer destruction.

But Patroklos first with a shining spear cast straight into the press, where most men were thronging, even by the stern of the ship of great-hearted Protesilaos, and he smote Pyraichmes, who led his Paionian horsemen out of Amydon, from the wide water of Axios; him he smote on the right shoulder, and he fell on his back in the dust with a groan, and his comrades around him, the Paionians, were afraid, for Patroklos sent fear among them all, when he slew their leader that was ever the best in fight. Then he drove them out from the ships, and quenched the burning fire. And the half-burnt ship was left there, and the Trojans fled, with a marvellous din, and the Danaans poured in among the hollow ships, and ceaseless was the shouting. And as when from the high crest of a great hill Zeus, the gatherer of the lightning, hath stirred a dense cloud, and forth shine all the peaks, and sharp promontories, and glades, and from heaven the infinite air breaks open, even so the Danaans, having driven the blazing fire from the ships, for a little while took breath, but there was no pause in the battle. For not yet were the Trojans driven in utter rout by the Achaians, dear to Ares, from the black ships, but they still stood up against them, and only perforce gave ground from the ships.

But even as robber wolves fall on the lambs or kids, choosing them out of the herds, when they are scattered on hills by the witlessness of the shepherd, and the wolves behold it, and speedily harry the younglings that have no heart of courage, — even so the Danaans fell on the Trojans, and they were mindful of ill-sounding flight, and forgot their impetuous valour.

But that great Aias ever was fain to cast his spear at Hector of the helm of bronze, but he, in his cunning of war, covered his broad shoulders with his shield of bulls' hide, and watched the hurtling of the arrows, and the noise of spears. And verily well he knew the change in the mastery of war, but even so he abode, and was striving to rescue his trusty comrades.

And as when from Olympus a cloud fares into heaven, from the sacred air, when Zeus spreadeth forth the tempest, even so from the ships came the war-cry and the rout, nor in order due did they cross the ditch again. But his swift-footed horses bare Hector forth with his arms, and he left the host of Troy, whom the delved trench restrained against their will. And in the trench did many swift steeds that draw the car break the fore-part of the pole, and leave the chariots of their masters.

But Patroklos followed after, crying fiercely to the Danaans, and full of evil will against the Trojans, while they with cries and flight filled all the ways, for they were scattered, and on high the storm of dust was scattered below the clouds, and the whole-hooved horses strained back towards the city, away from the ships and the huts.

But even where Patroklos saw the folk thickest in the rout, thither did he guide his horses with a cry, and under his axle-trees men fell prone from their chariots, and the cars were overturned with a din of shattering. But straight over the ditch, in forward flight, leaped the swift horses. And the heart of Patroklos urged him against Hector, for he was eager to smite him, but his swift steeds bore Hector forth and away. And even as beneath a tempest the whole black earth is oppressed, on an autumn day, when Zeus pours forth rain most vehemently, and all the rivers run full, and many a scaur the torrents tear away, and down to the dark sea they rush headlong from the hills, roaring mightily, and minished are the works of men, even so mighty was the roar of the Trojan horses as they ran.

Now Patroklos when he had cloven the nearest companies, drave them backward again to the ships, nor suffered them to approach the city, despite their desire, but between the ships, and the river, and the lofty wall, he rushed on them, and slew them, and avenged many a comrade slain. There first he smote Pronoos with a shining spear, where the shield left bare the breast, and loosened his limbs, and he fell with a crash. Then

Thestor the son of Enops he next assailed, as he sat crouching in the polished chariot, for he was struck distraught, and the reins flew from his hands. Him he drew near, and smote with the lance on the right jaw, and clean pierced through his teeth. And Patroklos caught hold of the spear and dragged him over the rim of the car, as when a man sits on a jutting rock, and drags a sacred fish forth from the sea, with line and glittering hook of bronze; so on the bright spear dragged he Thestor gaping from the chariot, and cast him down on his face and life left him as he fell. Next, as Euryalos came on, he smote him on the midst of the head with a stone, and all his head was shattered within the strong helmet, and prone on the earth he fell, and death that slayeth the spirit overwhelmed him. Next Erymas, and Amphoteros, and Epaltes and Tlepolemos son of Damastor, and Echios and Pyris, and Ipheus and Euippos, and Polymelos son of Argeas, all these in turn he brought low to the bounteous earth. But when Sarpedon beheld his comrades with ungirdled doublets, subdued beneath the hands of Patroklos son of Menoitios, he cried aloud, upbraiding the godlike Lykians: "Shame, ye Lykians, whither do ye flee? Now be ye strong, for I will encounter this man that I may know who he is that conquers here, and verily many evils hath he wrought the Trojans, in that he hath loosened the knees of many men and noble."

So spake he, and leaped with his arms from the chariot to the ground. But Patroklos, on the other side, when he beheld him leaped from his chariot. And they, like vultures of crooked talons and curved beaks, that war with loud yells on some high cliff, even so they rushed with cries against each other. And beholding then the son of Kronos of the crooked counsels took pity on them, and he spake to Hera, his sister and wife: "Ah woe is me for that it is fated that Sarpedon, the best-beloved of men to me, shall be subdued under Patroklos son of Menoitios. And in two ways my heart within my breast is divided, as I ponder whether I should catch him up alive out of the tearful war, and set him down in the rich land of Lykia, or whether I should now subdue him beneath the hands of the son of Menoitios."

Then the ox-eyed lady Hera made answer to him: "Most dread son of Kronos, what word is this thou hast spoken? A mortal man long doomed to fate dost thou desire to deliver again from death of evil name? Work thy will, but all we other gods will in no wise praise thee. And another thing I will tell thee, and do thou lay it up in thy heart; if thou dost send Sarpedon living to his own house, consider lest thereon some other god likewise desire to send his own dear son away out of the strong battle. For round the great citadel of Priam war many sons of the Immortals, and among the Immortals wilt thou send terrible wrath. But if he be dear to thee, and thy heart mourns for him, truly then suffer him to be subdued in the strong battle beneath the hands of Patroklos son of Menoitios, but when his soul and life leave that warrior, send Death and sweet Sleep to bear him, even till they come to the land of wide Lykia, there will his kindred and friends bury him, with a barrow and a pillar, for this is the due of the dead."

So spake she, nor did the father of gods and men disregard her. But he shed bloody raindrops on the earth, honouring his dear son, that Patroklos was about to slay in the deep-soiled land of Troia, far off from his own country. Now when they were come near each other in onset, there verily did Patroklos smite the renowned Thrasymelos, the good squire of the prince Sarpedon, on the lower part of the belly, and loosened his limbs. But Sarpedon missed him with his shining javelin, as he in turn rushed on, but wounded the horse Pedasos on the right shoulder with the spear, and he shrieked as he breathed his life away, and fell crying in the dust, and his spirit fled from him. But the other twain reared this way and that, and the yoke creaked, and the reins were confused on them, when their trace-horse lay in the dust. But thereof did Automedon, the spearman renowned, find a remedy, and drawing his long-edged sword from his stout thigh, he leaped forth, and cut adrift the horse, with no delay, and the pair righted themselves, and strained in the reins, and they met again in life-devouring war.

Then again Sarpedon missed with his shining dart, and the point of the spear flew over the left shoulder of Patroklos and smote him not, but he in turn arose with the bronze, and his javelin flew not vainly from his hand, but struck Sarpedon even where the midriff clasps the beating heart. And he fell as falls an oak, or a silver poplar, or a slim pine tree, that on the hills the shipwrights fell with whetted axes, to be timber for ship-building; even so before the horses and chariot he lay at length, moaning aloud, and clutching at the bloody dust. And as when a lion hath fallen on a herd, and slain a bull, tawny and high of heart, among the kine of trailing gait, and he perishes groaning beneath the claws of the lion, even so under Patroklos did the leader of the Lykian shieldmen rage, even in death, and he called to his dear comrade: "Dear Glaukos, warrior among warlike men, now most doth it behove thee to be a spearman, and a hardy fighter: now let baneful war be dear to thee, if indeed thou art a man of might. First fare all about and urge on the heroes that be leaders of the Lykians, to fight for Sarpedon, and thereafter thyself do battle for me with the sword. For to thee even in time to come shall I be shame and disgrace for ever, all thy days, if the Achaians strip me of mine armour, fallen in the gathering of the ships. Nay, hold out manfully, and spur on all the host."

Even as he spake thus, the end of death veiled over his eyes and his nostrils, but Patroklos, setting foot on his breast drew the spear out of his flesh, and the midriff followed with the spear, so that he drew forth together the spear point, and the soul of Sarpedon; and the Myrmidons held there his panting steeds, eager to fly afar, since the chariot was reft of its lords.

Then dread sorrow came on Glaukos, when he heard the voice of Sarpedon, and his heart was stirred, that he availed not to succour him. And with his hand he caught and held his arm, for the wound galled him, the wound of the arrow wherewith, as he pressed on towards the lofty wall, Teukros had smitten him, warding off destruction from his fellows Then in prayer spake Glaukos to far-darting Apollo: "Hear, O Prince that art somewhere in the rich land of Lykia, or in Troia, for thou canst listen everywhere to the man that is in need, as even now need cometh upon me. For I have this stark wound, and mine arm is thoroughly pierced with sharp pains, nor can my blood be stanched, and by the wound is my shoulder burdened, and I cannot hold my spear firm, nor go and fight against the enemy. And the best of men has perished, Sarpedon, the son of Zeus, and he succours not even his own child. But do thou, O Prince, heal me this stark wound, and lull my pains, and give me strength, that I may call on my Lykian kinsmen, and spur them to the war, and myself may fight about the dead man fallen."

So spake he in his prayer, and Phoebus Apollo heard him. Straightway he made his pains to cease, and in the grievous wound stanched the black blood, and put courage into his heart. And Glaukos knew it within him, and was glad, for that the great god speedily heard his prayer. First went he all about and urged on them that were leaders of the Lykians to fight around Sarpedon, and thereafter he went with long strides among the Trojans, to Polydamas son of Panthoös and noble Agenor, and he went after Aineias, and Hector of the helm of bronze, and standing by them spake winged words: "Hector, now surely art thou utterly forgetful of the allies, that for thy sake, far from their friends and their own country, breathe their lives away! but thou carest not to aid them!

Sarpedon lies low, the leader of the Lykian shieldmen, he that defended Lykia by his dooms and his might, yea him hath mailed Ares subdued beneath the spear of Patroklos. But, friends, stand by him, and be angry in your hearts lest the Myrmidons strip him of his harness, and dishonour the dead, in wrath for the sake of the Danaans, even them that perished, whom we slew with spears by the swift ships."

So spake he, and sorrow seized the Trojans utterly, ungovernable and not to be borne; for Sarpedon was ever the stay of their city, all a stranger as he was, for many people followed with him, and himself the best warrior of them all. Then they made straight for the Danaans eagerly, and Hector led them, being wroth for Sarpedon's sake. But the fierce heart of Patroklos son of Menoitios urged on the Achaians. And he spake first to the twain Aiantes that themselves were right eager: "Aiantes, now let defence be your desire, and be such as afore ye were among men, or even braver yet. That man lies low who first leaped on to the wall of the Achaians, even Sarpedon. Nay, let us strive to take him, and work his body shame, and strip the harness from his shoulders, and many a one of his comrades fighting for his sake let us subdue with the pitiless bronze."

So spake he, and they themselves were eager in defence. So on both sides they strengthened the companies, Trojans and Lykians, Myrmidons and Achaians, and they joined battle to fight around the dead man fallen; terribly they shouted, and loud rang the harness of men. And as the din ariseth of woodcutters in the glades of a mountain, and the sound thereof is heard far away, so rose the din of them from the wide-wayed earth, the noise of bronze and of well-tanned bulls' hides smitten with swords and double-pointed spears. And now not even a clear-sighted man could any longer have known noble Sarpedon, for with darts and blood and dust was he covered wholly from head to foot. And ever men thronged about the dead, as in a steading flies buzz around the full milk-pails, in the season of spring, when the milk drenches the bowls, even so thronged they about the dead. Nor ever did Zeus turn from the strong fight his shining eyes, but ever looked down on them, and much in his heart he debated of the slaying of Patroklos, whether there and then above divine Sarpedon glorious Hector should slay him likewise in strong battle with the sword, and strip his harness from his shoulders, or whether to more men yet he should deal sheer labour of war. And thus to him as he pondered it seemed the better way, that the gallant squire of Achilles, Peleus' son, should straightway drive the Trojans and Hector of the helm of bronze towards the city, and should rob many of their life. And in Hector first he put a weakling heart, and leaping into his car Hector turned in flight, and cried on the rest of the Trojans to flee, for he knew the turning of the sacred scales of Zeus. Thereon neither did the strong Lykians abide, but fled all in fear, when they beheld their king stricken to the heart, lying in the company of the dead, for many had fallen above him, when Kronion made fierce the fight. Then the others stripped from the shoulders of Sarpedon his shining arms of bronze, and these the strong son of Menoitios gave to his comrades to bear to the hollow ships. Then Zeus that gathereth the clouds spake to Apollo: "Prithee, dear Phoebus, go take Sarpedon out of range of darts, and cleanse the black blood from him, and thereafter bear him far away, and bathe him in the streams of the river, and anoint him with ambrosia, and clothe him in garments that wax not old, and send him to be wafted by fleet convoy, by the twin brethren Sleep and Death, that quickly will set him in the rich land of wide Lykia. There will his kinsmen and clansmen give him burial, with barrow and pillar, for such is the due of the dead."

So spake he, nor was Apollo disobedient to his father. He went down the hills of Ida to the dread battle din, and straightway bore goodly Sarpedon out of the darts, and carried him far away, and bathed him in the streams of the river, and anointed him with ambrosia, and clad him in garments that wax not old, and sent him to be wafted by fleet convoy, the twin brethren Sleep and Death, that swiftly set him down in the rich land of wide Lykia. But Patroklos cried to his horses and Automedon, and after the Trojans and Lykians went he, and so was blindly forgetful, in his witlessness, for if he had kept the saying of the son of Peleus, verily he should have escaped the evil fate of black death. But ever is the wit of Zeus stronger than the wit of men, so now he roused the spirit of Patroklos in his breast. There whom first, whom last didst thou slay, Patroklos, when the gods called thee deathward? Adrestos first, and Autonoos, and Echeklos, and Perimos, son of Megas, and Epistor, and Melanippos, and thereafter Elasos, and Moulios, and Pylartes; these he slew, but the others were each man of them fain of flight. Then would the sons of the Achaians have taken high-gated Troy, by the hands of Patroklos, for around and before him he raged with the spear, but that Phoebus Apollo stood on the well-built wall, with baneful thoughts towards Patroklos, and succouring the Trojans. Thrice clomb Patroklos on the corner of the lofty wall, and thrice did Apollo force him back and smote the shining shield with his immortal hands. But when for the fourth time he came on like a god, then cried far-darting Apollo terribly, and spake winged words: "Give back, Patroklos of the seed of Zeus! Not beneath thy spear is it fated that the city of the valiant Trojans shall fall, nay nor beneath Achilles, a man far better than thou."

So spake he, and Patroklos retreated far back, avoiding the wrath of far-darting Apollo. But Hector within the Skaian gates was restraining his whole-hooved horses, pondering whether he should drive again into the din and fight, or should call unto the host to gather to the wall. While thus he was thinking, Phoebus Apollo stood by him in the guise of a young

P

man and a strong, Asios, who was the mother's brother of horse-taming Hector, being own brother of Hekabe, and son of Dymas, who dwelt in Phrygia, on the streams of Sangarios. In his guise spake Apollo, son of Zeus, to Hector: "Hector, wherefore dost thou cease from fight? It doth not behove thee. Would that I were as much stronger than thou as I am weaker, thereon quickly shouldst thou stand aloof from war to thy hurt. But come, turn against Patroklos thy strong-hooved horses, if perchance thou mayst slay him, and Apollo give thee glory."

So spake the god, and went back again into the moil of men. But renowned Hector bade wise-hearted Kebriones to lash his horses into the war. Then Apollo went and passed into the press, and sent a dread panic among the Argives, but to the Trojans and Hector gave he renown. And Hector let the other Argives be, and slew none of them, but against Patroklos he turned his strong-hooved horses, and Patroklos on the other side leaped from his chariot to the ground, with a spear in his left hand, and in his other hand grasped a shining jagged stone, that his hand covered. Firmly he planted himself and hurled it, nor long did he shrink from his foe, nor was his cast in vain, but he struck Kebriones the charioteer of Hector, the bastard son of renowned Priam, on the brow with the sharp stone, as he held the reins of the horses. Both his brows the stone drave together, and his bone held not, but his eyes fell to the ground in the dust, there, in front of his feet. Then he, like a diver, fell from the well-wrought car, and his spirit left his bones. Then taunting him didst thou address him, knightly Patroklos: "Out on it, how nimble a man, how lightly he diveth! Yea, if perchance he were on the teeming deep, this man would satisfy many by seeking for oysters, leaping from the ship, even if it were stormy weather, so lightly now he diveth from the chariot into the plain. Verily among the Trojans too there be diving men."

So speaking he set on the hero Kebriones with the rush of a

lion, that while wasting the cattle-pens is smitten in the breast, and his own valour is his bane, even so against Kebriones, Patroklos, didst thou leap furiously. But Hector, on the other side, leaped from his chariot to the ground. And these twain strove for Kebriones like lions, that on the mountain peaks fight, both hungering, both high of heart, for a slain hind. Even so for Kebriones' sake these two masters of the war-cry, Patroklos son of Menoitios, and renowned Hector, were eager each to hew the other's flesh with the ruthless bronze.

Hector then seized him by the head, and slackened not hold, while Patroklos on the other side grasped him by the foot, and thereon the others, Trojans and Danaans, joined strong battle. And as the East wind and the South contend with one another in shaking a deep wood in the dells of a mountain, shaking beech, and ash, and smooth-barked cornel tree, that clash against each other their long boughs with marvellous din, and a noise of branches broken, so the Trojans and Achaians were leaping on each other and slaying, nor had either side any thought of ruinous flight. And many sharp darts were fixed around Kebriones, and winged arrows leaping from the bow-string, and many mighty stones smote the shields of them that fought around him. But he in the whirl of dust lay mighty and mightily fallen, forgetful of his chivalry.

Now while the sun was going about mid-heaven, so long the darts smote either side, and the host fell, but when the sun turned to the time of the loosing of oxen, lo, then beyond their doom the Achaians proved the better. The hero Kebriones drew they forth from the darts, out of the tumult of the Trojans, and stripped the harness from his shoulders, and with ill design against the Trojans, Patroklos rushed upon them. Three times then rushed he on, peer of swift Ares, shouting terribly, and thrice he slew nine men. But when the fourth time he sped on like a god, thereon to thee, Patroklos, did the end of life appear, for Phoebus met thee in the strong battle, in dreadful wise

And Patroklos was not ware of him coming through the press, for hidden in thick mist did he meet him, and stood behind him, and smote his back and broad shoulders with a down-stroke of his hand, and his eyes were dazed. And from his head Phoebus Apollo smote the helmet that rolled rattling away with a din beneath the hooves of the horses, the helm with upright socket, and the crests were defiled with blood and dust. And all the long-shadowed spear was shattered in the hands of Patroklos, the spear great and heavy and strong, and sharp, while from his shoulders the tasselled shield with the baldric fell to the ground.

And the prince Apollo, son of Zeus, loosed his corslet, and blindness seized his heart and his shining limbs were unstrung, and he stood in amaze, and at close quarters from behind a Dardanian smote him on the back, between the shoulders, with a sharp spear, even Euphorbos, son of Panthoös, who excelled them of his age in casting the spear, and in horsemanship, and in speed of foot. Even thus, verily, had he cast down twenty men from their chariots, though then first had he come with his car to learn the lesson of war. He it was that first smote a dart into thee, knightly Patroklos, nor overcame thee, but ran back again and mingled with the throng, first drawing forth from the flesh his ashen spear, nor did he abide the onset of Patroklos, unarmed as he was, in the strife. But Patroklos, being overcome by the stroke of the god, and by the spear, gave ground, and retreated to the host of his comrades, avoiding Fate. But Hector, when he beheld great-hearted Patroklos give ground, being smitten with the keen bronze, came nigh unto him through the ranks, and wounded him with a spear, in the lowermost part of the belly, and drave the bronze clean through. And he fell with a crash, and sorely grieved the host of Achaians. And as when a lion hath overcome in battle an untiring boar, they twain fighting with high heart on the crests of a hill, about a little well, and both are desirous to drink, and the lion hath by force overcome the boar that draweth difficult breath; so after that he had slain many did Hector son of Priam take the life away from the strong son of Menoitios, smiting him at close quarters with the spear; and boasting over him he spake winged words: "Patroklos, surely thou saidst that thou wouldst sack my town, and from Trojan women take away the day of freedom, and bring them in ships to thine own dear country: fool! nay, in front of these were the swift horses of Hector straining their speed for the fight; and myself in wielding the spear excel among the war-loving Trojans, even I who ward from them the day of destiny: but thee shall vultures here devour. Ah, wretch, surely Achilles for all his valour, availed thee not, who straitly charged thee as thou camest, he abiding there, saying, 'Come not to me, Patroklos lord of steeds, to the hollow ships, till thou hast torn the gory doublet of man-slaying Hector about his breast;' so, surely, he spake to thee, and persuaded the wits of thee in thy witlessness."

Then faintly didst thou answer him, knightly Patroklos: "Boast greatly, as now, Hector, for to thee have Zeus, son of Kronos, and Apollo given the victory, who lightly have subdued me; for themselves stripped my harness from my shoulders. But if twenty such as thou had encountered me, here had they all perished, subdued beneath my spear. But me have ruinous Fate and the son of Leto slain, and of men Euphorbos, but thou art the third in my slaying. But another thing will I tell thee, and do thou lay it up in thy heart; verily thou thyself art not long to live, but already doth Death stand hard by thee, and strong Fate, that thou art to be subdued by the hands of noble Achilles, of the seed of Aiakos."

Even as so he spake the end of death overshadowed him. And his soul, fleeting from his limbs, went down to the house of Hades, wailing its own doom, leaving manhood and youth.

Then renowned Hector spake to him even in his death:

"Patroklos, wherefore to me dost thou prophesy sheer destruction? who knows but that Achilles, the child of fair-tressed Thetis, will first be smitten by my spear, and lose his life?"

So spake he, and drew the spear of bronze from the wound, setting his foot on the dead, and cast him off on his back from the spear. And straightway with the spear he went after Automedon, the godlike squire of the swift-footed Aiakides, for he was eager to smite him; but his swift-footed immortal horses bare him out of the battle, horses that the gods gave to Peleus, a splendid gift.

BOOK XVII

Of the battle around the body of Patroklos.

But Atreus' son, Menelaos dear to Ares, was not unaware of the slaying of Patroklos by the Trojans in the fray. He went up through the front of the fight harnessed in flashing bronze, and strode over the body as above a first-born calf standeth lowing its mother. Thus above Patroklos strode fair-haired Menelaos, and before him held his spear and the circle of his shield, eager to slay whoever should encounter him. Then was Panthoös' son of the stout ashen spear not heedless of noble Patroklos as he lay, and he smote on the circle of the shield of Menelaos, but the bronze spear brake it not, but the point was bent back in the stubborn shield. And Menelaos Atreus' son in his turn made at him with his bronze spear, having prayed unto father Zeus, and as he gave back pierced the nether part of his throat, and threw his weight into the stroke, following his heavy hand; and sheer through the tender neck went the point of the spear. And he fell with a crash, and his armour rang upon him. In blood was his hair drenched that was like unto the hair of the Graces, and his tresses closely knit with bands of silver and gold.

Then easily would the son of Atreus have borne off the noble spoils of Panthoös' son, had not Phoebus Apollo grudged it to him, and aroused against him Hector peer of swift Ares, putting on the semblance of a man, of Mentes chief of the Kikones. And he spake aloud to him winged words : " Hector, now art thou hasting after things unattainable, even the horses of wise Aiakides ; for hard are they to be tamed or driven by mortal man, save only Achilles whom an immortal mother bare. Meanwhile hath warlike Menelaos Atreus' son stridden over Patroklos and slain the best of the Trojans there, even Panthoös' son Euphorbos, and hath stayed him in his impetuous might."

Thus saying the god went back into the strife of men, but dire grief darkened Hector's inmost soul, and then he gazed searchingly along the lines, and straightway was aware of the one man stripping off the noble arms, and the other lying on the earth ; and blood was flowing about the gaping wound. Then he went through the front of the fight harnessed in flashing bronze, crying a shrill cry, like unto Hephaistos' flame unquenchable. Not deaf to his shrill cry was Atreus' son, and sore troubled he spake to his great heart : " Ay me, if I shall leave behind me these goodly arms, and Patroklos who here lieth for my vengeance' sake, I fear lest some Danaan beholding it be wroth against me. But if for honour's sake I do battle alone with Hector and the Trojans, I fear lest they come about me many against one ; for all the Trojans is bright-helmed Hector leading hither. But if I might somewhere find Aias of the loud war-cry, then both together would we go and be mindful of battle even were it against the power of heaven, if haply we might save his dead for Achilles Peleus' son : that were best among these ills."

While thus he communed with his mind and heart, therewithal the Trojan ranks came onward, and Hector at their head

Then Menelaos gave backward, and left the dead man, turning himself ever about like a deep-maned lion which men and dogs chase from a fold with spears and cries; and his strong heart within him groweth chill, and loth goeth he from the steading; so from Patroklos went fair-haired Menelaos, and turned and stood, when he came to the host of his comrades, searching for mighty Aias Telamon's son. Him very speedily he espied on the left of the whole battle, cheering his comrades and rousing them to fight, for great terror had Phoebus Apollo sent on them; and he hasted him to run, and straightway stood by him and said: "This way, beloved Aias; let us bestir us for the dead Patroklos, if haply his naked corpse at least we may carry to Achilles, though his armour is held by Hector of the glancing helm."

Thus spake he, and aroused the heart of wise Aias. And he went up through the front of the fight, and with him fair-haired Menelaos. Now Hector, when he had stripped from Patroklos his noble armour, was dragging him thence that he might cut off the head from the shoulders with the keen bronze and carry his body to give to the dogs of Troy. But Aias came anigh, and the shield that he bare was as a tower; then Hector gave back into the company of his comrades, and sprang into his chariot; and the goodly armour he gave to the Trojans to carry to the city, to be great glory unto him. But Aias spread his broad shield over the son of Menoitios and stood as it were a lion before his whelps when huntsmen in a forest encounter him as he leadeth his young. And by his side stood Atreus' son, Menelaos dear to Ares, nursing great sorrow in his breast.

Then Hector called on the Trojans with a mighty shout: "Trojans and Lykians and Dardanians that fight hand to hand, be men, my friends, and bethink you of impetuous valour, until I do on me the goodly arms of noble Achilles that I stripped from brave Patroklos when I slew him."

Thus having spoken went Hector of the glancing helm forth

out of the strife of war, and ran and speedily with fleet feet
following overtook his comrades, not yet far off, who were
bearing to the city Peleides' glorious arms. And standing
apart from the dolorous battle he changed his armour; his own
he gave the warlike Trojans to carry to sacred Ilios, and he put
on the divine arms of Achilles, Peleus' son.

But when Zeus that gathereth the clouds beheld from afar
off Hector arming him in the armour of Peleus' godlike son, he
shook his head and spake thus unto his soul: "Ah, hapless
man, no thought is in thy heart of death that yet draweth nigh
unto thee; thou doest on thee the divine armour of a peerless
man before whom the rest have terror. His comrade, gentle
and brave, thou hast slain, and unmeetly hast stripped the
armour from his head and shoulders; yet now for a while at
least I will give into thy hands great might, in recompense
for this, even that nowise shalt thou come home out of the
battle, for Andromache to receive from thee Peleides' glorious
arms."

Thus spake the son of Kronos, and bowed his dark brows
therewithal.

But the armour fitted itself unto Hector's body, and Ares the
dread war-god entered into him, and his limbs were filled within
with valour and strength. Then he sped among the noble
allies with a mighty cry, and in the flashing of his armour he
seemed to all of them like unto Peleus' great-hearted son. And
he came to each and encouraged him with his words—
Mesthles and Glaukos and Medon and Thersilochos and Asteropaios and Deisenor and Hippothoös and Phorkys and Chromios
and the augur Ennomos—these encouraged he and spake to them
winged words: "Listen, ye countless tribes of allies that dwell
round about. It was not for mere numbers that I sought or
longed when I gathered each of you from your cities, but that
ye might zealously guard the Trojans' wives and infant little
ones from the war-loving Achaians. For this end am I weary

ing my people by taking gifts and food from them, and nursing thereby the courage of each of you. Now therefore let all turn straight against the foe and live or die, for such is the dalliance of war. And whoso shall drag Patroklos, dead though he be, among the horse-taming men of Troy, and make Aias yield, to him will I award half the spoils and keep half myself; so shall his glory be great as mine."

Thus spake he, and they against the Danaans charged with all their weight, levelling their spears, and their hearts were high of hope to drag the corpse from under Aias, Telamon's son. Fond men! from full many reft he life over that corpse. And then spake Aias to Menelaos of the loud warcry: "Dear Menelaos, fosterling of Zeus, no longer count I that we two of ourselves shall return home out of the war. Nor have I so much dread for the corpse of Patroklos, that shall soon glut the dogs and birds of the men of Troy, as for thy head and mine lest some evil fall thereon, for all is shrouded by a storm-cloud of war, even by Hector, and sheer doom stareth in our face. But come, call thou to the best men of the Danaans, if haply any hear."

Thus spake he, and Menelaos of the loud war-cry disregarded him not, but shouted unto the Danaans, crying a far-heard cry: "O friends, ye leaders and counsellors of the Argives, who by the side of the sons of Atreus, Agamemnon and Menelaos, drink at the common cost and are all commanders of the host, on whom wait glory and honour from Zeus, hard is it for me to distinguish each chief amid the press — such blaze is there of the strife of war. But let each go forward of himself and be wroth at heart that Patroklos should become a sport among the dogs of Troy."

Thus spake he, and Oïleus' son fleet Aias heard him clearly, and was first to run along the mellay to meet him, and after him Idomeneus, and Idomeneus' brother-in-arms, Meriones, peer of the man-slaying war-god. And who shall of his own thought tell the names of the rest, even of all that after these aroused the battle of the Achaians?

Now the Trojans charged forward in close array, and Hector led them. And as when at the mouth of some heaven-born river a mighty wave roareth against the stream, and arouseth the high cliffs' echo as the salt sea belloweth on the beach, so loud was the cry wherewith the Trojans came. But the Achaians stood firm around Menoitios' son with one soul all, walled in with shields of bronze. And over their bright helmets the son of Kronos shed thick darkness, for in the former time was Menoitios' son not unloved of him, while he was yet alive and squire of Aiakides. So was Zeus loth that he should become a prey of the dogs of his enemies at Troy, and stirred his comrades to do battle for him.

Now first the Trojans thrust back the glancing-eyed Achaians, who shrank before them and left the dead, yet the proud Trojans slew not any of them with spears, though they were fain, but set to hale the corpse. But little while would the Achaians hold back therefrom, for very swiftly Aias rallied them, Aias the first in presence and in deeds of all the Danaans after the noble son of Peleus. Right through the fighters in the forefront rushed he like a wild boar in his might that in the mountains when he turneth at bay scattereth lightly dogs and lusty young men through the glades. Thus did proud Telamon's son the glorious Aias press on the Trojan battalions and lightly scatter them, as they had bestrode Patroklos and were full fain to drag him to their city and win renown.

Then would the Trojans in their turn in their weakness overcome have been driven back into Ilios by the Achaians dear to Ares, and the Argives would have won glory even against the appointment of Zeus by their power and might. But Apollo himself aroused Aineias, putting on the semblance of Periphas the herald, the son of Epytos, who grew old with his old father in his heraldship, of friendly thought toward

Aineias. In his similitude spake Apollo, son of Zeus: "Aineias, how could ye ever guard high Ilios if it were against the will of God? Other men have I seen that trust in their own might and power and valour, and in their host, even though they have scant folk to lead. But here, albeit Zeus is fainer far to give victory to us than to the Danaans, yet ye are dismayed exceedingly and fight not."

Thus spake he, and Aineias knew far-darting Apollo when he looked upon his face, and spake unto Hector, shouting loud: "Hector and ye other leaders of the Trojans and their allies, shame were this if in our weakness overcome we were driven back into Ilios by the Achaians dear to Ares. Nay, thus saith a god, who standeth by my side: Zeus, highest Orderer, is our helper in this fight. Therefore let us go right onward against the Danaans. Not easily at least let them take the dead Patroklos to the ships."

Thus spake he, and leapt forth far before the fighters in the front. And the Trojans rallied and stood up against the Achaians. Thus strove they as it had been fire, nor wouldst thou have thought there was still sun or moon, for over all the battle where the chiefs stood around the slain son of Menoitios they were shrouded in darkness, while the other Trojans and well-greaved Achaians fought at ease in the clear air, and piercing sunlight was spread over them, and on all the earth and hills there was no cloud seen; and they ceased fighting now and again, avoiding each other's dolorous darts and standing far apart. But they who were in the midst endured affliction of the darkness and the battle, and all the best men of them were wearied by the pitiless weight of their bronze arms.

Thus all day long waxed the mighty fray of their sore strife, and unabatingly ever with the sweat of toil were the knees and legs and feet of each man and arms and eyes bedewed as the two hosts did battle around the brave squire of fleet Aiakides. And as when a man giveth the hide of a great bull to his folk to stretch, all soaked in fat, and they take and stretch it standing in a circle, and straightway the moisture thereof departeth and the fat entereth in under the haling of many hands, and it is all stretched throughout, — thus they on both sides haled the dead man this way and that in narrow space, for their hearts were high of hope, the Trojans that they should drag him to Ilios and the Achaians to the hollow ships; and around him the fray waxed wild, nor might Ares rouser of hosts nor Athene despise the sight thereof, albeit their anger were exceeding great.

Such was the grievous travail of men and horses over Patroklos that Zeus on that day wrought. But not as yet knew noble Achilles aught of Patroklos' death, for far away from the swift ships they were fighting beneath the wall of the men of Troy. Therefore never deemed he in his heart that he was dead, but that he should come back alive, after that he had touched the gates; for neither that other thought had he anywise, that Patroklos should sack the stronghold without his aid.

Now the rest continually around the dead man with their keen spears made onset relentlessly and slew each the other. And thus would one speak among the mail-clad Achaians: "Friends, it were verily not glorious for us to go back to the hollow ships; rather let the black earth yawn for us all beneath our feet. Far better were that straightway for us if we suffer the horse-taming Trojans to hale this man to their city and win renown."

And thus on the other side would one of the great-hearted Trojans say: "Friends, though it were our fate that all together we be slain beside this man, let none yet give backward from the fray."

Thus would one speak, and rouse the spirit of each. So they fought on, and the iron din went up through the high desert air unto the brazen heaven. But the horses of Aiakides that were apart from the battle were weeping, since first they were aware that their charioteer was fallen in the dust beneath the hand of man-slaying Hector. Verily Automedon, Diores' valiant son, plied them oft with blows of the swift lash, and oft with gentle words he spake to them and oft with chiding, yet would they neither go back to the ships at the broad Hellespont nor yet to the battle after the Achaians, but as a pillar abideth firm that standeth on the tomb of a man or woman dead, so abode they immovably with the beautiful chariot, abasing their heads unto the earth. And hot tears flowed from their eyes to the ground as they mourned in sorrow for their charioteer, and their rich manes were soiled as they drooped from beneath the yoke-cushion on both sides beside the yoke. And when the son of Kronos beheld them mourning he had compassion on them, and shook his head and spake to his own heart: "Ah, hapless pair, why gave we you to king Peleus, a mortal man, while ye are deathless and ever young? Was it that ye should suffer sorrows among ill-fated men? For methinketh there is nothing more piteous than a man among all things that breathe and creep upon the earth. But verily Hector Priam's son shall not drive you and your deftly-wrought car; that will I not suffer. Is it a small thing that he holdeth the armour and vaunteth himself vainly thereupon? Nay, I will put courage into your knees and heart that ye may bring Automedon also safe out of the war to the hollow ships. For yet further will I increase victory to the men of Troy, so that they slay until they come unto the well-timbered ships, and the sun set and divine night come down."

Thus saying he breathed good courage into the horses. And they shook to earth the dust from their manes, and lightly bare the swift car amid Trojans and Achaians. And behind them fought Automedon, albeit in grief for his comrade, swooping with his chariot as a vulture on wild geese; for lightly he would flee out of the onset of the Trojans and lightly charge, pursuing them through the thick mellay. Yet could he not slay any man as he hasted to pursue them, for it was impossible that being alone in his sacred car he should at once assail them with the spear and hold his fleet horses. Then at last espied him a comrade, even Alkimedon son of Laerkes, son of Haimon, and he halted behind the car and spake unto Automedon: "Automedon, what god hath put into thy breast unprofitable counsel and taken from thee wisdom, that thus alone thou art fighting against the Trojans in the forefront of the press? Thy comrade even now was slain, and Hector goeth proudly, wearing on his own shoulders the armour of Aiakides."

And Automedon son of Diores answered him, saying: "Alkimedon, what other Achaian hath like skill to guide the spirit of immortal steeds, save only Patroklos, peer of gods in counsel, while he yet lived? but now have death and fate overtaken him. But take thou the lash and shining reins, and I will get me down from my horses, that I may fight."

Thus spake he, and Alkimedon leapt on the fleet war-chariot and swiftly took the lash and reins in his hands, and Automedon leapt down. And noble Hector espied them, and straightway spake unto Aineias as he stood near: "Aineias, counsellor of mail-clad Trojans, I espy here the two horses of fleet Aiakides come forth to battle with feeble charioteers. Therefore might I hope to take them if thou in thy heart art willing, since they would not abide our onset and stand to do battle against us."

Thus spake he, and the brave son of Anchises disregarded him not. And they twain went right onward, their shoulders shielded by ox-hides dried and tough, and bronze thick overlaid. And with them went both Chromios and godlike Aretos, and their hearts were of high hope to slay the men and drive off the strong-necked horses — fond hope, for not without blood lost were they to get them back from Automedon. He praying to father Zeus was filled in his inmost heart with valour and strength. And straightway he spake to Alkimedon, his faithful comrade: "Alkimedon, hold the horses not far from me, but with their very breath upon my back; for I deem that Hector the son of Priam will not refrain him from his fury until he mount behind Achilles' horses of goodly manes after slaying us twain, and dismay the ranks of Argive men, or else himself fall among the foremost."

Thus said he, and called upon the Aiantes and Menelaos: "Aiantes, leaders of the Argives, and Menelaos, lo now, commit ye the corpse unto whoso may best avail to bestride it and resist the ranks of men, and come ye to ward the day of doom from us who are yet alive, for here in the dolorous war are Hector and Aineias, the best men of the Trojans, pressing hard. Yet verily these issues lie in the lap of the gods: I too will cast my spear, and the rest shall Zeus decide."

He said, and poised his far-shadowing spear and hurled it, and smote on the circle of the shield of Aretos, and the shield sustained not the spear, but right through went the bronze, and he forced it into his belly low down through his belt. And as when a strong man with a sharp axe smiting behind the horns of an ox of the homestead cleaveth the sinew asunder, and the ox leapeth forward and falleth, so leapt Aretos forward and fell on his back; and the spear in his entrails very piercingly quivering unstrung his limbs. And Hector hurled at Automedon with his bright spear, but he looked steadfastly on the bronze javelin as it came at him and avoided it, for he stooped forward, and the long spear fixed itself in the ground behind, and the javelin-butt quivered, and there dread Ares took away its force. And then had they lashed at each other with their swords hand to hand, had not the Aiantes parted them in their fury, when they were come through the mellay at their comrades' call. Before them Hector and Aineias and godlike Chromios shrank backward and gave ground and left Aretos wounded to the death as he lay. And Automedon, peer of swift Ares, stripped off the armour of the dead, and spake exultingly: "Verily, I have a little eased my heart of grief for the death of Menoitios' son, albeit a worse man than him have I slain."

Thus saying he took up the gory spoils and set them in his car, and gat him thereon, with feet and hands all bloody, as a lion that hath devoured a bull.

Now great-hearted Aias and Menelaos were aware of Zeus how he gave the Trojans their turn to victory. First of these to speak was great Aias son of Telamon: "Ay me, now may any man, even though he be a very fool, know that father Zeus himself is helping the Trojans. Come, let us ourselves devise some excellent means, that we may both hale the corpse away and ourselves return home to the joy of our friends, who grieve as they look hitherward and deem that no longer shall the fury of man-slaying Hector's unapproachable hand refrain itself, but fall upon the black ships. And would there were some comrade to carry tidings with all speed unto the son of Peleus, since I deem that he hath not even heard the grievous tidings, how his dear comrade is slain. But nowhere can I behold such an one among the Achaians, for themselves and their horses likewise are wrapped in darkness. O father Zeus, deliver thou the sons of the Achaians from the darkness, and make clear sky and vouchsafe sight unto our eyes. In the light be it that thou slayest us, since it is thy good pleasure that we die."

Then fair-haired Menelaos departed glancing everywhither, as an eagle which men say hath keenest sight of all birds under heaven, and though he be far aloft the fleet-footed hare eludeth him not by crouching beneath a leafy bush, but the eagle swoopeth thereon and swiftly seizeth her and taketh her life. Thus in that hour, Menelaos fosterling of Zeus, ranged thy shining eyes everywhither through the multitude of the host of thy comrades, if haply they might behold Nestor's son yet alive. Him quickly he perceived at the left of the whole battle, heartening his comrades and rousing them to fight. And fair-haired Menelaos came and stood nigh and said unto him: "Antilochos, fosterling of Zeus, come hither that thou mayest learn woful tidings — would it had never been. Ere now, I ween, thou too hast known by thy beholding that God rolleth mischief upon the Danaans, and with the Trojans is victory. And slain is the best man of the Achaians, Patroklos, and great sorrow is wrought for the Danaans. But run thou to the ships of the Achaians and quickly tell this to Achilles, if haply he may straightway rescue to his ship the naked corpse: but his armour is held by Hector of the glancing helmet."

Thus spake he, and Antilochos had horror of the word he heard. And long time speechlessness possessed him, and his eyes were filled with tears, and his full voice choked. Yet for all this disregarded he not the bidding of Menelaos, but set him to run, when he had given his armour to a noble comrade, Laodokos, who close anigh him was wheeling his whole-hooved horses.

So him his feet bare out of the battle weeping, to Achilles son of Peleus carrying an evil tale. But thy heart, Menelaos fosterling of Zeus, chose not to stay to aid the wearied comrades from whom Antilochos departed, and great sorrow was among the Pylians. But to them Menelaos sent noble Thrasymedes, and himself went again to bestride the hero Patroklos. And he hasted and stood beside the Aiantes and straightway spake to them: "So have I sent that man to the swift ships to go to fleet-footed Achilles. Yet deem I not that he will now come, for all his wrath against noble Hector, for he could not fight unarmed against the men of Troy. But let us ourselves devise some excellent means, both how we may hale the dead away, and how we ourselves may escape death and fate amid the Trojans' battle-cry."

Then answered him great Aias Telamon's son, saying: "All

this hast thou said well, most noble Menelaos. But do thou and Meriones put your shoulders beneath the dead and lift him and bear him swiftly out of the fray, while we twain behind you shall do battle with the Trojans and noble Hector, one in heart as we are in name, for from of old time we are wont to await fierce battle side by side."

Thus spake he, and the others took the dead man in their arms and lifted him mightily on high. But the Trojan host behind cried aloud when they saw the Achaians lifting the corpse, and charged like hounds that spring in front of hunter-youths upon a wounded wild boar, and for a while run in haste to rend him, but when he wheeleth round among them, trusting in his might, then they give ground and shrink back here and there. Thus for a while the Trojans pressed on with all their power, striking with swords and double-headed spears, but when the Aiantes turned about and halted over against them, then they changed colour, and none dared farther onset to do battle around the dead.

BOOK XVIII

How Achilles grieved for Patroklos, and how Thetis asked for him new armour of Hephaistos ; and of the making of the armour.

THUS fought the rest in the likeness of blazing fire, while to Achilles came Antilochos, a messenger fleet of foot. Him found he in front of his ships of upright horns, boding in his soul the things which even now were accomplished. And sore troubled he spake to his great heart : " Ay me, wherefore again are the flowing-haired Achaians flocking to the ships and flying in rout over the plain ? May the gods not have wrought against me the grievous fears at my heart, even as my mother revealed and told me that while I am yet alive the best man of the Myrmidons must by deed of the men of Troy forsake the light of the sun. Surely now must Menoitios' valiant son be dead — foolhardy! surely I bade him when he should have beaten off the fire of the foe to come back to the ships nor with Hector fight amain."

While thus he held debate in his heart and soul, there drew nigh unto him noble Nestor's son, shedding hot tears, and spake his grievous tidings: "Ay me, wise Peleus' son, very bitter tidings must thou hear, such as I would had never been. Fallen is Patroklos, and they are fighting around his body, naked, for his armour is held by Hector of the glancing helm."

Thus spake he, and a black cloud of grief enwrapped Achilles, and with both hands he took dark dust and poured it over his head and defiled his comely face, and on his fragrant doublet black ashes fell. And himself in the dust lay mighty and mightily fallen, and with his own hands tore and marred his hair. And the handmaidens, whom Achilles and Patroklos took captive, cried aloud in the grief of their hearts, and ran forth around valiant Achilles, and all beat on their breasts with their hands, and the knees of each of them were unstrung. And Antilochos on the other side wailed and shed tears, holding Achilles' hands while he groaned in his noble heart, for he feared lest he should cleave his throat with the sword. Then terribly moaned Achilles; and his lady mother heard him as she sate in the depths of the sea beside her ancient sire. And thereon she uttered a cry, and the goddesses flocked around her, all the daughters of Nereus that were in the deep of the sea. With these the bright cave was filled, and they all beat together on their breasts, and Thetis led the lament: "Listen, sister Nereids, that ye all hear and know well what sorrows are in my heart. Ay me unhappy, ay me that bare to my sorrow the first of men! For after I had borne a son noble and strong, the chief of heroes, and he shot up like a young branch, then when I had reared him as a plant in a very fruitful field

I sent him in beaked ships to Ilios to fight against the men of Troy ; but never again shall I welcome him back to his home, to the house of Peleus. And while he yet liveth in my sight and beholdeth the light of the sun, he sorroweth, neither can I help him any whit though I go unto him. But I will go, that I may look upon my dear child, and learn what sorrow hath come to him though he abide aloof from the war."

Thus spake she and left the cave; and the nymphs went with her weeping, and around them the surge of the sea was sundered. And when they came to deep-soiled Troy-land they went up upon the shore in order, where the ships of the Myrmidons were drawn up thickly around fleet Achilles. And as he groaned heavily his lady mother stood beside him, and with a shrill cry clasped the head of her child, and spake unto him winged words of lamentation: "My child, why weepest thou? what sorrow hath come to thy heart? Tell it forth, hide it not. One thing at least hath been accomplished of Zeus according to the prayer thou madest, holding up to him thy hands, that the sons of the Achaians should all be pent in at the ships, through lack of thee, and should suffer hateful things."

Then groaning heavily spake unto her Achilles fleet of foot: "My mother, that prayer truly hath the Olympian accomplished for me. But what delight have I therein, since my dear comrade is dead, Patroklos, whom I honoured above all my comrades as it were my very self! Him have I lost, and Hector that slew him hath stripped from him the armour great and fair, a wonder to behold, that the gods gave to Peleus a splendid gift, on the day when they laid thee in the bed of a mortal man. Would thou hadst abode among the deathless daughters of the sea, and Peleus had wedded a mortal bride! But now, that thou mayest have sorrow a thousand fold in thy heart for a dead son, never shalt thou welcome him back home, since my soul biddeth me also live no longer nor abide among men, if Hector be not first smitten by my spear and yield his life, and pay for his slaughter of Patroklos, Menoitios' son."

Then answered unto him Thetis shedding tears: "Short-lived, I ween, must thou be then, my child, by what thou sayest, for straightway after Hector is death appointed unto thee."

Then mightily moved spake unto her Achilles fleet of foot: "Straightway may I die, since I might not succour my comrade at his slaying. He hath fallen afar from his country and lacked my help in his sore need. Now therefore, since I go not back to my dear native land, neither have at all been succour to Patroklos nor to all my other comrades that have been slain by noble Hector, but I sit beside my ships a profitless burden of the earth, I that in war am such an one as is none else of the mail-clad Achaians, though in council are others better — may strife perish utterly among gods and men, and wrath that stirreth even a wise man to be vexed, wrath that far sweeter than trickling honey waxeth like smoke in the breasts of men, even as I was wroth even now against Agamemnon king of men. But bygones will we let be, for all our pain, curbing the heart in our breasts under necessity. Now go I forth, that I may light on the destroyer of him I loved, on Hector: then will I accept my death whensoever Zeus willeth to accomplish it and the other immortal gods. For not even the mighty Herakles escaped death, albeit most dear to Kronian Zeus the king, but Fate overcame him and Hera's cruel wrath. So also shall I, if my fate hath been fashioned likewise, lie low when I am dead. But now let me win high renown, let me set some Trojan woman, some deep-bosomed daughter of Dardanos, staunching with both hands the tears upon her tender cheeks and wailing bitterly; yea, let them know that I am come back, though I tarried long from the war. Hold not me then from the battle in thy love, for thou shalt not prevail with me."

Then Thetis the silver-footed goddess answered him, saying: "Yea verily, my child, no blame is in this, that thou ward sheer destruction from thy comrades in their distress. But thy fair glittering armour of bronze is held among the Trojans. Hector of the glancing helm beareth it on his shoulders in triumph, yet not for long, I ween, shall he glory therein, for death is hard anigh him. But thou, go not yet down into the mellay of war until thou see me with thine eyes come hither. In the morning will I return, at the coming up of the sun, bearing fair armour from the king Hephaistos."

Thus spake she and turned to go from her son, and as she turned she spake among her sisters of the sea: "Ye now go down within the wide bosom of the deep, to visit the Ancient One of the Sea and our father's house, and tell him all. I am going to high Olympus to Hephaistos of noble skill, if haply he will give unto my son noble armour shining gloriously."

Thus spake she, and they forthwith went down beneath the surge of the sea. And the silver-footed goddess Thetis went on to Olympus that she might bring noble armour to her son.

So her unto Olympus her feet bore. But the Achaians with terrible cries were fleeing before man-slaying Hector till they came to the ships and to the Hellespont. Nor might the well-greaved Achaians drag the corpse of Patroklos Achilles' squire out of the darts, for now again overtook him the host and the horses of Troy, and Hector son of Priam, in might as it were a flame of fire. Thrice did glorious Hector seize him from behind by the feet, resolved to drag him away, and mightily called upon the men of Troy. Thrice did the two Aiantes, clothed on with impetuous might, beat him off from the dead man, but he nathless, trusting in his might, anon would charge into the press, anon would stand and cry aloud, but he gave ground never a whit. As when shepherds in the field avail nowise to chase a fiery lion in fierce hunger away from a carcase, so availed not the two warrior Aiantes to scare Hector son of

Priam from the dead. And now would he have won the body and gained renown unspeakable, had not fleet wind-footed Iris come speeding from Olympus with a message to the son of Peleus to array him, unknown of Zeus and the other gods, for Hera sent her. And she stood anigh and spake to him winged words: "Rouse thee, son of Peleus, of all men most redoubtable! Succour Patroklos, for whose body is terrible battle afoot before the ships. There slay they one another, these guarding the dead corpse, while the men of Troy are fierce to hale him unto windy Ilios, and chiefliest noble Hector is fain to drag him, and his heart biddeth him fix the head on the stakes of the wall when he hath sundered it from the tender neck. But arise, lie thus no longer! let awe enter thy heart to forbid that Patroklos become the sport of dogs of Troy. Thine were the shame if he go down mangled amid the dead."

Then answered her fleet-footed noble Achilles: "Goddess Iris, what god sent thee a messenger unto me?"

And to him again spake wind-footed fleet Iris: "It was Hera that sent me, the wise wife of Zeus, nor knoweth the high-throned son of Kronos nor any other of the Immortals that on snowy Olympus have their dwelling-place."

And Achilles fleet of foot made answer to her and said: "And how may I go into the fray? The Trojans hold my arms; and my dear mother bade me forbear to array me until I behold her with my eyes returned, for she promised to bring fair armour from Hephaistos. Other man know I none whose noble armour I might put on, save it were the shield of Aias Telamon's son. But himself, I ween, is in the forefront of the press, dealing death with his spear around Patroklos dead."

Then again spake unto him wind-footed fleet Iris: "Well are we also aware that thy noble armour is held from thee. But go forth unto the trench as thou art and show thyself to the men of Troy, if haply they will shrink back and refrain them from battle, and the warlike sons of the Achaians take breath."

Thus spake fleet-footed Iris and went her way. But Achilles dear to Zeus arose, and around his strong shoulders Athene cast her tasselled aegis, and around his head the bright goddess set a crown of a golden cloud, and kindled therefrom a blazing flame. And as when a smoke issueth from a city and riseth up into the upper air, from an island afar off that foes beleaguer, while the others from their city fight all day in hateful war, — but with the going down of the sun blaze out the beacon-fires in line, and high aloft rusheth up the glare for dwellers round about to behold, if haply they may come with ships to help in need — thus from the head of Achilles soared that blaze toward the heavens. And he went and stood beyond the wall beside the trench, yet mingled not among the Achaians, for he minded the wise bidding of his mother. There stood he and shouted aloud, and afar off Pallas Athene uttered her voice, and spread terror unspeakable among the men of Troy. Clear as the voice of a clarion when it soundeth by reason of slaughterous foemen that beleaguer a city, so clear rang forth the voice of Aiakides. And when they heard the brazen voice of Aiakides, the souls of all of them were dismayed, and the horses of goodly manes were fain to turn the chariots backward, for they boded anguish in their hearts. And the charioteers were amazed when they saw the unwearying fire blaze fierce on the head of the great-hearted son of Peleus, for the bright-eyed goddess Athene made it blaze. Thrice from over the trench shouted mightily noble Achilles, and thrice were the men of Troy confounded and their proud allies. Yea there and then perished twelve men of their best by their own chariot wheels and spears. But the Achaians with joy drew Patroklos forth of the darts and laid him on a litter, and his dear comrades stood around lamenting him; and among them followed fleet-footed Achilles, shedding hot tears, for his true comrade he saw lying on the bier, mangled by the keen bronze. Him sent he forth with chariot and horses unto the battle, but home again welcomed never more.

Then Hera the ox-eyed queen sent down the unwearying Sun to be gone unwillingly unto the streams of Ocean. So the Sun set, and the noble Achaians made pause from the stress of battle and the hazardous war.

But the Achaians all night made moan in lamentation for Patroklos. And first of them in the loud lamentation was the son of Peleus, laying upon the breast of his comrade his man-slaying hands and moaning very sore, even as a deep-bearded lion whose whelps some stag-hunter hath snatched away out of a deep wood; and the lion coming afterward grieveth and through many glens he rangeth on the track of the footsteps of the man, if anywhere he might find him, for most bitter anger seizeth him; — thus Achilles moaning heavily spake among the Myrmidons: "Ay me, vain verily was the word I uttered on that day when I cheered the hero Menoitios in his halls and said that I would bring back to Opoeis his son in glory from the sack of Ilios with the share of spoil that should fall unto him. Not all the purposes of men doth Zeus accomplish for them. It is appointed that both of us redden the same earth with our blood here in Troy-land, for neither shall the old knight Peleus welcome me back home within his halls, nor my mother Thetis, but even here shall earth keep hold on me. Yet now, O Patroklos, since I follow thee under earth, I will not hold thy funeral till I have brought hither the armour and the head of Hector, thy high-hearted slayer, and before thy pyre I will cut the throats of twelve noble sons of the men of Troy, for mine anger thou art slain. Till then beside the beaked ships shalt thou lie as thou art, and around thee deep-bosomed women, Trojan and Dardanian, shall mourn thee weeping night and day, even they whom we toiled to win by our strength and our long spears when we sacked rich cities of mortal men."

Thus spake noble Achilles, and bade his comrades set a great tripod on the fire, that with all speed they might wash from Patroklos the bloody gore. So they set a tripod of ablution on the burning fire, and poured therein water and took wood and kindled it beneath; and the fire wrapped the belly of the tripod, and the water grew hot. And when the water boiled in the bright bronze, then washed they him and anointed with olive oil, and filled his wounds with fresh ointment, and laid him on a bier and covered him with soft cloth from head to foot, and thereover a white robe. Then all night around Achilles fleet of foot the Myrmidons made lament and moan for Patroklos.

Meanwhile Zeus spake unto Hera his sister and wife: "Thou hast accomplished this, O Hera, ox-eyed queen, thou hast aroused Achilles fleet of foot. Verily of thine own children must the flowing-haired Achaians be."

Then answered unto him Hera the ox-eyed queen: "Most dread son of Kronos, what is this word thou hast said? Truly even a man, I ween, is to accomplish what he may for another man, albeit he is mortal and hath not wisdom as we. How then was I who avow me the first of goddesses both by birth and for that I am called thy wife, and thou art king among all Immortals — how was I not in mine anger to devise evil against the men of Troy?"

So debated they on this wise with one another. But Thetis of the silver feet came unto the house of Hephaistos, imperishable, starlike, far seen among the dwellings of Immortals, a house of bronze, wrought by the crook-footed god himself. Him found she sweating in toil and busy about his bellows, for he was forging tripods twenty in all to stand around the wall of his stablished hall, and beneath the base of each he had set golden wheels, that of their own motion they might enter the assembly of the gods and again return unto his house, a marvel to look upon. Thus much were they finished that not yet were the ears of cunning work set thereon; these was he making ready, and welding chains. While hereat he was labouring with wise intent, then drew nigh unto him Thetis, goddess of the silver feet. And Charis went forward and beheld her, fair Charis of the shining chaplet whom the renowned lame god had wedded. And she clasped her hand in hers and spake and called her by her name : " Wherefore, long-robed Thetis, comest thou to our house, honoured that thou art and dear ? No frequent comer art thou hitherto. But come onward with me that I may set guest-cheer before thee."

Thus spake the bright goddess and led her on. Then set she her on a silver-studded throne, goodly, of cunning work, and a footstool was beneath her feet; and she called to Hephaistos, the famed artificer, and said unto him : " Hephaistos, come forth hither, Thetis hath need of thee."

And the renowned lame god made answer to her : " Verily a dread and honoured goddess in my sight is she that is within, seeing that she delivered me when pain came upon me from my great fall though the ill-will of my shameless mother who would fain have hid me away, for that I was lame. Then had I suffered anguish of heart had not Eurynome and Thetis taken me into their bosom — Eurynome daughter of Ocean that floweth back ever upon himself. Nine years with them I wrought much cunning work of bronze, brooches and spiral arm-bands and cups and necklaces, in the hollow cave, while around me the stream of Ocean with murmuring foam flowed infinite. Neither knew thereof any other of gods or of mortal men, save only Thetis and Eurynome who delivered me. And now cometh Thetis to our house; wherefore behoveth it me verily in all wise to repay fair-tressed Thetis for the saving of my life. But do thou now set beside her fair entertainment, while I put away my bellows and all my gear."

He said, and from the anvil rose limping, a huge bulk, but under him his slender legs moved nimbly. The bellows he set away from the fire, and gathered all his gear wherewith he worked into a silver chest; and with a sponge he wiped his face and hands and sturdy neck and shaggy breast, and did on his doublet, and took a stout staff and went forth limping; but there were handmaidens of gold that moved to help their lord, the semblances of living maids. In them is understanding at their hearts, in them are voice and strength, and they have skill of the immortal gods. These moved beneath their lord, and he gat him haltingly near to where Thetis was, and set him on a bright seat, and clasped her hand in his and spake and called her by her name: "Wherefore, long-robed Thetis, comest thou to our house, honoured that thou art and dear? No frequent comer art thou hitherto. Speak what thou hast at heart; my soul is fain to accomplish it, if accomplish it I can, and if it be appointed for accomplishment."

Then answered unto him Thetis shedding tears: "Hephaistos, hath there verily been any of all goddesses in Olympus that hath endured so many grievous sorrows at heart as are the woes that Kronian Zeus hath laid upon me above all others? He chose me from among the sisters of the sea to enthrall me to a man, even Peleus Aiakos' son, and with a man I endured wedlock sore against my will. Now lieth he in his halls forspent with grievous age, but other griefs are mine. A son he gave me to bear and nourish, the chief of heroes, and he shot up like a young branch. Like a plant in a very fruitful field I reared him and sent him forth on beaked ships to Ilios to fight against the men of Troy, but never again shall I welcome him back to his home within the house of Peleus. And while he yet liveth in my sight and beholdeth the light of the sun, he sorroweth, neither can I help him any whit though I go unto him. The maiden whom the sons of the Achaians chose out to be his prize, her hath the lord Agamemnon taken back out of his hands. In grief for her wasted he his heart, while the men of Troy were driving the Achaians on their ships, nor suffered them to come forth. And the elders of the Argives entreated him, and told over many noble gifts. Then albeit himself he refused to ward destruction from them, he put his armour on Patroklos and sent him to the war, and much people with him. All day they fought around the Skaian gates and that same day had sacked the town, but that when now Menoitios' valiant son had wrought much harm, Apollo slew him in the forefront of the battle, and gave glory unto Hector. Therefore now come I a suppliant unto thy knees, if haply thou be willing to give my short-lived son shield and helmet, and goodly greaves fitted with ankle-pieces, and cuirass. For the armour that he had erst, his trusty comrade lost when he fell beneath the men of Troy; and my son lieth on the earth with anguish in his soul."

Then made answer unto her the lame god of great renown: "Be of good courage, let not these things trouble thy heart. Would that so might I avail to hide him far from dolorous death, when dread fate cometh upon him, as surely shall goodly armour be at his need, such as all men afterward shall marvel at, whatsoever may behold."

Thus saying he left her there and went unto his bellows and turned them upon the fire and bade them work. And the bellows, twenty in all, blew on the crucibles, sending deft blasts on every side, now to aid his labour and now anon howsoever Hephaistos willed and the work went on. And he threw bronze that weareth not into the fire, and tin and precious gold and silver, and next he set on an anvil-stand a great anvil, and took in his hand a sturdy hammer, and in the other he took the tongs.

First fashioned he a shield great and strong, adorning it all over, and set thereto a shining rim, triple, bright-glancing, and therefrom a silver baldric. Five were the folds of the shield itself; and therein fashioned he much cunning work from his wise heart.

There wrought he the earth, and the heavens, and the sea,

and the unwearying sun, and the moon waxing to the full, and the signs every one wherewith the heavens are crowned, Pleiads and Hyads and Orion's might, and the Bear that men call also the Wain, her that turneth in her place and watcheth Orion, and alone hath no part in the baths of Ocean.

Also he fashioned therein two fair cities of mortal men. In the one were espousals and marriage feasts, and beneath the blaze of torches they were leading the brides from their chambers through the city, and loud arose the bridal song. And young men were whirling in the dance, and among them flutes and viols sounded high; and women standing each at her door were marvelling. But the folk were gathered in the assembly place; for there a strife was arisen, two men striving about the blood-price of a man slain; the one claimed to pay full atonement, expounding to the people, but the other denied him and would take naught. And the folk were cheering both, as they took part on either side. And heralds kept order among the folk, while the elders on polished stones were sitting in the sacred circle, and holding in their hands staves from the loud-voiced heralds. Then before the people they rose up and gave judgment each in turn. And in the midst lay two talents of gold, to be given unto him who should plead among them most righteously.

But around the other city were two armies in siege with glittering arms. And two counsels found favour among them, either to sack the town or to share all with the townsfolk even whatsoever substance the fair city held within. But the besieged were not yet yielding, but arming for an ambushment. On the wall there stood to guard it their dear wives and infant children, and with these the old men; but the rest went forth, and their leaders were Ares and Pallas Athene, both wrought in gold, and golden was the vesture they had on. Goodly and great were they in their armour, even as gods, far seen around, and the folk at their feet were smaller. And when they came where it seemed good to them to lay ambush, in a river bed where there was a common watering-place of herds, there they set them, clad in glittering bronze. And two scouts were posted by them afar off to spy the coming of flocks and of oxen with crooked horns. And presently came the cattle, and with them two herdsmen playing on pipes, that took no thought of the guile. Then the others when they beheld these ran upon them and quickly cut off the herds of oxen and fair flocks of white sheep, and slew the shepherds withal. But the besiegers, as they sat before the speech-places [1] and heard much din among the oxen, mounted forthwith behind their high-stepping horses, and came up with speed. Then they arrayed their battle and fought beside the river banks, and smote one another with bronze-shod spears. And among them mingled Strife and Tumult, and fell Death, grasping one man alive fresh-wounded, another without wound, and dragging another dead through the mellay by the feet; and the raiment on her shoulders was red with the blood of men. Like living mortals they hurled together and fought, and haled the corpses each of the other's slain.

Furthermore he set in the shield a soft fresh-ploughed field, rich tilth and wide, the third time ploughed; and many ploughers therein drave their yokes to and fro as they wheeled about. Whensoever they came to the boundary of the field and turned, then would a man come to each and give into his hands a goblet of sweet wine, while others would be turning back along the furrows, fain to reach the boundary of the deep tilth. And the field grew black behind and seemed as it were a-ploughing, albeit of gold, for this was the great marvel of the work.

Furthermore he set therein the demesne-land of a king, where hinds were reaping with sharp sickles in their hands. Some

---

[1] From which the orators spoke.

armfuls along the swathe were falling in rows to the earth, whilst others the sheaf-binders were binding in twisted bands of straw. Three sheaf-binders stood over them, while behind boys gathering corn and bearing it in their arms gave it constantly to the binders; and among them the king in silence was standing at the swathe with his staff, rejoicing in his heart. And henchmen apart beneath an oak were making ready a feast, and preparing a great ox they had sacrificed; while the women were strewing much white barley to be a supper for the hinds.

Also he set therein a vineyard teeming plenteously with clusters, wrought fair in gold; black were the grapes, but the vines hung throughout on silver poles. And around it he ran a ditch of cyanus, and round that a fence of tin; and one single pathway led to it, whereby the vintagers might go when they should gather the vintage. And maidens and striplings in childish glee bare the sweet fruit in plaited baskets. And in the midst of them a boy made pleasant music on a clear-toned viol, and sang thereto a sweet Linos-song [1] with delicate voice; while the rest with feet falling together kept time with the music and song.

Also he wrought therein a herd of kine with upright horns, and the kine were fashioned of gold and tin, and with lowing they hurried from the byre to pasture beside a murmuring river, beside the waving reed. And herdsmen of gold were following with the kine, four of them, and nine dogs fleet of foot came after them. But two terrible lions among the foremost kine had seized a loud-roaring bull that bellowed mightily as they haled him, and the dogs and the young men sped after him. The lions rending the great bull's hide were devouring his vitals and his black blood; while the herdsmen in vain tarred on their fleet dogs to set on, for they shrank from biting the lions but stood hard by and barked and swerved away.

---

[1] Probably a lament for departing summer.

Also the glorious lame god wrought therein a pasture in a fair glen, a great pasture of white sheep, and a steading, and roofed huts, and folds.

Also did the glorious lame god devise a dancing-place like unto that which once in wide Knosos Daidalos wrought for Ariadne of the lovely tresses. There were youths dancing and maidens of costly wooing, their hands upon one another's wrists. Fine linen the maidens had on, and the youths well-woven doublets faintly glistening with oil. Fair wreaths had the maidens, and the youths daggers of gold hanging from silver baldrics. And now would they run round with deft feet exceeding lightly, as when a potter sitting by his wheel that fitteth between his hands maketh trial of it whether it run : and now anon they would run in lines to meet each other. And a great company stood round the lovely dance in joy; and through the midst of them, leading the measure, two tumblers whirled.

Also he set therein the great might of the River of Ocean around the uttermost rim of the cunningly-fashioned shield.

Now when he had wrought the shield great and strong, then wrought he him a corslet brighter than a flame of fire, and he wrought him a massive helmet to fit his brows, goodly and graven, and set thereon a crest of gold, and he wrought him greaves of pliant tin.

So when the renowned lame god had finished all the armour, he took and laid it before the mother of Achilles. Then she like a falcon sprang down from snowy Olympus, bearing from Hephaistos the glittering arms.

THETIS BRINGING THE ARMOUR TO ACHILLES

BOOK XIX

How Achilles and Agamemnon were reconciled before the assembly of the Achaians, and Achilles went forth with them to battle.

Now Morning saffron-robed arose from the streams of Ocean to bring light to gods and men, and Thetis came to the ships, bearing his gift from the god. Her dear son she found fallen about Patroklos and uttering loud lament; and round him many of his company made moan. And the bright goddess stood beside him in their midst, and clasped her hand in his and spake and called upon his name: "My child, him who lieth here we must let be, for all our pain, for by the will of gods from the beginning was he brought low. But thou take from Hephaistos arms of pride, arms passing goodly, such as no man on his shoulders yet hath borne."

Thus spake the goddess and in front of Achilles laid the arms, and they rang all again in their glory. And awe fell on all the Myrmidons, nor dared any to gaze thereon, for they were awe-stricken. But when Achilles looked thereon, then came fury upon him the more, and his eyes blazed terribly forth as it were a flame beneath their lids: glad was he as he held in his hands that splendid gift of a god. But when he had satisfied his soul in gazing on the glory of the arms, straightway to his mother spake he winged words: "My mother, the arms the god has given are such as it beseemeth that the work of Immortals should be, and that no mortal man should have wrought. Now therefore will I arm me in them, but I have grievous fear lest meantime on the gashed wounds of Menoitios' valiant son flies light and breed worms therein, and defile his corpse — for the life is slain out of him — and so all his flesh shall rot."

Then answered him Thetis, goddess of the silver feet:

"Child, have no care for this within thy mind. I will see to ward from him the cruel tribes of flies which prey on men slain in fight: for even though he lie till a whole year's course be run, yet his flesh shall be sound continually, or better even than now. But call thou the Achaian warriors to the place of assembly, and unsay thy wrath against Agamemnon shepherd of the host, and then arm swiftly for battle, and clothe thee with thy strength."

Thus saying she filled him with adventurous might, while on Patroklos she shed ambrosia and red nectar through his nostrils, that his flesh might abide the same continually.

But noble Achilles went down the beach of the sea, crying his terrible cry, and roused the Achaian warriors. And they who before were wont to abide in the circle of the ships, and they who were helmsmen and kept the steerage of the ships, or were stewards there and dealt out food, even these came then to the place of assembly, because Achilles was come forth, after long ceasing from grievous war. Limping came two of Ares' company, Tydeus' son staunch in fight and noble Odysseus, each leaning on his spear, for their wounds were grievous still; and they went and sate them down in the forefront of the assembly. And last came Agamemnon king of men, with his wound upon him, for him too in the stress of battle Koön Antenor's son had wounded with his bronze-tipped spear. But when all the Achaians were gathered, then uprose fleet-footed Achilles and spake in their midst: "Son of Atreus, was this in any wise the better way for both thee and me, what time with grief at our hearts we waxed fierce in soul-devouring strife for the sake of a girl? Would that Artemis had slain her with her arrow at the ships, on the day whereon I took her to me, when I had spoiled Lyrnessos; so should not then so many Achaians have bitten the wide earth beneath their enemies' hands, by reason of my exceeding wrath. It hath been well for Hector and the Trojans, but the Achaians I

think shall long remember the strife that was betwixt thee
and me. But bygones will we let be, for all our pain, and
curb under necessity the spirit within our breasts. I now
will stay my anger: it beseems me not implacably for ever to
be wroth; but come rouse speedily to the fight the flowing-
haired Achaians, that I may go forth against the men of Troy
and put them yet again to the proof, if they be fain to couch
hard by the ships. Methinks that some among them shall be
glad to rest their knees when they are fled out of the fierceness of the battle, and from before our spear."

He spake, and the well-greaved Achaians rejoiced that the
great-hearted son of Peleus had made renouncement of his
wrath. Then among them spake Agamemnon king of men,
speaking from the place where he sat, not arisen to stand
forth in their midst: "O Danaan friends and heroes, to the
son of Peleus I will declare myself, but ye other Argives give
heed, and each mark well my word. Oft have the Achaians
spoken thus to me, and upbraided me; but it is not I who
am the cause, but Zeus and Destiny and Erinys that walketh
in the darkness, who put into my soul fierce madness on the
day when in the assembly I, even I, bereft Achilles of his
meed. But since thus blinded was I, and Zeus bereft me of
my wit, fain am I to make amends, and recompense manifold
for the wrong. Only arise thou to the battle and rouse the
rest of the host. Gifts am I ready to offer, even all that noble
Odysseus went yesterday to promise in thy hut. So, if thou
wilt, stay awhile, though eager, from battle, and squires shall
take the gifts from my ship and carry them to thee, that thou
mayest see that what I give sufficeth thee."

Then answered him Achilles swift of foot: "Most noble son
of Atreus, Agamemnon king of men, for the gifts, to give them
as it beseemeth, if so thou wilt, or to withhold, is in thy choice.
But now let us bethink us of battle with all speed; this is no
time to dally here with subtleties, for a great work is yet

undone. Once more must Achilles be seen in the forefront of the battle, laying waste with his brazen spear the battalions of the men of Troy. Thereof let each of you think as he fighteth with his man."

Then Odysseus of many counsels answered him and said: "Nay yet, for all thy valour, godlike Achilles, not against Ilios lead thou the sons of Achaians fasting to fight the men of Troy, since not of short spell shall the battle be, when once the ranks of men are met, and God shall breathe valour into both. But bid the Achaians taste at the swift ships food and wine; for thence is vigour and might."

Then to him spake Agamemnon king of men: "Let Achilles abide for a space, eager for battle though he be, and all ye others abide together, until the gifts come forth from my hut, and we make faithful oath with sacrifice. But thee thyself I thus charge and bid. Choose thee young men, princes of the Achaian folk, and bear my gifts from my ship, even all that we promised yesterday to Achilles, and take with thee the women. And let Talthybios speedily make me ready a boar-swine in the midst of the wide Achaian host, to sacrifice to Zeus and to the Sun."

And to him in answer swift-footed Achilles spake: "Most noble son of Atreus, Agamemnon king of men, at some other time were it even better ye should be busied thus, when haply there shall be some pause of war, and the spirit within my breast shall be less fierce. But now they lie mangled on the field — even they whom Hector son of Priam slew, when Zeus gave him glory — and ye call men to their food. Verily for my part I would bid the sons of the Achaians to fight now unfed and fasting, and with the setting sun make ready a mighty meal, when we shall have avenged the shame. Till then down my throat at least nor food nor drink shall go, since my comrade is dead, who in my hut is lying mangled by the sharp spear, with his feet toward the door, and round him our comrades mourn; wherefore in my heart is no thought of those matters, but of slaying, and blood, and grievous moans of men."

Then answered him Odysseus of many counsels: "O Achilles, Peleus' son, mightiest of Achaians far, better and mightier not a little art thou than I with the spear, but in counsel I may surpass thee greatly, since I was born first and know more things: wherefore let thy heart endure to listen to my speech. Quickly have men surfeit of battle, of that wherein the sword streweth most straw yet is the harvest scantiest,[1] when Zeus inclineth his balance, who is disposer of the wars of men. But it cannot be that the Achaians fast to mourn a corpse; for exceeding many and thick fall such on every day; when then should there be rest from toil? Nay, it behoveth to bury him who is dead, steeling our hearts, when once we have wept him for a day; but such as are left alive from hateful war must take thought of meat and drink, that yet more against our foes we may fight relentlessly ever, clad in unyielding bronze. Then let none of the host hold back awaiting other summons; this is the summons, and ill shall it be for whoso is left behind at the Argive ships; but all together as one we will rouse against the horse-taming Trojans the fury of war."

He spoke, and took with him the sons of noble Nestor, and Meges son of Phyleus, and Thoas, and Meriones, and Lykomedes son of Kreiontes, and Melanippos. And they went on their way to the hut of Agamemnon, Atreus' son. Forthwith as the word was spoken so was the deed done. Seven tripods they bare from the hut, as he promised him, and twenty bright caldrons, and twelve horses, and anon they led forth women skilled in goodly arts, seven, and the eighth was fair-faced Briseis. Then Odysseus, having weighed ten talents of gold in all, led the way, and with him young men of the Achaians bare the gifts. These they set in the midst of the place of

[1] *i.e.* in a pitched battle there is little plunder, the hope of which might help to sustain men's efforts in storming a town.

assembly, and Agamemnon rose up, and beside that shepherd of the host stood Talthybios, whose voice was like a god's, and held a boar between his hands. And the son of Atreus drawing with his hands his knife, which ever hung beside the mighty scabbard of his sword, cut off the first hairs from the boar, and lifting up his hands he prayed to Zeus, and cut the boar's throat with the pitiless knife. And the body Talthybios whirled and threw into the great wash of the hoary sea, to be the food of fishes; but Achilles arose up and spake in the midst of the warrior Argives: "Father Zeus, sore madness dealest thou verily to men. Never could the son of Atreus have stirred the soul within my breast, nor led off the damsel implacably against my will, had not Zeus willed that on many of the Achaians death should come. But now go forth to your meal, that we may join battle thereupon."

Thus he spake and dispersed the assembly with all speed. The rest were scattered each to his own ship, but the greathearted Myrmidons took up the gifts, and bare them to the ship of godlike Achilles. And they laid them in the huts and set the women there, and gallant squires drave the horses among their troop.

But Briseis that was like unto golden Aphrodite, when she beheld Patroklos mangled by the keen spear, fell about him and made shrill lament, and tore with her hands her breast and tender neck, and beautiful face. And she spake amid her weeping, that woman like unto goddesses: "Patroklos, dearest to my hapless heart, alive I left thee when I left this hut, but now, O prince of the people, I am come back to find thee dead; thus evil ever followeth evil in my lot. My husband, unto whom my father and lady mother gave me, I beheld before our city mangled with the keen spear, and my three brothers whom my own mother bore, my near and dear, who all met their day of doom. But thou, when swift Achilles slew my husband and wasted godlike Mynes' city, wouldst ever that I

should not even weep, and saidest that thou wouldst make
me godlike Achilles' wedded wife, and that ye would take me
in your ships to Phthia and make me a marriage feast among
the Myrmidons. Therefore with all my soul I mourn thy death,
for thou wert ever kind."

Thus spake she weeping, and thereon the women wailed, in
semblance for Patroklos, but each for her own woe. But round
Achilles gathered the elders of the Achaians, praying him that
he would eat; but he denied them with a groan: "I pray you,
if any kind comrade will hearken to me, bid me not sate my
heart with meat and drink, since terrible grief is come upon
me. Till the sun go down I will abide, and endure continually
until then."

Thus spake he weeping, and the elders mourned with him.
And when the son of Kronos beheld them sorrowing he pitied
them, and forthwith to Athene spake he winged words: "My
child, thou hast then left utterly the man of thy heart. Hath
Achilles then no longer a place within thy thought? He before
the steep-prowed ships sits mourning his dear comrade; the
rest are gone to their meal, but he is fasting and unfed. But
go, distil into his breast nectar and pleasant ambrosia, that no
pains of hunger come on him."

Thus saying he sped forward Athene who before was fain.
And she, like a falcon wide-winged and shrill-voiced, hurled
herself forth from heaven through the upper air. So while the
Achaians were arming presently throughout the camp, she in
Achilles' breast distilled nectar and pleasant ambrosia, that
grievous hunger might not assail his knees, and then herself
was gone to the firm house of her mighty father. Then the
Achaians poured forth from the swift ships. As when thick
snowflakes flutter down from Zeus, chill beneath the blast of
Boreas born in the upper air, so thick from the ships streamed
forth bright glittering helms and bossy shields, strong-plaited
cuirasses and ashen spears. And the sheen thereof went up to

heaven and all the earth around laughed in the flash of bronze, and there went a sound beneath the feet of the men, and in the midst of them noble Achilles harnessed him. His teeth gnashed together, and his eyes blazed as it were the flame of a fire, for into his heart was intolerable anguish entered in. Thus wroth against the men of Troy he put on the gift of the god, which Hephaistos wrought him by his art. First on his legs he set the fair greaves fitted with silver ankle-pieces, and next he donned the cuirass about his breast. Then round his shoulders he slung the bronze sword silver-studded; then lastly he took the great and strong shield, and its brightness shone afar off as the moon's. Or as when over the sea there appeareth to sailors the brightness of a burning fire, and it burneth on high among the mountains in some lonely steading — sailors whom storm-blasts bear unwilling over the sea, the home of fishes, afar from them they love: — so from Achilles' goodly well-dight shield the brightness thereof shot up toward heaven. And he lifted the stout helmet and set it on his head, and like a star it shone, the horse-hair crested helmet, and around it waved plumes of gold that Hephaistos had set thick about the crest. Then noble Achilles proved him in his armour to know whether it fitted unto him, and whether his glorious limbs ran free; and it became to him as it were wings, and buoyed up the shepherd of hosts.

And forth from its stand he drew his father's spear, heavy and great and strong: that spear could none other of the Achaians wield, but Achilles alone awaited to wield it, the Pelian ashen spear that Cheiron gave to his father dear, from a peak of Pelion, to be the death of warriors. And Automedon and Alkimos went about to yoke the horses, and put on them fair breast-straps, and bits within their jaws, and stretched the reins behind to the firm-built chariot. Then Automedon took the bright lash, fitted to his hand, and sprang up behind the horses, and after him mounted Achilles armed, effulgent in his armour like bright Hyperion. And terribly he called upon the horses of his sire: "Xanthos and Balios, famed children of Podarge, in other sort take heed to bring your charioteer safe back to the Danaan host, when we have done with battle, and leave him not as ye left Patroklos to lie there dead."

Then the horse Xanthos of glancing feet made answer unto him from beneath the yoke;—and he bowed with his head, and all his mane fell from the yoke-cushion beside the yoke and touched the ground;—for the white-armed goddess Hera gave him speech: "Yea verily for this hour, dread Achilles, we will still bear thee safe, yet is thy death day nigh at hand, neither shall we be cause thereof, but a mighty god, and forceful Fate. For not through sloth or heedlessness of ours did the men of Troy from Patroklos' shoulders strip his arms, but the best of the gods, whom bright-haired Leto bore, slew him in the forefront of the battle, and to Hector gave renown. We even with the wind of Zephyr, swiftest, they say, of all winds, well might run; nathless to thee thyself it is appointed to be slain in fight by a god and by a man."

Now when he had thus spoken the Erinyes stayed his voice. And sore troubled did fleet-footed Achilles answer him: "Xanthos, why prophesiest thou my death? nowise behoveth it thee. Well know I of myself that it is appointed me to perish here, far from my father dear and mother; howbeit anywise I will not refrain till I give the Trojans surfeit of war."

He said, and with a cry among the foremost held on his whole-hooved steeds.

BOOK XX

How Achilles made havoc among the men of Troy.

So by the beaked ships around thee, son of Peleus, hungry for war, the Achaians armed; and over against them the men of Troy, upon the high ground of the plain.

But Zeus bade Themis call the gods to council from many-folded Olympus' brow; and she ranged all about and bade them to the house of Zeus. There was no River came not up, save only Ocean, nor any nymph, of all that haunt fair thickets and springs of rivers and grassy water-meadows. And they came to the house of Zeus who gathereth the clouds, and sat them down in the polished colonnades which Hephaistos in the cunning of his heart had wrought for father Zeus.

Thus gathered they within the doors of Zeus; nor was the Earthshaker heedless of the goddess' call, but from the salt sea came up after the rest, and set him in the midst, and inquired concerning the purpose of Zeus: "Wherefore, O Lord of the bright lightning, hast thou called the gods again to council? Say, ponderest thou somewhat concerning the Trojans and Achaians? for lo, the war and the fighting of them are kindled very nigh."

And Zeus, who gathered the clouds, answered him, saying: "Thou knowest, O Earthshaker, the purpose within my breast, wherefor I gathered you hither; even in their perishing have I regard unto them. But for me I will abide here, sitting within a fold of Olympus, where I will gladden my heart with gazing; but go all ye forth that ye come among the Trojans and Achaians and succour these or those, howsoever each of you hath a mind. For if Achilles alone shall fight against the Trojans, not even a little while shall they hold back the son of Peleus, the fleet of foot. Nay, but even aforetime they trembled when they looked upon him; now therefore that his wrath for his friend is waxen terrible I fear me lest he overleap the bound of fate, and storm the wall."

Thus spake the son of Kronos, and roused unabating war. For on this side and on that the gods went forth to war: to the company of the ships went Hera, and Pallas Athene, and Poseidon, Earth-enfolder, and the Helper Hermes, pre-eminent in subtle thoughts; and with these went Hephaistos in the greatness of his strength, halting, but his shrunk legs moved nimbly under him: but to the Trojans went Ares of the glancing helm, and with him Phoebus of the unshorn hair, and archer Artemis, and Leto and Xanthos and laughter-loving Aphrodite.

Now for so long as gods were afar from mortal men, so long waxed the Achaians glorious, for that Achilles was come forth among them, and his long ceasing from grim battle was at an end. And the Trojans were smitten with sore trembling in the limbs of every one of them, in terror when they beheld the son of Peleus, fleet of foot, blazing in his arms, peer of man-slaying Ares. But when among the mellay of men the Olympians were come down, then leapt up in her might Strife, rouser of hosts, then sent forth Athene a cry, now standing by the hollowed trench without the wall, and now on the echoing shores she shouted aloud. And a shout uttered Ares against her, terrible as the blackness of the storm, now from the height of the city to the Trojans calling clear, or again along Simois shore over Kallikolonë he sped.

So urged the blessed gods both hosts to battle, then themselves burst into fierce war. And terribly thundered the father of gods and men from heaven above; and from beneath Poseidon made the vast earth shake and the steep mountain tops. Then trembled all the spurs of many-fountained Ida, and all her crests, and the city of the Trojans, and the ships of the Achaians. And the Lord of the Underworld, Aïdoneus, had terror in hell, and leapt from his throne in that terror and cried aloud, lest the world be cloven above him by Poseidon, Shaker of earth, and his dwelling-place be laid bare to mortals and immortals — grim halls, and vast, and lothly to the gods. So loud the roar rose of that battle of gods. For against King Poseidon stood Phoebus Apollo with his winged arrows, and against Enyalios stood Athene, bright-eyed goddess, and against Hera she of the golden shafts and echoing chase, even archer

Artemis, sister of the Far-darter; and against Leto the strong Helper Hermes, and against Hephaistos the great deep-eddying River, whom gods call Xanthos and men Skamandros.

Thus gods with gods were matched. Meanwhile Achilles yearned above all to meet Hector, son of Priam, in the fray; for with that blood chiefliest his spirit bade him sate Ares, stubborn lord of war. But straightway Apollo, rouser of hosts, moved Aineias to go to meet the son of Peleus, and filled him with brave spirit: and he made his own voice like the voice of Lykaon the son of Priam; in his semblance spake Apollo, son of Zeus: "Aineias, counsellor of Trojans, where now are thy threats wherewith thou didst boast to the Trojan lords over thy wine, saying thou wouldest stand up in battle against Achilles, Peleus' son?"

And to him Aineias answered and said: "Son of Priam, why biddest thou me thus face the fierce son of Peleus in battle, though I be not fain thereto? It is impossible for man to face Achilles in fight, for that ever some god is at his side to ward off death. Ay, and at any time his spear flieth straight, neither ceaseth till it have pierced through flesh of man. But if God once give us fair field of battle, not lightly shall he overcome me, not though he boast him made of bronze throughout."

And to him in answer spake Apollo son of Zeus: "Yea, hero, pray thou too to the everliving gods; for thou too, men say, wast born of Aphrodite daughter of Zeus, and Achilles' mother is of less degree among the gods. For thy mother is child of Zeus, his but of the Ancient One of the Sea. Come, bear up thy unwearying spear against him, let him nowise turn thee back with revilings and bitter words."

He said, and breathed high spirit into the shepherd of the host, and he went onward through the forefront of the fighting, harnessed in flashing bronze. But white-armed Hera failed not to discern Anchises' son as he went through the press of men to meet the son of Peleus, and gathering the gods about her she spake among them thus: "Consider ye twain, Poseidon and Athene, within your hearts, what shall come of these things that are done. Here is Aineias gone forth harnessed in flashing bronze, to meet the son of Peleus, and it is Phoebus Apollo that hath sent him. Come then, be it ours to turn him back straightway; or else let some one of us stand likewise beside Achilles and give him mighty power, so that he fail not in his spirit, but know that they who love him are the best of the Immortals, and that they who from of old ward war and fighting from the Trojans are vain as wind. All we from Olympus are come down to mingle in this fight that he take no hurt among the Trojans on this day — afterward he shall suffer whatsoever things Fate span for him with her thread, at his beginning, when his mother bare him. If Achilles learn not this from voice divine, then shall he be afraid when some god shall come against him in the battle; for gods revealed are hard to look upon."

Then to her made answer Poseidon, Shaker of the earth: "Hera, be not fierce beyond wisdom; it behoveth thee not. Not fain am I at least to match gods with gods in strife. Let us go now into some high place apart and seat us there to watch, and battle shall be left to men. Only if Ares or Phoebus Apollo fall to fighting, or put constraint upon Achilles and hinder him from fight, then straightway among us too shall go up the battle-cry of strife; right soon, methinks, shall they hie them from the issue of the fray back to Olympus to the company of the gods, overcome by the force of our hands."

Thus spake the blue-haired god, and led the way to the mounded wall of heaven-sprung Herakles. There sate them down Poseidon and the other gods, and clothed their shoulders with impenetrable cloud. And they of the other part sat down on the brows of Kallikolonë around thee, Archer Phoebus, and Ares waster of cities. Thus they on either side sat devising counsels, but shrank all from falling to grievous war, and Zeus from his high seat commanded them.

Meanwhile the whole plain was filled with men and horses, and ablaze with bronze; and the earth rang with the feet of them as they rushed together in the fray. Two men far better than the rest were meeting in the midst between the hosts, eager for battle, Aineias, Anchises' son, and noble Achilles. First came on Aineias threateningly, tossing his strong helm; his rapid shield he held before his breast, and brandished his bronze spear. And on the other side the son of Peleus rushed to meet him like a lion. And when they were come near against each other, then first to Aineias spake fleet-footed noble Achilles: "Aineias, wherefore hast thou so far come forward from the crowd to stand against me: doth thy heart bid thee fight with me in hope of holding Priam's honour and lordship among the horse-taming Trojans? Nay, though thou slay me, not for that will Priam lay his kingdom in thy hands, for he hath sons, and is sound and of unshaken mind. Or have the Trojans allotted thee some lot of ground more choice than all the rest, fair land of tilth and orchard, that thou mayest dwell therein, if thou slay me? But methinks thou wilt find the slaying hard; for once before, I ween, have I made thee flee before my spear. Hast thou forgotten the day when thou wert alone with the kine, and I made thee run swift-footed down Ida's steeps in haste?—then didst thou not look behind thee in thy flight. Thence fleddest thou to Lernessos, but I wasted it, having fought against it with the help of Athene and of father Zeus, and carried away women captive, bereaving them of their day of freedom: only thee Zeus shielded, and other gods. But not this time, methinks, shall they shield thee, as thou imaginest in thy heart: therefore I bid thee go back into the throng and come not forth against me, while as yet thou art unhurt — after the event even a fool is wise."

Then to him in answer again Aineias spake: "Son of Peleus, think not with words to affright me as a child, since I too well know myself how to speak taunts and unjust speech. We know each other's race and lineage in that we have heard the fame proclaimed by mortal men, but never hast thou set eyes on my parents, or I on thine. Thou, they say, art son of noble Peleus, and of Thetis of the fair tresses, the daughter of the sea: the sire I boast is Anchises great of heart, and my mother is Aphrodite. Of these shall one pair or the other mourn their dear son to-day; for verily not with idle words shall we two satisfy our strife and depart out of the battle."

He said, and against the other's dread and mighty shield hurled his great spear, and the shield rang loud beneath the spear-point. And the son of Peleus held away the shield from him with his stout hand, in fear, for he thought that the far-shadowing spear of Aineias great of heart would lightly pierce it through — fond man, and knew not in his mind and heart that not lightly do the glorious gifts of gods yield to force of mortal men. So did not the great spear of wise Aineias pierce that shield, for the gold resisted it, even the gift of the god. Yet through two folds he drave it, but three remained, for five folds had the lame god welded, two bronze, and two inside of tin, and one of gold; therein was stayed the ashen spear.

Then Achilles in his turn hurled his far-shadowing spear, and smote upon the circle of the shield of Aineias, beneath the edge of the rim, where the bronze ran thinnest round, and the bull-hide was thinnest thereon; and right through sped the Pelian ashen spear, and the shield cracked under it. And Aineias crouched and held up the shield away from him in dread; and the spear flew over his back and fixed itself in the earth, having divided asunder the two circles of the sheltering shield. And having escaped the long spear he stood still, and a vast anguish drowned his eyes, affrighted that the spear was planted by him so nigh. But Achilles drew his sharp sword and furiously made at him, crying his terrible cry: then Aineias grasped in his hand a stone (a mighty deed) such as two men, as men now are, would not avail to lift, but he with ease wielded it all alone. Then would Aineias have smitten him with the stone as he charged, either on helm or shield, which had warded from him bitter death, and then would the son of Peleus have closed and slain him with his sword, had not Poseidon, Shaker of earth, marked it with speed, and straightway spoken among the immortal gods: "Alas, woe is me for Aineias great of heart, who quickly will go down to Hades slain by the son of Peleus, for that he will obey the words of Apollo the far-darter, fond man, but nowise shall the god help him from grievous death. Come, let us guide him out of death's way, lest the son of Kronos be wroth, if Achilles slay him."

And him then answered Hera the ox-eyed queen: "Shaker of earth, thyself with thine own mind take counsel, whether thou wilt save Aineias, or leave him. For by many oaths among all the Immortals have we two sworn, even Pallas Athene and I, never to help the Trojans from their evil day, not even when all Troy shall burn in the burning of fierce fire, and they that burn her shall be the warlike sons of the Achaians."

Now when Poseidon Shaker of earth heard that, he went up amid the battle and the clash of spears, and came where Aineias and renowned Achilles were. Then presently he shed mist over the eyes of Achilles, Peleus' son, and drew the bronze-headed ashen spear from the shield of Aineias great of heart, and set it before Achilles' feet, and lifted Aineias and swung him high from off the earth. Over many ranks of warriors, of horses many, sprang Aineias soaring in the hand of the god, and lighted at the farthest verge of the battle of many onsets, where the Kaukones were arraying them for the fight. Then hard beside him came Poseidon, Shaker of earth, and spake aloud to him winged words: "Aineias, what god is it that biddeth thee fight infatuate against Peleus' vehement son, who is both a better man than thou and dearer to Immortals? Rather withdraw thee whensoever thou fallest in with him, lest even contrary to thy fate thou enter the house of Hades. But when Achilles shall have met his death and doom, then be thou of good courage to fight among the foremost, for there shall none other of the Achaians slay thee."

He spoke, and left him there, when he had shown him all these things. Then quickly from Achilles' eyes he purged the magic mist; and he stared with wide eyes, and in trouble spake unto his proud soul: "Ha! verily a great marvel behold I here with mine eyes. My spear lieth here upon the ground, nor can I anywise see the man at whom I hurled it with intent to slay him. Truly then is Aineias likewise dear to the immortal gods, howbeit I deemed that his boasting thereof was altogether vanity. Away with him! not again will he find heart to make trial of me, now that once more he has escaped death to his joy. But come, I will call on the warlike Danaans and go forth to make trial of some other Trojan face to face."

He said, and leapt along the lines, and called upon each man: "No longer stand afar from the men of Troy, noble Achaians, but come let man match man and throw his soul into the fight. Hard is it for me, though I be strong, to assail so vast a folk and fight them all: not even Ares, though an immortal god, nor Athene, could plunge into the jaws of such a fray and toil therein. But to my utmost power with hands and feet and strength no whit, I say, will I be slack, nay, never so little, but right through their line will I go forward, nor deem I that any Trojan shall be glad who shall come nigh my spear."

Thus spake he urging them. But to the Trojans glorious Hector called aloud, and proclaimed that he would go forth against Achilles: "High-hearted Trojans, fear not Peleus' son. I too in words could fight even Immortals, but with the spear it were hard, for they are stronger far. Neither shall Achilles accomplish all his talk, but part thereof he is to accomplish, and part to break asunder in the midst. And against him will I go forth, though the hands of him be even as fire, yea though his hands be as fire and his fierceness as the flashing steel."

Thus spake he urging them, and the Trojans raised their spears for battle ; and their fierceness was mingled confusedly, and the battle-cry arose. Then Phoebus Apollo stood by Hector and spake to him: "Hector, no longer challenge Achilles at all before the lines, but in the throng await him and from amid the roar of the battle, lest haply he spear thee or come near and smite thee with his sword."

Thus spake he, and Hector again fell back into the crowd of men, for he was amazed when he heard the sound of a god's voice.

But Achilles sprang in among the Trojans, his heart clothed with strength, crying his terrible cry, and fell upon godlike Polydoros, Priam's son. Him would his sire continually forbid to fight, for that among his children he was youngest born and best beloved, and overcame all in fleetness of foot. Just then in boyish folly, displaying the swiftness of his feet, he was rushing through the forefighters, until he lost his life. Him in the midst did fleet-footed noble Achilles smite with a javelin, in his back as he darted by, where his belt's golden buckles clasped, and the breast and back plates overlapped : and right through beside the navel went the spear-head, and he fell on his knee with a cry, and dark cloud covered him round about, and he clasped his bowels to him with his hands as he sank.

Then when Hector saw his brother Polydoros clasping his bowels with his hands, and sinking to the earth, a mist fell over his eyes, nor longer might he endure to range so far apart, but he came up against Achilles brandishing his sharp spear, and like flame of fire. And Achilles when he saw him, sprang up, and spake exultingly : "Behold the man who hath deepest stricken into my soul, who slew my dear prized friend;

not long shall we now shrink from each other along the highways of the war."

He said, and looking grimly spake unto goodly Hector:
"Come thou near, that the sooner thou mayest arrive at the
goal of death."

Then to him, unterrified, said Hector of the glancing helm:
"Son of Peleus, think not with words to affright me as a child,
since I too know myself how to speak taunts and unjust speech.
And I know that thou art a man of might, and a far better
man than I. Yet doth this issue lie in the lap of the gods,
whether I though weaker shall take thy life with my hurled
spear, for mine too hath been found keen ere now."

He said, and poised his spear and hurled it, and Athene with
a breath turned it back from glorious Achilles, breathing very
lightly; and it came back to goodly Hector, and fell there
before his feet. Then Achilles set fiercely upon him, eager to
slay him, crying his terrible cry. But Apollo caught Hector
up, very easily, as a god may, and hid him in thick mist.
Thrice then did fleet-footed noble Achilles make onset with his
spear of bronze, and thrice smote the thick mist. Then with
dread shout he spake to him winged words: "Dog, thou art
now again escaped from death; yet came ill very nigh thee;
but now hath Phoebus Apollo saved thee, to whom thou must
surely pray when thou goest forth amid the clash of spears.
Verily I will slay thee yet when I meet thee hereafter, if any
god is helper of me too. Now will I make after the rest,
whomsoever I may seize."

As through deep glens rageth fierce fire on some parched
mountain-side, and the deep forest burneth, and the wind
driving it whirleth every way the flame, so raged he every way
with his spear, as it had been a god, pressing hard on the men
he slew; and the black earth ran with blood. For even as
when one yoketh wide-browed bulls to tread white barley in a
stablished threshing-floor, and quickly is it trodden out beneath

the feet of the loud-lowing bulls, thus beneath great-hearted Achilles his whole-hooved horses trampled corpses and shields together; and with blood all the axletree below was sprinkled and the rims that ran around the car, for blood-drops from the horses' hooves splashed them, and blood-drops from the tires of the wheels. But the son of Peleus pressed on to win him glory, flecking with gore his irresistible hands.

BOOK XXI

How Achilles fought with the River, and chased the men of Troy within their gates.

BUT when now they came unto the ford of the fair-flowing river, even eddying Xanthos, whom immortal Zeus begat, there sundering them he chased the one part to the plain toward the city, even where the Achaians were flying in affright the day before, when glorious Hector was in his fury — thither poured some in flight, and Hera spread before them thick mist to hinder them: — but half were pent into the deep-flowing silver-eddied river, and fell therein with a mighty noise, and the steep channel sounded, and the banks around rang loudly; for with shouting they swam therein hither and thither, whirled round the eddies. And as when at the rush of fire locusts take wing to fly unto a river, and the unwearying fire flameth forth on them with sudden onset, and they huddle in the water; so before Achilles was the stream of deep-eddying Xanthos filled with the roar and the throng of horses and men.

Then the seed of Zeus left behind him his spear upon the bank, leant against tamarisk bushes, and leapt in, as it were a god, keeping his sword alone, and devised grim work at heart, and smote as he turned him every way about: and their groaning went up ghastly as they were stricken by the sword, and the water reddened with blood. As before a dolphin of huge maw fly other fish and fill the nooks of some fair-havened bay, in terror, for he devoureth amain whichsoever of them he may catch; so along the channels of that dread stream the Trojans crouched beneath the precipitous sides. And when his hands were weary of slaughter he chose twelve young men alive out of the river, an atonement for Patroklos, Menoitios' son that was dead. These brought he forth amazed like fawns, and bound behind them their hands with well-cut thongs, which they themselves wore on their pliant doublets, and gave them to his comrades to lead down to the hollow ships. Then again he made his onset, athirst for slaying.

But the River waxed ever more wroth in his heart, and sought in his soul how he should stay goodly Achilles from his work, and ward destruction from the Trojans. Meanwhile the son of Peleus with his far-shadowing spear leapt, fain to slay him, upon Asteropaios son of Pelegon, whom wide-flowing Axios begat of Periboia eldest of the daughters of Akessamenos. Upon him set Achilles, and Asteropaios stood against him from the river, holding two spears; for Xanthos put courage into his heart, being angered for the slaughtered youths whom Achilles was slaughtering along the stream and had no pity on them. Then when the twain were come nigh in onset on each other, unto him first spake fleet-footed noble Achilles: "Who and whence art thou of men, that darest to come against me? Ill-fated are they whose children match them with my might."

And to him made answer Pelegon's noble son: "High-hearted son of Peleus, why askest thou my lineage? I come from deep-soiled Paionia, a land far off, leading Paionian men with their long spears, and this now is the eleventh morn since I am come to Ilios. My lineage is of wide-flowing Axios, who begat Pelegon famous with the spear, and he, men say, was my father. Now fight we, noble Achilles!"

Thus spake he in defiance, and goodly Achilles lifted the Pelian ash: but the warrior Asteropaios hurled with both spears together, for he could use both hands alike, and with the one spear smote the shield, but pierced it not right through, for the gold stayed it, the gift of a god; and with the other he grazed the elbow of Achilles' right arm, and there leapt forth dark blood, but the point beyond him fixed itself in the earth, eager to batten on flesh. Then in his turn Achilles hurled on Asteropaios his straight-flying ash, fain to have slain him, but missed the man and struck the high bank, and quivering half its length in the bank he left the ashen spear. Then the son of Peleus drew his sharp sword from his thigh and leapt fiercely at him, and he availed not to draw with his stout hand Achilles' ashen shaft from the steep bank. Thrice shook he it striving to draw it forth, and thrice gave up the strain, but the fourth time he was fain to bend and break the ashen spear of the seed of Aiakos, but ere that Achilles closing on him reft him of life with his sword. For in the belly he smote him beside the navel, and all his bowels gushed out to the earth, and darkness covered his eyes as he lay gasping. Then Achilles trampling on his breast stripped off his armour and spake exultingly: "Lie there! It is hard to strive against children of Kronos' mighty son, even though one be sprung from a River-god. Thou truly declarest thyself the seed of a wide-flowing River, but I avow me of the lineage of great Zeus. My sire is a man ruling many Myrmidons, Peleus the son of Aiakos, and Aiakos was begotten of Zeus. As Zeus is mightier than seaward-murmuring rivers, so is the seed of Zeus made mightier than the seed of a river. Nay, there is hard beside thee a great river, if he may anywise avail; but against Zeus the son of Kronos it is not possible to fight."

He said, and from the steep bank drew his bronze spear, and left there Asteropaios whom he had slain, lying in the sands, and the dark water flooded him. Around him eels and fishes swarmed, tearing and gnawing the fat about his kidneys. But Achilles went on after the charioted Paiones who still along the

eddying river huddled in fear, when they saw their best man in
the stress of battle slain violently by the hands and the sword
of the son of Peleus. There slew he Thersilochos and Mydon
and Astypylos and Mnesos and Thrasios and Ainios and
Ophelestes; and more yet of the Paiones would swift Achilles
have slain, had not the deep-eddying River called unto him in
wrath, in semblance of a man, and from an eddy's depth sent
forth a voice: "O Achilles, thy might and thy evil work are
beyond the measure of men; for gods themselves are ever helping thee. If indeed the son of Kronos hath delivered thee all
the Trojans to destroy, at least drive them forth from me and
do thy grim deeds on the plain, for filled with dead men is my
pleasant bed, nor can I pour my stream to the great sea, being
choked with dead, and thou slayest ruthlessly. Come then, let
be; I am astonied, O captain of hosts."

And to him answered Achilles fleet of foot: "So be it,
heaven-sprung Skamandros, even as thou biddest. But the
proud Trojans I will not cease from slaying until I have driven
them into their city, and have made trial with Hector face to
face whether he is to vanquish me or I him."

Thus saying, he set upon the Trojans, like a god. Then unto
Apollo spake the deep-eddying River: "Out on it, lord of the
silver bow, child of Zeus, thou hast not kept the ordinance of
Kronos' son, who charged thee straitly to stand by the Trojans
and to help them, until eve come with light late-setting, and
darken the deep-soiled earth."

He said, and spear-famed Achilles sprang from the bank and
leapt into his midst; but he rushed on him in a furious wave,
and stirred up all his streams in tumult, and swept down the
many dead who lay thick in him, slain by Achilles; these out
to land he cast with bellowing like a bull, and saved the living
under his fair streams, hiding them within eddies deep and
wide. But terribly around Achilles arose his tumultuous wave,
and the stream smote violently against his shield, nor availed

he to stand firm upon his feet. Then he grasped a tall fair-grown elm, and it fell uprooted and tore away all the bank, and reached over the fair river bed with its thick shoots, and stemmed the River himself, falling all within him: and Achilles, struggling out of the eddy, made haste to fly over the plain with his swift feet, for he was afraid. But the great god ceased not, but arose upon him with darkness on his crest, that he might stay noble Achilles from slaughter, and ward destruction from the men of Troy. And the son of Peleus rushed away a spear's throw, with the swoop of a black eagle, the mighty hunter, strongest at once and swiftest of winged birds. Like him he sped, and on his breast the bronze rang terribly as he fled from beneath the onset, and behind him the River rushed on with a mighty roar. As when a field-waterer from a dark spring leadeth water along a bed through crops and garden grounds, a mattock in his hands, casting forth hindrances from the ditch, and as it floweth all pebbles are swept down, and swiftly gliding it murmureth down a sloping place, and outrunneth him that is its guide: — thus ever the river wave caught up Achilles for all his speed; for gods are mightier than men. For whensoever fleet-footed noble Achilles struggled to stand against it, and know whether all immortals be upon him who inhabit spacious heaven, then would a great wave of the heaven-sprung River beat upon his shoulders from above, and he sprang upward with his feet, sore vexed at heart; and the River was wearying his knees with violent rush beneath, and devouring the earth from under his feet. Then the son of Peleus cried aloud, looking up to the broad heaven: "Zeus, Father, how doth none of the gods take it on him in pity to save me from the River? after that let come to me what may. None other of the inhabitants of Heaven is chargeable so much, but only my dear mother, who beguiled me with false words, saying that under the wall of the mail-clad men of Troy I must die by the swift arrows of Apollo. Would that Hector had slain me, the best of men bred here:

then brave had been the slayer, and a brave man had he slain. But now by a sorry death am I doomed to die, pent in this mighty river, like a swineherd boy whom a torrent sweepeth down as he essayeth to cross it in a storm."

Thus spake he, and quickly Poseidon and Athene came near and stood beside him, in the likeness of men, and taking his hands in theirs pledged him in words. And the first that spake was Poseidon, Shaker of the earth: "Son of Peleus, tremble not, neither be afraid; such helpers of thee are we from the gods, approved of Zeus, even Pallas Athene and I, for to be vanquished of a river is not appointed thee, but he will soon give back, and thou wilt thyself perceive it: but we will give thee wise counsel, if thou wilt obey it; hold not thy hand from hazardous battle until within Ilios' famous walls thou have pent the Trojan host, even all that flee before thee. But do thou, when thou hast taken the life of Hector, go back unto the ships; this glory we give unto thee to win."

They having thus spoken departed to the immortals, but he toward the plain — for the bidding of gods was strong upon him — went onward; and all the plain was filled with waterflood, and many beautiful arms and corpses of slain youths were drifting there. So upward sprang his knees as he rushed against the stream right on, nor stayed him the wide-flowing River, for Athene put great strength in him. Neither did Skamandros slacken his fierceness, but yet more raged against the son of Peleus, and he curled crestwise the billow of his stream, lifting himself on high, and on Simoeis he called with a shout: "Dear brother, the strength of this man let us both join to stay, since quickly he will lay waste the great city of king Priam, and the Trojans abide not in the battle. Help me with speed, and fill thy streams with water from thy springs, and urge on all thy torrents, and raise up a great wave, and stir huge roaring of tree-stumps and stones, that we may stay the fierce man who now is lording it, and deeming himself match for gods. For neither, I ween, will strength avail him, nor comeliness anywise, nor that armour beautiful, which deep beneath the flood shall be o'erlaid with slime, and himself I will wrap him in my sands and pour round him countless shingle without stint, or shall the Achaians know where to gather his bones, so vast a shroud of silt will I heap over them. Where he dieth there shall be his tomb, neither shall he have need of any barrow to be raised, when the Achaians make his funeral."

He said, and rushed in tumult on Achilles, raging from on high, thundering with foam and blood and bodies of dead men. Then did a dark wave of the heaven-sprung River stand towering up and overwhelm the son of Peleus. But Hera cried aloud in terror of Achilles, lest the great deep-eddying River sweep him away, and straightway she called to Hephaistos, her dear son: "Rise, lame god, O my son; it was against thee we thought that eddying Xanthos was matched in fight. Help with all speed, put forth large blast of flame. Then will I go to raise a strong storm out of the sea of the west wind and the white south which shall utterly consume the dead Trojans and their armour, blowing the angry flame. Thou along Xanthos' banks burn up his trees and wrap himself in fire, nor let him anywise turn thee back by soft words or by threat, nor stay thy rage—only when I cry to thee with my voice, then hold the unwearying fire."

Thus spake she, and Hephaistos made ready fierce-blazing fire. First on the plain fire blazed, and burnt the many dead who lay there thick, slain by Achilles; and all the plain was parched and the bright water stayed. And as when in late summer the north wind swiftly parcheth a new watered orchard, and he that tilleth it is glad, thus was the whole plain parched, and Hephaistos consumed the dead; then against the river he turned his gleaming flame. Elms burnt and willow trees and tamarisks, and lotos burnt and rush and galingale which round the fair streams of the river grew in multitude. And the eels

and fishes beneath the eddies were afflicted, which through the
fair streams tumbled this way and that, in anguish at the blast
of crafty Hephaistos. And the strong River burned, and spake
and called to him by name: "Hephaistos, there is no god can
match with thee, nor will I fight thee thus ablaze with fire.
Cease strife, yea, let noble Achilles drive the Trojans forthwith
out of their city; what have I to do with strife and succour?"

Thus spake he, burnt with fire, for his fair streams were
bubbling. Then unto Hera, earnestly beseeching her, he spake
winged words: "Hera, wherefore hath thy son assailed my
stream to vex it above others? I am less chargeable than all
the rest that are helpers of the Trojans. But lo, I will give
over, if thou wilt, and let thy son give over too. And I further
will swear even this, that never will I ward the day of evil from
the Trojans, not even when all Troy is burning in the blaze of
hungry fire, and the warlike sons of Achaians are the burners
thereof."

Then when the white-armed goddess Hera heard his speech,
straightway she spake unto Hephaistos her dear son: "Hephaistos, hold, famed son; it befitteth not thus for mortals'
sake to do violence to an immortal god."

Thus said she and Hephaistos quenched the fierce-blazing
fire, and the wave once more rolled down the fair river-bed.

Now Achilles was still slaying the Trojans, both themselves
and their whole-hooved horses. And as when a smoke goeth
up to the broad heaven, when a city burneth, kindled by the
wrath of gods, and causeth toil to all, and griefs to many, thus
caused Achilles toil and griefs to the Trojans. And the old
man Priam stood on the sacred tower, and was aware of dread
Achilles, how before him the Trojans thronged in rout, nor
was any succour found of them. Then with a cry he went
down from the tower, to rouse the gallant warders along the
walls: "Hold open the gates in your hands until the folk come
to the city in their rout, for closely is Achilles chasing them—

now trow I there will be deadly deeds. And when they are gathered within the wall and are taking breath, then again shut back the gate-wings firmly builded; for I fear lest that murderous man spring in within the wall."

Thus spake he, and they opened the gates and thrust back the bolts; and the gates flung back gave safety. Then Apollo leapt forth to the front that he might ward destruction from the Trojans. They straight for the city and the high wall were fleeing, parched with thirst and dust-grimed from the plain, and Achilles chased them vehemently with his spear, for strong frenzy possessed his heart continually, and he thirsted to win him renown. Then would the sons of the Achaians have taken high-gated Troy, had not Phoebus Apollo aroused goodly Agenor, Antenor's son, a princely man and strong. In his heart he put good courage, and himself stood by his side that he might ward off the grievous visitations of death, leaning against the oak, and he was shrouded in thick mist. So when Agenor was aware of Achilles waster of cities, he halted, and his heart much wavered as he stood; and in trouble he spake to his great heart: "Ay me, if I flee before mighty Achilles, there where the rest are driven terror-struck, nathless will he overtake me and slaughter me as a coward. Or what if I leave these to be driven before Achilles the son of Peleus, and flee upon my feet from the wall by another way to the Ileian plain, until I come to the spurs of Ida, and hide me in the underwood? So then at evening, having bathed in the river and refreshed me of sweat, I might return to Ilios. Nay, why doth my heart debate thus within me? Lest he might be aware of me as I get me from the city for the plain, and speeding after overtake me with swift feet; then will it no more be possible to avoid the visitation of death, for he is exceeding mighty above all mankind. What then if in front of the city I go forth to meet him? Surely his flesh too is penetrable by sharp bronze, and there is but one life within, and men say he is mortal, howbeit Zeus the son of Kronos giveth him renown."

Thus saying, he gathered himself to await Achilles, and within him his stout heart was set to strive and fight. As a leopardess goeth forth from a deep thicket to affront a huntsman, nor is afraid at heart, nor fleeth when she heareth the bay of hounds; for albeit the man first smite her with thrust or throw, yet even pierced through with the spear she ceaseth not from her courage until she either grapple or be slain, so noble Antenor's son, goodly Agenor, refused to flee till he should put Achilles to the proof, but held before him the circle of his shield, and aimed at him with his spear, and cried aloud: "Doubtless thou hopest in thy heart, noble Achilles, on this day to sack the city of the proud men of Troy. Fond man, there shall many woful things yet be wrought before it, for within it we are many men and staunch, who in front of our parents dear and wives and sons keep Ilios safe; but thou shalt here meet death, albeit so redoubtable and bold a man of war."

He said, and hurled his sharp spear with weighty hand, and smote him on the leg beneath the knee, nor missed his mark, and the greave of new-wrought tin rang terribly on him; but the bronze bounded back from him it smote, nor pierced him, for the god's gift drave it back. Then the son of Peleus in his turn made at godlike Agenor, but Apollo suffered him not to win renown, but caught away Agenor, and shrouded him in thick mist, and sent him in peace to be gone out of the war. Then by wile he kept the son of Peleus away from the folk, for in complete semblance of Agenor himself he stood before the feet of Achilles, who hasted to run upon him and chase him. And while he chased him over the wheat-bearing plain, edging him toward the deep-eddying river Skamandros, as he ran but a little in front of him (for by wile Apollo beguiled him that he kept ever hoping to overtake him in the race), meantime the other Trojans in common rout came gladly unto their fastness, and the city was filled with the throng of them. Neither had they heart to await one another outside the city and wall, and to know who might have escaped and who had perished in the fight, but impetuously they poured into the city, whomsoever of them his feet and knees might save.

BOOK XXII

How Achilles fought with Hector, and slew him, and brought his body to the ships.

THUS they throughout the city, scared like fawns, were cooling their sweat and drinking and slaking their thirst, leaning on the fair battlements, while the Achaians drew near the wall, setting shields to shoulders. But Hector deadly fate bound to abide in his place, in front of Ilios and the Skaian gates. Then to the son of Peleus spake Phoebus Apollo: "Wherefore, son of Peleus, pursuest thou me with swift feet, thyself being mortal and I a deathless god? Thou hast not even yet known me, that I am a god, but strivest vehemently. Truly thou regardest not thy task among the affliction of the Trojans whom thou affrightedst, who now are gathered into the city, while thou hast wandered hither. Me thou wilt never slay, for I am not subject unto death."

Then mightily moved spake unto him Achilles fleet of foot: "Thou hast baulked me, Far-darter, most mischievous of all the gods, in that thou hast turned me hither from the wall: else should full many yet have bitten the dust or ever within Ilios had they come. Now hast thou robbed me of great renown, and lightly hast saved them, because thou hadst no vengeance to fear thereafter. Verily I would avenge me on thee, had I but the power."

Thus saying toward the city he was gone in pride of heart,

rushing like some victorious horse in a chariot, that runneth lightly at full speed over the plain; so swiftly plied Achilles his feet and knees. Him the old man Priam first beheld as he sped across the plain, blazing as the star that cometh forth at harvest-time, and plain seen his rays shine forth amid the host of stars in the darkness of night, the star whose name men call Orion's Dog. Even so on Achilles' breast the bronze gleamed as he ran. And the old man cried aloud and beat upon his head with his hands, raising them on high, and with a cry called aloud beseeching his dear son; for he before the gates was standing, all hot for battle with Achilles. And the old man spake piteously unto him, stretching forth his hands: "Hector, beloved son, I pray thee await not this man alone with none beside thee, lest thou quickly meet thy doom, slain by the son of Peleus, since he is mightier far, a merciless man. Would the gods loved him even as do I! then quickly would dogs and vultures devour him on the field — thereby would cruel pain go from my heart — the man who hath bereft me of many valiant sons, slaying them and selling them captive into far-off isles. Nay, come within the wall, my child, that thou preserve the men and women of Troy, neither give great triumph to the son of Peleus, and be thyself bereft of sweet life. Have compassion also on me, the helpless one, who still can feel, ill-fated; whom the father, Kronos' son, will bring to naught by a grievous doom in the path of old age, having seen full many ills, his sons perishing and his daughters carried away captive, and his chambers laid waste and infant children hurled to the ground in terrible war, and his sons' wives dragged away by the ruinous hands of the Achaians. Myself then last of all at the street door will ravening dogs tear, when some one by stroke or throw of the sharp bronze hath bereft my limbs of life — even the dogs I reared in my halls about my table and to guard my door, which then having drunk my blood, maddened at heart shall lie in the gateway. A young man all beseemeth, even to be slain in war, to be torn by the sharp bronze and lie on the field; though he be dead yet is all honourable to him, whate'er be seen: but when dogs defile the hoary head and hoary beard of an old man slain, this is the most piteous thing that cometh upon hapless men."

Thus spake the old man, and grasped his hoary hairs, plucking them from his head, but he persuaded not Hector's soul. Then his mother in her turn wailed tearfully, loosening the folds of her robe, while with the other hand she showed her breast; and through her tears spake to him winged words: "Hector, my child, have regard unto this bosom and pity me, if ever I gave thee consolation of my breast. Think of it, dear child, and from this side the wall drive back the foe, nor stand in front to meet him. He is merciless; if he slay thee it will not be on a bed that I or thy wife shall bewail thee, my own dear child, but far away from us by the ships of the Argives will swift dogs devour thee."

Thus they with wailing spake to their dear son, beseeching him sore, yet they persuaded not Hector's soul, but he stood awaiting Achilles as he drew nigh in giant might. As a serpent of the mountains upon his den awaiteth a man, having fed on evil poisons, and fell wrath hath entered into him, and terribly he glared as he coileth himself about his den, so Hector with courage unquenchable gave not back, leaning his shining shield against a jutting tower. Then sore troubled he spake to his great heart: "Ay me, if I go within the gates and walls, Polydamas will be first to bring reproach against me, since he bade me lead the Trojans to the city during this ruinous night, when noble Achilles arose. But I regarded him not, yet surely it had been better far. And now that I have undone the host by my wantonness, I am ashamed before the men of Troy and women of trailing robes, lest at any time some worse man than I shall say: 'Hector by trusting his own might undid the host.' So will they speak; then to me would it be better far to face Achilles and either slay him and go home, or myself die gloriously before the city. Or what if I lay down my bossy shield and my stout helm, and lean my spear against the wall, and go of myself to meet noble Achilles and promise him that Helen, and with her all possessions that Alexandros brought in hollow ships to Troy, the beginning of strife, we will give to the sons of Atreus to take away, and therewithal to divide in half with the Achaians all else that this city holdeth: and if thereafter I obtain from the Trojans an oath of the Elders that they will hide nothing but divide all in twain? But wherefore doth my heart debate thus? I might come unto him and he would not pity 'or regard me at all, but presently slay me unarmed as it were but a woman, if I put off my armour. Better is it to join battle with all speed: let us know upon which of us twain the Olympian shall bestow renown."

Thus pondered he as he stood, but nigh on him came Achilles, brandishing from his right shoulder the Pelian ash, his terrible spear; and all around the bronze on him flashed like the gleam of blazing fire or of the Sun as he ariseth. And trembling seized Hector as he was aware of him, nor endured he to abide in his place, but left the gates behind him and fled in fear. And the son of Peleus darted after him, trusting in his swift feet. As a falcon upon the mountains, swiftest of winged things, swoopeth fleetly after a trembling dove; and she before him fleeth, while he with shrill screams hard at hand still darteth at her, for his heart urgeth him to seize her; so Achilles in hot haste flew straight for him, and Hector fled beneath the Trojans' wall, and plied swift knees. They past the watch-place and wind-waved wild fig-tree sped ever, away from under the wall, along the waggon-track, and came to the two fair-flowing springs, where two fountains rise that feed deep-eddying Skamandros. Thereby they ran, he flying, he pursuing. Valiant was the flier but far mightier he who fleetly pursued him. For not for beast of sacrifice or for an oxhide were they striving, such as are prizes for men's speed of foot, but for the life of horse-taming Hector was their race. And as when victorious whole-hooved horses run rapidly round the turning-points, and some great prize lieth in sight, be it a tripod or a woman, in honour of a man that is dead, so thrice around Priam's city circled those twain with flying feet, and all the gods were gazing on them. Then among them spake first the father of gods and men: "Ay me, a man beloved I see pursued around the wall. My heart is woe for Hector, who hath burnt for me many thighs of oxen amid the crests of many-folded Ida, and other times on the city-height; but now is goodly Achilles pursuing him with swift feet round Priam's town. Come, give your counsel, gods, and devise whether we shall save him from death or now at last slay him, valiant though he be, by the hand of Achilles Peleus' son."

Then to him answered the bright-eyed goddess Athene: "O Father, Lord of the bright lightning and the dark cloud, what is this thou hast said? A man that is a mortal, doomed long ago by fate, wouldst thou redeem back from ill-boding death? Do it, but not all we other gods approve."

And unto her in answer spake cloud-gathering Zeus: "Be of good cheer, dear child: not in full earnest speak I, and I would fain be kind to thee. Do as seemeth good to thy mind, and draw not back."

Thus saying he roused Athene, that already was set thereon, and from the crests of Olympus she darted down.

But after Hector sped fleet Achilles chasing him vehemently. And as when on the mountains a hound hunteth the fawn of a deer, having started it from its covert, through glens and glades, and if it crouch to baffle him under a bush, yet scenting it out the hound runneth constantly until he find it; so Hector baffled not Peleus' fleet-footed son. Oft as he set himself to dart under the well-built walls over against the Dardanian gates, if haply from above they might succour him with darts, so oft would Achilles gain on him and turn him toward the plain, while himself he sped ever on the city-side. And as in a dream one faileth in chase of a flying man — the one faileth in his flight and the other in his chase — so failed Achilles to overtake him in the race, and Hector to escape. For to the host did noble Achilles sign with his head, and forbade them to hurl bitter darts against Hector, lest any smiting him should gain renown, and he himself come second. But when the fourth time they had reached the springs, then the Father hung his golden balances, and set therein two lots of dreary death, one of Achilles, one of horse-taming Hector, and held them by the midst and poised. Then Hector's fated day sank down, and fell to the house of Hades, and Phoebus Apollo left him. But to Peleus' son came the bright-eyed goddess Athene, and standing near spake to him winged words: "Now verily, glorious Achilles dear to Zeus, I have hope that we twain shall carry off great glory to the ships for the Achaians, having slain Hector, for all his thirst for fight. No longer is it possible for him to escape us, not even though far-darting Apollo should travail sore, grovelling before the Father, aegis-bearing Zeus. But do thou now stand and take breath, and I will go and persuade this man to confront thee in fight."

Thus spake Athene, and he obeyed, and was glad at heart, and stood leaning on his bronze-pointed ashen-spear. And she left him and came to noble Hector, like unto Deïphobos in shape and in strong voice, and standing near spake to him winged words: "Dear brother, verily fleet Achilles doth thee violence, chasing thee round Priam's town with swift feet: but come let us make a stand and await him on our defence."

Then answered her great Hector of the glancing helm: "Deïphobos, verily aforetime wert thou far dearest of my brothers, but now methinks I shall honour thee even more, in that thou hast dared for my sake, when thou sawest me, to come forth of the wall, while the others tarry within."

Then to him again spake the bright-eyed goddess Athene: "Dear brother, of a truth my father and lady mother and my comrades around besought me much, entreating me in turn, to tarry there, so greatly do they all tremble before him; but my heart within was sore with dismal grief. And now fight we with straight-set resolve and let there be no sparing of spears, that we may know whether Achilles is to slay us and carry our bloody spoils to the hollow ships, or whether he might be vanquished by thy spear."

Thus saying Athene in her subtlety led him on. And when they were come nigh in onset on one another, to Achilles first spake great Hector of the glancing helm: "No longer, son of Peleus, will I fly thee, as before I thrice ran round the great town of Priam, and endured not to await thy onset. Now my heart biddeth me stand up against thee; I will either slay or be slain. But come hither and let us pledge us by our gods, for they shall be best witnesses and beholders of covenants: I will entreat thee in no outrageous sort, if Zeus grant me to outstay thee, and if I take thy life, but when I have despoiled thee of thy glorious armour, O Achilles, I will give back thy dead body to the Achaians, and do thou the same."

But unto him with grim gaze spake Achilles fleet of foot: "Hector, talk not to me, thou madman, of covenants. As between men and lions there is no pledge of faith, nor wolves and sheep can be of one mind, but imagine evil continually against each other, so is it impossible for thee and me to be friends, neither shall be any pledge between us until one or other shall have fallen and glutted with blood Ares, the stubborn god of war. Bethink thee of all thy soldiership: now behoveth it thee to quit thee as a good spearman and valiant man of war. No longer is there way of escape for thee, but

Pallas Athene will straightway subdue thee to my spear; and now in one hour shalt thou pay back for all my sorrows for my friends whom thou hast slain in the fury of thy spear."

He said, and poised his far-shadowing spear and hurled. And noble Hector watched the coming thereof and avoided it; for with his eye on it he crouched, and the bronze spear flew over him, and fixed itself in the earth; but Pallas Athene caught it up and gave it back to Achilles, unknown of Hector shepherd of hosts. Then Hector spake unto the noble son of Peleus: "Thou hast missed, so nowise yet, godlike Achilles, has thou known from Zeus the hour of my doom, though thou thoughtest it. Cunning of tongue art thou and a deceiver in speech, that fearing thee I might forget my valour and strength. Not as I flee shalt thou plant thy spear in my reins, but drive it straight through my breast as I set on thee, if God hath given thee to do it. Now in thy turn avoid my spear of bronze. O that thou mightst take it all into thy flesh! Then would the war be lighter to the Trojans, if but thou wert dead, for thou art their greatest bane."

He said, and poised his long-shadowed spear and hurled it, and smote the midst of the shield of Peleus' son, and missed him not: but far from the shield the spear leapt back. And Hector was wroth that his swift weapon had left his hand in vain, and he stood downcast, for he had no second ashen spear. And he called with a loud shout to Deïphobos of the white shield, and asked of him a long spear, but he was nowise nigh. Then Hector knew the truth in his heart, and spake and said: "Ay me, now verily the gods have summoned me to death. I deemed the warrior Deïphobos was by my side, but he is within the wall, and it was Athene who played me false. Now therefore is evil death come very nigh me, not far off, nor is there way of escape. This then was from of old the pleasure of Zeus and of the far-darting son of Zeus, who yet before were fain to succour me: but now my fate hath found me. At least let me not die without a struggle or ingloriously, but in some great deed of arms whereof men yet to be born shall hear."

Thus saying he drew his sharp sword that by his flank hung great and strong, and gathered himself and swooped like a soaring eagle that darteth to the plain through the dark clouds to seize a tender lamb or crouching hare. So Hector swooped, brandishing his sharp sword. And Achilles made at him, for his heart was filled with wild fierceness, and before his breast he made a covering with his fair graven shield, and tossed his bright four-plated helm; and round it waved fair golden plumes. As a star goeth among stars in the darkness of night, Hesperos, fairest of all stars set in heaven, so flashed there forth a light from the keen spear Achilles poised in his right hand, devising mischief against noble Hector, eyeing his fair flesh to find the fittest place. Now for the rest of him his flesh was covered by the fair bronze armour he stripped from strong Patroklos when he slew him, but there was an opening where the collar bones coming from the shoulders clasp the neck, even at the gullet, where destruction of life cometh quickliest; there, as he came on, noble Achilles drave at him with his spear, and right through the tender neck went the point. Yet the bronze-weighted ashen spear clave not the windpipe, so that he might yet speak words of answer to his foe. And he fell down in the dust, and noble Achilles spake exultingly: "Hector, thou thoughtest, whilst thou wert spoiling Patroklos, that thou wouldst be safe, and didst reck nothing of me who was afar, thou fool. But away among the hollow ships his comrade, a mightier far, even I, was left behind, who now have unstrung thy knees. Thee shall dogs and birds tear foully, but his funeral shall the Achaians make."

Then with faint breath spake unto him Hector of the

glancing helm: "I pray thee by thy life and knees and
parents, leave me not for dogs of the Achaians to devour
by the ships, but take good store of bronze and gold, gifts
that my father and lady mother shall give to thee, and give
them home my body back again, that the Trojans and Trojans'
wives give me my due of fire after my death."

But unto him with grim gaze spake Achilles fleet of foot:
"Entreat me not, dog, by knees or parents. Would that
my heart's desire could so bid me myself to carve and eat raw
thy flesh, for the evil thou hast wrought me, as surely is there
none that shall keep the dogs from thee, not even should they
bring ten or twenty fold ransom and here weigh it out, and
promise even more, not even were Priam Dardanos' son to
bid pay thy weight in gold, not even so shall thy lady mother
lay thee on a bed to mourn her son, but dogs and birds shall
devour thee utterly."

Then dying spake unto him Hector of the glancing helm:
"Verily I know thee and behold thee as thou art, nor was
I destined to persuade thee; truly thy heart is iron in thy
breast. Take heed now lest I draw upon thee wrath of gods,
in the day when Paris and Phoebus Apollo slay thee, for all
thy valour, at the Skaian gate."

He ended, and the shadow of death came down upon him,
and his soul flew forth of his limbs and was gone to the house
of Hades, wailing her fate, leaving her vigour and youth.
Then to the dead man spake noble Achilles: "Die: for my
death, I will accept it whensoever Zeus and the other immortal
gods are minded to accomplish it."

He said, and from the corpse drew forth his bronze spear,
and set it aside, and stripped the bloody armour from the
shoulders. And other sons of Achaians ran up around, who
gazed upon the stature and marvellous goodliness of Hector.
Nor did any stand by but wounded him, and thus would many
a man say looking toward his neighbour: "Go to, of a truth

far easier to handle is Hector now than when he burnt the ships with blazing fire." Thus would many a man say, and wound him as he stood hard by. And when fleet noble Achilles had despoiled him, he stood up among the Achaians and spake winged words: "Friends, chiefs and counsellors of the Argives, since the gods have vouchsafed us to vanquish this man who hath done us more evil than all the rest together, come let us make trial in arms round about the city, that we may know somewhat of the Trojans' purpose, whether since he hath fallen they will forsake the citadel, or whether they are minded to abide, albeit Hector is no more. But wherefore doth my heart debate thus? There lieth by the ships a dead man unbewailed, unburied, Patroklos; him will I not forget, while I abide among the living and my knees can stir. Nay if even in the house of Hades the dead forget their dead, yet will I even there be mindful of my dear comrade. But come, ye sons of the Achaians, let us now, singing our song of victory, go back to the hollow ships and take with us our foe. Great glory have we won; we have slain the noble Hector, unto whom the Trojans prayed throughout their city, as he had been a god."

He said, and devised foul entreatment of noble Hector. The tendons of both feet behind he slit from heel to ankle-joint, and thrust therethrough thongs of ox-hide, and bound him to his chariot, leaving his head to trail. And when he had mounted the chariot and lifted therein the famous armour, he lashed his horses to speed, and they nothing loth flew on. And dust rose around him that was dragged, and his dark hair flowed loose on either side, and in the dust lay all his once fair head, for now had Zeus given him over to his foes to entreat foully in his own native land.

Thus was his head all grimed with dust. But his mother when she beheld her son, tore her hair and cast far from her her shining veil, and cried aloud with an exceeding bitter cry. And piteously moaned his father, and around them the folk fell to crying and moaning throughout the town. Most like it seemed as though all beetling Ilios were burning utterly in fire. Scarcely could the folk keep back the old man in his hot desire to get him forth of the Dardanian gates. For he besought them all, casting himself down in the mire, and calling on each man by his name: "Hold, friends, and though you love me leave me to get me forth of the city alone and go unto the ships of the Achaians. Let me pray this accursed horror-working man, if haply he may feel shame before his age-fellows and pity an old man. He also hath a father such as I am, Peleus, who begat and reared him to be a bane of Trojans — and most of all to me hath he brought woe. So many sons of mine hath he slain in their flower — yet for all my sorrow for the rest I mourn them all less than this one alone, for whom my sharp grief will bring me down to the house of Hades — even Hector. Would that he had died in my arms; then would we have wept and wailed our fill, his mother who bore him to her ill hap, and I myself."

Thus spake he wailing, and all the men of the city made moan with him. And among the women of Troy, Hekabe led the wild lament: "My child, ah, woe is me! wherefore should I live in my pain, now thou art dead, who night and day wert my boast through the city, and blessing to all, both men and women of Troy throughout the town, who hailed thee as a god, for verily an exceeding glory to them wert thou in thy life: — now death and fate have overtaken thee."

Thus spake she wailing. But Hector's wife knew not as yet, for no true messenger had come to tell her how her husband abode without the gates, but in an inner chamber of the lofty house she was weaving a double purple web, and broidering therein manifold flowers. Then she called to her goodly-haired handmaids through the house to set a great tripod on the fire, that Hector might have warm washing when he came home out of the battle — fond heart, and was unaware how, far from all washings, bright-eyed Athene had slain him by the hand of Achilles. But she heard shrieks and groans from the battlements, and her limbs reeled, and the shuttle fell from her hands to earth. Then again among her goodly-haired maids she spake: "Come two of ye this way with me that I may see what deeds are done. It was the voice of my husband's noble mother that I heard, and in my own breast my heart leapeth to my mouth and my knees are numbed beneath me: surely some evil thing is at hand against the children of Priam. Would that such word might never reach my ear! yet terribly I dread lest noble Achilles have cut off bold Hector from the city by himself and chased him to the plain and ere this ended his perilous pride that possessed him, for never would he tarry among the throng of men but ran out before them far, yielding place to no man in his hardihood."

Thus saying she sped through the chamber like one mad, with beating heart, and with her went her handmaidens. But when she came to the battlements and the throng of men, she stood still upon the wall and gazed, and beheld him dragged before the city: — swift horses dragged him recklessly toward the hollow ships of the Achaians. Then dark night came on her eyes and shrouded her, and she fell backward and gasped forth her spirit. From off her head she shook the bright attiring thereof, frontlet and net and woven band, and veil, the veil that golden Aphrodite gave her on the day when Hector of the glancing helm led her forth of the house of Eëtion, having given bride-gifts untold. And around her thronged her husband's sisters and his brothers' wives, who held her up among them, distraught even to death. But when at last she came to herself and her soul returned into her breast, then wailing with deep sobs she spake among the women of Troy: "O Hector, woe is me! to one fate then were we both born, thou in Troy in the house of Priam, and I in Thebe under woody Plakos, in the house of Eëtion, who reared me from a little one — ill-fated sire of cruel-fated child. Now thou to the house of Hades beneath the secret places of the earth departest, and me in bitter mourning thou leavest a widow in thy halls: and thy son is but an infant child — son of unhappy parents, thee and me — nor shalt thou profit him, Hector, since thou art dead, neither he thee."

Thus spake she wailing, and the women joined their moan.

BOOK XXIII

Of the funeral of Patroklos, and the funeral games.

THUS they throughout the city made moan: but the Achaians when they were come to the ships and to the Hellespont were scattered each to his own ship: only the Myrmidons Achilles suffered not to be scattered, but spake among his comrades whose delight was in war: " Fleet-horsed Myrmidons, my trusty comrades, let us not yet unyoke our whole-hooved steeds from their cars, but with horses and chariots let us go near and mourn Patroklos, for such is the honour of the dead. Then when we have our fill of grievous wailing, we will unyoke the horses and all sup here."

He said, and they with one accord made lamentation, and Achilles led their mourning. So thrice around the dead they drave their well-maned steeds, moaning; and Thetis stirred among them desire of wailing. Bedewed were the sands with tears, bedewed the warriors' arms; so great a lord of fear they sorrowed for. And Peleus' son led their loud wail, laying his man-slaying hands on his comrade's breast: "All hail, Patroklos, even in the house of Hades; for all that I promised thee before am I accomplishing, seeing I have dragged hither Hector to give raw unto dogs to devour, and twelve noble children of the Trojans to slaughter before thy pyre, because of mine anger at thy slaying."

He said, and devised foul entreatment of noble Hector, stretching him prone in the dust beside the bier of Menoitios' son. And the rest put off each his glittering bronze arms, and unyoked their high-neighing horses, and sate them down numberless beside the ship of fleet-footed Aiakides, and he gave them ample funeral feast. Many sleek oxen were stretched out, their throats cut with steel, and many sheep and bleating goats, and many white-tusked boars well grown in fat were spitted to singe in the flame of Hephaistos; so on all sides round the corpse in cupfuls blood was flowing.

But the fleet-footed prince, the son of Peleus, was brought to noble Agamemnon by the Achaian chiefs, hardly persuading him thereto, for his heart was wroth for his comrade. And when they were come to Agamemnon's hut, forthwith they bade clear-voiced heralds set a great tripod on the fire, if haply they might persuade the son of Peleus to wash from him the bloody gore. But he denied them steadfastly, and sware moreover an oath: "Nay, verily by Zeus, who is highest and best of gods, not lawful is it that water should come nigh my head or ever I shall have laid Patroklos on the fire, and heaped a barrow, and shaved my hair, since never again shall second grief thus reach my heart, while I remain among the living. Yet now for the present let us yield us to our mournful meal: but with the morning, O king of men Agamemnon, rouse the folk to bring wood and furnish all that it beseemeth a dead man to have when he goeth beneath the misty gloom, to the end that untiring fire may burn him quickly from sight, and the host betake them to their work."

Thus spake he, and they listened readily to him and obeyed, and eagerly making ready each his meal they supped, and no lack had their soul of equal feast. But when they had put off from them the desire of meat and drink, the rest went down each man to his tent to take his rest, but the son of Peleus upon the beach of the sounding sea lay groaning heavily, amid the host of Myrmidons, in an open place, where waves were breaking on the shore. Now when sleep took hold on him, easing the cares of his heart, deep sleep that fell about him, (for sore tired were his glorious knees with onset upon Hector toward windy Ilios), then came there unto him the spirit of hapless Patroklos, in all things like his living self, in stature, and fair eyes, and voice, and the raiment of his body was the same; and he stood above Achilles' head and spake to him: "Thou sleepest, and hast forgotten me, O Achilles. Not in my life wast thou ever unmindful of me, but in my death. Bury me with all speed, that I pass the gates of Hades. Far off the spirits banish me, the phantoms of men outworn, nor suffer me to mingle with them beyond the River, but vainly I wander along the wide-gated dwelling of Hades. Now give me, I pray pitifully of thee, thy hand, for never more again shall I come back from Hades, when ye have given me my due of fire. Never among the living shall we sit apart from our dear comrades and take counsel together, but me hath the harsh fate swallowed up which was appointed me even from my birth. Yea and thou too thyself, Achilles peer of gods, beneath the wall of the noble Trojans art doomed to die. Yet one thing will I say, and charge thee, if haply thou wilt have regard thereto. Lay not my bones apart from thine, Achilles, but together, even as we were nurtured in your house, when Menoitios brought me yet a little one from Opöeis to your country by reason of a grievous man-slaying, on the day when I slew Amphidamas' son, not willing it, in childish wrath over the dice. Then took me the knight Peleus into his house and reared me kindly and named me thy squire: so therefore let one coffer hide our bones."

Then made answer unto him Achilles fleet of foot: "Wherefore, O my brother, hast thou come hither, and chargest me everything that I should do? Verily I will accomplish all, and have regard unto thy bidding. But stand more nigh me; for one moment let us throw our arms around each other, and take our fill of dolorous lament."

He spake, and reached forth with his hands, but clasped him not; for like a vapour the spirit was gone beneath the earth with a faint shriek. And Achilles sprang up marvelling, and smote his hands together, and spake a word of woe: "Ay me, there remaineth then even in the house of Hades a spirit and phantom of the dead, albeit the life be not anywise therein: for all night long hath the spirit of hapless Patroklos stood over me, wailing and making moan, and charged me everything that I should do, and wondrous like his living self it seemed."

Thus said he, and stirred in all of them yearning to make lament; and rosy-fingered Morn shone forth on them while they still made moan around the piteous corpse. Then lord Agamemnon sped mules and men from all the huts to fetch wood; and a man of valour watched thereover, even Meriones, squire of kindly Idomeneus. And they went forth with wood-cutting axes in their hands and well-woven ropes, and before them went the mules, and uphill and downhill and sideways and across they went. But when they came to the spurs of many-fountained Ida, straightway they set them lustily to hew high-foliaged oaks with the long-edged bronze, and with loud noise fell the trees. Then splitting them asunder the Achaians bound them behind the mules, and they tore up the earth with their feet as they made for the plain through the thick underwood. And all the wood-cutters bare logs; for thus bade Meriones, squire of kindly Idomeneus. And on the shore they threw them down in line, where Achilles purposed a mighty tomb for Patroklos and for himself.

Then when they had laid down all about great piles of wood, they sate them down all together and abode. Then straightway Achilles bade the warlike Myrmidons gird on their arms, and each yoke the horses to his chariot; and they arose and put their armour on, and mounted their chariots, both fighting men and charioteers. In front were the men in chariots, and a cloud of footmen followed after, numberless; and in the midst his comrades bare Patroklos. And they heaped all the corpse with their hair that they cut off and threw thereon; and behind did goodly Achilles bear the head, sorrowing; for a noble comrade was he speeding forth unto the realm of Hades.

And when they came to the place where Achilles had bidden them, they set down the dead, and piled for him abundant wood. Then fleet-footed noble Achilles bethought him of one thing more: standing apart from the pyre he shore off a golden lock, the lock whose growth he nursed to offer unto the River Spercheios, and sore troubled spake he, looking forth over the wine-dark sea: "Spercheios, in other wise vowed my father Peleus unto thee that I returning thither to my native land should shear my hair for thee and offer a holy hecatomb, and fifty rams should sacrifice there above thy springs, where is thy sacred close and altar burning spice. So vowed the old man, but thou hast not accomplished him his desire. And now since I return not to my dear native land, unto the hero Patroklos I may give this hair to take away."

Thus saying he set the hair in the hands of his dear comrade, and stirred in all of them yearning to make lament. And so would the light of the sun have gone down on their lamentation, had not Achilles said quickly to Agamemnon as he stood beside him: "Son of Atreus — for to thy words most will the host of the Achaians have regard — of lamentation they may sate them to the full. But now disperse them from the burning and bid them make ready their meal, and we to whom the dead is dearest will take pains for these things; yet let the chiefs tarry nigh unto us."

Then when Agamemnon king of men heard that, he forthwith dispersed the host among the trim ships, but the nearest to the dead tarried there and piled the wood, and made a pyre a hundred feet this way and that, and on the pyre's top set the corpse, with anguish at their hearts. And many lusty sheep and shambling crook-horned oxen they flayed and made ready before the pyre ; and taking from all of them the fat, great-hearted Achilles wrapped the corpse therein from head to foot, and heaped the flayed bodies round. And he set therein two-handled jars of honey and oil, leaning them against the bier; and four strong-necked horses he threw swiftly on the pyre, and groaned aloud. Nine house-dogs had the dead chief: of them did Achilles slay twain and throw them on the pyre. And twelve valiant sons of great-hearted Trojans he slew with the sword — for he devised mischief in his heart — and he set to the merciless might of the fire, to feed thereon. Then moaned he aloud, and called on his dear comrade by his name : "All hail to thee, O Patroklos, even in the house of Hades, for all that I promised thee before am I now accomplishing. Twelve valiant sons of great-hearted Trojans, behold these all in company with thee the fire devoureth : but Hector son of Priam will I nowise give to the fire to feed upon, but to dogs."

Thus spake he threatening, but no dogs might deal with Hector, for day and night Aphrodite daughter of Zeus kept off the dogs, and anointed him with rose-sweet oil ambrosial that Achilles might not tear him when he dragged him. And over him Phoebus Apollo brought a dark cloud from heaven to earth and covered all that place whereon the dead man lay, lest meanwhile the sun's strength shrivel his flesh round about upon his sinews and limbs.

But the pyre of dead Patroklos kindled not. Then fleet-footed noble Achilles had a further thought : standing aside from the pyre he prayed to the two Winds of North and West, and promised them fair offerings, and pouring large libations from a golden cup besought them to come, that the corpses might blaze up speedily in the fire, and the wood make haste

THE FUNERAL PILE OF PATROKLOS

to be enkindled. Then Iris, when she heard his prayer, went swiftly with the message to the Winds. They within the house of the gusty West Wind were feasting all together at meat, when Iris sped thither, and halted on the threshold of stone. And when they saw her with their eyes, they sprang up and called to her every one to sit by him. But she refused to sit, and spake her word: "No seat for me; I must go back to the streams of Ocean, to the Ethiopians' land where they sacrifice hecatombs to the immortal gods, that I too may feast at their rites. But Achilles is praying the North Wind and the loud West to come, and promising them fair offerings, that ye may make the pyre be kindled whereon lieth Patroklos, for whom all the Achaians are making moan."

She having thus said departed, and they arose with a mighty sound, rolling the clouds before them. And swiftly they came blowing over the sea, and the wave rose beneath their shrill blast; and they came to deep-soiled Troy, and fell upon the pile, and loudly roared the mighty fire. So all night drave they the flame of the pyre together, blowing shrill; and all night fleet Achilles, holding a two-handled cup, drew wine from a golden bowl, and poured it forth and drenched the earth, calling upon the spirit of hapless Patroklos. As a father waileth when he burneth the bones of his son, new-married, whose death is woe to his hapless parents, so wailed Achilles as he burnt the bones of his comrade, going heavily round the burning pile, with many moans.

But at the hour when the Morning Star goeth forth to herald light upon the earth, the star that saffron-mantled Dawn cometh after, and spreadeth over the salt sea, then grew the burning faint, and the flame died down. And the Winds went back again to betake them home over the Thracian main, and it roared with a violent swell. Then the son of Peleus turned away from the burning and lay down wearied, and sweet sleep leapt on him. But they who were with Atreus' son gathered all together, and the noise and clash of their approach aroused him ; and he sate upright and spake a word to them : " Son of Atreus and ye other chiefs of the Achaians, first quench with gleaming wine all the burning so far as the fire's strength hath reached, and then let us gather up the bones of Patroklos, Menoitios' son, singling them well, and easy are they to discern, for he lay in the middle of the pyre, while the rest apart at the edge burnt confusedly, horses and men. And his bones let us put within a golden urn, and double-folded fat, until that I myself be hidden in Hades. But no huge barrow I bid you toil to raise — a seemly one, no more : then afterward do ye Achaians build it broad and high, whosoever of you after I am gone may be left in the benched ships."

Thus spake he, and they hearkened to the fleet-footed son of Peleus. First quenched they with gleaming wine the burning so far as the flame went, and the ash had settled deep : then with lamentation they gathered up the white bones of their gentle comrade into a golden urn and double-folded fat, and placed the urn in the hut and covered it with a linen veil. And they marked the circle of the barrow, and set the foundations thereof around the pyre, and straightway heaped thereon a heap of earth. Then when they had heaped up the barrow they were for going back. But Achilles stayed the folk in that place, and made them sit in wide assembly, and from his ships he brought forth prizes, caldrons and tripods, and horses and mules and strong oxen, and fair-girdled wómen, and grey iron.

First for fleet chariot-racers he ordained a noble prize, a woman skilled in fair handiwork for the winner to lead home, and an eared tripod that held two-and-twenty measures ; these for the first man ; and for the second he ordained a six-year-old mare unbroke ; and for the third he gave a goodly caldron yet untouched by fire, holding four measures, bright as when first made ; and for the fourth he ordained two talents of gold ; and for the fifth a two-handled urn untouched of fire. Then he stood up and spake a word among the Argives: "Son of Atreus and ye other well-greaved Achaians, for the chariot-racers these prizes lie awaiting them in the lists. If in some other's honour we Achaians were now holding our games, it would be I who should win the first prize and bear it to my hut; for ye know how far my pair of horses are first in excellence, for they are immortal, and Poseidon gave them to my father Peleus, and he again to me. But verily I will abide, I and my whole-hooved horses, so glorious a charioteer have they lost, and one so kind, who on their manes full often poured smooth oil, when he had washed them in clear water. For him they stand and mourn, and their manes are trailing on the ground, and there stand they with sorrow at their hearts. But ye others throughout the host get ye to your places, whosoever of the Achaians hath trust in his horses and firm-jointed car."

Thus spake the son of Peleus, and the fleet chariot-racers were gathered. First of all arose up Eumelos king of men, Admetos' son, a skilful charioteer; and next to him arose Tydeus' son, valiant Diomedes, and yoked his horses of the breed of Tros, which on a time he seized from Aineias, when Apollo saved their lord. And after him arose Atreus' son, fair-haired heaven-sprung Menelaos, and yoked him a swift pair, Aithe, Agamemnon's mare, and his own horse Podargos.

And Meriones was the fifth to make ready his sleek-coated steeds. Then went they up into their chariots, and cast in the lots: and Achilles shook them, and forth leapt the lot of Antilochos Nestor's son, and the next lot had lord Eumelos, and next to him the son of Atreus, spear-famed Menelaos, and next to him drew Meriones his place; then lastly Tydeides, far the best of all, drew his lot for his chariot's place. Then they stood side by side, and Achilles showed to them the turning-post, far off in the smooth plain; and beside it he placed an umpire, godlike Phoinix, his father's follower, that he might note the running and tell the truth thereof.

Then all together lifted the lash above their steeds, and smote them with the reins, and called on them eagerly with words: and they forthwith sped swiftly over the plain, leaving the ships behind; and beneath their breasts stood the rising dust like a cloud or whirlwind, and their manes waved on the blowing wind. And the chariots ran sometimes on the bounteous earth, and other whiles would bound into the air. And the drivers stood in the cars, and the heart of every man beat in desire of victory, and they called every man to his horses, that flew amid their dust across the plain.

But when the fleet horses were now running the last part of the course, back toward the grey sea, then was manifest the prowess of each, and the horses strained in the race; and presently to the front rushed the fleet mares of Pheres' grandson, and next to them Diomedes' stallions of the breed of Tros, not far apart, but hard anigh, for they seemed ever as they would mount Eumelos' car, and with their breath his back was warm and his broad shoulders, for they bent their heads upon him as they flew along. Thus would Tydeus' son have either outstripped the other or made it a dead heat, had not Phoebus Apollo been wroth with him and smitten from his hand the shining lash. Then from his eyes ran tears of anger, for that he saw the mares still at speed, even swiftlier than before, while his own horses were thrown out, as running without spur. But Athene was not unaware of Apollo's guile against Tydeides, and presently sped after the shepherd of hosts, and gave him back the lash, and put spirit into his steeds. Then in wrath after the son of Admetos was the goddess gone, and brake his steeds' yoke, and the mares ran sideways off the course, and the pole was twisted to the ground. And Eumelos was hurled out of the car beside the wheel, and his elbows and mouth and nose were flayed, and his forehead bruised above his eyebrows; and his eyes filled with tears and his lusty voice was choked. Then Tydeides held his whole-hooved horses on one side, darting far out before the rest, for Athene put spirit into his steeds and shed glory on himself. Now next after him came golden-haired Menelaos Atreus' son. But Antilochos called to his father's horses: "Go ye too in, strain to your fleetest pace. Truly I nowise bid you strive with those, the horses of wise Tydeides, unto which Athene hath now given speed, and shed glory on their charioteer. But overtake Atreides' horses with all haste, and be not outstripped by them, lest Aithe that is but a mare pour scorn on you. Why are ye outstripped, brave steeds? Thus will I tell you, and verily it shall be brought to pass — ye will find no tendance with Nestor shepherd of hosts, but straightway he will slay you with the edge of the sword if through heedlessness we win but the worse prize. Have after them at your utmost speed, and I for my part will devise a plan to pass them in the strait part of the course, and this shall fail me not."

Thus spake he, and they fearing the voice of the prince ran swiftlier some little while; and presently did the good warrior Antilochos espy a strait place in a sunk part of the way. There was a rift in the earth, where torrent water gathered and brake part of the track away, and hollowed all the place; there drave Menelaos, shunning the encounter of the wheels. But Antilochos turned his whole-hooved horses out of the track, and followed him a little at one side. And the son of Atreus took alarm and shouted to Antilochos: "Antilochos, thou art driving recklessly — hold in thy horses! The road is straitened, soon thou mayest pass me in a wider place, lest thou foul my chariot and undo us both."

Thus spake he, but Antilochos drave even fiercelier than before, plying his lash, as though he heard him not. As far as is the range of a disk swung from the shoulder when a young man hurleth it, making trial of his force, even so far ran they on; then the mares of Atreus' son gave back, for he ceased of himself to urge them on, lest the whole-hooved steeds should encounter on the track, and overset the well-knit cars, and the drivers fall in the dust in their zeal for victory. So upbraiding Antilochos spake golden-haired Menelaos: "Antilochos, no mortal man is more malicious than thou. Go thy mad way, since falsely have we Achaians called thee wise. Yet even so thou shalt not bear off the prize unchallenged to an oath."

Thus saying he called aloud to his horses: "Hold ye not back nor stand still with sorrow at heart. Their feet and knees will grow weary before yours, for they both lack youth."

Thus spake he, and they fearing the voice of the prince sped faster on, and were quickly close upon the others.

Now the Argives sitting in concourse were gazing at the horses, and they came flying amid their dust over the plain. And the first aware of them was Idomeneus, chief of the Cretans, for he was sitting outside the concourse in the highest place of view, and when he heard the voice of one that shouted, though afar off, he knew it; and he was aware of a horse showing plainly in the front, a chestnut all the rest of him, but in the forehead marked with a white star round like the moon. And he stood upright and spoke among the Argives: "Friends, chiefs, and counsellors of the Argives, is it I alone who see the horses, or do ye also? A new pair seem to me now to be in front, and a new charioteer appeareth; the mares which led in the outward course must have been thrown out there in the plain. For I saw them turning first the hither post, but now can see them nowhere, though my eyes are gazing everywhere along the Trojan plain. Did the reins escape the charioteer so that he could not drive aright round the post and failed in the turn? There, methinks, must he have been cast forth, and have broken his chariot, and the mares must have left the course, in the wildness of their heart. But stand up ye too and look, for myself I discern not certainly, but the first man seemeth to me one of Aitolian race, and he ruleth among Argives, the son of horse-taming Tydeus, stalwart Diomedes."

Then fleet Aias Oïleus' son rebuked him in unseemly sort: "Idomeneus, why art thou a braggart of old? As yet far off the high-stepping mares are coursing over the wide plain. Neither art thou so far the youngest among the Argives, nor do thy eyes look so far the keenliest from thy head, yet continually braggest thou. It beseemeth thee not to be a braggart, for there are here better men. And the mares leading are they that led before, Eumelos' mares, and he standeth and holdeth the reins within the car."

Then wrathfully in answer spake the chief of Cretans: "Aias, master of railing, ill-counselled, in all else art thou behind other Argives, for thy mind is unfriendly. Come then let us wager a tripod or caldron, and make Agamemnon Atreus' son our umpire, which mares are leading, that thou mayest pay and learn."

Thus said he, and straightway fleet Aias Oïleus' son arose angrily to answer with harsh words: and strife between the twain would have gone further, had not Achilles himself stood up and spake a word: "No longer answer each other with harsh words, Aias and Idomeneus, ill words, for it beseemeth not. Surely ye are displeased with any other who should do thus. Sit ye in the concourse and keep your eyes upon the horses; soon they in zeal for victory will come hither, and then shall ye know each of you the Argives' horses, which follow, and which lead."

He said, and the son of Tydeus came driving up, and with his lash smote now and again from the shoulder, and his horses were stepping high as they sped swiftly on their way. And sprinklings of dust smote ever the charioteer, and his chariot overlaid with gold and tin ran behind his fleet-footed steeds, and small trace was there of the wheel-tires behind in the fine dust, as they flew speeding on. Then he drew up in the mid concourse, and much sweat poured from the horses' heads and chests to the ground. And Diomedes leapt to earth from the shining car, and leant his lash against the yoke. Then stalwart Sthenelos tarried not, but promptly took the prize, and gave to his proud comrades the woman to lead and the eared tripod to bear away, and he loosed the horses from the yoke.

And next after him drave Neleian Antilochos his horses, by craft, not swiftness, having passed by Menelaos; yet even now Menelaos held his swift steeds hard anigh. As far as a horse is from the wheel, which draweth his master, straining with the car over the plain — his hindmost tail-hairs touch the tire, for the wheel runneth hard anigh nor is much space between, as he speedeth far over the plain — by so much was Menelaos behind high-born Antilochos, howbeit at first he was a whole disk-cast behind, but quickly he was catching Antilochos up, for the high mettle of Agamemnon's mare, sleek-coated Aithë, was rising in her. And if yet further both had had to run he would have passed his rival nor left it even a dead heat. But Meriones, stout squire of Idomeneus, came in a spear-throw behind famous Menelaos, for tardiest of all were his sleek-coated horses, and slowest he himself to drive a chariot in the race. Last of them all came Admetos' son, dragging his goodly car, driving his steeds in front. Him when fleet-footed noble Achilles beheld he pitied him, and he stood up and spake winged words among the Argives: "Last driveth his wholehooved horses the best man of them all. But come let us give him a prize, as is seemly, prize for the second place, but the first let the son of Tydeus take."

Thus spake he, and all applauded that he bade. And he would have given him the mare, for the Achaians applauded, had not Antilochos, son of great-hearted Nestor, risen up and answered Peleïan Achilles on behalf of his right: "O Achilles, I shall be sore angered with thee if thou accomplish this word, for thou art minded to take away my prize, because thou thinkest of how his chariot and fleet steeds miscarried, and himself withal, good man though he be. Nay, it behoved him to pray to the Immortals, then would he not have come in last of all in the race. But if thou pitiest him and he be dear to thy heart, there is much gold in thy hut, bronze is there and sheep, handmaids are there and whole-hooved horses. Thereof take thou and give unto him afterward even a richer prize, or even now at once, that the Achaians may applaud thee. But the mare I will not yield; for her let what man will essay the battle at my hands."

Thus spake he, and fleet-footed noble Achilles smiled, pleased with Antilochos, for he was his dear comrade; and spake in answer to him winged words: "Antilochos, if thou wouldst have me give Eumelos some other thing beside from out my house, that also will I do. I will give unto him a breast-plate that I took from Asteropaios, of bronze, whereon a casting of bright tin is overlaid, and of great worth will it be to him." He said, and bade his dear comrade Automedon bring it from the hut, and he went and brought it.

But Menelaos also arose among them, sore at heart, angered exceedingly against Antilochos; and the herald set the staff in his hand, and called for silence among the Argives; then spake among them that godlike man: "Antilochos, who once wert wise, what thing is this thou hast done? Thou hast shamed my skill and made my horses fail, thrusting thine own in front that are far worse. Come now, ye chiefs and counsellors of the Argives, give judgment between us both, and favour neither: lest some one of the mail-clad Achaians say at any time: 'By constraining Antilochos through false words hath Menelaos gone off with the mare, for his horses were far worse, howbeit he hath advantage in rank and power.' Nay, I myself will bring the issue about, and I deem that none other of the Danaans shall reproach me, for the trial shall be just. Antilochos, fosterling of Zeus, come thou hither and as it is ordained stand up before thy horses and chariot and take in thy hand the pliant lash wherewith thou dravest erst, and touching thy horses swear by the Enfolder and Shaker of the earth that not wilfully didst thou hinder my chariot by guile."

Then answered him wise Antilochos: "Bear with me now, for far younger am I than thou, king Menelaos, and thou art before me and my better. Thou knowest how a young man's transgressions come about, for his mind is hastier and his counsel shallow. So let thy heart suffer me, and I will of myself give to thee the mare I have taken. Yea, if thou shouldst ask some other greater thing from my house, I were fain to give it thee straightway, rather than fall for ever from my place in thy heart, O fosterling of Zeus, and become a sinner against the gods."

Thus spake great-hearted Nestor's son, and brought the mare and put her in the hand of Menelaos. And his heart was gladdened as when the dew cometh upon the ears of ripening harvest-corn, what time the fields are bristling. So gladdened was thy soul, Menelaos, within thy heart. And he spake unto Antilochos and uttered winged words: "Antilochos, now will I of myself put away mine anger against thee, since nowise formerly wert thou flighty or light-minded, howbeit now thy reason was overcome of youthfulness. Another time be loth to outwit better men. Not easily should another of the Achaians have persuaded me, but thou hast suffered and toiled greatly, and thy brave father and brother, for my sake: therefore will I hearken to thy prayer, and will even give unto thee the mare, though she is mine, that these also may know that my heart was never overweening or implacable."

He said, and gave the mare to Noëmon Antilochos' comrade to lead away, and then took the shining caldron. And Meriones took up the two talents of gold in the fourth place, as he had come in. So the fifth prize was left unclaimed, a two-handled cup; to Nestor gave Achilles this, bearing it to him through the concourse of Argives, and stood by him and said: "Lo now for thee too, old man, be this a treasure, a memorial of Patroklos' burying; for no more shalt thou behold him among the Argives. Now give I thee this prize unwon, for not in boxing shalt thou strive, neither wrestle, nor enter on the javelin match, nor race with thy feet; for grim old age already weigheth on thee."

Then he ordained prizes of the violent boxing match; a sturdy mule he led forth and tethered amid the assembly, a six-year mule unbroken, hardest of all to break; and for the loser set a two-handled cup. Then he stood up and spake a word among the Argives: "Son of Atreus and ye other well-greaved Achaians, for these rewards we summon two men of the best to lift up their hands to box amain. He to whom Apollo shall grant endurance to the end, and all the Achaians acknowledge it, let him take the sturdy mule and return with her to his hut; and the loser shall take with him the two-handled-cup."

Thus spake he, and forthwith arose a man great and valiant and skilled in boxing, Epeios son of Panopeus, and laid his hand on the sturdy mule and said aloud: "Let one come nigh to bear off the two-handled cup; the mule I say none other of the Achaians shall take for victory with his fists, for I claim to be the best man here. Sufficeth it not that I fall short of you in battle? Not possible is it that in all arts a man be skilled. Thus proclaim I, and it shall be accomplished: I will utterly bruise mine adversary's flesh and break his bones, so let his friends abide together here to bear him forth when vanquished by my hands."

Thus spake he, and they all kept deep silence. And alone arose against him Euryalos, a godlike man, son of king Mekisteus the son of Talaos. Thus Tydeides famous with the spear made ready Euryalos for the fight, cheering him with speech, and greatly desired for him victory. And first he cast about him a girdle, and next gave him well-cut thongs of the hide of an ox of the field. And the two boxers being girt went into

the midst of the ring, and both lifting up their stalwart hands
fell to, and their hands joined battle grievously. Then was
there terrible grinding of teeth, and sweat flowed from all their
limbs. And noble Epeios came on, and as the other spied for
an opening, smote him on the cheek, nor could he much more
stand, for his limbs failed straightway under him. And as
when beneath the North Wind's ripple a fish leapeth on a
tangle-covered beach, and then the black wave hideth it, so
leapt up Euryalos at that blow. But great-hearted Epeios
took him in his hands and set him upright, and his dear comrades stood around him, and led him through the ring with
trailing feet, spitting out clotted blood, drooping his head awry,
and they set him down in his swoon among them and themselves went forth and fetched the two-handled cup.

Then Peleus' son ordained straightway the prizes for a third
contest, offering them to the Danaans, for the grievous wrestling match: for the winner a great tripod for standing on the
fire, prized by the Achaians among them at twelve oxens' worth;
and for the loser he brought a woman into the midst, skilled
in manifold work, and they prized her at four oxen. And he
stood up and spake a word among the Argives: "Rise, ye who
will essay this match."

Thus said he, and there arose great Aias son of Telamon, and
Odysseus of many wiles stood up, the crafty-minded. And the
twain being girt went into the midst of the ring, and clasped
each the other in his arms with stalwart hands, like gable
rafters of a lofty house which some famed craftsman joineth,
that he may baffle the wind's force. And their backs creaked,
gripped firmly under the vigorous hands, and sweat ran down
in streams, and frequent weals along their ribs and shoulders
sprang up, red with blood, while ever they strove amain for
victory, to win the wrought tripod. Neither could Odysseus trip
Aias and bear him to the ground, nor Aias him, for Odysseus's
strength withheld him. But when they began to irk the well-

greaved Achaians, then said to Odysseus great Aias, Telamon's son: "Heaven-sprung son of Laertes, Odysseus of many wiles, or lift thou me, or I will thee, and the issue shall be with Zeus."

Having thus said he lifted him, but Odysseus was not unmindful of his craft. He smote deftly from behind the hollow of Aias' knee, and loosed his limbs, and threw him down backward, and Odysseus fell upon his chest, and the folk gazed and marvelled. Then in his turn much-enduring noble Odysseus tried to lift, and moved him a little from the ground, but lifted him not, so he crooked his knee within the other's, and both fell on the ground nigh to each other, and were soiled with dust. And now starting up again a third time would they have wrestled, had not Achilles himself arisen and held them back: "No longer press each the other, nor wear you out with pain. Victory is with both; take equal prizes and depart, that other Achaians may contend."

Thus spake he, and they were fain to hear and to obey, and wiped the dust from them and put their doublets on.

Then straightway the son of Peleus set forth other prizes for fleetness of foot; a mixing-bowl of silver, chased; six measures it held, and in beauty it was far the best in all the earth, for artificers of Sidon wrought it cunningly, and men of the Phoenicians brought it over the misty sea, and landed it in harbour, and gave it a gift to Thoas; and Euneos son of Jason gave it to the hero Patroklos a ransom for Lykaon Priam's son. Now this cup did Achilles set forth as a prize in honour of his friend, for whoso should be fleetest in speed of foot. For the second he set an ox great and very fat, and for the last prize half a talent of gold. And he stood up and spake a word among the Argives: "Rise, ye who will essay this match."

Thus spake he, and straightway arose fleet Aias Oïleus' son, and Odysseus of many wiles, and after them Nestor's son Antilochos, for he was best of all the youth in the foot-race. Then they stood side by side, and Achilles showed to them the goal. Right eager was the running from the start, but Oïleus' son forthwith shot to the front, and close behind him came noble Odysseus, as close as is a weaving-rod to a fair-girdled woman's breast when she pulleth it deftly with her hands, drawing the spool along the warp, and holdeth the rod nigh her breast — so close ran Odysseus behind Aias and trod in his footsteps or ever the dust had settled there, and on his head fell the breath of noble Odysseus as he ran ever lightly on, and all the Achaians applauded his struggle for the victory and called on him as he laboured hard. But when they were running the last part of the course, forthwith Odysseus prayed in his soul to bright-eyed Athene: "Hearken, goddess, come thou a good helper of my feet."

Thus prayed he, and Pallas Athene hearkened to him, and made his limbs feel light, both feet and hands. But when they were now nigh darting on the prize, then Aias slipped as he ran, for Athene marred his race, where filth was strewn from the slaughter of loud-bellowing oxen that fleet Achilles slew in honour of Patroklos: and Aias' mouth and nostrils were filled with that filth of oxen. So much-enduring noble Odysseus, as he came in first, took up the mixing-bowl, and famous Aias took the ox. And he stood holding in his hand the horn of the ox of the field, sputtering away the filth, and spake among the Argives: "Out on it, it was the goddess who marred my running, she who from of old like a mother standeth by Odysseus' side and helpeth him."

So spake he, but they all laughed pleasantly to behold him. Then Antilochos smiling bore off the last prize, and spake his word among the Argives: "Friends, ye will all bear me witness when I say that even herein also the immortals favour elder men. For Aias is a little older than I, but Odysseus of an earlier generation and earlier race of men. A green old age is his, they say, and hard were it for any Achaian to rival him in speed, save only Achilles."

HECTOR'S BODY DRAGGED AT THE CAR OF ACHILLES

Thus spake he, and gave honour to the fleet son of Peleus. And Achilles answered him and said: "Antilochos, not unheeded shall thy praise be given; a half-talent of gold I will give thee over and above." He said, and set it in his hands, and Antilochos received it gladly.

BOOK XXIV

How the body of Hector was ransomed, and of his funeral.

THEN the assembly was broken up, and the tribes were scattered to betake them each to their own swift ships. The rest bethought them of supper and sweet sleep to have joy thereof; but Achilles wept, remembering his dear comrade, nor did sleep that conquereth all take hold on him, but he kept turning him to this side and to that, yearning for Patroklos' manhood and excellent valour, and all the toils he achieved with him and the woes he bare, cleaving the battles of men and the grievous waves. As he thought thereon he shed big tears, now lying on his side, now on his back, now on his face; and then anon he would arise upon his feet and roam wildly beside the beach of the salt sea. Nor would he be unaware of the Dawn when she arose over the sea and shores. But when he had yoked the swift steeds to his car he would bind Hector behind his chariot to drag him withal; and having thrice drawn him round the barrow of the dead son of Menoitios he rested again in his hut, and left Hector lying stretched on his face in the dust. But Apollo kept away all defacement from his flesh, for he had pity on him even in death, and covered him all with his golden aegis, that Achilles might not tear him when he dragged him.

Thus Achilles in his anger entreated noble Hector shamefully; but the blessed gods when they beheld him pitied him, and urged the clear-sighted slayer of Argus to steal the corpse away. So to all the others seemed it good, yet not to Hera or Poseidon or the bright-eyed Maiden, but they continued as when at the beginning sacred Ilios became hateful to them, and Priam and his people, by reason of the sin of Alexandros in that he contemned those goddesses when they came to his steading, and preferred her who brought him deadly lustfulness. But when the twelfth morn from that day arose, then spake among the Immortals Phoebus Apollo: "Hard of heart are ye, O gods, and cruel. Hath Hector never burnt for you thigh-bones of unblemished bulls and goats? Now have ye not taken heart to rescue even his corpse for his wife to look upon and his mother and his child and his father Priam and his people, who speedily would burn him in the fire and make his funeral."

Then in anger spake unto him white-armed Hera: "Even thus mightest thou speak, O Lord of the silver bow, if ye are to give equal honour to Achilles and to Hector. Hector is but a mortal and was suckled at a woman's breast, but Achilles is child of a goddess whom I myself bred up and reared and gave to a man to be his wife, even to Peleus who was dearest of all men to the Immortals' heart. And all ye gods came to her bridal, and thou among them wert feasting with thy lyre, O lover of ill company, faithless ever."

Then to her in answer spake Zeus who gathereth the clouds: "Hera, be not wroth utterly with the gods: for these men's honour is not to be the same, yet Hector also was dearest to the gods of all mortals that are in Ilios. So was he to me at least, for nowise failed he in the gifts I loved. Never did my altar lack seemly feast, drink-offering and the steam of sacrifice, even the honour that falleth to our due. But verily we will say no more of stealing away brave Hector, for it cannot be hidden from Achilles, for his mother abideth ever nigh to him night and day. But I were fain that some one of the gods would call Thetis to come near to me, that I may speak unto her a wise word, so that Achilles may take gifts from Priam and give Hector back."

Thus spake he, and airy-footed Iris sped forth upon the errand and between Samothrace and rocky Imbros leapt into the black sea, and the waters closed above her with a noise. And she sped to the bottom like a weight of lead that mounted on horn of a field-ox goeth down bearing death to ravenous fishes. And she found Thetis in a hollow cave; about her sat gathered other goddesses of the sea, and she in their midst was wailing for the fate of her noble son who must perish in deep-soiled Troy, far from his native land. And standing near, fleet-footed Iris spake to her: "Rise, Thetis; Zeus of immortal counsels calleth thee."

And to her made answer Thetis the silver-footed goddess: "Wherefore biddeth me that mighty god? I shrink from mingling among the Immortals, for I have countless woes at heart. Yet go I, nor shall his word be in vain, whatsoever he saith."

Thus having said the noble goddess took to her a dark-hued robe, no blacker raiment was there found than that. Then she went forth, and wind-footed swift Iris led the way before her, and around them the surge of the sea was sundered. And when they had come forth upon the shore they sped up to heaven, and found the far-seeing son of Kronos, and round him sat gathered all the other blessed gods that are for ever. Then she sat down beside father Zeus, and Athene gave her place. And Hera set a fair golden cup in her hand and cheered her with words, and Thetis drank, and gave back the cup. Then began speech to them the father of gods and men: "Thou art come to Olympus, divine Thetis, in thy sorrow, with violent grief at thy heart; I know it of myself. Nevertheless will I tell thee wherefore I called thee hither. Nine days hath dispute arisen among the Immortals concerning the corpse of Hector and Achilles waster of cities. Fain are they to send clear-sighted Hermes to steal the body away, but now hear what glory I accord herein to Achilles, that I may keep through times to come thy honour and good will. Go with all speed to the host and bear to thy son my bidding. Say to him that the gods are displeased at him, and that I above all Immortals am wroth, because with furious heart he holdeth Hector at the beaked ships and hath not given him back, if haply he may fear me and give Hector back. But I will send Iris to great-hearted Priam to bid him go to the ships of the Achaians to ransom his dear son, and carry gifts to Achilles that may gladden his heart."

Thus spake he, and Thetis the silver-footed goddess was not disobedient to his word, and sped darting upon her way down from the peaks of Olympus. And she came to her son's hut; there found she him making grievous moan, and his dear comrades round were swiftly making ready and furnishing their early meal, and a sheep great and fleecy was being sacrificed in the hut. Then his lady-mother sate her down close beside him, and stroked him with her hand and spake to him by his name:. "My child, how long with lamentation and woe wilt thou devour thine heart, taking thought of neither food nor rest? good were even a woman's embrace, for not long shalt thou be left alive to me; already death and forceful fate are standing nigh thee. But hearken forthwith unto me, for I am the messenger of Zeus to thee. He saith that the gods are displeased at thee, and that himself above all Immortals is wroth, because with furious heart thou holdest Hector at the beaked ships and hast not given him back. But come restore him, and take ransom for the dead."

Then to her in answer spake fleet-footed Achilles: "So be it: whoso bringeth ransom let him take back the dead, if verily with heart's intent the Olympian biddeth it himself."

So they in the assembly of the ships, mother and son, spake to each other many winged words. But the son of Kronos thus bade Iris go to holy Ilios: "Go forth, fleet Iris, leave the abode of Olympus and bear my message within Ilios to great-hearted Priam that he go to the ships of the Achaians and ransom his dear son and carry gifts to Achilles that may gladden his heart; let him go alone, and no other man of the Trojans go with him. Only let some elder herald attend on him to guide the mules and smooth-wheeled waggon and carry back to the city the dead man whom noble Achilles slew. Let not death be in his thought nor any fear; such guide will we give unto him, even Hermes who shall lead him until his leading bring him to Achilles. And when he shall have led him within the hut, neither shall Achilles himself slay him nor suffer any other herein, for not senseless is he or unforeseeing or wicked, but with all courtesy he will spare a suppliant man."

Thus spake he, and airy-footed Iris sped forth upon the errand. And she came to the house of Priam, and found therein crying and moan. His children sitting around their father within the court were bedewing their raiment with their tears, and the old man in their midst was close wrapped all over in his cloak; and on his head and neck was much mire that he had gathered in his hands as he grovelled upon the earth. And his daughters and his sons' wives were wailing throughout the house, bethinking them of all those valiant men who had lost their lives at the hands of the Argives and were lying low. And the messenger of Zeus stood beside Priam and spake softly unto him, and trembling came upon his limbs: "Be of good cheer in thy heart, O Priam son of Dardanos, and be not dismayed for anything, for no evil come I hither to forebode to thee, but with good will. I am the messenger of Zeus to thee, who, though he be afar off, hath great care and pity for thee. The Olympian biddeth thee ransom noble Hector and carry gifts to Achilles that may gladden his heart: go thou alone, let none other of the Trojans go with thee. Only let some elder herald attend on thee to guide the mules and the smooth-wheeled waggon to carry back to the city the dead man whom noble Achilles slew. Let not death be in thy thought, nor any fear; such guide shall go with thee, even the slayer of Argus, who shall lead thee until his leading bring thee to Achilles. And when he shall have led thee into the hut, neither shall Achilles himself slay thee, nor suffer any other herein, for not senseless is he or unforeseeing or wicked, but with all courtesy he will spare a suppliant man."

Thus having spoken fleet Iris departed from him; and he bade his sons make ready the smooth-wheeled mule waggon, and bind the wicker carriage thereon. And himself he went down to his fragrant chamber, of cedar wood, high-roofed, that held full many jewels, and opened fair lids of chests wherefrom he chose twelve very goodly women's robes and twelve cloaks of single fold and of coverlets a like number and of fair sheets, and of doublets thereupon. And he weighed and brought forth talents of gold ten in all, and two shining tripods and four caldrons, and a goblet exceeding fair that men of Thrace had given him when he went thither on an embassy, a chattel of great price, yet not that even did the old man grudge from his halls, for he was exceeding fain at heart to ransom his dear son.

Then he called unto his sons, chiding Helenos and Paris and noble Agathon and Pammon and Antiphonos, and Polites of the loud war-cry, and Deïphobos and Hippothoos and proud Dios; nine were they whom the old man called and bade unto him: "Haste ye, ill sons, my shame; would that ye all in Hector's stead had been slain at the swift ships! Woe is me all unblest, since I begat sons the best men in wide Troy-land, but none of them is left for me to claim, neither godlike Mestor, nor Troilos with his chariot of war, nor Hector who was a god among men, neither seemed he as the son of a mortal man but of a god: — all these hath Ares slain, and here are my shames all left to me, false-tongued, light-heeled, the heroes of the dance, plunderers of your own people's sheep and kids. Will ye not make me ready a wain with all speed, and lay all these thereon, that we get us forward on our way?"

Thus spake he, and they fearing their father's voice brought forth the smooth-running mule chariot, fair and new, and bound the body thereof on the frame; and from its peg they took down the mule yoke, a boxwood yoke with knob well fitted with guiding-rings; and they brought forth the yoke-band of nine cubits with the yoke. The yoke they set firmly on the polished pole on the rest at the end thereof, and slipped the ring over the upright pin, which with three turns of the band they lashed to the knob, and then belayed it close round the pole and turned the tongue thereunder. Then they brought from the chamber and heaped on the polished wain the countless ransom of Hector's head, and yoked strong-hooved harness mules, which on a time the Mysians gave to Priam, a splendid gift. But to Priam's car they yoked the horses that the old man kept for his use and reared at the polished crib.

Then the old man made haste to go up into his car, and drave forth from the doorway and the echoing portico. In front the mules drew the four-wheeled wain, and wise Idaios drave them; behind came the horses which the old man urged with the lash at speed along the city: and his friends all followed lamenting loud as though he were faring to his death. And when they were come down from the city and were now on the plain, then went back again to Ilios his sons and marriage kin. But the two coming forth upon the plain were not unbeheld of far-seeing Zeus. But he looked upon the old man and had compassion on him, and straightway spake unto Hermes his dear son: "Hermes, since unto thee especially is it dear to companion men, and thou hearest whomsoever thou wilt, go forth and so guide Priam to the hollow ships of the Achaians that no man behold or be aware of him, among all the Danaans' host, until he come to the son of Peleus."

Thus spake he, and the Messenger, the slayer of Argus, was not disobedient unto his word. Straightway beneath his feet he bound on his fair sandals, golden, divine, that bare him over wet sea and over the boundless land with the breathings of the wind. And he took up his wand wherewith he entranceth the eyes of such men as he will, and others he likewise waketh out of sleep: this did the strong slayer of Argus take in his hand, and flew. And quickly came he to Troy-land and the Hellespont, and went on his way in semblance as a young man that is a prince, with the new down on his chin, as when the youth of men is the comeliest.

Now the others, when they had driven beyond the great barrow of Ilos, halted the mules and horses at the river to drink; for darkness was come down over the earth. Then the herald beheld Hermes from hard by, and marked him, and spake and said to Priam: "Consider, son of Dardanos; this is matter of prudent thought. I see a man, methinks we shall full soon be rent in pieces. Come, let us flee in our chariot, or else at least touch his knees and entreat him that he have mercy on us."

Thus spake he, and the old man was confounded, and he was dismayed exceedingly, and the hair on his pliant limbs stood up, and he stood still amazed. But the Helper came nigh of himself and took the old man's hand, and spake and questioned him: "Whither, father, dost thou thus guide these horses and mules through the divine night, when other mortals are asleep? Hadst thou no fear of the fierce-breathing Achaians, thy bitter foes that are hard anigh thee? If one of them should espy thee carrying such treasures through the swift black night, what then would be thy thought? Neither art thou young thyself, and thy companion here is old, that ye should make defence against a man that should assail thee first. But I will nowise harm thee, yea I will keep any other from thy hurt: for the similitude of my dear father I see in thee."

And to him in answer spake the old man, godlike Priam: "Even so, kind son, are all these things as thou sayest. Nevertheless hath some god stretched forth his hand even over me in that he hath sent a wayfarer such as thou to meet me, a bearer of good luck, by the nobleness of thy form and semblance; and thou art wise of heart and of blessed parents art thou sprung."

And to him again spake the Messenger, the slayer of Argus: "All this, old sire, hast thou verily spoken aright. But come say this and tell me truly whether thou art taking forth a great and goodly treasure unto alien men, where it may abide for thee in safety, or whether by this ye are all forsaking holy Ilios in fear; so far the best man among you hath perished, even thy son; for of battle with the Achaians abated he never a jot."

And to him in answer spake the old man, godlike Priam: "Who art thou, noble sir, and of whom art born? For meetly hast thou spoken of the fate of my hapless son."

And to him again spake the Messenger, the slayer of Argus: "Thou art proving me, old sire, in asking me of noble Hector. Him have I full oft seen with mine eyes in glorious battle, and when at the ships he was slaying the Argives he drave thither, piercing them with the keen bronze, and we stood still and marvelled thereat, for Achilles suffered us not to fight, being wroth against Atreus' son. His squire am I, and came in the same well-wrought ship. From the Myrmidons I come, and my father is Polyktor."

And the old man, godlike Priam, answered him, saying: "If verily thou art a squire of Achilles Peleus' son, come tell me all the truth, whether still my son is by the ships, or whether ere now Achilles hath riven him limb from limb and cast him to the dogs."

Then to him again spake the Messenger the slayer of Argus: "Old sire, not yet have dogs or birds devoured him, but there lieth he still by Achilles' ship, even as he fell, among the huts, and the twelfth morn now hath risen upon him, nor doth his flesh corrupt at all, neither worms consume it, such as devour men slain in war. Truly Achilles draggeth him recklessly around the barrow of his dear comrade so oft as divine day dawneth, yet marreth he him not; thou wouldst marvel if thou couldst go see thyself how dewy fresh he lieth, and is washed clean of blood, nor anywhere defiled; and all his wounds wherewith he was stricken are closed; howbeit many plunged their points in him. So careful are the blessed gods of thy son, though he be but a dead corpse, for they held him dear at heart."

Thus spake he, and the old man rejoiced, and answered him, saying: "My son, it is verily a good thing to give due offerings withal to the Immortals, for never did my child — if that child indeed I had — forget in our halls the gods who inhabit Olympus. Therefore have they remembered this for him, albeit his portion is death. But come now take from me this goodly goblet, and guard me myself and guide me, under Heaven, that I may come unto the hut of Peleus' son."

Then spake unto him again the Messenger the slayer of Argus: "Thou art proving me, old sire, who am younger than thou, but thou wilt not prevail upon me, in that thou biddest me take gifts from thee without Achilles' privity. I were afraid and shamed at heart to defraud him, lest some evil come to pass on me hereafter. But as thy guide I would go even unto famous Argos, accompanying thee courteously in swift ship or on foot. Not from scorn of thy guide would any assail thee then."

Thus spake the Helper, and leaping on the chariot behind the horses he swiftly took lash and reins into his hand, and breathed brave spirit into horses and mules. But when they were come to the towers and trench of the ships, there were the sentinels just busying them about their supper. Then the Messenger, the slayer of Argus, shed sleep upon them all, and straightway opened the gates and thrust back the bars, and brought within Priam and the splendid gifts upon his wain. And they came to the lofty hut of the son of Peleus, which the

Myrmidons made for their king and hewed therefor timber of the pine, and thatched it with downy thatching-rush that they mowed in the meadows, and around it made for him their lord a great court with close-set palisades ; and the door was barred by a single bolt of pine that three Achaians wont to drive home, and three drew back that mighty bar — three of the rest, but Achilles by himself would drive it home. Then opened the Helper Hermes the door for the old man, and brought in the splendid gifts for Peleus' fleet-footed son, and descended from the chariot to the earth and spake aloud : " Old sire, I that have come to thee am an immortal god, even Hermes, for my father sent me to companion thee on thy way. But now will I depart from thee nor come within Achilles' sight ; it were cause of wrath that an immortal god should thus show favour openly unto mortals. But thou go in and clasp the knees of Peleus' son and entreat him for his father's sake and his mother's of the lovely hair and for his child's sake that thou mayest move his soul."

Thus Hermes spake, and departed unto high Olympus. But Priam leapt from the car to the earth, and left Idaios in his place ; he stayed to mind the horses and mules ; but the old man made straight for the house where Achilles dear to Zeus was wont to sit. And therein he found the man himself, and his comrades sate apart : two only, the hero Automedon and Alkimos, of the stock of Ares, were busy in attendance ; and he was lately ceased from meat, even from eating and drinking : and still the table stood beside him. But they were unaware of great Priam as he came in, and so stood he anigh and clasped in his hands the knees of Achilles, and kissed his hands, terrible, man-slaying, that slew many of Priam's sons. And as when a grievous curse cometh upon a man who in his own country hath slain another and escapeth to a land of strangers, to the house of some rich man, and wonder possesseth them that look on him — so Achilles wondered when he saw godlike

Priam, and the rest wondered likewise, and looked upon one another. Then Priam spake and entreated him, saying: "Bethink thee, O Achilles like to gods, of thy father that is of like years with me, on the grievous pathway of old age. Him haply are the dwellers round about entreating evilly, nor is there any to ward from him ruin and bane. Nevertheless while he heareth of thee as yet alive he rejoiceth in his heart, and hopeth withal day after day that he shall see his dear son returning from Troy-land. But I, I am utterly unblest, since I begat sons the best men in wide Troy-land, but declare unto thee that none of them is left. Fifty I had, when the sons of the Achaians came. Now of the more part had impetuous Ares unstrung the knees, and he who was yet left and guarded city and men, him slewest thou but now as he fought for his country, even Hector. For his sake come I unto the ships of the Achaians that I may win him back from thee, and I bring with me untold ransom. Yea, fear thou the gods, Achilles, and have compassion on me, even me, bethinking thee of thy father. Lo, I am yet more piteous than he, and have braved what none other man on earth hath braved before, to stretch forth my hand toward the face of the slayer of my sons."

Thus spake he, and stirred within Achilles desire to make lament for his father. And he touched the old man's hand and gently moved him back. And as they both bethought them of their dead, so Priam for man-slaying Hector wept sore as he was fallen before Achilles' feet, and Achilles wept for his own father, and now again for Patroklos, and their moan went up throughout the house. But when noble Achilles had satisfied him with lament, and the desire thereof departed from his heart and limbs, straightway he sprang from his seat and raised the old man by his hand, pitying his hoary head and hoary beard, and spake unto him winged words and said: "Ah hapless! many ill things verily thou hast endured in thy heart. How durst thou come alone to the ships of the Achaians and to meet the eyes of the man who hath slain full many of thy brave sons? of iron verily is thy heart. But come then set thee on a seat, and we will let our sorrows lie quiet in our hearts, for all our pain, for no avail cometh of chill lament. This is the lot the gods have spun for miserable men, that they should live in pain; yet themselves are sorrowless. For two urns stand upon the floor of Zeus filled with his evil gifts, and one with blessings. To whomsoever Zeus whose joy is in the lightning dealeth a mingled lot, that man chanceth now upon ill and now again on good, but to whom he giveth but of the bad kind him he bringeth to scorn, and evil famine chaseth him over the goodly earth, and he is a wanderer honoured of neither gods nor men. Even thus to Peleus gave the gods splendid gifts from his birth, for he excelled all men in good fortune and wealth, and was king of the Myrmidons, and mortal though he was the gods gave him a goddess to be his bride. Yet even on him God brought evil, seeing that there arose to him no offspring of princely sons in his halls, save that he begat one son to an untimely death. Neither may I tend him as he groweth old, since very far from my country I am dwelling in Troy-land, to vex thee and thy children. And of thee, old sire, we have heard how of old time thou wert happy, even how of all that Lesbos, seat of Makar, boundeth to the north thereof and Phrygia farther up and the vast Hellespont — of all these folk, men say, thou wert the richest in wealth and in sons, but after that the Powers of Heaven brought this bane on thee, ever are battles and man-slayings around thy city. Keep courage, and lament not unabatingly in thy heart. For nothing wilt thou avail by grieving for thy son, neither shalt thou bring him back to life or ever some new evil come upon thee."

Then made answer unto him the old man, godlike Priam: "Bid me not to a seat, O fosterling of Zeus, so long as Hector lieth uncared for at the huts, but straightway give him back that I may behold him with mine eyes; and accept thou the great ransom that we bring. So mayest thou have pleasure thereof, and come unto thy native land, since thou hast spared me from the first."

Then fleet-footed Achilles looked sternly upon him and said: "No longer chafe me, old sire; of myself am I minded to give Hector back to thee, for there came to me a messenger from Zeus, even my mother who bare me, daughter of the Ancient One of the Sea. And I know, O Priam, in my mind, nor am unaware that some god it is that hath guided thee to the swift ships of the Achaians. For no mortal man, even though in prime of youth, would dare to come among the host, for neither could he escape the watch, nor easily thrust back the bolt of our doors. Therefore now stir my heart no more amid my troubles, lest I leave not even thee in peace, old sire, within my hut, albeit thou art my suppliant, and lest I transgress the commandment of Zeus."

Thus spake he, and the old man feared, and obeyed his word. And the son of Peleus leapt like a lion through the door of the house, not alone, for with him went two squires, the hero Automedon and Alkimos, they whom above all his comrades Achilles honoured, save only Patroklos that was dead. They then loosed from under the yoke the horses and mules, and led in the old man's crier-herald and set him on a chair, and from the wain of goodly felloes they took the countless ransom set on Hector's head. But they left two robes and a well-spun doublet, that Achilles might wrap the dead therein when he gave him to be carried home. And he called forth handmaids and bade them wash and anoint him when they had borne him apart, so that Priam should not look upon his son, lest he should not refrain the wrath at his sorrowing heart when he should look upon his son, and lest Achilles' heart be vexed thereat and he slay him and transgress the commandment of Zeus. So when the handmaids had washed the body and anointed it with oil, and had thrown over it a fair robe and a doublet, then Achilles himself lifted it and laid it on a bier, and his comrades with him lifted it on to the polished waggon. Then he groaned aloud and called on his dear comrade by his name: "Patroklos, be not vexed with me if thou hear even in the house of Hades that I have given back noble Hector unto his dear father, for not unworthy is the ransom he hath given me, whereof I will deal to thee again thy rightful share."

Thus spake noble Achilles, and went back into the hut, and sate him down on the cunningly-wrought couch whence he had arisen by the opposite wall, and spake a word to Priam: "Thy son, old sire, is given back as thou wouldest and lieth on a bier, and with the break of day thou shalt see him thyself as thou carriest him. But come let us, noble father, take thought of meat, and afterward thou shalt mourn over thy dear son as thou carriest him to Ilios; and many tears shall be his due."

Thus spake fleet Achilles, and sprang up, and slew a pure white sheep, and his comrades skinned and made it ready in seemly fashion, and divided it cunningly and pierced it with spits, and roasted it carefully and drew all off. And Automedon took bread and served it on a table in fair baskets, while Achilles dealt out the flesh. And they stretched forth their hands to the good cheer lying ready before them. But when they had put off the desire of meat and drink, then Priam son of Dardanos marvelled at Achilles to see how great he was and how goodly, for he was like a god to look upon. And Achilles marvelled at Priam son of Dardanos, beholding his noble aspect and hearkening to his words. But when they had gazed their fill upon one another, then first spake the old man, godlike Priam, to Achilles: "Now presently give me whereon to lie, fosterling of Zeus, that of sweet sleep also we may now take our fill at rest: for never yet have mine eyes closed beneath their lids since at thy hands my son lost his life, but I continually mourn and brood over countless griefs, grovelling in the courtyard-close amid the mire. Now at last have I tasted bread and poured bright wine down my throat, but till now I had tasted naught."

He said, and Achilles bade his comrades and handmaids to set a bedstead beneath the portico, and to cast thereon fair shining rugs and spread coverlets above and thereon to lay thick mantles to be a clothing over all. And the maids went forth from the inner hall with torches in their hands, and quickly spread two beds in haste. Then with bitter meaning[1] said fleet-footed Achilles unto Priam: "Lie thou without, dear sire, lest there come hither one of the counsellors of the Achaians, such as ever take counsel with me by my side, as custom is. If any of such should behold thee through the swift black night, forthwith he might haply tell it to Agamemnon shepherd of the host, and thus would there be delay in giving back the dead. But come say this to me and tell it true, how many days' space thou art fain to make funeral for noble Hector, so that for so long I may myself abide and may keep back the host."

And the old man, godlike Priam, answered him, saying: "If thou art verily willing that I accomplish noble Hector's funeral, by doing as thou sayest, O Achilles, thou wilt do me grace. For thou knowest how we are pent within the city, and wood from the mountain is far to fetch, and the Trojans are much in fear. Nine days will we make moan for him in our halls, and on the tenth we will hold funeral and the folk shall feast, and on the eleventh we will make a barrow over him, and on the twelfth we will do battle if need be."

Then again spake the fleet noble Achilles unto him, saying: "All this, O ancient Priam, shall be as thou biddest; for I will hold back the battle even so long a time as thou tellest me."

Thus speaking he clasped the old man's right hand at the

---

[1] In his reference to Agamemnon.

wrist, lest he should be anywise afraid at heart. So they in the forepart of the house laid them down, Priam and the herald, with wise thoughts at their hearts, but Achilles slept in a recess of the firm-wrought hut.

Now all other gods and warriors lords of chariots slumbered all night, by soft sleep overcome. But not on the Helper Hermes did sleep take hold as he sought within his heart how he should guide forth king Priam from the ships unespied of the trusty sentinels. And he stood above his head and spake a word to him: "Old sire, no thought then hast thou of any evil, seeing thou yet sleepest among men that are thine enemies, for that Achilles spared thee. Truly now hast thou won back thy dear son, and at great price. But for thy life will thy sons thou hast left behind be offering threefold ransom, if but Agamemnon Atreus' son be aware of thee, and aware be all the Achaians."

Thus spake he, and the old man feared, and roused the herald. And Hermes yoked the horses and mules for them, and himself drave them lightly through the camp, and none was aware of them.

But when they came to the ford of the fair-flowing river, then Hermes departed up to high Olympus, and Morning of the saffron robe spread over all the earth. And they with wail and moan drave the horses to the city, and the mules drew the dead. Nor marked them any man or fair-girdled woman until Kassandra, peer of golden Aphrodite, having gone up upon Pergamos, was aware of her dear father as he stood in the car, and the herald that was crier to the town. Then beheld she him that lay upon the bier behind the mules, and thereat she wailed and cried aloud throughout all the town: "O men and women of Troy, come ye hither and look upon Hector, if ever while he was alive ye rejoiced when he came back from battle, since great joy was he to the city and all the folk."

Thus spake she, nor was man or woman left within the city,

for upon all came unendurable grief. And near the gates they met Priam bringing home the dead. First bewailed him his dear wife and lady mother, as they cast them on the fair-wheeled wain and touched his head; and around them stood the throng and wept. So all day long unto the setting of the sun they had lamented Hector in tears without the gate, had not the old man spoken from the car among the folk: "Give me place for the mules to pass through; hereafter ye shall have your fill of wailing, when I have brought him unto his home."

Thus spake he and they parted asunder and gave place to the wain. And the others when they had brought him to the famous house, laid him on a fretted bed, and set beside him minstrel leaders of the dirge, who wailed a mournful lay, while the women made moan with them. And among the women white-armed Andromache led the lamentation, while in her hands she held the head of Hector slayer of men: "Husband, thou art gone young from life, and leavest me a widow in thy halls. And the child is yet but a little one, child of ill-fated parents, thee and me; nor methinks shall he grow up to manhood, for ere then shall this city be utterly destroyed. For thou art verily perished who didst watch over it, who guardedst it and keptest safe its noble wives and infant little ones. These soon shall be voyaging in the hollow ships, yea and I too with them, and thou, my child, shalt either go with me unto a place where thou shalt toil at unseemly tasks, labouring before the face of some harsh lord, or else some Achaian will take thee by the arm and hurl thee from the battlement, a grievous death, for that he is wroth because Hector slew his brother or father or son, since full many of the Achaians' in Hector's hands have bitten the firm earth. For no light hand had thy father in the grievous fray. Therefore the folk lament him throughout the city, and woe unspeakable and mourning hast thou left to thy parents, Hector, but with me chiefliest shall grievous pain abide. For neither didst thou stretch thy hands to me from a bed in thy death, neither didst speak to me some memorable word that I might have thought on evermore as my tears fall night and day."

Thus spake she wailing, and the women joined their moan. And among them Hekabe again led the loud lament : " Hector, of all my children far dearest to my heart, verily while thou wert alive dear wert thou to the gods, and even in thy doom of death have they had care for thee. For other sons of mine whom he took captive would fleet Achilles sell beyond the unvintaged sea unto Samos and Imbros and smoking Lemnos,[1] but when with keen-edged bronze he had bereft thee of thy life he was fain to drag thee oft around the tomb of his comrade, even Patroklos whom thou slewest, yet might he not raise him up thereby. But now all dewy and fresh thou liest in our halls, like one on whom Apollo, lord of the silver bow, hath descended and slain him with his gentle darts."

Thus spake she wailing, and stirred unending moan. Then thirdly Helen led their sore lament : " Hector, of all my brethren of Troy far dearest to my heart ! Truly my lord is godlike Alexandros who brought me to Troy-land — would I had died ere then. For this is now the twentieth year since I went thence and am gone from my own native land, but never yet heard I evil or despiteful word from thee; nay, if any other haply upbraided me in the palace-halls, whether brother or sister of thine or brother's fair-robed wife, or thy mother — but thy father is ever kind to me as he were my own — then wouldst thou soothe such with words and refrain them, by the gentleness of thy spirit and by thy gentle words. Therefore bewail I thee with pain at heart, and my hapless self with thee, for no more is any left in wide Troy-land to be my friend and kind to me, but all men shudder at me."

Thus spake she wailing, and therewith the great multitude

---

[1] A volcanic island.

of the people groaned. But the old man Priam spake a word among the folk: "Bring wood, men of Troy, unto the city, and be not anywise afraid at heart of a crafty ambush of the Achaians; for this message Achilles gave me when he sent me from the black ships, that they should do us no hurt until the twelfth morn arise."

Thus spake he, and they yoked oxen and mules to wains, and quickly then they flocked before the city. So nine days they gathered great store of wood. But when the tenth morn rose with light for men, then bare they forth brave Hector, weeping tears, and on a lofty pyre they laid the dead man, and thereon cast fire.

But when the daughter of Dawn, rosy-fingered Morning, shone forth, then gathered the folk around glorious Hector's pyre. First quenched they with bright wine all the burning, so far as the fire's strength went, and then his brethren and comrades gathered his white bones lamenting, and big tears flowed down their cheeks. And the bones they took and laid in a golden urn, shrouding them in soft purple robes, and straightway laid the urn in a hollow grave and piled thereon great close-set stones, and heaped with speed a barrow, while watchers were set everywhere around, lest the well-greaved Achaians should make onset before the time. And when they had heaped the barrow they went back, and gathered them together and feasted right well in noble feast at the palace of Priam, Zeus-fostered king.

Thus held they funeral for Hector tamer of horses.

PRONUNCIATION OF PROPER NAMES

In this volume the translators have spelled proper names as nearly as possible like the Greek originals.

Vowels. — Each vowel is pronounced separately, except in *ai, au, ei, eu, oi*, which have the following sounds: *ai* and *ei* are pronounced as *i* in *island*; *au*, as *ow* in *now*; *eu*, as *u* in *use*; *oi*, as in *boil*. When accented, *y* is pronounced as *i* in *island*; when unaccented, as *i* in *till*.

Consonants. — *Ch* is pronounced as *k*. *G* is always hard, as in *gas*.

Accents. — Words of two syllables are accented on the first syllable. Words of three or more syllables are accented on the antepenult, that is, the third syllable from the end, unless the penult, or syllable next to the end, is "long." A penult is long when it contains (1) a vowel followed by two consonants; (2) a diphthong (*ai, au, ei*). The following list includes all the proper names as to the accentuation of which the English reader would be in doubt after reading carefully the foregoing explanation. Each word in the list is accented on the penult, *i.e.* the next to the last syllable.

Admetos.	Aretos.	Deisenor.
Agelaos.	Athene.	Diomedes.
Agenor.		Dione.
Aidoneus.	Briseïs.	Diores.
Aisyetes.		
Alkmaon.	Chalkodon.	Elephenor.
Anchises.	Chryseïs.	Enyo.
Antenor.		Erinys.
Aphrodite.	Deïopites.	Eumedes.

Eumelos.	Lykaon.	Paieon.
Euneos.	Lykomedes.	Paiones.
		Polites.
Ganymede.	Machaon.	Polydorus.
	Menelaos.	Polymelos.
Hekamede.	Messeïs.	Polyphetes.
Hyperion.	Mykene.	Protesilaos.
		Sarpedon.
Kabesos.	Noëmon.	Sellëeis.
Kallikolone.		Thrasymedes.
Kaukones.	Opites.	Thersites.
Kronion.	Orion.	Thoötes.

The reader will perhaps also be helped by the following list of the Greek and Latin names of the gods and goddesses who play important parts in the narrative. When the Greek names are new to him, the corresponding Latin names may be more familiar.

Greek	*Latin*
Zeus.	Jupiter.
Hera.	Juno.
(Pallas) Athene.	Minerva.
Aphrodite.	Venus.
Poseidon.	Neptune.
Ares.	Mars.
Hephaestus.	Vulcan.

It should also be noted that the termination *des* means "son of"; *e.g.* Atreides, son of Atreus.

THE ODYSSEY OF HOMER

BY

S. H. BUTCHER, M.A.

HON. LL.D. GLASGOW, HON. LITT.D. DUBLIN
PROFESSOR OF GREEK IN THE UNIVERSITY OF EDINBURGH
FORMERLY FELLOW OF TRINITY COLLEGE, CAMBRIDGE
AND OF UNIVERSITY COLLEGE, OXFORD

AND

A. LANG, M.A.

HON. LL.D. ST. ANDREWS

COPYRIGHT, 1905,
BY THE MACMILLAN COMPANY.

Set up and electrotyped. Published January, 1905.
Reprinted July, 1906; March, 1907; December, 1908;
April, 1909.

As one that for a weary space has lain
  Lulled by the song of Circe and her wine
  In gardens near the pale of Proserpine,
Where that Ægæan isle forgets the main,
And only the low lutes of love complain,
  And only shadows of wan lovers pine,
  As such an one were glad to know the brine
Salt on his lips, and the large air again,
So gladly, from the songs of modern speech
  Men turn, and see the stars, and feel the free
    Shrill wind beyond the close of heavy flowers
    And through the music of the languid hours,
They hear like ocean on a western beach
  The surge and thunder of the Odyssey.

A. L.

THE ODYSSEY

BOOK I

In a Council of the Gods, Poseidon absent, Pallas procureth an order for the restitution of Odysseus; and appearing to his son Telemachus, in human shape, adviseth him to complain of the Wooers before the Council of the people, and then go to Pylos and Sparta to inquire about his father.

TELL me, Muse, of that man, so ready at need, who wandered far and wide, after he had sacked the sacred citadel of Troy. Many were the men whose towns he saw and whose mind he learnt, yea, and many the woes he suffered in his heart upon the deep, striving to win his own life and the return of his company. Even so he saved not his company, though he desired it sore.

Now all the rest of the princes who had fought at Troy were at home, and had escaped both war and sea, but Odysseus only, craving for his wife and for his homeward path, the nymph Calypso held in her hollow caves, longing to have him for her lord. All the gods had pity on him save Poseidon, who raged continually against godlike Odysseus. But when Poseidon had departed for the distant Ethiopians, the other gods were gathered in the halls of Zeus. Then among them the father of gods and men began to speak, for he bethought him in his heart of noble Aegisthus, whom the son of Agamemnon, far-famed Orestes, slew. Thinking upon him he spake out among the Immortals:

"Lo you now, how vainly mortal men do blame the gods! For of us they say comes evil, whereas they even of themselves, through the blindness of their own hearts, have sorrows beyond that which is ordained. Thus of late Aegisthus, beyond that which was ordained, took to him the wedded wife of Agamemnon and killed her lord on his return, and that with sheer doom before his eyes, since we had warned him by the embassy of Hermes the keen-sighted, that he should neither kill the man nor woo his wife."

And the goddess, grey-eyed Athene, answered him, saying: "O father, throned in the highest, that man assuredly lies in a death that is his due; so perish likewise all who work such deeds! But my heart is rent for wise Odysseus, the hapless one, who far from his friends this long while suffereth affliction in a seagirt isle, where is the navel of the sea, a woodland isle, and therein a goddess hath her habitation, the daughter of the wizard Atlas, who knows the depths of every sea, and himself upholds the tall pillars which keep earth and sky asunder. His daughter it is that holds the hapless man in sorrow: and ever with soft and guileful tales she is wooing him to forgetfulness of Ithaca. But Odysseus, yearning to see if it were but the smoke leap upwards from his own land, hath a desire to die. As for thee, thine heart regardeth it not at all! What! did not Odysseus by the ships of the Argives make thee free offering of sacrifice in the wide Trojan land? Wherefore wast thou then so wroth with him, O Zeus?"

And Zeus the cloud-gatherer answered her, and said: "My child, what word hath escaped the door of thy lips? Yea, how should I forget divine Odysseus, who in understanding is beyond mortals and beyond all men hath done sacrifice to the deathless gods, who keep the wide heaven? Nay, but it is Poseidon, the girdler of the earth, that hath been wroth continually with quenchless anger for the Cyclops' sake whom he blinded of his eye, even godlike Polyphemus whose power is

mightiest amongst all the Cyclôpes.[1] From that day forth
Poseidon the earth-shaker doth not indeed slay Odysseus, but
driveth him wandering from his own country. But come, let
us here one and all take good counsel as touching his returning,
that he may be got home; so shall Poseidon let go his displeasure, for he will in no wise be able to strive alone against
all, in despite of all the deathless gods."

Then the goddess, grey-eyed Athene, answered him, and
said: "O father, throned in the highest, if indeed this thing is
now well pleasing to the blessed gods, that wise Odysseus
should return to his own home, let us then speed Hermes the
Messenger, to the island of Ogygia. There with all speed let
him declare to the lady of the braided tresses our unerring
counsel, even the return of the patient Odysseus, that so he may
come to his home. But as for me I will go to Ithaca that I
may rouse his son yet the more, planting might in his heart, to
call an assembly of the long-haired Achaeans and speak out
to all the wooers who slaughter continually the sheep of his
thronging flocks, and his kine with trailing feet and shambling
gait. And I will guide him to Sparta and to sandy Pylos to
seek tidings of his dear father's return, if peradventure he may
hear thereof and that so he may be had in good report among
men."

She spake and bound beneath her feet her lovely golden
sandals, that wax not old, and bare her alike over the wet sea
and over the limitless land, swift as the breath of the wind.
And she seized her doughty spear, shod with sharp bronze,
weighty and huge and strong, wherewith she quells the ranks
of heroes with whomsoever she is wroth. Then from the
heights of Olympus she came glancing down, and she stood in
the land of Ithaca, at the entry of the gate of Odysseus, on the
threshold of the courtyard, holding in her hand the spear of

---

[1] [The adventure is related in Book ix.]

bronze, in the semblance of a stranger, Mentes the captain of Taphians. And there she found the lordly wooers: now they were taking their pleasure at draughts in front of the doors, sitting on hides of oxen, which themselves had slain. And of the henchmen and the ready squires, some were mixing for them wine and water in bowls, and some again were washing the tables with porous sponges and were setting them forth, and others were carving flesh in plenty.

And godlike Telemachus was far the first to descry her, for he was sitting with a heavy heart among the wooers dreaming on his good father, if haply he might come somewhence, and make a scattering of the wooers there throughout the palace, and himself get honour and bear rule among his own possessions. Thinking thereupon, as he sat among the wooers, he saw Athene—and he went straight to the outer porch, for he thought it blame in his heart that a stranger should stand long at the gates: and halting nigh her he clasped her right hand and took from her the spear of bronze, and uttered his voice and spake unto her winged words:

"Hail, stranger, with us thou shalt be kindly entreated, and thereafter, when thou hast tasted meat, thou shalt tell us that whereof thou hast need."

Therewith he led the way, and Pallas Athene followed. And when they were now within the lofty house, he set her spear that he bore against a tall pillar, within the polished spearstand, where stood many spears besides, even those of Odysseus of the hardy heart; and he led the goddess and seated her on a goodly carven chair, and spread a linen cloth thereunder, and beneath was a footstool for the feet. For himself he placed an inlaid seat hard by, apart from the company of the wooers, lest the stranger should be disquieted by the noise and should have a loathing for the meal, being come among overweening men, and also that he might ask him about his father that was gone from his home.

Then a handmaid bare water for the washing of hands in a goodly golden ewer, and poured it forth over a silver basin to wash withal, and drew to their side a polished table. And a grave dame bare wheaten bread and set it by them, and laid on the board many dainties, giving freely of such things as she had by her. And a carver lifted and placed by them platters of divers kinds of flesh, and nigh them he set golden bowls, and a henchman walked to and fro pouring out to them the wine.

Then in came the lordly wooers; and they sat them down in rows on chairs and on high seats, and henchmen poured water on their hands, and maidservants piled wheaten bread by them in baskets, and pages crowned the bowls with drink; and they stretched forth their hands upon the good cheer spread before them. Now when the wooers had put from them the desire of meat and drink, they minded them of other things, even of the song and dance: for these are the crown of the feast. And a henchman placed a beauteous lyre in the hands of Phemius, who was minstrel to the wooers despite his will. Yea and as he touched the lyre he lifted up his voice in sweet song.

But Telemachus spake unto grey-eyed Athene, holding his head close to her that those others might not hear: "Dear stranger, wilt thou of a truth be wroth at the word that I shall say? Yonder men verily care for such things as these, the lyre and song, lightly, as they that devour the livelihood of another without atonement, of that man whose white bones, it may be, lie wasting in the rain upon the mainland, or the billow rolls them in the brine. Were but these men to see him returned to Ithaca, they all would pray rather for greater speed of foot than for gain of gold and raiment. But now he hath perished, even so, an evil doom, and for us is no comfort, no, not though any of earthly men should say that he will come again. Gone is the day of his returning! But come declare me this, and tell me all plainly: Who art thou of the sons of men, and whence?

Where is thy city, where are they that begat thee? Say, on what manner of ship didst thou come, and how did sailors bring thee to Ithaca, and who did they avow themselves to be, for in no wise do I deem that thou camest hither by land. And herein tell me true, that I may know for a surety whether thou art a newcomer, or whether thou art a guest of the house, seeing that many were the strangers that came to our home, for that *he* too had voyaged much among men."

Then the goddess, grey-eyed Athene, answered him: "Yea now, I will plainly tell thee all. I avow me to be Mentes, son of wise Anchialus, and I bear rule among the Taphians, lovers of the oar. And now am I come to shore, as thou seest, with ship and crew, sailing over the wine-dark sea, unto men of strange speech, even to Temesa,[1] in quest of copper, and my cargo is shining iron. And there my ship is lying toward the upland, away from the city, in the harbour of Rheithron beneath wooded Neïon: and we declare ourselves to be friends one of the other, and of houses friendly, from of old. Nay, if thou wouldest be assured, go ask the old man, the hero Laertes, who they say no more comes to the city, but far away toward the upland suffers affliction, with an ancient woman for his handmaid, who sets by him meat and drink, whensoever weariness takes hold of his limbs, as he creeps along the knoll of his vineyard plot. And now am I come; for verily they said that *he*, thy father, was among his people; but lo, the gods withhold him from his way. For goodly Odysseus hath not yet perished on the earth; but still, methinks, he lives and is kept on the wide deep in a seagirt isle, and hard men constrain him, wild folk that hold him, it may be, sore against his will. But now of a truth will I utter my word of prophecy, as the Immortals bring it into my heart and as I deem it will be accomplished, though no soothsayer am I, nor skilled in the signs of birds. Henceforth indeed for no long while shall he be far from his own dear

[1] Tamasia, in the mountainous centre of Cyprus.

country, not though bonds of iron bind him; he will advise him of a way to return, for he is a man of many devices. But come, declare me this, and tell me all plainly, whether indeed, so tall as thou art, thou art sprung from the loins of Odysseus. Thy head surely and thy beauteous eyes are wondrous like to his, since full many a time have we held converse together ere he embarked for Troy, whither the others, aye the bravest of the Argives, went in hollow ships. From that day forth neither have I seen Odysseus, nor he me."

Then wise Telemachus answered her, and said: "Yea, sir, now will I plainly tell thee all. My mother verily saith that I am his; for myself I know not, for never man yet knew of himself his own descent. O that I had been the son of some blessed man, whom old age overtook among his own possessions!"

Then the goddess, grey-eyed Athene, spake unto him, and said: "Surely no nameless lineage have the gods ordained for thee in days to come, since Penelope bore thee so goodly a man. But come, declare me this, and tell it all plainly. What feast, nay, what rout is this? What hast thou to do therewith? Is it a clan drinking, or a wedding feast, for here we have no banquet where each man brings his share? In such wise, flown with insolence, do they seem to me to revel wantonly through the house: and well might any man be wroth to see so many deeds of shame."

Then wise Telemachus answered her, and said: "Sir, forasmuch as thou questionest me of these things and inquirest thereof, our house was once like to have been rich and honourable, while yet that man was among his people. But now the gods willed it otherwise, in evil purpose, who have made him pass utterly out of sight as no man ever before. Truly I would not even for his death make so great sorrow, had he fallen among his fellows in the land of the Trojans. Then would the whole Achaean host have built him a barrow,[1] and even for

[1] [Burial mound.]

his son would he have won great glory in the after days. But now the spirits of the storm have swept him away inglorious. He is gone, lost to sight and hearsay, but for me hath he left anguish and lamentation; nor henceforth is it for him alone that I mourn and weep, since the gods have wrought for me other sore distress. For all the noblest that are princes in the isles, in Dulichium and Same and wooded Zacynthus, and as many as lord it in rocky Ithaca, all these woo my mother and waste my house. But as for her she neither refuseth the hated bridal, nor hath the heart to make an end: so they devour and minish my house, and ere long will they make havoc likewise of myself."

Then in heavy displeasure spake unto him Pallas Athene: "God help thee! thou art surely sore in need of Odysseus that is afar, to stretch forth his hands upon the shameless wooers. If he could but come now and stand at the entering in of the gate, with helmet and shield and lances twain, as mighty a man as when first I marked him in our house drinking and making merry what time he came up out of Ephyra from Ilus son of Mermerus! For even thither had Odysseus gone on his swift ship to seek a deadly drug, that he might have wherewithal to smear his bronze-shod arrows: but Ilus would in no wise give it him, for he had in awe the everliving gods. But my father gave it him, for he bare him wondrous love. O that Odysseus might in such strength consort with the wooers: so should they all have swift fate and bitter wedlock! Howbeit these things surely lie on the knees of the gods, whether he shall return or not, and take vengeance in his halls. But I charge thee to take counsel how thou mayest thrust forth the wooers from the hall. Come now, mark and take heed unto my words. On the morrow call the Achaean lords to the assembly, and declare thy saying to all, and take the gods to witness. As for the wooers bid them scatter them each one to his own, and for thy mother, if her heart is moved to marriage, let her go back to the hall of

that mighty man her father, and her kinsfolk will furnish a
wedding feast, and array the gifts of wooing exceeding many,
all that should go back with a daughter dearly beloved. And
to thyself I will give a word of wise counsel, if perchance thou
wilt hearken. Fit out a ship, the best thou hast, with twenty
oarsmen, and go to inquire concerning thy father that is long
afar, if perchance any man shall tell thee aught, or if thou mayest hear the voice from Zeus, which chiefly brings tidings to men.
Get thee first to Pylos and inquire of goodly Nestor, and from
thence to Sparta to Menelaus of the fair hair, for he came home
the last of the mail-coated Achaeans. If thou shalt hear news
of the life and the returning of thy father, then verily thou mayest endure the wasting for yet a year. But if thou shalt hear
that he is dead and gone, return then to thine own dear country
and pile his mound, and over it pay burial rites, full many as is
due, and give thy mother to a husband. But when thou hast
done this and made an end, thereafter take counsel in thy mind
and heart, how thou mayest slay the wooers in thy halls, whether
by guile or openly; for thou shouldest not carry childish thoughts,
being no longer of years thereto. Hast thou not heard what renown the goodly Orestes gat him among all men in that he slew
the slayer of his father, guileful Aegisthus? And thou, too, my
friend, for I see that thou art very comely and tall, be valiant,
that even men unborn may praise thee. But I will now go
down to the swift ship and to my men, who methinks chafe
much at tarrying for me; and do thou thyself take heed and
give ear unto my words."

Then wise Telemachus answered her, saying: "Sir, verily
thou speakest these things out of a friendly heart, as a father
to his son, and never will I forget them. But now I pray thee
abide here, though eager to be gone, to the end that after thou
hast bathed and had all thy heart's desire, thou mayest wend
to the ship joyful in spirit, with a costly gift and very goodly, to
be an heirloom of my giving, such as dear friends give to friends."

Then the goddess, grey-eyed Athene, answered him: "Hold me now no longer, that am eager for the way. But whatsoever gift thine heart shall bid thee give me, when I am on my way back let it be mine to carry home: bear from thy stores a gift right goodly, and it shall bring thee the worth thereof in return."

So spake she and departed, the grey-eyed Athene, and like an eagle of the sea she flew away, but in his spirit she planted might and courage, and put him in mind of his father yet more than heretofore. And he marked the thing and was amazed, for he deemed that it was a god; and anon he went among the wooers, a godlike man.

Now the renowned minstrel was singing to the wooers, and they sat listening in silence; and his song was of the pitiful return of the Achaeans, that Pallas Athene laid on them as they came forth from Troy. And from her upper chamber the daughter of Icarius, wise Penelope, caught the glorious strain, and she went down the high stairs from her chamber, not alone, for two of her handmaids bare her company. Now when the fair lady had come unto the wooers, she stood by the door-post of the well-builded roof holding up her glistening tire before her face; and a faithful maiden stood on either side her. Then she fell a-weeping, and spake unto the divine minstrel:

"Phemius, since thou knowest many other charms for mortals, deeds of men and gods, which bards rehearse, some one of these do thou sing as thou sittest by them, and let them drink their wine in silence; but cease from this pitiful strain, that ever wastes my heart within my breast, since to me above all women hath come a sorrow comfortless. So dear a head do I long for in constant memory, namely, that man whose fame is noised abroad from Hellas to mid Argos."

Then wise Telemachus answered her, and said: "O my mother, why then dost thou grudge the sweet minstrel to gladden us as his spirit moves him? It is not minstrels who are in

fault, but Zeus, methinks, is in fault, who gives to men, that
live by bread, to each one as he will. As for him it is no blame
if he sings the ill-faring of the Danaans; for men always prize
that song the most which rings newest in their ears. But let
thy heart and mind endure to listen, for not Odysseus only lost
in Troy the day of his returning, but many another likewise
perished. Howbeit go to thy chamber and mind thine own
housewiferies, the loom and distaff, and bid thy handmaids ply
their tasks. But speech shall be for men, for all, but for me in
chief; for mine is the lordship in the house."

Then in a maze she went back to her chamber, for she laid
up the wise saying of her son in her heart. She ascended to
her upper chamber with the women her handmaids, and then
was bewailing Odysseus, her dear lord, till grey-eyed Athene
cast sweet sleep upon her eyelids.

Now the wooers clamoured throughout the shadowy halls.
And wise Telemachus first spake among them:

"Wooers of my mother, men despiteful out of measure, let
us feast now and make merry and let there be no brawling;
for, lo, it is a good thing to list to a minstrel such as him, like
to the gods in voice. But in the morning let us all go to the
assembly and sit us down, that I may declare my saying outright, to wit that ye leave these halls: and busy yourselves with
other feasts, eating your own substance, going in turn from
house to house. But if ye deem this a likelier and a better
thing, that one man's goods should perish without atonement,
then waste ye as ye will; and I will call upon the everlasting
gods, if haply Zeus may grant that acts of recompense be
made: so should ye hereafter perish within the halls without
atonement."

So spake he, and all that heard him bit their lips and marvelled at Telemachus, in that he spake boldly.

Then Antinous, son of Eupeithes, answered him: "Telemachus, in very truth the gods themselves instruct thee to be

proud of speech and boldly to harangue. Never may Cronion[1] make thee king in seagirt Ithaca, which thing is of inheritance thy right!"

Then wise Telemachus answered him, and said: "Antinous, wilt thou indeed be wroth at the word that I shall say? Yea, at the hand of Zeus would I be fain to take even this thing upon me. Howsoever, there are many other kings of the Achaeans in seagirt Ithaca, kings young and old; someone of them shall surely have this kingship since goodly Odysseus is dead. But as for me, I will be lord of our own house and thralls, that goodly Odysseus gat me with his spear."

Then Eurymachus, son of Polybus, answered him, saying: "Telemachus, on the knees of the gods it surely lies, what man is to be king over the Achaeans in seagirt Ithaca. But mayest thou keep thine own possessions and be lord in thine own house! Never may that man come who shall wrest from thee thy substance violently in thine own despite, while Ithaca yet stands. But I would ask thee, friend, concerning the stranger — whence he is, and of what land he avows him to be? Where are his kin and his native fields? Doth he bear some tidings of thy father on his road, or cometh he thus to speed some matter of his own? In such wise did he start up, and lo, he was gone, nor tarried he that we should know him; — and yet he seemed no mean man to look upon."

Then wise Telemachus answered him, and said: "Eurymachus, surely the day of my father's returning hath gone by. Therefore no more do I put faith in tidings, whencesoever they may come, neither have I regard unto any divination, whereof my mother may inquire at the lips of a diviner, when she hath bidden him to the hall. But as for that man, he is a friend of my house from Taphos, and he avows him to be Mentes, son of wise Anchialus, and he hath lordship among the Taphians, lovers of the oar."

[1] [The son of Cronos, that is, Zeus.]

So spake Telemachus, but in his heart he knew the deathless goddess. Now the wooers turned them to the dance and the delightsome song, and made merry, and waited till evening should come on. And as they made merry, dusk evening came upon them. Then they went each one to his own house to lie down to rest.

But Telemachus, where his chamber was builded high up in the fair court, in a place with wide prospect, thither betook him to his bed, pondering many thoughts in his mind; and with him went trusty Eurycleia, and bare for him torches burning. She was the daughter of Ops, son of Peisenor, and Laertes bought her on a time with his wealth, while as yet she was in her first youth, and gave for her the worth of twenty oxen. She went with Telemachus and bare for him the burning torches: and of all the women of the household she loved him most, and she had nursed him when a little one. Then he opened the doors of the well-builded chamber and sat him on the bed and took off his soft doublet, and put it in the wise old woman's hands. So she folded the doublet and smoothed it, and hung it on a pin by the jointed bedstead, and went forth on her way from the room, and pulled to the door with the silver handle, and drew home the bar with the thong. There, all night through, wrapt in a fleece of wool, he meditated in his heart upon the journey that Athene had showed him.

BOOK II

Telemachus complains in vain, and borrowing a ship, goes secretly to Pylos by night. And how he was there received.

Now so soon as early Dawn shone forth, the rosy-fingered, the dear son of Odysseus gat him up from his bed, and put on his raiment and cast his sharp sword about his shoulder, and beneath his smooth feet he bound his goodly sandals, and stept forth from his chamber in presence like a god. And straightway he bade the clear-voiced heralds to call the long-haired Achaeans to the assembly. And the heralds called the gathering, and the Achaeans were assembled quickly. Now when they were gathered and come together, he went on his way to the assembly holding in his hand a spear of bronze, — not alone he went, for two swift hounds bare him company. Then Athene shed on him a wondrous grace, and all the people marvelled at him as he came. And he sat him in his father's seat and the elders gave place to him.

Then the lord Aegyptus spake among them first; bowed was he with age, and skilled in things past number. Now for this reason he spake, that his dear son, the warrior Antiphus, had gone in the hollow ships to Ilios. So weeping for his sake he made harangue and spake among them:

"Hearken now to me, ye men of Ithaca, to the word that I shall say. Never hath our assembly or session been since the day that goodly Odysseus departed in the hollow ships. And now who was minded thus to assemble us? On what man hath such sore need come, of the young men or of the elder born? Hath he heard some tidings of the host now returning, which he might plainly declare to us, or doth he show forth and tell some other matter of the common weal? Methinks he is a true man — good luck be with him! Zeus vouchsafe him some good thing in his turn, even all his heart's desire!"

So spake he, and the dear son of Odysseus was glad at the omen of the word; nor sat he now much longer, but he burned to speak, and he stood in mid assembly; and the herald Peisenor, skilled in sage counsels, placed the staff in his hands. Then he spake, accosting the old man first:

"Old man, he is not far off, and soon shalt thou know it for thyself, he who called the folk together, even I: for sorrow hath come to me in chief. Neither have I heard any tidings of the host now returning, which I may plainly declare to you; neither do I show forth or tell any other matter of the common weal, but mine own need, for evil hath befallen my house, a double woe. First, I have lost my noble sire, who sometime was king among you here, and was gentle as a father; and now is there an evil yet greater far, which surely shall soon make grievous havoc of my whole house and ruin all my livelihood. My mother did certain wooers beset sore against her will, even the sons of those men that here are the noblest. They are too craven to go to the house of.her father Icarius, that he may himself set the bride-price for his daughter, and bestow her on whom he will, even on him who finds favour in his sight. But they resorting to our house day by day sacrifice oxen and sheep and fat goats, and keep revel, and drink the dark wine recklessly, and lo, our great wealth is wasted, for there is no man now alive such as Odysseus was, to keep ruin from the house. As for me I am nowise strong like him to ward mine own; verily to the end of my days shall I be a weakling and all unskilled in prowess. Truly I would defend me if but strength were mine; for deeds past sufferance have now been wrought, and now my house is wasted utterly beyond pretence of right. Resent it in your own hearts, and have regard to your neighbours who dwell around, and tremble ye at the anger of the gods, lest haply they turn upon you in wrath at your evil deeds. I pray you by Zeus and by Themis,[1] who looseth and gathereth the meetings of men, let be, my friends, and leave me alone to waste in bitter grief."

So spake he in wrath, and dashed the staff to the ground, and brake forth in tears; and pity fell on all the people. Then all the others held their peace, and none had the heart to answer Telemachus with hard words, but Antinous alone made answer, saying:

[1] [The goddess of law and order.]

"Telemachus, proud of speech and unrestrained in fury, what is this thou hast said to put us to shame, and wouldst fasten on us reproach? Behold the fault is not in the Achaean wooers, but in thine own mother, for she is the craftiest of women. For it is now the third year, and the fourth is fast going by, since she began to deceive the minds of the Achaeans in their breasts. She gives hope to all, and makes promises to every man, and sends them messages, but her mind is set on other things. And she hath devised in her heart this wile besides; she set up in her halls a mighty web, fine of woof and very wide, whereat she would weave, and anon she spake among us:

"'Ye princely youths, my wooers, now that the goodly Odysseus is dead, do ye abide patiently, how eager soever to speed on this marriage of mine, till I finish the robe. I would not that the threads perish to no avail, even this shroud for the hero Laertes, against the day when the ruinous doom shall bring him low, of death that lays men at their length. So shall none of the Achaean women in the land count it blame in me, as well might be, were he to lie without a winding-sheet, a man that had gotten great possessions.'

"So spake she, and our high hearts consented thereto. So then in the day time she would weave the mighty web, and in the night unravel the same, when she had let place the torches by her. Thus for the space of three years she hid the thing by craft and beguiled the minds of the Achaeans; but when the fourth year arrived and the seasons came round, then at the last one of her women who knew all declared it, and we found her unravelling the splendid web. Thus she finished it perforce and sore against her will. But as for thee, the wooers make thee answer thus, that thou mayest know it in thine own heart, thou and all the Achaeans! Send away thy mother, and bid her be married to whomsoever her father commands, and whoso is well pleasing unto her. But if she will continue

PENELOPE SURPRISED BY THE SUITORS

for long to vex the sons of the Achaeans, pondering in her heart those things that Athene hath given her beyond women, knowledge of all fair handiwork, yea, and cunning wit, and wiles —so be it! For in despite of her the wooers will devour thy living and thy substance, so long as she is steadfast in such purpose as the gods now put within her breast: great renown for herself she winneth, but for thee regret for thy much livelihood. But we will neither go to our own lands, nor otherwhere, till she marry that man whom she will of the Achaeans.'

Then wise Telemachus answered him, saying: "Antinous, I may in no wise thrust forth from the house, against her will, the woman that bare me, that reared me: while as for my father he is abroad on the earth, whether he be alive or dead. Moreover, it is hard for me to make heavy restitution to Icarius, as needs I must, if of mine own will I send my mother away. For I shall have evil at his hand, at the hand of her father, and some god will give me more besides, for my mother will call down the dire Avengers as she departs from the house, and I shall have blame of men; surely then I will never speak this word. Nay, if your own heart, even yours, is indignant, quit ye my halls, and busy yourselves with other feasts, eating your own substance, and going in turn from house to house. But if ye deem this a likelier and a better thing, that one man's goods should perish without atonement, then waste ye as ye will: and I will call upon the everlasting gods, if haply Zeus may grant that acts of recompense be made: so should ye hereafter perish in the halls without atonement."

So spake Telemachus, and in answer to his prayer did Zeus, of the far-borne voice, send forth two eagles in flight, from on high, from the mountain-crest. Awhile they flew as fleet as the blasts of the wind, side by side, with straining of their pinions. But when they had now reached the mid assembly, the place of many voices, there they wheeled about and flapped their strong wings, and looked down upon the heads of all, and destruction was in their gaze. Then tore they with their talons each the other's cheeks and neck on every side, and so sped to the right across the dwellings and the city of the people. And the men marvelled at the birds when they had sight of them, and pondered in their hearts the things that should come to pass. Yea and the old man, the lord Halitherses son of Mastor spake among them, for he excelled his peers in knowledge of birds, and in uttering words of fate. With good will he made harangue and spake among them:

"Hearken to me now, ye men of Ithaca, to the word that I shall say : and mainly to the wooers do I show forth and tell these things, seeing that a mighty woe is rolling upon them. For Odysseus shall not long be away from his friends, nay, even now, it may be, he is near, and sowing the seeds of death and fate for these men, every one ; and he will be a bane to many another likewise of us who dwell in clear-seen Ithaca. But long ere that falls out let us advise us how we may make an end of their mischief ; yea, let them of their ownselves make an end, for this is the better way for them, as will soon be seen."

And Eurymachus, son of Polybus, answered him, saying: "Go now, old man, get thee home and prophesy to thine own children, lest haply they suffer harm hereafter. And I myself will give a word of counsel to Telemachus in presence of you all. Let him command his mother to return to her father's house ; and her kinsfolk will furnish a wedding feast, and array the gifts of wooing, exceeding many, all that should go back with a daughter dearly beloved. For ere that, I trow, we sons of the Achaeans will not cease from our rough wooing, since, come what may, we fear not any man, no, not Telemachus, full of words though he be, nor soothsaying do we heed, whereof thou, old man, pratest idly, and art hated yet the more. His substance too shall be woefully devoured, nor shall recompense ever be made, so long as she shall put off the Achaeans in the matter of her marriage."

Then wise Telemachus answered him, saying: "Eurymachus, and ye others, that are lordly wooers, I entreat you no more concerning this nor speak thereof, for the gods have knowledge of it now and all the Achaeans. But come, give me a swift ship and twenty men, who shall accomplish for me my voyage to and fro. For I will go to Sparta and to sandy Pylos to inquire concerning the return of my father that is long afar, if perchance any man shall tell me aught, or if I may hear the voice from Zeus, that chiefly bring tidings to men. If I shall hear news of the life and the returning of my father, then verily I may endure the wasting for yet a year; but if I shall hear that he is dead and gone, let me then return to my own dear country, and pile his mound, and over it pay burial rights full many as is due, and I will give my mother to a husband."

So with that word he sat him down; then in the midst uprose Mentor, the companion of noble Odysseus. He it was to whom Odysseus, as he departed in the fleet, had given the charge over all his house, that it should obey the old man, and that he should keep all things safe. With good will he now made harangue and spake among them:

"Hearken to me now, ye men of Ithaca, to the word that I shall say. Henceforth let not any sceptred king be kind and gentle with all his heart, nor minded to do righteously, but let him alway be a hard man and work unrighteousness: for behold, there is none of the people whose lord he was that remembereth divine Odysseus, who was gentle as a father. Howsoever, it is not that I grudge the lordly wooers their deeds of violence in the evil devices of their heart. For at the hazard of their own heads they violently devour the household of Odysseus, and say of him that he will come no more again. But I am indeed wroth with the rest of the people, to see how ye all sit thus speechless, and do not cry shame upon the wooers, and put them down, ye that are so many and they so few."

And Leocritus, son of Euenor, answered him, saying: "Mentor infatuate, with thy wandering wits, what word hast thou spoken, that callest upon them to put us down? Nay, it is a hard thing to fight about a feast, and that with men who are even more in number than you. Though Odysseus of Ithaca himself should come and were eager of heart to drive forth from the hall the lordly wooers that feast throughout his house, yet should his wife have no joy of his coming, though she yearns for him; — but even there should he meet foul doom, if he fought with those that outnumbered him; so thou hast not spoken aright. But as for the people, come now, scatter yourselves each one to his own lands, but Mentor and Halitherses will speed this man's voyage, for they are friends of his house from of old. Yet after all, methinks that long time he will abide and seek tidings in Ithaca, and never accomplish this voyage."

Thus he spake, and in haste they broke up the assembly. So they were scattered each one to his own dwelling, while the wooers departed to the house of divine Odysseus.

Then Telemachus, going far apart to the shore of the sea, laved his hands in the grey sea water, and prayed unto Athene, saying: "Hear me, thou who yesterday didst come in thy godhead to our house, and badest me go in a ship across the misty seas, to seek tidings of the return of my father that is long gone: but all this my purpose do the Achaeans delay, and mainly the wooers in the naughtiness of their pride."

So spake he in prayer, and Athene drew nigh him in the likeness of Mentor, in fashion and in voice, and she spake and hailed him in winged words:

"Telemachus, hereafter thou shalt not be craven or witless, if indeed thou hast a drop of thy father's blood and a portion of his spirit. Nor shall thy voyage be vain or unfulfilled. Wherefore now take no heed of the counsel or the purpose of the senseless wooers, for they are in no way wise or just: neither know they aught of death and of black fate, which already is close upon them, that they are all to perish in one day. But the voyage on which thy heart is set shall not long be lacking to thee — so faithful a friend of thy father am I, who will furnish thee a swift ship and myself be thy companion. Go thou to the house, and consort with the wooers, and make ready corn, and bestow all in vessels, the wine in jars and barley-flour, the marrow of men, in well-sewn skins; and I will lightly gather in the township a crew that offer themselves willingly. There are many ships, new and old, in seagirt Ithaca; of these I will choose out the best for thee, and we will quickly rig her and launch her on the broad deep."

So spake Athene, daughter of Zeus, and Telemachus made no long tarrying, when he had heard the voice of the goddess. He went on his way towards the house, heavy at heart, and there he found the noble wooers in the halls, flaying goats and singeing swine in the court. And Antinous laughed out and went straight to Telemachus, and clasped his hand and spake and hailed him:

"Telemachus, proud of speech and unrestrained in fury, let no evil word any more be in thy heart, nor evil work, but let me see thee eat and drink as of old. And the Achaeans will make thee ready all things without fail, a ship and chosen oarsmen, that thou mayest come the quicker to fair Pylos, to seek tidings of thy noble father."

Then wise Telemachus answered him, saying, "Antinous, in no wise in your proud company can I sup in peace, and make merry with a quiet mind. Is it a little thing, ye wooers, that in time past ye wasted many good things of my getting, while as yet I was a child? But now that I am a man grown, and learn the story from the lips of others, and my spirit waxeth within me, I will seek to let loose upon you evil fates, as I may; going either to Pylos for help, or abiding here in this township. Yea, I will go, nor vain shall the voyage be whereof I speak; a passenger on another's ship go I, for I am not to have a ship nor oarsmen of mine own; so in your wisdom ye have thought it for the better."

He spake and snatched his hand from out the hand of Antinous, lightly, and all the while the wooers were busy feasting through the house; and they mocked him and sharply taunted him, and thus would some proud youth speak:

"In very truth Telemachus planneth our destruction. He will bring a rescue either from sandy Pylos, or even it may be from Sparta, so terribly is he set on slaying us. Or else he will go to Ephyra, a fruitful land, to fetch a poisonous drug that he may cast it into the bowl and make an end of all of us."

And again another proud youth would say: "Who knows but that he himself, if he goes hence on the hollow ship, may perish wandering far from his friends, even as Odysseus? So should we have yet more ado, for then must we divide among us all his substance, and moreover give the house to his mother to possess it, and to him whosoever should wed her."

So spake they; but he stepped down into the vaulted treasure-chamber of his father, a spacious room, where gold and bronze lay piled, and raiment in coffers, and fragrant olive oil in plenty. And there stood casks of sweet wine and old, full of the unmixed drink divine, all orderly ranged by the wall, ready if ever Odysseus should come home, albeit after travail and much pain. And the close-fitted doors, the folding doors, were shut, and night and day there abode within a dame in charge, who guarded all in the fulness of her wisdom, Eurycleia. Telemachus now called her into the chamber and spake unto her, saying:

"Mother, come draw off for me sweet wine in jars, the choicest next to that thou keepest mindful ever of that ill-fated one, Odysseus, if perchance he may come I know not whence, having avoided death and the fates. So fill twelve jars, and close each with his lid, and pour me barley-meal into well-sewn skins, and let there be twenty measures of the grain of bruised barley-meal. Let none know this but thyself! As for these things let them all be got together; for in the evening I will take them with me, at the time that my mother hath gone to her upper chamber and turned her thoughts to sleep. Lo, to Sparta I go and to sandy Pylos to seek tidings of my dear father's return, if haply I may hear thereof."

So spake he, and the good nurse Eurycleia wailed aloud, and making lament spake to him winged words: "Ah, wherefore, dear child, hath such a thought arisen in thine heart? How shouldst thou fare over wide lands, thou that art an only child and well-beloved? As for him he hath perished, far from his own country in the land of strangers. And yonder men, so soon as thou art gone, will devise mischief against thee thereafter, that thou mayest perish by guile, and they will share among them all this wealth of thine. Nay, abide here, settled on thine own lands: thou hast no need upon the deep unharvested to suffer evil and go wandering."

Then wise Telemachus answered her, saying: "Take heart, nurse, for lo, this my purpose came not but of a god. But swear to tell no word thereof to my dear mother, till at least it shall be the eleventh or twelfth day from hence, or till she miss me of herself, and hear of my departure, that so she may not mar her fair face with her tears."

Thus he spake, and the old woman sware a great oath by the gods not to reveal it. But when she had sworn that oath, straightway she drew off the wine for him in jars, and poured barley-meal into well-sewn skins, and Telemachus departed to the house and consorted with the wooers.

Then the goddess, grey-eyed Athene, turned to other thoughts. In the likeness of Telemachus she went all through the city, and stood by each one of the men and spake her saying, and bade them gather at even by the swift ship. Furthermore, she craved a swift ship of Noëmon, famous son of Phronius, and right gladly he promised it.

Now the sun sank and all the ways were darkened. Then at length she let drag the swift ship to the sea and stored within it all such tackling as decked ships carry. And she moored it at the far end of the harbour and the good company was gathered together, and the goddess cheered on all.

Then the goddess, grey-eyed Athene, turned to other thoughts. She went on her way to the house of divine Odysseus; and there she shed sweet sleep upon the wooers and made them distraught in their drinking, and cast the cups from their hands. And they arose up to go to rest throughout the city, nor sat they yet a long while, for slumber was falling on their eyelids. Now grey-eyed Athene spake unto Telemachus, and called him from out the fair-lying halls, taking the likeness of Mentor, both in fashion and in voice:

"Telemachus, thy goodly-greaved companions are sitting already at their oars, it is thy despatch they are waiting. Nay then, let us go, that we delay them not long from the way."

Therewith Pallas Athene led the way quickly, and he followed hard in the steps of the goddess. Now when they had come down to the ship and to the sea, they found the long-haired youths of the company on the shore; and the mighty prince Telemachus spake among them:

"Come hither, friends, let us carry the corn on board, for all is now together in the room, and my mother knows nought thereof, nor any of the maidens of the house: one woman only heard my saying."

Thus he spake and led the way, and they went with him. So they brought all and stowed it in the decked ship, according to the word of the dear son of Odysseus. Then Telemachus climbed the ship, and Athene went before him, and behold, she sat her down in the stern, and near her sat Telemachus. And the men loosed the hawsers and climbed on board themselves, and sat upon the benches. And grey-eyed Athene sent them a favourable gale, a fresh West Wind, singing over the wine-dark sea.

And Telemachus called unto his company and bade them lay hands on the tackling, and they hearkened to his call. So they raised the mast of pine tree and set it in the hole of the cross plank, and made it fast with forestays, and hauled up the white sails with twisted ropes of oxhide. And the wind filled the belly of the sail, and the dark wave seethed loudly round the stem of the running ship, and she fleeted over the wave, accomplishing her path. Then they made all fast in the swift black ship, and set mixing bowls brimmed with wine, and poured drink-offering to the deathless gods that are from everlasting, and in chief to the grey-eyed daughter of Zeus. So all night long and through the dawn the ship cleft her way.

BOOK III

Nestor entertains Telemachus at Pylos and tells him how the Greeks departed from Troy ; and sends him for further information to Sparta.

Now the sun arose and left the lovely mere, speeding to the brazen heaven, to give light to the immortals and to mortal men on the earth, the graingiver, and they reached Pylos, the stablished castle of Neleus. There the people were doing sacrifice on the sea shore, slaying black bulls without spot to the dark-haired god, the shaker of the earth. Nine companies there were, and five hundred men sat in each, and in every company they held nine bulls ready to hand. Just as they had tasted the inner parts, and were burning the slices of the thighs on the altar to the god, the others were bearing straight to land, and brailed up the sails of the gallant ship, and moored her, and themselves came forth. And Telemachus too stept forth from the ship, and Athene led the way. And the goddess, grey-eyed Athene, spake first to him, saying:

"Telemachus, thou needest not now be abashed, no, not one whit. For to this very end didst thou sail over the deep, that thou mightest hear tidings of thy father, even where the earth closed over him, and what manner of death he met. But come now, go straight to Nestor, tamer of horses: let us learn what counsel he hath in the secret of his heart. And beseech him thyself that he may give unerring answer; and he will not lie to thee, for he is very wise."

The wise Telemachus answered, saying: "Mentor, and how shall I go, how shall I greet him, I, who am untried in words of wisdom? Moreover a young man may well be abashed to question an elder."

Then the goddess, grey-eyed Athene, spake to him again: "Telemachus, thou shalt bethink thee of somewhat in thine own breast, and somewhat the god will give thee to say. For thou, methinks, of all men, wert not born and bred without the will of the gods."

So spake Athene and led the way quickly; and he followed hard in the steps of the goddess. And they came to the gathering and the session of the men of Pylos. There was Nestor seated with his sons, and round him his company making ready the feast, and roasting some of the flesh and spitting other. Now when they saw the strangers, they went all together, and clasped their hands in welcome, and would have them sit down. First Peisistratus, son of Nestor, drew nigh, and took the hands of each, and made them to sit down at the feast on soft fleeces upon the sea sand, beside his brother Thrasymedes and his father. And he gave them messes of the inner meat, and poured wine into a golden cup, and pledging her, he spake unto Pallas Athene, daughter of Zeus, lord of the aegis:[1]

"Pray now, my guest, to the lord Poseidon, even as it is his

---

[1] [The storm mantle of Zeus.]

feast whereon ye have chanced in coming hither. And when thou hast made drink-offering and prayed, as is due, give thy friend also the cup of honeyed wine to make offering thereof, inasmuch as he too, methinks, prayeth to the deathless gods, for all men stand in need of the gods. Howbeit he is younger and mine own equal in years, therefore to thee first will I give the golden chalice."

Therewith he placed in her hand the cup of sweet wine. And Athene rejoiced in the wisdom and judgment of the man, in that he had given to her first the chalice of gold. And straightway she prayed, and that instantly,[1] to the lord Poseidon:

"Hear me, Poseidon, girdler of the earth, and grudge not the fulfilment of this labour in answer to our prayer. To Nestor first and to his sons vouchsafe renown, and thereafter grant to all the people of Pylos a gracious recompense for this splendid hecatomb. Grant moreover that Telemachus and I may return, when we have accomplished that for which we came hither with our swift black ship."

Now as she prayed on this wise, herself the while was fulfilling the prayer. And she gave Telemachus the fair two-handled cup; and in like manner prayed the dear son of Odysseus. Then, when the others had roasted the outer parts and drawn them off the spits, they divided the messes and shared the glorious feast. But when they had put from them the desire of meat and drink, Nestor of Gerenia, lord of chariots, first spake among them:

"Now is the better time to inquire and ask of the strangers who they are, now that they have had their delight of food. Strangers, who are ye? Whence sail ye over the wet ways? On some trading enterprise, or at adventure do ye rove, even as sea-robbers, over the brine, for they wander at hazard of their own lives bringing bale to alien men?"

Then wise Telemachus answered him and spake with courage,

[1] [Earnestly.]

for Athene herself had put boldness in his heart, that he might ask about his father who was afar, and that he might be had in good report among men:

"Nestor, son of Neleus, great glory of the Achaeans, thou askest whence we are, and I will surely tell thee all. We have come forth out of Ithaca; and this our quest whereof I speak is a matter of mine own, and not of the common weal. I follow after the far-spread rumour of my father, if haply I may hear thereof, even of the goodly steadfast Odysseus, who upon a time, men say, fought by thy side and sacked the city of the Trojans. For none can surely declare the place where he hath perished, whether he was smitten by foemen on the mainland, or lost upon the deep. So now am I come hither to thy knees, if perchance thou art willing to tell me of his pitiful death, as one that saw it with thine own eyes, or heard the story from some other wanderer. And speak me no soft words in pity, but tell me plainly what sight thou didst get of him."

Then Nestor of Gerenia, lord of chariots, answered him: "My friend, since thou hast brought sorrow back to mind, behold, this is the story of the woe which we endured in that land, we sons of the Achaeans, unrestrained in fury, and of all that we bore in wanderings after spoil, sailing with our ships over the misty deep, wheresoever Achilles led; and of all our war round the mighty burg of king Priam. Yea and there the best of us were slain. There lies valiant Aias, and there Achilles, and there Patroclus, the peer of the gods in counsel, and there my own dear son, strong and noble, Antilochus, that excelled in speed of foot and in the fight. And many other ills we suffered beside these; who of mortal men could tell the tale? Nay none, though thou wert to abide here for five years, ay, and for six, and ask of all the ills which the goodly Achaeans then endured. Ere all was told thou wouldst be weary and turn to thine own country. For nine whole years we were busy about the Trojans, devising their ruin with all manner of craft; and

scarce did Zeus bring it to pass. There never a man durst
match with goodly Odysseus in wisdom, for he very far outdid
the rest in all manner of craft. Now look you, all the while
that myself and goodly Odysseus were there, we never spake
diversely either in the assembly or in the council, but always
were of one mind, and advised the Argives with understanding
and sound counsel, how all might be for the very best. But
after we had sacked the steep city of Priam, and had departed
in our ships, a god scattered the Achaeans, and Zeus devised in
his heart a pitiful returning for the Argives. So I came, dear
child, without tidings, nor know I aught of those others, which
of the Achaeans were saved and which were lost. But all that
I hear tell of as I sit in our halls, thou shalt learn as it is
meet, and I will hide nothing from thee. Safely, they say,
came the Myrmidons the wild spearsmen, whom the famous
son of high-souled Achilles led; and Idomeneus brought all his
company to Crete, all that escaped the war, and from him the
sea gat none. And of Agamemnon even yourselves have heard,
far apart though ye dwell, how he came, and how Aegisthus
devised his evil end; but verily he himself paid a terrible reckoning. So good a thing it is that a son of the dead should still
be left, even as that son also took vengeance on the slayer of
his father."

And wise Telemachus answered him, and said: "Nestor,
son of Neleus, great glory of the Achaeans, verily and indeed
he avenged himself, and the Achaeans shall noise his fame
abroad, that even those may hear who are yet for to be. Oh
that the gods would clothe me with such strength as his, that
I might take vengeance on the wooers for their cruel transgression, who wantonly devise against me infatuate deeds!"

Then Nestor, lord of chariots, made answer: "Dear friend,
seeing thou dost call these things to my remembrance and
speak thereof, they tell me that many wooers for thy mother's
hand plan mischief within the halls in thy despite. Say, dost

thou willingly submit thee to oppression, or do the people through the land hate thee, obedient to the voice of a god? Who knows but that Odysseus may some day come and requite their violence, either himself alone or all the host of the Achaeans with him? Ah, if but grey-eyed Athene were inclined to love thee, as once she cared exceedingly for the renowned Odysseus in the land of the Trojans, where we Achaeans were sore afflicted, — for never yet have I seen the gods show forth such manifest love, as then did Pallas Athene standing manifest by him, — if she would be pleased so to love thee and to care for thee, then might certain of them clean forget their marriage.''

And wise Telemachus answered him, saying: "Old man, in no wise methinks shall this word be accomplished. This is a hard saying of thine, awe comes over me. Not for my hopes shall this thing come to pass, not even if the gods so willed it."

Then the goddess, grey-eyed Athene, spake to him again: "Telemachus, what word hath escaped the door of thy lips? Lightly might a god, if so he would, bring a man safe home even from afar. Rather myself would I have travail and much pain ere I came home and saw the day of my returning, than come back and straightway perish on my own hearth-stone, even as Agamemnon perished by guile at the hands of his own wife and of Aegisthus."

Then said Nestor, lord of chariots: "My friend, wander not long far away from home, leaving thy substance behind thee and men in thy house so wanton, lest they divide and utterly devour all thy wealth, and thou shalt have gone on a vain journey. Rather I bid and command thee to go to Menelaus, for he hath lately come from a strange country, from the land of men whence none would hope in his heart to return, whom once the storms have driven wandering into so wide a sea. Thence not even the birds can make their way in the space of one year, so great a sea it is and terrible. But go now with thy ship and with thy company, or if thou hast a mind to fare by land, I have a chariot and horses at thy service, yea and my sons to do thy will, who will be thy guides to goodly Lacedaemon, where is Menelaus of the fair hair. Do thou thyself entreat him, that he may give thee unerring answer. He will not lie to thee, for he is very wise."

Thus he spake, and the sun went down and darkness came on. Then the goddess, grey-eyed Athene, spake among them, saying: "Come, cut up the tongues of the victims and mix the wine, that we may pour forth before Poseidon and the other deathless gods, and so may bethink us of sleep, for it is the hour for sleep. For already has the light gone beneath the west, and it is not seemly to sit long at a banquet of the gods, but to be going home."

So spake the daughter of Zeus, and they hearkened to her voice. And the henchmen poured water over their hands, and pages crowned the mixing bowls with drink, and served out the wine to all, after they had first poured for libation into each cup in turn; and they cast the tongues upon the fire, and stood up and poured the drink-offering thereon. But when they had poured forth and had drunken to their hearts' content, Athene and godlike Telemachus were both set on returning to the hollow ship; but Nestor would have stayed them, and accosted them, saying: "Zeus forfend it, and all the other deathless gods, that ye should depart from my house to the swift ship, as from the dwelling of one that is utterly without raiment or a needy man, who hath not rugs or blankets many in his house whereon to sleep softly, he or his guests. Nay not so, I have rugs and fair blankets by me. Never, methinks, shall the dear son of this man, even of Odysseus, lay him down upon the ship's deck, while as yet I am alive, and my children after me are left in my hall to entertain strangers, whoso may chance to come to my house."

Then the goddess, grey-eyed Athene, spake to him again: "Yea, herein hast thou spoken aright, dear father: and Telemachus may well obey thee, for before all things this is meet. Behold, he shall now depart with thee, that he may sleep in thy halls; as for me I will go to the black ship, that I may cheer my company and tell them all. For I avow me to be the one elder among them; those others are but younger men, who follow for love of him, all of them of like age with the high-souled Telemachus. There will I lay me down by the black hollow ship this night; but in the morning I will go to the Cauconians high of heart, where somewhat of mine is owing to me, no small debt nor of yesterday. But do thou send this man upon his way with thy chariot and thy son, since he hath come to thy house, and give him horses the lightest of foot and chief in strength."

Therewith grey-eyed Athene departed in the semblance of a sea-eagle; and amazement fell on all that saw it, and the old man he marvelled when his eyes beheld it. And he took the hand of Telemachus and spake and hailed him:

"My friend, methinks that thou wilt in no sort be a coward and a weakling, if indeed in thy youth the gods thus follow with thee to be thy guides. For truly this is none other of those who keep the mansions of Olympus, save only the daughter of Zeus, she that honoured thy good father too among the Argives. Nay be gracious, queen, and vouchsafe a goodly fame to me, even to me and to my sons and to my wife revered. And I in turn will sacrifice to thee a yearling heifer, broad of brow, unbroken, which man never yet hath led beneath the yoke. Such an one will I offer to thee, and gild her horns with gold."

Even so he spake in prayer, and Athene heard him. Then Nestor led them, even his sons and the husbands of his daughters, to his own fair house. But when they had reached this prince's famous halls, they sat down all orderly on seats and high chairs; and when they were come, the old man mixed well for them a bowl of sweet wine, which now in the eleventh year from the vintaging the housewife opened, and unloosed the string that fastened the lid. The old man let mix a bowl thereof, and prayed instantly to Athene as he poured forth before her.

But after they had poured forth and had drunken to their heart's content, these went each one to his own house to lie down to rest. But Nestor would needs have Telemachus, son of divine Odysseus, to sleep there on a jointed bedstead beneath the echoing gallery, and by him Peisistratus of the good ashen spear, leader of men, who alone of his sons was yet unwed in his halls.

So soon as early Dawn shone forth, the rosy-fingered, Nestor gat him up from his bed, and after they had sacrificed a heifer to Athene, and had put from them the desire of meat and drink, Nestor first spake among them:

"Lo now, my sons, yoke for Telemachus horses with flowing mane and lead them beneath the car, that he may get forward on his way."

Even so he spake, and they gave good heed and hearkened; and quickly they yoked the swift horses beneath the chariot. And the dame that kept the stores placed therein corn and wine and dainties, such as princes eat, the fosterlings of Zeus. So Telemachus stept up into the goodly car, and with him Peisistratus son of Nestor leader of men, likewise climbed the car and grasped the reins in his hands, and he touched the horses with the whip to start them, and nothing loth the pair flew toward the plain, and left the steep citadel of Pylos. So all day long they swayed the yoke they bore upon their necks.

Now the sun sank and all the ways were darkened. And they came to Pherae, to the house of Diocles. There they rested for the night, and by them he set the entertainment of strangers.

Now so soon as early Dawn shone forth, the rosy-fingered, they yoked the horses and mounted the inlaid car. And forth they drave from the gateway and the echoing gallery, and Peisistratus touched the horses with the whip to start them, and the pair flew onward nothing loth. So they came to the wheat-bearing plain, and thenceforth they pressed toward the end: in such wise did the swift horses speed forward. Now the sun sank and all the ways were darkened.

BOOK IV

Telemachus's entertainment at Sparta, where Menelaus tells him what befell many of the Greeks on their return; that Odysseus was with Calypso in the isle Ogygia, as he was told by Proteus.

AND they came to Lacedaemon lying low among the caverned hills, and drave to the dwelling of renowned Menelaus. Him they found giving a feast in his house to many friends of his kin, a feast for the wedding of his noble son and daughter. So they were feasting through the great vaulted hall, the neighbours and the kinsmen of renowned Menelaus, making merry; and among them a divine minstrel was singing to the lyre, and as he began the song two tumblers in the company whirled through the midst of them.

Meanwhile those twain, the hero Telemachus and the splendid son of Nestor, made halt at the entry of the gate, they and their horses. And the lord Eteoneus came forth and saw them, the ready squire of renowned Menelaus; and he went through the palace to bear the tidings to the shepherd of the people, and standing near spake to him winged words:

"Menelaus, fosterling of Zeus, here are two strangers, whosoever they be, two men like to the lineage of great Zeus. Say, shall we loose their swift horses from under the yoke, or send them onward to some other host who shall receive them kindly?"

Then in sore displeasure spake to him Menelaus of the fair hair: "Eteoneus, truly thou wert not a fool aforetime, but now for this once, like a child thou talkest folly. Surely ourselves ate much hospitable cheer of other men, ere we twain came hither, even if in time to come Zeus haply give us rest from affliction. Nay go, unyoke the horses of the strangers, and as for the men, lead them forward to the house to feast with us."

So spake he, and Eteoneus hasted from the hall, and called the other ready squires to follow with him. So they loosed the sweating horses from beneath the yoke, and fastened them at the stalls of the horses, and threw beside them spelt, and therewith mixed white barley, and tilted the chariot against the shining faces of the gateway, and led the men into the hall divine. And they beheld and marvelled as they gazed throughout the palace of the king, the fosterling of Zeus; for there was a gleam as it were of sun or moon through the lofty palace of renowned Menelaus. But after they had gazed their fill, they went to the polished baths and bathed them. Now when the maidens had bathed them and anointed them with olive oil, and cast about them thick cloaks and doublets, they sat on chairs by Menelaus, son of Atreus. And a handmaid bare water for the hands in a goodly golden ewer, and poured it forth over a silver basin to wash withal; and to their side she drew a polished table, and a grave dame bare food and set it by them, and laid upon the board many dainties, giving freely of such things as she had by her, and a carver lifted and placed by them platters of divers kinds of flesh, and nigh them he set golden bowls. So Menelaus of the fair hair greeted the twain and spake:

"Taste ye food and be glad, and thereafter when ye have supped, we will ask what men ye are; for the blood of your parents is not lost in you, but ye are of the line of men that are sceptred kings, the fosterlings of Zeus; for no churls could beget sons like you."

So spake he, and took and set before them the fat ox-chine roasted, which they had given him as his own mess by way of honour. And they stretched forth their hands upon the good cheer set before them. Now when they had put from them the desire of meat and drink Telemachus spake to the son of Nestor, holding his head close to him, that those others might not hear:

"Son of Nestor, delight of my heart, mark the flashing of bronze through the echoing halls, and the flashing of gold and of amber and of silver and of ivory. Such like, methinks, is the court of Olympian Zeus within, for the world of things that are here; wonder comes over me as I look thereon."

And as he spake Menelaus of the fair hair was ware of him, and uttering his voice spake to them winged words:

"Children dear, of a truth no one of mortal men may contend with Zeus, for his mansions and his treasures are everlasting: but of men there may be who will vie with me in treasure, or there may be none. Yea, for after many a woe and wanderings manifold, I brought my wealth home in ships, and in the eighth year came hither. I roamed over Cyprus and Phoenicia and Egypt, and reached the Aethiopians and Sidonians and Erembi and Libya, where lambs are horned from the birth. While I was yet roaming in those lands, gathering much livelihood, meantime another slew my brother privily, at unawares, by the guile of his accursed wife. Thus, look you, I have no joy of my lordship among these my possessions: and ye are like to have heard hereof from your fathers, whosoever they be, for I have suffered much and let a house go to ruin that was stablished fair, and had in it much choice substance. I would that I had but a third part of those my riches, and dwelt in my halls, and that those men were yet safe, who perished of old in the wide land of Troy, far from Argos, the pastureland of horses. Howbeit, though I bewail them all and sorrow oftentimes as I sit in our halls, yet for them all I make no such dole, despite my grief, as for one only, who causes me to loathe both sleep and meat, when I think upon him. For no one of the Achaeans toiled so greatly as Odysseus toiled and adventured himself: but to him it was to be but labour and trouble, and to me grief ever comfortless for his sake, so long as he is afar, nor know we aught, whether he be alive or dead. Yea methinks they lament him, even that old Laertes and the constant Penelope and Telemachus, whom he left a child new-born in his house."

So spake he, and in the heart of Telemachus he stirred a yearning to lament his father; and at his father's name he let a tear fall from his eyelids to the ground, and held up his purple mantle with both his hands before his eyes. And Menelaus marked him and mused in his mind and his heart whether he should leave him to speak of his father, or first question him and prove him in every word.

While yet he pondered these things in his mind and in his heart, Helen came forth from her fragrant vaulted chamber, like Artemis of the golden arrows; and with her came Adrastê and set for her the well-wrought chair, and Alcippê bare a rug of soft wool, and Phylo bare a silver basket which Alcandrê gave her, the wife of Polybus, who dwelt in Thebes of Egypt, where is the chiefest store of wealth in the houses. He gave two silver baths to Menelaus, and tripods twain, and ten talents of gold. And besides all this, his wife bestowed on Helen lovely gifts; a golden distaff did she give, and a silver basket with wheels beneath, and the rims thereof were finished with gold. This it was that the handmaid Phylo bare and set beside her, filled with dressed yarn, and across it was laid a distaff charged with wool of violet blue. So Helen sat her down in the chair, and beneath was a footstool for the feet. And anon she spake to her lord and questioned him of each thing:

"Menelaus, fosterling of Zeus, know we now who these men avow themselves to be that have come under our roof? Shall

I dissemble or shall I speak the truth? Nay, I am minded to tell it. None, I say, have I ever yet seen so like another, man nor woman — wonder comes over me as I look on him — as this man is like the son of great-hearted Odysseus, Telemachus, whom he left a new-born child in his house, when for the sake of me, shameless woman that I was, ye Achaeans came up under Troy with bold war in your hearts."

And Menelaus of the fair hair answered her, saying: "Now I too, lady, mark the likeness even as thou tracest it. For such as these were his feet, such his hands, and the glances of his eyes, and his head, and his hair withal. Yea, and even now I was speaking of Odysseus, as I remembered him, of all his woeful travail for my sake; when, lo, he let fall a bitter tear beneath his brows, and held his purple cloak up before his eyes."

And Peisistratus, son of Nestor, answered him, saying: "Menelaus, son of Atreus, fosterling of Zeus, leader of the host, assuredly this is the son of that very man, even as thou sayest. But he is of a sober wit, and thinketh it shame in his heart on this his first coming to make show of presumptuous words in the presence of thee, in whose voice we twain delight as in the voice of a god. Now Nestor, lord of chariots, sent me forth to be his guide on the way: for he desired to see thee that thou mightest put into his heart some word or work. For a son hath many griefs in his halls when his father is away, if perchance he hath none to stand by him. Even so it is now with Telemachus; his father is away, nor hath he others in the township to defend him from distress."

And Menelaus of the fair hair answered him, and said: "Lo now, in good truth there has come unto my house the son of a friend indeed, who for my sake endured many adventures. And I thought to welcome him on his coming more nobly than all the other Argives, if but Olympian Zeus had vouchsafed us a return over the sea in our swift ships. And in Argos I would have given him a city to dwell in, and stablished for him a

house, and brought him forth from Ithaca with his substance
and his son and all his people. Then ofttimes would we have
held converse here, and nought would have parted us, the welcoming and the welcomed, ere the black cloud of death overshadowed us."

So spake he, and in the hearts of all he stirred the desire of
lamentation. She wept, even Argive Helen the daughter of
Zeus, and Telemachus wept, and Menelaus the son of Atreus;
nay, nor did the son of Nestor keep tearless eyes.

Then Helen, daughter of Zeus, turned to new thoughts.
Presently she cast a drug into the wine whereof they drank,
a drug to lull all pain and anger, and bring forgetfulness of
every sorrow. Whoso should drink a draught thereof, when it
is mingled in the bowl, on that day he would let no tear fall
down his cheeks, not though his mother and his father died,
not though men slew his brother or dear son with the sword
before his face, and his own eyes beheld it. Now after she had
cast in the drug and bidden pour forth of the wine, she made
answer once again, and spake:

"Now, verily, sit ye down and feast in the halls, and take
ye joy in the telling of tales, and I will tell you one that fits
the time. Now all of them I could not tell or number, so
many as were the adventures of Odysseus of the hardy heart;
but, ah, what a deed was this he wrought and dared in his
hardiness in the land of the Trojans, where ye Achaeans suffered
affliction. He subdued his body with unseemly stripes, and a
sorry covering he cast about his shoulders, and in the fashion
of a servant he went down into the wide-wayed city of the foemen, and he hid himself in the guise of a beggar. In this
semblance he passed into the city of the Trojans, and they wist
not who he was, and I alone knew him in that guise, and I
kept questioning him, but in his subtlety he avoided me. But
when at last I was about washing him and anointing him with
olive oil, and had put on him raiment, and sworn a great oath

not to reveal Odysseus amid the Trojans, ere he reached the swift ships and the huts, even then he told me all the purpose of the Achaeans. And after slaying many of the Trojans with the long sword, he returned to the Argives and brought back word again of all. Then the other Trojan women wept aloud, but my soul was glad, for already my heart was turned to go back again even to my home: and I groaned for the blindness that Aphrodite gave me, when she led me thither away from mine own country, forsaking my child and my lord, that lacked not aught whether for wisdom or yet for beauty."

And Menelaus of the fair hair answered her, saying: "Verily all this tale, lady, thou hast duly told. Ere now have I learned the counsel and the thought of many heroes, and travelled over many a land, but never yet have mine eyes beheld any such man of heart as was Odysseus; such another deed as he wrought and dared in his hardiness even in the shapen horse,[1] wherein sat all we chiefs of the Argives, bearing to the Trojans death and doom. Anon thou camest thither, and sure some god must have bidden thee, who wished to bring glory to the Trojans. Yea and godlike Deiphobus went with thee on thy way. Thrice thou didst go round about the hollow ambush and handle it, calling aloud on the chiefs of the Argives by name, and making thy voice like the voices of the wives of all the Argives. Now I and the son of Tydeus and goodly Odysseus sat in the midst and heard thy call; and verily we twain had a desire to start up and come forth or presently to answer from within; but Odysseus stayed and held us there, despite our eagerness. Then all the other sons of the Achaeans held their peace, but Anticlus alone was still minded to answer thee. Howbeit Odysseus firmly closed his mouth with strong hands, and so saved all the Achaeans, and held him until such time as Pallas Athene led thee back."

[1] [The hollow horse of wood, which the Greeks used as a stratagem for the capture of Troy.]

Then wise Telemachus answered him, and said: "Menelaus, son of Atreus, fosterling of Zeus, leader of the host, all the more grievous it is! for in no way did this courage ward from him pitiful destruction, not though his heart within him had been very iron. But come, bid us to bed, that forthwith we may take our joy of rest beneath the spell of sleep."

So spake he, and Argive Helen bade her handmaids set out bedsteads beneath the gallery, and fling on them fair purple blankets and spread coverlets above, and thereon lay thick mantles to be a clothing over all. So they went from the hall with torch in hand, and spread the beds, and the henchman led forth the guests. Thus they slept there in the outer gallery of the house, the hero Telemachus and the splendid son of Nestor. But the son of Atreus slept, as his custom was, in the inmost chamber of the lofty house, and by him lay long-robed Helen, that fair lady.

Soon as early Dawn shone forth, the rosy-fingered, Menelaus of the loud war-shout gat him up from his bed and put on his raiment, and cast his sharp sword about his shoulder, and beneath his smooth feet bound his goodly sandals, and stept forth from his chamber, in presence like a god, and sat by Telemachus, and spake and hailed him:

"To what end hath thy need brought thee hither, hero Telemachus, unto fair Lacedaemon, over the broad back of the sea? Is it a matter of the common weal or of thine own? Herein tell me the plain truth."

Then wise Telemachus answered him, and said: "Menelaus, son of Atreus, fosterling of Zeus, leader of the host, I have come if perchance thou mayest tell me some tidings of my father. My dwelling is being devoured and my fat lands are ruined, and of unfriendly men my house is full, — who slaughter continually my thronging flocks, and my kine with trailing feet and shambling gait, — none other than the wooers of my mother, despiteful out of measure. So now am I come hither to thy knees, if haply thou art willing to tell me of his pitiful death, as one that saw it perchance with thine own eyes, or heard the story from some other wanderer. And speak me no soft words in pity, but tell me plainly how thou didst get sight of him."

Then in heavy displeasure spake to him Menelaus of the fair hair: "Out upon them, for truly in the bed of a brave-hearted man were they minded to lie, very cravens as they are! Even as when a hind hath couched her new-born fawns unweaned in a strong lion's lair, and searcheth out the mountain-knees and grassy hollows, seeking pasture, and afterward the lion cometh back to his bed, and sendeth forth unsightly death upon that pair, even so shall Odysseus send forth unsightly death upon the wooers. But for that whereof thou askest and entreatest me, be sure I will not swerve from the truth in aught that I say, nor deceive thee; but of all that the ancient one of the sea, whose speech is sooth,[1] declared to me, not a word will I hide or keep from thee.

"In the river Aegyptus,[2] though eager I was to press onward home, the gods they stayed me, for that I had not offered them the acceptable sacrifice of hecatombs, and the gods ever desired that men should be mindful of their commandments. Now there is an island in the wash of the waves over against Aegyptus, and men call it Pharos, within one day's voyage of a hollow ship, when shrill winds blow fair in her wake. And therein is a good haven, whence men launch the gallant ships into the deep when they have drawn a store of deep black water. There the gods held me twenty days, nor did the sea-winds ever show their breath, they that serve to waft ships over the broad back of the sea. And now would all our corn have been spent, and likewise the strength of the men, except some goddess had taken pity on me and saved me, Eidothëe, daughter of mighty Proteus, the ancient one of the sea. For most of all I moved

---

[1] [Truth, prophecy.]   [2] The only name for the Nile in Homer.

her heart, when she met me wandering alone apart from my company, who were ever roaming round the isle, fishing with bent hooks, for hunger was gnawing at their belly. So she stood by, and spake and uttered her voice, saying:

"'Art thou so very foolish, stranger, and feeble-witted, or art thou wilfully remiss, and hast pleasure in suffering? So long time art thou holden in the isle and canst find no issue therefrom, while the heart of thy company faileth within them?'

"Even so she spake, and I answered her saying: 'I will speak forth, what goddess soever thou art, and tell thee that in no wise am I holden here by mine own will, but it needs must be that I have sinned against the deathless gods, who keep the wide heaven. Howbeit, do thou tell me — for the gods know all things — which of the immortals it is that binds me here and hath hindered me from my way, and declare as touching my returning how I may go over the teeming deep.'

"So I spake, and straightway the fair goddess made answer: 'Yea now, sir, I will plainly tell thee all. Hither resorteth that ancient one of the sea, whose speech is sooth, the deathless Egyptian Proteus, who knows the depths of every sea, and is the thrall of Poseidon, and who, they say, is my father. If thou couldst but lay an ambush and catch him, he will surely declare to thee the way and the measure of thy path, and will tell thee of thy returning, how thou mayest go over the teeming deep. Yea, and he will show thee, O fosterling of Zeus, if thou wilt, what good thing and what evil hath been wrought in thy halls, whilst thou hast been faring this long and grievous way.'

"So she spake, but I answered and said unto her: 'Devise now thyself the ambush to take this ancient one divine, lest by any chance he see me first, or know of my coming, and avoid me. For a god is hard for mortal man to quell.'

"So spake I, and straightway the fair goddess made answer:

'Yea now, sir, I will plainly tell thee all. So often as the sun in his course hath reached the mid heaven, then forth from the brine comes the ancient one of the sea, whose speech is sooth, before the breath of the West Wind he comes, and the sea's dark ripple covers him. And when he is got forth, he lies down to sleep in the hollow of the caves. And around him the seals, the brood of the fair daughter of the brine, sleep all in a flock, stolen forth from the grey sea water, and bitter is the scent they breathe of the deeps of the salt sea. There will I lead thee at the breaking of the day, and couch you all orderly; so do thou choose diligently three of thy company, the best thou hast in thy decked ships. And I will tell thee all the magic arts of that old man. First, he will number the seals and go over them; but when he has told their tale and beheld them, he will lay him down in the midst, as a shepherd mid the sheep of his flock. So soon as ever ye shall see him couched, even then mind you of your might and strength, and hold him there, despite his eagerness and striving to be free. And he will make assay, and take all manner of shapes of things that creep upon the earth, of water likewise, and of fierce fire burning. But do ye grasp him steadfastly and press him yet the more, and at length when he questions thee in his proper shape, as he was when first ye saw him laid to rest, then, hero, hold thy strong hands, and let the ancient one go free, and ask him which of the gods is hard upon thee, and as touching thy returning, how thou mayest go over the teeming deep.'

"Therewith she dived beneath the heaving sea, but I betook me to the ships where they stood in the sand, and my heart was darkly troubled as I went. But after I had come down to the ship and to the sea, and we had made ready our supper and immortal night had come on, then did we lay us to rest upon the sea-beach. So soon as early Dawn shone forth, the rosy-fingered, in that hour I walked by the shore of the wide-wayed sea, praying instantly to the gods; and I took with me three of my company, in whom I trusted most for every enterprise.

"Meanwhile, so it was that she had plunged into the broad bosom of the sea, and had brought from the deep the skins of four sea-calves, and all were newly flayed, for she was minded to lay a snare for her father. She scooped lairs on the sea-sand, and sat awaiting us, and we drew very nigh her, and she made us all lie down in order, and cast a skin over each. There would our ambush have been most terrible, for the deadly stench of the sea-bred seals distressed us sore: nay, who would lay him down by a beast of the sea? But herself she wrought deliverance, and devised a great comfort. She took ambrosia of a very sweet savour, and set it beneath each man's nostril, and did away with the stench of the beast. So all the morning we waited with steadfast heart, and the seals came forth in troops from the brine, and then they couched them all orderly by the sea-beach. And at high day the ancient one came forth from out of the brine, and found his fatted seals, yea and he went along their line and told their tale; and first among the sea-beasts he reckoned us, and guessed not that there was guile, and afterward he too laid him down. Then we rushed upon him with a cry, and cast our hands about him, nor did that ancient one forget his cunning. Now behold, at the first he turned into a bearded lion, and thereafter into a snake, and a pard, and a huge boar; then he took the shape of running water, and of a tall and flowering tree. We the while held him close with steadfast heart. But when now that ancient one of the magic arts was aweary, then at last he questioned me and spake unto me, saying:

"'Which of the gods was it, son of Atreus, that aided thee with his counsel, that thou mightest waylay and take me perforce? What wouldest thou thereby?'

"Even so he spake, but I answered him saying: 'Old man, thou knowest all, wherefore dost thou question me thereof with crooked words? For lo, I am holden long time in this isle, neither can I find any issue therefrom, and my heart faileth within me. Howbeit do thou tell me — for the gods know all things — which of the immortals it is that bindeth me here, and hath hindered me from my way; and declare as touching my returning, how I may go over the teeming deep.'

"Even so I spake, and he straightway answered me saying: 'Nay, surely thou shouldest have done goodly sacrifice to Zeus and the other gods ere thine embarking, that with most speed thou mightest reach thy country, sailing over the wine-dark deep. For it is not thy fate to see thy friends, and come to thy stablished house and thine own country, till thou hast passed yet again within the waters of Aegyptus, the heaven-fed stream, and offered holy hecatombs to the deathless gods who keep the wide heaven. So shall the gods grant thee the path which thou desirest.'

"So spake he, but my spirit within me was broken, for that he bade me again to go to Aegyptus over the misty deep, a long and grievous way.

"Yet even so I answered him saying: 'Old man, all this will I do, according to thy word. But come, declare me this, and tell it all plainly. Did all those Achaeans return safe with their ships, all whom Nestor and I left as we went from Troy, or perished any by a shameful death aboard his own ship, or in the arms of his friends?'

"So spake I, and anon he answered me saying: 'Son of Atreus, why dost thou straitly question me hereof? Nay, it is not for thy good to know or learn my thought; for I tell thee thou shalt not long be tearless, when thou hast heard it all aright. For many of these were taken, and many were left; but two only of the leaders of the mail-coated Achaeans perished in returning. And one methinks is yet alive, and is holden on the wide deep. Aias in truth was smitten in the midst of his ships of the long oars. And Aegisthus slew thy brother Agamemnon.'

"So spake he, and my spirit within me was broken, and I wept as I sat upon the sand, nor was I minded any more to live and to see the light of the sun. But when I had taken my fill of weeping and grovelling on the ground, then spake the ancient one of the sea, whose speech is sooth:

"'No more, son of Atreus, hold this long weeping without cease, for we shall find no help therein. Rather with all haste make essay that so thou mayest come to thine own country. For either thou shalt find Aegisthus yet alive, or it may be Orestes was beforehand with thee and slew him; so mayest thou chance upon his funeral feast.'

"So he spake, and my heart and lordly soul again were comforted for all my sorrow, and I uttered my voice and I spake to him winged words:

"'Their fate I now know; but tell me of the third; who is it that is yet living and holden on the wide deep, or perchance is dead? and fain would I hear despite my sorrow.'

"So spake I, and straightway he answered, and said: 'It is the son of Laertes, whose dwelling is in Ithaca; and I saw him in an island shedding big tears in the halls of the nymph Calypso, who holds him there perforce; so he may not come to his own country, for he has by him no ships with oars, and no companions to send him on his way over the broad back of the sea.'

"But lo, now tarry in my halls till it shall be the eleventh day hence or the twelfth. Then will I send thee with all honour on thy way, and give thee splendid gifts, three horses and a polished car; and moreover I will give thee a goodly chalice, that thou mayest pour forth before the deathless gods, and be mindful of me all the days of thy life."

Then wise Telemachus answered him, saying: "Son of Atreus, nay, hold me not long time here. Yea even for a year would I be content to sit by thee, and no desire for home or parents would come upon me; for I take wondrous pleasure in thy tales and talk. But already my company wearieth in fair Pylos, and yet thou art keeping me long time here. And whatsoever gift thou wouldest give me, let it be a thing to treasure; but horses I will take none to Ithaca, but leave them here to grace thine own house, for thou art lord of a wide plain wherein is lotus great plenty, and therein is spear-reed and wheat and rye, and white and spreading barley. In Ithaca there are no wide courses, nor meadow land at all. It is a pasture-land of goats, and more pleasant in my sight than one that pastureth horses; for of the isles that lie and lean upon the sea, none are fit for the driving of horses, or rich in meadow land, and least of all is Ithaca."

But the wooers meantime were before the palace of Odysseus, taking their pleasure in casting of weights and spears, on a levelled place, as heretofore, in their insolence. And Antinous and god-like Eurymachus were seated there, the chief men of the wooers, who were far the most excellent of all. And Noemon, son of Phromius, drew nigh to them and spake unto Antinous and questioned him, saying:

"Antinous, know we at all, or know we not, when Telemachus will return from sandy Pylos? He hath departed with a ship of mine, and I have need thereof, to cross over into spacious Elis, where I have twelve brood mares with hardy mules unbroken at the teat; I would drive off one of these and break him in."

So spake he, and they were amazed, for they deemed not that Telemachus had gone to Pylos, but that he was at home somewhere in the fields, whether among the flocks, or with the swineherd.

Then Antinous, son of Eupeithes, spake to him in turn: "Tell me the plain truth; when did he go, and what noble youths went with him? Were they chosen men of Ithaca or hirelings and thralls of his own? He was in case to bring even that about. And tell me this in good sooth, that I may know for a surety: did he take thy black ship from thee perforce against thy will? or didst thou give it him of free will at his entreaty?"

Then Noemon, son of Phromius, answered him saying: "I gave it him myself of free will. What can any man do, when such an one, so bestead with care, begs a favour? it were hard to deny the gift. The youths who next to us are noblest in the land, even these have gone with him; and I marked their leader on board ship, Mentor, or a god who in all things resembled Mentor. But one matter I marvel at: I saw the goodly Mentor here yesterday toward dawn, though already he had embarked for Pylos."

He spake and withal departed to his father's house. And the proud spirits of these twain were angered, and they made the wooers sit down together and cease from their games. And among them spake Antinous, son of Eupeithes, in displeasure; and his black heart was wholly filled with rage, and his eyes were like flaming fire:

"Out on him, a proud deed hath Telemachus accomplished with a high hand, even this journey, and we thought that he would never bring it to pass! This lad hath clean gone without more ado, in spite of us all; his ship he hath let haul to the sea, and chosen the noblest in the township. He will begin to be our bane even more than heretofore; but may Zeus destroy his might, not ours, ere he reach the measure of manhood! But come, give me a swift ship and twenty men, that I may lie in watch and wait even for him on his way home, in the strait between Ithaca and rugged Samos, that so he may have a woeful end of his cruising in quest of his father."

So spake he, and they all assented thereto, and bade him to the work. And thereupon they arose and went to the house of Odysseus.

Now it was no long time before Penelope heard of the counsel that the wooers had devised in the deep of their heart. For the henchman Medon told her thereof, who stood without the court and heard their purposes, while they were weaving their plot within. So he went on his way through the halls to bring the news to Penelope; and as he stept down over the threshold, Penelope spake unto him:

"Henchman, wherefore have the noble wooers sent thee forth? Was it to tell the handmaids of divine Odysseus to cease from their work, and prepare a banquet for them? Nay, after thus much wooing, never again may they come together, but here this day sup for their last and latest time; all ye who assemble so often, and waste much livelihood, the wealth of wise Telemachus!"

Then Medon, wise of heart, answered her: "Would, oh queen, that this were the crowning evil! But the wooers devise another far greater and more grievous, which I pray the son of Cronos may never fulfil! They are set on slaying Telemachus with the edge of the sword on his homeward way; for he is gone to fair Pylos and goodly Lacedaemon, to seek tidings of his father."

So spake he, but her knees were loosened where she stood, and her heart melted within her, and long time was she speechless, and lo, her eyes were filled with tears and the voice of her utterance was stayed. And at the last she answered him and said:

"Henchman, wherefore I pray thee is my son departed? There is no need that he should go abroad on swift ships, that serve men for horses on the sea, and that cross the great wet waste. Is it that even his own name may no more be left upon earth?"

Then Medon, wise of heart, answered her: "I know not whether some god set him on, or whether his own spirit stirred him to go to Pylos to seek tidings of his father's return, or to hear what end he met."

He spake, and departed through the house of Odysseus, and on her fell a cloud of consuming grief; so that she might no more endure to seat her on a chair, whereof there were many in the house, but there she crouched on the threshold of her well-built chamber, wailing piteously, and her handmaids round her made low moan, as many as were in the house with her, young and old. And Penelope spake among them pouring forth her lamentation:

"Hear me, my friends, for the Olympian sire hath given me pain exceedingly beyond all women who were born and bred in my day. For erewhile I lost my noble lord of the lion heart, adorned with all perfection among the Danaans, my good lord, whose fame is noised abroad from Hellas to mid Argos. And now again the storm-winds have snatched away my well-beloved son without tidings from our halls, nor heard I of his departure. Oh, women, hard of heart, that even ye did not each one let the thought come into your minds, to rouse me from my couch when he went to the black hollow ship, though ye knew full well thereof! For had I heard that he was purposing this journey, verily he should have stayed here still, though eager to be gone, or have left me dead in the halls."

Then the good nurse Eurycleia answered her: "Dear lady, aye, slay me if thou wilt with the pitiless sword or let me yet live on in the house, — yet will I not hide my saying from thee. I knew all this, and gave him whatsoever he commanded, bread and sweet wine. And he took a great oath of me not to tell thee till at least the twelfth day should come, or thou thyself shouldst miss him and hear of his departure, that thou mightest not mar thy fair flesh with thy tears. But now, wash thee in water, and take to thee clean raiment and ascend to thy upper chamber with the women thy handmaids, and pray to Athene, daughter of Zeus. For so may she save him even from death."

So spake she, and lulled her queen's lamentation, and made her eyes to cease from weeping. So she washed her in water, and took to her clean raiment, and ascended to the upper chamber with the women her handmaids, and placed the meal for sprinkling in a basket, and prayed unto Athene:

"Hear me, child of Zeus, lord of the aegis, unwearied maiden! If ever wise Odysseus in his halls burnt for thee fat slices of the thighs of heifer or of sheep, these things, I pray thee, now remember, and save my dear son, and ward from him the wooers in the naughtiness of their pride."

Now the goddess, grey-eyed Athene, turned to other thoughts. She made a phantom, and fashioned it after the likeness of a woman, Iphthime, daughter of great-hearted Icarius, whose dwelling was in Pherae. And she sent it to the house of divine Odysseus to bid Penelope, amid her sorrow and lamenting, to cease from her weeping and tearful lamentation. So the phantom passed into the chamber by the thong of the bolt, and stood above her head and spake unto her, saying:

"Sleepest thou, Penelope, stricken at heart? Nay, even the gods who live at ease suffer thee not to wail or be afflicted, seeing that thy son is yet to return; for no sinner is he in the eyes of the gods."

Then wise Penelope made her answer as she slumbered very softly at the gates of dreams:

"Wherefore, sister, hast thou come hither, that before wert not wont to come; for thou hast thine habitation very far away? Biddest thou me indeed to cease from the sorrows and pains, so many that disquiet my heart and soul? Erewhile I lost my noble lord of the lion heart, whose fame is noised abroad from Hellas to mid Argos. And now, again, my well-beloved son is departed on his hollow ship, poor child, not skilled in toils or in the gatherings of men. For him I sorrow yet more than for my lord, and I tremble and fear for him lest aught b all him, whether, it may be, amid that folk where he is gone, or in the deep. For many foemen devise evil against him, and go about to kill him, or ever he come to his own country."

And the dim phantom answered her, and said: "Take courage, and be not so sorely afraid. For lo, such a friend goes to guide him, as all men pray to stand by them, for that she hath the power, even Pallas Athene. And she pitieth thee in thy sorrow, and now hath sent me forth to speak these words to thee."

And wise Penelope answered her, saying: "If thou art indeed a god, and hast heard the word of a god, come, I pray thee, and tell me tidings concerning that ill-fated man, whether perchance he is yet alive and sees the light of the sun, or hath already died, and is a dweller in the house of Hades."

And the dim phantom answered her and said: "Concerning him I will not tell thee all the tale, whether he be alive or dead; it is ill to speak words light as wind."

Therewith the phantom slipped away by the bolt of the door and passed into the breath of the wind. And the daughter of Icarius started up from sleep, and her heart was cheered, so clear was the vision that sped toward her in the dead of the night.

Meanwhile the wooers had taken ship and were sailing over the wet ways, pondering in their hearts sheer death for Telemachus. Now there is a rocky isle in the mid sea, midway between Ithaca and rugged Samos, Asteris, a little isle; and there is a harbour therein with a double entrance, where ships may ride. There the Achaeans abode lying in wait for Telemachus.

BOOK V

The gods in council command Calypso by Hermes to send away Odysseus on a raft of trees; and Poseidon, returning from Ethiopia and seeing him on the coast of Phaeacia, scattered his raft; and how by the help of Ino he was thrown ashore, and slept on a heap of dry leaves till the next day.

Now the Dawn arose from her couch, from the side of the lordly Tithonus, to bear light to the immortals and to mortal men. And lo, the gods were gathering to session, and among them Zeus, that thunders on high, whose might is above all. And Athene told them the tale of the many woes of Odysseus, recalling them to mind; for near her heart was he that then abode in the dwelling of the nymph:

"Father Zeus, and all ye other blessed gods that live for ever, henceforth let not any sceptred king be kind and gentle with all his heart, nor minded to do righteously, but let him always be a hard man and work unrighteousness, for behold, there is none of the people whose lord he was that remembereth divine Odysseus, who was gentle as a father. Now he lieth in an island, suffering strong pains, in the halls of the nymph Calypso, who holdeth him perforce; so he may not reach his own country, for he hath no ships with oars, and no companions to send him on his way over the broad back of the sea. And now, again, they are set on slaying his beloved son on his homeward way, for he is gone to fair Pylos and to goodly Lacedaemon, to seek tidings of his father."

And Zeus, gatherer of the clouds, answered and spake unto her: "My child, what word hath escaped the door of thy lips! Didst thou not thyself plan this device, that Odysseus may assuredly take vengeance on those men at his coming? As for

Telemachus, do thou guide him by thine art, as well thou mayest, that so he may come to his own country all unharmed, and the wooers may return in their ship with their labour all in vain."

Therewith he spake to Hermes, his dear son: "Hermes, forasmuch as thou art our herald, tell unto the nymph of the braided tresses my unerring counsel, even the return of the patient Odysseus, how he is to come to his home, with no furtherance of gods or of mortal men. He shall sail on a well-bound raft, in sore distress, and on the twentieth day arrive at fertile Scheria, even at the land of the Phaeacians, who are near of kin to the gods. And they shall give him all worship heartily as to a god, and send him on his way in a ship to his own dear country, with gifts of bronze and gold, and raiment in plenty, such as never would Odysseus have won for himself out of Troy, yea, though he had returned unhurt with the share of the spoil that fell to him. On such wise is he fated to see his friends, and come to his high-roofed home and his own country."

So spake he, nor heedless was the messenger. Straightway he bound beneath his feet his lovely golden sandals, that wax not old, that bare him alike over the wet sea and over the limitless land, swift as the breath of the wind. And he took the wand wherewith he lulls the eyes of whomso he will, while others again he even wakes from out of sleep. With this rod in his hand flew the strong slayer of Argos. Above Pieria he passed and leapt from the upper air into the deep. Then he sped along the wave like the cormorant, that chaseth the fishes through the perilous gulfs of the unharvested sea, and wetteth his thick plumage in the brine. Such like did Hermes ride upon the press of the waves. But when he had now reached that far-off isle, he went forth from the sea of violet blue to get him up into the land, till he came to a great cave, wherein dwelt the nymph of the braided tresses: and he found her within. And on the hearth there was a great fire burning, and from afar through the isle was smelt the fragrance of cleft cedar blazing, and of sandal wood. And the nymph within was singing with a sweet voice as she fared to and fro before the loom, and wove with a shuttle of gold. And round about the cave there was a wood blossoming, alder and poplar and sweet-smelling cypress. And therein roosted birds long of wing, owls and falcons and chattering sea-crows, which have their business in the waters. And lo, there about the hollow cave trailed a gadding garden vine, all rich with clusters. And fountains four set orderly were running with clear water, hard by one another, turned each to his own course. And all around soft meadows bloomed of violets and parsley, yea, even a deathless god who came thither might wonder at the sight and be glad at heart. There the messenger, the slayer of Argos, stood and wondered. Now when he had gazed at all with wonder, anon he went into the wide cave; nor did Calypso, that fair goddess, fail to know him, when she saw him face to face; for the gods use not to be strange one to another, the immortals, not though one have his habitation far away. But he found not Odysseus, the great-hearted, within the cave, who sat weeping on the shore even as aforetime, straining his soul with tears and groans and griefs, and as he wept he looked wistfully over the unharvested deep. And Calypso, that fair goddess, questioned Hermes, when she had made him sit on a bright shining seat:

"Wherefore, I pray thee, Hermes, of the golden wand, hast thou come hither, worshipful and welcome, whereas as of old thou wert not wont to visit me? Tell me all thy thought; my heart is set on fulfilling it, if fulfil it I may, and if it hath been fulfilled in the counsel of fate. But now follow me further, that I may set before thee the entertainment of strangers."

Therewith the goddess spread a table with ambrosia and set it by him, and mixed the ruddy nectar. So the messenger, the slayer of Argos, did eat and drink. Now after he had supped and comforted his soul with food, at the last he answered, and spake to her on this wise:

"Thou makest question of me on my coming, a goddess of a god, and I will tell thee this my saying truly, at thy command. 'Twas Zeus that bade me come hither, by no will of mine; nay, who of his free will would speed over such a wondrous space of brine, whereby is no city of mortals that do sacrifice to the gods, and offer choice hecatombs? He saith that thou hast with thee a man most wretched beyond his fellows, beyond those men that round the burg of Priam for nine years fought, and in the tenth year sacked the city and departed homeward. Yet on the way they sinned against Athene, and she raised upon them an evil blast and long waves of the sea. Then all the rest of his good company was lost, but it came to pass that the wind bare and the wave brought him hither. And now Zeus biddeth thee send him hence with what speed thou mayest, for it is not ordained that he die away from his friends, but rather it is his fate to look on them even yet, and to come to his high-roofed home and his own country."

So spake he, and Calypso, that fair goddess, shuddered and uttered her voice, and spake unto him winged words: "Hard are ye gods and jealous exceeding, who grudge that a mortal man should dwell with me. Him I saved as he went all alone bestriding the keel of a bark, for Zeus had cleft his swift ship with a white bolt in the midst of the wine-dark deep. There all the rest of his good company was lost, but it came to pass that the wind bare and the wave brought him hither. And him have I loved and cherished, and I said that I would make him to know not death and age for ever. Yet forasmuch as it is in no wise possible for another god to go beyond, or make void the purpose of Zeus, lord of the aegis, let him away over the unharvested seas, if the summons and the bidding be of Zeus. But I will give him no despatch, not I, for I have no ships by me with oars, nor company to bear him on his way over the broad back of the sea. Yet will I be forward to put this in his mind, and will hide nought, that all unharmed he may come to his own country."

Then the messenger, the slayer of Argos, answered her: "Yea, speed him now upon his path and have regard unto the wrath of Zeus, lest haply he be angered and bear hard on thee hereafter."

Therewith the great slayer of Argos departed, but the nymph went on her way to the great-hearted Odysseus, when she had heard the message of Zeus. And there she found him sitting on the shore, and his eyes were never dry of tears, and his sweet life was ebbing away as he mourned for his return; for the nymph no more found favour in his sight. So standing near him that fair goddess spake to him:

"Hapless man, sorrow no more I pray thee in this isle, nor let thy good life waste away, for even now will I send thee hence with all my heart. Nay, arise and cut long beams, and fashion a wide raft with the axe, and lay deckings high thereupon, that it may bear thee over the misty deep. And I will place therein bread and water, and red wine to thy heart's desire, to keep hunger far away. And I will put raiment upon thee, and send a fair gale in thy wake, that so thou mayest come all unharmed to thine own country, if indeed it be the good pleasure of the gods who hold wide heaven, who are stronger than I am both to will and to do."

So she spake, and the steadfast goodly Odysseus shuddered, and uttering his voice spake to her winged words: "Herein, goddess, thou hast plainly some other thought, and in no wise my furtherance, for that thou biddest me to cross in a raft the great gulf of the sea so dread and difficult, which not even the swift gallant ships pass over rejoicing in the breeze of Zeus. Nor would I go aboard a raft to displeasure thee, unless thou wilt deign, O goddess, to swear a great oath not to plan any hidden guile to mine own hurt."

So spake he, and Calypso, the fair goddess, smiled and caressed him with her hand, and spake and hailed him:

"Let earth be now witness hereto, and the wide heaven above, and that falling water of the Styx, the greatest oath and the most terrible to the blessed gods, that I will not plan any hidden guile to thine own hurt. Nay, but my thoughts are such, and such will be my counsel, as I would devise for myself, if ever so sore a need came over me. For I too have a righteous mind, and my heart within me is not of iron, but pitiful even as thine."

Therewith the fair goddess led the way quickly, and he followed hard in the steps of the goddess. And they reached the hollow cave, the goddess and the man; so he sat him down upon the chair whence Hermes had arisen, and the nymph placed by him all manner of food to eat and drink, such as is meat for men. As for her she sat over against divine Odysseus, and the handmaids placed by her ambrosia and nectar. So they put forth their hands upon the good cheer set before them. But after they had taken their fill of meat and drink, Calypso, the fair goddess, spake first and said:

"Son of Laertes, of the seed of Zeus, Odysseus of many devices, so it is indeed thy wish to get thee home to thine own dear country even in this hour? Good fortune go with thee even so! Yet didst thou know in thine heart what a measure of suffering thou art ordained to fulfil, or ever thou reach thine own country, here, even here, thou wouldst abide with me and keep this house, and wouldst never taste of death, though thou longest to see thy wife, for whom thou hast ever a desire day by day. Not in sooth that I avow me to be less noble than she in form or fashion, for it is in no wise meet that mortal women should match them with immortals, in shape and comeliness."

And Odysseus of many counsels answered, and spake unto her: "Be not wroth with me hereat, goddess and queen. My·

self I know it well, how wise Penelope is meaner to look upon than thou, in comeliness and stature. But she is mortal and thou knowest not age nor death. Yet even so, I wish and long day by day to fare homeward and see the day of my returning. Yea, and if some god shall wreck me in the wine-dark deep, even so I will endure, with a heart within me patient of affliction. For already have I suffered full much, and much have I toiled in perils of waves and war; let this be added to the tale of those."

So spake he, and the sun sank and darkness came on.

So soon as early Dawn shone forth, the rosy-fingered, anon Odysseus put on him a mantle and doublet, and the nymph clad her in a great shining robe, light of woof and gracious, and about her waist she cast a fair golden girdle, and a veil withal upon her head. Then she considered of the sending of Odysseus, the great-hearted. She gave him a great axe, fitted to his grasp, an axe of bronze double-edged, and with a goodly handle of olive wood fastened well. Next she gave him a polished adze, and she led the way to the border of the isle where tall trees grew, alder and poplar, and pine that reacheth unto heaven, seasoned long since and sere, that might lightly float for him. Now after she had shown him where the tall trees grew, Calypso, the fair goddess, departed homeward. And he set to cutting timber, and his work went busily. Twenty trees in all he felled, and then trimmed them with the axe of bronze, and deftly smoothed them, and over them made straight the line. Meanwhile Calypso, the fair goddess, brought him augers, so he bored each piece and jointed them together, and then made all fast with trenails and dowels. Wide as is the floor of a broad ship of burden, which some man well skilled in carpentry may trace him out, of such beam did Odysseus fashion his broad raft. And thereat he wrought, and set up the deckings, fitting them to the close-set uprights, and finished them off with long gunwales, and therein he set a mast, and a yard-arm fitted thereto, and moreover he made him a rudder to guide the craft. And he fenced it with

wattled osier withies from stem to stern, to be a bulwark against
the wave, and piled up wood to back them. Meanwhile Calypso,
the fair goddess, brought him web of cloth to make him sails;
and these too he fashioned very skilfully. And he made fast
therein braces and halyards and sheets, and at last he pushed
the raft with levers down to the fair salt sea.

It was the fourth day when he had accomplished all. And,
lo, on the fifth, the fair Calypso sent him on his way from the
island, when she had bathed him and clad him in fragrant attire.
Moreover, the goddess placed on board the ship two skins, one
of dark wine, and another, a great one, of water, and corn too
in a wallet, and she set therein a store of dainties to his heart's
desire, and sent forth a warm and gentle wind to blow. And
goodly Odysseus rejoiced as he set his sails to the breeze. So
he sate and cunningly guided the craft with the helm, nor did
sleep fall upon his eyelids, as he viewed the Pleiads and Boötes,
that setteth late, and the Bear, which they likewise call the
Wain, which turneth ever in one place, and keepeth watch upon
Orion, and alone hath no part in the baths of Ocean. This
star, Calypso, the fair goddess, bade him to keep ever on the
left as he traversed the deep. Ten days and seven he sailed
traversing the deep, and on the eighteenth day appeared the
shadowy hills of the land of the Phaeacians, at the point where
it lay nearest to him; and it showed like a shield in the misty
deep.

Now the lord, the shaker of the earth, on his way from the
Ethiopians espied him afar off from the mountains of the Solymi:
even thence he saw Odysseus as he sailed over the deep; and he
was yet more angered in spirit, and shaking his head he communed
with his own heart. "Lo now, it must be that the gods at the
last have changed their purpose concerning Odysseus, while I
was away among the Ethiopians. And now he is nigh to the
Phaeacian land, where it is ordained that he escape the great
issues of the woe which hath come upon him. But methinks

that even yet I will drive him far enough in the path of suffering."

With that he gathered the clouds and troubled the waters of the deep, grasping his trident in his hands; and he roused all storms of all manner of winds, and shrouded in clouds the land and sea: and down sped night from heaven. The East Wind and the South Wind clashed, and the stormy West, and the North, that is born in the bright air, rolling onward a great wave. Then were the knees of Odysseus loosened and his heart melted, and heavily he spake to his own great spirit:

"Oh, wretched man that I am! what is to befall me at the last? I fear that indeed the goddess spake all things truly, who said that I should fill up the measure of sorrow on the deep, or ever I came to mine own country; and lo, all these things have an end. In such wise doth Zeus crown the wide heaven with clouds, and hath troubled the deep, and the blasts rush on of all the winds; yea, now is utter doom assured me. Thrice blessed those Danaans, yea, four times blessed, who perished on a time in wide Troy-land, doing a pleasure to the sons of Atreus! Would to God that I too had died, and met my fate on that day when the press of Trojans cast their bronze-shod spears upon me, fighting for the body of the son of Peleus! So should I have gotten my dues of burial, and the Achaeans would have spread my fame; but now it is my fate to be overtaken by a pitiful death."

Even as he spake, the great wave smote down upon him, driving on in terrible wise, that the raft reeled again. And far therefrom he fell, and lost the helm from his hand; and the fierce blast of the jostling winds came and brake his mast in the midst, and sail and yard-arm fell afar into the deep. Long time the water kept him under, nor could he speedily rise from beneath the rush of the mighty wave: for the garments hung heavy which fair Calypso gave him. But late and at length he came up, and spat forth from his mouth the bitter salt water,

which ran down in streams from his head. Yet even so forgat
he not his raft, for all his wretched plight, but made a spring
after it in the waves, and clutched it to him, and sat in the midst
thereof, avoiding the issues of death; and the great wave swept
it hither and thither along the stream. And as the North
Wind in the harvest tide sweeps the thistle-down along the
plain, and close the tufts cling each to other, even so the winds
bare the raft hither and thither along the main. Now the
South would toss it to the North to carry, and now again the
East would yield it to the West to chase.

But the daughter of Cadmus marked him, Ino of the fair
ankles, Leucothea, who in time past was a maiden of mortal
speech, but now in the depths of the salt sea she had gotten her
share of worship from the gods. She took pity on Odysseus in
his wandering and travail, and she rose, like a sea-gull on the
wing, from the depth of the mere, and sat upon the well-bound
raft and spake saying:

"Hapless one, wherefore was Poseidon, shaker of the earth,
so wondrous wroth with thee, seeing that he soweth for thee
the seeds of many evils? Yet shall he not make a full end
of thee, for all his desire. But do even as I tell thee, and methinks thou art not witless. Cast off these garments, and
leave the raft to drift before the winds, but do thou swim with
thine hands and strive to win a footing on the coast of the
Phaeacians, where it is decreed that thou escape. Here, take
this veil imperishable and wind it about thy breast; so is there
no fear that thou suffer aught or perish. But when thou hast
laid hold of the mainland with thy hands, loose it from off thee
and cast it into the wine-dark deep far from the land, and thyself turn away."

With that the goddess gave the veil, and for her part dived
back into the heaving deep, like a sea-gull: and the dark wave
closed over her. But the steadfast goodly Odysseus pondered,
and heavily he spake to his own brave spirit:

"Ah, woe is me! Can it be that some one of the immortals is weaving a new snare for me, that she bids me quit my raft? Nay verily, I will not yet obey, for I had sight of the shore yet a long way off, where she told me that I might escape. I am resolved what I will do;—and methinks on this wise it is best. So long as the timbers abide in the dowels, so long will I endure steadfast in affliction, but so soon as the wave hath shattered my raft asunder, I will swim, for meanwhile no better counsel may be."

While yet he pondered these things in his heart and soul, Poseidon, shaker of the earth, stirred against him a great wave, terrible and grievous, and vaulted from the crest, and therewith smote him. And as when a great tempestuous wind tosseth a heap of parched husks, and scatters them this way and that, even so did the wave scatter the long beams of the raft. But Odysseus bestrode a single beam, as one rideth on a courser, and stript him of the garments which fair Calypso gave him. And presently he wound the veil beneath his breast, and fell prone into the sea, outstretching his hands as one eager to swim. And the lord, the shaker of the earth, saw him and shook his head, and communed with his own soul. "Even so, after all thy sufferings, go wandering over the deep, till thou shalt come among a people, the fosterlings of Zeus. Yet for all that I deem not that thou shalt think thyself too lightly afflicted." Therewith he lashed his steeds of the flowing manes, and came to Aegae, where is his lordly home.

But Athene, daughter of Zeus, turned to new thoughts. Behold, she bound up the courses of the other winds, and charged them all to cease and be still; but she roused the swift North and brake the waves before him, that so Odysseus, of the seed of Zeus, might mingle with the Phaeacians, lovers of the oar, avoiding death and the fates.

So for two nights and two days he was wandering in the swell of the sea, and much his heart boded of death. But

when at last the fair-tressed Dawn brought the full light of
the third day, thereafter the breeze fell, and lo, there was a
breathless calm, and with a quick glance ahead, (he being up-
borne on a great wave,) he saw the land very near. And even
as when most welcome to his children is the sight of a father's
life, who lies in sickness and strong pains long wasting away,
some angry god assailing him; and to their delight the gods
have loosed him from his trouble; so welcome to Odysseus
showed land and wood; and· he swam onward being eager to
set foot on the strand. But when he was within earshot of
the shore, and heard now the thunder of the sea against the
reefs — for the great wave crashed against the dry land belch-
ing in terrible wise, and all was covered with foam of the sea,
— for there were no harbours for ships nor shelters, but jutting
headlands and reefs and cliffs; then at last the knees of Odysseus were loosened and his heart melted, and in heaviness he
spake to his own brave spirit:

"Ah me! now that beyond all hope Zeus hath given me
sight of land, and withal I have cloven my way through this
gulf of the sea, here there is no place to land on from out of
the grey water. For without are sharp crags, and round them
the wave roars surging, and sheer the smooth rock rises, and
the sea is deep thereby, so that in no wise may I find firm foot-
hold and escape my bane, for as I fain would go ashore, the
great wave may haply snatch and dash me on the jagged rock
— and a wretched endeavour that would be. But if I swim
yet further along the coast to find, if I may, spits that take
the waves aslant and havens of the sea, I fear lest the storm-
winds catch me again and bear me over the teeming deep, making heavy moan; or else some god may even send forth against
me a monster from out of the shore water; and many such
pastureth the renowned Amphitrite. For I know how wroth
against me hath been the great Shaker of the Earth."

Whilst yet he pondered these things in his heart and mind,

a great wave bore him to the rugged shore. There would he have been stript of his skin and all his bones been broken, but that the goddess, grey-eyed Athene, put a thought into his heart. He rushed in, and with both his hands clutched the rock, whereto he clung till the great wave went by. So he escaped that peril, but again with backward wash it leapt on him and smote him and cast him forth into the deep. And as when the cuttlefish is dragged forth from his chamber, the many pebbles clinging to his suckers, even so was the skin stript from his strong hand against the rocks, and the great wave closed over him. There of a truth would luckless Odysseus have perished beyond that which was ordained, had not grey-eyed Athene given him sure counsel. He rose from the line of the breakers that belch upon the shore, and swam outside, ever looking landwards, to find, if he might, spits that take the waves aslant, and havens of the sea. But when he came in his swimming over against the mouth of a fair-flowing river, whereby the place seemed best in his eyes, smooth of rocks, and withal there was a covert from the wind, Odysseus felt the river running, and prayed to him in his heart:

"Hear me, O king, whosoever thou art; unto thee am I come, as to one to whom prayer is made, while I flee the rebukes of Poseidon from the deep. Yea, reverend even to the deathless gods is that man who comes as a wanderer, even as I now have come to thy stream and to thy knees after much travail. Nay pity me, O king; for I avow myself thy suppliant."

So spake he, and the god straightway stayed his stream and withheld his waves, and made the water smooth before him, and brought him safely to the mouths of the river. And his knees bowed and his stout hands fell, for his heart was broken by the brine. And his flesh was all swollen and a great stream of sea water gushed up through his mouth and nostrils. So he lay without breath or speech, swooning, such terrible weariness came upon him. But when now his breath returned and his spirit came to him again, he loosed from off him the veil of the goddess, and let it fall into the salt flowing river. And the great wave bare it back down the stream, and lightly Ino caught it in her hands. Then Odysseus turned from the river, and fell back in the reeds, and kissed earth, the grain-giver, and heavily he spake unto his own brave spirit:

"Ah, woe is me! what is to betide me? what shall happen unto me at the last? If I watch in the river bed all through the careful night, I fear that the bitter frost and fresh dew may overcome me, as I breathe forth my life for faintness, for the river breeze blows cold betimes in the morning. But if I climb the hill-side up to the shady wood, and there take rest in the thickets, though perchance the cold and weariness leave hold of me, and sweet sleep may come over me, I fear lest of wild beasts I become the spoil and prey."

So as he thought thereon this seemed to him the better way. He went up to the wood, and found it nigh the water in a place of wide prospect. So he crept beneath twin bushes that grew from one stem, both olive trees, one of them wild olive. Through these the force of the wet winds blew never, neither did the bright sun light on it with his rays, nor could the rain pierce through, so close were they twined either to other; and thereunder crept Odysseus, and anon he heaped together with his hands a broad couch; for of fallen leaves there was great plenty, enough to cover two or three men in winter time, however hard the weather. And the steadfast goodly Odysseus beheld it and rejoiced, and he laid him in the midst thereof and flung over him the fallen leaves. And as when a man hath hidden away a brand in the black embers at an upland farm, one that hath no neighbours nigh, and so saveth the seed of fire, that he may not have to seek a light otherwhere, even so did Odysseus cover him with the leaves. And Athene shed sleep upon his eyes, that so it might soon release him from his weary travail, overshadowing his eyelids.

BOOK VI

Nausicaa, going to a river near that place to wash the clothes of her father, mother, and brethren, while the clothes were drying played with her maids at ball; and Odysseus coming forth is fed and clothed, and led on his way to the house of her father, King Alcinous.

So there he lay asleep, the steadfast goodly Odysseus, fordone with toil and drowsiness. Meanwhile Athene went to the land and the city of the Phaeacians, to the house of King Alcinous. She betook her to the rich-wrought bower, wherein was sleeping a maiden like to the gods in form and comeliness, Nausicaa, the daughter of Alcinous, high of heart. Beside her on either hand of the pillars of the door were two handmaids, dowered with beauty from the Graces, and the shining doors were shut.

But the goddess, fleet as the breath of the wind, swept towards the couch of the maiden, and stood above her head, and spake to her in the semblance of the daughter of a famous seafarer, Dymas, a girl of like age with Nausicaa, who had found grace in her sight. In her shape the grey-eyed Athene spake to the princess, saying:

"Nausicaa, how hath thy mother so heedless a maiden to her daughter? Lo, thou hast shining raiment that lies by thee uncared for, and thy marriage-day is near at hand, when thou thyself must needs go beautifully clad, and have garments to give to them who shall lead thee to the house of the bridegroom! And, behold, these are the things whence a good report goes abroad among men, wherein a father and lady mother take delight. But come, let us arise and go a-washing with the breaking of the day, and I will follow with thee to be thy mate in the toil, that without delay thou mayst get thee ready, since truly thou art not long to be a maiden. Lo, already they are wooing thee, the noblest youths of all the Phaeacians, among that people whence thou thyself dost draw thy lineage. So come, beseech thy noble father betimes in the morning to furnish thee with mules and a wain to carry the men's raiment, and the robes, and the shining coverlets. Yea and for thyself it is seemlier far to go thus than on foot, for the places where we must wash are a great way off the town."

So spake the grey-eyed Athene, and departed to Olympus, where, as they say, is the seat of the gods that standeth fast for ever. Not by winds is it shaken, nor ever wet with rain, nor doth the snow come nigh thereto, but most clear air is spread about it cloudless, and the white light floats over it. Therein the blessed gods are glad for all their days, and thither Athene went when she had shown forth all to the maiden.

Anon came the throned Dawn, and awakened Nausicaa of the fair robes, who straightway marvelled on the dream, and went through the halls to tell her parents, her father dear and her mother. And she found them within, her mother sitting by the hearth with the women her handmaids, spinning yarn of sea-purple stain, but her father she met as he was going forth to the renowned kings in their council, whither the noble Phaeacians called him. Standing close by her dear father she spake, saying: "Father, dear, couldst thou not lend me a high waggon with strong wheels, that I may take the goodly raiment to the river to wash, so much as I have lying soiled? Yea and it is seemly that thou thyself, when thou art with the princes in council, shouldst have fresh raiment to wear. Also, there are five dear sons of thine in the halls, two married, but three are lusty bachelors, and these are always eager for new-washen garments wherein to go to the dances; for all these things have I taken thought."

This she said, because she was ashamed to speak of glad marriage to her father; but he saw all and answered, saying:

"Neither the mules nor aught else do I grudge thee, my child. Go thy ways, and the thralls shall get thee ready a high waggon with good wheels, and fitted with an upper frame."

Therewith he called to his men, and they gave ear, and without the palace they made ready the smooth-running mule-wain, and led the mules beneath the yoke, and harnessed them under the car, while the maiden brought forth from her bower the shining raiment. This she stored in the polished car, and her mother filled a basket with all manner of food to the heart's desire, dainties too she set therein, and she poured wine into a goat-skin bottle, while Nausicaa climbed into the wain. And her mother gave her soft olive oil also in a golden cruse, that she and her maidens might anoint themselves after the bath. Then Nausicaa took the whip and the shining reins, and touched the mules to start them; then there was a clatter of hoofs, and on they strained without flagging, with their load of the raiment and the maiden. Not alone did she go, for her attendants followed with her.

Now when they were come to the beautiful stream of the river, where truly were the unfailing cisterns, and bright water welled up free from beneath, and flowed past, enough to wash the foulest garments clean, there the girls unharnessed the mules from under the chariot, and turning them loose they drove them along the banks of the eddying river to graze on the honey-sweet clover. Then they took the garments from the wain, in their hands, and bore them to the black water, and briskly trod them down in the trenches, in busy rivalry. Now when they had washed and cleansed all the stains, they spread all out in order along the shore of the deep, even where the sea, in beating on the coast, washed the pebbles clean. Then having bathed and anointed them well with olive oil, they took their mid-day meal on the river's banks, waiting till the clothes should dry in the brightness of the sun. Anon, when they were satisfied with food, the maidens and the princess, they fell to playing at ball.

But when now she was about going homewards, after yoking the mules and folding up the goodly raiment, then grey-eyed Athene turned to other thoughts, that so Odysseus might awake, and see the lovely maiden, who should be his guide to the city of the Phaeacian men. So then the princess threw the ball at one of her company; she missed the girl, and cast the ball into the deep eddying current, whereat they all raised a piercing cry. Then the goodly Odysseus awoke and sat up, pondering in his heart and spirit:

"Woe is me! to what men's land am I come now? say, are they froward, and wild, and unjust, or are they hospitable, and of God-fearing mind? How shrill a cry of maidens rings round me, of the nymphs that hold the steep hill-tops, and the river-springs, and the grassy water meadows! It must be, methinks, that I am near men of human speech. Go to, I myself will make trial and see."

Therewith the goodly Odysseus crept out from under the coppice, having broken with his strong hand a leafy bough from the thick wood, to hold athwart his body, that it might hide his nakedness withal. And forth he sallied like a lion mountain-bred, trusting in his strength, who fares out blown and rained upon, with flaming eyes; amid the kine he goes or amid the sheep or in the track of the wild deer; yea, his belly bids him go even to the good homestead to make assay upon the flocks. Even so Odysseus was fain to ·draw nigh to the fair-tressed maidens, all naked as he was, such need had come upon him. But he was terrible in their eyes, being marred with the salt sea foam, and they fled cowering here and there about the jutting spits of shore. And the daughter of Alcinous alone stood firm, for Athene gave her courage of heart, and took all trembling from her limbs. So she halted and stood over against him, and Odysseus considered whether he should clasp the knees of the lovely maiden, and so make his prayer, or should stand as he was, apart, and beseech her with smooth words, if haply she might show him the town, and give him raiment. And as he thought within himself, it seemed better to stand apart, and beseech her with smooth words, lest the maiden should be angered with him if he touched her knees: so straightway he spake a sweet and cunning word:

"I supplicate thee, O queen, whether thou art a goddess or a mortal! If indeed thou art a goddess of them that keep the wide heaven; to Artemis, then, the daughter of great Zeus, I mainly liken thee, for beauty and stature and shapeliness. But if thou art one of the daughters of men who dwell on earth, thrice blessed are thy father and thy lady mother, and thrice blessed thy brethren. Surely their souls ever glow with gladness for thy sake, each time they see thee entering the dance, so fair a flower of maidens. But he is of heart the most blessed beyond all other who shall prevail with gifts of wooing, and lead thee to his home. Never have mine eyes beheld such an one among mortals, neither man nor woman; great awe comes upon me as I look on thee. Yesterday, on the twentieth day, I escaped from the wine-dark deep, but all that time continually the wave bare me, and the vehement winds drave, from the isle Ogygia. And now some god has cast me on this shore, that here too, methinks, some evil may betide me; for I trow not that trouble will cease; the gods ere that time will yet bring many a thing to pass. But, queen, have pity on me, for after many trials and sore to thee first of all am I come, and of the other folk, who hold this city and land, I know no man. Nay show me the town, give me an old garment to cast about me, if thou hadst, when thou camest here, any wrap for the linen. And may the gods grant thee all thy heart's desire: a husband and a home, and a mind at one with his may they give — a good gift, for there is nothing mightier and nobler than when man and wife are of one heart and mind in a house, a grief to their foes, and to their friends great joy, but their own hearts know it best."

Then Nausicaa of the white arms answered him, and said:

"Stranger, forasmuch as thou seemest no evil man nor foolish — and it is Olympian Zeus himself that giveth weal to men, to the good and to the evil, to each one as he will, and this thy lot doubtless is of him, and so thou must in any wise endure it: — and now, since thou hast come to our city and our land, thou shalt not lack raiment, nor aught else that is the due of a hapless suppliant, when he has met them who can befriend him. And I will show thee the town, and name the name of the people. The Phaeacians hold this city and land, and I am the daughter of Alcinous, great of heart, on whom all the might and force of the Phaeacians depend."

Thus she spake, and called to her maidens of the fair tresses: "Halt, my maidens, whither flee ye at the sight of a man? Ye surely do not take him for an enemy? That mortal breathes not, and never will be born, who shall come with war to the land of the Phaeacians, for they are very dear to the gods. For apart we live in the wash of the waves, the outermost of men, and no other mortals are conversant with us. Nay, but this man is some helpless one come hither in his wanderings, whom now we must kindly entreat, for all strangers and beggars are from Zeus, and a little gift is dear. So, my maidens, give the stranger meat and drink, and bathe him in the river, where withal is a shelter from the winds."

So she spake, but they had halted and called each to the other, and they brought Odysseus to the sheltered place, and made him sit down, as Nausicaa bade them, the daughter of Alcinous, high of heart. Beside him they laid a mantle, and a doublet for raiment, and gave him soft olive oil in the golden cruse, and bade him wash in the streams of the river. Then goodly Odysseus spake among the maidens, saying: "I pray you stand thus apart, while I myself wash the brine from my shoulders, and anoint me with olive oil, for truly oil is long a stranger to my skin. But in your sight I will not bathe, for I am ashamed to make me naked in the company of fair-tressed maidens.'

Then they went apart and told all to their lady. But with the river water the goodly Odysseus washed from his skin the salt scurf that covered his back and broad shoulders, and from his head he wiped the crusted brine of the barren sea. But when he had washed his whole body, and anointed him with olive oil, and had clad himself in the raiment that the unwedded maiden gave him, then Athene, the daughter of Zeus, made him greater and more mighty to behold, and from his head caused deep curling locks to flow, like the hyacinth flower. And as when some skilful man overlays gold upon silver, even so did Athene shed grace about his head and shoulders.

Then to the shore of the sea went Odysseus apart, and sat down, glowing in beauty and grace, and the princess marvelled at him, and spake among her fair-tressed maidens, saying:

"Listen, my white-armed maidens, and I will say somewhat. Not without the will of all the gods who hold Olympus hath this man come among the godlike Phaeacians. Erewhile he seemed to me uncomely, but now he is like the gods that keep the wide heaven. Would that such an one might be called my husband, dwelling here, and that it might please him here to abide! But come, my maidens, give the stranger meat and drink."

Thus she spake, and they gave ready ear and hearkened, and set beside Odysseus meat and drink, and the steadfast goodly Odysseus did eat and drink eagerly, for it was long since he had tasted food.

Now Nausicaa of the white arms had another thought. She folded the raiment and stored it in the goodly wain, and yoked the mules strong of hoof, and herself climbed into the car. Then she called on Odysseus, and spake and hailed him: "Up now, stranger, and rouse thee to go to the city, that I may convey thee to the house of my wise father, where, I promise thee, thou shalt get knowledge of all the noblest of the Phaeacians. But do thou even as I tell thee, and thou seemest a discreet

ODYSSEUS FOLLOWING THE CAR OF NAUSICAA

man enough. So long as we are passing along the fields and
farms of men, do thou fare quickly with the maidens behind
the mules and the chariot, and I will lead the way. But when
we set foot within the city,—whereby goes a high wall with
towers, and there is a fair haven on either side of the town, and
narrow is the entrance, and curved ships are drawn up on either
hand of the mole, for all the folk have stations for their vessels,
each man one for himself. And there is the place of assembly
about the goodly temple of Poseidon, furnished with heavy
stones, deep bedded in the earth. There men look to the gear
of the black ships, hawsers and sails, and there they fine down
the oars. For the Phaeacians care not for bow nor quiver, but
for masts, and oars of ships, and gallant barques, wherein
rejoicing they cross the grey sea. Their ungracious speech it
is that I would avoid, lest some man afterward rebuke me, and
there are but too many insolent folk among the people. And
some one of the baser sort might meet me and say : 'Who is
this that goes with Nausicaa, this tall and goodly stranger?
Where found she him? Her husband he will be, her very own.
Either she has taken in some shipwrecked wanderer of strange
men,—for no men dwell near us; or some god has come in
answer to her instant prayer; from heaven has he descended,
and will have her to wife for evermore. Better so, if herself
she has ranged abroad and found a lord from a strange land, for
verily she holds in no regard the Phaeacians here in this country,
the many men and noble who are her wooers.' So will they
speak, and this would turn to my reproach. Yea, and I myself
would think it blame of another maiden who did such things in
despite of her friends, her father and mother being still alive,
and was conversant with men before the day of open wedlock.
But, stranger, heed well what I say, that as soon as may be
thou mayest gain at my father's hands an escort and a safe return.
Thou shalt find a fair grove of Athene, a poplar grove near the
road, and a spring wells forth therein, and a meadow lies all

around. There is my father's demesne, and his fruitful close, within the sound of a man's shout from the city. Sit thee down there and wait until such time as we may have come into the city, and reached the house of my father. But when thou deemest that we are got to the palace, then go up to the city of the Phaeacians, and ask for the house of my father Alcinous, high of heart. It is easily known, and a young child could be thy guide, for nowise like it are builded the houses of the Phaeacians, so goodly is the palace of the hero Alcinous. But when thou art within the shadow of the halls and the court, pass quickly through the great chamber, till thou comest to my mother, who sits at the hearth in the light of the fire, weaving yarn of sea-purple stain, a wonder to behold. Her chair is leaned against a pillar, and her maidens sit behind her. And there my father's throne leans close to hers, wherein he sits and drinks his wine, like an immortal. Pass thou by him, and cast thy hands about my mother's knees, that thou mayest see quickly and with joy the day of thy returning, even if thou art from a very far country. If but her heart be kindly disposed toward thee, then is there hope that thou shalt see thy friends, and come to thy well-builded house, and to thine own country."

She spake, and smote the mules with the shining whip, and quickly they left behind them the streams of the river. And well they trotted and well they paced, and she took heed to drive in such wise that the maidens and Odysseus might follow on foot, and cunningly she plied the lash. Then the sun set, and they came to the famous grove, the sacred place of Athene; so there the goodly Odysseus sat him down. Then straightway he prayed to the daughter of mighty Zeus: "Listen to me, child of Zeus, lord of the aegis, unwearied maiden; hear me even now, since before thou heardest not when I was smitten on the sea, when the renowned Earth-shaker smote me. Grant me to come to the Phaeacians as one dear, and worthy of pity."

So he spake in prayer, and Pallas Athene heard him; but she did not yet appear to him face to face, for she had regard unto her father's brother, who furiously raged against the godlike Odysseus, till he should come to his own country.

BOOK VII

Odysseus being received at the house of the king Alcinous, the queen after supper, taking notice of his garments, gives him occasion to relate his passage thither on the raft. Alcinous promises him a convoy for the morrow.

So he prayed there, the steadfast goodly Odysseus, while the two strong mules bare the princess to the town. And when she had now come to the famous palace of her father, she halted at the gateway, and round her gathered her brothers, men like to the immortals, and they loosed the mules from under the car, and carried the raiment within.

At that same hour Odysseus roused him to go to the city, and Athene shed a deep mist about Odysseus for the favour that she bare him, lest any of the Phaeacians, high of heart, should meet him and mock him in sharp speech, and ask him who he was. But when he was now about to enter the pleasant city, then the goddess, grey-eyed Athene, met him, in the fashion of a young maiden carrying a pitcher, and she stood over against him, and goodly Odysseus inquired of her:

"My child, couldst thou not lead me to the palace of the lord Alcinous, who bears sway among this people? Lo, I am come here, a stranger travel-worn from afar, from a distant land; wherefore of the folk who possess this city and country I know not any man."

Then the goddess, grey-eyed Athene, answered him saying: "Yea now, father and stranger, I will show thee the house that thou bidst me declare, for it lies near the palace of my noble father; behold, be silent as thou goest, and I will lead the way. And look on no man, nor question any. For these men do not gladly suffer strangers, nor lovingly entreat whoso cometh from a strange land. They trust to the speed of their swift ships, wherewith they cross the great gulf, for the Earth-shaker hath vouchsafed them this power. Their ships are swift as the flight of a bird, or as a thought."

Therewith Pallas Athene led the way swiftly, and he followed hard in the footsteps of the goddess. And it came to pass that the Phaeacians, mariners renowned, marked him not as he went down the city through their midst, for the fair-tressed Athene suffered it not, that awful goddess, who shed a wondrous mist about him, for the favour that she bare him in her heart. And Odysseus marvelled at the havens and the gallant ships, yea and the places of assembly of the heroes, and the long high walls crowned with palisades, a marvel to behold. But when they had now come to the famous palace of the king, the goddess, grey-eyed Athene, spake first and said:

"Lo, here, father and stranger, is the house that thou wouldst have me show thee: and thou shalt find kings at the feast, the fosterlings of Zeus; enter then, and fear not in thine heart, for the dauntless man is the best in every adventure, even though he come from a strange land. Thou shalt find the queen first in the halls: Arete is the name whereby men call her. If but her heart be kindly disposed to thee, then is there good hope that thou mayest see thy friends, and come to thy high-roofed home and thine own country."

Therewith grey-eyed Athene departed over the unharvested seas. Meanwhile Odysseus went to the famous palace of Alcinous, and his heart was full of many thoughts as he stood there or ever he had reached the threshold of bronze. For there was a gleam as it were of sun or moon through the high-roofed hall of great-hearted Alcinous. Brazen were the walls which ran this way and that from the threshold to the inmost chamber, and round them was a frieze of blue, and golden were the doors that closed in the good house. Silver were the door-posts that were set on the brazen threshold, and silver the lintel thereupon, and the hook of the door was of gold. And on either side stood golden hounds and silver, which Hephaestus wrought by his cunning, to guard the palace of great-hearted Alcinous, being free from death and age all their days. And within were seats arrayed against the wall this way and that, from the threshold even to the inmost chamber, and thereon were spread light coverings finely woven, the handiwork of women. There the Phaeacian chieftains were wont to sit eating and drinking, for they had continual store. Yea, and there were youths fashioned in gold, standing on firm-set bases, with flaming torches in their hands, giving light through the night to the feasters in the palace. And he had fifty handmaids in the house, and some grind the yellow grain on the millstone, and others weave webs and turn the yarn as they sit, restless as the leaves of the tall poplar tree: and the soft olive oil drops off that linen, so closely is it woven. For as the Phaeacian men are skilled beyond all others in driving a swift ship upon the deep, even so are the women the most cunning at the loom, for Athene hath given them notable wisdom in all fair handiwork and cunning wit.

There the steadfast goodly Odysseus stood and gazed. But when he had gazed at all and wondered, he passed quickly over the threshold within the house. And he found the captain and the counsellors of the Phaeacians pouring forth wine to the keen-sighted god, the slayer of Argos; for to him they poured the last cup when they were minded to take rest. Now the steadfast goodly Odysseus went through the house, clad in a thick mist, which Athene shed around him, till he came to Arete and the king Alcinous. And Odysseus cast his hands about the knees of Arete, and then it was that the wondrous mist melted from off him, and a silence fell on them that were within the house at the sight of him, and they marvelled as they beheld him. Then Odysseus began his prayer:

"Arete, after many toils am I come to thy husband and to thy knees and to these guests, and may the gods vouchsafe them a happy life, and may each one leave to his children after him his substance in his halls and whatever dues of honour the people have rendered unto him. But speed, I pray you, my parting, that I may come the more quickly to mine own country, for already too long do I suffer affliction far from my friends."

Therewith he sat him down by the hearth in the ashes at the fire, and behold, a dead silence fell on all. And at the last the ancient lord Echeneus spake among them, an elder of the Phaeacians, excellent in speech and skilled in much wisdom of old time. With good will he made harangue and spake among them :

"Alcinous, this truly is not the more seemly way, nor is it fitting that the stranger should sit upon the ground in the ashes by the hearth. Nay come, bid the stranger arise, and set him on a chair inlaid with silver, and command the henchmen to mix the wine, that we may pour forth likewise before Zeus, whose joy is in the thunder, who attendeth upon reverend suppliants. And let the housewife give supper to the stranger out of such stores as be within."

Now when the mighty king Alcinous heard this saying, he took Odysseus, the wise and crafty, by the hand, and raised him from the hearth, and set him on a shining chair, whence he bade his son give place, valiant Laodamas, who sat next him and was his dearest. And a handmaid bare water for the hands in a goodly golden ewer, and poured it forth over a silver basin to wash withal, and drew to his side a polished table. And a grave dame bare wheaten bread and set it by him and laid upon the board many dainties, giving freely of such things as she had by her. So the steadfast goodly Odysseus did eat and drink, and then the mighty Alcinous spake unto the henchman:

"Pontonous, mix the bowl and serve out the wine to all in the hall, that we may pour forth likewise before Zeus, whose joy is in the thunder, who attendeth upon reverend suppliants."

So spake he, and Pontonous mixed the honey-hearted wine, and served it out to all, when he had poured for libation into each cup in turn. But when they had poured forth and had drunken to their hearts' content, Alcinous made harangue and spake among them:

"Hear me, ye captains and counsellors of the Phaeacians, that I may speak as my spirit bids me. Now that the feast is over, go ye home and lie down to rest; and in the morning we will call yet more elders together, and entertain the stranger in the halls and do fair sacrifice to the gods, and thereafter we will likewise bethink us of the convoy, that so without pain or grief yonder stranger may by our convoy reach his own country speedily and with joy, even though he be from very far away. So shall he suffer no hurt or harm in mid passage, ere he set foot on his own land; but thereafter he shall endure such things as Fate and the stern spinning women drew off the spindles for him at his birth when his mother bare him. But if he is some deathless god come down from heaven, then do the gods herein imagine some new device against us. For always heretofore the gods appear manifest amongst us, whensoever we offer glorious hecatombs, and they feast by our side, sitting at the same board; yea, and even if a wayfarer going all alone has met with them, they use no disguise, since we are near of kin to them, even as are the Cyclôpes and the wild tribes of the Giants."

And Odysseus of many counsels answered him, saying: "Alcinous, that thought be far from thee! for I bear no likeness either in form or fashion to the deathless gods, who keep wide heaven, but to men that die. Whomsoever ye know of human kind the heaviest laden with sorrow, to them might I liken myself in my griefs. Yea, and I might tell of yet other woes, even the long tale of toil that by the gods' will I endured. But as for me, suffer me to sup, afflicted as I am; for nought is there more shameless than a ravening belly, which biddeth a man perforce be mindful of him, though one be worn and sorrowful in spirit, even as I have sorrow of heart; yet evermore he biddeth me eat and drink and maketh me utterly to forget all my sufferings, and commandeth me to take my fill. But do ye bestir you at the breaking of the day, that so ye may set me, hapless as I am, upon my country's soil, albeit after much suffering. Ah, and may life leave me when I have had sight of mine own possessions, my thralls, and my dwelling that is great and high!"

So spake he, and they all assented thereto, and bade send the stranger on his way, for that he had spoken aright. Now when they had poured forth and had drunken to their hearts' content, they went each one to his house to lay them to rest. But goodly Odysseus was left behind in the hall, and by him sat Arete and godlike Alcinous; and the maids cleared away the furniture of the feast; and white-armed Arete first spake among them. For she knew the mantle and the doublet, when she saw the goodly raiment that she herself had wrought with the women her handmaids. So she uttered her voice and spake to him winged words:

"Sir, I am bold to ask thee first of this. Who art thou of the sons of men, and whence? Who gave thee this raiment? Didst thou not say indeed that thou camest hither wandering over the deep?"

Then Odysseus of many counsels answered her, telling her of Calypso and the raft and his meeting with Nausicaa.

And Alcinous answered again, and spake saying: "Sir, surely this was no right thought of my daughter, in that she brought thee not to our house with the women her handmaids, though thou didst first entreat her grace."

And Odysseus of many counsels answered, and said unto

him: "My lord, chide not, I pray thee, for this the blameless maiden. For indeed she bade me follow with her company, but I would not for fear and very shame, lest perchance thine heart might be clouded at the sight; for a jealous race upon the earth are we, the tribes of men."

And Alcinous answered yet again, and spake saying: "Sir, my heart within me is not of such temper as to have been wroth without a cause: due measure in all things is best. Would to father Zeus, and Athene, and Apollo, would that so goodly a man as thou art, and like-minded with me, thou wouldst wed my daughter, and be called my son, here abiding: so would I give thee house and wealth, if thou wouldst stay of thine own will: but against thy will shall none of the Phaeacians keep thee: never be this well-pleasing in the eyes of father Zeus! And now I ordain an escort for thee on a certain day, that thou mayst surely know, and that day the morrow. Then shalt thou lay thee down overcome by sleep, and they the while shall smite the calm waters, till thou come to thy country and thy house, and whatsoever place is dear to thee. And thou shalt know for thyself how far my ships are the best, and how my young men excel at tossing the salt water with the oar-blade."

So spake he, and the steadfast goodly Odysseus rejoiced; and then he uttered a word in prayer, and called aloud to Zeus: "Father Zeus, oh that Alcinous may fulfil all that he hath said, so may his fame never be quenched upon the earth, the grain-giver, and I should come to mine own land!"

Thus they spake one to the other. And white-armed Arete bade her handmaids set out bedsteads beneath the gallery, and cast fair purple blankets over them, and spread coverlets above, and thereon lay thick mantles to be a clothing over all. So they went from the hall with torch in hand. But when they had busied them and spread the good bedstead, they stood by Odysseus and called unto him, saying:

"Up now, stranger, and get thee to sleep, thy bed is made."

So spake they, and it seemed to him that rest was wondrous good. So he slept there, the steadfast goodly Odysseus, on the jointed bedstead, beneath the echoing gallery.

BOOK VIII

The next day's entertainment of Odysseus, where he sees them contend in wrestling and other exercises, and upon provocation took up a greater stone than that which they were throwing, and overthrew them all. Alcinous and the lords give him presents. And how the king asked his name, his country, and his adventures.

Now when early Dawn shone forth, the rosy-fingered, then the mighty king Alcinous gat him up from his bed; and Odysseus, of the seed of Zeus, likewise uprose, the waster of cities. And the mighty king Alcinous led the way to the assembly place of the Phaeacians, which they had stablished hard by the ships. So when they had come thither, and sat them down on the polished stones close by each other, Pallas Athene went on her way through the town, in the semblance of the herald of wise Alcinous, devising a return for the great-hearted Odysseus. Then standing by each man she spake, saying:

"Hither now get ye to the assembly, ye captains and counsellors of the Phaeacians, that ye may learn concerning the stranger, who hath lately come to the palace of wise Alcinous, in his wanderings over the deep, and his form is like the deathless gods."

Therewith she aroused the spirit and desire of each one, and speedily the meeting-places and seats were filled with men that came to the gathering: yea, and many an one marvelled at the sight of the wise son of Laertes, for wondrous was the grace Athene poured upon his head and shoulders, and she made him

greater and more mighty to behold, that he might win love and
worship and honour among all the Phaeacians, and that he
might accomplish many feats, wherein the Phaeacians made
trial of Odysseus. Now when they were gathered and come
together, Alcinous made harangue and spake among them:

"Hearken, ye captains and counsellors of the Phaeacians,
and I will say that which my spirit within me bids me utter.
This stranger, I know not who he is, hath come to my house
in his wandering, whether from the men of the dawning or the
westward, and he presses for a convoy, and prays that it be
assured to him. So let us, as in time past, speed on the convoy. For never, nay never, doth any man who cometh to my
house, abide here long in sorrow for want of help upon his way.
Nay, come let us draw down a black ship to the fair salt sea,
for her first voyage, and let them choose fifty and two noble
youths throughout the township, who have been proved heretofore the best. And when ye have made fast the oars upon the
benches, step all ashore, and thereafter come to our house, and
quickly fall to feasting; and I will make good provision for all.
To the noble youths I give this commandment; but ye others,
sceptred kings, come to my fair dwelling, that we may entertain the stranger in the halls, and let no man make excuse.
Moreover, bid hither the divine minstrel, Demodocus, for the
god hath given minstrelsy to him as to none other, to make
men glad in what way soever his spirit stirs him to sing."

He spake and led the way, and the sceptred kings accom-
panied him, while the henchman went for the divine minstrel.
And chosen youths, fifty and two, departed at his command,
to the shore of the unharvested sea. But after they had gone
down to the ship and to the sea, first of all they drew the ship
down to the deep water, and placed the mast and sails in the
black ship, and fixed the oars in leathern loops, all orderly, and
spread forth the white sails. And they moored her high out in
the shore water, and thereafter went on their way to the great

palace of the wise Alcinous. Now the galleries and the courts and the rooms were thronged with men that came to the gathering, for there were many, young and old. Then Alcinous sacrificed twelve sheep among them, and eight boars with flashing tusks, and two oxen with trailing feet. These they flayed and made ready, and dressed a goodly feast.

Then the henchman drew near, leading with him the beloved minstrel, whom the muse loved dearly, and she gave him both good and evil; of his sight she reft him, but granted him sweet song. Then Pontonous, the henchman, set for him a high chair inlaid with silver, in the midst of the guests, leaning it against the tall pillar, and he hung the loud lyre on a pin, close above his head, and showed him how to lay his hands on it. And close by him he placed a basket, and a fair table, and a goblet of wine by his side, to drink when his spirit bade him. So they stretched forth their hands upon the good cheer spread before them. But after they had put from them the desire of meat and drink, the Muse stirred the minstrel to sing the songs of famous men, even that lay whereof the fame had then reached the wide heaven, namely, the quarrel between Odysseus and Achilles, son of Peleus; how once on a time they contended in fierce words at a rich festival of the gods.

This song it was that the famous minstrel sang; but Odysseus caught his great purple cloak with his stalwart hands, and drew it down over his head, and hid his comely face, for he was ashamed to shed tears beneath his brows in presence of the Phaeacians. Yea, and oft as the divine minstrel paused in his song, Odysseus would wipe away the tears, and draw the cloak from off his head, and take the two-handled goblet and pour forth before the gods. But whensoever he began again, and the chiefs of the Phaeacians stirred him to sing, in delight at the lay, again would Odysseus cover up his head and make moan. Now none of all the company marked him weeping, but Alcinous alone noted it and was ware thereof as he sat by him and heard him groaning heavily. And presently he spake among the Phaeacians, masters of the oar:

"Hearken, ye captains and counsellors of the Phaeacians; now have our souls been satisfied with the good feast, and with the lyre, which is the mate of the rich banquet. Let us go forth anon, and make trial of divers games, that the stranger may tell his friends, when home he returneth, how greatly we excel all men in boxing, and wrestling, and leaping, and speed of foot."

He spake, and led the way, and they went with him. And the henchman hung the loud lyre on the pin, and took the hand of Demodocus, and led him forth from the hall, and guided him by the same way, whereby those others, the chiefs of the Phaeacians, had gone to gaze upon the games. So they went on their way to the place of assembly, and with them a great company innumerable; and many a noble youth stood up to play. Now when they had all taken their pleasure in the games, Laodamas, son of Alcinous, spake among them:

"Come, my friends, let us ask the stranger whether he is skilled or practised in any sport. Ill fashioned, at least, he is not in his thighs and sinewy legs and hands withal, and his stalwart neck and mighty strength: yea and he lacks not youth, but is crushed by many troubles. For I tell thee there is nought else worse than the sea to confound a man, how hardy soever he may be."

And Euryalus in turn made answer, and said: "Laodamas, verily thou hast spoken this word in season. Go now thyself and challenge him, and declare thy saying."

Now when the good son of Alcinous heard this, he went and stood in the midst, and spake unto Odysseus: "Come, do thou too, father and stranger, try thy skill in the sports, if haply thou art practised in any; and thou art like to have knowledge of games, for there is no greater glory for a man while yet he lives, than that which he achieves by hand and foot. Come then, make essay, and cast away care from thy soul: thy journey shall not now be long delayed; lo, thy ship is even now drawn down to the sea, and the men of thy company are ready."

And Odysseus of many counsels answered him, saying: "Laodamas, wherefore do ye mock me, requiring this thing of me? Sorrow is far nearer my heart than sports, for much have I endured and laboured sorely in time past, and now I sit in this your gathering, craving my return, and making my prayer to the king and all the people."

And Euryalus answered, and rebuked him to his face: "No truly, stranger, nor do I think thee at all like one that is skilled in games, whereof there are many among men; rather art thou such an one as comes and goes in a benched ship, a master of sailors that are merchantmen, one with a memory for his freight, or that hath the charge of a cargo homeward bound, and of greedily gotten gains; thou seemest not a man of thy hands."

Then Odysseus of many counsels looked fiercely on him and said: "Stranger, thou hast not spoken well; thou art like a man presumptuous. So true it is that the gods do not give every gracious gift to all, neither shapeliness, nor wisdom, nor skilled speech. Yea, thou hast stirred my spirit in my breast by speaking thus amiss. I am not all unversed in sports, as thy words go, but methinks I was among the foremost while as yet I trusted in my youth and my hands, but now I am holden in misery and pains: for I have endured much in passing through the wars of men and the grievous waves of the sea. Yet even so, for all my affliction, I will essay the games, for thy word hath bitten to the quick, and thou hast roused me with thy saying."

He spake, and clad even as he was in his mantle leaped to his feet, and caught up a weight larger than the rest, a huge weight heavier far than those wherewith the Phaeacians contended in casting. With one whirl he sent it from his stout hand, and the stone flew hurtling: and the Phaeacians, of the long oars, those mariners renowned, crouched to earth beneath the rushing of the stone. Beyond all the marks it flew, so lightly it sped from his hand, and Athene in the fashion of a man marked the place, and spake and hailed him:

"Yea, even a blind man, stranger, might discern that token if he groped for it, for it is in no wise lost among the throng of the others, but is far the first; for this bout then take heart: not one of the Phaeacians shall attain thereunto or overpass it."

So spake she; and the steadfast goodly Odysseus rejoiced and was glad, for that he saw a true friend in the lists. Then with a lighter heart he spake amid the Phaeacians:

"Now reach ye this throw, young men, if ye may; and soon, methinks, will I cast another after it, as far or yet further. And whomsoever of the rest his heart and spirit stir thereto, hither let him come and try the issue with me, in boxing or in wrestling or even in the foot race, I care not which, for ye have greatly angered me: let any of all the Phaeacians come save Laodamas alone, for he is mine host: who would strive with one that entreated him kindly? But for the rest, I refuse none and hold none lightly, but I fain would know and prove them face to face. For I am no weakling in all sports, even in the feats of men. I know well how to handle the polished bow, and ever the first would I be to shoot and smite my man in the press of foes, even though many of my company stood by, and were aiming at the enemy. Alone Philoctetes in the Trojan land surpassed me with the bow in our Achaean archery. But I avow myself far more excellent than all besides, of the mortals that are now upon the earth and live by bread. And with the spear I can throw further than any other man can shoot an arrow. Only I doubt that in the foot race some of the Phaeacians may outstrip me, for I have been shamefully broken in many waters, seeing that there was no continual sustenance on board; wherefore my knees are loosened.'

So spake he and all kept silence; and Alcinous alone answered him, saying:

"We are no perfect boxers, nor wrestlers, but speedy runners, and the best of seamen; and dear to us ever is the banquet, and the harp, and the dance, and changes of raiment, and the warm bath, and love, and sleep. Lo, now arise, ye dancers of the Phaeacians, the best in the land, and make sport, that so the stranger may tell his friends, when he returneth home, how far we surpass all men besides in seamanship, and speed of foot, and in the dance and song."

So spake Alcinous the godlike, and the henchman rose to bear the hollow lyre from the king's palace. Then stood up nine chosen men in all, the judges of the people, who were wont to order all things in the lists aright. So they levelled the place for the dance, and made a fair ring and a wide. And the henchman drew near bearing the loud lyre to Demodocus, who gat him into the midst, and round him stood boys in their first bloom, skilled in the dance, and they smote the good floor with their feet. And Odysseus gazed at the twinklings of the feet, and marvelled in spirit.

Then goodly Odysseus spake unto Alcinous: "My lord Alcinous, thou didst boast thy dancers to be the best in the world, and lo, thy words are fulfilled; I wonder as I look on them."

So spake he, and the mighty king Alcinous rejoiced and spake at once among the Phaeacians, masters of the oar:

"Hearken ye, captains and counsellors of the Phaeacians, this stranger seems to me a wise man enough. Come then, let us give him a stranger's gift, as is meet. Behold, there are twelve glorious princes who rule among this people and bear sway, and I myself am the thirteenth. Now each man among you bring a fresh robe and a doublet, and a talent of fine gold, and let us speedily carry all these gifts together, that the stranger may take them in his hands, and go to supper with a glad heart.

As for Euryalus let him yield amends to the man himself with soft speech and with a gift, for his was no gentle saying."

So spake he, and they all assented thereto, and would have it so. And each one sent forth his henchman to fetch his gift, and Euryalus answered the king and spake, saying:

"My lord Alcinous, most notable among all the people, I will make atonement to thy guest according to thy word. I will give him a hanger all of bronze, with a silver hilt thereto, and a sheath of fresh-sawn ivory covers it about, and it shall be to him a thing of price."

Therewith he puts into his hands the hanger dight with silver, and uttering his voice spake to him winged words: "Hail, stranger and father; and if aught grievous hath been spoken, may the storm-winds soon snatch and bear it away. But may the gods grant thee to see thy wife and to come to thine own country, for all too long hast thou endured affliction away from thy friends."

And Odysseus of many counsels answered him saying: "Thou too, my friend, all hail; and may the gods vouchsafe thee happiness, and mayest thou never miss this sword which thou hast given me, thou that with soft speech hast yielded me amends."

He spake and hung about his shoulders the silver-studded sword. And the sun sank, and the noble gifts were brought him. Then the proud henchmen bare them to the palace of Alcinous, and the sons of noble Alcinous took the fair gifts, and set them by their reverend mother. And the mighty king Alcinous led the way, and they came in and sat them down on the high seats. And the mighty Alcinous spake unto Arete:

"Bring me hither, my lady, a choice coffer, the best thou hast, and thyself place therein a fresh robe and a doublet, and heat for our guest a cauldron on the fire, and warm water, that after the bath the stranger may see all the gifts duly arrayed which the noble Phaeacians bare hither, and that he may have joy in the feast, and in hearing the song of the minstrelsy. Also

I will give him a beautiful golden chalice of mine own, that he may be mindful of me all the days of his life when he poureth the drink-offering to Zeus and to the other gods."

So spake he, and Arete bade her handmaids to set a great cauldron on the fire with what speed they might. And they set the cauldron for the filling of the bath on the blazing fire, and poured water therein, and took faggots and kindled them beneath. So the fire began to circle round the belly of the cauldron, and the water waxed hot. Meanwhile Arete brought forth for her guest the beautiful coffer from the treasure chamber, and bestowed fair gifts therein, raiment and gold, which the Phaeacians gave him. And with her own hands she placed therein a robe and goodly doublet, and uttering her voice spake to him winged words:

"Do thou now look to the lid, and quickly tie the knot, lest any man spoil thy goods by the way, when presently thou fallest on sweet sleep travelling in thy black ship."

Now when the steadfast goodly Odysseus heard this saying, forthwith he fixed on the lid, and quickly tied the curious knot, which the lady Circe on a time had taught him. Then straightway the housewife bade him go to the bath and bathe him; and he saw the warm water and was glad, for he was not wont to be so cared for, from the day that he left the house of fair-tressed Calypso.

Now after the maids had bathed him and anointed him with olive oil, and had cast a fair mantle and a doublet upon him, he stept forth from the bath, and went to be with the chiefs at their wine. And Nausicaa, dowered with beauty by the gods, stood by the doorpost of the well-builded hall, and marvelled at Odysseus, beholding him before her eyes, and she uttered her voice and spake to him winged words:

"Farewell, stranger, and even in thine own country bethink thee of me upon a time, for that to me first thou owest the ransom of life."

And Odysseus of many counsels answered her saying: "Nausicaa, daughter of great-hearted Alcinous, yea, may Zeus, the thunderer, the lord of Here, grant me to reach my home and see the day of my returning; so would I, even there, do thee worship as to a god, all my days for evermore, for thou, lady, hast given me my life."

He spake and sat him in the high seat by king Alcinous. And now they were serving out the portions and mixing the wine. Then the henchman drew nigh leading the sweet minstrel, Demodocus, that was had in honour of the people. So he set him in the midst of the feasters, and made him lean against a tall column. Then to the henchman spake Odysseus of many counsels, for he had cut off a portion of the chine of a white-toothed boar, whereon yet more was left, with rich fat on either side:

"Lo, henchman, take this mess, and hand it to Demodocus, that he may eat, and I will bid him hail, despite my sorrow. For minstrels from all men on earth get their meed of honour and worship; inasmuch as the Muse teacheth them the paths of song, and loveth the tribe of minstrels."

Thus he spake, and the henchman bare the mess, and set it upon the knees of the lord Demodocus, and he took it, and was glad at heart. Then they stretched forth their hands upon the good cheer set before them. Now after they had put from them the desire of meat and drink, then Odysseus of many counsels spake to Demodocus, saying:

"Come now, change thy strain, and sing of the fashioning of the horse of wood, which Epeius made by the aid of Athene, even the guileful thing, that goodly Odysseus led up into the citadel, when he had laden it with the men who wasted Ilios. If thou wilt indeed rehearse me this aright, so will I be thy witness among all men, how the god of his grace hath given thee the gift of wondrous song."

So spake he, and the minstrel, being stirred by the god, began and showed forth his minstrelsy. He took up the tale where it tells how the Argives of the one part set fire to their huts, and went aboard their decked ships and sailed away, while those others, the fellowship of renowned Odysseus, were now seated in the assembly-place of the Trojans, all hidden in the horse, for the Trojans themselves had dragged him to the citadel. So the horse stood there, while seated all around him the people spake many things confusedly and three ways their counsel looked; either to cleave the hollow timber with the pitiless spear, or to drag it to the brow of the hill, and hurl it from the rocks, or to leave it as a mighty offering to appease the gods. And on this wise it was to be at the last. For the doom was on them to perish when their city should have closed upon the great horse of wood, wherein sat all the bravest of the Argives, bearing to the Trojans death and destiny. And he sang how the sons of the Achaeans poured forth from the horse, and left the hollow lair, and sacked the burg. And he sang how and where each man wasted the town, and of Odysseus, how he went like Ares to the house of Deiphobus with godlike Menelaus. It was there, he said, that Odysseus adventured the most grievous battle, and in the end prevailed, by grace of great-hearted Athene.

This was the song that the famous minstrel sang. But the heart of Odysseus melted, and the tear wet his cheeks beneath the eyelids. Now none of all the company marked him weeping; but Alcinous alone noted it, and was ware thereof, as he sat nigh him and heard him groaning heavily. And presently he spake among the Phaeacians, masters of the oar:

"Hearken, ye captains and counsellors of the Phaeacians, and now let Demodocus hold his hand from the loud lyre, for this song of his is nowise pleasing alike to all. From the time that we began to sup, and that the divine minstrel was moved to sing, ever since hath yonder stranger never ceased from woeful lamentation: sore grief, methinks, hath encompassed his heart

ODYSSEUS WEEPS AT THE SONG OF DEMODOCUS

Nay, but let the minstrel cease, that we may all alike make merry, hosts and guest, since it is far meeter so. Wherefore do thou too hide not now with crafty purpose aught whereof I ask thee; it were more meet for thee to tell it out. Say, what is the name whereby they call thee at home, even thy father and thy mother, and others thy townsmen and the dwellers round about? For there is none of all mankind nameless, neither the mean man nor yet the noble, from the first hour of his birth, but parents bestow a name on every man so soon as he is born. Tell me too of thy land, thy township, and thy city, that our ships may conceive of their course to bring thee thither. But come now, declare me this and plainly tell it all; whither wast thou borne wandering, and to what shores of men thou camest; tell me of the people and of their fair-lying cities, of those whoso are hard and wild and unjust, and of those likewise who are hospitable and of a god-fearing mind. Declare, too, wherefore thou dost weep and mourn in spirit at the tale of the faring of the Argive Danaans and the lay of Ilios. All this the gods have fashioned, and have woven the skein of death for men, that there might be a song in the ears even of the folk of after-time. Hadst thou even a kinsman by marriage that fell before Ilios, a true man, a daughter's husband or wife's father, such as are nearest us after those of our own stock and blood? Or else, maybe, some loving friend, a good man and true; for a friend with an understanding heart is no whit worse than a brother."

BOOK IX

Odysseus relates, first, what befell him amongst the Cicones at Ismarus; secondly, amongst the Lotophagi; thirdly, how he was used by the Cyclops Polyphemus.

AND Odysseus of many counsels answered him saying: "Now, first will I tell my name, that ye too may know it, and that I, when I have escaped the pitiless day, may yet be your host, though my home is in a far country. I am ODYSSEUS, SON OF LAERTES, who am in men's minds for all manner of wiles, and my fame reaches unto heaven. And I dwell in clear-seen Ithaca, wherein is a mountain Neriton, with trembling forest leaves, standing manifest to view, and many islands lie around, very near one to the other, Dulichium and Same, and wooded Zacynthus. Now Ithaca lies low, furthest up the sea-line toward the darkness, but those others face the dawning and the sun: a rugged isle, but a good nurse of noble youths; and for myself I can see nought beside sweeter than a man's own country. But come, let me tell thee too of the troubles of my journeying, which Zeus laid on me as I came from Troy.

"The wind that bare me from Ilios brought me nigh to the Cicones, even to Ismarus, whereupon I sacked their city and slew the people. And from out the city we took their wives and much substance, and divided them amongst us, that none through me might go lacking his proper share. Howbeit, thereafter I commanded that we should flee with a swift foot, but my men in their great folly hearkened not. There was much wine still a-drinking, and still they slew many flocks of sheep by the sea shore and kine with trailing feet and shambling gait. Meanwhile the Cicones went and raised a cry to other Cicones their neighbours, dwelling inland, who were more in number than they and braver withal: skilled they were to fight with men from chariots, and when need was on foot. So they gathered in the early morning as thick as leaves and flowers that spring in their season — yea and in that hour an evil doom of Zeus stood by us, ill-fated men, that so we might be sore afflicted. They set their battle in array by the swift ships, and the hosts cast at one another with their bronze-shod spears. So long as it was morn and the sacred day waxed stronger, so long we abode their assault and beat them off, albeit they outnumbered us. But when the sun was wending to the time of the loosing of cattle, then at last the Cicones drave in the Achaeans and overcame them, and six of my goodly-greaved company perished from each ship: but the remnant of us escaped death and destiny.

"Thence we sailed onward stricken at heart, yet glad as men saved from death, albeit we had lost our dear companions. Nor did my curved ships move onward ere we had called thrice on each of those our hapless fellows, who died at the hands of the Cicones on the plain. Now Zeus, gatherer of the clouds, aroused the North Wind against our ships with a terrible tempest, and covered land and sea alike with clouds, and down sped night from heaven. Thus the ships were driven headlong, and their sails were torn to shreds by the might of the wind. So we lowered the sails into the hold, in fear of death, but rowed the ships landward apace. There for two nights and two days we lay continually, consuming our hearts with weariness and sorrow. But when the fair-tressed Dawn had at last brought the full light of the third day, we set up the masts and hoisted the white sails and sat us down, while the wind and the helmsman guided the ships. And now I should have come to mine own country all unhurt, but the wave and the stream of the sea and the North Wind swept me from my course as I was doubling Malea, and drave me wandering past Cythera.

"Thence for nine whole days was I borne by ruinous winds over the teeming deep; but on the tenth day we set foot on the land of the lotus-eaters, who eat a flowery food. So we stepped ashore and drew water, and straightway my company took their midday meal by the swift ships. Now when we had tasted meat and drink I sent forth certain of my company to go and make search what manner of men they were who here live upon the earth by bread, and I chose out two of my fellows, and sent a third with them as herald. Then straightway they went and mixed with the men of the lotus-eaters, and so it was that the lotus-eaters devised not death for our fellows, but gave them of the lotus to taste. Now whosoever of them did eat the honey-sweet fruit of the lotus had no more wish to bring tidings nor to come back, but there he chose to abide with the lotus-eating men, ever feeding on the lotus, and forgetful of his homeward way. Therefore I led them back to the ships weeping, and sore against their will, and dragged them beneath the benches, and bound them in the hollow barques. But I commanded the rest of my well-loved company to make speed and go on board the swift ships, lest haply any should eat of the lotus and be forgetful of returning. Right soon they embarked and sat upon the benches, and sitting orderly they smote the grey sea water with their oars.

"Thence we sailed onward stricken at heart. And we came to the land of the Cyclôpes, a froward and a lawless folk, who trusting to the deathless gods plant not aught with their hands, neither plough: but, behold, all these things spring for them in plenty, unsown and untilled, wheat, and barley, and vines, which bear great clusters of the juice of the grape, and the rain of Zeus gives them increase. These have neither gatherings for council nor oracles of law, but they dwell in hollow caves on the crests of the high hills, and each one utters the law to his children and his wives, and they reck not one of another.

"Now there is a waste isle stretching without the harbour of the land of the Cyclôpes, neither nigh at hand nor yet afar off, a woodland isle, wherein are wild goats unnumbered, for no path of men scares them, nor do hunters resort thither who suffer hardships in the wood, as they range the mountain crests. Thither we sailed, and some god guided us through the night, for it was dark and there was no light to see, a mist lying deep about the ships, nor did the moon show her light from heaven, but was shut in with clouds. No man then beheld that island, neither saw we the long waves rolling to the beach, till we had run our decked ships ashore. And when our ships were beached, we took down all their sails, and ourselves too stept forth upon the strand of the sea, and there we fell into sound sleep and waited for the bright Dawn.

"So soon as early Dawn shone forth, the rosy-fingered, in wonder at the island we roamed over the length thereof: and the Nymphs, the daughters of Zeus, lord of the aegis, started the wild goats of the hills, that my company might have wherewith to sup. Anon we took to us our curved bows from out the ships and long spears, and arrayed in three bands we began shooting at the goats; and the god soon gave us game in plenty. Now twelve ships bare me company, and to each ship fell nine goats for a portion, but for me alone they set ten apart.

"Thus we sat there the livelong day until the going down of the sun, feasting on abundant flesh and on sweet wine. For the red wine was not yet spent from out the ships, but somewhat was yet therein, for we had each one drawn off large store thereof in jars, when we took the sacred citadel of the Cicones. And we looked across to the land of the Cyclôpes who dwell nigh, and to the smoke, and to the voice of the men, and of the sheep and of the goats. And when the sun had sunk and darkness had come on, then we laid us to rest upon the sea-beach. So soon as early Dawn shone forth, the rosy-fingered, then I called a gathering of my men, and spake among them all :

"'Abide here all the rest of you, my dear companions; but I will go with mine own ship and my ship's company, and make proof of these men, what manner of folk they are, whether froward, and wild, and unjust, or hospitable and of god-fearing mind.'

"So I spake, and I climbed the ship's side, and bade my company themselves to mount, and to loose the hawsers. So they soon embarked and sat upon the benches, and sitting orderly smote the grey sea water with their oars. Now when we had come to the land that lies hard by, we saw a cave on the border near to the sea, lofty and roofed over with laurels and there many flocks of sheep and goats were used to rest. And about it a high outer court was built with stones, deep bedded, and with tall pines and oaks with their high crown of leaves. And a man was wont to sleep therein, of monstrous size, who shepherded his flocks alone and afar, and was not conversant with others, but dwelt apart in lawlessness of mind. Yea, for he was a monstrous thing and fashioned marvellously, nor was he like to any man that lives by bread, but like a wooded peak of the towering hills, which stands out apart and alone from others.

"Then I commanded the rest of my well-loved company to tarry there by the ship, and to guard the ship, but I chose out twelve men, the best of my company, and sallied forth. Now I had with me a goat-skin of the dark wine and sweet, which Maron, son of Euanthes, had given me, the priest of Apollo, the god that watched over Ismarus. And he gave it, for that we had protected him with his wife and child reverently; for he dwelt in a thick grove of Phoebus Apollo. And he made me splendid gifts; he gave me seven talents of gold well wrought, and he gave me a mixing bowl of pure silver, and furthermore wine which he drew off in twelve jars in all, sweet wine unmingled, a draught divine; nor did any of his servants or of his handmaids in the house know thereof, but himself and his dear wife and one housedame only. And as often as they drank that red wine honey sweet, he would fill one cup and pour it into twenty measures of water, and a marvellous sweet smell went up from the mixing bowl: then truly it was no pleasure to refrain.

"With this wine I filled a great skin, and bare it with me, and corn too I put in a wallet, for my lordly spirit straightway had a boding that a man would come to me, a strange man, clothed in mighty strength, one that knew not judgment and justice.[1]

[1] Literally, knowing neither dooms, nor ordinances of law.

"Soon we came to the cave, but we found him not within ; he was shepherding his fat flocks in the pastures. So we went into the cave, and gazed on all that was therein. The baskets were well laden with cheeses, and the folds were thronged with lambs and kids ; each kind was penned by itself, the firstlings apart, and the summer lambs apart, apart too the younglings of the flock. Now all the vessels swam with whey, the milkpails and the bowls, the well-wrought vessels whereinto he milked. My company then spake and besought me first of all to take of the cheeses and to return, and afterwards to make haste and drive off the kids and lambs to the swift ships from out the pens, and to sail over the salt sea water. Howbeit I hearkened not (and far better would it have been), but waited to see the giant himself, and whether he would give me gifts as a stranger's due. Yet was not his coming to be with joy to my company.

"Then we kindled a fire, and made burnt-offering, and ourselves likewise took of the cheeses, and did eat, and sat waiting for him within till he came back, shepherding his flocks. And he bore a grievous weight of dry wood, against supper time. This log he cast down with a din inside the cave, and in fear we fled to the secret place of the rock. As for him, he drave his fat flocks into the wide cavern, even all that he was wont to milk ; but the males both of the sheep and of the goats he left without in the deep yard. Thereafter he lifted a huge door-stone and weighty, and set it in the mouth of the cave, such an one as two and twenty good four-wheeled wains could not raise from the ground, so mighty a sheer rock did he set against the doorway. Then he sat down and milked the ewes and bleating goats all orderly, and beneath each ewe he placed her young. And anon he curdled one half of the white milk, and massed it together, and stored it in wicker-baskets, and the other half he let stand in pails, that he might have it to take and drink against supper time. Now when he had done all his work busily, then he kindled the fire anew, and espied us, and made question:

"'Strangers, who are ye? Whence sail ye over the wet ways? On some trading enterprise or at adventure do ye rove, even as sea-robbers over the brine, for at hazard of their own lives they wander, bringing bale to alien men?'

"So spake he, but as for us our heart within us was broken for terror of the deep voice and his own monstrous shape; yet despite all I answered and spake unto him, saying:

"'Lo, we are Achaeans, driven wandering from Troy, by all manner of winds over the great gulf of the sea; seeking our homes we fare, but another path have we come, by other ways: even such, methinks, was the will and the counsel of Zeus. And we avow us to be the men of Agamemnon, son of Atreus, whose fame is even now the mightiest under heaven, so great a city did he sack, and destroyed many people; but as for us we have lighted here, and come to these thy knees, if perchance thou wilt give us a stranger's gift, or make any present, as is the due of strangers. Nay, lord, have regard to the gods, for we are thy suppliants; and Zeus is the avenger of suppliants and sojourners, Zeus, the god of the stranger, who fareth in the company of reverend strangers.'

"So I spake, and anon he answered out of his pitiless heart: 'Thou art witless, my stranger, or thou hast come from afar, who biddest me either to fear or shun the gods. For the Cyclôpes pay no heed to Zeus, lord of the aegis, nor to the blessed gods, for verily we are better men than they. Nor would I, to shun the enmity of Zeus, spare either thee or thy company, unless my spirit bade me. But tell me where thou didst stay thy well-wrought ship on thy coming? Was it perchance at the far end of the island, or hard by, that I may know?'

"So he spake tempting me, but he cheated me not, who knew full much, and I answered him again with words of guile:

"'As for my ship, Poseidon, the shaker of the earth, brake it to pieces, for he cast it upon the rocks at the border of your country, and brought it nigh the headland, and a wind bare it thither from the sea. But I with these my men escaped from utter doom.'

"So I spake, and out of his pitiless heart he answered me not a word, but sprang up, and laid his hands upon my fellows, and clutching two together dashed them, as they had been whelps, to the earth, and the brain flowed forth upon the ground, and the earth was wet. Then cut he them up piecemeal, and made ready his supper. So he ate even as a mountain-bred lion, and ceased not, devouring entrails and flesh and bones with their marrow. And we wept and raised our hands to Zeus, beholding the cruel deeds; and we were at our wits' end. And after the Cyclops had filled his huge maw with human flesh and the milk he drank thereafter, he lay within the cave, stretched out among his sheep.

"So I took counsel in my great heart, whether I should draw near, and pluck my sharp sword from my thigh, and stab him in the breast, where the midrib holds the liver, feeling for the place with my hand. But my second thought withheld me, for so should we too have perished even there with utter doom. For we should not have prevailed to roll away with our hands from the lofty door the heavy stone which he set there. So for that time we made moan, awaiting the bright Dawn.

"Now when early Dawn shone forth, the rosy-fingered, again he kindled the fire and milked his goodly flocks all orderly, and beneath each ewe set her lamb. Anon when he had done all his work busily, again he seized yet other two men and made ready his mid-day meal. And after the meal, lightly he moved away the great door-stone, and drave his fat flocks forth from the cave, and afterwards he set it in its place again, as one might set the lid on a quiver. Then with a loud whoop, the Cyclops turned his fat flocks towards the hills; but I was left devising evil in the deep of my heart, if in any wise I might avenge me, and Athene grant me renown.

"And this was the counsel that showed best in my sight

There lay by a sheep-fold a great club of the Cyclops, a club of olive wood, yet green, which he had cut to carry with him when it should be seasoned. Now when we saw it we likened it in size to the mast of a black ship of twenty oars, a wide merchant vessel that traverses the great sea gulf, so huge it was to view in bulk and length. I stood thereby and cut off from it a portion as it were a fathom's length, and set it by my fellows, and bade them fine it down, and they made it even, while I stood by and sharpened it to a point, and straightway I took it and hardened it in the bright fire. Then I laid it well away, and hid it beneath the dung, which was scattered in great heaps in the depths of the cave. And I bade my company cast lots among them, which of them should risk the adventure with me, and lift the bar and turn it about in his eye, when sweet sleep came upon him. And the lot fell upon those four whom I myself would have been fain to choose, and I appointed myself to be the fifth among them. In the evening he came shepherding his flocks of goodly fleece, and presently he drave his fat flocks into the cave each and all, nor left he any without in the deep court-yard, whether through some foreboding, or perchance that the god so bade him do. Thereafter he lifted the huge doorstone and set it in the mouth of the cave, and sitting down he milked the ewes and bleating goats, all orderly, and beneath each ewe he placed her young. Then when he had done all his work busily, again he seized yet other two and made ready his supper. Then I stood by the Cyclops and spake to him, holding in my hands an ivy bowl of the dark wine:

"'Cyclops, take and drink wine after thy feast of man's meat, that thou mayest know what manner of drink this was that our ship held. And lo, I was bringing it thee as a drink offering, if haply thou mayest take pity and send me on my way home, but thy mad rage is past all sufferance. O hard of heart, how may another of the many men there be come ever to thee again, seeing that thy deeds have been lawless?'

ODYSSEUS GIVING WINE TO THE CYCLOPS

"So I spake, and he took the cup and drank it off, and found great delight in drinking the sweet draught, and asked me for it yet a second time:

"'Give it me again of thy grace, and tell me thy name straightway, that I may give thee a stranger's gift, wherein thou mayest be glad. Yea, for the earth, the grain-giver, bears for the Cyclôpes the mighty clusters of the juice of the grape, and the rain of Zeus gives them increase, but this is a rill of very nectar and ambrosia.'

"So he spake, and again I handed him the dark wine. Thrice I bare and gave it him, and thrice in his folly he drank it to the lees. Now when the wine had got about the wits of the Cyclops, then did I speak to him with soft words:

"'Cyclops, thou askest me my renowned name, and I will declare it unto thee, and do thou grant me a stranger's gift, as thou didst promise. Noman is my name, and Noman they call me, my father and my mother and all my fellows.'

"So I spake, and straightway he answered me out of his pitiless heart:

"'Noman will I eat last in the number of his fellows, and the others before him: that shall be thy gift.'

"Therewith he sank backwards and fell with face upturned, and there he lay with his great neck bent round, and sleep, that conquers all men, overcame him. And the wine and the fragments of men's flesh issued forth from his mouth, and he vomited, being heavy with wine. Then I thrust in that stake under the deep ashes, until it should grow hot, and I spake to my companions comfortable words, lest any should hang back from me in fear. But when that bar of olive wood was just about to catch fire in the flame, green though it was, and began to glow terribly, even then I came nigh, and drew it from the coals, and my fellows gathered about me, and some god breathed great courage into us. For their part they seized the bar of olive wood, that was sharpened at the point, and thrust it into his eye, while I from my place aloft turned it about, as when a man bores a ship's beam with a drill, while his fellows below spin it with a strap, which they hold at either end, and the auger runs round continually. Even so did we seize the fiery-pointed brand and whirled it round in his eye, and the blood flowed about the heated bar. And the breath of the flame singed his eyelids and brows all about, as the ball of the eye burnt away, and the roots thereof crackled in the flame. And as when a smith dips an axe or adze in chill water with a great hissing, when he would temper it — for hereby anon comes the strength of iron — even so did his eye hiss round the stake of olive. And he raised a great and terrible cry, that the rock rang around, and we fled away in fear, while he plucked forth from his eye the brand bedabbled in much blood. Then maddened with pain he cast it from him with his hands, and called with a loud voice on the Cyclôpes, who dwelt about him in the caves along the windy heights. And they heard the cry and flocked together from every side, and gathering round the cave asked him what ailed him:

"'What hath so distressed thee, Polyphemus, that thou criest thus aloud through the immortal night, and makest us sleepless? Surely no mortal driveth off thy flocks against thy will: surely none slayeth thyself by force or craft?'

"And the strong Polyphemus spake to them again from out the cave: 'My friends, Noman is slaying me by guile, nor at all by force.'

"And they answered and spake winged words: 'If then no man is violently handling thee in thy solitude, it can in no wise be that thou shouldest escape the sickness sent by mighty Zeus. Nay, pray thou to thy father, the lord Poseidon.'

"On this wise they spake and departed; and my heart within me laughed to see how my name and cunning counsel had beguiled them. But the Cyclops, groaning and travailing in pain, groped with his hands, and lifted away the stone from the door of the cave, and himself sat in the entry, with arms outstretched to catch, if he might, any one that was going forth with his sheep, so witless, methinks, did he hope to find me. But I advised me how all might be for the very best, if perchance I might find a way of escape from death for my companions and myself, and I wove all manner of craft and counsel, as a man will for his life, seeing that great mischief was nigh. And this was the counsel that showed best in my sight. The rams of the flock were well nurtured and thick of fleece, great and goodly, with wool dark as the violet. Quietly I lashed them together with twisted withies, whereon the Cyclops slept, that lawless monster. Three together I took: now the middle one of the three would bear each a man, but the other twain went on either side, saving my fellows. Thus every three sheep bear their man. But as for me I laid hold of the back of a young ram who was far the best and the goodliest of all the flock, and curled beneath his shaggy belly there I lay, and so clung face upward, grasping the wondrous fleece with a steadfast heart. So for that time making moan we awaited the bright Dawn.

"So soon as early Dawn shone forth, the rosy-fingered, then did the rams of the flock hasten forth to pasture, but the ewes bleated unmilked about the pens, for their udders were swollen to bursting. Then their lord, sore stricken with pain, felt along the backs of all the sheep as they stood up before him, and guessed not in his folly how that my men were bound beneath the breasts of his thick-fleeced flocks. Last of all the sheep came forth the ram, cumbered with his wool, and the weight of me and my cunning. And the strong Polyphemus laid his hands on him and spake to him, saying:

"'Dear ram, wherefore, I pray thee, art thou the last of all the flocks to go forth from the cave, who of old wast not wont to lag behind the sheep, but wert ever the foremost to pluck the tender blossom of the pasture, faring with long strides, and wert still the first to come to the streams of the rivers, and first didst long to return to the homestead in the evening? But now art thou the very last. Surely thou art sorrowing for the eye of thy lord, which an evil man blinded, with his accursed fellows, when he had subdued my wits with wine, even Noman, whom I say hath not yet escaped destruction. Ah, if thou couldst feel as I, and be endued with speech, to tell me where he shifts about to shun my wrath; then should he be smitten, and his brains be dashed against the floor here and there about the cave, and my heart be lightened of the sorrows which Noman, nothing worth, hath brought me!'

"Therewith he sent the ram forth from him, and when we had gone but a little way from the cave and from the yard, first I loosed myself from under the ram and then I set my fellows free. And swiftly we drave on those stiff-shanked sheep, so rich in fat, and often turned to look about, till we came to the ship. And a glad sight to our fellows were we that had fled from death, but the others they would have bemoaned with tears; howbeit I suffered it not, but with frowning brows forbade each man to weep. Rather I bade them to cast on board the many sheep with goodly fleece, and to sail over the salt sea water. So they embarked forthwith, and sate upon the benches, and sitting orderly smote the grey sea water with their oars. But when I had not gone so far but that a man's shout might be heard, then I spoke unto the Cyclops taunting him:

"'Cyclops, so thou wert not to eat the company of a weakling by main might in thy hollow cave! Thine evil deeds were very sure to find thee out, thou cruel man, who hadst no shame to eat thy guests within thy gates, wherefore Zeus hath requited thee, and the other gods.'

"So I spake, and he was yet the more angered at heart, and he brake off the peak of a great hill and threw it at us, and it fell in front of the dark-prowed ship. And the sea

heaved beneath the fall of the rock, and the backward flow of
the wave bare the ship quickly to the dry land, with the wash
from the deep sea, and drave it to the shore. Then I caught
up a long pole in my hands, and thrust the ship from off the
land, and roused my company, and with a motion of the head
bade them dash in with their oars, that so we might escape
our evil plight. So they bent to their oars and rowed on. But
when we had now made twice the distance over the brine,
I would fain have spoken to the Cyclops, but my company
stayed me on every side with soft words, saying:

"'Foolhardy that thou art, why wouldst thou rouse a wild
man to wrath, who even now hath cast so mighty a throw
towards the deep and brought our ship back to land, yea and
we thought that we had perished even there? If he had heard
any of us utter sound or speech he would have crushed our
heads and our ship timbers with a cast of a rugged stone, so
mightily he hurls.'

"So spake they, but they prevailed not on my lordly spirit,
and I answered him again from out an angry heart:

"'Cyclops, if any one of mortal men shall ask thee of the
unsightly blinding of thine eye, say that it was Odysseus that
blinded it, the waster of cities, son of Laertes, whose dwelling
is in Ithaca.'

"So I spake, and with a moan he answered me, saying:

"'Lo now, in very truth the ancient oracles have come
upon me. There lived here a soothsayer, a noble man and
a mighty, Telemus, son of Eurymus, who surpassed all men
in soothsaying, and waxed old as a seer among the Cyclôpes.
He told me that all these things should come to pass in the
aftertime, even that I should lose my eyesight at the hand of
Odysseus. But I ever looked for some tall and goodly man to
come hither, clad in great might, but behold now one that is a
dwarf, a man of no worth and a weakling, hath blinded me of
my eye after subduing me with wine. Nay, come hither,

Odysseus, that I may set by thee a stranger's cheer, and speed thy parting hence, that so the Earth-shaker may vouchsafe it thee, for his son am I, and he avows him for my father. And he himself will heal me, if it be his will; and none other of the blessed gods or of mortal men.'

"Even so he spake, but I answered him, and said: 'Would God that I were as sure to rob thee of soul and life, and send thee within the house of Hades, as I am that not even the Earth-shaker will heal thine eye!'

"So I spake, and then he prayed to the lord Poseidon stretching forth his hands to the starry heaven: 'Hear me, Poseidon, girdler of the earth, god of the dark hair, if indeed I be thine, and thou avowest thee my sire, — grant that he may never come to his home, even Odysseus, waster of cities, the son of Laertes, whose dwelling is in Ithaca; yet if he is ordained to see his friends and come unto his well-builded house, and his own country, late may he come in evil case, with the loss of all his company, in the ship of strangers, and find sorrows in his house.'

"So he spake in prayer, and the god of the dark locks heard him. And once again he lifted a stone, far greater than the first, and with one swing he hurled it, and he put forth a measureless strength, and cast it but a little space behind the dark-prowed ship, and all but struck the end of the rudder. And the sea heaved beneath the fall of the rock, but the wave bare on the ship and drave it to the further shore.

"But when we had now reached that island, where all our other decked ships abode together, and our company were gathered sorrowing, expecting us evermore, on our coming thither we ran our ship ashore upon the sand, and ourselves too stept forth upon the sea beach. Next we took forth the sheep of the Cyclops from out the hollow ship, and divided them, that none through me might go lacking his proper share. But the ram for me alone my goodly-greaved company chose out, in the dividing of the sheep, and on the shore I offered him up to Zeus, even to the son of Cronos, who dwells in the dark clouds, and is lord of all, and I burnt the slices of the thighs. But he heeded not the sacrifice, but was devising how my decked ships and my dear company might perish utterly. Thus for that time we sat the livelong day, until the going down of the sun, feasting on abundant flesh and sweet wine. And when the sun had sunk and darkness had come on, then we laid us to rest upon the sea beach. So soon as early Dawn shone forth, the rosy-fingered, I called to my company, and commanded them that they should themselves climb the ship and loose the hawsers. So they soon embarked and sat upon the benches, and sitting orderly smote the grey sea water with their oars.

"Thence we sailed onward stricken at heart, yet glad as men saved from death, albeit we had lost our dear companions."

BOOK X

Odysseus's entertainment by Aeolus, of whom he received a fair wind for the present, and all the rest of the winds tied up in a bag; which his men untying, flew out, and carried him back to Aeolus, who refused to receive him. His adventure at Lestrygonia with Antiphates, where of twelve ships he lost eleven, men and all. How he went thence to the Isle of Aea, where half of his men were turned by Circe into swine, and how he went himself, and by the help of Hermes recovered them and stayed with Circe a year.

"THEN we came to the isle Aeolian, where dwelt Aeolus, son of Hippotas, dear to the deathless gods, in a floating island, and all about it is a wall of bronze unbroken, and the cliff runs up sheer from the sea. His twelve children too abide there in his halls, six daughters and six lusty sons. And they feast evermore by their dear father and their kind mother, and dainties innumerable lie ready to their hands. The king entreated me kindly for a whole month, and sought out each thing, Ilios and the ships of the Argives, and the return of the Achaeans. So I told him all the tale in order duly. But when I in turn took the word and asked of my journey, and bade him send me on my way, he too denied me not, but furnished an escort. He gave me a wallet, made of the hide of an ox of nine seasons old, which he let flay, and therein he bound the ways of all the noisy winds; for him the son of Cronos made keeper of the winds, either to lull or to rouse what blasts he will. And he made it fast in the hold of the ship with a shining silver thong, that not the faintest breath might escape. Then he sent forth the blast of the West Wind to blow for me, to bear our ships and ourselves upon our way; but this he was never to bring to pass, for we were undone through our own heedlessness.

"For nine whole days we sailed by night and day continually, and now on the tenth day my native land came in sight, and already we were so near that we beheld the folk tending the beacon fires. Then over me there came sweet slumber in my weariness, for all the time I was holding the sheet, nor gave it to any of my company, that so we might come quicker to our own country. Meanwhile my company held converse together, and said that I was bringing home for myself gold and silver, gifts from Aeolus the high-hearted son of Hippotas. And thus would they speak looking each man to his neighbour:

"'Lo now, how beloved he is and highly esteemed among all men, to the city and land of whomsoever he may come. Many are the goodly treasures he taketh with him out of the spoil from Troy, while we who have fulfilled like journeying with him return homeward bringing with us but empty hands. And now Aeolus hath given unto him these things freely in his love. Nay, come, let us quickly see what they are, even what wealth of gold and silver is in the wallet.'

"So they spake, and the evil counsel of my company pre

vailed. They loosed the wallet, and all the winds brake forth.
And the violent blast seized my men, and bare them towards
the high seas weeping, away from their own country; but as
for me, I awoke and communed with my great heart, whether I
should cast myself from the ship and perish in the deep, or
endure in silence and abide yet among the living. Howbeit I
hardened my heart to endure, and muffling my head I lay still
in the ship. But the vessels were driven by the evil storm-
wind back to the isle Aeolian, and my company made moan.

"There we stepped ashore and drew water, and my company
presently took their midday meal by the swift ships. Now
when we had tasted bread and wine, I took with me a herald
and one of my company, and went to the famous dwelling of
Aeolus: and I found him feasting with his wife and children.
So we went in and sat by the pillars of the door on the threshold, and they all marvelled and asked us:

"'How hast thou come hither, Odysseus? What evil god
assailed thee? Surely we sent thee on thy way with all diligence, that thou mightest get thee to thine own country and
thy home, and whithersoever thou wouldest.'

"Even so they said, but I spake among them heavy at heart:
'My evil company hath been my bane, and sleep thereto remorse-
less. Come, my friends, do ye heal the harm, for yours is the
power.'

"So I spake, beseeching them in soft words, but they held
their peace. And the father answered, saying: 'Get thee
forth from the island straightway, thou that art the most
reprobate of living men. Far be it from me to help or to
further that man whom the blessed gods abhor! Get thee
forth, for lo, thy coming marks thee hated by the deathless
gods.'

"Therewith he sent me forth from the house making heavy
moan. Thence we sailed onwards stricken at heart. And the
spirit of the men was spent beneath the grievous rowing by

reason of our vain endeavour, for there was no more any sign of a wafting wind. So for the space of six days we sailed by night and day continually, and on the seventh we came to the steep stronghold of Lamos, Telepylos of the Laestrygons, where herdsman hails herdsman as he drives in his flock, and the other who drives forth answers the call. There might a sleepless man have earned a double wage, the one as neat-herd,[1] the other shepherding white flocks: so near are the outgoings of the night and of the day. Thither when we had come to the fair haven, whereabout on both sides goes one steep cliff unbroken, and jutting headlands over against each other stretch forth at the mouth of the harbour, and strait is the entrance; thereinto all the others steered their curved ships. Now the vessels were bound within the hollow harbour each hard by other, for no wave ever swelled within it, great or small, but there was a bright calm all around. But I alone moored my dark ship without the harbour, at the uttermost point thereof, and made fast the hawser to a rock. And I went up a craggy hill, a place of out-look, and stood thereon: thence there was no sign of the labour of men or oxen, only we saw the smoke curling upward from the land. Then I sent forth certain of my company to go and search out what manner of men they were who here live upon the earth by bread, choosing out two of my company and sending a third with them as herald. Now when they had gone ashore, they went along a level road whereby wains were wont to draw down wood from the high hills to the town. And without the town they fell in with a damsel drawing water, the noble daughter of Laestrygonian Antiphates. She had come down to the clear-flowing spring Artacia, for thence it was custom to draw water to the town. So they stood by her and spake unto her, and asked who was king of that land, and who they were he ruled over. Then at once she showed

---

[1] [Cattle-herd.]

them the high-roofed hall of her father. Now when they had entered the renowned house, they found his wife therein: she was huge of bulk as a mountain peak and was loathly in their sight. Straightway she called the renowned Antiphates, her lord, from the assembly-place, and he contrived a pitiful destruction for my men. Forthwith he clutched up one of my company and made ready his mid-day meal, but the other twain sprang up and came in flight to the ships. Then he raised the war cry through the town, and the valiant Laestrygons at the sound thereof flocked together from every side, a host past number, not like men but like the Giants. They cast at us from the cliffs with great rocks, each of them a man's burden, and anon there arose from the fleet an evil din of men dying and ships shattered withal. And like folk spearing fishes they bare home their hideous meal. While as yet they were slaying my friends within the deep harbour, I drew my sharp sword from my thigh, and with it cut the hawsers of my dark-prowed ship. Quickly then I called to my company, and bade them dash in with the oars, that we might clean escape this evil plight. And all with one accord they tossed the sea water with the oar-blade, in dread of death, and to my delight my barque flew forth to the high seas away from the beetling rocks, but those other ships were lost there, one and all.

"Thence we sailed onward stricken at heart, yet glad as men saved from death, albeit we had lost our dear companions. And we came to the isle Aeaean, where dwelt Circe of the braided tresses, an awful goddess of mortal speech, own sister to the wizard Aeetes. Both were begotten of Helios,[1] who gives light to all men, and their mother was Perse, daughter of Oceanus. There on the shore we put in with our ship into the sheltering haven silently, and some god was our guide. Then we stept ashore, and for two days and two nights

[1] [The sun.]

lay there, consuming our own hearts for weariness and pain. But when now the fair-tressed Dawn had brought the full light of the third day, then did I seize my spear and my sharp sword, and quickly departing from the ship I went up unto a place of wide prospect, if haply I might see any sign of the labour of men and hear the sound of their speech. So I went up a craggy hill, a place of out-look, and I saw the smoke rising from the broadwayed earth in the halls of Circe, through the thick coppice and the woodland. Then I mused in my mind and heart whether I should go and make discovery, for that I had seen the smoke and flame. And as I thought thereon this seemed to me the better counsel, to go first to the swift ship and to the sea-banks, and give my company their mid-day meal, and then send them to make search. But as I came and drew nigh to the curved ship, some god even then took pity on me in my loneliness, and sent a tall antlered stag across my very path. He was coming down from his pasture in the woodland to the river to drink, for verily the might of the sun was sore upon him. And as he came up from out of the stream, I smote him on the spine in the middle of the back, and the brazen shaft went clean through him, and with a moan he fell in the dust, and his life passed from him. Then I set my foot on him and drew forth the brazen shaft from the wound, and laid it hard by upon the ground and let it lie. Next I broke withies and willow twigs, and wove me a rope a fathom in length, well twisted from end to end, and bound together the feet of the huge beast, and went to the black ship bearing him across my neck, and leaning on a spear, for it was in no wise possible to carry him on my shoulder with the one hand, for he was a mighty quarry. And I threw him down before the ship and roused my company with soft words, standing by each man in turn:

"'Friends, for all our sorrows we shall not yet a while go down to the house of Hades, ere the coming of the day of destiny; go to then, while as yet there is meat and drink in the swift ship, let us take thought thereof, that we be not famished for hunger.'

" Even so I spake, and they speedily hearkened to my words. They unmuffled their heads, and there on the shore of the unharvested sea gazed at the stag, for he was a mighty quarry. But after they had delighted their eyes with the sight of him, they washed their hands and got ready the glorious feast. So for that time we sat the livelong day till the going down of the sun, feasting on abundant flesh and sweet wine. But when the sun sank and darkness had come on, then we laid us to rest upon the sea beach. So soon as early Dawn shone forth, the rosy-fingered, I called a gathering of my men and spake in the ears of them all:

"'Hear my words, my fellows, despite your evil case. My friends, lo, now we know not where is the place of darkness or of dawning, nor where the Sun, that gives light to men, goes beneath the earth, nor where he rises; therefore let us advise us speedily if any counsel yet may be: as for me, I deem there is none. For I went up a craggy hill, a place of out-look, and saw the island crowned about with the circle of the endless sea, the isle itself lying low; and in the midst thereof mine eyes beheld the smoke through the thick coppice and the woodland.'

"Even so I spake, but their spirit within them was broken, as they remembered the deeds of Antiphates the Laestrygonian, and all the evil violence of the haughty Cyclops, the man-eater. So they wept aloud shedding big tears. Howbeit no avail came of their weeping.

"Then I numbered my goodly-greaved company in two bands, and appointed a leader for each, and I myself took the command of the one part, and godlike Eurylochus of the other. And anon we shook the lots in a brazen-fitted helmet, and out leapt the lot of proud Eurylochus. So he went on his way, and with him two and twenty of my fellowship all weeping;

and we were left behind making lament. In the forest glades they found the halls of Circe builded, of polished stone, in a place with wide prospect. And all around the palace mountain-bred wolves and lions were roaming, whom she herself had bewitched with evil drugs that she gave them. Yet the beasts did not set on my men, but lo, they ramped about them and fawned on them, wagging their long tails. And as when dogs fawn about their lord when he comes from the feast, for he always brings them the fragments that soothe their mood, even so the strong-clawed wolves and the lions fawned around them; but they were affrighted when they saw the strange and terrible creatures. So they stood at the outer gate of the fair-tressed goddess, and within they heard Circe singing in a sweet voice, as she fared to and fro before the great web imperishable, such as is the handiwork of goddesses, fine of woof and full of grace and splendour. Then Polites, a leader of men, the dearest to me and the trustiest of all my company, first spake to them:

"'Friends, forasmuch as there is one within that fares to and fro before a mighty web singing a sweet song, so that all the floor of the hall makes echo, a goddess she is or a woman; come quickly and cry aloud to her.'

"He spake the word and they cried aloud and called to her. And straightway she came forth and opened the shining doors and bade them in, and all went with her in their heedlessness. But Eurylochus tarried behind, for he guessed that there was some treason. So she led them in and set them upon chairs and high seats, and made them a mess of cheese and barley-meal and yellow honey with Pramnian wine, and mixed harmful drugs with the food to make them utterly forget their own country. Now when she had given them the cup and they had drunk it off, presently she smote them with a wand, and in the styes of the swine she penned them. So they had the head and voice, the bristles and the shape of swine, but their mind abode even as of old. Thus were they penned there weeping, and Circe flung them acorns and mast and fruit of the cornel tree to eat, whereon wallowing swine do always batten.

"Now Eurylochus came back to the swift black ship to bring tidings of his fellows, and of their unseemly doom. Not a word could he utter, for all his desire, so deeply smitten was he to the heart with grief, and his eyes were filled with tears and his soul was fain of lamentation. But when we all had pressed him with our questions in amazement, even then he told the fate of the remnant of our company.

"Then I cast about my shoulder my silver-studded sword, a great blade of bronze, and slung my bow about me and bade him lead me again by the way that he came. But he caught me with both hands, and by my knees he besought me, and bewailing him spake to me winged words:

"'Lead me not thither against my will, oh fosterling of Zeus, but leave me here! For well I know thou shalt thyself return no more, nor bring any one of all thy fellowship; nay, let us flee the swifter with those that be here, for even yet may we escape the evil day.'

"On this wise he spake, but I answered him, saying: 'Eurylochus, abide for thy part here in this place, eating and drinking by the black hollow ship: but I will go forth, for a strong constraint is laid on me.'

"With that I went up from the ship and the sea shore. But lo, when in my faring through the sacred glades I was now drawing near to the great hall of the enchantress Circe, then did Hermes, of the golden wand, meet me as I approached the house, in the likeness of a young man with the first down on his lip, the time when youth is most gracious. So he clasped my hand and spake and hailed me:

"'Ah, hapless man, whither away again, all alone through the wolds, thou that knowest not this country? And thy company yonder in the hall of Circe are penned in the guise of swine, in their deep lairs abiding. Is it in hope to free them that thou art come hither? Nay, methinks, thou thyself shalt never return but remain there with the others. Come, then, I will redeem thee from thy distress, and bring deliverance. Lo, take this herb of virtue, and go to the dwelling of Circe, that it may keep from thy head the evil day. And I will tell thee all the magic sleight of Circe. She will mix thee a potion and cast drugs into the mess; but not even so shall she be able to enchant thee; so helpful is this charmed herb that I shall give thee, and I will tell thee all. When it shall be that Circe smites thee with her long wand, even then draw thou thy sharp sword from thy thigh, and spring on her, as one eager to slay her. And she will shrink away. But command her to swear a mighty oath by the blessed gods, that she will plan nought else of mischief to thine own hurt.'

"Therewith the slayer of Argos gave me the plant that he had plucked from the ground, and he showed me the growth thereof. It was black at the root, but the flower was like to milk. Moly the gods call it, but it is hard for mortal men to dig; howbeit with the gods all things are possible.

"Then Hermes departed toward high Olympus, up through the woodland isle, but as for me I held on my way to the house of Circe, and my heart was darkly troubled as I went. So I halted in the portals of the fair-tressed goddess; there I stood and called aloud and the goddess heard my voice, who presently came forth and opened the shining doors and bade me in, and I went with her heavy at heart. So she led me in and set me on a chair with studs of silver, a goodly carven chair, and beneath was a footstool for the feet. And she made me a potion in a golden cup, that I might drink, and she also put a charm therein, in the evil counsel of her heart. Now when she had given it and I had drunk it off and was not bewitched, she smote me with her wand and spake and hailed me:

"'Go thy way now to the stye, couch thee there with the rest of thy company.'

"So spake she, but I drew my sharp sword from my thigh and sprang upon Circe, as one eager to slay her. But with a great cry she slipped under, and clasped my knees, and bewailing herself spake to me winged words:

"'Who art thou of the sons of men, and whence? Where is thy city? Where are they that begat thee? I marvel to see how thou hast drunk of this charm, and wast nowise subdued. Nay, for there lives no man else that is proof against this charm, whoso hath drunk thereof, and once it hath passed his lips. But thou hast, methinks, a mind within thee that may not be enchanted. Verily thou art Odysseus, ready at need, whom he of the golden wand, the slayer of Argos, full often told me was to come hither, on his way from Troy with his swift black ship. Nay, come, put thy sword into the sheath, that we may trust each the other.'

"So spake she, but I answered her, saying: 'Nay, Circe, how canst thou bid me be gentle to thee, who hast turned my company into swine within thy halls, except thou wilt deign, goddess, to swear a mighty oath, that thou wilt plan nought else of mischief to mine own hurt.'

"So I spake, and she straightway swore the oath not to harm me, as I bade her.

"Now all this while her handmaids busied them in the halls, four maidens that are her serving women in the house. They are born of the wells and of the woods and of the holy rivers, that flow forward into the salt sea. Of these one cast upon the chairs goodly coverlets of purple above, and spread a linen cloth thereunder. And lo, another drew up silver tables to the chairs, and thereon set for them golden baskets. And a third mixed sweet honey-hearted wine in a silver bowl, and set out cups of gold. And a fourth bare water, and kindled a great fire beneath the mighty cauldron. So the water waxed warm; but when it boiled in the bright brazen vessel, she set me in a bath and bathed me with water from out a great cauldron, pouring it over head and shoulders, when she had mixed it to a pleasant warmth, till from my limbs she took away the consuming weariness. Now after she had bathed me and anointed me well with olive oil, and cast about me a fair mantle and a doublet, she led me into the halls and set me on a chair with studs of silver, a goodly carven chair, and beneath was a footstool for the feet. And a handmaid bare water for the hands in a goodly golden ewer, and poured it forth over a silver basin to wash withal; and to my side she drew a polished table, and a grave dame bare wheaten bread and set it by me, and laid on the board many dainties, giving freely of such things as she had by her. And she bade me eat, but my soul found no pleasure therein. I sat with other thoughts, and my heart had a boding of ill.

"Now when Circe saw that I sat thus, and that I put not forth my hands to the meat, and that I was mightily afflicted, she drew near to me and spake to me winged words:

"'Wherefore thus, Odysseus, dost thou sit there like a speechless man, consuming thine own soul, and dost not touch meat nor drink? Dost thou indeed deem there is some further guile? Nay, thou hast no cause to fear, for already I have sworn thee a strong oath not to harm thee.'

"So spake she, but I answered her, saying: 'Oh, Circe, what righteous man would have the heart to taste meat and drink ere he had redeemed his company, and beheld them face to face? But if in good faith thou biddest me eat and drink, then let them go free, that mine eyes may behold my dear companions.'

"So I spake, and Circe passed out through the hall with the wand in her hand, and opened the doors of the stye, and drave them forth in the shape of swine of nine seasons old. There they stood before her, and she went through their midst, and anointed each one of them with another charm. And lo, from their limbs the bristles dropped away, wherewith the venom had erewhile clothed them, that lady Circe gave them. And they became men again, younger than before they were, and goodlier far, and taller to behold. And they all knew me again and each one took my hands, and wistful was the lament that sank into their souls, and the roof around rang wondrously. And even the goddess herself was moved with compassion.

"Then standing nigh me the fair goddess spake unto me: 'Son of Laertes, of the seed of Zeus, Odysseus of many devices, depart now to thy swift ship and the sea-banks. And first of all, draw ye up the ship ashore, and bestow the goods in the caves and all the gear. And thyself return again, and bring with thee thy dear companions.'

"So spake she, and my lordly spirit consented thereto. So I went on my way to the swift ship and the sea-banks, and there I found my dear company on the swift ship lamenting piteously, shedding big tears. And as when calves of the homestead gather round the droves of kine that have returned to the yard, when they have had their fill of pasture, and all with one accord frisk before them, and the folds may no more contain them, but with a ceaseless lowing they skip about their dams, so flocked they all about me weeping, when their eyes beheld me. Yea, and to their spirit it was as though they had got to their dear country, and the very city of rugged Ithaca where they were born and reared.

"Meanwhile Circe bathed the rest of my company in her halls with all care, and anointed them well with olive oil; and cast thick mantles and doublets about them. And we found them all feasting nobly in the halls. And when they saw and knew each other face to face, they wept and mourned, and the house rang around. Then she stood near me, that fair goddess, and spake, saying:

"'Son of Laertes, of the seed of Zeus, Odysseus of many devices, no more now wake this plenteous weeping: myself I know of all the pains ye endured upon the teeming deep, and the great despite done you by unkindly men upon the land. Nay, come, eat ye meat and drink wine, till your spirit shall return to you again, as it was when first ye left your own country of rugged Ithaca, but now are ye wasted and wanting heart, mindful evermore of your sore wandering, nor has your heart ever been merry, for very grievous hath been your trial.'

"So spake she, and our lordly spirit consented thereto. So there we sat day by day for the full circle of a year, feasting on abundant flesh and sweet wine. But when now a year had gone, and the seasons returned as the months waned, and the long days came in their course, then did my dear company call me forth, and say:

"'Good sir, now is it high time to mind thee of thy native land, if it is ordained that thou shalt be saved, and come to thy lofty house and thine own country.'

"So spake they and my lordly spirit consented thereto. So for that time we sat the livelong day till the going down of the sun, feasting on abundant flesh and sweet wine. But when the sun sank and darkness came on, they laid them to rest throughout the shadowy halls.

"Then I besought Circe by her knees, and the goddess heard my speech, and uttering my voice I spake to her winged words: 'Circe, fulfil for me the promise which thou madest me to send me on my homeward way. Now is my spirit eager to be gone, and the spirit of my company, that wear away my heart as they mourn around me, when haply thou art gone from us.'

"So spake I, and the fair goddess answered me anon: 'Son of Laertes, of the seed of Zeus, Odysseus of many devices, tarry ye now no longer in my house against your will; but first must ye perform another journey, and reach the dwelling of Hades and of dread Persephone[1] to seek the spirit of

[1] [Goddess of the lower world.]

Theban Teiresias, the blind soothsayer, whose wits abide steadfast. To him Persephone hath given judgment, even in death, that he alone should have understanding; but the other souls sweep shadow-like around.'

"Thus spake she, but as for me, my heart was broken, and my soul had no more care to live and to see the sunlight. But when I had my fill of weeping and grovelling, then at the last I answered and spake unto her saying: 'And who, Circe, will guide us on this way? for no man ever yet sailed to hell in a black ship.'

"So spake I, and the fair goddess answered me anon: 'Son of Laertes, of the seed of Zeus, Odysseus of many devices, nay, trouble not thyself for want of a guide, by thy ship abiding, but set up the mast and spread abroad the white sails and sit thee down; and the breeze of the North Wind will bear thy vessel on her way. But when thou hast now sailed in thy ship across the stream Oceanus, where is a waste shore and the groves of Persephone, even tall poplar trees and willows that shed their fruit before the season, there beach thy ship by deep eddying Oceanus, but go thyself to the dank house of Hades. So, hero, draw nigh thereto, as I command thee, and dig a trench as it were a cubit in length and breadth, and about it pour a drink-offering to all the dead, first with mead and thereafter with sweet wine, and for the third time with water, and sprinkle white meal thereon; and entreat with many prayers the strengthless heads of the dead, and promise that on thy return to Ithaca thou wilt offer in thy halls a barren heifer, the best thou hast, and wilt fill the pyre with treasure, and wilt sacrifice apart, to Teiresias alone, a black ram without spot, the fairest of your flock. But when thou hast with prayers made supplication to the lordly races of the dead, then offer up a ram and a black ewe, bending their heads towards Erebus and thyself turn thy back, with thy face set for the shore of the river. Then will many spirits come to thee of the dead that be departed. Thereafter thou shalt call to thy company and command them to flay the sheep which even now lie slain by the pitiless sword, and to consume them with fire, and to make prayer to the gods, to mighty Hades and to dread Persephone. And thyself draw the sharp sword from thy thigh and sit there, suffering not the strengthless heads of the dead to draw nigh to the blood, ere thou hast word of Teiresias. Then the seer will come to thee quickly, leader of the people; he will surely declare to thee the way and the measure of thy path, and as touching thy returning, how thou mayst go over the teeming deep.'

"So spake she, and anon came the golden-throned Dawn. Then she put on me a mantle and a doublet for raiment, and the nymph clad herself in a great shining robe, light of woof and gracious, and about her waist she cast a fair golden girdle, and put a veil upon her head. But I passed through the halls and roused my men with smooth words, standing by each one in turn:

"'Sleep ye now no more nor breathe sweet slumber; but let us go on our way, for surely she hath shown me all, the lady Circe.'

"So spake I, and their lordly soul consented thereto. Yet even thence I led not my company safe away. There was one, Elpenor, the youngest of us all, not very valiant in war neither steadfast in mind. He was lying apart from the rest of my men on the housetop of Circe's sacred dwelling, very fain of the cool air, as one heavy with wine. Now when he heard the noise of the voices and of the feet of my fellows as they moved to and fro, he leaped up of a sudden and minded him not to descend again by the way of the tall ladder, but fell right down from the roof, and his neck was broken from the bones of the spine, and his spirit went down to the house of Hades.

"Then I spake among my men as they went on their

ODYSSEUS TERRIFIED BY THE GHOSTS

way, saying: 'Ye deem now, I see, that ye are going to your own dear country; but Circe hath showed us another way, even to the dwelling of Hades and of dread Persephone, to seek to the spirit of Theban Teiresias.'

"Even so I spake, but their heart within them was broken, and they sat them down even where they were, and made lament and tore their hair. Howbeit no help came of their weeping.

"But as we were now wending sorrowful to the swift ship and the sea-banks, shedding big tears, Circe meanwhile had gone her ways and made fast a ram and a black ewe by the dark ship, lightly passing us by: who may behold a god against his will, whether going to or fro?"

BOOK XI

Odysseus descends into hell and discourses with the ghosts of the deceased heroes.

"Now when we had gone down to the ship and to the sea, first of all we drew the ship unto the fair salt water, and placed the mast and sails in the black ship, and took those sheep and put them therein, and ourselves too climbed on board, sorrowing, and shedding big tears. And in the wake of our dark-prowed ship she sent a favouring wind that filled the sails, a kindly escort,—even Circe of the braided tresses, a dread goddess of human speech. And we set in order all the gear throughout the ship and sat us down; and the wind and the helmsman guided our barque. And all day long her sails were stretched in her seafaring; and the sun sank and all the ways were darkened.

"She came to the limits of the world, to the deep-flowing

Oceanus. There is the land and the city of the Cimmerians, shrouded in mist and cloud, and never does the shining sun look down on them with his rays, neither when he climbs up the starry heavens, nor when again he turns earthward from the firmament, but deadly night is outspread over miserable mortals. Thither we came and ran the ship ashore and took out the sheep; but for our part we held on our way along the stream of Oceanus, till we came to the place which Circe had declared to us.

"There Perimedes and Eurylochus held the victims, but I drew my sharp sword from my thigh, and dug a pit, as it were a cubit in length and breadth, and about it poured a drink-offering to all the dead, first with mead and thereafter with sweet wine, and for the third time with water. And I sprinkled white meal thereon, and entreated with many prayers the strengthless heads of the dead, and promised that on my return to Ithaca I would offer in my halls a barren heifer, the best I had, and fill the pyre with treasure, and apart unto Teiresias alone sacrifice a black ram without spot, the fairest of my flock. But when I had besought the tribes of the dead with vows and prayers, I took the sheep and cut their throats over the trench, and the dark blood flowed forth, and lo, the spirits of the dead that be departed gathered them from out of Erebus. Brides and youths unwed, and old men of many and evil days, and tender maidens with grief yet fresh at heart; and many there were, wounded with bronze-shod spears, men slain in fight with their bloody mail about them. And these many ghosts flocked together from every side about the trench with a wondrous cry, and pale fear gat hold on me. Then did I speak to my company and command them to flay the sheep that lay slain by the pitiless sword, and to consume them with fire, and to make prayer to the gods, to mighty Hades and to dread Persephone, and myself I drew the sharp sword from my thigh and sat there, suffering not the strengthless heads of the dead to draw nigh to the blood, ere I had word of Teiresias.

"And first came the soul of Elpenor, my companion, that had not yet been buried beneath the wide-wayed earth; for we left the corpse behind us in the hall of Circe, unwept and unburied, seeing that another task was instant on us. At the sight of him I wept and had compassion on him, and uttering my voice spake to him winged words: 'Elpenor, how hast thou come beneath the darkness and the shadow? Thou hast come fleeter on foot than I in my black ship.'

"So spake I, and with a moan he answered me, saying: 'Son of Laertes, of the seed of Zeus, Odysseus of many devices, an evil doom of some god was my bane and wine out of measure. When I laid me down on the housetop of Circe I minded me not to descend again by the way of the tall ladder, but fell right down from the roof, and my neck was broken off from the bones of the spine, and my spirit went down to the house of Hades. And now I pray thee in the name of those whom we left, who are no more with us, thy wife, and thy sire who cherished thee when as yet thou wert a little one, and Telemachus, whom thou didst leave in thy halls alone; forasmuch as I know that on thy way hence from out the dwelling of Hades, thou wilt stay thy well-wrought ship at the isle Aeaean, even then, my lord, I charge thee to think on me. Leave me not unwept and unburied as thou goest hence, nor turn thy back upon me, lest haply I bring on thee the anger of the gods. Nay, burn me there with mine armour, all that is mine, and pile me a barrow on the shore of the grey sea, the grave of a luckless man, that even men unborn may hear my story. Fulfil me this and plant upon the barrow mine oar, wherewith I rowed in the days of my life, while yet I was among my fellows.'

"Even so he spake, and I answered him, saying: 'All this, luckless man, will I perform for thee and do.'

"Even so we twain were sitting holding sad discourse, I on the one side, stretching forth my sword over the blood, while on the other side the ghost of my friend told all his tale.

"Anon came up the soul of my mother dead, Anticleia, the daughter of Autolycus the great-hearted, whom I left alive when I departed from sacred Ilios. At the sight of her I wept, and was moved with compassion, yet even so, for all my sore grief, I suffered her not to draw nigh to the blood, ere I had word of Teiresias.

"Anon came the soul of Theban Teiresias, with a golden sceptre in his hand, and he knew me and spake unto me: 'Son of Laertes, of the seed of Zeus, Odysseus of many devices, what seekest thou *now*, wretched man, wherefore hast thou left the sunlight and come hither to behold the dead and a land desolate of joy? Nay, hold off from the ditch and draw back thy sharp sword, that I may drink of the blood and tell thee sooth.'[1]

"So spake he and I put up my silver-studded sword into the sheath, and when he had drunk the dark blood, even then did the noble seer speak unto me, saying: 'Thou art asking of thy sweet returning, great Odysseus, but that will the god make hard for thee; for methinks thou shalt not pass unheeded by the Shaker of the Earth, who hath laid up wrath in his heart against thee, for rage at the blinding of his dear son. Yet even so, through many troubles, ye may come home, if thou wilt restrain thy spirit and the spirit of thy men so soon as thou shalt bring thy well-wrought ship nigh to the isle Thrinacia, fleeing the sea of violet blue, when ye find the herds of Helios grazing and his brave flocks, of Helios who overseeth all and overheareth all things. If thou doest these no hurt, being heedful of thy return, so may ye yet reach Ithaca, albeit in evil case. But if thou hurtest them, I foreshow ruin for thy ship and for thy men, and even though thou shalt thyself escape,

---

[1] [True prophecy.]

late shalt thou return in evil plight, with the loss of all thy company, on board the ship of strangers, and thou shalt find sorrows in thy house, even proud men that devour thy living, while they woo thy godlike wife and offer the gifts of wooing. Yet I tell thee, on thy coming thou shalt avenge their violence. But when thou hast slain the wooers in thy halls, whether by guile, or openly with the edge of the sword, thereafter go thy way, taking with thee a shapen oar, till thou shalt come to such men as know not the sea, neither eat meat savoured with salt; yea, nor have they knowledge of ships of purple cheek, nor shapen oars which serve for wings to ships. And I will give thee a most manifest token, which cannot escape thee. In the day when another wayfarer shall meet thee and say that thou hast a winnowing fan on thy stout shoulder, even then make fast thy shapen oar in the earth and do goodly sacrifice to the lord Poseidon, even with a ram and a bull and a boar, the mate of swine, and depart for home and offer holy hecatombs to the deathless gods that keep the wide heaven, to each in order due. And from the sea shall thine own death come, the gentlest death that may be, which shall end thee foredone with smooth old age, and the folk shall dwell happily around thee. This that I say is sooth.'

"So spake he, and I answered him, saying: 'Teiresias, all these threads, methinks, the gods themselves have spun. But come, declare me this and plainly tell me all. I see here the spirit of my mother dead; lo, she sits in silence near the blood, nor deigns to look her son in the face nor speak to him! Tell me, prince, how may she know me again that I am he?'

"So spake I, and anon he answered me, and said: 'I will tell thee an easy saying, and will put it in thy heart. Whomsoever of the dead that be departed thou shalt suffer to draw nigh to the blood, he shall tell thee sooth; but if thou shalt grudge any, that one shall go to his own place again.' Therewith the spirit of the prince Teiresias went back within the house of

Hades, when he had told all his oracles. But I abode there steadfastly, till my mother drew nigh and drank the dark blood; and at once she knew me, and bewailing herself spake to me winged words:

"'Dear child, how didst thou come beneath the darkness and the shadow, thou that art a living man? Grievous is the sight of these things to the living, for between us and you are great rivers and dreadful streams; first, Oceanus, which can nowise be crossed on foot, but only if one have a well-wrought ship. Art thou but now come hither with thy ship and thy company in thy long wanderings from Troy? and hast thou not yet reached Ithaca, nor seen thy wife in thy halls?'

"Even so she spake, and I answered her, and said: 'O my mother, necessity was on me to come down to the house of Hades to seek the spirit of Theban Teiresias. For not yet have I drawn near to the Achaean shore, nor yet have I set foot on mine own country, but have been wandering evermore in affliction, from the day that first I went with goodly Agamemnon to Ilios of the fair steeds, to do battle with the Trojans. But come, declare me this and plainly tell it all. What doom overcame thee of death that lays men at their length? Was it a slow disease, or did Artemis the archer slay thee with the visitation of her gentle shafts? And tell me of my father and my son, that I left behind me; doth my honour yet abide with them, or hath another already taken it, while they say that I shall come home no more? And tell me of my wedded wife, of her counsel and her purpose, doth she abide with her son and keep all secure, or hath she already wedded the best of the Achaeans?'

"Even so I spake, and anon my lady mother answered me: 'Yea, verily, she abideth with steadfast spirit in thy halls; and wearily for her the nights wane always and the days in shedding of tears. But the fair honour that is thine no man hath yet taken; but Telemachus sits at peace on his demesne, and feasts at equal banquets, whereof it is meet that a judge partake, for all men bid him to their house. And thy father abides there in the field, and goes not down to the town, nor lies he on bedding or rugs or shining blankets, but all the winter he sleeps, where sleep the thralls in the house, in the ashes by the fire, and is clad in sorry raiment. But when the summer comes and the rich harvest-tide, his beds of fallen leaves are strewn lowly all about the knoll of his vineyard plot. There he lies sorrowing and nurses his mighty grief, for long desire of thy return, and old age withal comes heavy upon him. Yea and even so did I too perish and meet my doom. It was not the archer goddess of the keen sight, who slew me in my halls with the visitation of her gentle shafts, nor did any sickness come upon me, such as chiefly with a sad wasting draws the spirit from the limbs; nay, it was my sore longing for thee, and for thy counsels, great Odysseus, and for thy loving-kindness, that reft me of sweet life.'

"So spake she, and I mused in my heart and would fain have embraced the spirit of my mother dead. Thrice I sprang towards her, and was minded to embrace her; thrice she flitted from my hands as a shadow or even as a dream, and grief waxed ever the sharper at my heart. And uttering my voice I spake to her winged words:

"'Mother mine, wherefore dost thou not abide me who am eager to clasp thee, that even in Hades we twain may cast our arms each about the other, and have our fill of chill lament? Is this but a phantom that the high goddess Persephone hath sent me, to the end that I may groan for more exceeding sorrow?'

"So spake I, and my lady mother answered me anon: 'Ah me, my child, of all men most ill-fated, Persephone, the daughter of Zeus, doth in no wise deceive thee, but even on this wise it is with mortals when they die. For the sinews no more bind together the flesh and the bones, but the great force of burning fire abolishes these, so soon as the life hath left the white bones, and the spirit like a dream flies forth and hovers near. But haste with all thine heart toward the sunlight, and mark all this, that even hereafter thou mayest tell it to thy wife.'

"Straightway then I went to the ship, and bade my men mount the vessel, and loose the hawsers. So speedily they went on board, and sat upon the benches. And the wave of the flood bore the barque down the stream of Oceanus, we rowing first, and afterwards the fair wind was our convoy."

BOOK XII

Odysseus's passage by the Sirens, and by Scylla and Charybdis. The sacrilege committed by his men in the isle Thrinacia. The destruction of his ships and men. How he swam on a plank nine days together, and came to Ogygia, where he stayed seven years with Calypso.

"Now after the ship had left the stream of the river Oceanus, and was come to the wave of the wide sea, and the isle Aeaean, where is the dwelling place of early Dawn and her dancing grounds, and the land of sunrising, upon our coming thither we beached the ship in the sand, and ourselves too stept ashore on the sea beach. There we fell on sound sleep and awaited the bright Dawn.

"So soon as early Dawn shone forth, the rosy-fingered, I sent forth my fellows to the house of Circe to fetch the body of the dead Elpenor. And speedily we cut billets of wood and sadly we buried him, where the furthest headland runs out into the sea, shedding big tears. But when the dead man was burned and the arms of the dead, we piled a barrow and dragged up thereon a pillar, and on the topmost mound we set the shapen oar.

"Now all that task we finished, and our coming from out of

Hades was not unknown to Circe, but she arrayed herself and speedily drew nigh, and her handmaids with her bare flesh and bread in plenty and dark red wine. And the fair goddess stood in the midst and spake in our ears, saying:

"'Men overbold, who have gone alive into the house of Hades, to know death twice, while all men else die once for all. Nay, come, eat ye meat and drink wine here all day long; and with the breaking of the day ye shall set sail, and myself I will show you the path and declare each thing, that ye may not suffer pain or hurt through any grievous ill-contrivance by sea or on the land.'

"So spake she, and our lordly souls consented thereto. Thus for that time we sat the livelong day, until the going down of the sun, feasting on abundant flesh and on sweet wine. Now when the sun sank and darkness came on, my company laid them to rest by the hawsers of the ship. Then she took me by the hand and led me apart from my dear company, and made me to sit down and laid herself at my feet, and asked all my tale. And I told her all in order duly. Then at the last the lady Circe spake unto me, saying:

"'Even so, now all these things have an end; do thou then hearken even as I tell thee, and the god himself shall bring it back to thy mind. To the Sirens first shalt thou come, who bewitch all men, whosoever shall come to them. Whoso draws nigh them unwittingly and hears the sound of the Sirens' voice, never doth he see wife or babes stand by him on his return, nor have they joy at his coming; but the Sirens enchant him with their clear song, sitting in the meadow, and all about is a great heap of bones of men, corrupt in death, and round the bones the skin is wasting. But do thou drive thy ship past, and knead honey-sweet wax, and anoint therewith the ears of thy company, lest any of the rest hear the song; but if thou thyself art minded to hear, let them bind thee in the swift ship hand and foot, upright in the mast-stead, and from the mast let rope-ends be tied, that with delight thou mayest hear the voice of the Sirens. And if thou shalt beseech thy company and bid them to loose thee, then let them bind thee with yet more bonds. But when thy friends have driven thy ship past these, I will not tell thee fully which path shall thenceforth be thine, but do thou thyself consider it, and I will speak to thee of either way. On the one side there are beetling rocks, and against them the great wave roars of dark-eyed Amphitrite. These, ye must know, are they the blessed gods call the Rocks Wandering. By this way even winged things may never pass, nay, not even the cowering doves that bear ambrosia to Father Zeus, but the sheer rock evermore takes away one even of these, and the Father sends in another to make up the tale. Thereby no ship of men ever escapes that comes thither, but the planks of ships and the bodies of men confusedly are tossed by the waves of the sea and the storms of ruinous fire.

" 'On the other part are two rocks, whereof the one reaches with sharp peak to the wide heaven, and a dark cloud encompasses it; this never streams away, and there is no clear air about the peak neither in summer nor in harvest tide. No mortal man may scale it or set foot thereon, not though he had twenty hands and feet. For the rock is smooth and sheer, as it were polished. And in the midst of the cliff is a dim cave turned to Erebus, towards the place of darkness, whereby ye shall even steer your hollow ship, noble Odysseus. Not with an arrow from a bow might a man in his strength reach from his hollow ship into that deep cave. And therein dwelleth Scylla, yelping terribly. Her voice indeed is no greater than the voice of a new-born whelp, but a dreadful monster is she, nor would any look on her gladly, not if it were a god that met her. Verily she hath twelve feet all dangling down, and six necks exceeding long, and on each a hideous head, and therein three rows of teeth set thick and close, full of black death. Up to her middle is she sunk far down in the hollow cave, but forth she holds her heads from the dreadful gulf, and there she fishes, swooping round the rock, for dolphins or sea-dogs, or whatso greater beast she may anywhere take, whereof the deep-voiced Amphitrite feeds countless flocks. Thereby no sailors boast that they have fled scatheless ever with their ship, for with each head she carries off a man, whom she hath snatched from out the dark-prowed ship.

"'But that other cliff, Odysseus, thou shalt note, lying lower, hard by the first: thou couldest send an arrow across. And thereon is a great fig-tree growing, in fullest leaf, and beneath it mighty Charybdis sucks down black water, for thrice a day she spouts it forth, and thrice a day she sucks it down in terrible wise. Never mayest thou be there when she sucks the water, for none might save thee then from thy bane, not even the Earth-shaker! But take heed and swiftly drawing nigh to Scylla's rock drive the ship past, since of a truth it is far better to mourn six of thy company in the ship, than all in the self-same hour.'

"So spake she, but I answered, and said unto her: 'Come, I pray thee, goddess, tell me true, if there be any means whereby I might escape from the deadly Charybdis and avenge me on that other, when she would prey upon my company.'

"So spake I, and that fair goddess answered me: 'Man overbold, lo, now again the deeds of war are in thy mind and the travail thereof. Wilt thou not yield thee even to the deathless gods? As for her, she is no mortal, but an immortal plague, dread, grievous, and fierce, and not to be fought with; and against her there is no defence; flight is the bravest way. For if thou tarry to do on thine armour by the cliff, I fear lest once again she sally forth and catch at thee with so many heads, and seize as many men as before. So drive past with all thy force, and call on Cratais, mother of Scylla, which bore her for a bane to mortals. And she will then let her from darting forth thereafter.

"'Then thou shalt come unto the isle Thrinacia; there are the many kine of Helios and his brave flocks feeding, seven herds of kine and as many goodly flocks of sheep, and fifty in each flock. If thou doest these no hurt, being heedful of thy return, truly ye may even yet reach Ithaca, albeit in evil case. But if thou hurtest them, I foreshow ruin for thy ship and for thy men, and even though thou shouldest thyself escape, late shalt thou return in evil plight with the loss of all thy company.'

"So spake she, and anon came the golden-throned Dawn. Then the fair goddess took her way up the island. But I departed to my ship and roused my men themselves to mount the vessel and loose the hawsers. And speedily they went aboard and sat upon the benches, and sitting orderly smote the grey sea water with their oars. And in the wake of our dark-prowed ship she sent a favouring wind that filled the sails, a kindly escort, — even Circe of the braided tresses, a dread goddess of human speech. And straightway we set in order the gear throughout the ship and sat us down and the wind and the helmsman guided our barque.

"Then I spake among my company with a heavy heart: 'Friends, forasmuch as it is not well that one or two alone should know of the oracles that Circe, the fair goddess, spake unto me, therefore will I declare them, that with foreknowledge we may die, or haply shunning death and destiny escape. First she bade us avoid the sound of the voice of the wondrous Sirens, and their field of flowers, and me only she bade listen to their voices. So bind ye me in a hard bond, that I may abide unmoved in my place, upright in the mast-stead, and from the mast let rope-ends be tied, and if I beseech and bid you to set me free, then do ye straiten me with yet more bonds.'

"Thus I rehearsed these things one and all, and declared them to my company. Meanwhile our good ship quickly came to the island of the Sirens twain, for a gentle breeze sped her on her way. Then straightway the wind ceased, and lo, there was a windless calm, and some god lulled the waves. Then my company rose up and drew in the ship's sails, and stowed them in the hold of the ship, while they sat at the oars and whitened the water with their polished pine blades. But I with my sharp sword cleft in pieces a great circle of wax, and with my strong hands kneaded it. And soon the wax grew warm, for that my great might constrained it, and the beam of the lord Helios, son of Hyperion. And I anointed therewith the ears of all my men in their order, and in the ship they bound me hand and foot upright in the mast-stead, and from the mast they fastened rope-ends and themselves sat down, and smote the grey sea water with their oars. But when the ship was within the sound of a man's shout from the land, we fleeing swiftly on our way, the Sirens espied the swift ship speeding toward them, and they raised their clear-toned song:

"'Hither, come hither, renowned Odysseus, great glory of the Achaeans, here stay thy barque, that thou mayest listen to the voice of us twain. For none hath ever driven by this way in his black ship, till he hath heard from our lips the voice sweet as the honeycomb, and hath had joy thereof and gone on his way the wiser. For lo, we know all things, all the travail that in wide Troy-land the Argives and Trojans bare by the gods' designs, yea, and we know all that shall hereafter be upon the fruitful earth.'

"So spake they uttering a sweet voice, and my heart was fain to listen, and I bade my company unbind me, nodding at them with a frown, but they bent to their oars and rowed on. Then straight uprose Perimedes and Eurylochus and bound me with more cords and straitened me yet the more. Now when we had driven past them, nor heard we any longer the sound of the Sirens or their song, forthwith my dear company took away the wax wherewith I had anointed their ears and loosed me from my bonds.

"But so soon as we left that isle, thereafter presently I saw smoke and a great wave, and heard the sea roaring. Then for very fear the oars flew from their hands, and down the stream they all splashed, and the ship was holden there, for my company no longer plied with their hands the tapering oars. But I paced the ship and cheered on my men, as I stood by each one and spake smooth words:

"'Friends, forasmuch as in sorrow we are not all unlearned, truly this is no greater woe that is upon us than when the Cyclops penned us by main might in his hollow cave; yet even thence we made escape by my manfulness, even by my counsel and my wit, and some day I think that this adventure too we shall remember. Come now, therefore, let us all give ear to do according to my word. Do ye smite the deep surf of the sea with your oars, as ye sit on the benches, if peradventure Zeus may grant us to escape from and shun this death. And as for thee, helmsman, thus I charge thee, and ponder it in thine heart, seeing that thou wieldest the helm of the hollow ship. Keep the ship well away from this smoke and from the wave and hug the rocks, lest the ship, ere thou art aware, start from her course to the other side, and so thou hurl us into ruin.'

"So I spake, and quickly they hearkened to my words. But of Scylla I told them nothing more, a bane none might deal with, lest haply my company should cease from rowing for fear, and hide them in the hold. In that same hour I suffered myself to forget the hard behest of Circe, in that she bade me in no wise be armed; but I did on my glorious harness and caught up two long lances in my hands, and went on to the decking of the prow, for thence methought that Scylla of the rock would first be seen, who was to bring woe on my company. Yet could I not spy her anywhere, and my eyes waxed weary for gazing all about toward the darkness of the rock.

"Next we began to sail up the narrow strait lamenting. For on the one hand lay Scylla, and on the other mighty

SCYLLA

Charybdis in terrible wise sucked down the salt sea water. As often as she belched it forth, like a cauldron on a great fire she would seethe up through all her troubled deeps, and overhead the spray fell on the tops of either cliff. But oft as she gulped down the salt sea water, within she was all plain to see through her troubled deeps, and the rock around roared horribly and beneath the earth was manifest swart with sand, and pale fear gat hold on my men. Toward her, then, we looked fearing destruction; but Scylla meanwhile caught from out my hollow ship six of my company, the hardiest of their hands and the chief in might. And looking into the swift ship to find my men, even then I marked their feet and hands as they were lifted on high, and they cried aloud in their agony, and called me by my name for that last time of all. Even as when a fisher on some headland lets down with a long rod his baits for a snare to the little fishes below, casting into the deep the horn of an ox of the homestead, and as he catches each flings it writhing ashore, so writhing were they borne upward to the cliff. And there she devoured them shrieking in her gates, they stretching forth their hands to me in the dread death-struggle. And the most pitiful thing was this that mine eyes have seen of all my travail in searching out the paths of the sea.

"Now when we had escaped the Rocks and dread Charybdis and Scylla, thereafter we soon came to the fair island of the god; where were the goodly kine, broad of brow, and the many brave flocks of Helios Hyperion. Then while as yet I was in my black ship upon the deep, I heard the lowing of the cattle being stalled and the bleating of the sheep, and on my mind there fell the saying of the blind seer, Theban Teiresias, and of Circe of Aia, who charged me very straitly to shun the isle of Helios, the gladdener of the world. Then I spake out among my company in sorrow of heart:

"'Hear my words, my men, albeit in evil plight, that I may

declare unto you the oracles of Teiresias and of Circe of Aia, who very straitly charged me to shun the isle of Helios, the gladdener of the world. For there she said the most dreadful mischief would befall us. Nay, drive ye then the black ship beyond and past that isle.'

"So spake I, and their heart was broken within them. And Eurylochus straightway answered me sadly, saying:

"'Hardy art thou, Odysseus, of might beyond measure, and thy limbs are never weary; verily thou art fashioned all of iron, that sufferest not thy fellows, foredone with toil and drowsiness, to set foot on shore, where we might presently prepare us a good supper in this sea-girt island. But even as we are thou biddest us fare blindly through the sudden night, and from the isle go wandering on the misty deep. And strong winds, the bane of ships, are born of the night. How could a man escape from utter doom, if there chanced to come a sudden blast of the South Wind, or of the boisterous West, which mainly wreck ships, beyond the will of the gods, the lords of all? Howbeit for this present let us yield to the black night, and we will make ready our supper abiding by the swift ship, and in the morning we will climb on board, and put out into the broad deep.'

"So spake Eurylochus, and the rest of my company consented thereto. Then at the last I knew that some god was indeed imagining evil, and I uttered my voice and spake unto him winged words:

"'Eurylochus, verily ye put force upon me, being but one among you all. But come, swear me now a mighty oath, one and all, to the intent that if we light on a herd of kine or a great flock of sheep, none in the evil folly of his heart may slay any sheep or ox; but in quiet eat ye the meat which the deathless Circe gave.'

"So I spake, and straightway they swore to refrain as I commanded them. Now after they had sworn and done that oath, we stayed our well-builded ship in the hollow harbour near to a well of sweet water, and my company went forth from out the ship and deftly got ready supper. But when they had put from them the desire of meat and drink, thereafter they fell a-weeping as they thought upon their dear companions whom Scylla had snatched from out the hollow ship and so devoured. And deep sleep came upon them amid their weeping. And when it was the third watch of the night, and the stars had crossed the zenith, Zeus the cloud-gatherer roused against them an angry wind with wondrous tempest, and shrouded in clouds land and sea alike, and from heaven sped down the night. Now when early Dawn shone forth, the rosy-fingered, we beached the ship, and dragged it up within a hollow cave, where were the fair dancing grounds of the nymphs and the places of their session. Thereupon I ordered a gathering of my men and spake in their midst, saying:

"'Friends, forasmuch as there is yet meat and drink in the swift ship, let us keep our hands off those kine, lest some evil thing befall us. For these are the kine and the brave flocks of a dread god, even of Helios, who overseeth all and overheareth all things.'

"So I spake, and their lordly spirit hearkened thereto. Then for a whole month the South Wind blew without ceasing, and no other wind arose, save only the East and the South.

"Now so long as my company still had corn and red wine, they refrained them from the kine, for they were fain of life. But when the corn was now all spent from out the ship, and they went wandering with barbed hooks in quest of game, as needs they must, fishes and fowls, whatsoever might come to their hand, for hunger gnawed at their belly, then at last I departed up the isle, that I might pray to the gods, if perchance some one of them might show me a way of returning. And now when I had avoided my company on my way through the island, I laved my hands where was a shelter from the wind, and prayed to all the gods that hold Olympus. But they shed sweet sleep upon my eyelids. And Eurylochus the while set forth an evil counsel to my company:

"'Hear my words, my friends, though ye be in evil case. Truly every shape of death is hateful to wretched mortals, but to die of hunger and so meet doom is most pitiful of all. Nay, come, we will drive off the best of the kine of Helios and will do sacrifice to the deathless gods who keep wide heaven. And if we may yet reach Ithaca, our own country, forthwith will we rear a rich shrine to Helios Hyperion, and therein would we set many a choice offering. But if he be somewhat wroth for his cattle with straight horns, and is fain to wreck our ship, and the other gods follow his desire, rather with one gulp at the wave would I cast my life away, than be slowly straitened to death in a desert isle.'

"So spake Eurylochus, and the rest of the company consented thereto. Forthwith they drave off the best of the kine of Helios that were nigh at hand, for the fair kine of shambling gait and broad of brow were feeding no great way from the dark-prowed ship. Then they stood around the cattle and prayed to the gods, plucking the fresh leaves from an oak of lofty boughs, for they had no white barley on board the decked ship. Now after they had prayed and cut the throats of the kine and flayed them, they cut out slices of the thighs and wrapped them in the fat, making a double fold, and thereon they laid raw flesh. Yet had they no pure wine to pour over the flaming sacrifices, but they made libation with water and roasted the entrails over the fire. Now after the thighs were quite consumed and they had tasted the inner parts, they cut the rest up small and spitted it on spits. In the same hour deep sleep sped from my eyelids and I sallied forth to the swift ship and the sea-banks. But on my way as I drew near to the curved ship, the sweet savour of the fat came all about me; and I groaned and spake out before the deathless gods:

"'Father Zeus, and all ye other blessed gods that live for ever, verily to my undoing ye have lulled me with a ruthless sleep, and my company abiding behind have imagined a monstrous deed.'

"Then swiftly to Helios Hyperion came the nymph Lampetie of the long robes, with the tidings that we had slain his kine. And straight he spake with angry heart amid the Immortals:

"'Father Zeus, and all ye other blessed gods that live for ever, take vengeance I pray you on the company of Odysseus, son of Laertes, that have insolently slain my cattle, wherein I was wont to be glad as I went toward the starry heaven, and when I again turned earthward from the firmament. And if they pay me not full atonement for the cattle, I will go down to Hades and shine among the dead.'

"And Zeus the cloud-gatherer answered him, saying: 'Helios, do thou, I say, shine on amidst the deathless gods, and amid mortal men upon the earth, the grain-giver. But as for me, I will soon smite their swift ship with my white bolt, and cleave it in pieces in the midst of the wine-dark deep.'

"But when I had come down to the ship and to the sea, I went up to my companions and rebuked them one by one; but we could find no remedy, the cattle were dead and gone. And soon thereafter the gods showed forth signs and wonders to my company. The skins were creeping, and the flesh bellowing upon the spits, both the roast and raw, and there was a sound as the voice of kine.

"Then for six days my dear company feasted on the best of the kine of Helios which they had driven off. But when Zeus, son of Cronos, had added the seventh day thereto, thereafter the wind ceased to blow with a rushing storm, and at once we climbed the ship and launched into the broad deep, when we had set up the mast and hoisted the white sails.

"But now when we left that isle nor any other land appeared, but sky and sea only, even then the son of Cronos stayed a dark cloud above the hollow ship, and beneath it the deep darkened. And the ship ran on her way for no long while, for of a sudden came the shrilling West, with the rushing of a great tempest, and the blast of wind snapped the two forestays of the mast, and the mast fell backward and all the gear dropped into the bilge. And behold, on the hind part of the ship the mast struck the head of the pilot and brake all the bones of his skull together, and like a diver he dropt down from the deck, and his brave spirit left his bones. In that same hour Zeus thundered and cast his bolt upon the ship, and she reeled all over, being stricken by the bolt of Zeus, and was filled with sulphur, and lo, my company fell from out the vessel. Like sea-gulls they were borne round the black ship upon the billows, and the god reft them of returning.

"But I kept pacing through my ship, till the surge loosened the sides from the keel, and the wave swept her along stript of her tackling, and brake her mast clean off at the keel. Now the backstay fashioned of an oxhide had been flung thereon; therewith I lashed together both keel and mast, and sitting thereon I was borne by the ruinous winds.

"Then verily the West Wind ceased to blow with a rushing storm, and swiftly withal the South Wind came, bringing sorrow to my soul, that so I might again measure back that space of sea, the way to deadly Charybdis. All the night was I borne, but with the rising of the sun I came to the rock of Scylla, and to dread Charybdis. Now she had sucked down her salt sea water, when I was swung up on high to the tall fig-tree whereto I clung like a bat, and could find no sure rest for my feet nor place to stand, for the roots spread far below and the branches hung aloft out of reach, long and large, and overshadowed Charybdis. Steadfast I clung till she should spew forth mast and keel again; and late they came to my desire. At the hour when a man rises up from the assembly and goes to supper, one who judges the many quarrels of the young men that seek him for law, at that same hour those timbers came forth to view from out Charybdis. And I let myself drop down hands and feet, and plunged heavily in the midst of the waters beyond the long timbers, and sitting on these I rowed hard with my hands. But the father of gods and of men suffered me no more to behold Scylla, else I should never have escaped from utter doom.

"Thence for nine days was I borne, and on the tenth night the gods brought me nigh to the isle of Ogygia, where dwells Calypso of the braided tresses, an awful goddess of mortal speech, who took me in and entreated me kindly. But why rehearse all this tale? For even yesterday I told it to thee and to thy noble wife in thy house; and it liketh me not twice to tell a plain-told tale."

BOOK XIII

Odysseus, sleeping, is set ashore at Ithaca by the Phaeacians, and waking knows it not. Pallas, in the form of a shepherd, helps to hide his treasure. The ship that conveyed him is turned into a rock, and Odysseus by Pallas is instructed what to do, and transformed into an old beggarman.

So spake he, and dead silence fell on all, and they were spell-bound throughout the shadowy halls. Thereupon Alcinous answered him, and spake, saying:

"Odysseus, now that thou hast come to my high house with floor of bronze, never, methinks, shalt thou be driven from thy way ere thou returnest, though thou hast been sore afflicted. And for each man among you, that in these halls of mine drink evermore the dark wine of the elders, and hearken to the minstrel, this is my word and command. Garments for the stranger are already laid up in a polished coffer, with gold curiously wrought, and all other such gifts as the counsellors of the Phaeacians bare hither. Come now, let us each of us give him a great tripod and a cauldron, and we in turn will gather goods among the people and get us recompense; for it were hard that one man should give without return."

So spake Alcinous, and the saying pleased them well. Then they went each one to his house to lay him down to rest; but so soon as early Dawn shone forth, the rosy-fingered, they hasted to the ship and bare the bronze, the joy of men. And the mighty king Alcinous himself went about the ship and diligently bestowed the gifts beneath the benches, that they might not hinder any of the crew in their rowing, when they laboured at their oars. Then they betook them to the house of Alcinous and fell to feasting. And the mighty king Alcinous sacrificed before them an ox to Zeus, the son of Cronos, that dwells in the dark clouds, who is lord of all. And when they had burnt the pieces of the thighs, they shared the glorious feast and made merry, and among them harped the divine minstrel Demodocus, whom the people honoured. But Odysseus would ever turn his head toward the splendour of the sun, as one fain to hasten his setting: for verily he was most eager to return. And as when a man longs for his supper, for whom all day long two dark oxen drag through the fallow field the jointed plough, yea and welcome to such an one the sunlight sinketh, that so he may get him to supper, for his knees wax faint by the way, even so welcome was the sinking of the sunlight to Odysseus. Then straight he spake among the Phaeacians, masters of the oar, and to Alcinous in chief he made known his word, saying:

"My lord Alcinous, most notable of all the people, pour ye the drink offering, and send me safe upon my way, and as for you, fare ye well. For now have I all that my heart desired, an escort and loving gifts. May the gods of heaven give me good fortune with them, and may I find my noble wife in my home with my friends unharmed, while ye, for your part, abide here and make glad your wedded wives and children; and may the gods vouchsafe all manner of good, and may no evil come nigh the people!"

So spake he, and they all consented thereto and bade send the stranger on his way, in that he had spoken aright. Then the mighty Alcinous spake to the henchman: "Pontonous, mix the bowl and serve out the wine to all in the hall, that we may pray to Father Zeus, and send the stranger on his way to his own country."

So spake he, and Pontonous mixed the honey-hearted wine, and served it to all in turn. And they poured forth before the blessed gods that keep wide heaven, even there as they sat. Then goodly Odysseus uprose, and placed in Arete's hand the two-handled cup, and uttering his voice spake to her winged words:

"Fare thee well, O queen, all the days of thy life, till old age come and death, that visit all mankind. But I go homeward, and do thou in this thy house rejoice in thy children and thy people and Alcinous the king."

Therewith goodly Odysseus stept over the threshold. And with him the mighty Alcinous sent forth a henchman to guide him to the swift ship and the sea-banks. And Arete sent in his train certain maidens of her household, one bearing a fresh robe and a doublet, and another she joined to them to carry the strong coffer, and yet another bare bread and red wine. Now when they had come down to the ship and to the sea, straightway the good men of the escort took these things and laid them by in the hollow ship, even all the meat and drink. Then they strewed for Odysseus a rug and a sheet of linen, on the decks of the hollow ship in the hinder part thereof, that he might sleep sound. Then he too climbed aboard and laid him down in silence, while they sat upon the benches, every man in order, and unbound the hawser from the pierced stone. So soon as they leant backwards and tossed the sea water with the oar blade, a deep sleep fell upon his eyelids, a sound sleep, very sweet, and next akin to death. And even as on a plain a yoke of four stallions comes springing all together beneath the lash, leaping high and speedily accomplishing the way, so leaped the stern of that ship, and the dark wave of the sounding sea rushed mightily in the wake, and she ran ever surely on her way, nor could a circling hawk keep pace with her, of winged things the swiftest. Even thus she lightly sped and cleft the waves of the sea, bearing a man whose counsel was as the counsel of the gods, one that erewhile had suffered much sorrow of heart, in passing through the wars of men, and the grievous waves; but for that time he slept in peace, forgetful of all that he had suffered.

So when the star came up, that is brightest of all, and goes ever heralding the light of early Dawn, even then did the seafaring ship draw nigh the island. There is in the land of Ithaca a certain haven of Phorcys, the ancient one of the sea, and thereby are two headlands of sheer cliff, which slope to the sea on the haven's side and break the mighty wave that ill winds roll without, but within, the decked ships ride unmoored when once they have attained to that landing place. Now at the harbour's head is a long-leaved olive tree, and hard by is a pleasant cave and shadowy, sacred to the nymphs, that are called the Naiads. And therein are mixing bowls and jars of stone, and there moreover do bees hive. And there are great looms of stone, whereon the nymphs weave raiment of purple stain, a marvel to behold, and therein are waters welling evermore. Two gates there are to the cave, the one set toward the North Wind whereby men may go down, but the portals toward the South pertain rather to the gods, whereby men may not enter: it is the way of the immortals.

Thither they, as having knowledge of that place, let drive their ship; and now the vessel in full course ran ashore, half her keel's length high; so well was she sped by the hands of the oarsmen. Then they alighted from the benched ship upon the land, and first they lifted Odysseus from out the hollow ship, all as he was in the sheet of linen and the bright rug, and laid him yet heavy with slumber on the sand. And they took forth the goods which the lordly Phaeacians had given him on his homeward way by grace of the great-hearted Athene. These they set in a heap by the trunk of the olive tree, a little aside from the road, lest some wayfaring man, before Odysseus awakened, should come and spoil them. Then themselves departed homeward again. But the shaker of the earth forgat not the threats, wherewith at the first he had threatened god-like Odysseus, and he inquired into the counsel of Zeus, saying:

"Father Zeus, I for one shall no longer be of worship among the deathless gods, when mortal men hold me in no regard, even Phaeacians, who moreover are of mine own lineage. Lo, now I said that after much affliction Odysseus should come home, for I had no mind to rob him utterly of his return, when once thou hadst promised it and given assent; but behold, in his sleep they have borne him in a swift ship over the sea, and set him down in Ithaca, and given him gifts out of measure, bronze and gold in plenty and woven raiment, much store, such as never would Odysseus have won for himself out of Troy; yea, though he had returned unhurt with the share of the spoil that fell to him."

And Zeus, the cloud gatherer, answered him, saying: "Lo now, shaker of the earth, of widest power, what a word hast thou spoken! The gods nowise dishonour thee; hard would it be to bring into dishonour our eldest and our best. But if any man, giving place to his own hardihood and strength, holds thee not in worship, thou hast always thy revenge for the same, even in the time to come. Do thou as thou wilt, and as seems to thee good."

Then Poseidon, shaker of the earth, answered him: "Lightly would I have done as thou sayest, O god of the dark clouds; but always do I hold in awe and avoid thy wrath

Howbeit, now I fain would smite a fair ship of the Phaeacians, as she comes home from a convoy on the misty deep, that thereby they may learn to hold their hands, and cease from giving escort to men; and I would overshadow their city with a great mountain."

And Zeus the gatherer of the clouds, answered him, saying: "Friend, learn now what seems best in my sight. At an hour when the folk are all looking forth from the city at the ship upon her way, smite her into a stone hard by the land; a stone in the likeness of a swift ship, that all mankind may marvel, and do thou overshadow their city with a great mountain."

Now when Poseidon, shaker of the earth, heard this saying, he went on his way to Scheria, where the Phaeacians dwell. There he abode awhile; and lo, she drew near, the sea-faring ship, lightly sped upon her way. Then nigh her came the shaker of the earth, and he smote her into a stone, and rooted her far below with the down-stroke of his hand; and he departed thence again.

Then one to the other they spake winged words, the Phaeacians of the long oars, mariners renowned. And thus would they speak, looking each man to his neighbour:

"Ah me! who is this that hath bound our swift ship on the deep as she drave homewards? Even now she stood all plain to view."

Even so they would speak; but they knew not how these things were ordained. And Alcinous made harangue and spake among them:

"Lo now, in very truth the ancient oracles of my father have come home to me. He was wont to say that Poseidon was jealous of us, for that we give safe escort to all men. He said that the day would come when the god would smite a fair ship of the Phaeacians, as she came home from a convoy on the misty deep, and overshadow our city with a great mountain. Thus that ancient one would speak; and lo, all these things now have an end. But come, let us all give ear and do according to my word. Cease ye from the convoy of mortals, whensoever any shall come unto our town, and let us sacrifice to Poseidon twelve choice bulls, if perchance he may take pity, neither overshadow our city with a great mountain."

So spake he, and they were dismayed and got ready the bulls. Thus were they praying to the lord Poseidon, the princes and counsellors of the land of the Phaeacians, as they stood about the altar.

Even then the goodly Odysseus awoke where he slept on his native land; nor knew he the same again, having now been long afar, for around him the goddess had shed a mist, even Pallas Athene, daughter of Zeus, to the end that she might make him undiscovered for that he was, and might expound to him all things, that so his wife should not know him, neither his townsmen and kinsfolk, ere the wooers had paid for all their transgressions. Wherefore each thing showed strange to the lord of the land, the long paths and the sheltering havens and the steep rocks and the trees in their bloom. So he started up, and stood and looked upon his native land, and then he made moan withal, and smote on both his thighs with the down-stroke of his hands, and making lament, he spake, saying:

"Oh, woe is me, unto what mortals' land am I now come? Say, are they froward, and wild, and unjust, or hospitable and of a god-fearing mind? Whither shall I bear all this wealth? Yea, where shall I myself go wandering? Oh! that it had abided with the Phaeacians where it was, and that I had gone to some other of the mighty princes, who would have entreated me kindly and sent me on my way. But now I know not where to bestow my treasure, and yet I will not leave it here behind, lest haply other men make spoil of it. Lo now, they were not wholly wise or just, the princes and counsellors of the Phaeacians, who carried me to a strange land. Verily they promised to bring me to clear-seen Ithaca, but they performed it not. May Zeus requite them, the god of suppliants, seeing that he watches over all men and punishes the transgressor! But come, I will reckon up these goods and look to them, lest the men be gone, and have taken back of their gifts upon their hollow ship."

Therewith he set to number the fair tripods and the cauldrons and the gold and the goodly woven raiment; and of all these he lacked not aught, but he bewailed him for his own country, as he walked downcast by the shore of the sounding sea, and made sore lament. Then Athene came nigh him in the guise of a young man, the herdsman of a flock, a young man most delicate, such as are the sons of kings. And she had a well-wrought mantle that fell in two folds about her shoulders, and beneath her smooth feet she had sandals bound, and a javelin in her hands. And Odysseus rejoiced as he saw her, and came over against her, and uttering his voice spake to her winged words:

"Friend, since thou art the first that I have chanced on in this land, hail to thee, and with no ill-will mayest thou meet me! Nay, save this my substance and save me too, for to thee as to a god I make prayer, and to thy dear knees have I come. And herein tell me true, that I may surely know. What land, what people is this? what men dwell therein? Surely, methinks, it is some clear-seen isle, or a shore of the rich mainland that lies and leans upon the deep."

Then the goddess, grey-eyed Athene, spake to him again: "Thou art witless, stranger, or thou art come from afar, if indeed thou askest of this land; nay, it is not so very nameless but that many men know it, both all those who dwell toward the dawning and the sun, and they that abide over against the light toward the shadowy west. Verily it is rough and not fit for the driving of horses, yet is it not a very sorry isle, though narrow withal. For herein is corn past telling, and herein too wine is found, and the rain is on it evermore, and the fresh dew. And it is good for feeding goats and feeding kine; all manner of wood is here, and watering places unfailing are herein. Wherefore, stranger, the name of Ithaca hath reached even unto Troyland, which men say is far from this Achaean shore."

So spake she, and the steadfast goodly Odysseus was glad, and had joy in his own country, according to the word of Pallas Athene, daughter of Zeus, lord of the aegis. And he uttered his voice and spake unto her winged words; yet he did not speak the truth, but wrested the word into guile, for he had a gainful and a nimble wit within his breast:

"Of Ithaca have I heard tell, even in broad Crete, far over the seas; and now have I come hither myself with these my goods. And I left as much again to my children, when I turned outlaw for the slaying of the dear son of Idomeneus, Orsilochus, swift of foot, who in wide Crete was the swiftest of all men that live by bread. Now he would have despoiled me of all that booty of Troy, for the which I had endured pain of heart, in passing through the wars of men, and the grievous waves of the sea, for this cause that I would not do a favour to his father, and make me his squire in the land of the Trojans, but commanded other fellowship of mine own. So I smote him with a bronze-shod spear as he came home from the field, lying in ambush for him by the wayside, with one of my companions. And dark midnight held the heavens, and no man marked us, but privily I took his life away. Now after I had slain him with the sharp spear, straightway I went to a ship and besought the lordly Phoenicians, and gave them spoil to their hearts' desire. I charged them to take me on board, and land me at Pylos or at goodly Elis where the Epeans bear rule. Howbeit of a truth, the might of the wind drave them out of their course, sore against their will, nor did they wilfully play me false. Thence we were driven wandering, and came hither by night. And with much ado we rowed onward into harbour, nor took we any thought of supper, though we stood sore in need thereof, but even as we were we stept ashore and all lay down. Then over me there came sweet slumber in my weariness, but they took forth my goods from the hollow ship, and set them by me where I myself lay upon the sands. Then they went on board, and departed for the fair-lying land of Sidon; while as for me I was left stricken at heart."

So spake he and the goddess, grey-eyed Athene, smiled, and caressed him with her hand; and straightway she changed to the semblance of a woman, fair and tall, and skilled in splendid handiwork. And uttering her voice she spake unto him winged words:

"Crafty must he be, and knavish, who would outdo thee in all manner of guile, even if it were a god encountered thee. Hardy man, subtle of wit, of guile insatiate, so thou wast not even in thine own country to cease from thy sleights and knavish words, which thou lovest from the bottom of thine heart! But come, no more let us tell of these things, being both of us practised in deceits, for that thou art of all men far the first in counsel and in discourse, and I in the company of all the gods win renown for my wit and wile. Yet thou knewest not me, Pallas Athene, daughter of Zeus, who am always by thee and guard thee in all adventures. Yea, and I made thee to be beloved of all the Phaeacians. And now am I come hither to contrive a plot with thee and to hide away the goods, that by my counsel and design the noble Phaeacians gave thee on thy homeward way. And I would tell thee how great a measure of trouble thou art ordained to fulfil within thy well-builded house. But do thou harden thy heart, for so it must be, and tell none neither man nor woman of all the folk, that thou hast indeed returned from wandering, but in silence endure much sorrow, submitting thee to the despite of men."

And Odysseus of many counsels answered her, saying: "Hard is it, goddess, for a mortal man that meets thee to discern thee, howsoever wise he be; for thou takest upon thee every shape. But this I know well, that of old thou wast kindly to me, so long as we sons of the Achaeans made war in Troy. But so soon as we had sacked the steep city of Priam and had gone on board our ships, and the god had scattered the Achaeans, thereafter I have never beheld thee, daughter of Zeus, nor seen thee coming on board my ship, to ward off sorrow from me. But I wandered evermore with a stricken heart, till the gods delivered me from my evil case, even till the day when, within the fat land of the men of Phaeacia, thou didst comfort me with thy words, and thyself didst lead me to their city. And now I beseech thee in thy father's name to tell me: for I deem not that I am come to clear-seen Ithaca, but I roam over some other land, and methinks that thou speakest thus to mock me and beguile my mind. Tell me whether in very deed I am come to mine own dear country."

Then the goddess, grey-eyed Athene, answered him: "Yea, such a thought as this is ever in thy breast. Wherefore I may in no wise leave thee in all thy grief, so wary art thou, so ready of wit and so prudent. Right gladly would any other man on his return from wandering have hasted to behold his children and his wife in his halls; but thou hast no will to learn or to hear aught, till thou hast furthermore made trial of thy wife, who sits as ever in her halls, and wearily for her the nights wane always and the days, in shedding of tears. But of this I never doubted, but ever knew it in my heart that thou wouldest come home with the loss of all thy company. Yet, I tell thee, I had no mind to be at strife with Poseidon, my own father's brother, who laid up wrath in his heart against thee, being angered at the blinding of his dear son. But come, and I will show thee the place of the dwelling of Ithaca, that thou mayst be assured. Lo, here is the haven of Phorcys, the ancient one of the sea, and here at the haven's head is the olive tree with spreading leaves, and hard by it is the pleasant cave and shadowy, sacred to the nymphs that are called the Naiads. Yonder, behold, is the roofed cavern, where thou offeredst many an acceptable sacrifice of hecatombs to the nymphs; and lo, this hill is Neriton, all clothed in forest."

Therewith the goddess scattered the mist, and the land appeared. Then the steadfast goodly Odysseus was glad, rejoicing in his own land, and he kissed the earth, the grain-giver.

Then the goddess, grey-eyed Athene, spake to him again: "Be of good courage. Come, let us straightway set thy goods in the secret place of the wondrous cave, that there they may abide for thee safe. And let us for ourselves advise us how all may be for the very best."

Therewith the goddess plunged into the shadowy cave, searching out the chambers of the cavern. Meanwhile Odysseus brought up his treasure, the gold and the unyielding bronze and fair woven raiment, which the Phaeacians gave him. And these things he laid by with care, and Pallas Athene, daughter of Zeus, lord of the aegis, set a stone against the door of the cave. Then they twain sat down by the trunk of the sacred olive tree, and devised death for the froward wooers. And the goddess, grey-eyed Athene, spake first, saying:

"Son of Laertes, of the seed of Zeus, Odysseus of many devices, advise thee how thou mayest stretch forth thine hands upon the shameless wooers, who now these three years lord it through thy halls, as they woo thy godlike wife and proffer the gifts of wooing. And she, that is ever bewailing her for thy return, gives hope to all and makes promises to every man and sends them messages, but her mind is set on other things."

And Odysseus of many counsels answered her, saying:

"Lo now, in very truth I was like to have perished in my halls by the evil doom of Agamemnon, son of Atreus, hadst not thou, goddess, declared me each thing aright. Come, then, weave some counsel whereby I may requite them; and thyself stand by me, and put great boldness of spirit within me, even as in the day when we loosed the shining coronal[1] of Troy. If but thou wouldest stand by me with such eagerness, thou grey-eyed goddess, I would war even with three hundred men, with thee my lady and goddess, if thou of thy grace didst succour me the while."

Then the goddess, grey-eyed Athene, answered him: "Yea, verily I will be near thee nor will I forget thee, whensoever we come to this toil: and methinks that certain of the wooers that devour thy livelihood shall bespatter the boundless earth with blood and brains. But come, I will make thee such-like that no man shall know thee. Thy fair skin I will wither on thy supple limbs, and make waste thy yellow hair from off thy head, and wrap thee in a foul garment, such that one would shudder to see a man therein. And I will dim thy two eyes, erewhile so fair, in such wise that thou mayest be unseemly in the sight of all the wooers and of thy wife and son, whom thou didst leave in thy halls. And do thou thyself first of all go unto the swineherd, who tends thy swine, and is loyal to thee as of old, and loves thy son and constant Penelope. Him shalt thou find sitting by the swine, as they are feeding near the rock of Corax and the spring Arethusa, and there they eat abundance of acorns and drink the black water, things that make in good case the rich flesh of swine. There do thou abide and sit by the swine, and find out all, till I have gone to Sparta, the land of fair women, to call Telemachus thy dear son, Odysseus, who hath betaken himself to spacious Lacedaemon, to the house of Menelaus to seek tidings of thee, whether haply thou art yet alive."

And Odysseus of many counsels answered her, saying: "Nay,

---

[1] [The battlements.]

wherefore then didst thou not tell him, seeing thou hast knowledge of all? Was it, perchance, that he too may wander in sorrow over the unharvested seas, and that others may consume his livelihood?"

Then the goddess, grey-eyed Athene, answered him: "Nay, let him not be heavy on thy heart. I myself was his guide, that by going thither he might win a good report. Lo, he knows no toil, but he sits in peace in the palace of the son of Atreus, and has boundless store about him. Truly, the young men with their black ship they lie in wait, and are eager to slay him ere he come to his own country. But this, methinks, shall never be. Yea, sooner shall the earth close over certain of the wooers that devour thy livelihood."

Therewith Athene touched him with her wand. His fair flesh she withered on his supple limbs, and made waste his yellow hair from off his head, and over all his limbs she cast the skin of an old man, and dimmed his two eyes, erewhile so fair. And she changed his raiment to a vile wrap and a doublet, torn garments and filthy, stained with foul smoke. And over all she clad him with the great bald hide of a swift stag, and she gave him a staff and a mean tattered scrip, and a cord therewith to hang it.

And after they twain had taken this counsel together, they parted; and she now went to goodly Lacedaemon to fetch the son of Odysseus.

BOOK XIV

Odysseus, in the form of a beggar, goes to Eumaeus, the master of his swine, where he is well used and tells a feigned story, and informs himself of the behaviour of the wooers.

But Odysseus fared forth from the haven by the rough track; up the wooded country and through the heights, where Athene

BOOK XIV 161

had shown him that he should find the goodly swineherd, who cared most for his substance of all the thralls that goodly Odysseus had gotten.

Now he found him sitting at the front entry of the house, where his courtyard was builded high, in a place with wide prospect; a great court it was and a fair, with free range round it. This the swineherd had builded by himself for the swine of his lord who was afar, and his mistress and the old man Laertes knew not of it. With stones dragged thither had he builded it, and coped it with a fence of white thorn, and he had split an oak to the dark core, and without he had driven stakes the whole length thereof on either side, set thick and close; and within the courtyard he made twelve styes hard by one another to be beds for the swine, and in each stye fifty grovelling swine were penned, brood swine; but the boars slept without. Now these were far fewer in number, the godlike wooers minishing them at their feasts, for the swineherd ever sent in the best of all the fatted hogs. And their tale was three hundred and three-score. And by them always slept four dogs, as fierce as wild beasts, which the swineherd had bred, a master of men. Now he was fitting sandals to his feet, cutting a good brown oxhide, while the rest of his fellows, three in all, were abroad this way and that, with the droves of swine; while the fourth he had sent to the city to take a boar to the proud wooers, as needs he must, that they might sacrifice it and satisfy their soul with flesh.

And of a sudden the baying dogs saw Odysseus, and they ran at him yelping, but Odysseus in his wariness sat him down, and let the staff fall from his hand. There by his own homestead would he have suffered foul hurt, but the swineherd with quick feet hasted after them, and sped through the outer door, and let the skin fall from his hand. And the hounds he chid and drave them this way and that, with a shower of stones, and he spake unto his lord, saying:

M

"Old man, truly the dogs went nigh to be the death of thee all of a sudden, so shouldest thou have brought shame on me. Yea, and the gods have given me other pains and griefs enough. Here I sit, mourning and sorrowing for my godlike lord, and foster the fat swine for others to eat, while he in lack of food, it may be, wanders over some land and city of men of a strange speech, if haply he yet lives and beholds the sunlight. But come with me, let us to the inner steading, old man, that when thy heart is satisfied with bread and wine, thou too mayest tell thy tale and declare whence thou art, and how many woes thou hast endured."

Therewith the goodly swineherd led him to the steading, and took him in and set him down and strewed beneath him thick brushwood, and spread thereon the hide of a shaggy wild goat, wide and soft, which served himself for a mattress. And Odysseus rejoiced that he had given him such welcome, and spake and hailed him:

"May Zeus, O stranger, and all the other deathless gods grant thee thy dearest wish, since thou hast received me heartily!"

Then, O swineherd Eumaeus, didst thou answer him, saying: "Guest of mine, it were an impious thing for me to slight a stranger, even if there came a meaner man than thou; for from Zeus are all strangers and beggars; and a little gift from such as we, is dear; for this is the way with thralls, who are ever in fear when young lords like ours bear rule over them. For surely the gods have stayed the returning of my master, who would have loved me diligently, and given me somewhat of my own, a house and a parcel of ground, and a comely wife, such as a kind lord gives to his man, who hath laboured much for him and the work of whose hands God hath likewise increased, even as he increaseth this work of mine whereat I abide. Therefore would my lord have rewarded me greatly, had he grown old at home. But he hath perished, as I would that all the stock of Helen had perished utterly, forasmuch as she hath caused the loosening of many a man's knees. For he too departed to Ilios of the goodly steeds, to get atonement for Agamemnon, that so he might war with the Trojans."

Therewith he quickly bound up his doublet with his girdle, and went his way to the styes, where the tribes of the swine were penned. Thence he took and brought forth two, and sacrificed them both, and singed them and cut them small, and spitted them. And when he had roasted all, he bare and set it by Odysseus, all hot as it was upon the spits, and he sprinkled thereupon white barley-meal. Then in a bowl of ivywood he mixed the honey-sweet wine, and himself sat over against him and bade him fall to:

"Eat now, stranger, such fare as thralls have to hand, even flesh of sucking pigs; but the fatted hogs the wooers devour, for they know not the wrath of the gods nor any pity. For every day and every night that comes from Zeus, they make sacrifice not of one victim only, nor of two, and wine they draw and waste it riotously. For surely his livelihood was great past telling, no lord in the dark mainland had so much, nor any in Ithaca itself; nay, not twenty men together have wealth so great, and I will tell thee the sum thereof. Twelve herds of kine upon the mainland, as many flocks of sheep, as many droves of swine, as many ranging herds of goats, that his own shepherds and strangers pasture. And ranging herds of goats, eleven in all, graze here by the extremity of the island with trusty men to watch them. And day by day each man of these ever drives one of the flock to the wooers, whichsoever seems the best of the fatted goats. But as for me I guard and keep these swine and I choose out for them, as well as I may, the best of the swine and send it hence."

So spake he, but Odysseus ceased not to eat flesh and drink wine right eagerly and in silence, and the while was sowing the seeds of evil for the wooers. Now when he had well eaten and comforted his heart with food, then the herdsman filled him the bowl out of which he was wont himself to drink, and he gave it him brimming with wine, and he took it and was glad at heart, and uttering his voice spake to him winged words:

"My friend, who was it then that bought thee with his wealth, a man so exceeding rich and mighty as thou declarest? Thou saidest that he perished to get atonement for Agamemnon; tell me, if perchance I may know him, being such an one as thou sayest. For Zeus, methinks, and the other deathless gods know whether I have seen him and may bring tidings of him; for I have wandered far."

Then the swineherd, a master of men, answered him: "Old man, no wanderer who came hither and brought tidings of him could win the ear of his wife and his dear son; but lightly do vagrants lie when they need entertainment, and care not to tell truth. Whosoever comes straying to the land of Ithaca, goes to my mistress and speaks words of guile. And she receives him kindly and lovingly and inquires of all things, and the tears fall from her eyelids for weeping, as is meet for a woman when her lord hath died afar. And quickly enough wouldst thou too, old man, forge a tale, if any would but give thee a mantle and a doublet for raiment. But as for him, dogs and swift fowls are like already to have torn his skin from the bones, and his spirit hath left him. Or the fishes have eaten him in the deep, and there lie his bones swathed in sand-drift on the shore. Yonder then hath he perished, but for his friends nought is ordained but care, for all, but for me in chief. For never again shall I find a lord so gentle, how far soever I may go, not though again I attain unto the house of my father and my mother, where at first I was born, and they nourished me themselves and with their own hands they reared me. Nor henceforth it is not for these that I sorrow so much, though I long to behold them with mine eyes in mine own country, but desire takes hold of me for Odysseus who is afar. His name, stranger, even though he is not here, it shameth me to speak, for he loved me exceedingly, and cared for me at heart; nay, I call him 'worshipful,' albeit he is far hence."

Then the steadfast goodly Odysseus spake to him again: "My friend, forasmuch as thou utterly beliest me, and sayest that henceforth he will not come again, and thine heart is ever slow to believe, therefore will I tell thee not lightly but with an oath, that Odysseus shall return. And let me have the wages of good tidings as soon as ever he in his journeying shall come hither to his home. Then clothe me in a mantle and a doublet, goodly raiment. But ere that, albeit I am sore in need I will not take aught, for hateful to me even as the gates of hell, is that man, who under stress of poverty speaks words of guile. Now be Zeus my witness before any god, and the hospitable board and the hearth of noble Odysseus whereunto I am come, that all these things shall surely be accomplished even as I tell thee. In this same year Odysseus shall come hither; as the old moon wanes and the new is born shall he return to his home, and shall take vengeance on all who here dishonour his wife and noble son."

Then didst thou make answer, swineherd Eumaeus: "Old man, it is not I, then, that shall ever pay thee these wages of good tidings, nor henceforth shall Odysseus ever come to his home. Nay, drink at ease, and let us turn our thoughts to other matters, and bring not these to my remembrance, for surely my heart within me is sorrowful whenever any man puts me in mind of my true lord. But come, old man, do thou tell me of thine own troubles. And herein tell me true, that I may surely know. Who art thou of the sons of men, and whence? Where is thy city, where are they that begat thee? Say on what manner of ship didst thou come, and how did sailors bring thee to Ithaca, and who did they avow them to be? For in no wise do I deem that thou camest hither by land."

And Odysseus of many counsels answered him, saying: "Yea, now, I will tell thee all most plainly. Might we have food and sweet wine enough to last for long, while we abide within thy hut to feast thereon in quiet, and others betake them to their work; then could I easily speak for a whole year, nor yet make a full end of telling all the troubles of my spirit, all the travail I have wrought by the will of the gods."

Then he told him a feigned tale, that he came from Crete and had fought with the Achaeans at Troy, and then wandered far and wide, and had been cast by the waves on the land of the Thesprotians. "There," he said, "I heard tidings of Odysseus, for the king told me that he had entertained him, and kindly entreated him on his way to his own country; and he showed me all the wealth that Odysseus had gathered, bronze and gold and well-wrought iron; yea, it would suffice for his children after him even to the tenth generation, so great were the treasures he had stored in the chambers of the king. He had gone, he said, to Dodona to hear the counsel of Zeus, from the high leafy oak tree of the god, how he should return to the fat land of Ithaca after long absence, whether openly or by stealth. Moreover, he sware, in mine own presence, as he poured the drink offering in his house, that the ship was drawn down to the sea and his company were ready, who were to convey him to his own dear country. But ere that, he sent me off, for it chanced that a ship of the Thesprotians was starting for Dulichium, a land rich in grain. Thither he bade them guide me with all diligence to the king Acastus. But an evil counsel concerning me found favour in their sight, that even yet I might reach the extremity of sorrow. When the seafaring ship had sailed a great way from the land, anon they sought how they might compass for me the day of slavery. They stript me of my garments, my mantle and a doublet, and changed my raiment to a vile wrap and doublet, tattered garments, even those thou seest now before thee; and in the evening they reached the fields of clear-seen Ithaca. There in the decked ship they bound me closely with a twisted rope, and themselves went ashore, and hasted to take supper by the sea-banks. Meanwhile the gods themselves lightly unclasped my bands, and muffling my head with the wrap I slid down the smooth ladder at the stern, and set my breast to the sea and rowed hard with both hands as I swam, and very soon I was out of the water and beyond their reach. Then I went up where there was a thicket, a wood in full leaf, and lay there crouching. And they went hither and thither making great moan; but when now it seemed to them little avail to go further on their quest, they departed back again aboard their hollow ship. And the gods themselves hid me easily and brought me nigh to the homestead of a wise man; for still, methinks, I am ordained to live on."

Then didst thou make answer to him, swineherd Eumaeus: "Ah! wretched guest, verily thou hast stirred my heart with the tale of all these things, of thy sufferings and thy wanderings. Yet herein, methinks, thou speakest not aright, and never shalt thou persuade me with the tale about Odysseus; why should one in thy plight lie vainly? Well I know of mine own self, as touching my lord's return, that he was utterly hated by all the gods, in that they smote him not among the Trojans nor in the arms of his friends, when he had wound up the clew of war. So should the whole Achaean host have builded him a barrow; yea, and for his son would he have won great glory in the after days; but now all ingloriously the spirits of the storm have snatched him away. But as for me I dwell apart by the swine and go not to the city, unless perchance wise Penelope summons me thither, when tidings of my master are brought I know not whence. Now all the people sit round and straitly question the news-bearer, both such as grieve for their lord that is long gone, and such as rejoice in devouring his living without atonement. But I have no care to ask or to inquire, since the day that an Aetolian cheated me with his story, one who had slain his man and wandered over wide lands and came to my steading, and I dealt lovingly with him. He said that he had seen my master among the Cretans at the house of Idomeneus, mending his ships which the storms had broken. And he said that he would come home either by the summer or the harvest-tide, bringing much wealth with the godlike men of his company. And thou too, old man of many sorrows, seeing that some god hath brought thee to me, seek not my grace with lies, nor give me any such comfort; not for this will I have respect to thee or hold thee dear, but only for the fear of Zeus, the god of strangers, and for pity of thyself."

And Odysseus of many counsels answered him, saying: "Verily thy heart within thee is slow to believe, seeing that even with an oath I have not won thee, nor find credence with thee. But come now, let us make a covenant; and we will each one have for witnesses the gods above, who hold Olympus. If thy lord shall return to this house, put on me a mantle and doublet for raiment, and send me on my way to Dulichium, whither I had a desire to go. But if thy lord return not according to my word, set thy thralls upon me, and cast me down from a mighty rock, that another beggar in his turn may beware of deceiving."

And the goodly swineherd answered him, saying: "Yea, stranger, even so should I get much honour and good luck among men both now and ever hereafter, if after bringing thee to my hut and giving thee a stranger's cheer, I should turn again and slay thee and take away thy dear life. With good heart thereafter would I pray to Zeus the son of Cronos! But now it is supper-time, and would that my fellows may speedily be at home, that we may make ready a dainty supper within the hut."

Thus they spake one to the other. And lo, the swine and the swineherds drew nigh. And the swine they shut up to

sleep in their lairs, and a mighty din arose as the swine were
being stalled. Then the goodly swineherd called to his fellows,
saying :
"Bring the best of the swine, that I may sacrifice it for a
guest of mine from a far land : and we too will have good cheer
therewith, for we have long suffered and toiled by reason of the
white-tusked swine, while others devour the fruit of our labour
without atonement."

Now after they had put from them the desire of meat and
drink, a thrall cleared away the bread, and they, now that they
had eaten enough of bread and flesh, were moved to go to rest.

Now it was so that night came on foul with a blind moon, and
Zeus rained the whole night through, and still the great West
Wind, the rainy wind, was blowing. Then Odysseus spake
among them that he might make trial of the swineherd, and
see whether he would take off his own mantle and give it to
him or bid one of his company strip, since he cared for him so
greatly :

"Listen now, Eumaeus, and all of you his companions, I will
utter a prayer and then tell my tale; so bids me witless wine,
which drives even the wisest to sing and to laugh softly, and
rouses him to dance, yea and makes him to speak out a word
which were better unspoken. Howbeit, now that I have
broken into speech, I will not hide aught. Oh, that I were
young, and my might were steadfast, as in the day when we
arrayed our ambush and led it beneath Troy town! And
Odysseus, and Menelaus son of Atreus, were leaders and with
them I was a third in command; for so they bade me. Now
when we had come to the city and the steep wall, we lay about
the citadel in the thick brushwood, crouching under our arms
among the reeds and the marsh land, and behold, the night came
on foul, with frost, as the North Wind went down, while the
snow fell from above, and crusted like rime, bitter cold, and the
ice set thick about our shields. Now the others all had man

tles and doublets, and slept in peace with their shields buckled close about their shoulders ; but I as I went forth had left my mantle behind with my men, in my folly, thinking that even so I should not be cold : so I came with my shield alone, and my shining doublet. But when it was now the third watch of the night and the stars had passed the zenith, in that hour I spake unto Odysseus who was nigh me, and thrust him with my elbow, and he listened straightway :

"'Son of Laertes, of the seed of Zeus, Odysseus of many devices, verily I shall cease from among living men, for this wintry cold is slaying me, seeing that I have no mantle. Some god beguiled me to wear a doublet only, and henceforth is no way of escape.'

"So I spake, and he apprehended a thought in his heart, such an one as he was in counsel and in fight. So he whispered and spake to me, saying :

"'Be silent now, lest some other Achaeans hear thee.' Therewith he raised his head upon his elbow, and spake, saying: 'Listen, friends, a vision from a god came to me in my sleep. Lo, we have come very far from the ships ; I would there were one to tell it to Agamemnon, son of Atreus, shepherd of the host, if perchance he may send us hither a greater company from the ships.'

"So spake he, and Thoas, son of Andraemon, rose up quickly and cast off his purple mantle. And he started to run unto the ships, but I lay gladly in his garment, and the golden-throned Dawn showed her light. Oh, that I were young as then and my might steadfast ! Then should some of the swineherds in the homestead give me a mantle, alike for love's sake and for pity of a good warrior. But now they scorn me for that sorry raiment is about my body."

Then didst thou make answer, O swineherd Eumaeus : "Old man, the tale that thou hast told in his praise is very good, and so far thou hast not misspoken aught, nor uttered a word unprofitably. Wherefore for this night thou shalt lack neither raiment nor aught else that is the due of a hapless suppliant, when he has met them that can befriend him. But in the morning thou shalt go shuffling in thine own rags, for there are not many mantles here or changes of doublet; for each man hath but one coat. But when the dear son of Odysseus comes, he himself will give thee a mantle and doublet for raiment, and send thee whithersoever thy heart and spirit bid."

With that he sprang up and set a bed for Odysseus near the fire, and thereon he cast skins of sheep and goats. There Odysseus laid him down and Eumaeus cast a great thick mantle over him, which he had ever by him for a change of covering, when any terrible storm should arise.

So there Odysseus slept, and the young men slept beside him. But the swineherd had no mind to lie there in a bed away from the boars. So he made him ready to go forth and Odysseus was glad, because he had a great care for his master's substance while he was afar. First he cast his sharp sword about his strong shoulders, then he clad him in a very thick mantle, to keep the wind away; and he caught up the fleece of a great and well-fed goat, and seized his sharp javelin, to defend him against dogs and men. Then he went to lay him down even where the white-tusked boars were sleeping, beneath the hollow of the rock, in a place of shelter from the North Wind.

BOOK XV

Pallas sends home Telemachus from Lacedaemon with the presents given him by Menelaus. Telemachus landed, goes first to Eumaeus.

Now Pallas Athene went to the wide land of Lacedaemon, to put the noble son of the great-hearted Odysseus in mind of his return, and to make him hasten his coming. And she found Telemachus, and the glorious son of Nestor, couched at the entry of the house of famous Menelaus. The son of Nestor truly was overcome with soft sleep, but sweet sleep gat not hold of Telemachus, but, through the night divine, careful thoughts for his father kept him wakeful. And grey-eyed Athene stood nigh him and spake to him, saying:

"Telemachus, it is no longer meet that thou shouldest wander far from thy home, leaving thy substance behind thee, and men in thy house so wanton, lest they divide and utterly devour all thy wealth, and thou shalt have gone on a vain journey. But come, rouse with all haste Menelaus, of the loud war cry, to send thee on thy way, that thou mayest even yet find thy noble mother in her home. For even now her father and her brethren bid her wed Eurymachus, for he outdoes all the wooers in his presents, and hath been greatly increasing his gifts of wooing. Now another word will I tell thee, and do thou lay it up in thine heart. The noblest of the wooers lie in wait for thee of purpose, in the strait between Ithaca and rugged Samos, eager to slay thee before thou come to thine own country. But this, methinks, will never be; yea, sooner shall the earth close over certain of the wooers that devour thy livelihood. Nay, keep thy well-wrought ship far from those isles, and sail by night as well as day, and he of the immortals who hath thee in his keeping and protection will send thee a fair breeze in thy wake. But when thou hast touched the nearest shore of Ithaca, send thy ship and all thy company forward to the city, but for thy part seek first the swineherd who keeps thy swine, and is loyal to thee as of old. There do thou rest the night, and bid him go to the city to bear tidings of thy coming to the wise Penelope, how that she hath got thee safe, and thou art come up out of Pylos."

Therewith she departed to high Olympus. But Telemachus woke the son of Nestor out of sweet sleep, touching him with his heel, and spake to him, saying:

"Awake, Peisistratus, son of Nestor, bring up thy horses

of solid hoof, and yoke them beneath the car, that we may get forward on the road."

Then Peisistratus, son of Nestor, answered him, saying: "Telemachus, we may in no wise drive through the dark night, how eager soever to be gone; nay, soon it will be dawn. Tarry then, till the hero, the son of Atreus, spear-famed Menelaus, brings gifts, and sets them on the car, and bespeaks thee kindly, and sends thee on thy way. For of him a guest is mindful all the days of his life, even of the host that shows him loving-kindness."

So spake he, and anon came the golden-throned Dawn. And Menelaus, of the loud war cry, drew nigh to them, new risen from his bed, by fair-haired Helen. Now when the dear son of Odysseus marked him, he made haste and girt his shining doublet about him, and the hero cast a great mantle over his mighty shoulders, and went forth at the door, and Telemachus, dear son of divine Odysseus, came up and spake to Menelaus, saying:

"Menelaus, son of Atreus, fosterling of Zeus, leader of the people, even now do thou speed me hence, to mine own dear country; for even now my heart is fain to come home again."

Then Menelaus, of the loud war cry, answered him: "Telemachus, as for thee, I will not hold thee a long time here, that art eager to return. But abide till I bring fair gifts and set them on the car and thine own eyes behold them, and I bid the women to prepare the mid-day meal in the halls, out of the good store thay have within. Honour and glory it is for us, and gain withal for thee, that ye should have eaten well ere ye go on your way, over vast and limitless lands."

Then the prince went down into the fragrant treasure chamber, not alone, for Helen went with him, and Megapenthes. Now, when they came to the place where the treasures were stored, then Atrides took a two-handled cup, and bade his son Megapenthes to bear a mixing bowl of silver. And Helen stood by the coffers, wherein were her robes of curious needlework which she herself had wrought. Then Helen, the fair lady, lifted one and brought it out, the widest and most beautifully embroidered of all, and it shone like a star, and lay far beneath the rest.

Then they went forth through the house till they came to Telemachus. And the strong Megapenthes bare the shining silver bowl and set it before him. And Helen came up, beautiful Helen, with the robe in her hands, and spake and hailed him:

"Lo! I too give thee this gift, dear child, a memorial of the hands of Helen, against the day of thy desire, even of thy bridal, for thy bride to wear it. But meanwhile let it lie by thy dear mother in her chamber. And may joy go with thee to thy well-builded house, and thine own country."

Now when they had put from them the desire of meat and drink, then did Telemachus and the glorious son of Nestor yoke the horses and climb into the inlaid car. And they drave forth from the gateway and the echoing gallery. After these Menelaus, of the fair hair, son of Atreus, went forth bearing in his right hand a golden cup of honey-hearted wine, that they might pour a drink-offering ere they departed. And he stood before the horses and spake his greeting:

"Farewell, knightly youths, and salute in my name Nestor, the shepherd of the people; for truly he was gentle to me as a father, while we sons of the Achaeans warred in the land of Troy."

And wise Telemachus answered him, saying: "Yea verily, O fosterling of Zeus, we will tell him all on our coming even as thou sayest. Would God I were so sure to find Odysseus in his home when I return to Ithaca and to tell him how I have met with all manner of loving-kindness at thy hands ere my departure, and now take with me treasures many and goodly!"

And even as he spake a bird flew forth at his right hand, an eagle that bare in his claws a great white goose, a tame fowl from the yard, and men and women followed shouting. But the bird drew near them and flew off to the right, across the horses, and they that saw it were glad, and their hearts were all comforted within them. And Peisistratus, son of Nestor, first spake among them:

"Consider, Menelaus, fosterling of Zeus, leader of the people, whether god hath showed forth this sign for us twain, or for thee thyself."

So spake he, and the warrior Menelaus pondered thereupon, how he should take heed to answer, and interpret it aright.

And long-robed Helen took the word and spake, saying: "Hear me, and I will prophesy as the immortals put it into my heart, and as I deem it will be accomplished. Even as yonder eagle came down from the hill, the place of his birth and kin, and snatched away the goose that was fostered in the house, even so shall Odysseus return home after much trial and long wanderings and take vengeance; yea, or even now is he at home and sowing the seeds of evil for all the wooers."

Then wise Telemachus answered her, saying: "Now may Zeus ordain it so, Zeus the thunderer and the lord of Here. Then would I do thee worship, as to a god, even in my home afar."

He spake and smote the horses with the lash, and they sped quickly towards the plain, in eager course through the city. So all day long they swayed the yoke they bore upon their necks. And the sun sank, and all the ways were darkened. And they came to Pherae, to the house of Diocles. There they rested for the night, and by them he set the entertainment of strangers.

Now so soon as early Dawn shone forth, the rosy-fingered, they yoked the horses and mounted the inlaid car. And forth they drave from the gateway and the echoing gallery. And he touched the horses with the whip to start them, and the pair flew onward nothing loth. And soon thereafter they reached the steep hold of Pylos. Then Telemachus spake unto the son of Nestor, saying:

"Take me not hence past my ship, O fosterling of Zeus, but leave me there, lest that old man keep me in his house in my despite, out of his eager kindness, for I must go right quickly home."

So spake he, and the son of Nestor communed with his own heart how he might make promise, and duly fulfil the same. So as he thought thereon, in this wise it seemed to him best. He turned back his horses toward the swift ship and the sea-banks, and took forth the fair gifts and set them in the hinder part of the ship, the raiment and the gold which Menelaus gave him. And he called to Telemachus and spake to him winged words:

"Now climb the ship with all haste, and bid all thy company do likewise, ere I reach home and bring the old man word. For well I know in my mind and heart that, being so wilful of heart, he will not let thee go, but he himself will come hither to bid thee to his house, and methinks that he will not go back without thee; for very wroth will he be despite thine excuse."

Thus he spake, and drave the horses with the flowing manes back to the town of the Pylians, and came quickly to the halls. And Telemachus called to his companions and commanded them, saying:

"Set ye the gear in order, my friends, in the black ship, and let us climb aboard that we may make way upon our course."

So spake he, and they gave good heed and hearkened. Then straightway they loosed the hawsers, and raised the mast of pine tree, and set it in the hole of the cross plank and made it fast with forestays, and hauled up the white sails with twisted ropes of ox-hide. And grey-eyed Athene sent them a favouring breeze, rushing violently through the clear sky that the ship might speedily finish her course over the salt water of the sea.

Now Odysseus and the goodly swineherd were supping in the hut, and the other men sat at meat with them. So when they had put from them the desire of meat and drink, Odysseus spake among them, to prove the swineherd, whether he would still entertain him diligently, and bid him abide there in the steading or send him forward to the city:

"Listen now, Eumaeus, and all the others of the company. In the morning I would fain be gone to the town to go a-begging, that I be not ruinous to thyself and thy fellows. Now advise me well, and lend me a good guide by the way to lead me thither; and through the city will I wander alone as needs I must, if perchance one may give me a cup of water and a morsel of bread. Moreover I would go to the house of divine Odysseus and bear tidings to the wise Penelope, and consort with the wanton wooers, if haply they might grant me a meal out of the boundless store that they have by them. Lightly might I do good service among them, even all that they would. For lo! I will tell thee and do thou mark and listen. By the favour of Hermes, the messenger, who gives grace and glory to all men's work, no mortal may vie with me in the business of a serving-man, in piling well a fire, in cleaving dry faggots, and in carving and roasting flesh and in pouring of wine, those offices wherein meaner men serve their betters."

Then didst thou speak to him in heaviness of heart, swineherd Eumaeus: "Ah! wherefore, stranger, hath such a thought arisen in thine heart? Surely thou art set on perishing utterly there, if thou wouldest indeed go into the throng of the wooers, whose outrage and violence reacheth even to the iron heaven! Not such as thou are their servants; they that minister to them are young and gaily clad in mantles and in doublets, and their heads are anointed with oil and they are fair of face, and the polished boards are laden with bread and flesh and wine. Nay, abide here, for none is vexed by thy presence, neither I nor any of my fellows that are with me. But when the dear son of Odysseus comes, he himself will give thee a mantle and a doublet for raiment, and will send thee whithersoever thy heart and spirit bid thee go."

Then the steadfast goodly Odysseus answered him: "Oh, that thou mayst so surely be dear to father Zeus as thou art to me, in that thou didst make me to cease from wandering and dread woe! For there is no other thing more mischievous to men than roaming; yet for their cursed belly's need men endure sore distress, to whom come wandering and tribulation and pain. But behold now, since thou stayest me here, and biddest me wait his coming, tell me of the mother of divine Odysseus, and of the father whom at his departure he left behind him on the threshold of old age; are they, it may be, yet alive beneath the sunlight, or already dead and within the house of Hades?"

Then spake to him the swineherd, a master of men: "Yea now, stranger, I will plainly tell thee all. Laertes yet lives, and prays evermore to Zeus that his life may waste from out his limbs within his halls. For he has wondrous sorrow for his son that is far away, and for the wedded lady his wise wife, whose death afflicted him in chief and brought him to old age before his day. Now she died of very grief for her son renowned, by an evil death, so may no man perish who dwells here and is a friend to me in word and deed!"

Thus they spake one with the other. Then they laid them down to sleep for no long while, but for a little space, for soon came the throned Dawn. But on the shore the company of Telemachus were striking their sails, and took down the mast quickly and rowed the ship on to anchorage. And they cast anchors and made fast the hawsers, and themselves too stept forth upon the strand of the sea, and made ready the mid-day meal, and mixed the dark wine. Now when they had put from them the desire of meat and drink, wise Telemachus first spake among them:

"Do ye now drive the black ship to the city, while I will go to the fields and to the herdsmen, and at even I will return to the city, when I have seen my lands. And in the morning I will set by you the wages of the voyage, a good feast of flesh and of sweet wine."

And Telemachus bound his goodly sandals beneath his feet, and seized a mighty spear, shod with sharp bronze, from the deck of the ship and his men loosed the hawsers. So they thrust off and sailed to the city, as Telemachus bade them, the dear son of divine Odysseus. But swiftly his feet bore him on his forward way, till he came to the court, where were his swine out of number; and among them the good swineherd slept, a man loyal to his lords.

BOOK XVI

Telemachus sends Eumaeus to the city to tell his mother of his return. And how, in the meantime, Odysseus discovers himself to his son.

Now these twain, Odysseus and the goodly swineherd, within the hut had kindled a fire, and were making ready breakfast at the dawn, and had sent forth the herdsmen with the droves of swine. And round Telemachus the hounds, that love to bark, fawned and barked not, as he drew nigh. And goodly Odysseus took note of the fawning of the dogs, and the noise of footsteps fell upon his ears. Then straight he spoke to Eumaeus winged words:

"Eumaeus, verily some friend or some other of thy familiars will soon be here, for the dogs do not bark but fawn around, and I catch the sound of footsteps."

While the word was yet on his lips, his own dear son stood at the entering in of the gate. Then the swineherd sprang up in amazement, and out of his hands fell the vessels wherewith he was busied in mingling the dark wine. And he came over against his master and kissed his head and both his beautiful eyes and both his hands, and he let a great tear fall. And even as a loving father welcomes his son that has come in the tenth year from a far country, his only son and well-beloved, for whose sake he has had great sorrow and travail, even so did the goodly swineherd fall upon the neck of godlike Telemachus, and kiss him all over as one escaped from death, and he wept aloud and spake to him winged words:

"Thou art come, Telemachus, sweet light of mine eyes; methought I should see thee never again, after thou hadst gone in thy ship to Pylos. Nay, now enter, dear child, that my heart may be glad at the sight of thee in mine house, who hast newly come from afar. For thou dost not often visit the field and the herdsmen, but abidest in the town; so it seems has thy good pleasure been, to look on the ruinous throng of the wooers."

Then wise Telemachus answered him, saying: "So be it, father, as thou sayest; and for thy sake am I come hither to see thee with mine eyes, and to hear from thy lips whether my mother yet abides in the halls or another has already wedded her, and the couch of Odysseus, perchance, lies in lack of bedding and deep in foul spider-webs."

Then the swineherd, a master of men, answered him: "Yea verily, she abides with patient spirit in thy halls, and wearily for her the nights wane always and the days, in shedding of tears."

So he spake and took from him the spear of bronze. Then Telemachus passed within and crossed the threshold of stone. As he came near, his father Odysseus arose from his seat to give him place; but Telemachus, on his part, stayed him and spake, saying:

"Be seated, stranger, and we will find a seat some other where in our steading, and there is a man here to set it for us."

So he spake, and Odysseus went back and sat him down again. And the swineherd strewed for Telemachus green brushwood below, and a fleece thereupon, and there presently the dear son of Odysseus sat him down. Next the swineherd set by them platters of roast flesh, the fragments that were left from the meal of yesterday. And wheaten bread he briskly heaped up in baskets, and mixed the honey-sweet wine in a goblet of ivy wood, and himself sat down over against divine Odysseus. So they stretched forth their hands upon the good cheer set before them. Now when they had put from them the desire of meat and drink, Telemachus spake to the goodly swineherd, saying:

"Father, whence came this stranger to thee? How did sailors bring him to Ithaca? and who did they avow them to be? For in no wise, I deem, did he come hither by land."

Then didst thou make answer, swineherd Eumaeus: "Yea now, my son, I will plainly tell thee all. Of wide Crete he avows him to be by lineage, and he says that round many cities of mortals he has wandered at adventure; even so has some god spun for him the thread of fate. But now, as a runaway from a ship of the Thesprotians, has he come to my steading, and I will give him to thee for thy man; do with him as thou wilt; he avows him for thy suppliant."

Then wise Telemachus answered him, saying: "Eumaeus, verily a bitter word is this that thou speakest. How indeed shall I receive this guest in my house? Myself I am young, and trust not yet to my strength of hands to defend me against the man who is angered without a cause. And my mother has divisions of heart, whether to abide here with me and keep the house, respecting the bed of her lord and the voice of the people, or straightway to go with whomsoever of the Achaeans that woo her in the halls is the best man, and gives most bridal gifts. But behold, as for this guest of thine, now that he has come to thy house, I will clothe him in a mantle and a doublet, goodly raiment, and I will give him a two-edged sword, and shoes for his feet, and send him on his way, whithersoever his heart and his spirit bid him go. Or, if thou wilt, hold him here in the steading and take care of him, and raiment I will send hither, and all manner of food to eat, that he be not ruinous to thee and to thy fellows. But thither into the company of the wooers would I not suffer him to go, for they are exceeding full of infatuate insolence, lest they mock at him, and that would be a sore grief to me. And hard it is for one man, how valiant soever, to achieve aught among a multitude, for verily they are far the stronger."

Then the steadfast goodly Odysseus answered him: "My friend, since it is indeed my right to answer thee withal, of a truth my heart is rent as I hear your words, such infatuate deeds ye say the wooers devise in the halls, in despite of thee, a man so noble. Say, dost thou willingly submit thee to oppression, or do the people through the township hate thee, obedient to the voice of a god? Or hast thou cause to blame thy brethren, in whose battle a man puts trust, even if a great feud arise?"

Then wise Telemachus answered him, saying: "Yea now, stranger, I will plainly tell thee all. There is no grudge and hatred borne me by the whole people, neither have I cause to blame my brethren, in whose battle a man puts trust, even if a great feud arise. For thus, as thou seest, Cronion has made us a house of but one heir. Arceisius got him one only son Laertes, and one only son Odysseus was begotten of his father, and Odysseus left me the only child of his getting in these halls, and had no joy of me; wherefore now are foemen innumerable in the house. For all the noblest that are princes in the islands, in Dulichium and Same and wooded Zacynthus, and as many as lord it in rocky Ithaca, all these woo my mother and waste my house. But as for her she neither refuseth the hated bridal, nor hath the heart to make an end; so they devour and minish my house; and ere long will they make havoc likewise of myself. Howbeit these things surely lie on the knees of the gods. Nay, father, but do thou go with haste and tell the constant Penelope that she hath got me safe and that I am come up out of Pylos. As for me, I will tarry here, and do thou return hither when thou hast told the tidings to her alone; but of the other Achaeans let no man learn it, for there be many that devise mischief against me."

Then didst thou make answer, swineherd Eumaeus: "I mark, I heed, all this thou speakest to one with understanding. But come, declare me this and tell it plainly; whether or no I shall go the same road with tidings to Laertes, that hapless man, who till lately, despite his great sorrow for Odysseus' sake, yet had oversight of the tillage, and did eat and drink with the thralls in his house, as often as his heart within him bade him. But now, from the day that thou wentest in thy ship to Pylos, never to this hour, they say, hath he eaten and drunken as before, nor looked to the labours of the field, but with groaning and lamentation he sits sorrowing, and the flesh wastes away about his bones."

Then wise Telemachus answered him, saying: "All the more grievous it is! yet will we let him be, though we sorrow thereat. For if men might in any wise have all their will we should before aught else choose the day of my father's returning. But do thou when thou hast told the tidings come straight back, and go not wandering through the fields after Laertes. But speak to my mother that with all speed she send forth the house-dame her handmaid, secretly, for she might bear tidings to the old man."

With that word he roused the swineherd, who took his sandals in his hands and bound them beneath his feet and departed for the city. Now Athene noted Eumaeus the swineherd pass from the steading, and she drew nigh in the semblance of a woman fair and tall, and skilled in splendid handiwork. And she stood in presence manifest to Odysseus over against the doorway of the hut; but it was so that Telemachus saw her not before him and marked her not; for the gods in no wise appear visible to all. But Odysseus was ware of her and the dogs likewise, which barked not, but with a low whine shrank cowering to the far side of the steading. Then she nodded at him with bent brows, and goodly Odysseus perceived it, and came forth from the room, past the great wall of the yard, and stood before her, and Athene spake to him, saying:

"Son of Laertes, of the seed of Zeus, Odysseus of many devices, now is the hour to reveal thy word to thy son, and hide it not, that ye twain having framed death and doom for the wooers, may fare to the famous town. Nor will I, even I, be long away from you, being right eager for battle."

Therewith Athene touched him with her golden wand. First she cast about his breast a fresh linen robe and a doublet, and she increased his bulk and bloom. Dark his colour grew again, and his cheeks filled out, and the black beard spread thick around his chin.

Now she, when she had so wrought, withdrew again, but Odysseus went into the hut, and his dear son marvelled at him and looked away for very fear lest it should be a god, and he uttered his voice and spake to him winged words:

"Even now, stranger, thou art other in my sight than that thou wert a moment since, and other garments thou hast, and the colour of thy skin is no longer the same. Surely thou art a god of those that keep the wide heaven. Nay, then, be gracious, that we may offer to thee well-pleasing sacrifices and golden gifts, beautifully wrought; and spare us I pray thee."

Then the steadfast goodly Odysseus answered him, saying: "Behold, no god am I; why likenest thou me to the immortals? nay, thy father am I, for whose sake thou sufferest many pains and groanest sore, and submittest thee to the despite of men."

At the word he kissed his son, and from his cheeks let a tear fall to earth: before, he had stayed the tears continually. But Telemachus (for as yet he believed not that it was his father) answered in turn and spake, saying:

"Thou art not Odysseus my father, but some god beguiles me, that I may groan for more exceeding sorrow. For it cannot be that a mortal man should contrive this by the aid of his own wit, unless a god were himself to visit him, and lightly of his own will to make him young or old. For truly, but a moment gone, thou wert old and foully clad, but now thou art like the gods who keep the wide heaven."

Then Odysseus of many counsels answered him, saying:

"Telemachus, it fits thee not to marvel overmuch that thy father is come home, or to be amazed. Nay, for thou shalt find no other Odysseus come hither any more; but lo, I, all as I am, after sufferings and much wandering have come in the twentieth year to mine own country. Behold, this is the work of Athene, driver of the spoil, who makes me such manner of man as she will, — for with her it is possible, — now like a beggar, and now again like a young man, and one clad about in rich raiment. Easy it is for the gods who keep the wide heaven to glorify or to abase a mortal man."

With this word then he sat down again; but Telemachus, flinging himself upon his noble father's neck, mourned and shed tears, and in both their hearts arose the desire of lamentation. And they wailed aloud, more ceaselessly than birds, sea-eagles or vultures of crooked claws, whose younglings the country folk have taken from the nest, ere yet they are fledged. Even so pitifully fell the tears beneath their brows. And now would the sunlight have gone down upon their sorrowing, had not Telemachus spoken to his father suddenly :

"And in what manner of ship, father dear, did sailors at length bring thee hither to Ithaca? and who did they avow them to be? For in no wise, I deem, didst thou come hither by land."

And the steadfast goodly Odysseus answered him : "Yea now, my child, I will tell thee all the truth. The Phaeacians brought me hither, mariners renowned, who speed other men too upon their way, whosoever comes to them. Asleep in the swift ship they bore me over the seas and set me down in Ithaca, and gave me splendid gifts, bronze and gold in plenty and woven raiment. And these treasures are lying by the gods' grace in the caves. But now I am come hither by the promptings of Athene, that we may take counsel for the slaughter of the foemen. But come, tell me all the tale of the wooers and their number, that I may know how many and what men they be, and that so I may commune with my good heart and advise me, whether we twain shall be able alone to make head against them without aid, or whether we should even seek succour of others."

Then wise Telemachus answered him, saying : "Verily, father, I have ever heard of thy great fame, for a warrior hardy of thy hands, and sage in counsel. But this is a hard saying of thine : awe comes over me ; for it may not be that two men should do battle with many men and stalwart. For of the wooers there are not barely ten nor twice ten only, but many a decad more : and straight shalt thou learn the tale of them ere we part. From Dulichium there be two and fifty chosen lords, and six serving men go with them ; and out of Same four and twenty men ; and from Zacynthus there are twenty lords of the Achaeans ; and from Ithaca itself full twelve men of the best, and with them Medon the henchman, and the divine minstrel, and two squires skilled in carving viands. If we shall encounter all these within the halls, see thou to it, lest bitter and baneful for us be the vengeance thou takest on their violence at thy coming. But do thou, if thou canst think of some champion, advise thee of any that may help us with all his heart."

Then the steadfast goodly Odysseus answered him, saying:

"Yea now, I will tell thee, and do thou mark and listen to me, and consider whether Athene with Father Zeus will suffice for us twain, or whether I shall cast about for some other champion."

Then wise Telemachus answered him, saying: "Verily the best of champions are these two thou namest, though high in the clouds is their seat, and they rule among all men and among the deathless gods."

Then the steadfast goodly Odysseus answered him : " Verily these twain will not keep aloof from the strong tumult of war, when between the wooers and us in my halls is held the trial of the might of Ares. But as now, do thou go homeward at the breaking of the day, and consort with the proud wooers. As for me, the swineherd will lead me to the town later in the day, in the likeness of a beggar, a wretched man and an old. And if they shall evil entreat me in the house, let thy heart harden itself to endure while I am shamefully handled, yea, even if they drag me by the feet through the house to the doors, or cast at me and smite me : still do thou bear the sight. Yet another thing will I tell thee, and do thou ponder it in thy heart. When Athene, of deep counsel, shall put it into my heart, I will nod to thee with my head and do thou note it, and carry away all thy weapons of war that lie in the halls, and lay them down every one in the secret place of the lofty chamber. And when the wooers miss them and ask thee concerning them, thou shalt beguile them with soft words, saying:

"'Out of the smoke have I laid them by, since they are no

longer like those that Odysseus left behind him of old when he went to Troy, but they are wholly marred: so mightily hath passed upon them the vapour of fire. Moreover Cronion hath put into my heart this other and greater care, that perchance, when ye are heated with wine, ye set a quarrel between you and wound one the other and thereby shame the feast and the wooing; for iron of itself draws a man thereto.' But for us twain alone leave two swords and two spears and two shields of ox-hide to grasp, that we may rush upon the arms and seize them; and then shall Pallas Athene and Zeus the counsellor enchant the wooers to their ruin. Yet another thing will I tell thee, and do thou ponder it in thy heart. If in very truth thou art my son and of our blood, then let no man hear that Odysseus is come home; neither let Laertes know it, nor the swineherd nor any of the household nor Penelope herself, but let me and thee alone discover the intent of the women. Yea, and we would moreover make trial of certain of the men among the thralls, and learn who of them chances to honour us and to fear us heartily, and who regards us not at all and holds even thee in no esteem, so noble a man as thou art."

Then his renowned son answered him, and said: "O my father, of a truth thou shalt learn, methinks, even hereafter what spirit I am of, for no whit doth folly possess me. But I deem not that this device of thine will be gainful to us twain, so I bid thee to give heed. For thou shalt be long time on thy road to little purpose, making trial of each man, while thou visitest the farm lands; but at ease in thy halls the wooers devour thy goods with insolence, and now there is no sparing. Howbeit I would have thee take knowledge of the women, who they be that dishonour thee, and who are guiltless. But of the men I would not that we should make trial in the steadings, but that we should see to this task afterwards, if indeed thou knowest some sign from Zeus, lord of the aegis."

Thus they spake one to the other. And now the well-builded

ship was being brought to land at Ithaca, the ship that bare Telemachus from Pylos with all his company. When they were now come within the deep harbour, the men drew up the black ship on the shore, while squires, haughty of heart, bare away their weapons, and straightway carried the glorious gifts to the house of Clytius. Anon they sent forward a herald to the house of Odysseus to bear the tidings to prudent Penelope, namely, how Telemachus was in the field, and had bidden the ship sail to the city, lest the noble queen should be afraid, and let the round tears fall. So these two met, the herald and the goodly swineherd, come on the same errand to tell all to the lady. Now when they were got to the house of the divine king, the herald spake out among all the handmaids, saying:

"Verily, O queen, thy son hath come out of Pylos."

But the swineherd went up to Penelope, and told her all that her dear son had bidden him say. So, when he had declared all that had been enjoined him, he went on his way to the swine and left the enclosure and the hall.

Now the wooers were troubled and downcast in spirit, and forth they went from the hall past the great wall of the court, and there in front of the gates they sat them down. And Eurymachus son of Polybus first spake among them, saying:

"Verily, friends, a proud deed hath Telemachus accomplished with a high hand, even this journey, and we said that he should never bring it to pass. But come, launch we a black ship, the best there is, and let us get together oarsmen of the sea, who shall straightway bear word to our friends to return home with speed."

The word was yet on his lips, when Amphinomus turned in his place and saw the ship within the deep harbour, and the men lowering the sails and with the oars in their hands. Then sweetly he laughed out and spake among his fellows:

"Nay, let us now send no message any more, for lo, they are come home. Either some god has told them all or they themselves have seen the ship of Telemachus go by, and have not been able to catch her."

Thus he spake, and they arose and went to the sea-banks. Swiftly the men drew up the black ship on the shore, and squires, haughty of heart, bare away their weapons. And the wooers all together went to the assembly place, and suffered none other to sit with them, either of the young men or of the elders. Then Antinous spake among them, the son of Eupeithes:

"Lo now, how the gods have delivered this man from his evil case! All day long did scouts sit along the windy headlands, ever in quick succession, and at the going down of the sun we never rested for a night upon the shore, but sailing with our swift ship on the high seas we awaited the bright Dawn, as we lay in wait for Telemachus, that we might take and slay the man himself; but meanwhile some god has brought him home. But even here let us devise an evil end for him, even for Telemachus, and let him not escape out of our hands, for methinks that while he lives we shall never achieve this task of ours. For he himself has understanding in counsel and wisdom, and the people no longer show us favour in all things. Nay, come, before he assembles all the Achaeans to the gathering; for methinks that he will in no wise be slack, but will be exceeding wroth, and will stand up and speak out among them all, and tell how we plotted against him sheer destruction but did not overtake him. Then will they not approve us, when they hear these evil deeds. Beware then lest they do us a harm, and drive us forth from our country, and we come to the land of strangers. Nay, but let us be beforehand and take him in the field far from the city, or by the way; and let us ourselves keep his livelihood and his possessions, making fair division among us, but the house we would give to his mother to keep and to whomsoever marries her. But if this saying likes you not, but ye choose rather that he should live and keep the heritage of his father, no longer then let us gather here and eat all his store of pleasant substance, but let each one from his own hall woo her with his bridal gifts and seek to win her; so should she wed the man that gives the most and comes as the chosen of fate."

So he spake, and they all held their peace. Then Amphinomus made harangue and spake out among them; he was the famous son of Nisus the prince, the son of Aretias, and he led the wooers that came from out Dulichium, a land rich in wheat and in grass, and more than all the rest his words were pleasing to Penelope, for he was of an understanding mind. And now of his good will he made harangue, and spake among them:

"Friends, I for one would not choose to kill Telemachus; it is a fearful thing to slay one of the stock of kings! Nay, first let us seek the counsel of the gods, and if the oracles of great Zeus approve, myself I will slay him and bid all the rest to aid. But if the gods are disposed to avert it, I bid you to refrain."

So spake Amphinomus, and his saying pleased them well. Then straightway they arose and went to the house of Odysseus and entering in sat down on the polished seats.

Then the wise Penelope had a new thought, namely, to show herself to the wooers, so despiteful in their insolence; for she had heard of the death of her son that was to be in the halls, seeing that Medon the henchman had told her of it, who heard their counsels. So she went on her way to the hall, with the women her handmaids. Now when that fair lady had come unto the wooers, she stood by the doorpost of the well-built roof, holding up her glistening tire before her face, and rebuked Antinous and spake and hailed him:

"Antinous, full of all insolence, deviser of mischief! and yet they say that in the land of Ithaca thou art chiefest among thy peers in counsel and in speech. Nay, no such man dost thou show thyself. Fool! why indeed dost thou contrive death and doom for Telemachus, and hast no regard unto suppliants who have Zeus to witness? Nay, but it is an impious thing to contrive evil one against another. What! knowest thou not of the day when thy father fled to this house in fear of the people, for verily they were exceeding wroth against him, because he had followed with Taphian sea robbers and harried the Thesprotians, who were at peace with us? So they wished to destroy thy father and wrest from him his dear life, and utterly to devour all his great and abundant livelihood; but Odysseus stayed and withheld them, for all their desire. His house thou now consumest without atonement, and his wife thou wooest, and wouldst slay his son, and dost greatly grieve me. But I bid thee cease, and command the others to do likewise."

Then Eurymachus, son of Polybus, answered her, saying: "Daughter of Icarius, wise Penelope, take courage, and let not thy heart be careful for these things. The man is not, nor shall be, nor ever shall be born, that shall stretch forth his hands against Telemachus, thy son, while I live and am on earth and see the light. For thus will I declare to thee, and it shall surely come to pass. Right quickly shall the black blood of such an one flow about my spear; for Odysseus, waster of cities, of a truth did many a time set me too upon his knees, and gave me roasted flesh into my hand, and held the red wine to my lips. Wherefore Telemachus is far the dearest of all men to me, and I bid him have no fear of death, not from the wooers' hands; but from the gods none may avoid it."

Thus he spake comforting her, but was himself the while framing death for her son.

Now she ascended to her shining upper chamber, and then was bewailing Odysseus, her dear lord, till grey-eyed Athene cast sweet sleep upon her eyelids.

And in the evening the goodly swineherd came back to Odysseus and his son, and they went about to make ready the supper, when they had sacrificed a swine of a year old. Then

Athene drew near Odysseus, son of Laertes, and smote him with her wand, and made him into an old man again. In sorry raiment she clad him about his body, lest the swineherd should look on him and know him, and depart to tell the constant Penelope, and not keep the matter in his heart.

Then Telemachus spake first to the swineherd, saying: "Thou hast come, goodly Eumaeus. What news is there in the town? Are the lordly wooers now come home from their ambush, or do they still watch for me yonder, to take me on my way home?"

Then didst thou make answer, swineherd Eumaeus: "I had no mind to go about the city asking and inquiring hereof; my heart bade me get me home again, as quick as might be, when once I had told the tidings. And the swift messenger from thy company joined himself unto me, the henchman, who was the first to tell the news to thy mother. Yet this, too, I know, if thou wouldest hear; for I beheld it with mine eyes. Already had I come in my faring above the city, where is the hill Hermaean, when I marked a swift ship entering our haven, and many men there were in her, and she was laden with shields and two-headed spears, and methought they were the wooers, but I know not at all."

So spake he, and the mighty prince Telemachus smiled, and glanced at his father, while he shunned the eye of the swineherd.

Now when they had ceased from the work and got supper ready, they fell to feasting, and their hearts lacked not aught of the equal banquet. But when they had put from them the desire of meat and drink, they bethought them of rest, and took the boon of sleep.

BOOK XVII

Telemachus relates to his mother what he had heard at Pylos and Sparta.

So soon as early Dawn shone forth, the rosy-fingered, then Telemachus, the dear son of divine Odysseus, bound beneath his feet his goodly sandals, and took up his mighty spear that fitted his grasp, to make for the city; and he spake to his swineherd, saying:

"Verily, father, I am bound for the city, that my mother may see me, for methinks that she will not cease from grievous wailing and tearful lament, until she beholds my very face. But this command I give thee: Lead this stranger, the hapless one, to the city, that there he may beg his meat, and whoso chooses will give him a morsel of bread and a cup of water. As for myself, I can in no wise suffer every guest who comes to me, so afflicted am I in spirit. But if the stranger be sore angered hereat, the more grievous will it be for himself; howbeit I for one love to speak the truth."

And Odysseus of many counsels answered him, saying: "I, too, my friend, have no great liking to be left behind here. It is better that a beggar should beg his meat in the town than in the fields, and whoso chooses will give it me. For I am not now of an age to abide at the steading, and to obey in all things the word of the master. Nay, go, and this man that thou biddest will lead me, so soon as I shall be warmed with the fire, and the sun waxes hot. For woefully poor are these garments of mine, and I fear lest the hoar frost of the dawn overcome me; moreover ye say the city is far away."

So he spake, and Telemachus passed out through the steading, stepping forth at a quick pace, and was sowing the seeds of evil for the wooers. Now when he was come to the fair-lying house, he set his spear against the tall pillar and leaned it there, and himself went in and crossed the threshold of stone.

And the nurse Eurycleia saw him far before the rest, as she was strewing skin coverlets upon the carven chairs, and straightway she drew near him, weeping, and all the other maidens of Odysseus, of the hardy heart, were gathered about him, and kissed him lovingly on the head and shoulders. Now wise Penelope came forth from her chamber, like Artemis or golden Aphrodite, and cast her arms about her dear son, and fell a-weeping, and kissed his face and both his beautiful eyes, and wept aloud, and spake to him winged words:

"Thou art come, Telemachus, sweet light of mine eyes; methought I should see thee never again, after thou hadst gone in thy ship to Pylos, secretly and without my will, to seek tidings of thy dear father. Come now, tell me, what sight thou didst get of him."

And wise Telemachus answered her, saying: "Yea now, mother, I will tell thee all the truth. We went to Pylos and to Nestor, the shepherd of the people, and he received me in his lofty house, and was diligent to entreat me lovingly, as a father might his son that had but newly come from strange lands after many years; even so diligently he cared for me with his renowned sons. Yet he said that he had heard no word from any man on earth concerning Odysseus, of the hardy heart, whether alive or dead. But he sent me forward on my way with horses and a chariot, well compact, to Menelaus, son of Atreus, spearsman renowned. There I saw Argive Helen, for whose sake the Argives and Trojans bore much travail by the gods' designs. Then straightway Menelaus, of the loud war cry, asked me on what quest I had come to goodly Lacedaemon. And I told him all the truth. Then he made answer, and spake, saying:

"'For that whereof thou askest and entreatest me, be sure I will not swerve from the truth in aught that I say, nor deceive thee; but of all that the ancient one of the sea, whose speech is sooth, declared to me, not a word will I hide or keep from thee. He said that he saw Odysseus in an island, suffering strong pains in the halls of the nymph Calypso, who holds him there perforce; so that he may not come to his own country, for he has by him no ships with oars, and no companions to send him on his way over the broad back of the sea.' So spake Menelaus, son of Atreus, spearsman renowned. Then having fulfilled all, I set out for home, and the deathless gods gave me a fair wind, and brought me swiftly to mine own dear country."

But the wooers meantime were before the palace of Odysseus, taking their pleasure in casting of weights and of spears on a levelled place, as heretofore, in their insolence. But when it was now the hour for supper, and the sheep came home from the fields all around, and the men led them whose custom it was, then Medon, who of all the henchmen was most to their mind, and was ever with them at the feast, spake to them, saying:

"Noble youths, now that ye have had sport to your hearts' content, get you into the house, that we may make ready a feast; for truly it is no bad thing to take meat in season."

Even so he spake, and they rose up and departed, and were obedient to his word. Now when they were come into the fair-lying house, they laid aside their mantles on the chairs and high seats, and they sacrificed great sheep and stout goats, yea, and the fatlings of the boars and an heifer of the herd, and got ready the feast.

Now all this while Odysseus and the goodly swineherd were bestirring them to go from the field to the city; and the swineherd, a master of men, spake first, saying:

"Well, my friend, forasmuch as I see thou art eager to be going to the city to-day, even as my master gave command, — though myself I would well that thou shouldest be left here to keep the steading, but I hold him in reverence and fear, lest he chide me afterwards, and grievous are the rebukes of masters, — come then, let us go on our way, for lo, the day is far spent, and soon wilt thou find it colder toward evening."

Then Odysseus of many counsels answered him, saying: "I mark, I heed: all this thou speakest to one with understanding. But let us be going, and be thou my guide withal to the end. And if thou hast anywhere a staff ready cut, give it me to lean upon, for truly ye said that slippery was the way."

Therewith he cast about his shoulders a mean scrip, all tattered, and a cord withal to hang it, and Eumaeus gave him a staff to his mind. So these twain went on their way, and the dogs and the herdsmen stayed behind to guard the steading. And the swineherd led his lord to the city in the guise of a beggar, a wretched man and an old, leaning on a staff; and sorry was the raiment wherewith he was clothed upon. But as they fared along the rugged path they drew near to the town, and came to the fair flowing spring, with a basin fashioned, whence the people of the city drew water. This well Ithacus and Neritus and Polyctor had builded. And around it was a thicket of alders that grow by the waters, all circlewise, and down the cold stream fell from a rock on high, and above was reared an altar to the Nymphs, whereat all wayfarers made offering. In that place Melanthius, son of Dolius, met them, leading his goats to feast the wooers, the best goats that were in all the herds; and two herdsmen bare him company. Now when he saw them he reviled them, and spake and hailed them, in terrible and evil fashion, and stirred the heart of Odysseus, saying:

"Now in very truth the vile is leading the vile, for god brings ever like to like! Say, whither art thou leading this glutton, — thou wretched swineherd, — this plaguy beggar, a kill-joy of the feast? He is one to stand about and rub his shoulders against many doorposts, begging for scraps of meat.

not for swords or cauldrons. If thou wouldst give me the fellow to watch my steading and sweep out the stalls, and carry young branches to the kids, then he might drink whey and get him a stout thigh. Howbeit, since he is practised only in evil, he will not care to betake him to the labour of the farm, but rather chooses to go louting through the land asking alms to fill his insatiate belly. But now I will speak out and my word shall surely be accomplished. If ever he fares to the house of divine Odysseus, many a stool that men's hands hurl shall fly about his head, and break upon his ribs, as they pelt him through the house."

Therewith, as he went past, he kicked Odysseus on the hip, in his witlessness, yet he drave him not from the path, but he abode steadfast. And Odysseus pondered whether he should rush upon him and take away his life with the staff, or lift him in his grasp and smite his head to the earth. Yet he hardened his heart to endure and refrained himself.

And they walked slowly on. But Melanthius stepped forth, and came very speedily to the house of the prince, and straightway he went in and sat down among the wooers, over against Eurymachus, for he loved him above all the rest. And they that ministered set by him a portion of flesh, and the grave dame brought wheaten bread and set it by him to eat. Now Odysseus and the goodly swineherd drew near and stood by, and the sound of the hollow lyre rang around them, for Phemius was lifting up his voice amid the company in song, and Odysseus caught the swineherd by the hand, and spake, saying:

"Eumaeus, verily this is the fair house of Odysseus, and right easily might it be known and marked even among many. There is building beyond building, and the court of the house is cunningly wrought with a wall and battlements, and well fenced are the folding doors; no man may hold it in disdain. And I see that many men keep revel within, for the savour of the fat rises upward, and the voice of the lyre is heard there, which the gods have made to be the mate of the feast."

Then didst thou make answer, swineherd Eumaeus: "Easily thou knowest it, for indeed thou never lackest understanding. But come, let us advise us how things shall fall out here. Either do thou go first within the fair-lying halls, and join the company of the wooers, so will I remain here, or if thou wilt, abide here, and I will go before thy face, and tarry not long, lest one see thee without, and hurl at thee or strike thee. Look well to this, I bid thee."

Then the steadfast goodly Odysseus answered him, saying: "I mark, I heed, all this thou speakest to one with understanding. Do thou then go before me, and I will remain here, for well I know what it is to be smitten and hurled at. My heart is full of hardiness, for much evil have I suffered in perils of waves and war; let this be added to the tale of those."

Thus they spake one to the other. And lo, a hound raised up his head and pricked his ears, even where he lay, Argos, the hound of Odysseus of the hardy heart, which of old himself had bred, but had got no joy of him, for ere that he went to sacred Ilios. Now in time past the young men used to lead the hound against wild goats and deer and hares; but as then, despised he lay (his master being afar) in the deep dung of mules and kine, whereof an ample bed was spread before the doors, till the thralls of Odysseus should carry it away to dung therewith his wide demesne. There lay the dog Argos, full of vermin. Yet even now when he was ware of Odysseus standing by, he wagged his tail and dropped both his ears, but nearer to his master he had not now the strength to draw. But Odysseus looked aside and wiped away a tear that he easily hid from Eumaeus, and straightway he asked him, saying:

"Eumaeus, verily this is a great marvel, this hound lying here in the dung. Truly he is goodly of growth, but I know not certainly if he have speed with this beauty, or if he be comely only, like as are men's trencher dogs that their lords keep for the pleasure of the eye."

Then didst thou make answer, swineherd Eumaeus: "In very truth this is the dog of a man that has died in a far land. If he were what once he was in limb and in the feats of the chase, when Odysseus left him to go to Troy, soon wouldst thou marvel at the sight of his swiftness and his strength. There was no beast that could flee from him in the deep places of the wood, when he was in pursuit; for even on a track he was the keenest hound. But now he is holden in an evil case, and his lord hath perished far from his own country, and the careless women take no charge of him. Nay, thralls are no more inclined to honest service when their masters have lost the dominion, for Zeus, of the far-borne voice, takes away the half of a man's virtue, when the day of slavery comes upon him."

Therewith he passed within the fair-lying house, and went straight to the hall, to the company of the proud wooers. But upon Argos came the fate of black death even in the hour that he beheld Odysseus again, in the twentieth year.

Now godlike Telemachus was far the first to behold the swineherd as he came through the hall, and straightway then he beckoned and called him to his side. So Eumaeus looked about and took a settle that lay by him, where the carver was wont to sit dividing much flesh among the wooers that were feasting in the house. This seat he carried and set by the table of Telemachus over against him, and there sat down himself. And the henchman took a mess and served it him, and wheaten bread out of the basket.

And close behind him Odysseus entered the house in the guise of a beggar, a wretched man and an old, leaning on his staff, and clothed on with sorry raiment. And he sat down on the ashen threshold within the doorway, leaning against a pillar of cypress wood, which the carpenter on a time had deftly planed, and thereon made straight the line. And

Telemachus called the swineherd to him, and took a whole loaf out of the fair basket, and of flesh so much as his hands could hold in their grasp, saying:

"Take and give this to the stranger, and bid him go about and beg himself of all the wooers in their turn, for shame is an ill mate of a needy man."

So he spake, and the swineherd went when he heard that saying, and stood by and spake to him winged words:

"Stranger, Telemachus gives thee these and bids thee go about and beg of all the wooers in their turn, for, he says, 'shame ill becomes a beggar man.'"

Then Odysseus of many counsels answered him and said: "King Zeus, grant me that Telemachus may be happy among men, and may he have all his heart's desire!"

Therewith he took the gift in both hands, and set it there before his feet on his unsightly scrip. Then he ate meat so long as the minstrel was singing in the halls. When he had done supper, and the divine minstrel was ending his song, then the wooers raised a clamour through the halls; but Athene stood by Odysseus, son of Laertes, and moved him to go gathering morsels of bread among the wooers, and learn which were righteous and which unjust. Yet not even so was she minded to redeem one man of them from an evil fate. So he set out, beginning on the right, to ask of each man, stretching out his hand on every side, as though he were a beggar from of old. And they pitied him, and gave him somewhat, and were amazed at him, asking one another who he was and whence he came?

Then Melanthius, the goatherd, spake among them:

"Listen, ye wooers of the renowned queen, concerning this stranger, for verily I have seen him before. The swineherd truly was his guide hither, but of him I have no certain knowledge, whence he avows him to be born."

So spake he, but Antinous rebuked the swineherd, saying: "Oh, notorious swineherd, wherefore, I pray thee, didst thou bring this man to the city? Have we not vagrants enough besides, plaguy beggars, kill-joys of the feast? Dost thou count it a light thing that they assemble here and devour the living of thy master, but thou must needs call in this man too?"

Then didst thou make answer, swineherd Eumaeus: "Antinous, no fair words are these of thine, noble though thou art. For who himself ever seeks out and bids to the feast a stranger from afar, save only one of those that are craftsmen of the people, a prophet or a healer of ills, or a shipwright, or even a godlike minstrel, who can delight all with his song? Nay, these are the men that are welcome over all the wide earth. But none would call a beggar to the banquet, to be a torment to himself. But thou art ever hard above all the other wooers to the servants of Odysseus, and, beyond all, to me; but behold, I care not, so long as my mistress, the constant Penelope, lives in the halls and godlike Telemachus."

Then wise Telemachus answered him, saying: "Be silent, answer him not, I pray thee, with many words, for Antinous is wont ever to chide us shamefully with bitter speech, yea, and urges the others thereto."

Therewithal he spake winged words to Antinous: "Antinous, verily thou hast a good care for me, as it were a father for his son, thou that biddest me drive our guest from the hall with a harsh command. God forbid that such a thing should be! Take somewhat and give it him: lo, I grudge it not; nay, I charge thee to do it. And herein regard not my mother, nor any of the thralls that are in the house of divine Odysseus. Nay, but thou hast no such thought in thy heart, for thou art far more fain to eat thyself than to give to another."

Then Antinous answered him and spake, saying: "Telemachus, proud of speech, and unrestrained in fury, what word hast thou spoken? If all the wooers should vouchsafe him as much as I, this house would keep him far enough aloof even for three months' space."

So he spake, and seized the footstool whereon he rested his smooth feet as he sat at the feast, and showed it from beneath the table where it lay. But all the others gave somewhat and filled the wallet with bread and flesh; yea, and Odysseus was even now going back to the threshold, presently to taste of the bounty of the Achaeans, but he halted by Antinous, and spake to him, saying:

"Friend, give me somewhat; for methinks thou art not the basest of the Achaeans, but the best man of them all, for thou art like a king. Wherefore thou shouldest give me a portion of bread, and that a better than the others; so would I make thee renowned over all the wide earth. For I too once had a house of mine own among men, a rich man with a wealthy house, and many a time would I give to a wanderer, what manner of man soever he might be, and in whatsoever need he came. And I had thralls out of number, and all else in plenty, wherewith folk live well and have a name for riches. But Zeus, the son of Cronos, made me desolate of all, — for surely it was his will, — who sent me with wandering sea-robbers to go to Egypt and Cyprus, a far road, to my ruin."

Then Antinous answered, and spake, saying: "What god hath brought this plague hither to trouble the feast? Stand forth thus in the midst, away from my table, lest thou come soon to a bitter Egypt and a sad Cyprus; for a bold beggar art thou and a shameless. Thou standest by all in turn and recklessly they give to thee, for they hold not their hand nor feel any ruth in giving freely of others' goods, for that each man has plenty by him."

Then Odysseus of many counsels drew back and answered him: "Lo now, I see thou hast not wisdom with thy beauty! From out of thine own house thou wouldest not give even so much as a grain of salt to thy suppliant, thou who now even at another's board dost sit, and canst not find it in thy heart to take of the bread and give it me, where there is plenty to thy hand."

He spake, and Antinous waxed yet more wroth at heart, and looked fiercely on him and spake winged words:

"Henceforth, methinks, thou shalt not get thee out with honour from the hall, seeing thou dost even rail upon me."

Therewith he caught up the footstool and smote Odysseus on the right shoulder, at the upper end of the back. But he stood firm as a rock, nor reeled he beneath the blow of Antinous, but shook his head in silence, brooding evil in the deep of his heart. Then he went back to the threshold, and sat him there, and laid down his well-filled scrip, and spake among the wooers:

"Hear me, ye wooers of the renowned queen, and I will say what my spirit within me bids me. Verily there is neither pain nor grief of heart, when a man is smitten in battle fighting for his own possessions, whether cattle or white sheep. But now Antinous hath stricken me for my wretched belly's sake, a thing accursed, that works much ill for men. Ah, if indeed there be gods and Avengers of beggars, may the issues of death come upon Antinous before his wedding!"

Then Antinous, son of Eupeithes, answered him: "Sit and eat thy meat in quiet, stranger, or get thee elsewhere, lest the young men drag thee by hand or foot through the house for thy evil words, and strip all thy flesh from off thee."

Even so he spake, and they were all exceeding wroth at his word. And on this wise would one of the lordly young men speak:

"Antinous, thou didst ill to strike the hapless wanderer, doomed man that thou art, — if indeed there be a god in heaven. Yea and the gods, in the likeness of strangers from far countries, put on all manner of shapes, and wander through the cities, beholding the violence and the righteousness of men."

So the wooers spake, but he heeded not their words. Now Telemachus nursed in his heart a mighty grief at the smiting of Odysseus, yet he let no tear fall from his eyelids to the ground, but shook his head in silence, brooding evil in the deep of his heart.

Now when wise Penelope heard of the stranger being smitten in the halls, she spake among her maidens, saying:

"Oh that Apollo, the famed archer, may so smite thee thyself, Antinous!"

And the house-dame, Eurynome, answered her, saying: "Oh that we might win fulfilment of our prayers! So should not one of these men come to the fair-throned Dawn."

And wise Penelope answered her: "Nurse, they are all enemies, for they all devise evil continually, but of them all Antinous is the most like to black fate. Some hapless stranger is roaming about the house, begging alms of the men, as his need bids him; and all the others filled his wallet and gave him somewhat, but Antinous smote him between his right shoulder and the back with the stool."

So she spake among her maidens, sitting in her chamber, while goodly Odysseus was at meat. Then she called to her the goodly swineherd and spake, saying:

"Go thy way, goodly Eumaeus, and bid the stranger come hither, that I may speak him a word of greeting, and ask him if haply he has heard tidings of Odysseus of the hardy heart, or seen him with his eyes; for he seems like one that has wandered far."

Then didst thou make answer, swineherd Eumaeus: "Queen, oh that the Achaeans would hold their peace! so would he charm thy very heart, such things doth he say. For I kept him three nights and three days I held him in the steading, for to me he came first when he fled from the ship, yet he had not made an end of the tale of his affliction. Even as when a man gazes on a singer, whom the gods have taught to sing words of yearning joy to mortals, and they have a ceaseless desire to hear him, so long as he will sing; even so he charmed me, sitting by me in the halls. He says that he is a friend of Odysseus and of his house, one that dwells in Crete, where is the race of Minos. Thence he has come hither even now, with sorrow by the way, onward and yet onward wandering; and he stands to it that he has heard tidings of Odysseus nigh at hand and yet alive in the fat land of the men of Thesprotia; and he is bringing many treasures to his home."

Then wise Penelope answered him, saying: "Go, call him hither, that he may speak to me face to face. And if I shall find that he has spoken nought but truth, I will clothe him with a mantle and a doublet, goodly raiment."

So she spake, and the swineherd departed when he heard that saying, and stood by the stranger and spake winged words:

"Father and stranger, wise Penelope, the mother of Telemachus, is calling for thee, and her mind bids her inquire as touching her lord, albeit she has sorrowed much already. And if she shall find that thou hast spoken nought but truth, she will clothe thee in a mantle and a doublet, whereof thou standest most in need. Moreover thou shalt beg thy bread through the land and shalt fill thy belly, and whosoever will, shall give to thee."

Then the steadfast goodly Odysseus answered him, saying: "Eumaeus, soon would I tell all the truth to the daughter of Icarius, wise Penelope, for well I know his story, and we have borne our travail together. But somewhat I fear the throng of the froward wooers, whose outrage and violence reach even to the iron heaven. For even now, as I was going through the house, when this man struck and pained me sore, and that for no ill deed, neither Telemachus nor any other kept off the blow. Wherefore now, bid Penelope tarry in the halls, for all her eagerness, till the going down of the sun, and then let her ask me concerning her lord, as touching the day of his returning, and let her give me a seat yet nearer to the fire, for behold, I have sorry raiment, and thou knowest it thyself, since I made my supplication first to thee."

Even so he spake, and the swineherd departed when he heard that saying. And as he crossed the threshold Penelope spake to him:

"Thou bringest him not, Eumaeus: what means the wanderer hereby? Can it be that he fears some one out of measure, or is he even ashamed of tarrying in the house? A shamefaced man makes a bad beggar."

Then didst thou make answer, swineherd Eumaeus: "He speaks aright, and but as another would deem, in that he shuns the outrage of overweening men. Rather would he have thee wait till the going down of the sun. Yea, and it is far meeter for thyself, O queen, to utter thy word to the stranger alone, and to listen to his speech."

Then the wise Penelope answered: "The stranger deems as a man of understanding, and it may well be even so. For there are no mortal men, methinks, so wanton as these, and none that devise such infatuate deeds."

So she spake, and the goodly swineherd departed into the throng of the wooers, when he had shown her all his message. And straightway he spake to Telemachus winged words, holding his head close to him, that the others might not hear:

"Friend, I am going hence to look after thy swine and the things of the farm, thy livelihood and mine; but do thou take charge of all that is here. Yet first look to thyself and take heed that no evil comes nigh thee, for many of the Achaeans have ill will against us, whom may Zeus confound before their mischief falls on us!"

And wise Telemachus answered him, and said: "Even so shall it be, father; and do thou get thee on thy way, when thou hast supped. And in the morning come again, and bring fair victims for sacrifice. And all these matters will be a care to me and to the deathless gods."

Thus he spake, and the other sat down again on the polished settle; and when he had satisfied his heart with meat and drink, he went on his way to the swine, leaving the courts and the hall full of feasters; and they were making merry with dance and song, for already it was close on eventide.

BOOK XVIII

The fighting at fists of Odysseus with Irus. His admonitions to Amphinomus. Penelope appears before the wooers, and draws presents from them.

THEN up came a common beggar, who was wont to beg through the town of Ithaca, one that was known among all men for ravening greed, for his endless eating and drinking, yet he had no force or might, though he was bulky enough to look on. Arnaeus was his name, for so had his good mother given it him at his birth, but all the young men called him Irus, because he ran on errands, whensoever any might bid him. So now he came, and would have driven Odysseus from his own house, and began reviling him, and spake winged words:

"Get thee hence, old man, from the doorway, lest thou be even haled out soon by the foot. Seest thou not that all are now giving me the wink, and bidding me drag thee forth? Nevertheless, I feel shame of the task. Nay, get thee up, lest our quarrel soon pass even to blows."

Then Odysseus of many counsels looked fiercely on him, and spake, saying: "Sir, neither in deed nor word do I harm thee, nor do I grudge that any should give to thee, yea though it were a good handful. But this threshold will hold us both, and thou hast no need to be jealous for the sake of other men's goods. Thou seemest to me to be a wanderer, even as I am, and the gods it is that are like to give us gain. Only provoke me not overmuch to buffeting, lest thou anger me, and old though I be I defile thy breast and lips with blood. Thereby should I have the greater quiet to-morrow, for methinks that thou shalt never again come to the hall of Odysseus, son of Laertes."

Then the beggar Irus spake unto him in anger: "Lo now, how trippingly and like an old cinder-wife this glutton speaks, on whom I will work my evil will, and smite him right and left, and drive all the teeth from his jaws to the ground, like the tusks of a swine that spoils the corn. Gird thyself now, that even these men all may know our mettle in fight. Nay, how shouldst thou do battle with a younger man than thou?"

Thus did they whet each the other's rage right manfully before the lofty doors upon the polished threshold. And the mighty prince Antinous heard the twain, and sweetly he laughed out, and spake among the wooers:

"Friends, never before has there been such a thing; such goodly game has a god brought to this house. The stranger yonder and Irus are bidding each other to buffets. Quick, let us match them one against the other."

Then all at the word leaped up laughing, and gathered round the ragged beggars, and Antinous, son of Eupeithes, spake among them, saying: "Hear me, ye lordly wooers, and I will say somewhat. Here are goats' bellies lying at the fire, that we laid by at supper-time and filled with fat and blood. Now whichsoever of the train wins, and shows himself the better man, let him stand up and take his choice of these puddings. And further, he shall always eat at our feasts, nor will we suffer any other beggar to come among us and ask for alms."

So spake Antinous, and the saying pleased them well. Then Odysseus of many counsels spake among them craftily:

"Friends, an old man and foredone with travail may in no wise fight with a younger. But my belly's call is urgent on me, that evil-worker, to the end that I may be subdued with stripes. But come now, swear me all of you a strong oath, so that none, for the sake of showing a favour to Irus, may strike

P

me a foul blow with heavy hand and subdue me by violence to my foe."

So he spake, and they all swore not to strike him, as he bade them. Now when they had sworn and done that oath, the mighty prince Telemachus once more spake among them:

"Stranger, if thy heart and lordly spirit urge thee to rid thee of this fellow, then fear not any other of the Achaeans, for whoso strikes thee shall have to fight with many. Thy host am I, and the princes consent with me, Antinous and Eurymachus, men of wisdom both."

So spake he and they all consented thereto. Then Odysseus girt his rags about his loins, and let his thighs be seen, goodly and great, and his broad shoulders and breast and mighty arms were manifest. And Athene came nigh and made greater the limbs of the shepherd of the people. Then the wooers were exceedingly amazed, and thus would one speak looking to his neighbour:

"Right soon will Irus, un-Irused, have a bane of his own bringing, such a thigh as that old man shows from out his rags!"

So they spake, and the mind of Irus was pitifully stirred; but even so the servants girded him and led him out perforce in great fear, his flesh trembling on his limbs. Then Antinous chid him, and spake and hailed him:

"Thou braggart, better for thee that thou wert not now, nor ever hadst been born, if indeed thou tremblest before this man, and art so terribly afraid; an old man too he is, and foredone with the travail that is come upon him."

So he spake, and yet greater trembling gat hold of the limbs of Irus, and they led him into the ring, and the twain put up their hands. Then the steadfast goodly Odysseus mused in himself whether he should smite him in such wise that his life should leave his body, even there where he fell, or whether he should strike him lightly, and stretch him on the earth. And as he thought thereon, this seemed to him the better way, to strike lightly, that the Achaeans might not know him, who he was. Then the twain put up their hands, and Irus struck at the right shoulder, but the other smote him on his neck beneath the ear, and crushed in the bones, and straightway the red blood gushed up through his mouth, and with a moan he fell in the dust, and drave together his teeth as he kicked the ground. But the proud wooers threw up their hands, and died outright for laughter. Then Odysseus seized him by the foot, and dragged him forth through the doorway, till he came to the courtyard and the gates of the gallery, and he set him down and rested him against the courtyard wall, and put his staff in his hands, and uttering his voice spake to him winged words :

"Sit thou there now, and scare off swine and dogs, and let not such an one as thou be lord over strangers and beggars, pitiful as thou art, lest haply some worse thing befall thee."

Thus he spake, and cast about his shoulders his mean scrip all tattered, and the cord therewith to hang it, and he gat him back to the threshold, and sat him down there again. Now the wooers went within laughing sweetly, and greeted him, saying:

"May Zeus, stranger, and all the other deathless gods give thee thy dearest wish, even all thy heart's desire, seeing that thou hast made that insatiate one to cease from his begging in the land!"

So they spake, and goodly Odysseus rejoiced in the omen of the words. And Antinous set by him the great pudding, stuffed with fat and blood, and Amphinomus took up two loaves from the basket, and set them by him and pledged him in a golden cup, and spake saying:

"Father and stranger, hail! may happiness be thine in the time to come; but as now, thou art fast holden in many sorrows."

And Odysseus of many counsels answered him, saying: "Amphinomus, verily thou seemest to me a prudent man enough; for such too was the father of whom thou art sprung, for I have heard the fair fame of him, how that Nisus of Dulichium was a good man and a rich, and his son they say thou art, and thou seemest a man of understanding. Wherefore I will tell thee, and do thou mark and listen to me. Nought feebler doth the earth nurture than man, of all the creatures that breathe and move upon the face of the earth. Lo, he thinks that he shall never suffer evil in time to come, while the gods give him happiness, and his limbs move lightly. But when again the blessed gods have wrought for him sorrow, even so he bears it, as he must, with a steadfast heart. For the spirit of men upon the earth is even as their day, that comes upon them from the father of gods and men. Yea, and I too once was like to have been prosperous among men, but many an infatuate deed I did, giving place to mine own hardihood and strength, and trusting to my father and my brethren. Wherefore let no man for ever be lawless any more, but keep quietly the gifts of the gods, whatsoever they may give. Such infatuate deeds do I see the wooers devising, as they waste the wealth, and hold in no regard the wife of a man, who, methinks, will not much longer be far from his friends and his own land; nay, he is very near. But for thee, may some god withdraw thee hence to thy home, and mayst thou not meet him in the day when he returns to his own dear country! For not without blood, as I deem, will they be sundered, the wooers and Odysseus, when once he shall have come beneath his own roof."

Thus he spake, and poured an offering and then drank of the honey-sweet wine, and again set the cup in the hands of the arrayer of the people. But the other went back through the house, sad at heart and bowing his head; for verily his soul boded evil. Yet even so he avoided not his fate, for

Athene had bound him likewise to be slain outright at the hands and by the spear of Telemachus. So he sat down again on the high seat whence he had arisen.

Now the goddess, grey-eyed Athene, put it into the heart of the daughter of Icarius, wise Penelope, to show herself to the wooers, that she might make their heart greatly to swell for joy, and that she might win yet more worship from her lord and her son than heretofore. So she laughed an idle laugh, and spake to the nurse, and hailed her, saying:

"Eurynome, my heart yearns, though before I had no such desire, to show myself to the wooers, hateful as they are. I would also say a word to my son, that will be for his weal, namely, that he should not for ever consort with the proud wooers, who speak friendly with their lips, but imagine evil in the latter end."

Then the housewife, Eurynome, spake to her, saying: 'Yea, my child, all this thou hast spoken as is meet. Go then, and declare thy word to thy son and hide it not, but first wash thee and anoint thy face, and go not as thou art with thy cheeks all stained with tears. Go, for it is little good to sorrow always, and never cease. And lo, thy son is now of an age to hear thee, he whom thou hast above all things prayed the gods that thou mightest see with a beard upon his chin."

Then wise Penelope answered her, saying: "Eurynome, speak not thus comfortably to me, for all thy love, bidding me to wash and be anointed with ointment. For the gods that keep Olympus destroyed my bloom, since the day that he departed in the hollow ships. But bid Autonoe and Hippodameia come to me, to stand by my side in the halls. Alone I will not go among men, for I am ashamed."

So she spake, and the old woman passed through the chamber to tell the maidens, and hasten their coming.

Thereon the goddess, grey-eyed Athene, had another thought.

She shed a sweet slumber over the daughter of Icarius, who sank back in sleep, and all her joints were loosened as she lay in the chair, and the fair goddess the while was giving her gifts immortal, that all the Achaeans might marvel at her. Her fair face first she steeped with beauty imperishable, such as that wherewith the crowned Cytherea is anointed, when she goes to the lovely dances of the Graces. And she made her taller and greater to behold, and made her whiter than new-sawn ivory. Now when she had wrought thus, that fair goddess departed, and the white-armed handmaidens came forth from the chamber and drew nigh with a sound of voices. Then sweet sleep left hold of Penelope, and she rubbed her cheeks with her hands, and said:

"Surely soft slumber wrapped me round, most wretched though I be. Oh! that pure Artemis would give me so soft a death even now, that I might no more waste my life in sorrow of heart, and longing for the manifold excellence of my dear lord, for that he was foremost of the Achaeans."

With this word she went down from the shining upper chamber, not alone, for two handmaidens likewise bare her company. But when the fair lady had now come to the wooers, she stood by the doorpost of the well-builded room, holding her glistening tire before her face, and on either side of her stood a faithful handmaid. And straightway the knees of the wooers were loosened, and their hearts were enchanted with love. But she spake to Telemachus, her dear son:

"Telemachus, thy mind and thy thoughts are no longer stable as they were. While thou wast still a child, thou hadst a yet nimbler and more gainful wit, but now that thou art great of growth, and art come to the measure of manhood, and a stranger looking to thy stature and thy beauty might say that thou must be some rich man's son, thy mind and thy thoughts are no longer right as of old. For lo, what manner of deed has been done in these halls, in that thou hast suffered thy guest to be thus shamefully dealt with! How would it be now, if the stranger sitting in our house, were thus to come to some harm all through this evil handling? Shame and disgrace would be thine henceforth among men."

Then wise Telemachus answered her: "Mother mine, as to this matter I count it no blame that thou art angered. Yet have I knowledge and understanding of each thing, of the good and of the evil; but heretofore I was a child. Howbeit I cannot devise all things according to wisdom, for these men in their evil counsel drive me from my will, on this side and on that, and there is none to aid me. Howsoever this battle between Irus and the stranger did not fall out as the wooers would have had it, but the stranger proved the better man. Would to Father Zeus and Athene and Apollo, that the wooers in our halls were even now thus vanquished, and wagging their heads, some in the court, and some within the house, and that the limbs of each man were loosened in such fashion as Irus yonder sits now, by the courtyard gates wagging his head, like a drunken man, and cannot stand upright on his feet, nor yet get him home to his own place, seeing that his limbs are loosened!"

Thus they spake one to another. But Eurymachus spake to Penelope, saying:

"Daughter of Icarius, wise Penelope, if all the Achaeans in Iasian Argos could behold thee, even a greater press of wooers would feast in your halls from to-morrow's dawn, since thou dost surpass all women in beauty and stature, and within in wisdom of mind."

Then wise Penelope answered him: "Eurymachus, surely my excellence, both of face and form, the gods destroyed in the day when the Argives embarked for Ilios, and with them went my lord Odysseus. If but he might come and watch over this my life, greater thus would be my fame and fairer! But now am I in sorrow; such a host of ills some god has sent against me. Ah, well do I remember, when he set forth and left his own country, how he took me by the right hand at the wrist and spake, saying :

"'Lady, methinks that all the goodly-greaved Achaeans will not win a safe return from Troy ; for the Trojans too, they say, are good men at arms, as spearsmen, and bowmen, and drivers of fleet horses, such as ever most swiftly determine the great strife of equal battle. Wherefore I know not if the gods will suffer me to return, or whether I shall be cut off there in Troy ; so do thou have a care for all these things. Be mindful of my father and my mother in the halls, even as now thou art, or yet more than now, while I am far away. But when thou seest thy son a bearded man, marry whom thou wilt and leave thine own house.'

" Even so did he speak, and now all these things have an end. The night shall come when a hateful marriage shall find me out, me most luckless, whose good hap Zeus has taken away. But furthermore this sore trouble has come on my heart and soul ; for this was not the manner of wooers in time past. Whoso wish to woo a good lady and the daughter of a rich man, and vie one with another, themselves bring with them oxen of their own and goodly flocks, a banquet for the friends of the bride, and they give the lady splendid gifts, but do not devour another's livelihood without atonement."

Thus she spake, and the steadfast goodly Odysseus rejoiced because she drew from them gifts, and beguiled their souls with soothing words, while her heart was set on other things.

Then Antinous, son of Eupeithes, answered her again : "Daughter of Icarius, wise Penelope, the gifts which any of the Achaeans may choose to bring hither, do thou take ; for it is not well to refuse a gift. But we for our part will neither go to our lands nor otherwhere, before thou art wedded to the best man of the Achaeans."

So spake Antinous, and the saying pleased them well, and each man sent a henchman to bring his gifts. For Antinous his henchman bare a broidered robe, great and very fair, wherein were golden brooches, twelve in all, fitted with well-bent clasps. And the henchman straightway bare Eurymachus a golden chain of curious work, strung with amber beads, shining like the sun. And his squires bare for Eurydamas a pair of ear-rings, with three drops well wrought, and much grace shone from them. And out of the house of Peisander the prince, the son of Polyctor, the squire brought a necklet, a very lovely jewel. And likewise the Achaeans brought each one some other beautiful gift.

Then the fair lady went aloft to her upper chamber, and her attendant maidens bare for her the lovely gifts, while the wooers turned to dancing and the delight of song, and therein took their pleasure, and awaited the coming of eventide. And dark evening came on them at their pastime. Anon they set up three braziers in the halls, to give them light, and on these they laid firewood all around, faggots seasoned long since and sere, and new split with the axe, and to them they set burning pine-brands. And the maids of Odysseus, of the hardy heart, in turn were rousing the light of the flames. Then the prince Odysseus of many counsels himself spake among them, saying:

"Ye maidens of Odysseus, the lord so long afar, get ye into the chambers where the honoured queen abides, and twist the yarn at her side, and gladden her heart as ye sit in the chamber, or card the wools with your hands; but I will minister light to all these that are here. For even if they are minded to wait the throned Dawn, they shall not outstay me, so long enduring am I."

So he spake, but they laughed and looked one at the other. And the fair Melantho chid him shamefully, Melantho that Dolius begat, but Penelope reared, and entreated her tenderly as she had been her own child, and gave her playthings to her heart's desire. Yet, for all that, the sorrow of Penelope touched not her heart, but she loved Eurymachus and was his paramour. Now she chid Odysseus with railing words:

"Wretched guest, surely thou art some brain-struck man, seeing that thou dost not choose to go and sleep at a smithy, or at some place of common resort, but here thou pratest much and boldly among many lords and hast no fear at heart. Verily wine has got about thy wits, or perchance thou art always of this mind, and so thou dost babble idly. Art thou beside thyself for joy, because thou hast beaten the beggar Irus? Take heed lest a better man than Irus rise up presently against thee, to lay his mighty hands about thy head and bedabble thee with blood, and send thee hence from the house."

Then Odysseus of many counsels looked fiercely on her, and said: "Yea, straight will I go yonder and tell Telemachus hereof, thou shameless thing, for this thy speech, that forthwith he may cut thee limb from limb."

So he spake, and with his saying scared away the women, who fled through the halls, and the knees of each were loosened for fear, for they deemed that his words were true. But Odysseus took his stand by the burning braziers, tending the lights, and gazed on all the men: but far other matters he pondered in his heart, things not to be unfulfilled.

Now Athene would in no wise suffer the lordly wooers to abstain from biting scorn, that the pain might sink yet the deeper into the heart of Odysseus, son of Laertes. So Eurymachus, son of Polybus, began to speak among them, girding at Odysseus, and so made mirth for his friends:

"Hear me, ye wooers of the queen renowned, that I may say that which my spirit within me bids me. Not without the gods' will has this man come to the house of Odysseus; methinks at least that the torchlight flares forth from that head of his, for there are no hairs on it, nay, never so thin."

He spake and withal addressed Odysseus, waster of cities: "Stranger, wouldest thou indeed be my hireling, if I would take thee for my man, at an upland farm, and thy wages shall be assured thee, and there shalt thou gather stones for dykes and plant tall trees? There would I provide.thee bread continual, and clothe thee with raiment, and give thee shoes for thy feet. Howbeit, since thou art practised only in evil, thou wilt not care to go to the labours of the field, but wilt choose rather to go louting through the land, that thou mayst have wherewithal to feed thy insatiate belly."

Then Odysseus of many counsels answered him and said: "Eurymachus, would that there might be a trial of labour between us twain, in the season of spring, when the long days begin! In the deep grass might it be, and I should have a crooked scythe, and thou another like it, that we might try each the other in the matter of labour, fasting till late eventide, and grass there should be in plenty. Or would again, that there were oxen to drive, the best there may be, large and tawny, both well filled with fodder, of equal age and force to bear the yoke and of strength untiring! And it should be a field of four ploughgates, and the clod should yield before the ploughshare. Then shouldest thou see me, whether or no I would cut a clean furrow unbroken before me. Or would that this very day Cronion might waken war whence he would, and that I had a shield and two spears, and a helmet all of bronze, close fitting on my temples! Then shouldest thou see me mingling in the forefront of the battle, nor speak and taunt me with this my belly. Nay, thou art exceeding wanton and thy heart is hard, and thou thinkest thyself some great one and mighty, because thou consortest with few men and feeble. Ah, if Odysseus might but return and come to his own country, right soon would yonder doors, full wide as they are, prove all too strait for thee in thy flight through the doorway!"

Thus he spake, and Eurymachus waxed yet the more wroth at heart, and looking fiercely on him spake to him winged words:

"Ah, wretch that thou art, right soon will I work thee

mischief, so boldly thou pratest among many lords, and hast no fear at heart. Verily wine has got about thy wits, or perchance thou art always of this mind, and so thou dost babble idly. Art thou beside thyself for joy, because thou hast beaten the beggar Irus?"

Therewith he caught up a footstool, but Odysseus sat him down at the knees of Amphinomus of Dulichium, in dread of Eurymachus. And Eurymachus cast and smote the cup-bearer on the right hand, and the ladle cup dropped to the ground with a clang, while the young man groaned and fell backwards in the dust. Then the wooers clamoured through the shadowy halls, and thus one would say, looking to his neighbour:

"Would that our wandering guest had perished otherwhere, or ever he came hither; so should he never have made all this tumult in our midst! But now we are all at strife about beggars, and there will be no more joy of the good feast, for worse things have their way."

Then the mighty prince Telemachus spake among them:

"Sirs, ye are mad; now ye no longer hide it that ye have eaten and drunken; some one of the gods is surely moving you. Nay, now that ye have feasted well, go home and lay you to rest, whenso your spirit bids; for as for me, I drive no man hence."

Thus he spake, and they all bit their lips and marvelled at Telemachus, in that he spake boldly. Then Amphinomus made harangue, and spake among them, Amphinomus, the famous son of Nisus the prince, the son of Aretias:

"Friends, when a righteous word has been spoken, none surely would rebuke another with hard speech and be angry. Misuse ye not this stranger, neither any of the thralls that are in the house of godlike Odysseus. But come, let the wine-bearer pour for libation into each cup in turn, that after the drink-offering we may get us home to bed. But the stranger let us leave in the halls of Odysseus for a charge to Telemachus: for to his home has he come."

Thus he spake, and his word was well-pleasing to them all. Then the lord Mulius mixed for them the bowl, the henchman out of Dulichium, who was squire of Amphinomus. And he stood by them all and served it to them in their turn; and they poured forth before the blessed gods, and drank the honey-sweet wine. Now when they had poured forth and had drunken to their hearts' content, they departed to lie down, each one to his own house.

BOOK XIX

Telemachus removes the arms out of the hall. Odysseus discourseth with Penelope. And is known by his nurse, but concealed.

Now the goodly Odysseus was left behind in the hall, devising with Athene's aid the slaying of the wooers, and straightway he spake winged words to Telemachus:

"Telemachus, we must needs lay by the weapons of war within, every one; and when the wooers miss them and ask thee concerning them, thou shalt beguile them with soft words."

Thus he spake, and Telemachus hearkened to his dear father, and called forth to him the nurse Eurycleia and spake to her, saying:

"Nurse, come now, I pray thee, shut up the women in their chambers till I shall have laid by in the armoury the goodly weapons of my father, which all uncared for the smoke dims in the hall, since my father went hence, and I was still but a child. Now I wish to lay them by where the vapour of the fire will not reach them."

Then the good nurse Eurycleia answered him, saying: "Ah, my child, if ever thou wouldest but take careful thought in such wise as to mind the house, and guard all this wealth! But come, who shall attend thee and bear the light, if thou hast thy way, since thou wouldest not that the maidens, who might have given light, should go before thee?"

Then wise Telemachus made answer to her: "This stranger here, for I will keep no man in idleness who eats of my bread, even if he have come from afar."

Thus he spake, and his word unwinged abode with her, and she closed the doors of the fair-lying chambers. Then they twain sprang up, Odysseus and his renowned son, and set to carry within the helmets and the bossy shields, and the sharp-pointed spears; and before them Pallas Athene bare a golden cresset and cast a most lovely light. Thereon Telemachus spake to his father suddenly:

"Father, surely a great marvel is this that I behold with mine eyes; meseems, at least, that the walls of the hall and the fair main-beams of the roof and the cross-beams of pine, and the pillars that run aloft, are bright as it were with flaming fire. Verily some god is within, of those that hold the wide heaven."

And Odysseus of many counsels answered him and said: "Hold thy peace and keep all this in thine heart and ask not hereof. Lo, this is the wont of the gods that hold Olympus. But do thou go and lay thee down, and I will abide here, that I may yet further provoke the maids and thy mother to answer; and she in her sorrow will ask me concerning each thing, one by one."

So he spake, and Telemachus passed out through the hall to his chamber to lie down, by the light of the flaming torches, even to the chamber where of old he took his rest, when sweet sleep came over him. There now too he lay down and awaited the bright Dawn. But goodly Odysseus was left behind in the hall, devising with Athene's aid the slaying of the wooers.

Now forth from her chamber came the wise Penelope, like

Artemis or golden Aphrodite, and they set a chair for her hard by before the fire, where she was wont to sit, a chair well wrought and inlaid with ivory and silver, which on a time the craftsman Icmalius had fashioned, and had joined thereto a footstool, that was part of the chair, whereon a great fleece was used to be laid. Here, then, the wise Penelope sat her down, and next came white-armed handmaids from the women's chamber, and began to take away the many fragments of food, and the tables and the cups whence the proud lords had been drinking, and they cast the embers from the braziers on the floor, and piled many fresh logs upon them, to give light and warmth.

Then Melantho began to revile Odysseus yet a second time, saying: "Stranger, wilt thou still be a plague to us here, wandering through the house in the night, and spying the women? Nay, get thee forth, thou wretched thing, and be content with thy supper, or straightway shalt thou even be smitten with a torch and so fare out of the doors."

Then Odysseus of many counsels looked fiercely on her, and said: "Good woman, what possesses thee to assail me thus out of an angry heart? Is it because I go filthy and am clothed about in sorry raiment, and beg through the land, for necessity is laid on me? This is the manner of beggars and of wandering men. For I too once had a house of mine own among men, a rich man with a wealthy house, and many a time would I give to a wanderer, what manner of man soever he might be, and in whatsoever need he came. And I had countless thralls, and all else in plenty, whereby folk live well and have a name for riches. But Zeus, the son of Cronos, made me desolate of all, for surely it was his will. Wherefore, woman, see that thou too lose not all the glory wherewith thou art now preëminent among the handmaids, as well may chance, if thy mistress be provoked to anger with thee, or if Odysseus come home, for there is yet a place for hope. And even if he hath perished as ye deem, and is never more to return, yet by Apollo's grace he hath so goodly a son, Telemachus, and none of the women works wantonness in his halls without his knowledge, for he is no longer of an age not to mark it."

Thus he spake, and the wise Penelope heard him, and rebuked the handmaid, and spake and hailed her:

"Thou shameless thing and unabashed, thy great sin is in no wise hidden from me, and thy blood shall be on thine own head for the same! For thou knewest right well, in that thou hadst heard it from my lips, how that I was minded to ask the stranger in my halls for tidings of my lord; for I am grievously afflicted."

Therewith she spake likewise to the housedame, Eurynome, saying:

"Eurynome, bring hither a settle with a fleece thereon, that the stranger may sit and speak with me and hear my words, for I would ask him all his story."

So she spake, and the nurse made haste and brought a polished settle, and cast a fleece thereon; and then the steadfast goodly Odysseus sat him down there, and the wise Penelope spake first, saying:

"Stranger, I will make bold first to ask thee this: who art thou of the sons of men, and whence? Where is thy city, and where are they that begat thee?"

And Odysseus of many counsels answered her and said: "Lady, no one of mortal men in the wide world could find fault with thee, for thy fame goes up to the wide heaven, as doth the fame of a blameless king, one that fears the gods and reigns among many men and mighty, maintaining right, and the black earth bears wheat and barley, and the trees are laden with fruit, and the sheep bring forth and fail not, and the sea gives store of fish, and all out of his good guidance, and the people prosper under him. Wherefore do thou ask me now in thy house all else that thou wilt, but inquire not concerning my race and mine own country, lest as I think thereupon thou fill my heart the more with pains, for I am a man of many sorrows. Moreover, it beseems me not to sit weeping and wailing in another's house, for it is little good to mourn always without ceasing, lest perchance one of the maidens, or even thyself, be angry with me and say that I swim in tears, as one that is heavy with wine."

Then wise Penelope answered him, and said: "Stranger, surely my goodliness both of face and form the gods destroyed, in the day when the Argives embarked for Ilios, and with them went my lord Odysseus. If but he might come and watch over this my life, greater and fairer thus would be my fame! But now am I in sorrow, such a host of ills some god has sent against me. For all the noblest that are princes in the isles, in Dulichium and Same and wooded Zacynthus, and they that dwell around even in clear-seen Ithaca, these are wooing me against my will, and devouring the house. Wherefore I take no heed of strangers, nor suppliants, nor at all of heralds, the craftsmen of the people. But I waste my heart away in longing for Odysseus; so they speed on my marriage and I weave a web of wiles. But even so tell me of thine own stock, whence thou art, for thou art not sprung of oak or rock, whereof old tales tell."

And Odysseus of many counsels answered her and said:

"O wife revered of Odysseus, son of Laertes, thou wilt never have done asking me about mine own race. Nay, but I will tell thee: yet surely thou wilt give me over to sorrows yet more than those wherein I am holden, for so it ever is when a man has been afar from his own country for so long as now I am, wandering in sore pain to many cities of mortals."

So he told many a false tale in the likeness of truth, and her tears flowed as she listened, and her flesh melted. And even as the snow melts in the high places of the hills, the snow that the South-East wind has thawed, when the West has scattered it abroad, and as it wastes the river streams run full, even so her fair cheeks melted beneath her tears, as she wept her own lord, who even then was sitting by her. Now Odysseus had compassion of heart upon his wife in her lamenting, but his eyes kept steadfast between his eyelids as it were horn or iron, and craftily he hid his tears. But she, when she had taken her fill of tearful lamentation, answered him in turn and spake, saying:

"Friend as thou art, even now I think to make trial of thee, and learn whether in very truth thou didst entertain my lord there in thy halls with his godlike company, as thou sayest. Tell me what manner of raiment he was clothed in about his body, and what manner of man he was himself, and tell me of his fellows that went with him."

Then Odysseus of many counsels answered her, saying: "Lady, it is hard for one so long parted from him to tell thee all this, for it is now the twentieth year since he went thither and left my country. Yet even so I will tell thee as I see him in spirit. Goodly Odysseus wore a thick purple mantle, two-fold, which had a brooch fashioned in gold, with a double covering for the pins, and on the face of it was a curious device: a hound in his forepaws held a dappled fawn and gazed on it as it writhed. And all men marvelled at the workmanship, how, wrought as they were in gold, the hound was gazing on the fawn and strangling it, and the fawn was writhing with his feet and striving to flee. Moreover, I marked the shining doublet about his body, as it were the skin of a dried onion, so smooth it was, and glistering as the sun; truly many women looked thereon and wondered. I know not if Odysseus was thus clothed upon at home, or if one of his fellows gave him the raiment as he went on board the swift ship, or even it may be some stranger, seeing that to many men was Odysseus dear, for few of the Achaeans were his peers. I, too, gave him a sword of bronze, and a fair purple mantle with double fold, and a tasseled doublet, and I sent him away with all honour on his decked ship. Moreover, a henchman bare him company, somewhat older than he, and I will tell thee of him too, what manner of man he was. He was round-shouldered, brown-skinned, and curly-haired, his name Eurybates; and Odysseus honoured him above all his company, because in all things he was like-minded with himself."

So he spake, and in her heart he stirred yet more the desire of weeping, as she knew the certain tokens that Odysseus showed her. So when she had taken her fill of tearful lament, then she answered him, and spake, saying:

"Now verily, stranger, thou that even before wert held in pity, shalt be dear and honourable in my halls, for it was I who gave him these garments, even such as thou namest, and folded them myself, and brought them from the chamber, and added besides the shining brooch to be his jewel. But him I shall never welcome back, returned home to his own dear country. Wherefore with an evil fate it was that Odysseus went hence in the hollow ship to see that evil Ilios, never to be named."

And Odysseus of many counsels answered her, saying: "Wife revered of Odysseus, son of Laertes, destroy not now thy fair flesh any more, nor waste thy heart with weeping for thy lord; — not that I count it any blame in thee, for many a woman weeps that has lost her wedded lord, to whom she has borne children in her love, — albeit a far other man than Odysseus, who, they say, is like the gods. Nay, cease from thy lamenting, and lay up my word in thy heart; for I will tell thee without fail, and will hide nought, how but lately I heard tell of the return of Odysseus, that he is nigh at hand, and yet alive in the fat land of the men of Thesprotia, and is bringing with him many choice treasures, as he begs through the land. But he has lost his dear companions and his hollow ship on the wine-dark sea, on his way from the isle Thrinacia: for Zeus and Helios had a grudge against him, because his company had slain the kine of Helios. They for their part all perished in the wash of the sea, but the wave cast him on the keel of the ship out upon the coast, on the land of the Phaeacians that are near of kin to the gods, and they did him all honour heartily as unto a god, and gave him many gifts, and themselves would fain have sent him scathless home. Yea, and Odysseus would have been here long since, but he thought it more profitable to gather wealth, as he journeyed over wide lands; so truly is Odysseus skilled in gainful arts above all men upon earth, nor may any mortal men contend with him. So Pheidon king of the Thesprotians told me. Moreover, he sware, in mine own presence, as he poured the drink-offering in his house, that the ship was drawn down to the sea and his company were ready, who were to convey him to his own dear country. But me he first sent off, for it chanced that a ship of the Thesprotians was on her way to Dulichium, a land rich in grain. And he showed me all the wealth that Odysseus had gathered, yea, it would suffice for his children after him, even to the tenth generation, so great were the treasures he had stored in the chambers of the king. As for him he had gone, he said, to Dodona to hear the counsel of Zeus, from the high leafy oak tree of the god, how he should return to his own dear country, having now been long afar, whether openly or by stealth.

"In this wise, as I tell thee, he is safe and will come shortly, and very near he is and will not much longer be far from his friends and his own country; yet withal I will give thee my oath on it. Zeus be my witness first, of gods the highest and best, and the hearth of noble Odysseus whereunto I am come, that all these things shall surely be accomplished even as I tell thee. In this same year Odysseus shall come hither, as the old moon wanes and the new is born."

Then wise Penelope answered him: "Ah, stranger, would that this word may be accomplished! Soon shouldst thou be aware of kindness and many a gift at my hands, so that whoso met with thee would call thee blessed. But on this wise my heart has a boding, and so it shall be. Neither shall Odysseus come home any more, nor shalt thou gain an escort hence, since there are not now such masters in the house as Odysseus was among men, — if ever such an one there was, — to welcome guests revered and speed them on their way. But do ye, my handmaids, wash this man's feet and lay a bed for him, mattress and mantles and shining blankets, that well and warmly he may come to the time of golden-throned Dawn. And very early in the morning bathe him and anoint him, that within the house beside Telemachus he may eat meat, sitting quietly in the hall. And it shall be the worse for any hurtful man of the wooers, that vexes the stranger, yea, he shall not henceforth profit himself here, for all his sore anger. For how shalt thou learn concerning me, stranger, whether indeed I excel all women in wit and thrifty device, if all unkempt and evil clad thou sittest at supper in my halls? Man's life is brief enough! And if any be a hard man and hard at heart, all men cry evil on him for the time to come, while yet he lives, and all men mock him when he is dead. But if any be a blameless man and blameless of heart, his guests noise his wide fame abroad, and many call him excellent."

Then Odysseus of many counsels answered her and said : " O wife revered of Odysseus, son of Laertes, mantles verily and shining blankets are hateful to me, since first I left behind me the snowy hills of Crete, voyaging in the long-oared galley ; nay, I will lie as in time past I was used to rest through the sleepless nights. For full many a night I have lain on an unsightly bed, and awaited the bright-throned Dawn. And baths for the feet are no longer my delight, nor shall any women of those who are serving maidens in thy house touch my foot, unless there chance to be some old wife, true of heart, one that has borne as much trouble as myself; I would not grudge such an one to touch my feet."

Then wise Penelope answered him: "Dear stranger, for there has been none ever so discreet as thou, nor dearer, of all the strangers from afar that have come to my house, so clearly thou speakest all things prudently; I have such an ancient woman of an understanding heart, that diligently nursed that hapless man my lord, and cherished him and took him in her arms, in the hour when his mother bare him. She will wash thy feet, albeit she is weak with age. Up now, wise Eurycleia, and wash this man, who is of like age with thy master. Yea, and perchance such even now are the feet of Odysseus, and such too his hands, for men quickly age in evil fortune."

So she spake, and the old woman covered her face with her hands and shed warm tears, and spake a word of lamentation, saying:

"Ah, woe is me, child, for thy sake, all helpless that I am! Surely Zeus hated thee above all men, though thou hadst a god-fearing spirit! For never yet did any mortal burn so many fat pieces of the thigh and so many choice hecatombs to Zeus, whose joy is in the thunder, as thou didst give to him, with prayers that so thou mightest grow to a smooth old age and rear thy renowned son. But now from thee alone hath Zeus wholly cut off the day of thy returning. Haply at him too did the women mock in a strange land afar, whensoever he came to the famous palace of any lord, even as here these shameless ones all mock at thee. To shun their insults and many taunts it is that thou sufferest them not to wash thy feet, but the daughter of Icarius, wise Penelope, hath bidden me that am right willing to this task. Wherefore I will wash thy feet, both for Penelope's sake and for thine own, for that my heart within me is moved with pity. But come, mark the word that I shall speak. Many strangers travel-worn have ere now come hither, but I say that I have never seen any so like another, as thou art like Odysseus, in fashion, in voice and in feet."

Then Odysseus of many counsels answered her, saying: "Old

wife, even so all men declare, that have beheld us twain, that we favour each other exceedingly, even as thou dost mark and say."

Thereupon the crone took the shining cauldron, which she used for the washing of feet, and poured in much cold water and next mingled therewith the warm. Now Odysseus sat aloof from the hearth, and of a sudden he turned his face to the darkness, for anon he had a misgiving of heart lest when she handled him she might know the scar again, and all should be revealed. Now she drew near her lord to wash him, and straightway she knew the scar of the wound, that the boar had dealt him with his white tusk long ago.

Now the old woman took the scarred limb and passed her hands down it, and knew it by the touch and let the foot drop suddenly, so that the knee fell into the bath, and the brazen vessel rang, being turned over on the other side, and behold, the water was spilled on the ground. Then grief and joy came on her in one moment, and both her eyes filled up with tears, and the voice of her utterance was stayed, and touching the chin of Odysseus she spake to him, saying:

"Yea verily, thou art Odysseus, my dear child, and I knew thee not before, till I handled the body of my lord."

Therewithal she looked towards Penelope, as minded to make a sign that her husband was now home. But Penelope could not meet her eyes nor take note of her, for Athene had bent her thoughts to other things. But Odysseus feeling for the old woman's throat seized it with his right hand and with the other drew her closer to him and spake, saying:

"Woman, why wouldest thou indeed destroy me? It was thou that didst nurse me there at thine own breast, and now after travail and much pain I am come in the twentieth year to mine own country. But since thou art ware of me, and the god has put this in thy heart, be silent, lest another learn the matter in the halls. For on this wise I will declare it, and it shall surely be accomplished: — if the gods subdue the lordly wooers unto me, I will not hold my hand from thee, my nurse though thou art, when I slay the other handmaids in my halls."

Then wise Eurycleia answered, saying: "My child, what word hath escaped the door of thy lips? Thou knowest how firm is my spirit and unyielding, and I will keep me close as hard stone or iron. Yet another thing will I tell thee, and do thou ponder it in thine heart. If the gods subdue the lordly wooers to thy hand, then will I tell thee all the tale of the women in the halls, which of them dishonour thee and which be guiltless."

Then Odysseus of many counsels answered her, saying: "Nurse, wherefore, I pray thee, wilt thou speak of these? Thou needest not, for even I myself will mark them well and take knowledge of each. Nay, do thou keep thy saying to thyself, and leave the rest to the gods."

Even so he spake, and the old woman passed forth from the hall to bring water for his feet, for that first water was all spilled. So when she had washed him and anointed him well with olive-oil, Odysseus again drew up his settle nearer to the fire to warm himself, and covered up the scar with his rags. Then the wise Penelope spake first, saying:

"Stranger, there is yet a little thing I will make bold to ask thee, for soon will it be the hour for pleasant rest, for him on whomsoever sweet sleep falls, though he be heavy with care. But to me has the god given sorrow, yea, sorrow measureless, for all the day I have my fill of wailing and lamenting, as I look to mine own housewiferies and to the tasks of the maidens in the house. But when night comes and sleep takes hold of all, I lie on my couch, and shrewd cares, thick thronging about my inmost heart, disquiet me in my sorrowing. Even as when the daughter of Pandareus, the brown bright nightingale, sings sweet in the first season of the spring, from her place in the thick leafage of the trees, and with many a turn and trill she pours forth her full-voiced music bewailing her child, dear Itylus, whom on a time she slew with the sword unwitting, Itylus the son of Zethus the prince; even as her song, my troubled soul sways to and fro. Shall I abide with my son, and keep all secure, all the things of my getting, my thralls and great high-roofed home, having respect unto the bed of my lord and the voice of the people, or even now follow with the best of the Achaeans that woos me in the halls, and gives a bride-price beyond reckoning? Now my son, so long as he was a child and light of heart, would not suffer me to marry and leave the house of my husband; but now that he is great of growth, and is come to the full measure of manhood, even now he prays me to go back again from these halls, being vexed for his possessions that the Achaeans devour before his eyes. But come now, hear a dream of mine and tell me the interpretation thereof. Twenty geese I have in the house, that eat wheat out of the water-trough, and it gladdens me to look on them. Now a great eagle of crooked beak came forth from the mountain, and brake all their necks and slew them; and they lay strewn in a heap in the halls, while he was borne aloft to the bright air. Thereon I wept and wailed, in a dream though it was, and around me were gathered the fair-tressed Achaean women as I made piteous lament, for that the eagle had slain my geese. But he came back and sat him down on a jutting point of the roof-beam, and with the voice of a man he spake, and stayed my weeping:

" 'Take heart, O daughter of renowned Icarius; this is no dream but a true vision, that shall be accomplished for thee. The geese are the wooers, and I that before was the eagle am now thy husband come again, who will let slip unsightly death upon all the wooers.' With that word sweet slumber let me go, and I looked about, and beheld the geese in the court devouring the wheat by the trough, where they had been before."

Then Odysseus of many counsels answered her and said: "Lady, none may turn aside the dream to interpret it otherwise, seeing that Odysseus himself is showing thee how he will fulfil it. For the wooers destruction is clearly boded, for all and every one; not a man shall avoid death and the fates."

Then wise Penelope answered him: "Stranger, verily dreams are hard, and hard to be discerned; nor are all things therein fulfilled for men. Twain are the gates of shadowy dreams, the one is fashioned of horn and one of ivory. Such dreams as pass through the portals of sawn ivory are deceitful, and bear tidings that are unfulfilled. But the dreams that come forth through the gates of polished horn bring a true issue, whosoever of mortals beholds them. Yet methinks my strange dream came not thence; of a truth that would be most welcome to me and to my son. But another thing will I tell thee, and do thou ponder it in thy heart. Lo, even now draws nigh the morn of evil name, that is to sever me from the house of Odysseus, for now I am about to ordain for a trial those axes that he was wont to set up in his halls, like the stays of oak in shipbuilding, twelve in all, and he would stand far apart and shoot his arrow through them all.[1] And now I will offer this contest to the wooers: whoso shall most easily string the bow in his hands, and shoot through all twelve axes, with him will I go and forsake this house, this house of my wedlock, so fair and filled with all livelihood, which methinks I shall yet remember, aye, in a dream."

Then Odysseus of many counsels answered her and said: "Wife revered of Odysseus, son of Laertes, no longer delay this contest in thy halls; for, lo, Odysseus of many counsels will be here, before these men, for all their handling of the polished bow, shall have strung it, and shot the arrow through the iron."

Then the wise Penelope answered him: "Stranger, if only

---

[1] [That is, through the holes in the openwork of the blades.]

thou wert willing still to sit beside me in the halls and to delight me, not upon my eyelids would sleep be shed. But men may in no wise abide sleepless ever, for the immortals have made a time for all things for mortals on the earth, the grain-giver. Howbeit I will go aloft to my upper chamber, and lay me on my bed, the place of my groanings, that is ever watered by my tears, since the day that Odysseus went to see that evil Ilios, never to be named. There will I lay me down, but do thou lie in this house; either strew thee somewhat on the floor, or let them lay bedding for thee."

Therewith she ascended to her shining upper chamber, not alone, for with her likewise went her handmaids. So she went aloft to her upper chamber with the women her handmaids, and there was bewailing Odysseus, her dear lord, till grey-eyed Athene cast sweet sleep upon her eyelids.

BOOK XX

Pallas and Odysseus consult of the killing of the wooers.

Now the goodly Odysseus laid him down to sleep in the outer gallery of the house. He spread an undressed bull's hide on the ground and above it many fleeces of sheep, that the Achaeans were wont to slay in sacrifice, and Eurynome threw a mantle over him where he lay. But Odysseus himself lay tossing this way and that. And as when a man by a great fire burning takes a paunch full of fat and blood, and turns it this way and that and longs to have it roasted most speedily, so Odysseus tossed from side to side, musing how he might stretch forth his hands upon the shameless wooers, being but one man against so many. Then down from heaven came Athene and drew nigh him, fashioned in the likeness of a woman. And she stood over his head and spake to him, saying:

"Lo now again, wherefore art thou watching, most luckless of all men living? Is not this thy house and is not thy wife there within and thy child, such a son as men wish to have for their own?"

Then Odysseus of many counsels answered her, saying: "Yea, goddess, all this thou hast spoken as is meet. But my heart within me muses in some measure upon this, how I may stretch forth my hands upon the shameless wooers, being but one man, while they abide ever in their companies within. Moreover, this other and harder matter I ponder in my heart: even if I were to slay them by thy will and the will of Zeus, whither should I flee from the avengers? Look well to this, I pray thee."

Then answered the goddess, grey-eyed Athene: "O hard of belief! yea, many there be that trust even in a weaker friend than I am, in one that is a mortal and knows not such craft as mine; but I am a god, that preserve thee to the end, in all manner of toils. And now I will tell thee plainly; even should fifty companies of mortal men compass us about eager to slay us in battle, even their kine shouldst thou drive off and their brave flocks. But let sleep in turn come over thee; to wake and to watch all night, this too is vexation of spirit; and soon shalt thou rise from out thy troubles."

So she spake and poured slumber upon his eyelids, but for her part the fair goddess went back to Olympus.

While sleep laid hold of him loosening the cares of his soul, sleep that loosens the limbs of men, his good wife awoke and wept as she sat on her soft bed. But when she had taken her fill of weeping, to Artemis first the fair lady made her prayer:

"Artemis, lady and goddess, daughter of Zeus, would that even now thou wouldst plant thy shaft within my breast and take my life away, even in this hour! Or else, would that the storm-wind might snatch me up, and bear me hence down the dusky ways, and cast me forth where the back-flowing Oceanus mingles with the sea. Would that in such wise they that hold the mansions of·Olympus would take me from the sight of men, or that fair-tressed Artemis would strike me, that so with a vision of Odysseus before mine eyes I might even pass beneath the dreadful earth, nor ever make a baser man's delight! But herein is an evil that may well be borne, namely, when a man weeps all the day long in great sorrow of heart, but sleep takes him in the night, for sleep makes him forgetful of all things, of good and evil, when once it has overshadowed his eyelids. But as for me, even the dreams that the gods send upon me are evil. For furthermore, this very night one seemed to lie by my side, in the likeness of my lord, as he was when he went with the host, and then was my heart glad, since methought it was no vain dream but a clear vision at the last."

So she spake, and anon came the golden-throned Dawn. Now goodly Odysseus caught the voice of her weeping, and then he fell a-musing, and it seemed to him that even now she knew him and was standing by his head. So he took up the mantle and the fleeces whereon he was lying, and set them on a high seat in the hall, and bare out the bull's hide out of doors and laid it there, and lifting up his hands he prayed to Zeus:

"Father Zeus, if ye gods of your good will have led me over wet and dry, to mine own country, after ye had plagued me sore, let some one, I pray, of the folk that are waking show me a word of good omen within, and without let some other sign be revealed to me from Zeus."

So he spake in prayer, and Zeus, the counsellor, heard him. Straightway he thundered from shining Olympus, from on high from the place of clouds; and goodly Odysseus was glad. Moreover, a woman, a grinder at the mill, uttered a voice of omen from within the house hard by, where stood the mills of the shepherd of the people. At these handmills twelve women in all were wont to bestir themselves, making meal of barley and of wheat, the marrow of men. Now all the others were asleep, for they had ground out their task of grain, but this one alone rested not yet, being the weakest of all. She now stayed her quern [1] and spake a word, a sign to her lord:

"Father Zeus, who rulest over gods and men, loudly hast thou thundered from the starry sky, yet nowhere is there a cloud to be seen: this surely is a portent thou art showing to some mortal. Fulfil now, I pray thee, even to miserable me, the word that I shall speak. May the wooers, on this day, for the last and latest* time make their sweet feasting in the halls of Odysseus! They that have loosened my knees with cruel toil to grind their barley meal, may they now sup their last!"

Thus she spake, and goodly Odysseus was glad in the omen of the voice and in the thunder of Zeus; for he thought that he had gotten his vengeance on the guilty.

Now the other maidens in the fair halls of Odysseus had gathered, and were kindling on the hearth the never-resting fire. And Telemachus rose from his bed, a godlike man, and put on his raiment, and slung a sharp sword about his shoulders, and beneath his shining feet he bound his goodly sandals. And he caught up his mighty spear shod with sharp bronze, and went and stood by the threshold, and spake to Eurycleia:

"Dear nurse, have ye honoured our guest in the house with food and couch, or does he lie uncared for, as he may? For this is my mother's way, wise as she is: blindly she honours one of mortal men, even the worse, but the better she sends without honour away."

Then the prudent Eurycleia answered: "Nay, my child, thou shouldst not now blame her where no blame is. For the stranger sat and drank wine, so long as he would, and of food

[1] [Mill.]

he said he was no longer fain, for thy mother asked him. Moreover, against the hour when he should bethink him of rest and sleep, she bade the maidens strew for him a bed. But he, as one utterly wretched and ill-fated, refused to lie on a couch and under blankets, but on an undressed hide and on the fleeces of sheep he slept in the outer gallery, and we cast a mantle over him."

So she spake, and Telemachus passed out through the hall with his lance in his hand, and two fleet dogs bare him company. He went on his way to the assembly place to join the goodly-greaved Achaeans. But the good lady Eurycleia called aloud to her maidens:

"Come hither, let some of you go busily and sweep the hall, and sprinkle it, and on the fair-fashioned seats throw purple coverlets, and others with sponges wipe all the tables clean, and cleanse the mixing bowls and well-wrought double beakers, and others again go for water to the well, and return with it right speedily. For the wooers will not long be out of the hall but will return very early, for it is a feast day, yea for all the people."

So she spake, and they all gave ready ear and hearkened. Twenty of them went to the well of dark water, and the others there in the halls were busy with skilful hands.

Then in came the serving men of the Achaeans. Thereon they cleft the faggots well and cunningly, while, behold, the women came back from the well. Then the swineherd joined them, leading three fatted boars, the best in all the flock. These he left to feed at large in the fair courts, but as for him he spake to Odysseus gently, saying:

"Tell me, stranger, do the Achaeans at all look on thee with more regard, or do they dishonour thee in the halls, as heretofore?"

Then Odysseus of many counsels answered him, saying:

"Oh, that the gods, Eumaeus, may avenge the scorn wherewith these men deal insolently, and devise infatuate deeds in another's house, and know no touch of shame!"

On such wise they spake one to another. And Melanthius drew near them, the goatherd, leading the goats that were most excellent in all the herds to be a dinner for the wooers, and two shepherds bare him company. So he tethered the goats beneath the echoing gallery, and himself spake to Odysseus and taunted him, saying:

"Stranger, wilt thou still be a plague to us here in the hall, with thy begging of men, and wilt not get thee gone? In no wise do I think we twain will be sundered, till we taste each the other's fists, for thy begging is out of all order. Also there are elsewhere other feasts of the Achaeans."

So he spake, but Odysseus of many counsels answered him not a word, but in silence he shook his head, brooding evil in the deep of his heart.

Moreover, a third man came up, Philoetius, a master of men, leading a barren heifer for the wooers and fatted goats. The cattle he tethered carefully beneath the echoing gallery, and himself drew close to the swineherd, and began to question him:

"Swineherd, who is this stranger but newly come to our house? From what men does he claim his birth? Where are his kin and his native fields? Hapless is he, yet in fashion he is like a royal lord; but the gods mar the goodliness of wandering men, when even for kings they have woven the web of trouble."

So he spake, and came close to him offering his right hand in welcome, and uttering his voice spake to him winged words:

"Father and stranger, hail! may happiness be thine in the time to come; but as now, thou art fast holden in many sorrows! Father Zeus, none other god is more baneful than thou; thou hast no compassion on men, that are of thine own begetting, but makest them to have fellowship with evil and with bitter pains. The sweat brake out on me when I beheld him, and mine eyes stand full of tears for memory of Odysseus, for he too, methinks, is clad in such vile raiment as this, and is wandering among men, if haply he yet lives and sees the sunlight. But if he be dead already and in the house of Hades, then woe is me for the noble Odysseus, who set me over his cattle while I was but a lad in the land of the Cephallenians. And now these wax numberless; in no better wise could the breed of broad-browed cattle of any mortal increase, even as the ears of corn. But strangers command me to be ever driving these for themselves to devour, and they care nothing for the heir in the house, nor tremble at the vengeance of the gods, for they are eager even now to divide among themselves the possessions of our lord who is long afar. Now my heart within my breast often revolves this thing. Truly it were an evil deed, while a son of the master is yet alive, to get me away to the land of strangers, and go off, with cattle and all, to alien men. But this is more grievous still, to abide here in affliction watching over the herds of other men. Yea, long ago I would have fled and gone forth to some other of the proud kings, for things are now past sufferance; but still my thought is of that hapless one, if he might come I know not whence, and make a scattering of the wooers in the halls."

Then Odysseus of many counsels answered him, saying:

"Neatherd, seeing thou art not like to an evil man or a foolish, and of myself I mark how that thou hast gotten understanding of heart, therefore I will tell thee somewhat, and swear a great oath to confirm it. Be Zeus now my witness before any god, and the hospitable board and the hearth of noble Odysseus, whereunto I am come, that while thou art still in this place Odysseus shall come home, and thou shalt see with thine eyes, if thou wilt, the slaying of the wooers who lord it here."

Then the neatherd made answer, saying:

"Ah, would, stranger, that Cronion may accomplish this word! So shouldst thou know what my might is, and how my hands follow to obey."

In like manner Eumaeus prayed to all the gods, that wise Odysseus might return to his own home.

On such wise they spake one to the other, but the wooers at that time were framing death and doom for Telemachus. Even so there came by them a bird on their left, an eagle of lofty flight, with a cowering dove in his clutch. Then Amphinomus made harangue and spake among them:

"Friends, this counsel of ours will not go well, namely, the slaying of Telemachus; rather let us bethink us of the feast."

So spake Amphinomus, and his saying pleased them well. They passed into the halls of godlike Odysseus and laid by their mantles on the chairs and high seats, and sacrificed great sheep and stout goats and the fatlings of the boars and the heifer of the herd; then they roasted the entrails and served them round and mixed wine in the bowl, and the swineherd set a cup by each man. And Philoetius, a master of men, handed them wheaten bread in beautiful baskets, and Melanthius poured out the wine. So they put forth their hands on the good cheer set before them.

Now Telemachus, in his crafty purpose, made Odysseus to sit down within the established hall by the threshold of stone, and placed for him a mean settle and a little table. He set by him his mess of the entrails, and poured wine into a golden cup and spake to him, saying:

"There, sit thee down, drinking thy wine among the lords, and the taunts and buffets of all the wooers I myself will ward off from thee, for this is no house of public resort, but the very house of Odysseus, and for me he won it. But, ye wooers, refrain your minds from rebukes and your hands from buffets, that no strife and feud may arise."

So he said, and they all bit their lips and marvelled at Telemachus, in that he spake boldly. Then Antinous, son of Eupeithes, spake among them, saying:

"Hard though the word be, let us accept it, Achaeans, even the word of Telemachus, though mightily he threatens us in his speech. For Zeus Cronion hath hindered us of our purpose, else would we have silenced him in our halls, shrill orator as he is."

So spake Antinous, but Telemachus took no heed of his words. Now the henchmen were leading through the town the holy hecatomb of the gods, and lo, the long-haired Achaeans were gathered beneath the shady grove of Apollo, the prince of archery.

Now when they had roasted the outer flesh and drawn it off the spits, they divided the messes and shared the glorious feast. And beside Odysseus they that waited set an equal share, the same as that which fell to themselves, for so Telemachus commanded, the dear son of divine Odysseus.

Now Athene would in no wise suffer the lordly wooers to abstain from biting scorn, that the pain might sink yet the deeper into the heart of Odysseus, son of Laertes. There was among the wooers a man of a lawless heart, Ctesippus was his name, and in Same was his home, who, trusting, forsooth, to his vast possessions, was wooing the wife of Odysseus the lord long afar. And now he spake among the proud wooers:

"Hear me, ye lordly wooers, and I will say somewhat. The stranger verily has long had his due portion, as is meet, an equal share; for it is not fair nor just to rob the guests of Telemachus of their right, whosoever they may be that come to this house. Go to then, I also will bestow on him a stranger's gift, that he in turn may give a present either to the bath-woman, or to any other of the thralls within the house of godlike Odysseus."

Therewith he caught up an ox's foot from the dish, where it lay, and hurled it with strong hand. But Odysseus lightly avoided it with a turn of his head, and smiled right grimly in his heart, and the ox's foot smote the well-builded wall. Then Telemachus rebuked Ctesippus, saying:

"Verily, Ctesippus, it has turned out happier for thy heart's pleasure as it is! Thou didst not smite the stranger, for he himself avoided that which was cast at him, else surely would I have struck thee through the midst with the sharp spear, and in place of wedding banquet thy father would have had to busy him about a funeral feast in this place. Wherefore let no man make show of unseemly deeds in this my house, for now I have understanding to discern both good and evil, but in time past I was yet a child. But as needs we must, we still endure to see these deeds, while sheep are slaughtered and wine drunken and bread devoured, for hard it is for one man to restrain many. But come, no longer work me harm out of an evil heart; but if ye be set on slaying me, even me, with the sword, even that would I rather endure, and far better would it be to die than to witness for ever these unseemly deeds — strangers shamefully entreated, and men haling the handmaidens in foul wise through the fair house."

So he spake, and they were all hushed in silence. And late and at last spake among them Agelaus, son of Damastor:

"Friends, when a righteous word has been spoken, none surely would rebuke another with hard speech and be angry. Misuse ye not this stranger, nor any of the thralls that are in the house of godlike Odysseus. But to Telemachus himself I would speak a soft word and to his mother, if perchance it may find favour with the mind of those twain. So long as your hearts within you had hope of the wise Odysseus returning to his own house, so long none could be wroth that ye waited and held back the wooers in the halls, for better had it been if Odysseus had returned and come back to his own home. But now the event is plain, that he will return no more. Go then, sit by thy mother and tell her all, namely, that she must wed the best man that woos her, and whoso gives most gifts; so shalt thou with gladness live on the heritage of thy father, eating and drinking, while she cares for another's house."

Then wise Telemachus answered, and said: "Nay, by Zeus, Agelaus, and by the griefs of my father, who far away methinks from Ithaca has perished or goes wandering, in no wise do I delay my mother's marriage; nay, I bid her be married to what man she will, and withal I offer gifts without number. But I do indeed feel shame to drive her forth from the hall, despite her will, by a word of compulsion; God forbid that ever this should be."

So spake Telemachus, but among the wooers Pallas Athene roused laughter unquenchable, and drave their wits wandering. And now they were laughing with alien lips, and blood-bedabbled was the flesh they ate, and their eyes were filled with tears and their soul was fain of lamentation.

Now the daughter of Icarius, wise Penelope, had set her fair chair over against them, and heard the words of each one of the men in the halls. For in the midst of laughter they had got ready the mid-day meal, a sweet meal and abundant, for they had sacrificed many cattle. But never could there be a banquet less gracious than that supper, such an one as the goddess and the brave man were soon to spread for them; for that they had begun the devices of shame.

BOOK XXI

Penelope bringeth forth her husband's bow, which the suitors could not bend, but was bent by Odysseus.

Now the goddess, grey-eyed Athene, put it into the heart of the daughter of Icarius, wise Penelope, to set the bow and the axes of grey iron, for the wooers in the halls of Odysseus, to be the weapons of the contest, and the beginning of death. So she climbed the tall staircase of her chamber, and took the well-bent key in her strong hand, a goodly key of bronze, whereon was a handle of ivory. And she betook her, with her handmaidens, to the treasure-chamber in the uttermost part of the house, where lay the treasures of her lord, bronze and gold and well-wrought iron. And there lay the back-bent bow and the quiver for the arrows, and many shafts were therein, winged for death, gifts of a friend of Odysseus, that met with him in Lacedaemon, Iphitus son of Eurytus, a man like to the gods.

Now when the fair lady had come even to the treasure-chamber, and had stept upon the threshold of oak, which the carpenter had on a time planed cunningly, and over it had made straight the line, — doorposts also had he fitted thereby, whereon he set shining doors, — anon she quickly loosed the strap from the handle of the door, and thrust in the key, and with a straight aim shot back the bolts. And even as a bull roars that is grazing in a meadow, so mightily roared the fair doors smitten by the key; and speedily they flew open before her. Then she stept on to the high floor, where the coffers stood, wherein the fragrant raiment was stored. Thence she stretched forth her hand, and took the bow from off the pin, all in the bright case which sheathed it around. And there she sat down, and set the case upon her knees, and cried aloud and wept, and took out the bow of her lord. Now when she had her fill of tearful lament, she set forth to go to the hall to the company of the proud wooers, with the back-bent bow in her hands, and the quiver for the arrows, and many shafts were therein winged for death. And her maidens along with her bare a chest, wherein lay much store of iron and bronze, the gear of combat of their lord. Now when the fair lady had come unto the wooers, she stood by the doorpost of the well-builded roof, holding up her glistening tire before her face; and a faithful maiden stood on either side of her, and straight-

PENELOPE CARRYING THE BOW OF ODYSSEUS TO THE SUITORS

way she spake out among the wooers and declared her word, saying:

"Hear me, ye lordly wooers, who have vexed this house, that ye might eat and drink here evermore, forasmuch as the master is long gone, nor could ye find any other mark for your speech, but all your desire was to wed me and take me to wife. Nay, come now, ye wooers, seeing that this is the prize that is put before you. I will set forth for you the great bow of divine Odysseus, and whoso shall most easily string the bow in his hands, and shoot through all twelve axes, with him will I go and forsake this house, this house of my wedlock, so fair and filled with all livelihood, which methinks I shall yet remember, aye, in a dream."

So spake she, and commanded Eumaeus, the goodly swineherd, to set the bow for the wooers and the axes of grey iron. And Eumaeus took them with tears, and laid them down; and otherwhere the neatherd wept, when he beheld the bow of his lord. Then Antinous rebuked them, and spake and hailed them:

"Foolish boors, whose thoughts look not beyond the day, ah, wretched pair, wherefore now do ye shed tears, and stir the soul of the lady within her, when her heart already lies low in pain, for that she has lost her dear lord? Nay, sit and feast in silence, or else get ye forth and weep, and leave the bow here behind, to be a terrible contest for the wooers, for methinks that this polished bow does not lightly yield itself to be strung. For there is no man among all these present such as Odysseus was, and I myself saw him, yea, I remember it well, though I was still but a child."

So spake he, but his heart within him hoped that he would string the bow, and shoot through the iron. Yet verily, he was to be the first that should taste the arrow at the hands of the noble Odysseus, whom but late he was dishonouring as he sat in the halls, and was inciting all his fellows to do likewise

Then the mighty prince Telemachus spake among them, saying: "Lo now, in very truth, Cronion has robbed me of my wits! My dear mother, wise as she is, declares that she will go with a stranger and forsake this house; yet I laugh and in my silly heart I am glad. Nay, come now, ye wooers, seeing that this is the prize which is set before you, a lady, the like of whom there is not now in the Achaean land, neither in sacred Pylos, nor in Argos, nor in Mycenae, nor yet in Ithaca, nor in the dark mainland. Nay, but ye know all this yourselves, — why need I praise my mother? Come, therefore, delay not the issue with excuses, nor hold much longer aloof from the drawing of the bow, that we may see the thing that is to be. Yea, and I myself would make trial of this bow. If I shall string it, and shoot through the iron, my lady mother will not quit these halls to my grief, and go with a stranger while I am left behind, being now well able to lift my father's goodly gear of combat."

Therewith he cast from off his neck his cloak of scarlet, and sprang to his full height, and put away the sword from his shoulders. First he dug a good trench and set up the axes, one long trench for them all, and over it he made straight the line and round about stamped in the earth. And amazement fell on all that beheld how orderly he set the axes, though never before had he seen it so. Then he went and stood by the threshold and began to prove the bow. Thrice he made it to tremble in his great desire to draw it, and thrice he rested from his effort, though still he hoped in his heart to string the bow, and shoot through the iron. And now at last he might have strung it, mightily straining thereat for the fourth time, but Odysseus nodded frowning and stayed him, for all his eagerness. Then the strong prince Telemachus spake among them again:

"Lo you now, even to the end of my days I shall be a coward and a weakling, or it may be I am too young, and have as yet no trust in my hands to defend me from such an one as is angry with me without a cause. But come now, ye who are mightier men than I, essay the bow and let us make an end of the contest."

Therewith he put the bow from him on the ground, leaning it against the smooth and well-compacted doors, and the swift shaft he propped hard by against the fair bow-tip, and then he sat down once more on the high seat, whence he had risen.

Then Antinous, son of Eupeithes, spake among them, saying: "Rise up in order, all my friends, beginning from the left, even from the place whence the wine is poured."

So spake Antinous, and the saying pleased them well. Then first stood up Leiodes, son of Oenops, who was their soothsayer and ever sat by the fair mixing bowl at the extremity of the hall; he alone hated their infatuate deeds and was indignant with all the wooers. He now first took the bow and the swift shaft, and he went and stood by the threshold, and began to prove the bow; but he could not bend it; or ever that might be, his hands grew weary with the straining, his unworn, delicate hands; so he spake among the wooers, saying:

"Friends, of a truth I cannot bend it, let some other take it. Ah, many of our bravest shall this bow rob of spirit and of life, since truly it is far better for us to die, than to live on and to fail of that for which we assemble evermore in this place, day by day expecting the prize. Many there be even now that hope in their hearts and desire to wed Penelope, the bedfellow of Odysseus: but when such an one shall make trial of the bow and see the issue, thereafter let him woo some other fair-robed Achaean woman with his bridal gifts and seek to win her. So may our lady wed the man that gives most gifts, and comes as the chosen of fate."

So he spake, and put from him the bow leaning it against the smooth and well-compacted doors, and the swift shaft he propped hard by against the fair bow-tip, and then he sat down once more on the high seat, whence he had risen.

But Antinous rebuked him, and spake and hailed him: "Leiodes, what word hath escaped the door of thy lips; a hard word, and a grievous? Nay, it angers me to hear it, and to think that a bow such as this shall rob our bravest of spirit and of life, and all because thou canst not draw it. For I tell thee that thy lady mother bare thee not of such might as to draw a bow and shoot arrows: but there be others of the proud wooers that shall draw it soon."

So he spake and commanded Melanthius, the goatherd, saying: "Up now, light a fire in the halls, Melanthius; and place a great settle by the fire and a fleece thereon, and bring forth a great ball of lard that is within, that we young men may warm and anoint the bow therewith and prove it, and make an end of the contest."

So he spake, and Melanthius soon kindled the never-resting fire, and drew up a settle and placed it near, and put a fleece thereon, and he brought forth a great ball of lard that was within. Therewith the young men warmed the bow, and made essay, but could not string it, for they were greatly lacking of such might. But Antinous still abode in his place and godlike Eurymachus, chief men among the wooers, who were far the most excellent of all.

Now those other twain had gone forth both together from the house, the neatherd and the swineherd of godlike Odysseus; and Odysseus went forth after them. But when they had now passed without the gates and the courtyard, he uttered his voice and spake to them in gentle words:

"Neatherd and thou swineherd, shall I say somewhat or keep it to myself? Nay, my spirit bids me declare it. What manner of men would ye be to help Odysseus, if he should come thus suddenly, I know not whence, and some god were to bring him? Would ye stand on the side of the wooers or of Odysseus? Tell me even as your heart and spirit bid you."

Then the neatherd answered him, saying: "Father Zeus, if

but thou wouldst fulfil this wish:—oh, that that man might come, and some god lead him hither! So shouldest thou know what my might is, and how my hands follow to obey."

In like manner Eumaeus prayed to all the gods that wise Odysseus might return to his own home.

Now when he knew for a surety what spirit they were of, once more he answered and spake to them, saying:

"Behold, home am I come, even I; after much travail and sore am I come in the twentieth year to mine own country. And I know how that my coming is desired by you alone of all my thralls, for from none besides have I heard a prayer that I might return once more to my home. And now I will tell you all the truth, even as it shall come to pass. If the god shall subdue the proud wooers to my hands, I will bring you each one a wife, and will give you a heritage of your own and a house builded near to me, and ye twain shall be thereafter in mine eyes as the brethren and companions of Telemachus. But behold, I will likewise show you a most manifest token, that ye may know me well and be certified in heart, even the wound that the boar dealt me with his white tusk long ago, when I went to Parnassus with the sons of Autolycus."

Therewith he drew aside the rags from the great scar. And when the twain had beheld it and marked it well, they cast their arms about the wise Odysseus, and fell a-weeping; and kissed him lovingly on head and shoulders. And in like manner Odysseus too kissed their heads and hands. And now would the sunlight have gone down upon their sorrowing, had not Odysseus himself stayed them, saying:

"Cease ye from weeping and lamentation, lest some one come forth from the hall and see us, and tell it likewise in the house. Nay, go ye within one by one and not both together, I first and you following, and let this be the token between us. All the rest, as many as are proud wooers, will not suffer that I should be given the bow and quiver; do thou then, goodly Eumaeus, as thou bearest the bow through the hall, set it in my hands and speak to the women that they bar the well-fitting doors of their chamber. And if any of them hear the sound of groaning or the din of men within our walls, let them not run forth but abide where they are in silence at their work. But on thee, goodly Philoetius, I lay this charge, to bolt and bar the outer gate of the court and swiftly to tie the knot."

Therewith he passed within the fair-lying halls, and went and sat upon the settle whence he had risen. And likewise the two thralls of divine Odysseus went within.

And now Eurymachus was handling the bow, warming it on this side and on that at the light of the fire; yet even so he could not string it, and in his great heart he groaned mightily; and in heaviness of spirit he spake and called aloud, saying:

"Lo you now, truly am I grieved for myself and for you all! Not for the marriage do I mourn so greatly, afflicted though I be; there are many Achaean women besides, some in sea-begirt Ithaca itself and some in other cities. Nay, but I grieve, if indeed we are so far worse than godlike Odysseus in might, seeing that we cannot bend the bow. It will be a shame even for men unborn to hear thereof."

Then Antinous, son of Eupeithes, answered him: "Eurymachus, this shall not be so, and thou thyself too knowest it. For to-day the feast of the archer god is held in the land, a holy feast. Who at such a time would be bending bows? Nay, set it quietly by; what and if we should let the axes all stand as they are? None methinks will come to the hall of Odysseus, son of Laertes, and carry them away. Go to now, let the wine-bearer pour for libation into each cup in turn, that after the drink-offering we may set down the curved bow. And in the morning bid Melanthius, the goatherd, to lead hither the very best goats in all his herds, that we may lay pieces of the thighs on the altar of Apollo the archer, and assay the bow and make an end of the contest."

So spake Antinous, and the saying pleased them well. Then the henchmen poured water on their hands, and pages crowned the mixing bowls with drink, and served out the wine to all, when they had poured for libation into each cup in turn. But when they had poured forth and had drunken to their hearts' desire, Odysseus of many counsels spake among them out of a crafty heart, saying:

"Hear me, ye wooers of the renowned queen, that I may say that which my heart within me bids. And mainly to Eurymachus I make my prayer and to the godlike Antinous, forasmuch as he has spoken even this word aright, namely, that for this present ye cease from your archery and leave the issue to the gods; and in the morning the god will give the victory to whomsoever he will. Come therefore, give me the polished bow, that in your presence I may prove my hands and strength, whether I have yet any force such as once was in my supple limbs, or whether my wanderings and needy fare have even now destroyed it."

So spake he and they all were exceeding wroth, for fear lest he should string the polished bow. And Antinous rebuked him, and spake and hailed him:

"Wretched stranger, thou hast no wit, nay, never so little. Art thou not content to feast at ease in our high company, and to lack not thy share of the banquet, but to listen to our speech and our discourse, while no guest and beggar beside thee hears our speech? Wine it is that wounds thee, honey-sweet wine, that is the bane of others too, even of all who take great draughts and drink out of measure. Nay then, drink at thine ease, and strive not still with men that are younger than thou."

Then wise Penelope answered him: "Antinous, truly it is not fair nor just to rob the guests of Telemachus of their due, whosoever he may be that comes to this house. Dost thou think if yonder stranger strings the great bow of Odysseus, in the pride of his might and of his strength of arm, that he will lead me to his home and make me his wife? Nay, he himself, methinks, has no such hope in his breast; so, as for that, let not any of you fret himself while feasting in this place; that were indeed unmeet."

Then Eurymachus, son of Polybus, answered her, saying: "Daughter of Icarius, wise Penelope, it is not that we deem that he will lead thee to his home, — far be such a thought from us, — but we dread the speech of men and women, lest some day one of the baser sort among the Achaeans say: 'Truly, men far too mean are wooing the wife of one that is noble, nor can they string the polished bow. But a stranger and a beggar came in his wanderings, and lightly strung the bow, and shot through the iron.' Thus will they speak, and these things will turn to our reproach."

Then wise Penelope answered him: "Eurymachus, never can there be fair fame in the land for those that devour and dishonour the house of a prince. Why then do ye count such speech as a reproach? But, behold, our guest is great of growth and well-knit, and avows him to be born the son of a good father. Come then, give ye him the polished bow, that we may see that which is to be. For thus will I declare my saying, and it shall surely come to pass. If he shall string the bow and Apollo grant him renown, I will clothe him in a mantle and a doublet, goodly raiment, and I will give him a sharp javelin to defend him against dogs and men, and a two-edged sword and sandals to bind beneath his feet, and I will send him whithersoever his heart and spirit bid him go."

Then wise Telemachus answered her, saying: "My mother, as for the bow, no Achaean is mightier than I to give or to deny it to whomso I will, neither as many as are lords in rocky Ithaca nor in the isles on the side of Elis, the pastureland of horses. Not one of these shall force me in mine own despite, if I choose to give this bow, yea, once and for all, to the stranger to bear away with him. But do thou go to thine own chamber and mind thine own housewiferies, the loom and distaff, and bid thine handmaids ply their tasks. But the bow shall be for men, for all, but for me in chief, for mine is the lordship in the house."

Then in amaze she went back to her chamber, for she laid up the wise saying of her son in her heart. She ascended to her upper chamber with the women her handmaids, and then was bewailing Odysseus, her dear lord, till grey-eyed Athene cast sweet sleep upon her eyelids.

Now the goodly swineherd had taken the curved bow, and was bearing it, when the wooers all cried out upon him in the halls. And thus some one of the haughty youths would speak : " Whither now art thou bearing the curved bow, thou vagabond, thou wretched swineherd? Lo, soon shall the swift hounds of thine own breeding eat thee hard by thy swine, alone and away from men, if Apollo will be gracious to us and the other deathless gods."

Even so they spake, and he took and set down the bow in that very place, being affrighted because many cried out on him in the halls. Then Telemachus from the other side spake threateningly, and called aloud:

"Father, bring hither the bow, soon shalt thou rue it that thou servest many masters. Take heed, lest I that am younger than thou pursue thee to the field, and pelt thee with stones, for in might I am the better. If only I were so much mightier in strength of arm than all the wooers that are in the halls, soon would I send many an one forth on an evil road from out our house, for they imagine mischief against us."

So he spake, and all the wooers laughed sweetly at him,

and ceased now from their cruel anger toward Telemachus. Then the swineherd bare the bow through the hall, and went up to wise Odysseus, and set it in his hands. And he called forth the nurse Eurycleia from the chamber and spake to her:

"Wise Eurycleia, Telemachus bids thee bar the well-fitting doors of thy chamber, and if any of the women hear the sound of groaning or the din of men within our walls, let them not go forth, but abide where they are in silence at their work."

So he spake, and the word unwinged abode with her, and she barred the doors of the fair-lying halls.

Then Philoetius hasted forth silently from the house, and barred the outer gates of the fenced court. Now there lay beneath the gallery the cable of a curved ship, fashioned of the byblus plant, wherewith he made fast the gates, and then himself passed within. Then he went and sat on the settle whence he had risen, and gazed upon Odysseus. He already was handling the bow, turning it every way about, and proving it on this side and on that, lest the worms might have eaten the horns when the lord of the bow was away. And thus men spake looking each one to his neighbour:

"Verily he has a good eye, and a shrewd turn for a bow! It must be, methinks, that he himself has the like lying by at home or else he is set on making one, in such wise does he turn it hither and thither in his hands, this evil-witted beggar."

And another again of the haughty youths would say: "Oh, that the fellow may get wherewith to profit withal, just in such measure as he shall ever prevail to bend the bow!"

So spake the wooers, but Odysseus of many counsels had lifted the great bow and viewed it on every side, and even as when a man that is skilled in the lyre and in minstrelsy, easily stretches a cord about a new peg, after tying at either end the twisted sheep-gut, even so Odysseus straightway bent the great bow, all without effort, and took it in his right hand and proved the bow-string, which rang sweetly at the touch, in tone like a swallow. Then great grief came upon the wooers, and the colour of their countenance was changed, and Zeus thundered loud showing forth his tokens. And the steadfast goodly Odysseus was glad thereat, in that the son of deep-counselling Cronos had sent him a sign. Then he caught up a swift arrow which lay by his table, bare, but the other shafts were stored within the hollow quiver, those whereof the Achaeans were soon to taste. He took and laid it on the bridge of the bow, and held the notch and drew the string, even from the settle whereon he sat, and with straight aim shot the shaft and missed not one of the axes, beginning from the first axe-handle, and the bronze-weighted shaft passed clean through and out at the last. Then he spake to Telemachus, saying:

"Telemachus, thy guest that sits in the halls does thee no shame. In no wise did I miss my mark, nor was I wearied with long bending of the bow. Still is my might steadfast — not as the wooers say scornfully to slight me. But now is it time that supper too be got ready for the Achaeans, while it is yet light, and thereafter must we make other sport with the dance and the lyre, for these are the crown of the feast."

Therewith he nodded with bent brows, and Telemachus, the dear son of divine Odysseus, girt his sharp sword about him and took the spear in his grasp, and stood by his high seat at his father's side, armed with the gleaming bronze.

BOOK XXII

The killing of the wooers.

THEN Odysseus of many counsels stripped him of his rags and leaped on to the great threshold with his bow and quiver full of arrows, and poured forth all the swift shafts there before his feet, and spake among the wooers:

"Lo, now is this terrible trial ended at last; and now will I make for another mark, which never yet man has smitten, if perchance I may strike it and Apollo grant me renown."

With that he pointed the bitter arrow at Antinous. Now he was about raising to his lips a fair two-eared chalice of gold, and behold, he was handling it to drink of the wine, and death was far from his thoughts. For who among men at feast would deem that one man amongst so many, how hardy soever he were, would bring on him foul death and black fate? But Odysseus aimed and smote him with the arrow in the throat, and the point passed clean out through his delicate neck, and he fell back and the cup dropped from his hand as he was smitten, and at once through his nostrils there came up a thick jet of slain man's blood, and quickly he spurned the table from him with his foot, and spilt the food on the ground, and the bread and the roast flesh were defiled. Then the wooers raised a clamour through the halls when they saw the man fallen, and they leaped from their high seats, as men stirred by fear, all through the hall, peering everywhere along the well-builded walls, and nowhere was there a shield or mighty spear to lay hold on. Then they reviled Odysseus with angry words:

"Stranger, thou shootest at men to thy hurt. Never again shalt thou enter other lists, now is utter doom assured thee. Yea, for now hast thou slain the man that was far the best of all the noble youths in Ithaca; wherefore vultures shall devour thee here."

So each one spake, for indeed they thought that Odysseus had not slain him wilfully; but they knew not in their folly that on their own heads, each and all of them, the bands of death had been made fast. Then Odysseus of many counsels looked fiercely on them, and spake:

"Ye dogs, ye said in your hearts that I should never more

come home from the land of the Trojans, in that ye wasted my house, and traitorously wooed my wife while I was yet alive, and ye had no fear of the gods, that hold the wide heaven, nor of the indignation of men hereafter. But now the bands of death have been made fast upon you one and all."

Even so he spake, and pale fear gat hold on the limbs of all, and each man looked about, where he might shun utter doom. And Eurymachus alone answered him, and spake: "If thou art indeed Odysseus of Ithaca, come home again, with right thou speakest thus, of all that the Achaeans have wrought, many infatuate deeds in thy halls and many in the field. Howbeit, he now lies dead that is to blame for all, Antinous; for he brought all these things upon us, not as longing very greatly for the marriage nor needing it sore, but with another purpose, that Cronion has not fulfilled for him, namely, that he might himself be king over all the land of stablished Ithaca, and he was to have lain in wait for thy son and killed him. But now he is slain after his deserving, and do thou spare thy people, even thine own; and we will hereafter go about the township and yield thee amends for all that has been eaten and drunken in thy halls, each for himself bringing atonement of twenty oxen worth, and requiting thee in gold and bronze till thy heart is softened, but till then none may blame thee that thou art angry."

Then Odysseus of many counsels looked fiercely on him, and said: "Eurymachus, not even if ye gave me all your heritage, all that ye now have, and whatsoever else ye might in any wise add thereto, not even so would I henceforth hold my hands from slaying, ere the wooers had paid for all their transgressions. And now the choice lies before you, whether to fight in fair battle or to fly, if any may avoid death and the fates. But there be some, methinks, that shall not escape from utter doom."

He spake, and their knees were straightway loosened and

their hearts melted within them. And Eurymachus spake among them yet again:

"Friends, it is plain that this man will not hold his unconquerable hands, but now that he has caught up the polished bow and quiver, he will shoot from the smooth threshold, till he has slain us all; wherefore let us take thought for the delight of battle. Draw your blades, and hold up the tables to ward off the arrows of swift death, and let us all have at him with one accord, and drive him, if it may be, from the threshold and the doorway and then go through the city, and quickly would the cry be raised. Thereby should this man soon have shot his latest bolt."

Therewith he drew his sharp two-edged sword of bronze, and leapt on Odysseus with a terrible cry, but in the same moment goodly Odysseus shot the arrow forth and struck him on the breast by the pap, and drave the swift shaft into his liver. So he let the sword fall from his hand, and grovelling over the table he bowed and fell, and spilt the food and the two-handled cup on the floor. And in his agony he smote the ground with his brow, and spurning with both his feet he overthrew the high seat, and the mist of death was shed upon his eyes.

Then Amphinomus made at renowned Odysseus, setting straight at him, and drew his sharp sword, if perchance he might make him give ground from the door. But Telemachus was beforehand with him, and cast and smote him from behind with a bronze-shod spear between the shoulders, and drave it out through the breast, and he fell with a crash and struck the ground full with his forehead. Then Telemachus sprang away, leaving the long spear fixed in Amphinomus, for he greatly dreaded lest one of the Achaeans might run upon him with his blade, and stab him as he drew forth the spear, or smite him with a down stroke of the sword. So he started and ran and came quickly to his father, and stood by him, and spake winged words:

ODYSSEUS KILLING THE SUITORS

"Father, lo, now I will bring thee a shield and two spears and a helmet all of bronze, close fitting on the temples, and when I return I will arm myself, and likewise give arms to the swineherd and to the neatherd yonder: for it is better to be clad in full armour."

And Odysseus of many counsels answered him, saying: "Run and bring them while I have arrows to defend me, lest they thrust me from the doorway, one man against them all."

So he spake, and Telemachus obeyed his dear father, and went forth to the chamber, where his famous weapons were lying. Thence he took out four shields and eight spears, and four helmets of bronze, with thick plumes of horse hair, and he started to bring them and came quickly to his father. Now he girded the gear of bronze about his own body first, and in like manner the two thralls did on the goodly armour, and stood beside the wise and crafty Odysseus. Now he, so long as he had arrows to defend him, kept aiming and smote the wooers one by one in his house, and they fell thick one upon another. But when the arrows failed the prince in his archery, he leaned his bow against the doorpost of the stablished hall, against the shining faces of the entrance. As for him he girt his four-fold shield about his shoulders and bound on his mighty head a well-wrought helmet, with horse hair crest, and terribly the plume waved aloft. And he grasped two mighty spears tipped with bronze.

Now there was in the well-builded wall a certain postern raised above the floor, and there, by the topmost level of the threshold of the stablished hall, was a way into an open passage, closed by well-fitted folding doors. So Odysseus bade the goodly swineherd stand near thereto and watch the way, for thither was there but one approach. Then Agelaus spake among them, and declared his word to all:

"Friends, will not some man climb up to the postern, and

give word to the people, and a cry would be raised straightway; so should this man soon have shot his latest bolt?"

Then Melanthius, the goatherd, answered him, saying: "It may in no wise be, prince Agelaus; for the fair doors toward the court are grievously near to the postern, and perilous is the entrance to the passage, and one mighty man would keep back a host. But come, let me bring you armour from the inner chamber, that ye may be clad in hauberks, for methinks it is in that room and no other, that Odysseus and his renowned son laid by the arms."

Therewith Melanthius, the goatherd, climbed up by the clerestory of the hall to the inner chambers of Odysseus, whence he took twelve shields and as many spears, and as many helmets of bronze with thick plumes of horse hair, and he came forth and brought them speedily, and gave them to the wooers. Then the knees of Odysseus were loosened and his heart melted within him, when he saw them girding on the armour and brandishing the long spears in their hands, and great, he saw, was the adventure. Quickly he spake to Telemachus winged words:

"Telemachus, sure I am that one of the women in the halls is stirring up an evil battle against us, or perchance it is Melanthius."

Then wise Telemachus answered him: "My father, it is I that have erred herein and none other is to blame, for I left the well-fitted door of the chamber open, and there has been one of them but too quick to spy it. Go now, goodly Eumaeus, and close the door of the chamber, and mark if it be indeed one of the women that does this mischief, or Melanthius, as methinks it is."

Even so they spake one to the other. And Melanthius, the goatherd, went yet again to the chamber to bring the fair armour. But the goodly swineherd was ware thereof, and quickly he spake to Odysseus who stood nigh him:

"'Son of Laertes, of the seed of Zeus, Odysseus, of many devices, lo, there again is that baleful man, whom we ourselves suspect, going to the chamber; do thou tell me truly, shall I slay him if I prove the better man, or bring him hither to thee, that he may pay for the many transgressions that he has devised in thy house?"

Then Odysseus of many counsels answered, saying: "Verily, I and Telemachus will keep the proud wooers within the halls, for all their fury, but do ye twain tie his feet and arms behind his back and cast him into the chamber, and close the doors after you, and make fast to his body a twisted rope, and drag him up the lofty pillar till he be near the roof beams, that he may hang there and live for long, and suffer grievous torment."

So he spake, and they gave good heed and hearkened. So they went forth to the chamber, but the goatherd who was within knew not of their coming. Now he was seeking for the armour in the secret place of the chamber, but they twain stood in waiting on either side the doorposts. And when Melanthius, the goatherd, was crossing the threshold with a goodly helm in one hand, and in the other a wide shield and an old, stained with rust, the shield of the hero Laertes that he bare when he was young, — but at that time it was laid by, and the seams of the straps were loosened, — then the twain rushed on him and caught him, and dragged him in by the hair, and cast him on the floor in sorrowful plight, and bound him hand and foot in a bitter bond, tightly winding each limb behind his back, even as the son of Laertes bade them, the steadfast goodly Odysseus. And they made fast to his body a twisted rope, and dragged him up the lofty pillar till he came near the roof beams. Then didst thou speak to him and gird at him, swineherd Eumaeus:

"Now in good truth, Melanthius, shalt thou watch all night, lying in a soft bed as beseems thee, nor shall the early-born Dawn escape thy ken, when she comes forth from the streams of Oceanus, on her golden throne, in the hour when thou art wont to drive the goats to make a meal for the wooers in the halls."

So he was left there, stretched tight in the deadly bond. But they twain got into their harness, and closed the shining door, and went to Odysseus, wise and crafty chief. There they stood breathing fury, four men by the threshold, while those others within the halls were many and good warriors. Then Athene, daughter of Zeus, drew nigh them, like Mentor in fashion and in voice, and Odysseus was glad when he saw her and spake, saying:

"Mentor, ward from us hurt, and remember me, thy dear companion, that befriended thee often, and thou art of like age with me."

So he spake, deeming the while that it was Athene, summoner of the host. But the wooers on the other side shouted in the halls, and first Agelaus, son of Damastor, rebuked Athene, saying:

"Mentor, let not the speech of Odysseus beguile thee to fight against the wooers, and to succour him. For methinks that on this wise we shall work our will. When we shall have slain these men, father and son, thereafter shalt thou perish with them, such deeds thou art set on doing in these halls; nay, with thine own head shalt thou pay the price. But when with the sword we shall have overcome your violence, we will mingle all thy possessions, all that thou hast at home or in the field, with the wealth of Odysseus, and we will not suffer thy sons nor thy daughters to dwell in the halls, nor thy good wife to gad about in the town of Ithaca."

So spake he, and Athene waxed yet the more wroth at heart, and chid Odysseus with angry words: "Odysseus, thou hast no more steadfast might nor any prowess, as when for nine whole years continually thou didst battle with the Trojans for high-born Helen, of the white arms, and many men thou slewest in terrible warfare, and by thy device the wide-wayed city of Priam was taken. How then, now that thou art come to thy house and thine own possessions, dost thou bewail the need of courage to stand before the wooers? Nay, come hither, friend, and stand by me, and I will show thee a thing, that thou mayest know what manner of man is Mentor, son of Alcimus, to repay good deeds in the ranks of foemen."

She spake, and gave him not yet clear victory in full, but still for a while made trial of the might and prowess of Odysseus and his renowned son. As for her she flew up to the roof timber of the murky hall, in such fashion as a swallow flies, and there sat down.

Now Agelaus, son of Damastor, urged on the wooers, and likewise Eurynomus and Amphimedon and Demoptolemus and Peisandrus son of Polyctor, and wise Polybus, for these were in valiancy far the best men of the wooers, that still lived and fought for their lives; for the rest had fallen already beneath the bow and the thick rain of arrows. Then Agelaus spake among them, and made known his word to all:

"Friends, now at last will this man hold his unconquerable hands. Lo, now has Mentor left him and spoken but vain boasts, and these remain alone at the entrance of the doors. Wherefore now, throw not your long spears all together, but come, do ye six cast first, if perchance Zeus may grant us to smite Odysseus and win renown. Of the rest will we take no heed, so soon as that man shall have fallen."

So he spake and they all cast their javelins, as he bade them, eagerly; but behold, Athene so wrought that they were all in vain. One man smote the doorpost of the stablished hall, and another the well-fastened door, and the ashen spear of yet another wooer, heavy with bronze, stuck fast in the wall. So when they had avoided all the spears of the wooers, the steadfast goodly Odysseus began first to speak among them:

"Friends, now my word is that we too cast and hurl into the press of the wooers, that are mad to slay and strip us beyond the measure of their former iniquities."

So he spake, and they all took good aim and threw their sharp spears, and Odysseus smote Demoptolemus, and Telemachus Euryades, and the swineherd slew Elatus, and the neatherd Peisandrus. Thus they all bit the wide floor with their teeth, and the wooers fell back into the inmost part of the hall. But the others dashed upon them, and drew forth the shafts from the bodies of the dead.

Then once more the wooers threw their sharp spears eagerly; but behold, Athene so wrought that many of them were in vain. One man smote the doorpost of the stablished hall, and another the well-fastened door, and the ashen spear of another wooer, heavy with bronze, struck in the wall. Yet Amphimedon hit Telemachus on the hand by the wrist lightly, and the shaft of bronze wounded the surface of the skin. And Ctesippus grazed the shoulder of Eumaeus with a long spear high above the shield, and the spear flew over and fell to the ground. Then again Odysseus, the wise and crafty, he and his men cast their swift spears into the press of the wooers, and now once more Odysseus, waster of cities, smote Eurydamas, and Telemachus Amphimedon, and the swineherd slew Polybus, and last, the neatherd struck Ctesippus in the breast and boasted over him, saying:

"O son of Polytherses, thou lover of jeering, never give place at all to folly to speak so big, but leave thy case to the gods, since in truth they are far mightier than thou. This gift is thy recompense for the ox-foot that thou gavest of late to the divine Odysseus, when he went begging through the house."

So spake the keeper of the shambling kine. Next Odysseus wounded the son of Damastor in close fight with his long spear, and Telemachus wounded Leocritus son of Euenor, right in the flank with his lance, and drave the bronze point clean through, that he fell prone and struck the ground full with his forehead. Then Athene held up her destroying aegis on high from the roof, and their minds were scared, and they fled through the hall, like a drove of kine that the flitting gadfly falls upon and scatters hither and thither in springtime, when the long days begin. But the others set on like vultures of crooked claws and curved beak, that come forth from the mountains and dash upon smaller birds, and these scour low in the plain, stooping in terror from the clouds, while the vultures pounce on them and slay them, and there is no help nor way of flight, and men are glad at the sport; even so did the company of Odysseus set upon the wooers and smite them right and left through the hall; and there rose a hideous moaning as their heads were smitten, and the floor all ran with blood.

Now Leiodes took hold of the knees of Odysseus eagerly, and besought him and spake winged words: "I entreat thee by thy knees, Odysseus, and do thou show mercy on me and have pity. For never yet, I say, have I wronged a maiden in thy halls by froward word or deed, nay, I bade the other wooers refrain, whoso of them wrought thus. But they hearkened not unto me to keep their hands from evil. Wherefore they have met a shameful death through their own infatuate deeds. Yet I, the soothsayer among them, that have wrought no evil, shall fall even as they, for no gratitude survives for good deeds done."

Then Odysseus of many counsels looked askance at him, and said: "If indeed thou dost avow thee to be the soothsayer of these men, thou art like to have often prayed in the halls that the issue of a glad return might be far from me, and that my dear wife should follow thee and bear thee children; wherefore thou shalt not escape the bitterness of death."

Therewith he caught up a sword in his strong hand, that lay where Agelaus had let it fall to the ground when he was slain, and drave it clean through his neck, and as he yet spake his head fell even to the dust.

But the son of Terpes, the minstrel, still sought how he might shun black fate, Phemius, who sang among the wooers of necessity. He stood with the loud lyre in his hand hard by the postern gate, and his heart was divided within him, whether he should slip forth from the hall and sit down by the well-wrought altar of great Zeus of the household court, whereon Laertes and Odysseus had burnt many pieces of the thighs of oxen, or should spring forward and beseech Odysseus by his knees. And as he thought thereupon this seemed to him the better way, to embrace the knees of Odysseus, son of Laertes. So he laid the hollow lyre on the ground between the mixing bowl and the high seat inlaid with silver, and himself sprang forward and seized Odysseus by the knees, and besought him and spake winged words:

"I entreat thee by thy knees, Odysseus, and do thou show mercy on me and have pity. It will be a sorrow to thyself in the aftertime if thou slayest me who am a minstrel, and sing before gods and men. Yea, none has taught me but myself, and the god has put into my heart all manner of lays, and methinks I sing to thee as to a god, wherefore be not eager to cut off my head. And Telemachus will testify of this, thine own dear son, that not by mine own will or desire did I resort to thy house to sing to the wooers after their feasts; but being so many and stronger than I they led me by constraint."

So he spake, and the mighty prince Telemachus heard him and quickly spake to his father at his side: "Hold thy hand, and wound not this blameless man with the sword; and let us save also the henchman Medon, that ever had charge of me in our house when I was a child, unless perchance Philoetius or the swineherd have already slain him, or he hath met thee in thy raging through the house."

So he spake, and Medon, wise of heart, heard him. For he lay crouching beneath a high seat, clad about in the new-flayed hide of an ox and shunned black fate. So he rose up quickly from under the seat, and cast off the ox-hide, and sprang forth and caught Telemachus by the knees, and besought him and spake winged words :

"Friend, here am I; prithee stay thy hand and speak to thy father, lest he harm me with the sharp sword in the greatness of his strength, out of his anger for the wooers that wasted his possessions in the halls, and in their folly held thee in no honour."

And Odysseus of many counsels smiled on him and said: "Take courage, for lo, he has saved thee and delivered thee, that thou mayst know in thy heart, and tell it even to another, how far more excellent are good deeds than evil. But go forth from the halls and sit down in the court apart from the slaughter, thou and the full-voiced minstrel, till I have accomplished all that I must needs do in the house."

Therewith the two went forth and gat them from the hall. So they sat down by the altar of great Zeus, peering about on every side, still expecting death. And Odysseus peered all through the house, to see if any man was yet alive and hiding away to shun black fate. But he found all the sort of them fallen in their blood in the dust, like fishes that the fishermen have drawn forth in the meshes of the net into a hollow of the beach from out the grey sea, and all the fish, sore longing for the salt sea waves, are heaped upon the sand, and the sun shines forth and takes their life away; so now the wooers lay heaped upon each other. Then Odysseus of many counsels spake to Telemachus :

"Telemachus, go, call me the nurse Eurycleia, that I may tell her a word that is on my mind."

So he spake, and Telemachus obeyed his dear father, and smote at the door, and spake to the nurse Eurycleia: "Up now, aged wife, that overlookest all the women servants in our halls, come hither, my father calls thee and has somewhat to say to thee."

Even so he spake, and his word unwinged abode with her, and she opened the doors of the fair-lying halls, and came forth, and Telemachus led the way before her. So she found Odysseus among the bodies of the dead, stained with blood and soil of battle, like a lion that has eaten of an ox of the homestead and goes on his way, and all his breast and his cheeks on either side are flecked with blood, and he is terrible to behold; even so was Odysseus stained, both hands and feet. Now the nurse, when she saw the bodies of the dead and the great gore of blood, made ready to cry aloud for joy, beholding so great an adventure. But Odysseus checked and held her in her eagerness, and uttering his voice spake to her winged words:

"Within thine own heart rejoice, old nurse, and be still, and cry not aloud; for it is an unholy thing to boast over slain men. Now these hath the destiny of the gods overcome, and their own cruel deeds, for they honoured none of earthly men, neither the good nor yet the bad, that came among them. Wherefore they have met a shameful death through their own infatuate deeds. But come, tell me the tale of the women in my halls, which of them dishonour me, and which be guiltless."

Then the good nurse Eurycleia answered him: "Yea now, my child, I will tell thee all the truth. Thou hast fifty women-servants in thy halls, that we have taught the ways of housewifery, how to card wool and to bear bondage. Of these twelve in all have gone the way of shame, and honour not me, nor their lady Penelope. And Telemachus hath but newly come to his strength, and his mother suffered him not to take command over the women in this house. But now, let me go aloft to the shining upper chamber, and tell all to thy wife, on whom some god hath sent a sleep."

And Odysseus of many counsels answered her, saying: "Wake her not yet, but bid the women come hither, who in time past behaved themselves unseemly."

So he spake, and the old wife passed through the hall, to

tell the women and to hasten their coming. Then Odysseus called to him Telemachus, and the neatherd, and the swineherd, and spake to them winged words:

"Begin ye now to carry out the dead, and bid the women help you, and thereafter cleanse the fair high seats and the tables with water and porous sponges. And when ye have set all the house in order, lead the maidens without the stablished hall, between the vaulted room and the goodly fence of the court, and there slay them with your long blades, till they shall have all given up the ghost and forgotten the love that of old they had at the bidding of the wooers."

Even so he spake, and the women came all in a crowd together, making a terrible lament and shedding big tears. So first they carried forth the bodies of the slain, and set them beneath the gallery of the fenced court, and propped them one on another; and Odysseus himself hasted the women and directed them, and they carried forth the dead perforce. Thereafter they cleansed the fair high seats and the tables with water and porous sponges. And Telemachus, and the neatherd, and the swineherd scraped with spades the floor of the well-builded house, and, behold, the maidens carried all forth and laid it without the doors.

Now when they had made an end of setting the hall in order, they led the maidens forth from the stablished hall, and drove them up in a narrow space between the vaulted room and the goodly fence of the court, whence none might avoid; and wise Telemachus began to speak to his fellows, saying:

"God forbid that I should take these women's lives by a clean death, these that have poured dishonour on my head and on my mother."

With that word he tied the cable of a dark-prowed ship to a great pillar and flung it round the vaulted room, and fastened it aloft, that none might touch the ground with her feet. And even as when thrushes, long of wing, or doves fall into a net that is set in a thicket, as they seek their roosting-place, and a hateful bed harbours them, even so the women held their heads all in a row, and about all their necks nooses were cast, that they might die by the most pitiful death. And they writhed with their feet for a little space, but for no long while.

Then they led out Melanthius through the gateway and the court, and cut off his nostrils and his ears with the pitiless sword, and drew forth his vitals for the dogs to devour raw, and cut off his hands and feet in their cruel anger.

Thereafter they washed their hands and feet, and went into the house to Odysseus, and all the adventure was over. So Odysseus called to the good nurse Eurycleia: "Bring sulphur, old nurse, that cleanses all pollution and bring me fire, that I may purify the house with sulphur, and do thou bid Penelope come here with her handmaidens, and tell all the women in the house to speed them hither."

Then the good nurse Eurycleia made answer: "Yea, my child, herein thou hast spoken aright. But go to, let me bring thee a mantle and a doublet for raiment, and stand not thus in the halls with thy broad shoulders wrapped in rags; it were blame in thee so to do."

And Odysseus of many counsels answered her, saying: "First let a fire now be made me in the hall."

So he spake, and the good nurse Eurycleia was not slow to obey, but brought fire and brimstone; and Odysseus thoroughly purged the women's chamber and the great hall and the court.

Then the old wife went through the fair halls of Odysseus to tell the women, and to hasten their coming. So they came forth from their chamber with torches in their hands, and fell about Odysseus, and embraced him and kissed and clasped his head and shoulders and his hands lovingly, and a sweet longing came on him to weep and moan, for he remembered them every one.

BOOK XXIII

Odysseus maketh himself known to Penelope, tells his adventures briefly, and in the morning goes to Laertes and makes himself known to him.

THEN the ancient woman went up into the upper chamber laughing aloud, to tell her mistress how her dear lord was within, and her knees moved fast for joy, and her feet stumbled one over the other; and she stood above the lady's head and spake to her, saying:

"Awake, Penelope, dear child, that thou mayest see with thine own eyes that which thou desirest day by day. Odysseus hath come, and hath got him to his own house, though late hath he come, and hath slain the proud wooers that troubled his house, and devoured his substance, and oppressed his child."

Then wise Penelope answered her: "Dear nurse, the gods have made thee distraught, the gods that can make foolish even the wisdom of the wise, and that stablish the simple in understanding. They it is that have marred thy reason, though heretofore thou hadst a prudent heart. Why dost thou mock me, who have a spirit full of sorrow, to speak these wild words, and rousest me out of sweet slumber, that had bound me and overshadowed mine eyelids? Never yet have I slept so sound since the day that Odysseus went forth to see that evil Ilios, never to be named. Go to now, get thee down and back to the women's chamber, for if any other of the maids of my house had come and brought me such tidings, and wakened me from sleep, straightway would I have sent her back woefully to return within the women's chamber; but this time thine old age shall stand thee in good stead."

Then the good nurse Eurycleia answered her: "I mock thee not, dear child, but in very deed Odysseus is here, and hath come home, even as I tell thee. He is that guest on whom all men wrought such dishonour in the halls. But long ago Telemachus was ware of him, that he was within the house, yet in his prudence he hid the counsels of his father, that he might take vengeance on the violence of the haughty wooers."

Thus she spake, and then was Penelope glad, and leaping from her bed she fell on the old woman's neck, and let fall the tears from her eyelids, and uttering her voice spake to her winged words: "Come, dear nurse, I pray thee, tell me all the truth, if indeed he hath come home as thou sayest, how he hath laid his hands on the shameless wooers, he being but one man, while they abode ever in their companies within the house."

Then the nurse Eurycleia answered her: "I saw not, I wist not, only I heard the groaning of men slain. And we in an inmost place of the well-built chambers sat all amazed, and the close-fitted doors shut in the room, till thy son called me from the chamber, for his father sent him out to that end. Then I found Odysseus standing among the slain, who around him, stretched on the hard floor, lay one upon the other; it would have comforted thy heart to see him, all stained like a lion with blood and soil of battle. And now are all the wooers gathered in a heap by the gates of the court, while he is purifying his fair house with brimstone, and hath kindled a great fire, and hath sent me forth to call thee. So come with me, that ye may both enter into your hearts' delight, for ye have suffered much affliction. And even now hath this thy long desire been fulfilled; thy lord hath come alive to his own hearth, and hath found both thee and his son in the halls; and the wooers that wrought him evil he hath slain, every man of them in his house."

Then wise Penelope answered her: "Dear nurse, boast not yet over them with laughter. Thou knowest how welcome the sight of him would be in the halls to all, and to me in chief, and to his son that we got between us. But this is no true tale, as thou declarest it, nay, but it is one of the deathless gods that hath slain the proud wooers, in wrath at their bitter insolence and evil deeds. For they honoured none of earthly men, neither the good nor yet the bad, that came among them. Wherefore they have suffered an evil doom through their own infatuate deeds. But Odysseus, far away, hath lost his homeward path to the Achaean land, and himself is lost."

Then the good nurse Eurycleia made answer to her: "My child, what word hath escaped the door of thy lips, in that thou saidest that thy lord, who is even now within, and by his own hearth-stone, would return no more? Nay, thy heart is ever hard of belief. Go to now, and I will tell thee besides a most manifest token, even the scar of the wound that the boar on a time dealt him with his white tusk. This I spied while washing his feet, and fain I would have told it even to thee, but he laid his hand on my mouth, and in the fulness of his wisdom suffered me not to speak. But come with me and I will stake my life on it; and, if I play thee false, do thou slay me by a death most pitiful."

Then wise Penelope made answer to her: "Dear nurse, it is hard for thee, how wise soever, to spy out the purposes of the everlasting gods. None the less let us go to my child, that I may see the wooers dead, and him that slew them."

With that word she went down from the upper chamber, and much her heart debated, whether she should stand apart, and question her dear lord or draw nigh, and clasp and kiss his head and hands. But when she had come within and had crossed the threshold of stone, she sat down over against Odysseus, in the light of the fire, by the further wall. Now he was sitting by the tall pillar, looking down and waiting to know if perchance his noble wife would speak to him, when her eyes beheld him. But she sat long in silence, and amazement came upon her soul, and now she would look upon him steadfastly with her eyes, and now again she knew him not, for that he was clad in vile raiment. And Telemachus rebuked her, and spake and hailed:

"Mother mine, ill mother, of an ungentle heart, why turnest thou thus away from my father, and dost not sit by him and question him and ask him all? No other woman in the world would harden her heart to stand thus aloof from her lord, who after much travail and sore had come to her in the twentieth year to his own country. But thy heart is ever harder than stone."

Then wise Penelope answered him, saying: "Child, my mind is amazed within me, and I have no strength to speak, nor to ask him aught, nay, nor to look on him face to face. But if in truth this be Odysseus, and he hath indeed come home, verily we shall be ware of each other the more surely, for we have tokens that we twain know, even we, secret from all others."

So she spake, and the steadfast goodly Odysseus smiled, and quickly he spake to Telemachus winged words: "Telemachus, leave now thy mother to make trial of me within the chambers; so shall she soon come to a better knowledge than heretofore. But now I go filthy, and am clad in vile raiment, wherefore she has me in dishonour, and as yet will not allow that I am he. Let us then advise us how all may be for the very best. For whoso has slain but one man in a land, even one that leaves not many behind him to take up the feud for him, turns outlaw and leaves his kindred and his own country; but we have slain the very stay of the city, the men who were far the best of all the noble youths in Ithaca. So this I bid thee consider."

Then wise Telemachus answered him, saying: "Father, see thou to this, for they say that thy counsel is far the best among men, nor might any other of mortal men contend with thee. But right eagerly will we go with thee now, and I think we shall not lack prowess, so far as might is ours."

And Odysseus of many counsels answered him, saying: "Yea now, I will tell on what wise methinks it is best. First, go ye to the bath and array you in your doublets, and bid the maidens in the chambers to take to them their garments. Then let the divine minstrel, with his loud lyre in hand, lead off for us the measure of the mirthful dance. So shall any man that hears the sound from without, whether a wayfarer or one of those that dwell around, say that it is a wedding feast. And thus the slaughter of the wooers shall not be noised abroad through the town before we go forth to our well-wooded farm land. Thereafter shall we consider what gainful counsel the Olympian may vouchsafe us."

So he spake, and they gave good ear and hearkened to him. So first they went to the bath, and arrayed them in doublets, and the women were apparelled, and the divine minstrel took the hollow harp, and aroused in them the desire of sweet song and of the happy dance. Then the great hall rang round them with the sound of the feet of dancing men and of fair-girdled women. And whoso heard it from without would say:

"Surely some one has wedded the queen of many wooers. Hard of heart was she, nor had she courage to keep the great house of her wedded lord continually till his coming."

Even so men spake, and knew not how these things were ordained. Meanwhile, the housedame Eurynome had bathed the great-hearted Odysseus within his house, and anointed him with olive-oil, and cast about him a goodly mantle and a doublet. Moreover, Athene shed great beauty from his head downwards, and made him greater and more mighty to behold, and from his head caused deep curling locks to flow, like the hyacinth flower. And as when some skilful man overlays gold upon silver, one that Hephaestus and Pallas Athene have taught all manner of craft, and full of grace is his handiwork, even so did Athene shed grace about his head and shoulders, and forth from the bath he came, in form like to the Immortals. Then he sat down again on the high seat, whence he had arisen, over against his wife, and spake to her, saying:

"Strange lady, surely to thee above all womankind the Olympians have given a heart that cannot be softened. No other woman in the world would harden her heart to stand thus aloof from her husband, who after much travail and sore had come to her, in the twentieth year, to his own country. Nay come, nurse, strew a bed for me to lie all alone, for assuredly her spirit within her is as iron."

Then wise Penelope answered him again: "Strange man, I have no proud thoughts nor do I think scorn of thee, nor am I too greatly astonied, but I know right well what manner of man thou wert, when thou wentest forth out of Ithaca, on the long-oared galley. But come, Eurycleia, spread for him the good bedstead outside the stablished bridal chamber that he built himself. Thither bring ye forth the good bedstead and cast bedding thereon, even fleeces and rugs and shining blankets."

So she spoke and made trial of her lord, but Odysseus in sore displeasure spake to his true wife, saying: "Verily a bitter word is this, lady, that thou hast spoken. Who has set my bed otherwise? Hard it would be for one, how skilled soever, unless a god were to come that might easily set it in another place, if so he would. But of men there is none living, howsoever strong in his youth, that could lightly upheave it, for a great marvel is wrought in the fashion of the bed, and it was I that made it and none other. There was growing a bush of olive, long of leaf, and most goodly of growth, within the inner court, and the stem as large as a pillar. Round about this I built the chamber, till I had finished it, with stones close set, and I roofed it over well and added thereto compacted doors fitting well. Next I sheared off all the light wood of the long-cleaved olive, and rough-hewed the trunk upwards from the root, and smoothed it around with the adze, well and skilfully, and made straight the line thereto and so fashioned it into the bedpost, and I bored it all with the auger. Beginning from this bedpost, I wrought at the bedstead till I had finished it, and made it fair with inlaid work of gold and of silver and of ivory. Then I made fast therein a bright purple band of ox-hide. Even so I declare to thee this token, and I know not, lady, if the bedstead be yet fast in its place, or if some man has cut away the stem of the olive tree, and set the bedstead otherwhere."

So he spake, and at once her knees were loosened, and her heart melted within her, as she knew the sure tokens that Odysseus showed her. Then she fell a-weeping, and ran straight toward him and cast her hands about his neck, and kissed his head and spake, saying:

"Murmur not against me, Odysseus, for thou wert ever at other times the wisest of men. It is the gods that gave us sorrow, the gods who were jealous that we should abide together and have joy of our youth, and come to the threshold of old age. So now be not wroth with me hereat nor full of indignation, because I did not welcome thee gladly as now, when first I saw thee. For always my heart within my breast shuddered, for fear lest some man should come and deceive me with his words, for many they be that devise gainful schemes and evil. Nay, even Argive Helen, daughter of Zeus, would not have taken a stranger for a lover, had she known that the warlike sons of the Achaeans would bring her home again to her own dear country. Howsoever, it was the god that set her upon this shameful deed; nor ever, ere that, did she lay up in her heart the thought of this folly, a bitter folly, whence on us too first came sorrow. But now that thou hast told all the sure tokens of our bed, which never was seen by mortal man, save by thee and me and one maiden only, the daughter of Actor, that my father gave me ere yet I had come hither, she who kept the doors of our strong bridal chamber, even now dost thou bend my soul, all ungentle as it is."

Thus she spake, and in his heart she stirred yet a greater longing to lament, and he wept as he embraced his beloved wife and true. And even as when the sight of land is welcome to swimmers, whose well-wrought ship Poseidon hath smitten on the deep, all driven with the wind and swelling waves, and but a remnant hath escaped the grey sea-water and swum to the shore, and their bodies are all crusted with the brine, and gladly have they set foot on land and escaped an evil end; so welcome to her was the sight of her lord, and her white arms she would never quite let go from his neck. And now would the rosy-fingered Dawn have risen upon their weeping, but the goddess, grey-eyed Athene, had other thoughts. The night she held long in the utmost West, and on the other side she stayed the golden-throned Dawn by the stream Oceanus, and suffered her not to harness the swift-footed steeds that bear light to men, Lampus and Phaethon, the steeds ever young, that bring the morning.

Then at the last, Odysseus of many counsels spake to his wife, saying: "Lady, we have not yet come to the issue of all our labours; but still there will be toil unmeasured, long and difficult, that I must needs bring to a full end. Even so the spirit of Teiresias foretold to me, on that day when I went down into the house of Hades, to inquire after a returning for myself and my company. Wherefore come, lady, let us to bed, that forthwith we may take our joy of rest beneath the spell of sweet sleep."

Then wise Penelope answered him: "Thy bed verily shall be ready whensoever thy soul desires it, forasmuch as the gods have indeed caused thee to come back to thy stablished home and thine own country. But now that thou hast noted it and the god has put it into thy heart, come, tell me of this ordeal, for methinks the day will come when I must learn it, and timely knowledge is no hurt."

And Odysseus of many counsels answered her, saying: "Ah, why now art thou so instant with me to declare it? Yet I will tell thee all and hide nought. Howbeit thy heart shall have no joy of it, as even I myself have no pleasure therein. For Teiresias bade me fare to many cities of men, carrying a shapen oar in my hands, till I should come to such men as know not the sea, neither eat meat savoured with salt, nor have they knowledge of ships of purple cheek nor of shapen oars, which serve for wings to ships. And he told me this manifest token, which I will not hide from thee. In the day when another wayfarer should meet me and say that I had a winnowing fan on my stout shoulder, even then he bade me make fast my shapen oar in the earth, and do goodly sacrifice to the lord Poseidon, even with a ram and a bull and a boar, the mate of swine, and depart for home, and offer holy hecatombs to the deathless gods, that keep the wide heaven, to each in order due. And from the sea shall mine own death come, the gentlest death that may be, which shall end me, foredone with smooth old age, and the folk shall dwell happily around. All this, he said, was to be fulfilled."

Then wise Penelope answered him, saying: "If indeed the gods will bring about for thee a happier old age at the last, then is there hope that thou mayest yet have an escape from evil."

Thus they spake one to the other. Meanwhile, Eurynome and the nurse spread the bed with soft coverlets, by the light of the torches burning. But when they had busied them and spread the good bed, the ancient nurse went back to her chamber to lie down, and Eurynome, the bower-maiden, guided them on their way to the couch, with torches in her hands, and when she had led them to the bridal chamber she departed. But Telemachus, and the neatherd, and the swineherd stayed their feet from dancing, and made the women to cease, and themselves gat them to rest through the shadowy halls.

Then the goddess, grey-eyed Athene, turned to new thoughts. When she conceived that Odysseus had taken his fill of sleep, straightway she aroused from out Oceanus the golden-throned

Dawn, to bear light to men. Then Odysseus gat him up from his soft bed, and laid this charge on his wife, saying:

"Lady, already have we had enough of labours, thou and I; thou, in weeping here, and longing for my troublous return, I, while Zeus and the other gods bound me fast in pain, despite my yearning after home, away from mine own country. But now that we both have come to our desire, take thou thought for the care of my wealth within the halls. But as for the sheep that the proud wooers have slain, I myself will lift many more as spoil, and others the Achaeans will give, till they fill all my folds. But now, behold, I go to the well-wooded farm land, to see my good father, who for love of me has been in sorrow continually. And this charge I lay on thee, lady, too wise though thou art to need it. Quickly will the bruit go forth with the rising sun, the bruit concerning the wooers, whom I slew in the halls. Wherefore ascend with the women thy handmaids into the upper chamber, and sit there and look on no man, nor ask any question."

Therewith he girded on his shoulder his goodly armour, and roused Telemachus and the neatherd and the swineherd, and bade them all take weapons of war in their hands. So they were not disobedient to his word, but clad themselves in mail, and opened the doors and went forth, and Odysseus led the way. And now there was light over all the earth; but them Athene hid in night, and quickly conducted out of the town.

BOOK XXIV

The Ithacans bury the wooers, and sitting in council resolve on revenge. And coming near the house of Laertes, they are met by Odysseus and Laertes with Telemachus and servants, the whole number twelve, and are overcome, and submit.

Now when they had gone down from the city, quickly they came to the rich and well-ordered farm land of Laertes, that he had won for himself of old, as the prize of great toil in war. There was his house, and all about it ran the huts wherein the thralls were wont to eat and dwell and sleep, bondsmen that worked his will. And in the house there was an old Sicilian woman, who diligently cared for the old man, in the upland far from the city. There Odysseus spake to his thralls and to his son, saying: .

"Do ye now get you within the well-builded house, and quickly sacrifice the best of the swine for the mid-day meal, but I will make trial of my father, whether he will know me again and be aware of me when he sees me, or know me not, so long have I been away."

Therewith he gave the thralls his weapons of war. Then they went speedily to the house, while Odysseus drew near to the fruitful vineyard to make trial of his father. Now he found not Dolius there, as he went down into the great garden, nor any of the thralls nor of their sons. It chanced that they had all gone to gather stones for a garden fence, and the old man at their head. So he found his father alone in the terraced vineyard, digging about a plant. He was clothed in a filthy doublet, patched and unseemly, with clouted leggings of ox-hide bound about his legs, against the scratches of the thorns, and long sleeves over his hands by reason of the brambles, and on his head he wore a goatskin cap, and so he nursed his sorrow. Now when the steadfast goodly Odysseus saw his father thus wasted with age and in great grief of heart, he stood still beneath a tall pear tree and let fall a tear. Then he communed with his heart and soul, whether he should fall on his father's neck and kiss him, and tell him all, how he had returned and come to his own country, or whether he should first question him and prove him in every word. And as he thought within himself, this seemed to him the better way, namely, first to prove his father and speak to him sharply. So with this intent the goodly Odysseus went up to him. Now he was holding his head down and kept digging about the plant, while his renowned son stood by him and spake, saying:

"Old man, thou hast no lack of skill in tending a garden; lo, thou carest well for all, nor is there aught whatsoever, either plant or fig tree, or vine, yea, or olive, or pear, or garden-bed in all the close, that is not well seen to. Yet another thing will I tell thee and lay not up wrath thereat in thy heart. Thyself art scarce so well cared for, but a pitiful old age is on thee, and withal thou art withered and unkempt, and clad unseemly. It cannot be to punish thy sloth that thy master cares not for thee; there shows nothing of the slave about thy face and stature, for thou art like a kingly man, even like one who should lie soft, when he has washed and eaten well, as is the manner of the aged. But come, declare me this and plainly tell it all. Whose thrall art thou, and whose garden dost thou tend? Tell me moreover truly, that I may surely know, if it be indeed to Ithaca that I am now come, as one yonder told me who met with me but now on the way hither. He was but of little understanding, for he deigned not to tell me all nor to heed my saying, when I questioned him concerning my friend, whether indeed he is yet alive or is even now dead and within the house of Hades. For I will declare it and do thou mark and listen: once did I kindly entreat a man in mine own dear country, who came to our home, and never yet has any mortal been dearer of all the strangers that have drawn to my house from afar. He declared him to be by lineage from out of Ithaca, and said that his own father was Laertes son of Arceisius. So I led him to our halls and gave him good entertainment, with all loving-kindness, out of the plenty that was within. Such gifts too I gave him as are the due of guests; of well-wrought gold I gave him seven talents, and a mixing bowl of flowered work, all of silver, and twelve cloaks of single fold, and as many coverlets, and as many goodly mantles and doublets to boot, and besides all these, four women skilled in all fair works and most comely, the women of his choice."

Then his father answered him, weeping: "Stranger, thou art verily come to that country whereof thou askest, but outrageous men and froward hold it. And these thy gifts, thy countless gifts, thou didst bestow in vain. For if thou hadst found that man yet living in the land of Ithaca he would have sent thee on thy way with good return of thy presents, and with all hospitality, as is due to the man that begins the kindness. But come, declare me this and plainly tell me all; how many years are passed since thou didst entertain him, thy guest ill-fated and my child, — if ever such an one there was, — hapless man, whom, far from his friends and his country's soil, the fishes, it may be, have devoured in the deep sea, or on the shore he has fallen the prey of birds and beasts. His mother wept not over him nor clad him for burial, nor his father, we that begat him. Nor did his bride, whom men sought with rich gifts, the constant Penelope, bewail her lord upon the bier, as was meet, nor closed his eyes, as is the due of the departed. Moreover, tell me this truly, that I may surely know, who art thou and whence of the sons of men? Where is thy city and where are they that begat thee? Where now is thy swift ship moored, that brought thee thither with thy godlike company? Hast thou come as a passenger on another's ship, while they set thee ashore and went away?"

Then Odysseus of many counsels answered him, saying: "Yea now, I will tell thee all most plainly. From out of Alybas I come, where I dwell in a house renowned, and am the son of Apheidas the son of Polypemon, the prince, and my own name is Eperitus. But some god drave me wandering hither from Sicania against my will, and yonder my ship is moored toward the upland away from the city. But for Odysseus, this is now the fifth year since he went thence and departed out of my country. Ill-fated was he, and yet he had birds of good omen when he fared away, birds on the right; wherefore I sped him gladly on his road, and gladly he departed, and the heart of us twain hoped yet to meet in friendship on a day and to give splendid gifts."

So he spake, and on the old man fell a black cloud of sorrow. With both his hands he clutched the dust and ashes and showered them on his gray head, with ceaseless groaning. Then the heart of Odysseus was moved, and up through his nostrils throbbed anon the keen sting of sorrow at the sight of his dear father. And he sprang towards him and fell on his neck and kissed him, saying:

"Behold, I here, even I, my father, am the man of whom thou askest; in the twentieth year am I come to mine own country. But stay thy weeping and tearful lamentation, for I will tell thee all clearly, though great need there is of haste. I have slain the wooers in our halls and avenged their bitter scorn and evil deeds."

Then Laertes answered him and spake, saying: "If thou art indeed Odysseus, mine own child, that art come hither, show me now a manifest token, that I may be assured."

Then Odysseus of many counsels answered him, saying: "Look first on this scar and consider it, that the boar dealt me with his white tusk on Parnassus, whither I had gone, and thou didst send me forth, thou and my lady mother, to Autolycus my mother's father, to get the gifts which when he came hither he promised and covenanted to give me. But come, and I will even tell thee the trees through all the terraced garden, which thou gavest me once for mine own, and I was begging of thee this and that, being but a little child, and following thee through the garden. Through these very trees we were going, and thou didst tell me the names of each of them. Pear trees thirteen thou gavest me and ten apple trees and figs two-score, and, as we went, thou didst name the fifty rows of vines thou wouldest give me, whereof each one ripened at divers times, with all manner of clusters on their boughs, when the seasons of Zeus wrought mightily on them from on high."

So he spake, and straightway his knees were loosened, and his heart melted within him, as he knew the sure tokens that Odysseus showed him. About his dear son he cast his arms, and the steadfast goodly Odysseus caught him fainting to his breast. Now when he had got breath and his spirit came to him again, once more he answered and spake, saying:

"Father Zeus, verily ye gods yet bare sway on high Olympus, if indeed the wooers have paid for their infatuate pride! But now my heart is terribly afraid, lest straightway all the men of Ithaca come up against us here, and haste to send messengers everywhere to the cities of the Cephallenians."

Then Odysseus of many counsels answered him, saying: "Take courage, and let not thy heart be careful about these matters. But come, let us go to the house that lies near the garden, for thither I sent forward Telemachus and the neatherd and the swineherd to get ready the meal as speedily as may be."

After these words the twain set out to the goodly halls. Now when they had come to the fair-lying house, they found Telemachus and the neatherd and the swineherd carving much flesh, and mixing the dark wine. Meanwhile the Sicilian handmaid bathed high-hearted Laertes in his house, and anointed him with olive-oil, and cast a fair mantle about him. Then Athene drew nigh, and made greater the limbs of the shepherd of the people, taller she made him than before and mightier to behold. Then he went forth from the bath, and his dear son marvelled at him, beholding him like to the deathless gods in presence. And uttering his voice he spake to him winged words:

"Father, surely one of the gods that are from everlasting hath made thee goodlier and greater to behold."

Then wise Laertes answered him, saying: "Ah, would to father Zeus and Athene and Apollo, that such as I was when I took Nericus, the stablished castle on the foreland of the continent, being then the prince of the Cephallenians, would that in such might, and with mail about my shoulders, I had stood to aid thee yesterday in our house, and to beat back the wooers; so should I have loosened the knees of many an one of them in the halls, and thou shouldest have been gladdened in thine inmost heart!"

So they spake each with the other. But when the others had ceased from their task and made ready the feast, they sat down all orderly on chairs and on high seats. Then they began to put forth their hands on the meat, and the old man Dolius drew nigh, and the old man's sons withal came tired from their labour in the fields, for their mother, the aged Sicilian woman, had gone forth and called them, she that saw to their living and diligently cared for the old man, now that old age had laid hold on him. So soon as they looked on Odysseus and took knowledge of him, they stood still in the halls in great amazement. But Odysseus addressed them in gentle words, saying:

"Old man, sit down to meat and do ye forget your marvelling, for long have we been eager to put forth our hands on the food, as we abode in the hall alway expecting your coming."

So he spake, and Dolius ran straight toward him stretching

forth both his hands, and he grasped the hand of Odysseus and
kissed it on the wrist, and uttering his voice spake to him
winged words:

"Beloved, forasmuch as thou hast come back to us who sore
desired thee, and no longer thought to see thee, and the gods
have led thee home again;— hail to thee and welcome manifold, and may the gods give thee all good fortune! Moreover,
tell me this truly, that I may be assured, whether wise
Penelope yet knows well that thou hast come back hither, or
whether we shall despatch a messenger."

Then Odysseus of many counsels answered, saying: "Old
man, already she knows all; what need to busy thyself
herewith?"

Thereon the other sat him down again on his polished settle.
And in like wise the sons of Dolius gathered about the renowned Odysseus, and greeted him well and clasped his hands,
and then sat down all orderly by Dolius their father.

So they were busy with the meal in the halls. Now Rumour
the messenger went swiftly all about the city, telling the tale
of the dire death and fate of the wooers. And the people heard
it all at once, and thronged together from every side with sigh-
ing and groaning, before the house of Odysseus. And each
brought forth his dead from the halls, and buried them; but
those that came out of other cities they placed on swift ships,
and sent to fisher-folk to carry, each corpse to his own home.
As for them they all fared together to the assembly place, in
sorrow of heart. When they were all gathered and come
together, Eupeithes arose and spake among them, for a comfortless grief lay heavy on his heart for his son Antinous, the
first man that goodly Odysseus had slain. Weeping for him
he made harangue and spake among them:

"Friends, a great deed truly hath this man devised against
the Achaeans. Some with his ships he led away, many men
and noble, and his hollow ships hath he lost, and utterly lost

of his company, and others again, and those far the best of the Cephallenians he hath slain on his coming home. Up now, before ever he gets him swiftly either to Pylos or to fair Elis, where the Epeians bear sway, let us go forth; else even hereafter shall we have shame of face for ever. For a scorn this is even for the ears of men unborn to hear, if we avenge not ourselves on the slayers of our sons and of our brethren. Life would no more be sweet to me, but rather would I die straightway and be with the departed. Up, let us be going, lest these fellows be beforehand with us and get them over the sea."

Thus he spake weeping, and pity fell on all the Achaeans. Then came near to them Medon and the divine minstrel, forth from the halls of Odysseus, for that sleep had let them go. They stood in the midst of the gathering, and amazement seized every man. Then Medon, wise of heart, spake among them, saying:

"Hearken to me now, ye men of Ithaca, for surely Odysseus planned not these deeds without the will of the gods. Nay, I myself beheld a god immortal, who stood hard by Odysseus, in the perfect semblance of Mentor; now as a deathless god was he manifest in front of Odysseus, cheering him, and yet again scaring the wooers he stormed through the hall, and they fell thick one on another."

Thus he spake, and pale fear gat hold of the limbs of all Then the old man, the lord Halitherses, spake among them, the son of Mastor, for he alone saw before and after. Out of his good will he made harangue and spake among them, saying:

"Hearken to me now, ye men of Ithaca, to the word that I will say. Through your own cowardice, my friends, have these deeds come to pass. For ye obeyed not me, nor Mentor, the shepherd of the people, to make your sons cease from their foolish ways. A great villainy they wrought in their evil infatuation, wasting the wealth and holding in no regard the wife of a prince, while they deemed that he would never more come home. And now let things be on this wise, and obey my counsel. Let us not go forth against him, lest haply some may find a bane of their own bringing."

So he spake, but they leapt up with a great cry, the more part of them, while the rest abode there together: for his counsel was not to the mind of the more part, but they gave ear to Eupeithes, and swiftly thereafter they rushed for their armour. So when they had arrayed them in shining mail, they assembled together in front of the spacious town. And Eupeithes led them in his witlessness, for he thought to avenge the slaying of his son, yet himself was never to return, but then and there to meet his doom.

Now Athene spake to Zeus, the son of Cronos, saying: "O Father, our father Cronides, throned in the highest, answer and tell me what is now the hidden counsel of thy heart? Wilt thou yet further rouse up evil war and the terrible din of battle, or art thou minded to set them at one again in friendship?"

Then Zeus, the gatherer of the clouds, answered her, saying: "My child, why dost thou thus straitly question me, and ask me this? Nay, didst not thou thyself devise this very thought, namely, that Odysseus should indeed take vengeance on these men at his coming? Do as thou wilt, but I will tell thee of the better way. Now that goodly Odysseus hath wreaked vengeance on the wooers, let them make a firm covenant together with sacrifice, and let him be king all his days, and let us bring about oblivion of the slaying of their children and their brethren; so may both sides love one another as of old, and let peace and wealth abundant be their portion."

Therewith he roused Athene to yet greater eagerness, and from the peaks of Olympus she came glancing down.

Now when they had put from them the desire of honey-sweet food, the steadfast goodly Odysseus began to speak among them, saying:

"Let one go forth and see, lest the people be already drawing near against us."

So he spake, and the son of Dolius went forth at his bidding, and stood on the outer threshold and saw them all close at hand. Then straightway he spake to Odysseus winged words:

"Here they be, close upon us! Quick, let us to arms!"

Thereon they rose up and arrayed them in their harness, Odysseus and his men being four, and the six sons of Dolius, and likewise Laertes and Dolius did on their armour, greyheaded as they were, warriors through stress of need. Now when they had clad them in shining mail, they opened the gates and went forth and Odysseus led them.

Then Athene, daughter of Zeus, drew near them in the likeness of Mentor, in fashion and in voice. And the steadfast goodly Odysseus beheld her and was glad, and straightway he spake to Telemachus his dear son:

"Telemachus, soon shalt thou learn this, when thou thyself art got to the place of the battle where the best men try the issue — namely, not to bring shame on thy father's house, on us who in time past have been eminent for might and hardihood over all the world."

Then wise Telemachus answered him, saying: "Thou shalt see me, if thou wilt, dear father, in this my mood no whit disgracing thy line, according to thy word."

So spake he, and Laertes was glad and spake, saying: "What a day has dawned for me, kind gods; yea, a glad man am I! My son and my son's son are vying with one another in valour."

Then grey-eyed Athene stood beside Laertes, and spake to him: "O son of Arceisius that art far the dearest of all my friends, pray first to the grey-eyed maid and to father Zeus, then swing thy long spear aloft and hurl it straightway."

Therewith Pallas Athene breathed into him great strength. Then he prayed to the daughter of mighty Zeus, and straightway swung his long spear aloft and hurled it, and smote Eupeithes through his casque with the cheek-piece of bronze. The armour kept not out the spear that went clean through, and he fell with a crash, and his arms rattled about his body. Then Odysseus and his renowned son fell on the fore-fighters, and smote them with swords and two-headed spears. And now would they have slain them all and cut off their return, had not Athene called aloud, the daughter of Zeus lord of the aegis, and stayed all the host of the enemy, saying:

"Hold your hands from fierce fighting, ye men of Ithaca, that so ye may be parted quickly, without bloodshed."

So spake Athene, and pale fear gat hold of them all. The arms flew from their hands in their terror and fell all upon the ground, as the goddess uttered her voice. To the city they turned their steps, as men fain of life, and the steadfast goodly Odysseus with a terrible cry gathered himself together and hurled in on them, like an eagle of lofty flight. Then in that hour the son of Cronos cast forth a flaming bolt, and it fell at the feet of the grey-eyed goddess, the daughter of the mighty Sire. Then grey-eyed Athene spake to Odysseus, saying:

"Son of Laertes, of the seed of Zeus, Odysseus of many devices, refrain thee now and stay the strife of even-handed war, lest perchance the son of Cronos be angry with thee, even Zeus of the far-borne voice."

So spake Athene, and he obeyed and was glad at heart. And thereafter Pallas Athene set a covenant between them with sacrifice, she, the daughter of Zeus lord of the aegis, in the likeness of Mentor, both in fashion and in voice.

PRONUNCIATION OF PROPER NAMES

Vowels. — Each vowel is pronounced separately, except in *ae, ai, au, ei, eus, oe,* which have the following sounds: *ae* and *oe* are pronounced as *ae* in *Caesar; ai* and *ei,* as *i* in *island; au,* as *ow* in *now; eu,* as *u* in *use.* When accented, *y* is pronounced as *i* in *island;* when unaccented, as *i* in *till.*

Consonants. — *Ch* is pronounced as *k.* *C* and *g* are soft (as *s* and *j*) before *e, i, y, ae, oe, eu;* otherwise, as *k* and *g* in *gas.*

Accents. — Words of two syllables are accented on the first syllable. Words of three or more syllables are accented on the antepenult, that is, the third syllable from the end, unless the penult, or syllable next to the end, is "long." A penult is long when it contains (1) a vowel followed by two consonants; (2) a diphthong (*ae, ai, oe*). In the following list the accent is indicated for all proper names as to which the English reader would be in doubt after reading carefully the foregoing explanation.

A-chae'-ans.	Ar-nae'-us.	El-do'-the-e.
Ae-ae'-an.	A-the'-ne.	El-phe'-nor.
Ae-e'-tes.	Au-ton'-o-e.	Ep-e'-ans.
Ae'-o-lus.		Ep-ei'-us.
A-ge-la'-us.	Ceph-al-le'-ni.	Et-e-o'-neus.
Am-phi-tri'-te.	Cy-clo'-pes.	Eu-e'-nor.
An-drae'-mon.	Cy-the'-ra.	Eu-mae'-us.
An-ti-clei'-a.		Eu-pei'-thes.
Aph-ro-di'-te.	De-iph'-o-bus.	Eu-ry-clei'-a
A-re'-te.	Do-do'-na.	
A-re-thu'-sa.		He-phaes'-tus.
Ar-gives.	Ech-e-ne'-us.	He-re.

295

Hip-po-da-mei'-a.   Nau-sic'-a-a.   Per-seph'-o-ne.
Hy-pe-ri'-on.   No-e'-mon.   Phil-oc-te'-tes.
                                       Po-li'-tes.
Lac-e-dae'-mon.   O-ce'-a-nus.   Pol-y-phe'-mus.
La-er'-tes.   Po-sei'-don.
                    Pei-se'-nor.
Ma-le'-a.   Pe-nel'-o-pe.   Te-lem'-a-chus.
Men-e-la'-us.   Per-i-me'-des.   Ti-tho'-nus.

The reader will perhaps also be helped by the following list of the Greek and Latin names of the gods and goddesses who play important parts in the narrative. When the Greek names are new to him, the corresponding Latin names may be more familiar.

Greek	Latin
Zeus.	Jupiter.
Hera.	Juno.
(Pallas) Athene.	Minerva.
Aphrodite.	Venus.
Poseidon.	Neptune.
Ares.	Mars.
Hephaestus.	Vulcan.

✓ U

Milton Keynes UK
Ingram Content Group UK Ltd.
UKHW021943121124
451129UK00007B/195